Urban Systems

Contemporary Approaches to Modelling

Edited by

C. S. Bertuglia, G. Leonardi, S. Occelli,
G. A. Rabino, R. Tadei and
A. G. Wilson

Routledge Revivals

Urban Systems

This edited collection, first published in 1987, provides a comparative analysis of different approaches to urban modelling. The first part contextualises the development of the field of urban systems modelling, focusing on the variety of approaches and possible implications of this on the future of research and methodology. Next, the editors consider economic and 'non-economic' approaches, followed by an analysis of spatial-interaction-based approaches. Providing an overview to the field and research literature, the overarching argument is that there should be an integrated methodological approach to urban system modelling.

First published in 1987
by Croom Helm Ltd

This edition first published in 2013 by Routledge
2 Park Square, Milton Park, Abingdon, Oxon, OX14 4RN

Simultaneously published in the USA and Canada
by Routledge
711 Third Avenue, New York, NY 10017

Routledge is an imprint of the Taylor & Francis Group, an informa business

A Library of Congress record exists under LC control number: 86032764

ISBN 13: 978-0-415-71460-0 (hbk)
ISBN 13: 978-1-315-88254-3 (ebk)
ISBN 13: 978-0-415-71461-7 (pbk)

URBAN SYSTEMS:

Contemporary approaches to modelling

Edited by
C.S. Bertuglia, G. Leonardi, S. Occelli, G.A. Rabino,
R. Tadei, A.G. Wilson

CROOM HELM
London • New York • Sydney

Croom Helm Ltd, Provident House, Burrell Row, Beckenham, Kent, BR3 1AT

Croom Helm Australia, 44-50 Waterloo Road, North Ryde, 2113, New South Wales

British Library Cataloguing in Publication Data

Urban systems: contemporary approaches
to modelling.
1. City planning — Mathematical models
I. Bertuglia, C.S.
307'.12'0724 HT166

ISBN 0-7099-3971-X

Published in the USA by
Croom Helm
in association with Methuen, Inc.
29 West 35th Street
New York, NY 10001

Library of Congress Cataloging-in-Publication Data

Urban systems.

Bibliography: p.
Includes index.
1. Cities and towns — Mathematical models. 2. Urban economics. 3. Spatial systems. I. Bertuglia, Cristoforco Sergio.
HT153.U745 1987 307.7'6'0724 86-32764
ISBN 0-7099-3971-X

Printed and bound in Great Britain by
Biddles Ltd, Guildford and King's Lynn

CONTENTS

FIGURES AND TABLES

List of Figures

List of Tables

ACKNOWLEDGEMENTS

The research which is the foundation of this book was part of a major transport project sponsored by the Italian Consiglio Nazionale delle Ricerche (CNR) and we are grateful for their support. The study was carried out under contract no. CNR-IRES 82.00450.93. Excellent facilities for carrying out the work were provided by the Istituto Ricerche Economico-Sociale (IRES) in Turin, and the research was implemented and integrated within IRES. The book conforms with the research diffusion policies of the CNR.

We are grateful to Carla Aragno of IRES for her help, particularly with the task of compiling the bibliography. We would also like to thank Mandy Smith for the tremendous effort involved in producing the final typescript and Jane Senior for her help in the preparation of the index.

The Editors

Part One

URBAN SYSTEMS MODELLING: THE CONTEXT

Chapter 1

INTRODUCTION

C.S. Bertuglia and A.G. Wilson

If Lowry's (1964) *Model of metropolis* is taken as an established 'beginning' of urban modelling, then the field is now over 21 years old. It can perhaps be said to have matured, to have come of age in a more than arithmetical sense, in that very high levels of skill have been developed, but also a range of quite different styles of approach. This has drawbacks as well as advantages. Many students of urban modelling, for example, are taught within the confines of one 'school'. A similar point can be made about approaches to research. This makes it difficult to evaluate effectively the strengths and weaknesses of the different styles of approach. There is very little 'comparative' literature. The aim of this book is to fill that gap. This both helps to provide a basis for the evaluation of different approaches but also most importantly, lays the foundations for the possibility of integration in a number of respects and the development of a more unified field.

The strategy we have used to achieve this objective can be described as follows. First, in the remainder of Part One, we present a substantial historical review of the development of urban modelling, focusing in turn on the variety of approaches on the one hand and the implications of this history for future research policy on the other. Secondly, we subdivide the approaches into three main categories, two of which are then further subdivided. The first category is 'economic', and the next two could be labelled 'non-economic'; the first of these labelled 'operational research', the next a variety of approaches to 'spatial interaction'. The labels will ultimately be seen to be too restrictive. For example, there are economic approaches to spatial interaction, and many operational research and spatial interaction models can be given an economic interpretation. Indeed, in Chapter 10 of Part Five, arguments and theorems are presented which demonstrate formally that there is a considerable degree of equivalence at a basic level between the various approaches. In the remainder of this chapter, however, we discuss briefly the different approaches considered within each of the main Parts.

Economic contributions to urban modelling can be considered to have a long history through the 'classical' contributions to location theory of such authors as von Thünen and Weber. This tradition has proved rich in insight in contemporary research and Martin Beckmann (Chapter 3) is a distinguished exponent. The contribution of Beckmann is, of course, developed strictly according to the principles of the New Urban Economics, and therefore it trades off power of analysis with realism, by introducing the standard simplifying assumptions which are typical of that school.

In order to remove some of these assumptions and build operational models which remain consistent with economic theory, several approaches have been developed, such as disaggregate choice theory and random utility theory. Such a contribution is made by Leonardi (Chapter 4). Much effort in these approaches has been devoted to the behavioural side of the models, by introducing heterogeneity of preferences and imperfect information in the choices of urban actors. Interestingly enough, many of the models obtained in this way bear strong similarities with those derived by entropy maximising, a non-economic approach to be discussed in Part

Four (Chapter 7). A different kind of difficulty is exposed in at least some views by another critique: that the underlying assumptions of neo-classical economics are unsound and an analysis which relates back to Marxist economic theory is to be preferred. These alternative assumptions generate new kinds of urban models which are represented here in the chapter by Sheppard (Chapter 5).

Since the second world war, there has been a largely separate set of developments under the heading of operational research with a number of techniques being obviously relevant to locational analysis. Most applications have been to problems which are smaller in scale - such as those of a single firm - than those of urban modelling, but nonetheless there are lessons to be learned. This is particularly important now that there is beginning to be some conceptual integration between some of the models of operational research and the rest of urban modelling (cf Wilson, Coelho, Macgill and Williams, 1981). The history and these more recent developments are reviewed by Colorni in Chapter 6, which constitutes the whole of Part Three since it is distinctive relative to the other approaches.

In Part Four, a number of spatial-interaction-based approaches are presented. We have already mentioned entropy-maximising. When such ideas are combined with the more recent developments of dynamical systems theory, an approach is available which can be used to develop dynamic versions of most of the models needed in the urban field. These are presented by Wilson (Chapter 7). Random utility models, as an alternative to entropy-maximising, have already been discussed in relation to Chapter 4. A further alternative is the cost-efficiency theory of Smith (Chapter 8). His contribution is a good example of the restrictiveness of the classification into 'economic' or 'non-economic' approaches. Although it is true that it is closely related to entropy maximising, it is also true that it starts from economic justifications which relate it to approaches like random utility theory. The main difference is that while in the latter a disaggregate approach is used, in cost-efficiency theory aggregate assumptions about economic regularities are used. It is also possible to take a more explicitly dynamic view of flows (as well as locational behaviour) and a broad foundation for this approach is provided through compartment models and master equations. These techniques are described by de Palma and Lefèvre (Chapter 9).

As noted earlier, some formal integration is achieved in Chapter 10. However, we hope that the book as a whole will provide foundations for readers to carry out their own assessment of different approaches. Moreover, it is worth emphasising that integration is not just a formal task, nor does it leave complete freedom to assemble different elements from different approaches eclectically. It is something in-between which requires a balance between formal rigour and skilful use of the best contributions from various disciplines. This argument suggests that readers should use the book as a tool to achieve this balance in a way which is consistent with their own modelling styles. This is the way the book was conceived and the main goal underlying the research project which generated it.

Once again, it should be stressed that not all approaches are good for everything, not everything is best treated by all approaches. It is an ambition of this book to assess the achievements and limitations of such diverse approaches as classical space economics, recent behavioural economics, operational research, spatial interaction, and dynamical systems theory. It is an even more ambitious goal for the book, however, to outline paths towards consistent (that is, theoretically sound and operationally feasible) integration of the different contributions. The task of integration is of course a difficult one, and more needs to be done. In Chapter

2, this theme will be brought into a sharper focus in terms of emerging strands for future development. Chapter 10, as mentioned already, will provide some examples of what can be achieved at a purely formal level. Further steps towards building a truly integrated dynamic urban modelling framework will be reported as further research progresses.

Chapter 2

AN HISTORICAL REVIEW OF APPROACHES TO URBAN MODELLING

C.S. Bertuglia, G. Leonardi, S. Occelli, G.A. Rabino and R. Tadei

2.1 Introduction

The aim of this chapter is to offer an historical review of urban modelling involving location, transport and the relationships between them and to assess the most important directions for future research in this field. The emphasis on location-transport relationships provides a useful basis for structuring an analysis. Our intention is to: (a) describe the state-of-the-art (beginning in Section 2.2); (b) identify the main directions in which this work is advancing; and (c) look at the most promising avenues of research, with the aim of establishing how research efforts can be most effectively channelled in the future (in Section 2.3).

The interrelationships of location and transport are highly complex and consequently any description of the phenomena involved necessarily takes various forms and cannot claim to be exhaustive. Our classification of studies is clearly not the only one possible, but appears to correspond by and large to the main themes emerging from research in this field (and from the authors' experience seems the most useful). We maintain, in any case, that other classifications are likely to differ only marginally. The categories we have adopted for the purpose of this study are therefore: (a) interrelations between location of economic activities and commodity flows

(Section 2.4); (b) interrelations between services and the journeys generated by their use (Section 2.5); (c) interrelations between residential location and journeys to work (Section 2.6); (d) interrelations between location and transport in the urban system (Section 2.7); (e) interrelations between urban form and transport (Section 2.8).

There are clearly a large number of theoretical, methodological and practical problems involved in the exploration of these interrelationships. Later in the review we describe the new trends emerging in this field. It is possible, however, at the outset, to identify the three main streams which appear to be the most promising: (a) models of spatial choice behaviour; (b) mechanisms of the dynamics and evolution of location-transport systems; and (c) the application of various economic paradigms to the analysis of location-transport interrelationships.

The conclusions about research priorities are sketched in Section 2.9.

2.2 The Most Important Existing Approaches

The obligatory starting point for a study aiming to describe the most important contributions to the understanding of the interrelationships between location and transport, is that of classical urban economics of the 19th century and in particular that emanating from the German school. More precisely, we must go back to von Thünen (1826) and later Weber (1909), Hoover (1948) and Isard (1956, pages 77-142 and 221-287), who wrote specifically about the interrelationships of location and transport; and to Christaller (1933), Palander (1935), Lösch (1940) and more recently Isard (1956) - again, Lefeber (1958) and Greenhut (1963) who have contributed to the question of a general location theory which implicitly takes into account transport costs as well. The most natural 'descendant' of this line of research is Beckmann (summarised in his 1968 book - and see also the bibliography) who managed to combine systematically geographical theory and urban economics with the methods and techniques which operational research had made available from the late 1940s on (cf Chapter 6 below).

This alliance of geographic theory and urban economics forged ahead thanks to the work of, among others, Wingo (1961), Alonso (1964-A), Richardson (1969-A, 1969-B, 1973-A, 1973-C, 1977-B, 1978), Papageorgiou (ed) (1976-A), Fujita (1978), Puu (1978, 1979-B, 1981-A, 1981-B, 1981-C, 1982-C) and Kanemoto (1980-B). In all these cases, additional references are cited in the bibliography.

From the 1960s onwards there was a parallel development of powerful mathematical models. Unlike the types of study referred to above, each based on specific interpretative paradigms, usually from economics, this branch had its roots in quantitative formulations of empirical regularities which (at least initially) did not have economic underpinnings. These developments were built on two objectives: the building and testing of tools for direct application in town planning; and the construction of an alternative to strictly neo-classical approaches. The models constructed for planning purposes were inspired initially by the pioneering work of Hansen (1959) and found their mainstay in the Lowry model (1964). In fact Lowry's model can be taken as the foundation stone and point of departure for this whole style of model development. The models developed by the Penn Jersey Transportation Study (Seidmann, 1964, 1969) can be considered as having originated from Lowry's model, together with sectoral studies such as Herbert and Stevens' model of the housing market (1960), the industrial and service locations model and those related to transport infrastructure (cf Merlin, 1968, pages 37-39). Other models developed at the same time as Lowry's, though less global in their range, were those of Huff (1963, 1964), Harris

(1964-A) and Lakshmanan and Hansen (1965). None of these models, however, provided anything like the impulse generated by Lowry's model, the influence of which has been described fully by Goldner (1971). Garin (1966) gave a matrix version of Lowry's model which is frequently referred to. Although Garin's version facilitated computation and hence accelerated its diffusion, it overshadowed for a long time certain potential general developments of the model such as the non-linearity deriving from the presence of spatial constraints (which cannot be easily dealt with in a linear algebra version). Lowry's model itself was in fact immediately applied and extended. Among the early modifications were those of Crecine (1964), Brotchie (1965), Goldner and Graybeal (1965), the Bay Area Simulation Study (1968), Crecine (1968), Goldner (1968), Echenique, Crowther and Lindsay (1969), Wilson (1971-B), Batty (1971-A), Echenique, Crowther and Lindsay (1971) and Goldner, Rosenthal and Meredith (1971). For a review of the first modifications and developments of Lowry's model, see Goldner (1971) and with reference to Great Britain, Batty (1972-C). Many other models, including certain of Wilson's (cf 1969-A), can be seen as having originated from that of Lowry. In listing them in this way we do not wish, however, to over-emphasise the aspect of 'continuity' or to lose sight of important innovations which certain models introduced. The applications of Lowry's model (and its variants) were numerous and of different levels of complexity. Among the first, we have those of Batty (1969-A, 1969-B), Echenique, Crowther and Lindsay (1969), Echenique et al (1969), Batty (1970-A), Cripps and Foot (1970), Echenique and Domeyko (1970), Masser (1970), Stubbs and Barber (1970), Barras et al (1971), Echenique et al (1973), Batty et al (1974), Bertuglia and Rabino (1975), Christiansen (1975), Ayeni (1976-A), IRES (1976), Piasentin, Costa and Foot (1978). Certain of the modifications and applications cited tend towards a dynamic version and are therefore dealt with later on. Alongside the models which were directly or indirectly inspired by Lowry there are others which are often forgotten. We wish here to mention at least one of these, the statistical/econometric approach exemplified by the POLIMETRIC model (Traffic Research Corporation, 1964) and EMPIRIC (Hill, 1965, Hill, Brand and Hansen, 1966). Both of these models are described more fully in Merlin (1968, page 39). Criticisms have inevitably been levelled at Lowry's model and with the experience of those who have applied it certain limitations and oversimplifications have been brought to light and suggestions for overcoming them proposed. The earliest modifications came from Cripps and Foot (1969), Batty (1970-B) and Broadbent (1970).

The second aspect of model development referred to (that of the formulation of alternatives to the traditional neo-classic approaches), was stimulated by the work of Wilson. The impact of his work can be attributed to his innovative vigour, the result of which can be seen in the profound influence it has on later research. We are referring here to his introduction of the entropy maximising principle. The fundamental message conveyed by Wilson was the need to steer away from the determinism and perfect rationality implied in neo-classic theory and to introduce more realistic (and even stochastic) aspects. Wilson's early work adopted this theme, Wilson (1967, 1969-A, 1969-B, 1969-C), which was later developed further (1970-A, 1971-A, 1974). Several new directions of research were pursued, often involving the implementation of models of spatial interaction, but also sometimes purely for the sake of furthering understanding. Among the first developments orientated towards implementation were those concerned with calibration: Mackie (1971), Batty and Mackie (1972), Batty et al (1973), Cesario (1973), Massey (1973), Kirby (1974), Baxter and Williams (1975), Putman (1977), Putman and Ducca (1978-A, 1978-B); and those involving the zoning of study areas:

Broadbent (1969-A, 1969-B, 1970), Batty (1973), Batty et al (1973), Batty and Masser (1975), Beardwood and Kirby (1975), Masser, Batey and Brown (1975), Openshaw (1977, 1978-A). A work which represented an important advance and systematic reorganisation in this respect is that of Batty (1976). Among the first contributions to the better understanding of the models were those concerning the interpretation of spatial interaction models in terms of mathematical programming: Wilson and Senior (1974), Nijkamp (1975-A), Brotchie, Lesse and Roy (1979); those involving the extension of the principle of entropy maximisation in new sectors: Macgill (1977-A), Macgill and Wilson (1979); and those which reconciled classical urban economics and models of spatial interaction: Anas (1978-B, 1979, 1982).

Another important development involved the various economic interpretations of spatial interaction models, which by and large can be divided into two groups: (a) macro-economic approaches and (b) micro-economic approaches. In the first case, we have the models derived from the maximisation of consumer surplus and those based on cost efficiency. The second consists of the family of models based on random utility theory. The principle of maximisation of consumer surplus was introduced by Neuburger (1971-B) and Cochrane (1975) and developed principally in Coelho and Wilson (1976), Coelho and Williams (1978) and in Coelho (1979). Another approach which is very similar to the maximisation of consumer surplus is the maximisation of accessibility developed by Leonardi (1978). The principle of cost efficiency was developed by Smith (1978-A, 1978-B, 1983-A).

Random utility theory, which is perhaps the most important attempt to give spatial interaction models an economic base, is (both because of the number of models produced and the range of possible applications) that most closely comparable to the entropy approach of Wilson. This theory had its origins in the work of Thurstone (1927) and Luce (1959) and was extended to transport and the urban context in general in the work of McFadden (1973), Manski (1973), Ben-Akiva (1974), McFadden (1974), Domencich and McFadden (1975), Lerman (1975), Manski (1975), McFadden (1976), Manski (1977), Manski and Lerman (1977), Williams (1977-A), Brotchie (1978), McFadden (1978), Ben-Akiva and Lerman (1979), Brotchie (1979), Daganzo (1979), Lerman and Manski (1979), Manski and McFadden (1979), de Palma and Ben Akiva (1981), Leonardi (1981-C, 1982-A, 1982-B), Smith (1982-B). The axiomatic theory of choice (Smith, 1975-A, 1975-B, 1976-A, 1976-B) was proposed alongside random utility theory. For the relationship between the two see Williams and Wilson (1980), who trace them back to their origins: Thurstone (1927) in the case of random utility theory and Luce (1959) for the axiomatic theory of choice. There is also another version of random utility theory which was traced by Williams and Wilson (1980) back to Quandt (1968), Niedercorn and Bechdolt (1969), Beckmann (1971), Beckmann and Golob (1971), Golob and Beckmann (1971) and Golob, Gustafsson and Beckmann (1973).

Despite the differences, sometimes considerable, which exist in their theoretical base, the approaches derived from the theories described above can be considered equivalent to each other and equivalent also to those derived from the entropy maximisation principle. In fact, all of the approaches discussed so far, including the maximisation of entropy, lead, under fairly general hypotheses, to choice models and spatial interaction models in the form known as the logit model. It follows that the logit model is consistent with aggregated non-economic hypotheses such as the maximisation of entropy in its statistical mechanics interpretation (Wilson, 1970-A, Leonardi, 1977), with macro-economic hypotheses, such as the principle of maximisation of consumer surplus and cost efficiency and also with micro-economic hypotheses such as those underlying random utility theory. This equivalence has been proved by various authors, among whom are Coelho and Wilson (1977), Williams (1977-A), van Lierop and Nijkamp (1979) and Coelho (1983). (The statistical mechanics analogy is not the only interpretation of the entropy maximising principle. Wilson himself (1970-A) discusses the interpretation in terms of the theory of information. This latter interpretation was preferred and developed by various authors, among them Erlander (1977, 1980) and Webber (1979). Entropy is also used, without real theoretical justification, as an empirical device to introduce a realistic dispersion into location and transport models. The best example can be found in the work of Boyce et al, 1981.)

Many of those involved in location and transport studies have made attempts to 'relax' one of the restrictive assumptions of the neo-classical approach, in particular the equilibrium condition which is shared by many spatial interaction models. The static approach ignores not so much the time dimension of problems so much as the causal factors of evolution over time. There have been two different ways of tackling the problem of transformation. In the first, the dynamics of interacting phenomena are considered in linear terms (in other words, the variation in one quantity is seen as a linear function of other quantities). In the second, the dynamics of interacting phenomena are considered in non-linear terms (the variation in one quantity is seen as a non-linear function of other quantities). The relaxation of the hypothesis of equilibrium and the introduction of mechanisms of change, gave rise to the production of models in which the time dimension appears only as a descriptive feature of a process of comparative statics - in fact comparative analysis compares different equilibrium states without considering how the transitions from one to the other occur. This was what was done initially with the Lowry model (Crecine, 1964, 1968, 1969-A, 1969-B, Seidmann, 1969, Dickey, Leone and Schwarte, 1971, Batty, 1972-A, 1972-B, Sharpe et al, 1974, Bertuglia and Rabino, 1975, Sharpe,

Brotchie and Ahern, 1975, Ayeni, 1976-A and IRES, 1976). For an analysis of the passage from comparative statics to dynamics see Wilson (1978-A, 1978-C). A more detailed discussion of the meaning and significance of the expression 'dynamic' is given in Martin, Thrift and Bennett (eds) (1978) particularly in the introduction by the editors. This development was stimulated by the need to analyse the endogenous mechanisms responsible for the interactions between the various actors and tensions between various processes which are fundamental features of an urban system and from which the non-linearities of the structure of the changes of state derive.

For a discussion of fundamental issues and general problems in the building of dynamic models we refer to Batty (1971-B), Cordey-Hayes (1972), Wilson (1974), Nijkamp (1975-B), Wilson (1976-B, 1977), Williams and Wilson (1978) and Wilson and Macgill (1978). Forrester (1969) and others who applied Forrester's model made important contributions to the problem of dynamics. Modifications to this model and subsequent developments were introduced by Kain (1969), Babcock (1970), Garn and Wilson (1970), Kadanoff (1971), Batty (1972-A), Burdekin and Marshall (1972), the authors of the Special Issue on Urban Dynamics of *IEEE Transactions on Systems, Man and Cybernetics* (April 1972), Chen (ed) (1972), Chen (1973), Mass (ed) (1974), Schroeder III, Sweeny and Alfeld (1975), Alfeld and Graham (1976), Beumer et al (1978) and others. We can also include in this group the Dortmund model (Wegener, 1981, 1982, 1983) and the Turin model (Bertuglia et al, 1980, 1982, Bertuglia, Gallino et al, 1983-A, 1983-B, Bertuglia, Occelli et al, 1983) although the treatment of the residential subsystem in the latter has more in common with the second approach. Important work has been done by Rogers (1971, 1975) and his school on population studies, which are those more closely associated with our present study.

We can distinguish a number of different influences, in relation to both approach and subject-matter, in the treatment of non-linearities. Some models make use of dynamical generalisations which come directly from geography and regional science: central place theory (Curry, 1969, White, 1977, 1978, Wilson, 1978-B, Allen and Sanglier, 1979-A, 1981-A), or diffusion theory in its various forms (Curry, 1978, 1982, Ralston, 1983, Sonis, 1983) and the dynamic version of optimum land use (Isard and Liossatos, 1972, Domanski, 1973, Isard and Liossatos, 1975, 1979). Others make use of recent mathematical or physico-mathematical theories which have been applied to the analysis of the dynamics of spatial phenomena. It is interesting to note in this connection that those involved in producing such models tend to be regional scientists or physicists and mathematicians interested in urban problems. A predominant role is played here by the vast group of studies inspired by catastrophe theory which was applied at urban level by Amson (1974, 1975), Casti and Swain (1975), Amson (1977), Wilson (1976-A, 1981-A) and Clarke and Wilson (1983, 1985) and to the analysis of economic development and decline by Casetti (1981-A, 1981-B). The most important development was, however, the analysis of the dynamics of urban subsystems, particularly that of the service subsystem, undertaken by Wilson (1976-A, 1978-B, 1978-C, 1979-B, 1979-C, 1981-A, 1981-C), Poston and Wilson (1977), Harris and Wilson (1978), Wilson and Clarke (1979), Beaumont, Clarke and Wilson (1981-A, 1981-B), Harris, Choukroun and Wilson (1982) and also Lombardo and Rabino (1983-A, 1983-B) and Rijk and Vorst (1983). A group of studies derived from 'ecological' models, concerning in particular competition between species, where emphasis was placed on aspects of structural stability or instability includes the work of Dendrinos (1977, 1978, 1979, 1980-A, 1980-B, 1981-B, 1982), Dendrinos and Mullally (1981-A, 1981-B), also Day (1981) and Monaco and Rabino (1984). The theory of dissipative processes developed by the Brussels school inspired another group to extend their ideas to the analysis of urban systems (Allen et al, 1978, 1979-A, 1979-B, 1982, Allen and Sanglier, 1978, 1979-B, 1981-B, Allen, Boon and Sanglier, 1980, and Crosby, 1983). A further group developed from the theory of synergetic processes, which was extended to the analysis of the dynamics of social and spatial interactions. We include in this group the work of authors not only from the field of synergetics but also regional scientists who show a great similarity of approach. The essential difference between the kind of dynamic processes considered by this last group and the preceding one is the speed of the processes - those in the former group being essentially slow processes (such as changes in housing stock or services) and those in the latter being relatively rapid (such as mobility of population). We cite here by way of example Bertuglia and Leonardi (1979), Weidlich and Haag (1980-A), Leonardi and Campisi (1981), Haag and Weidlich (1983), Leonardi (1983), Weidlich and Haag (1983). From the point of view of treatment of the residential subsystem we can include in this group the Turin model (Bertuglia et al, 1980, 1982, Bertuglia, Gallino et al, 1983-A, 1983-B, Bertuglia, Occelli et al, 1983), and the Dortmund model (Wegener, 1981, 1982, 1983). Population studies can also be included in this group: Rees and Wilson (1977), Ledent (1978), Okabe (1979), Sikdar and Karmeshu (1982) and Sheppard (1983-E).

The application of new mathematical techniques has been a major stimulus in this group of studies. Particularly significant are differential topology (Chillingworth, 1976) which includes several important theories, including catastrophe theory (Thom, 1972), and also the theory of dissipative processes (Nicolis and Prigogine, 1977) and the theory of synergetic processes (Haken, 1977).

A general criticism of neo-classic assumptions has been made by the urban economists who have proposed alternative economic paradigms for urban analyses in general and also for transport-location analyses. The most prodigious of these seem to be the neo-Marxian (or neo-Ricardian) paradigms deriving from the essentially non-spatial theories of Sraffa (1960), Garegnani (1970), Spaventa (1970), Morishima (1973), Pasinetti (1974, 1977-A), Steedman (1977), Pasinetti (1981), Steedman and Sweezy (eds) (1981) and recently, covering spatial aspects, Scott (1976, 1979, 1980, 1982) and Sheppard (1981-B, 1983-C, 1983-D). There is also another group of neo-classic non-Walrasian approaches which includes the static models of Drèze (1975) and Benassy (1975), the dynamic models of Varian (1975), Kornai and Weibull (1978) and Weibull (1984-B) but these do not as yet incorporate the spatial dimension explicitly.

There has also been a notable growth of normative techniques involving optimisation and testing. First, there is the extremely important contribution of Operational Research. Various reviews illustrate the approach: (i) models based exclusively on transport costs (Eilon, Watson-Gandy and Christofides, 1971, Handler and Mirchandani, 1979, Halpern and Maimon, 1982, Coelho, 1983, Hansen and Thisse, 1983); (ii) models based on plant costs with increasing returns (ReVelle, Marks and Liebman, 1970, Francis and Goldstein, 1974, Bartezzaghi, 1979, Coelho, 1983) and models with technological constraints (Salkin, 1975, ReVelle, Cohon and Shobrys, 1981, Coelho, 1983); (iii) models taking into account non-perfect rationality on the part of the decision-maker (Leonardi, 1978, 1981-B, Palermo, 1981, Wilson et al, 1981, *Sistemi Urbani*, *3*, *3*, 1981, Coelho, 1983); and (iv) models with multiple objectives (Haimes, 1977, Nijkamp, 1977, Nijkamp and Spronk, 1981, ReVelle, Cohon and Shobrys, 1981, and the special issue *Sistemi Urbani*, *3*, *3*, 1981).

There has also been a growth of methods designed as aids in decision-making and evaluation in location processes.

There is not space here to describe these in full but certain aspects deserve to be mentioned - in particular those methods which attempt to link efficiency and optimisation with the satisfaction of decision-makers (Simon, 1955). These include goal programming (Charnes and Cooper, 1961) and more recently vector optimisation (Geoffrion, 1968, Zeleny, 1974), methods based on non-dominated structures (Yu, 1973-A) and methods based on outranking and the new axiomatics of Roy (1973, 1974, 1975, 1976, 1977, 1979-A, 1979-B). Although it is based on satisfaction, goal programming can be considered more a modification of rational strategy than a pluralistic approach and in addition does not seem to take the behaviour of decision-makers fully into account (cf Ostanello, 1980). The interactive methods are moving explicitly in this new direction and are part of the so-called 'hybrid approach' with the decision-makers' behaviour being inserted in the model (Aubin and Naslund, 1972, Geoffrion, Dyer and Feinberg, 1972, Steuer, 1977, Nijkamp and Spronk, 1979). A common strategy of these methods is that of presenting the decision-maker with a succession of new alternatives, asking him to express his preferences. They place emphasis on the decision-making process rather than the decision itself. The convergence on a solution is facilitated in many of these methods by having a 'point of reference' eg. the 'perfect solution' of Geoffrion and Dyer (Geoffrion, Dyer and Feinberg, 1972), the 'utopia point' of Yu (1973-B), the 'target' of Roy (1975), the 'ideal' of Zeleny (1976). This point of reference may be redefined with the interactive process, eg. the 'evolutive target' of Roy (1975) and the 'displaced ideal' of Zeleny (1976). The model is seen as a method of support to the process of solving the decision-maker's problem.

2.3 The Most Promising Themes From Current Research

From the above survey, three broad aspects of current research emerge as the most productive and promising for the future: (a) from the behavioural point of view, the progress from deterministic models to stochastic models; (b) for representing spatial and time structures, the development of dynamic models; and (c) from the point of view of economic theory, the contrast between neo-classic theory and the new urban economics and neo-Marxian (or neo-Ricardian) theory. These three aspects, if followed up, are likely to bring changes both in the way of analysing the various phenomena connected with location and transport interrelations and in the approaches traditionally used for solving the inherent theoretical and methodological problems. We shall in the following section look at these phenomena according to the classification introduced in 2.1, attempting not only to describe the state-of-the-art but also to assess the possible impact of new development. In addition we have selected from the vast range of theoretical and methodological problems, three which can be considered 'key' points in the understanding of static and dynamic behaviour of systems of location and transport: (a) spatial choice behaviour models; (b) mechanisms for the formation and spatial differentiation of prices; and (c) the technological structure of intersectoral transactions and mechanisms of production and consumption. These various themes are treated in subsequent sections of this review.

2.4 Location of Economic Activities and Commodity Flows

2.4.1 Introduction

While the study of the relationships between location and flows of people (especially for residential and commercial activities) can be considered relatively developed and with recognisable unifying elements among the different approaches (see Sections 2.5 and 2.6), the interrelations between economic activities and commodity flows has received relatively little attention. The work which has been done appears not to have a common thread and is rather difficult to fit into a general scheme. There are differences in the ways the various disciplines have approached the problem and in the depth to which they have explored the subject. Without doubt those who have done more than anyone else are the economists, though often they have ignored the question of space, or introduced it at a highly aggregated level (usually regional). Geographers and those regional scientists orientated towards physical planning have tended to introduce a more refined spatial disaggregation but at the cost of an exogenous treatment of the structure of intersectoral flows, considering them as given. In order to make a systematic survey of the possibility of building a general theory of location-commodity flows, and also to identify directions for future research, it will be useful to introduce a broad classification of problems, based on some qualitative differences in the type of commodity flows to be considered.

We distinguish first of all flows of goods towards consumption and flows of goods towards production. The former can be further broken down into flows of a single good and flows of multiple goods. For the latter no subdivision is necessary. There is, however, a third aspect, distinct from but closely linked to, this basic subdivision: the relationships between flows of goods, the location of economic activities and the labour market. An integrated analysis of the connections between these three phenomena is fundamental to the understanding of the structure and dynamics of a system of settlements. Economic activities receive as inputs not only products from other sectors but also labour from working populations. In addition, as they sell finished products to consumers, they condition and are conditioned by residential location.

A comprehensive model of the inter-relations described above does not exist, but given their complexity this is understandable. It is surprising, however, that two modelling traditions such as inter-regional flows of goods and urban models of the Lowry type have practically never been fully brought together. Their integration could be extremely useful for future developments, a theme which we shall take up again later.

2.4.2 Model of flows of a single commodity towards consumption

The models of which we shall speak briefly here go back to the formation proposed by Samuelson (1952) and are discussed in another chapter of this book by Beckmann. The basic Samuelson model has been subject to various developments and critical revisions (for example, Takayama and Judge, 1964, Sheppard and Curry, 1982). It is based on two main assumptions: (a) the existence at each point (or in each zone) in space of a net demand function (local consumption minus local production) which depends exclusively on local prices; and (b) the embedding of market equilibrium into an optimisation problem in which the total benefit (consumer surplus plus producer's surplus) is maximised. While the second assumption is less open to criticism, at least from a neo-classical viewpoint, the first needs to be looked at more closely.

First of all we should note that these models, even though they have been classified as involving flows 'towards consumers', deal in fact with an aggregation of all functions of production and final consumption in a single demand function. The net demand in each zone is not necessarily the final consumption, but includes in a single expression all intermediate and final consumption in that zone, both for the productive system and the consumers. The technological structure of production is therefore ignored, as assumptions on intersectoral transactions (for a single product) do not appear explicitly. The level of consumption in each zone is determined exclusively by the local price. This assumption seems to be reasonable as far as consumption is concerned, if the delivery costs are paid by the producer. In this case the consumer effectively pays the local consumer price, which becomes the determinant factor for the consumption level. It must not be forgotten, however, that the net demand is defined as the difference between consumption and local production and even if the hypothesis of dependence on local price is acceptable for consumption it will not be so for local production. In such systems the production is, by definition, orientated towards export to other zones. In addition it is the producer who pays the delivery costs of commodities. It therefore seems reasonable, though, contrary to what is accepted in the classic model, to assume that local production is a function not of local prices but all prices in all zones, plus the relative transport costs.

The only logical way of accepting a supply function which depends only on local price seems to be by reversing the classic assumption (that transport and delivery costs are paid by the exporter) and taking them to be paid by the importer, i.e. the consumer. In this case it is the exporter who fixes the local price, and this plus the transport costs in the zone of consumption must be paid by the consumer at the final destination.

At this point another contradiction emerges. If supply can be a function of local price only, it is not so for the demand. In fact if the consumer may buy the product in the various zones of production paying the respective local prices plus transport costs, the demand in each zone is a function of all the prices in all the zones as well as transport costs and not only the local price. An intrinsic contradiction, therefore, seems implicit in the very concept of net demand and the way in which it is represented in the classic model. This underlines the fact that it is necessary to introduce an explicit representation of the productive structure and producer behaviour and that the latter cannot be aggregated with that of the consumer without losing information fundamental to the understanding of the system.

2.4.3 Models of flows towards consumers for multiple goods

The same criticisms which have been levelled at the case of single commodity flows naturally hold also in the case of multiple commodity flows and need not be repeated. However, accepting for a moment the idea of a function of net demand depending only on local price, there can be a number of different models, according to the different assumptions made about the interactions between the different products either at the time of consumption or production. From the point of view of consumption, which is our main interest here, there are two distinct cases according to whether we assume the net demand for each product is exclusively a function of local price for the product or a function of all local prices for all products. In the first case, in the absence of other constraints, the problem of multiple products can simply be reduced to several independent problems involving a single product. In the second case we have a system of demand equations in which all products have interdependent consumptions and the problem becomes more complex. While systems of demand equations for bundles of multiple products have already been proposed in studies in the economic literature, their combination with the spatial dimension through a structure of inter-zonal imports and exports has received little attention. These models need, therefore, to be further developed if they are to be useful in this context.

The existence of multiple products underlines even more the need to distinguish clearly between final consumption and intermediate consumption. The latter, if formulated for more than one product, is the same as the disaggregated specification of functions of production for each sector, and is connected with the analysis of intersectoral interdependencies, which is generally treated as being a separate problem from that of inter-regional commercial flows. This theme is discussed in Section 2.4.4.

2.4.4 Flows of goods towards production, and sectoral interdependencies

The analysis of intersectoral transactions is dominated by the input-output approach which postulates the existence of a constant matrix of transaction coefficients or, in other words, linear technology. The subject is already too well known to require a detailed description here. We limit ourselves to a brief mention of the attempts to introduce multizonal spatial disaggregation into the input-output approach, thus making the relationships between the structure of the production system, the location of production units and the interzonal flows of goods explicit.

The first and simplest way in which spatial disaggregation can be introduced is that of extending the concept of constant intersectoral coefficients to that of constant intersectoral-interzonal coefficients. This purely descriptive approach is the oldest and is explained in Isard (1960). A more recent and more explanatory approach involves the combination of the input-output structure with a model of spatial interaction of the type commonly used in the analysis of movements of people. An example is the work of Macgill and Wilson (1979), in which spatial disaggregation is obtained by applying the maximisation-of-entropy method and using sectoral interdependence as constraints. A similar approach is proposed in Bertuglia and Leonardi (1980-A) and in Batty (1983). The same kind of spatial disaggregation, by means of a logit-type model is used by Sheppard in this book. What seems to be missing is a model in which the linear technology of input-output models is effectively combined with an economic model of interzonal flows of the Samuelson type. Even though the construction of such a model must obviously be left to future research, we suggest here a possible structure. Accepting the two paradigms of linear technology and the maximisation of total surplus, an integrated model could be devised incorporating the following elements. (a) A function of final demand (or consumption) should be defined for each zone. This replaces the concept of net demand, the contradictions of which have already been discussed. (b) The linear technology is imposed as a constraint on total intersectoral transactions. This constraint involves both production levels and final demand. (c) Spatial disaggregation, both for intersectoral transactions and delivery to final demand, is obtained by subtracting total transport costs from the total benefit function as in the classic Samuelson model. (d) A dispersion term (such as entropy) should be added to total benefit. In this way the function to be maximised contains a term of net surplus dependent on the function of final demand, a term of transport costs dependent on intersectoral-interzonal transactions and delivery flows to final demand, and a term of dispersion dependent also on intersectoral-interzonal export flows. In such a model the equilibrium state is obtained by maximising total surplus, subject to the constraints specified in (b) above.

We can predict certain salient features of the structure of the solution of this conjectured model. Above all the dual solution (shadow prices associated with the constraint (b)) would provide a mechanism of price formation in which the relations between consumer prices and intersectoral transactions would appear. This, to a certain extent, would combine a mechanism of price propagation of the type described by Sraffa (1960), Morishima (1976) and Sheppard (in his chapter in this book) with the classic concept of demand. The fundamental difference between the Sraffa-type models and the kind of solution proposed here is that while in the former even consumption is treated through linear technology, in our case it is described by a demand function, which is in general non-linear.

Secondly, the presence of the dispersion term associated with interzonal flows would produce models of a similar structure to classic spatial interaction models (such as logit models), containing, however, prices as well as transport costs. This, apart from the theoretical improvements, is a great advantage when it comes to application, because of the relative simplicity of the calculations required by such models.

Finally, from the point of view of the understanding of the spatial structure of a multi-sector economy, the proposed model would be a definite advance on the purely physical models of the Lowry type. Besides information on location and spatial interaction, it would also provide information on prices, on their formation and spatial differentiation. In addition, a factor which should not be underestimated, it would provide all this through a precise economic interpretation, something which was lacking in the Lowry type models (with the exception of certain recent developments proposed by Anas, 1983).

2.4.5 Commodity flows, location of economic activities and the labour market

The model outlined in 2.4.4, even though it promises to overcome various gaps and contradictions in existing models, is still deficient in one fundamental aspect. The resident population is seen solely as consumers and not as labour force and part of the productive process. It is important that this relationship between population and production should be taken into account since: (a) for production, manpower is an input as much as any other factor of production. It also constitutes the main feedback in the wage-profit cycle. Wages paid to workers determine final consumption and hence production. And (b) for the resident population the wage deriving from labour in a productive activity determines the demand for all goods and services including those associated with his ability to settle in a given zone, hence affecting housing and transport.

Naturally, the role of labour is contained in both traditional input-output models and their neo-Marxian version and in the Lowry model and its extensions. However, in all the cases mentioned here, labour is treated as a linear function in the same way as any other productive sector. Prices and wages in these models do not play a fundamental role in determining levels of employment and consumption (they are in fact either ignored or assumed to be exogenous).

Here we wish to put forward a generalisation of the model proposed in 2.4.4, which integrates labour and endogenously generates wages and prices. Basically such a generalisation is simple. In the same way that final demand functions and prices were introduced previously, it is possible to introduce wages and demand functions for labour for each productive sector. Naturally, the demand functions for final consumption will have to be reformulated in order to take account of the constraint on consumption set by disposable income i.e. wages. The total surplus function would contain two additional terms - the producer's surplus, related to the demand for labour, and the cost of transport, associated with journeys to work, paid by the population. Both the labour input and final demand would appear explicitly in the constraints on intersectoral transactions.

It is important to note that the system described above would be essentially governed by production rather than by consumption. Consumers partly control prices through the final demand functions, but are constrained by wages. Producers control wages through the labour demand functions but are not directly constrained by consumer prices. In fact, through the constraints on intersectoral transactions, producers control to a considerable extent both wages and prices.

The solution of this modified version of the model would have two additional advantages. First, its dual solution would provide a joint mechanism not only for prices, but for price and wage formation. Secondly, a model relating journeys to work, transport costs and wages would be generated, probably with a structure similar to a classic spatial interaction model. In conclusion, the model obtained should provide all the information of a classic Lowry model plus commodity flows, prices and wages.

2.5 Location of Services and Journeys Generated by Their Use

In this section we intend to outline the development of theory relating to location of services and to identify the most important stages in this development. The starting point from which location theory and especially service location theory grew is the neo-classic approach (Beckmann, 1968). This approach forms the nucleus of the economic activity equilibrium theory (see Beckmann's chapter in this book). The basic characteristic of this theory is the achievement of an equilibrium state where 'firms' (here the suppliers of services) maximise profits and users of services maximise utility. We can see here in the concept of optimal location the influence of Hotelling (1929). According to him the location of a service was optimal when the costs of its use were in equilibrium. The principal limitation of the economic activity equilibrium theory is that it is necessarily founded on the idea of equilibrium. This is a condition rarely achieved in reality and even if it occurs, it cannot be said to be always essential.

Other disadvantages are the impossibility of dealing with indivisibilities, externalities and imperfect rationality of decision-makers. Service location in fact involves indivisibilities such as fixed costs of provision or capacity constraints of facilities. These factors lead to combinatorial allocation problems: how to locate m service facilities choosing between w (w > m) possible locations. The equilibrium approach cannot resolve such problems unless we assume homogeneity of space. Then, optimum location can be found using 'marginal' analysis.

As we have said above, externalities are another element that the economic activity equilibrium theory cannot deal with. By externalities here we mean such factors as spill-over, diffusion, economies of agglomeration and environmental effects. It must be recognised however, that the introduction of externalities would not compromise the fundamental assumption of the theory, the equilibrium state, but would make this equilibrium non-optimal. A further limitation of this approach is the assumption that decision-makers are rational. It assumes for example that users of services seek to maximise their expected utility and that suppliers of services seek to maximise their profits. In addition it is supposed that all the decision-makers have the same tastes and preferences, which is clearly unrealistic in most cases. To conclude this rather brief description we should add that the economic activity equilibrium theory is of course static. It can be used to describe equilibrium situations and for comparative analysis of such situations but cannot explain how equilibrium is reached. Despite these limitations, the theory has nevertheless been a reference point for a number of developments in location theory which have succeeded in overcoming the problems mentioned and opened new fields of research. These we now describe in chronological order.

We begin with the observation that numerous methods of operational research still in use for service-location make use of the approach described above. These methods are characterised by the type of objective function employed which is typical of the neo-classic approach and is based on the concept of 'efficiency' (minisum). According to this concept the function to be minimised is some measure of disutility for the whole system such as total travel cost. Objective functions of another type came from the consideration of the 'worst case' (minimax). Here the function to be minimised is a measure of disutility of the user in the least favourable conditions. More recently a new formulation of the objective function was based on the concept of 'equity', eg. the redistribution of profits or income.

Following Colorni (1982 and his chapter in this book) we list a summary of other models which have been developed from these origins, classified according to type of location factor:

(a) Location based on transport costs (a review of these can be found in Eilon, Watson-Gandy and Christofides, 1971 and Coelho, 1983). Further assumptions include: (1) a single indicator of preference, based on costs; (2) perfect rationality of decision-makers; (3) no technological constraints (eg. minimum or maximum capacity); (4) no plant costs. These, it can be seen, are typically neo-classical models. They have been used both in continuous space (Hansen and Thisse, 1983) and discrete space (among others, Handler and Mirchandani, 1979).

(b) Location based on transport and plant costs (a review can be found in Francis and Goldstein, 1974 and Coelho, 1983). The following assumptions still hold: (1) a single indicator of preference based on costs; (2) perfect rationality of decision-makers; (3) no technological constraints. This kind of model is no longer strictly in the neo-classic mould. The presence of plant costs generates indivisibilities which the economic activity equilibrium theory cannot deal with for the reasons explained above.

(c) Location with technological constraints (for a review of these models see ReVelle, Cohon and Shobrys, 1981, and Coelho, 1983). The following assumptions remain valid: (1) a single indicator of preference, based on costs; (2) perfect rationality of decision-makers. These models resolve the so-called location-allocation problem.

(d) Location with non-perfectly rational decision-makers (Wilson et al, 1981, Leonardi, 1981-B). The following assumption remains valid: (1) a single indicator of preference, based on costs. In order to introduce non-perfect rationality of decision-makers and differentiation of their tastes and preferences, a random component is introduced in the utility function of decision-makers. Another interesting and more recent development is the introduction of a random component not only in decision-makers' behaviour but also in the transport network. In this way we can take into account stochastic aspects of the network which are analysed using probability graphs (Berman and Odoni, 1982). Another way of introducing a certain dispersion into decision-makers' behaviour is through the entropy models (Wilson, 1974). These models, other than including dispersion, could almost be considered multiple objective models. Their objective function consists of minimisation of costs (as first objective) and maximisation of decision-makers' surplus (as second objective) or, which is analogous, maximisation of accessibility (Coelho, 1983).

(e) Location with multiple objectives (Nijkamp and Spronk, 1981, ReVelle, Cohon and Shobrys, 1981). In these models we have an objective function with more than one objective and these objectives may even be conflicting. They can be quantitative or qualitative. Very often the function in fact consists of two objectives, one quantitative (minimisation of total travel costs, eg. based on the efficiency criterion) and one qualitative (improvement of the service quality, based on the worst case criterion). Together with these models we can consider the multi-criteria models. These, as they are able to deal with qualitative and quantitative information simultaneously, are useful for the determination of planning policy.

In addition to the developments outlined above there have been others which have originated from them:

(1) The use of methods of random search and global optimisation to solve combinatorial problems such as those mentioned in (b) above (Camerini, Colorni and Maffioli, 1983).

(2) The subdivision of the decision-making structure into levels. Here the phenomena of competition between decision-makers are considered and game theory is also used. This development derives in particular from the models with multiple objectives referred to in (e) above.

(3) Disaggregation of the model variables. This disaggregation (see Wilson's chapter in this book) is achieved according to: (a) type of good or service; (b) type of structure for the provision of goods or services; (c) type of user; (d) mode of transport. Of these, the most interesting and most recent is the second, the type of structure for the provision of goods or services. By taking into account differences in structure it makes it possible to analyse different and competitive location behaviour. A further disaggregation is

recognisable in the costs borne by the suppliers of goods or services. They can be split down into fixed costs of provision and running costs. The introduction of disaggregation makes the models far more complex both from the computational and data collection point of view. To reduce this disadvantage, at least in part, techniques of micro-simulation can be used (Clarke and Spowage, 1982). A final observation here is that the higher the level of disaggregation of the model, the more numerous are likely to be the phenomena of bifurcation of which we shall speak in the next paragraph. This arises from the non-linearity and large number of interdependencies present in highly disaggregated models.

(4) Dynamics of building stock. Despite its acknowledged importance (Wilson, in this book) the analysis of stock dynamics is still relatively under-developed. The need for an analysis of this kind derives from the fact that service facilities are located in an already structured environment in which the major problem is how to deal with existing stock - whether to expand, demolish or relocate. The dynamics of the stock can in its turn cause bifurcation and instability (Wilson, 1981-A). These phenomena appear when small changes in a parameter near a critical point bring about large structural changes. Only dynamic analysis is able to take account of this type of phenomenon. For the planner the existence of bifurcation and instabilities has the following implications: (a) negative - if the system is about to reach an undesired state, a modification of the parameters is required to prevent this; (b) it is possible to guide the system to a desired state with small adjustments (such as small investments). These are sufficient to bring the parameters to the critical value at which the desired state of the system is reached.

(5) Multi-level systems (Leonardi, 1981-B, Leonardi and Tadei, 1981, Bertuglia, Leonardi and Tadei, 1983). The consideration

of multi-level service systems is made necessary when for example the hypothesis of the single-purpose trip no longer holds. The single-purpose trip (home → services → home) is frequently and more realistically replaced by the multiple-purpose trip (home → service 1 → service 2 → ... → service n → home). The analysis of multi-level services is also necessary for studying the interrelations which exist between different kinds of services and the effects that different organisational and functional scenarios have on the overall spatial configuration. Multi-level services are usually studied using 'nested logit' models (McFadden, 1978).

Having examined the work done up to the present in the field of service location we shall now suggest two features which could possibly be included in a programme of future research: (a) the introduction of dynamic models of information diffusion (de Palma and Lefèvre, chapter in this book) into the analysis of services, with the aim of modelling the spatial behaviour of service demand and its dynamics. In this case too, bifurcations and instabilities worth analysing may arise; (b) the use of the cost-efficiency theory (Smith, chapter in this book) which is applied to the study of congestion phenomena in a transport network. However, it could easily be extended to deal with a different kind of congestion, like for example the congestion of services or housing makets. Probably the generalisation of the classic spatial price equilibrium models with the introduction of congestion effects in the network of commodity flows, proposed in this book by Smith, could be extended to the problem of service location by considering congestion as well as travel and use of services as a price.

2.6 Residential Location and Journeys to Work

We present here a brief review of the development of residential location theory and identify the most important contributions to the theory. In the final part we describe a number of possible future developments.

The most important first steps are the models of Alonso (1964-A) and Muth (1969), which are an extension of the work of von Thünen (1826) to the urban context. Alonso and Muth deal with the problem of urban land use in which residential development obviously plays an important part. They describe the spatial equilibrium of the city arising from a competitive market for urban land. In addition, in their definition of spatial structure of residential areas, special emphasis is given to the effects of trade-off between accessibility and space. These models are static and, at equilibrium, produce a spatial structure in which both residential density and land rents decrease monotonically outwards from the city centre. Land development is dense (there is no vacant land) and residential areas are structured in concentric rings characterised by different kinds of housing.

Alongside the models of Alonso and Muth (which are so similar that we shall from now on refer to the Alonso and Muth model) is the model of Herbert and Stevens (1960). This, unlike the Alonso and Muth model, is an operational model, determining residential location through linear programming. It is an extension of Alonso's theory to a policentric market in which households, divided into numerous groups with different tastes and preferences, choose their residential location. Herbert and Stevens' model was further developed by Harris, Nathanson and Rosenburg (1966) and later reinterpreted by Wheaton and Harris (1970).

Other contributions to residential location theory have been made by Wingo (1961), Wheaton (1972) and Mills (1967,

1972) among others. Alongside these we must not forget the more operational models such as those of Lowry (1964), the TOMM model (Time Oriented Metropolitan Model) (Crecine, 1964, 1969-B), the BASS model (Bay Area Simulation Study) (Goldner and Graybeal, 1965, Bay Area Simulation Study, 1968), and the PLUM model (Projected Land Use Model) (Goldner, 1968, Goldner, Rosenthal and Meredith, 1971). What was lacking until the beginning of the seventies was a model capable of bringing together the two different modelling approaches then emerging - the theoretical one and the descriptive operational one. Only the NBER model (National Bureau of Economic Research) (Kain, Ingram and Ginn, 1972) managed to achieve such an integration. This model which has a detailed breakdown both of the demand (households) and the supply (building stock) has been for many years the most important point of reference for the analysis of residential location.

Before we look at more recent models it would be useful to recall the theoretical foundations of the models of Alonso, Muth, Herbert and Stevens. All of these models are based on the theory of micro-economic behaviour. They assume that: (a) there are different kinds of household, each of which is homogenous in relation to the utility functions; (b) each household has a certain level of expected utility and is willing to pay a price for housing in the various zones consistent with its expected utility; and (c) the competition between different kinds of households modifies the levels of expected utility so that all the households are allocated. From this, it is clear they assume the housing market to be in a state of perfect competition, which is of course not realistic. In fact we find situations of disequilibrium in which not all households find their optimal residential location - some remaining below their level of expected utility, others exceeding it. In order to take this into account, Anas (1973) constructed a model of dynamic disequilibrium. This model gives a measure of disequilibrium expressed as a deviation from the global optimal solution of Herbert's and Stevens' model. Anas in fact reinterpreted their model in terms of entropy maximisation. This is similar to what was done by Senior and Wilson (1974-A) as we shall discuss later. What characterises Anas' model and differentiates it from the work mentioned here is his interpretation of the residential choice behaviour of households, justifying it in micro-economic terms and not in terms of entropy. In addition this model is the only one mentioned so far which is not static.

It is interesting to see how, using Alonso's theory as a base, other dynamic models of residential location have evolved. Some of the most important work has been done by Fujita (1976-B), whose first contribution was to give a dynamic version of Alonso's and Muth's and Herbert's and Stevens' models. In the dynamic version of Alonso's and Muth's model, the working of the land-use market was described, and in the dynamic version of Herbert's and Stevens' model this working, in some interpretations, became normative in order to reach an optimal situation. Fujita showed that it is possible to develop a unifying theory capable of including both descriptive and normative aspects of the dynamics of urban land-use. Senior and Wilson (1974-A) introduced entropy to what had until then been a purely neo-classical approach. They use the principle of entropy maximisation to assign a set of households to a set of residences, both sets being broken down into categories. It can be argued that Herbert and Stevens' model is a special case of Senior and Wilson's disaggregate spatial interaction model. A similar approach comes from Los (1978). He too uses entropy models, but the principal innovation is the use of endogenous prices.

The models of residential location described up to now, with the exception of the Bay Area Simulation Study (1968), determine the allocation of households to a housing stock which is given and fixed. In other words, we have dynamic demand but not dynamic supply. We shall see next how the problem of treating the dynamics of demand and supply jointly has been tackled in recent years and how it could be the subject of useful future research.

Another and new approach to residential location analysis came from the introduction of the concept of scarcity (Kornai and Weibull, 1978, Kornai, 1980). This approach grew out of the study of planned economic systems and focused on the analysis of a housing market in conditions of chronic shortage, making use of models based on queuing theory. A dynamic model of the housing market taking into account a dynamic stock as well as a dynamic demand was developed by Snickars (1978). His model, which was certainly inspired by Kornai's and Weibull's work, is deterministic and has exogenously fixed prices.

Finally, an approach to the problem of residential location, developed in parallel to the entropy approach, consists of the analysis of behaviour at micro-level using random utility theory (Lerman, 1975, 1979, McFadden, 1978, de Palma and Ben-Akiva, 1981). The most well-known product of this approach is the multinomial logit model used to describe choice behaviour of a user faced with a set of alternatives. An interesting application was made by de Palma and Ben-Akiva (1981). They construct a dynamic model of residential choice in which the transition rates are given by logit models. One limitation of this model, however, is that the attraction factors, used in the formation of transition rates are assumed to be exogenous and not time dependent. This has been overcome by Leonardi (see his chapter in this book), who makes the factors involved in the evaluation of alternatives on the demand side endogenous (as well as prices) and gives a dynamic version of the evaluation process based on future expectations. In addition he constructs a joint model of residential and labour mobility which produces, even in conditions of equilibrium, a flow structure rather different from the gravitational type.

As previously said, relatively little attention has been paid until now to the interactions between stock and demand dynamics. This could well be a fruitful theme for future research, in particular if a way were found of introducing dynamic stock and dynamic demand jointly within the framework of random utility theory. More specifically, it would be interesting to see if Wilson's dynamic equations for housing stock and Leonardi's dynamic equations for demand, both proposed in this book, could be combined.

2.7 Location and Transport in the Urban System

2.7.1 Introduction

As indicated in the heading to this section we are mainly interested here in the city as a system. The relationship between location and transport in the city (considered as a whole without stressing its internal structure) is dealt with in the next section, 2.8.

Most of what has already been said about transport and location in industry, housing and services pertains also to the urban system, as these subsystems are obviously fundamental components: what holds for each of them individually in general holds for the whole system. We proceed by showing how an urban model can be expressed in terms of mathematical programming (Macgill and Wilson, 1979). The well-known Lowry model will be taken as a reference-model and, from among the various different programming versions, the maximisation of consumer's surplus has been chosen. (Much of the discussion in this book, in fact, refers to the possibility of formulating different equivalent mathematical programming versions for spatial interaction models.)

First of all we must formulate the function to be optimised for the joint processes of residential and service location:

$$\max_{\{T_{ij}, S_{ij}\}} Z = -\frac{1}{\beta_1} \sum_{ij} T_{ij} \ln T_{ij} + \sum_{ij} T_{ij} \left(\frac{\alpha_1}{\beta_1} \ln W_i^{res} - c_{ij}\right) - $$

$$- \frac{1}{\beta_2} \sum_{ij} S_{ji} \ln S_{ij} + \sum_{ij} S_{ij} \left(\frac{\alpha_2}{\beta_2} \ln W_j^{ser} - c_{ij}\right) \tag{2.1}$$

where T_{ij} and S_{ij} are, respectively, the number of journeys to work from i to j and journeys to services from i to j; W_i^{res} and W_j^{ser} are, respectively, the residential and service attractiveness factors; c_{ij} are generalised transport costs; α_1, α_2, β_1, β_2 are Lagrange multipliers. The constraint equations of the two location processes, taking into account their reciprocal interdependence (according to Lowry) are:

$$\sum_j T_{ij} - \gamma_{1i} \sum_j S_{ij} = 0$$

$$\sum_i T_{ij} - \gamma_2 \sum_i S_{ij} = E_j \tag{2.2}$$

where E_i are jobs in the base sector; γ_{1j} and γ_2 are parameters defined according to urban economic base theory (cf Wilson, Coelho, Macgill and Williams, 1981, page 88).

Equations (2.1) and (2.2) provide the mathematical programming version of the Lowry model we are looking for. To this result, we can apply the same equivalence considerations which exist between the version derived from the methods of entropy-maximising, random utility, cost-efficiency, and so on. In addition we can modify the equations to make the attractiveness factors endogenous, as in the Harris and Wilson model (1978) and the static model can be embedded within a dynamic context.

All these extensions, far from being academic exercises, are of considerable interest for two reasons:

(a) The behaviour of individual submodels can be different when inserted in a global model and when they are considered separately because of the feedback which may occur. For example, the model of Lakshmanan and Hansen (1965), a production-constrained spatial interaction model, when introduced into a Lowry model behaves quite differently, as it becomes a model in which the production is in some complex way derived from the output of the model itself (Lombardo and Rabino, 1983-A).

(b) The generalisations themselves can stimulate new thinking on the urban model. We can see how Beaumont (1984), beginning with a mathematical programming version of the Lowry model reformulated in incremental terms (variations in numbers of jobs, housing and services) created a model for the optimisation of urban developments.

2.7.2 From static urban models to dynamic non-linear models

This section focuses on current developments in urban modelling and on the contribution made by certain chapters of this book. The works referred to represent only a small part of the wealth of inventive thought distinguishing this field but allow us to identify the logical thread passing through the history of urban modelling.

The starting point of this analysis is of course the Lowry model (1964). Although soon after its formulation it was considered above all a spatial version of economic base theory and for this reason was also greatly criticised, its fundamental role in urban modelling history is linked to a basic 'message' of the model: the city is a system, made up of a set of different subsystems (associated with certain socio-economic quantities such as population and jobs, plus certain spatial elements) all interacting with each other through spatial and socio-economic interrelationships. In this respect, it can be said that the Lowry model has played in its own field a role similar to that of input-output models in the analysis of economic structures. This is not altogether surprising if we consider that the Lowry model is really a special kind of input-output model (Macgill, 1977-B). This similarity between the Lowry model and normal input-output models is true also for the way in which they deal with both economic and spatial interrelations. Both treat them as being static and linear. That is true at least for Garin's matrix version of the model (1966) which is the one most frequently used. If we look closely at Lowry's original model we find in fact implicit elements of non-linearity, such as those associated with land-use constraints. Anyone who has worked with models of this kind will recall the complications these elements introduce into the resolution of an otherwise simple model.

The reference to the Lowry model recalls another famous model of the late 1960s, the dynamic urban model of Forrester (1969). Without diminishing its many positive qualities and the important role it played in introducing a dynamic view of urban systems we should underline that unlike the Lowry model which has a simple basic form but was capable of progressive and more refined extensions, the Forrester model (using the Dynamo language), attempted somewhat presumptuously to deal in an elementary way with the whole complexity of the urban system (using, for example, numerical tables for complex functions) but did not stimulate refinements of the model itself. In fact, despite its initial success, the Forrester model has had relatively few applications compared with the great number of models originating from the Lowry prototype.

Many of the most important developments of the Lowry model were made by Wilson (1974). These can be divided into three groups, including: (a) a more rigorous foundation of the theoretical aspects of spatial interaction, with the introduction of stochastic elements; (b) a more general treatment of spatial interaction, with the introduction of non-linear elements; (c) a development of the Lowry scheme through disaggregation.

As far as the first group is concerned, we find the use of the entropy-maximising methods according to which the observed interaction is the modal value of a multinomial probability distribution which is almost always discrete, limited by a given set of constraints corresponding to empirical evidence (Shannon and Weaver, 1949). This modal value is calculated using Lagrange multipliers:

$$\max_{\underline{x}} Z = -\sum_i x_i \ln x_1 + \sum_n \sum_i \lambda_n g_n(x_i) \qquad (2.3)$$

where $\underline{x}$ is the probability distribution; λ_n is the Lagrange multiplier associated with the nth constraint; and $g_n(x_i)$ is the nth constraint function.

Apart from the acknowledged importance of a sound theoretical base and the fact that (2.3) is the basis for the construction and calibration of a broad family of spatial interaction models (from the four elementary models to the variously disaggregate models from group (c) above), equation (2.3) has also been the stimulus for other new theoretical interpretations of spatial interaction models. The main characteristic, however, which should be emphasised here is that the underlying theory is developed from probability theory which is certainly more suitable for the analysis of economic and social phenomena than the deterministic (or analogue) approach which was used prior to this. Later we shall come back to the question of the superiority of the stochastic approach to the deterministic approach, observing for the moment simply that Wilson and many successive researchers undoubtedly failed to develop the full potential approach by taking into account only the mean (or mode) of the probability distribution and treating models as if they were deterministic (for example, in the treatment of structural stability problems).

As far as group (b) above is concerned the non-linearity is clearly an improvement on the original model (linearity frequently entails poor approximations, especially as many urban phenomena such as congestion, saturation etc are intrinsically non-linear). It appears in three types of phenomena: (i) that associated with the relationship between flow size and attractiveness factor (eg. economies of scale); (ii) that associated with flow constraints (eg. the family of models with different constraints at the origin and at the destination); and (iii) that where the attractiveness factor is in some way related to the flows arriving at the zone (a subset of the first type above). The most interesting is this last, described in the Harris and Wilson model (1978):

$$T_{ij} = A_i O_i D_j^{\alpha} f(c_{ij}) \text{ with } D_j = k_j \sum_i T_{ij} \qquad (2.4)$$

where T_{ij} are flows from i to j; O_i is the constrained origin; A_i is a normalising factor; D_j is the attractiveness term (a function of T_{ij}); $f(c_{ij})$ is the impedance of distance; and α and k_j are parameters.

It can be shown for certain values of the parameters that this model has multiple solutions, the number of which is also related to changes in parameters. This multiplicity of solutions, which reflects the multi-modality of the function (2.3), is one of the most notable characteristics of non-linearity. It means that the function (2.3) is not strictly concave within its domain of definition, and it poses serious problems for model resolution (Phiri, 1980). Its relevance is associated with the fact that it introduces differential topology into modelling (concerning the structural stability of systems and processes of the catastrophe type). This, as well as being of theoretical interest, is very important in planning (Wilson, 1981-A).

As far as the models in group (c) are concerned we should point out that the process of disaggregation, besides allowing a more detailed analysis of the urban system, is a process strictly associated with the entropy concept according to which each stage of disaggregation, corresponds to the introduction of new constraints in (2.3).

A further stage of development involved the passage from static non-linear models to dynamic non-linear models - the model formulated by the Brussels school (Allen et al, 1978). The innovative feature of this model was not simply the fact that it was dynamic (after all, many post-Lowry models were dynamic, see, for example, the TOMM model, Crecine, 1964), but that it was also non-linear. In this model the activities, which are the same as those used in the Lowry model, evolve in time according to a non-linear logistic growth dynamic:

$$x_i = \varepsilon_i[D_i - x_i]x_i \qquad (2.5)$$

where x_i is the activity x in zone i; D_i is the carrying capacity for activity x in zone i; and ε_i is a proportionality factor. The carrying capacity for an activity in a given zone is defined as a function of the values of the other activities in the other zones according to economic and spatial relations of the Lowry type. There is a close relationship between this model and the Lotka-Volterra model (Volterra, 1927) of the growth of different interacting animal populations.

An important aspect of this model is that in the processes of spatial differentiation, that is the occurrence of different possible urban spatial patterns (associated with catastrophic processes deriving from non-linearity), stochastic elements are considered. It is the random fluctuations of the system which, in proximity to the bifurcation points (in the evolution of the system itself), determine the path that will be followed.

Wilson was responsible for another important contribution to the development of dynamic non-linear models. This is the embedding in a dynamic context of the model of Harris and Wilson previously mentioned. Model (2.4) is considered the equilibrium state of a system which tends to move towards this state with a speed proportional to the distance from equilibrium:

$$\dot{D}_j = \varepsilon[\sum_i T_{ij} - k_j D_j]D_j^n \tag{2.6}$$

where n may take different values such as -1, 0, 1, 2, ... Model (2.6) is, like the preceding one, a logistic growth model of interacting populations and the function (2.3) from which it is derived plays in this case the role of 'potential' function of the system whose gradient determines the dynamic ($\dot{D}_j = \partial Z/\partial D_j$). It is important to note that an economic interpretation can be given to the dynamic process which arises from the disequilibrium between demand $\sum_i T_{ij}$ and supply $k_j D_j$.

Wilson in this book investigates the potential of this kind of dynamic approach very fully, suggesting ways of achieving a more refined analysis of the demand and, in particular the supply side and a more extensive application to a number of subsystems as well as to the urban systems as a whole. One of these suggestions, of particular interest here, is the application of a model like (2.6) to the transport system, as discussed in Wilson (1983).

A totally different approach is offered by the model of Leonardi and Campisi (1981), even though like Wilson's model it uses micro-economic aspects of spatial interaction, or more precisely random utility theory. They obtain the following expression for the transition rates (which are non-linear and non-constant) between different zones of a spatial system:

$$r_{ij}(t) = \lambda[Q_j - P_j(t)]f_{ij}e^{-\beta[V_j(t) - V_i(t)]} \qquad (2.7)$$

where r_{ij} is the transition rate from i to j; Q_j is the carrying capacity of zone j; P_j is the population of zone j; V_i is a measure of the utility of staying in zone i; f_{ij} is an impedance function of distance; and λ and β are parameters. Associated with (2.7), the following conservation equation gives the levels of $P_j(t)$ in the various zones:

$$\dot{P}_j(t) = \sum_i P_i(t)r_{ij} - P_j(t)\sum_i r_{ji} \qquad (2.8)$$

The non-linearity of (2.7) derives from the term V_i associated with utilities, which are complex functions of the populations P_i and, given (2.8) also of the rates r_{ij}, through the differential equations of the type:

$$\alpha V_i - \dot{V}_i = a_i + \frac{\lambda}{\beta}(\phi_i - \psi_i) \qquad (2.9)$$

where ϕ_i is the total accessibility in i at $(Q_j - P_j)$; ψ_i is the potential of the population in i; and α and a_i are constants.

Leonardi in this book explores all the aspects of the model described above from its derivation (from random utility theory) and 'catastrophic' characteristics (stability, bifurcation, etc) to its application to residential mobility (and to joint-residential mobility) also discussing its possible further developments. One development of particular interest is the relaxation of the assumption that the carrying capacities Q_j are constant and the modelling of their evolution. Some indications on how to proceed are contained in the IIASA Research Programme on 'Nested Urban Dynamics' (Johansson et al, 1983), an important research project with the aim of developing urban modelling, both theoretically and experimentally, exploring many of the aspects which in this section are considered important for future progress.

The above problem of carrying capacities is interesting and stimulating as it involves the study of interaction between dynamic processes with different speeds of change (eg. the dynamics of stocks, i.e. of carrying capacities, and the dynamics of activities). In this respect the models of Wilson and Leonardi represent two extreme cases. Wilson's model considers local dynamics (eg. stock dynamics) interacting through static spatial interaction models which are the equilibrium solution of a dynamic process (eg. activity dynamics) which is so fast that the equilibrium assumption is reasonable. Leonardi's model takes the dynamics of flows (eg. activity dynamics) occurring in constant 'compartments', which represent the state of a dynamic at a given moment (eg. the stock dynamic) which is so slow that it is reasonable to assume it is constant. Thus the study of dynamic processes of different speeds can also be seen as the problem of the integration of these two models.

Leonardi's model in particular can be considered a recent evolution from the multi-state models of population (Rogers, 1975), a particular kind of compartmental model. These models originating from the model of Leslie (1945) (with constant transition rates) have gradually become more complicated, first with systematic disaggregation (multi-regional and multi-state models) then with the introduction of non-linearity (Ledent, 1978, Okabe, 1979, Sheppard, 1983-E). Even though Leonardi's model is basically conceived in probabilistic terms this aspect is not fully developed in its treatment. This is also true for the other models discussed above. A more complete stochastic treatment is found in the model of Weidlich and Haag (1983), where the differential equations are expressed in terms of probability distributions of different states (even though only the mean value of the distributions are then treated analytically). The model is also a multi-state model in which the transitions are determined from the non-linear interaction of the populations in different states. An even more complete stochastic treatment is found in the model of Sikdar and Karmeshu (1982). This is a compartmental, multi-regional demographic, urban model with non-constant linear rates of transition, derived from the Okabe model (1979) referred to previously. An equally complex treatment is in the Monaco and Rabino model (1984) of interacting populations with constant non-linear rates of transition. Both of the models consider not only the mean but also other moments in the stochastic process.

All the above argument points to stochastic analysis as being one of the most promising aspects of research on urban models. Certain progress has already been made but much remains to be done. De Palma and Lefèvre (chapter in this book) provide a broad theoretical contribution on the state-of-the-art of compartmental systems (both deterministic and stochastic approaches) also describing the theorems of Lehoczky (1980) and Kurtz (1978) which define the conditions for which the results obtained from the deterministic approach continue to hold even in a stochastic context.

2.8 Urban Form and Transport

2.8.1 Introduction

A common element running through the preceding analyses, though not explicitly highlighted, concerns the effects which interrelationships between the location of socio-economic activities and transport have on the structure of urban space. More exactly it concerns the way in which location behaviour of socio-economic activities determines the urban form as a function of a given transport network and how, in its turn, the transport network is structured as a function of a certain pattern of socio-economic activities (i.e. as a function of the urban form). In this section the analysis is therefore carried out at a more general level, looking in particular at the relationships which exist at an aggregated level between urban patterns and transport. (The terms 'spatial structure' and 'urban form' are used interchangeably in the present discussion.)

2.8.2 Spatial structure and transport: state-of-the-art

There have been two completely different approaches to this subject. One is an economic approach, the well-known 'New Urban Economics' (Mills and Mackinnon, 1973), and the other, which could be called a functionalist approach, is based on spatial interaction models (Wilson, 1974).

New Urban Economics Approach

We define as New Urban Economics (NUE) any systematic theoretical explanation of urban spatial structure based on neo-classic economic principles, which describes the structure of urban space as a result of a market process. The precursors to NUE were two theoretical paradigms - von Thünen's theory of rent (von Thünen, 1826) and Lösch's central place theory (Lösch, 1940). Other authors who can be considered precursors of NUE include those from the Chicago school (Park, Burgess and McKenzie, 1925, Hoyt, 1939, Harris and Ullman, 1945) and certain other urban economists (Hurd, 1903, Haig, 1926, Ratcliff, 1949). In the development of NUE we can distinguish two modelling phases (cf Anas and Dendrinos, 1976).

The first phase, which occurred mainly in the sixties, saw the extension of von Thünen's model to the urban context. Fundamental contributions were made by Beckmann (1957-A, 1969), Alonso (1960, 1964-A), Muth (1961, 1969) and Wingo (1961). There has been a vast amount written on NUE but for reasons of space we have limited our references to those which are felt to be fundamental. For a more complete review, see Richardson (1971, 1977-B), Mills, Mackinnon (1973), Anas and Dendrinos (1976).

A common characteristic of these works is the use of a utility-maximising approach through which the individual's choice of location and decision on the amount of urban land to be consumed are examined. The underlying hypotheses of this approach can be summarised as follows: (a) the city has a single centre, the central business district (CBD), in which all the productive activities are concentrated, and an external ring in which all the residents are located. Space is considered uniform, i.e. homogeneous and isotropic; (b) perfect competition exists between individuals, whose behaviour is rational and based on perfect knowledge of the market. In addition, at equilibrium, demand is always satisfied and supply completely consumed.

The approach assumes that individuals maximise the utility associated with the goods and services to be consumed, subject to the condition that their level of consumption is limited by a given available income. In general utility is defined on the basis of: (a) the quantity of consumption goods produced in the city (in the CBD) and available in location d; (b) the residential services offered in location d by housing suppliers; (c) unit prices, of consumption goods (which do not vary spatially) and residential services respectively in location d; (d) transport costs associated with location d (which constitute a negative component of utility). In general in the first phase NUE models it is assumed that transport costs increase more slowly than (or at the same speed as) distance (the elasticity of transport costs in relation to distance is less than or equal to 1). This hypothesis is necessary in order to arrive at the results on price structure and density. The relaxation of this hypothesis and its consequent implications on urban form are discussed by Papageorgiou (1985).

For the individual, maximising utility means, first of all, determining his or her optimum residential location (in terms of distance from the CBD) given transport costs and housing prices (which constitute the spatial problem) and then, at the optimum location, selecting the optimum set of goods and services which can be consumed given total available income. If h(d) are the residential services (housing) in a location d and p(d) are the relative prices, the condition that expresses the equilibrium location of the consumer is:

$$\frac{h(d)\partial p(d)}{\partial d} = -p_e(d)t \qquad (2.10)$$

where $p_e(d)$ is the monetised value of the marginal utility of leisure time (or, in other words, the opportunity cost of travel time) and t is the travel time. (2.10) describes the trade-off relationships which must exist between housing prices (rents) and distance (transport costs) so that the consumer is in equilibrium and his location is optimum. From this equation we find that $\partial p(d)/\partial d < 0$, i.e. that a reduction in residential prices (rents) is necessary to compensate the increase in travel costs as distance from the CBD increases.

For a stable equilibrium in the city, all individuals, if characterised by the same income and same preferences, must have the same level of utility in the different locations. Thus the rent gradient $(\partial p(d)/\partial d)$ will have a monotonically decreasing curve, as shown in Figure 2.1. To determine the rent gradient see the figure in which the curve has been traced between d_0 (radius of CBD) and d_1 (the radius of the city). As the cost of housing in d_1, $p(d_1)$ is known, being equal to the cost of production of housing on agricultural land, and all individuals have the same utility, the value $U(d_1)$ can be determined and defines the level of utility in the whole city.

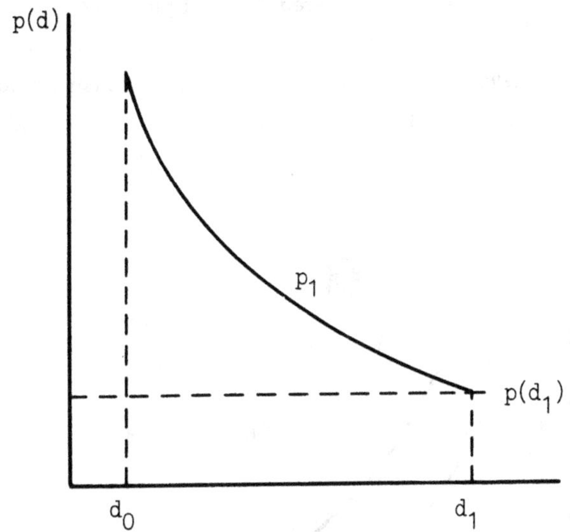

Figure 2.1: Rent gradient for consumers with identical income

For any location of d_i it is, therefore, possible to determine the value of $p(d_i)$ as U and the associated cost of transport are known.

In addition, since p(d) decreases as distance increases and utility remains constant as prices and locations vary, housing consumption, h(d), increases with distance ($\partial h(d)/\partial p(d) > 0$). In order to have spatial equilibrium in the whole city the above results must be valid for all radii from the CBD. That is, at a given distance from the CBD, residential prices must be equal.

From the above analysis we obtain a result which is fundamental to the NUE approach: that given the assumptions of uniformity, homogeneity and isotropy of space, the urban form will be circular. This holds even in the case where individuals are not identical for reasons of taste, preference or income. In this case, the bid-rent (bid-rent functions) of different consumers are considered (see Figure 2.2). The curves (F_1, F_2, F_3) represent the hypothetical price, which for a certain level of utility (U_1, U_2, U_3) a consumer would be willing to pay in different locations so as to be indifferent about these locations.

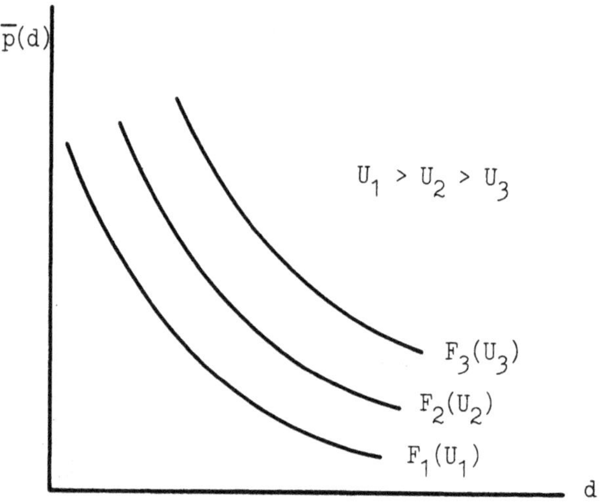

Figure 2.2: Bid-rent functions for consumers with non-identical incomes

(An interesting expression of the bid-rent function for individuals with identical tastes and preferences, where a relationship of inverse proportionality emerges between utility and bid-price is described by Beckmann in this book.)

In general the bid-rent curve or, more specifically, the gradient of this curve changes as the income of consumers varies (i.e. $h(u)$ and $p_e(u)$ change with income). If, for example, we assume that the quantity of residential services consumed, h(d) increases with respect to the marginal value of leisure time $p_e(d)$ as income increases, we find that the inclination of the bid-price curve increases (i.e. the gradient becomes less steep) (cf Figure 2.3).

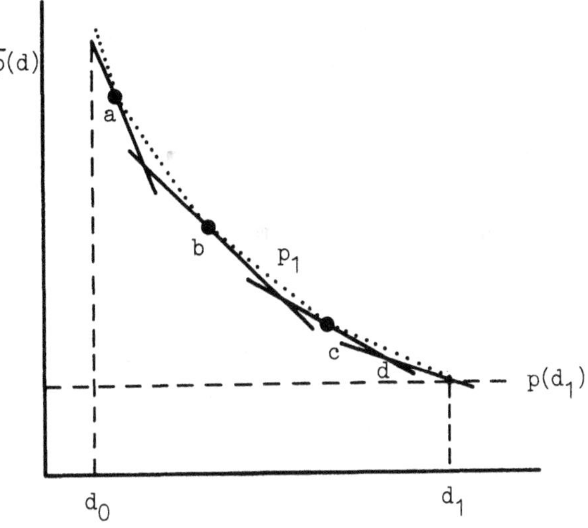

Figure 2.3: Bid-rent curves and gradient of equilibrium prices

The curve of equilibrium prices P_1 (market prices), which defines the spatial equilibrium pattern of the city, is obtained by 'enveloping' the bid-rent curves (a, b, c, d) of the different individuals. Along these curves of course consumers are in locations which maximise their utility.

Some general conclusions reached through this approach are: (a) land rents and density decrease monotonically from the city centre outwards; (b) no portion of the land within the city is left undeveloped; (c) land uses are structured in concentric rings around the city centre determined by the intensity of land-use (residential density, capital intensity per unit of land) which decreases monotonically outwards from the city centre. Hence, two different land-uses cannot be found at the same distance from the centre.

These conclusions, which are common to all first phase NUE studies, constitute axiomatic characteristics which define the overall spatial configuration of the city and hence its form. From the methodological point of view, the essential characteristic of NUE models, and in particular those of the first phase, is the static nature of the approach. It is assumed that the equilibrium configuration of the city (derived from the bid-rent mechanism) does not depend on past configurations nor on expectations of possible future forms and that, in addition, market land prices do not influence in determining that form.

To further clarify the static nature of this approach it may be useful to mention three different definitions of the city derived from the above assumptions (Fujita, 1983): (a) the instant city: the whole city is constructed at a given moment in time and subsequently is not subject to any change; (b) the malleable city: the adjustment costs of the land-use pattern (i.e. building costs and other urban infrastructure costs) are nil, so that at each time interval the urban spatial structure coincides with the static equilibrium spatial structure at that time; (c) the long-run equilibrium city: while recognising the fact that in the short-run the land-use pattern in an urban area is rigid, it is assumed that in the long-term the spatial structure of the city coincides (or almost coincides) with that predicted by the static model.

A final aspect of these models is the use, except in a few cases (eg. Herbert and Stevens' model, 1960) of a continuous spatial representation. This is connected with the basic hypotheses, especially the assumption of uniformity of space and the possibility of the use of standard mathematical tools already widely employed in economic analysis.

The second phase of development of NUE which began at the end of the sixties is characterised by the efforts to introduce a greater degree of realism into the analysis of the city's spatial structure. It was recognised that the axioms used gave an excessively simplified and largely unrealistic view of the city. In fact the spatial structure cannot be reduced in such a simple way to a monocentric and circular form but tends in fact to spread in an 'oil spot' fashion and have an irregular outline. The land rents and densities often increase in proximity to certain centres in the urban space as there are poles of concentration of population and activities. Lastly, at a given distance from the city centre it is likely that a mixture of land-uses will be found. Thus it is obvious that the structuring of urban space results from factors and mechanisms far more complex than those so far considered in the analysis. It emerges above all that urban structure is the result of the interacting behaviour of a number of actors (households, manufacturers, public bodies, etc). These interactions take place in a non-uniform space, the differentiations of which are to a certain extent both determined by and the cause of the interactions themselves.

The principal new elements of the second phase can be summarised as follows. First, the greater attention paid to the existence of externalities in urban space: the formation and effects of externalities are recognised as playing a determining role in the spatial structure of the city (cf Papageorgiou, 1983, for a review). For example, it is made clear that the presence of spatial differentiations in an urban area such as poles and environmental quality can create effects of agglomeration or increase in utility and thereby generate increasing rent functions. (For an analysis of the polycentric city see Casetti and Papageorgiou, 1971, Papageorgiou, 1974, 1976-B, and for an analysis of environmental effects see Papageorgiou, 1976-B, 1985.) The existence of economies of scale and externalities can induce firms and individuals to concentrate in particular zones of the urban space until the effects of congestion, which eventually occur, nullify the advantages produced by concentration (cf Lave, 1970, Mirlees, 1972, Dixit, 1973). It is the analysis of congestion which is of particular interest in this phase of development. From the acknowledged fact that congestion makes the city more compact, limiting its spatial extension (Strotz, 1965) later studies (eg. Mills and de Ferranti, 1971, Solow and Vickrey, 1971, Solow, 1972) come to the conclusion that land area destined for the transport infrastructure and the level of congestion are decreasing functions (linear or concave) of the distance from the city centre.

Secondly, efforts are made to introduce the time dimension more explicitly. Even though these efforts have been channelled principally into comparative statics approaches, the main aim of which were to analyse the effects that changes in income, population and transport costs produce on urban spatial equilibrium (and, in particular, bid-rent curves), it was stimulated by the recognition that the city is by nature dynamic.

We can distinguish two kinds of approach to the analysis of the dynamics of the spatial structure of the city (cf Miyao, 1981) which are however closely interconnected. They are: (i) the analysis of the stability of the equilibrium of a static spatial configuration (stability analysis) and (ii) the analysis of the evolution of the spatial configuration (growth analysis). Interesting examples of these two types of approach are given by Papageorgiou (1985), even though as far as the second type is concerned he seems to be relatively entrenched in the comparative statics approach. Arguing that at an aggregate level the urban spatial structure can be considered to be in a state of dynamic equilibrium, Papageorgiou examines how urban form is determined and evolves in time. More precisely, he examines the variation of dimension (population and utility) and the form of the city (land values, quantity of land consumed and density) relative to changes in income, technological level, agricultural land prices and interaction costs in the urban area. It is therefore (like Beckmann's contribution in this book) a general analysis of equilibrium, in which the aim is to find out to what extent variations in the socio-economic structure of the city influence the form of the urban space and vice versa. In this respect Papageorgiou's work belongs indisputably to the second phase of development of NUE to which it provides a very valuable contribution.

Even in this second phase the dynamic analysis of urban spatial structure appears relatively little developed, due above all to the difficulty of introducing both time and space into a continuous model as it involves an operation of simultaneous integration (cf Pines, 1976). One way of resolving this problem is to introduce discontinuities into the continuous model like those which characterise the discrete model. Three types of model are therefore possible (cf Richardson, 1977-B): (a) models discrete in terms of space and time (for example, Herbert and Stevens, 1960, Ripper and Varaiya, 1974); (b) models which are continuous in space but discrete in time (for example, Pines, 1976, Anas, 1976); (c) models which are continuous in time but discrete in space (for example, Hochman and Pines, 1973).

A last approach is to develop non-spatial models of urban growth (eg. for the residential sector), which can provide useful elements nevertheless for the analysis of evolution of land-use patterns over time (for example: Evans, 1975, Muth, 1976).

Although a truly dynamic model of urban spatial structure is yet to be developed, the studies referred to above represent some first and promising steps in that direction. Further advances, although not yet sufficiently consolidated nor completely operational (in that they are not ready for immediate empirical testing) can be found in Papageorgiou (1980, 1985), Miyao (1981) and Fujita (1983).

The Functionalist Approach

Unlike the economic approach, the *functionalist approach* - as the spatial interaction approach has been called - draws its concepts from the observation of empirical regularities which manifest themselves in the form of spatial interdependencies in the distribution of socio-economic activities in urban space. These interdependencies appear in the intensity of flows of goods and people between the various activity locations - the flows being more intense when the generation (attraction) capacity of activities is greater (due, for example, to a larger land area occupied) and the distance between locations is less. Unlike the NUE approach where there is a direct relationship between the mechanism of distribution of goods and people in urban space and the resulting structure of that space, in the spatial interaction approach this relationship is less immediate and not so axiomatic. Urban form is seen as the result of a set of interactions of goods and people occurring in an urban space which is not conditioned or predetermined by any hypothesis, but which is essentially a function of the interdependence observable in the spatial distribution of activities (and hence the use of the term functionalist). Thus, given the structure of interactions in an urban area, one can draw a 'map' of the accessibilities (or potentials) of that area which can be interpreted as a representation of its spatial structure.

From Reilly (1931) to Hansen (1959), Lowry (1964) and Wilson (1970-A, 1971-A, 1974), to mention only some of the most outstanding contributions, the spatial interaction approach has been widely applied in urban and regional studies, not so much for the analysis of spatial structure but for the location of activities.

The theoretical and methodological refinements, in particular the introduction of entropy-maximisation (Wilson, 1970-A) and the use of various forms of utility-maximising models (Williams, 1977-A) in the seventies, gave new potential for the explanation of urban form, making it possible for not only spatial but also economic interactions to be described. The relationship between the entropy version and the economic version (in particular the random utility version) will be explored in Chapter 10. We are thinking here, for example, of the improvements made in the formulation of terms for expressing potential and accessibility (Williams and Senior, 1978, Leonardi, 1979-B, Wilson in this book).

From the point of view of the analytical formulation, two well-known features characterise the spatial interaction model. The first is flexibility: the relative ease with which one can go from simple to more complex formulations, by disaggregating for example the variables of the model by household type, housing type, means of transport etc (Wilson, 1974), by incorporating more complex attraction terms (see the retail services model of Harris and Wilson, 1978) or principles of individual economic behaviour (Coelho and Williams, 1978, Coelho, 1979), by integrating several spatial interaction models of subsystems in a general urban model (Lowry, 1964, Wilson, 1974 and in this book) or by integrating different transport models in a system of integrated transport models (Wilson, 1974, Wilson et al, 1981), all make it possible to analyse specific problems such as the 'efficiency' of the spatial structure from the energy point of view. Beaumont (1984) for example, points out that the calculation of the energy efficiency of a spatial structure should be an integral part of the definition of land-uses and the overall journey patterns and not an ex-post operation made after the model has been run or simply based on transport costs minimisation, as is generally done in energy studies. In this respect the problems which must be taken into account are: (i) the treatment of the problem at the micro-level, implying the consideration of the individual's decision process (see, the mathematical programming version of Lowry's model, by Coelho and Williams, 1978); (ii) the explicit consideration of the existing infrastructure (cf Beaumont and Keys, 1982, and again Coelho and Williams' model, 1978); (iii) the inclusion of variables in the analysis of energy efficiency other than those relating to journeys (i.e. consideration of variables which take account of the in-place energy consumption of the different activities, cf Beaumont and Keys, 1981); (iv) the use of a dynamic approach.

Secondly, there is ease of operation: the fact that the spatial interaction model is relatively simple to apply (probably easier than the typical economic model) makes it a useful aid to planning. For a discussion of this point see Batty, 1979-B, Webber, 1981-B, and Wilson, in this book.

The introduction of the time dimension into the functionalist approach (Wilson, 1976-A) occurred more or less at the same time that a dynamic version of the NUE model was being experimented with, around the second half of the seventies. Mathematical techniques belonging to system dynamics, especially catastrophe theory (Thom, 1972) and bifurcation theory (Jordan and Smith, 1977), showed themselves to be fundamental tools for this kind of analysis. For a review of these see Beaumont, Clarke and Wilson (1981-A), Wilson (1981-A, 1981-D) and Beaumont (1982). Beaumont (1984) suggests that Q-analysis (Atkin, 1974, 1981) which is a special technique for the dynamic analysis of structural interrelationships, can be a useful tool for describing the evolution of the relationship between behaviour and structure of a system. He shows how, by developing the existing connections between bifurcation theory based on differential topology and Q-analysis based on algebraic topology it is possible to achieve a better description of structural changes in a dynamic system. Compared with NUE models, dynamic spatial interaction models (even if they are partial) are relatively easy to operate and have probably been applied more widely especially in simulation experiments (for example, Wilson and Clarke, 1979, Lombardo and Rabino, 1983-A). As already mentioned, Wilson's chapter in this book is particularly relevant to dynamic analysis, showing how by introducing supply and competition between demand and supply in a simple spatial interaction model, the system can produce different and unexpected behaviour (eg. multiple equilibrium solutions, oscillations, instability etc) even for very small variations in the parameters. His chapter therefore contains all the basic elements for the analysis of dynamic processes in the structuring of urban space, although many of these elements incorporate concepts and mechanisms belonging to the economic approach.

2.8.3 Conclusions

New Urban Economics and spatial interaction models constitute two alternative but complementary approaches for the analysis of the relationships of transport and urban form especially at an aggregate level. We have tried above to highlight the essential theoretical and methodological features of the two approaches making reference to the contributions in this book which are relevant to the subject. We now discuss directions in which research could proceed in the future and where we feel there lies undeveloped potential. First of all we deal with theory and methodology and then briefly mention some operational aspects.

Any advance in theory and methodology of the analysis and interpretation of a phenomenon will be rooted in the existing and already consolidated body of studies. We therefore look first at possible developments of the two main approaches above, and then at developments which may ensue from their integration with approaches from outside the immediate field.

The following six aspects of the NUE and functionalist approaches seem to offer scope for useful future research. First, consider the analysis of externalities. As we have seen previously, the phenomenon of externalities in the urban area is one of the questions most widely discussed at present, especially in New Urban Economics. Although a considerable number of theoretical and applied studies exist on the effects of externalities (cf Papageorgiou, 1983) there is still a need for an analysis of the processes of their formation, in particular of externalities deriving from agglomeration processes. We argue that the NUE approach provides the fundamental conceptual apparatus. As the formation of externalities is closely connected with the growth of urban structure, an explanatory theory of the formation of externalities requires the explicit consideration of the time dimension and therefore involves the analysis of the dynamics of spatial structure. The work of Miyao and Shapiro (1979), Kanemoto (1980-A, 1980-B), Miyao, Shapiro and Knapp (1980) and Miyao (1981) are particularly promising in this respect.

Secondly, consider partial versus global analysis. Full comprehension of the relationship between urban form and transport requires a global approach which takes account of all the components and interactions in the system. However, most existing studies, both economic and functionalist, are partial analyses which concentrate in general on the analysis of the interactions between two subsystems at most (usually transport and one other). There are many comprehensive studies which although still cumbersome and not as systematic as models are nevertheless promising for future development. In this respect the descriptive function of urban morphology obtained by Papageorgiou (1985, equation 30) and the formulation of comprehensive or integrated models of the urban system by Wilson (in this book) and Nakamura, Hayashi and Miyamoto (1983) deserve mention. In most existing formulations, the relationship between transport and urban form has been explored unidirectionally. In general, they concentrate on the analysis of the implications of transport facilities (measured in terms of distance, travel costs, travel times etc which are given exogenously) on spatial organisation, or else the analysis of the effects on the transport structure of a given spatial form (measured in terms of jobs, population etc also given exogenously). Thus an important improvement could be obtained by refining the modelling of these interrelationships. This would mean a close integration of transport submodels with other submodels (in both partial and global analysis), by making the determination of travel costs endogenous and introducing the supply side into the transport system, as suggested by Wilson (1983), or (for a given transport cost function) as illustrated by Puu (1979-B).

Thirdly, we turn to dynamic analysis. The need for a dynamic approach in the analysis of urban form has already emerged many times in the course of this discussion and clearly constitutes one of the priorities for future research. A dynamic analysis is fundamental in order: (i) to give a full interpretation of socio-economic processes which over time have produced a given spatial structure; (ii) to provide elements for the evaluation of the efficiency of those processes; (iii) to suggest ways and means of controlling them; (iv) to delineate possible future configurations of the spatial structure and the various directions of development which are likely to produce those configurations. Although dynamic models are a relatively recent development in this field, a certain number of studies have already reached a relatively advanced level (cf Papageorgiou, 1980, 1985, Wilson 1981-A and in this book). Of the NUE type studies, the work of Anas (1978-A), Mills (1981), Miyao (1981), Wheaton (1982) and in particular Fujita (1976-B), Dendrinos (1981-A) and Fujita (1983) are excellent starting points. For example Fujita (1976-B) presents a dynamic version of Alonso's model and Fujita (1983) shows how the dynamic modelling of future land-use price expectations, can justify the existence of high land prices on the outskirts of the city and help to explain the 'oil spot' effect. Dendrinos (1981-A) uses structural stability analysis (Thom, 1972, Zeeman, 1977) to examine from the qualitative point of view the dynamic processes which determine the evolution of the urban form. Among the functionalist studies the various works of Wilson (1978-C, 1981-A, 1983 and his contribution to this book) highlight a number of topics on which future research efforts could well be focused. The most important are the following: (i) the introduction of supply, and suggestions on how it can be modelled dynamically in particular in single-constrained spatial interaction models; (ii) a methodological framework for the building of dynamic comprehensive models of the urban system; (iii) suggestions for the use of the dynamic approach for exploring the formation of new spatial configurations leading towards a study of morphogenesis of the spatial structure (see the fourth point below). With respect to the implications of the energy crisis on the organisation of the human environment (Beaumont and Keys, 1982) dynamic analysis offers great potential for the determination of an energy-efficient spatial structure and the evaluation of the impact of alternative energy policies (Beaumont, 1984). As already mentioned above, important stimuli for the analysis of the relationship between urban form and transport have come also from other disciplines. In the field of urban and regional science the use of models taken directly or indirectly by analogy from other branches of the physical and human sciences has been fairly common and has often contributed considerably to progress in theory and methodology. Recently systems approaches from biology, ecology, chemistry and economics in particular have been applied successfully to socio-economic and spatial systems. We therefore add to the three points above a further two containing the elements from these other disciplines which appear to offer the most positive stimulus to further progress.

Fourthly, therefore, we pursue other disciplines. From biology, ecology and chemistry the most important contribution seems to be the dynamic aspect of systems analysis (see Wilson, 1981-A, Beaumont, 1982, for a review). There have been interesting biological studies on the evolution of highly complex systems and on the evolutionary behaviour of organisms and systems in interaction with their environment (cf Maynard Smith, 1978, Mayr, 1978). In the field of ecology interesting work has been done on competition between species (cf May, 1978, and for a review Jørgensen, 1983). Some applications of ecological concepts to urban analysis can be found in Dendrinos and Mullally (1981-A) in which Lotka-Volterra's prey-predator model is applied to population growth in some North American cities, and in Wilson (1981-A) where a spatially disaggregated version of the above model is presented. Although the full implications of the application of this kind of approach to spatial structure have still to be assessed, it is clear that the analysis of human behaviour in space can be of help in understanding the spatial structure which derives from it. The work of Prigogine and his school in the field of chemistry (cf Nicolis and Prigogine, 1977) on the evolution of dissipative structures offer new ideas on how interdependence of variables may result in the self-organisation of the system itself, where new structures and organisation can be generated or destroyed as the system evolves. The application of these concepts to the analysis of spatial evolution and in particular urban growth can help to explain and predict, above all from a topological point of view, the appearance of new nuclei (and disappearance of old nuclei) for example and can therefore be useful in exploring the formation of new spatial configurations (Allen et al, 1978, Allen and Sanglier, 1979-A, 1981-B). With reference to compartmental models, de Palma and Lefèvre (chapter in this book) present a survey of the most recent developments and the possibility of application to urban and regional science of dynamic approaches formulated in other scientific disciplines.

Fifthly, consider alternative economic approaches. Recently some new theoretical and methodological developments have been made by neo-Marxian economists offering interesting alternatives to the more traditional neo-classic approaches to spatial problems. Whereas in the past Marxian analysis mostly consisted of an interpretation of spatial problems couched in Marxist terms and strongly influenced by ideology, an effort has been made in the last ten years to produce a more general interpretation which is more consistent with spatial analysis (cf Lefebvre, 1972, Castells, 1973, Harvey, 1973-A, Shoukry and Scott, 1981). This effort has concentrated recently on the development of a theory of production and accumulation (containing elements of Marxian, Ricardian and Keynesian thought), which comes in answer to the criticism that the neo-classical production function was inconsistent when a disaggregate formulation was considered (Sheppard, in this book). The approach, which is based on the model of Sraffa (1960), has already been applied in geography in the works of Scott (1976) who shows the interrelationship which exists between Sraffa's model of the production process and von Thünen's rent model and the possibility of their integration. Scott (1978) also analyses the impact of investment in transport on profit, salary and rent distribution in an urban area and later (Scott, 1980) presents an application of this approach to urbanisation and planning processes. The article by Sheppard in this book in which he proposes a spatial extension of Sraffa's model (the Morishima version, 1973) using the theory of geographical potentials is particularly promising in this connection. Although his approach has been developed at a macro (regional) scale, it could be extended to the urban scale, introducing the consideration of stock (disaggregating capital) and the mechanism of formation of urban rents. This approach offers new potential for explaining the structure of economic interactions in the city and the resulting spatial implications in more realistic terms. In addition the social dimension underlying this approach constitutes a new point of view from which to tackle the problem of externalities.

Sixthly, and finally, we turn to operational aspects. In contrast to the considerable amount of effort made to develop the theoretical aspects of analysis of the relationships between transport and spatial structure the problem of the practical application of the models produced has been relatively neglected. It is obviously desirable that the functional relations that describe these relationships should be not only recognised but also quantified. It emerges that the New Urban Economics models, although providing a sound conceptual base for defining the relationships are particularly difficult to operate when it comes to experimental verification. The spatial interaction models on the other hand have proved to be rather more easily converted into operative tools and more easily used in planning. This results from the nature of the two approaches - more markedly orientated towards theory and methodology in the NUE studies, more orientated towards experimentation in the spatial interaction models - and the characteristics of the analytical formulation - in continuum in NUE models and in discrete form in spatial interaction models. Greater difficulty in quantifying variables has been encountered by the NUE models, and has led to the use of simplifying but unrealistic assumptions. However there seems to have been a recent tendency for NUE models to adopt forms which can be more easily tested empirically (see, for example Papageorgiou, 1985 and Fujita, 1982-B) and for functionalist models to incorporate economic principles of behaviour (cf Coelho and Wilson, 1976, Wilson, 1981-A, Lesse, 1982, Wilson in this book). How feasible the complete integration of the two approaches would be is difficult to say.

There remain many theoretical problems still to solve (for example that of interaction between micro- and macro-level, or that of the aggregation of individual behaviour). What is clear, however, is that in both approaches, there are important advances to make both in the theory and methodology as suggested above in points one to four and in the practical application of models. It is to be hoped that feedback from application to theory will help to refine the conceptual aspects and may eventually contribute to such an integration, or at least the development of a more rigorous theoretical base and more operational models.

2.9 The Most Promising Directions for Future Research

In this final section we look at the emerging areas of research which we feel deserve to be given a certain priority and on which efforts need to be concentrated in the future if significant progress is to be made. These areas, all relating of course to the whole variety of aspects of location-transport systems, are the following: (a) the analysis of dynamic structure; (b) the evaluation and testing of performance; (c) the relationship between individual and collective behaviour. We will briefly examine each of these aspects considering the need for: (i) an identification of the problems (in the light of the current state-of-the-art) and establishment of a general framework for the study programme; (ii) the developments necessary in methodology; (iii) the organisation of the research programme. The three main areas are taken in turn.

The analysis of dynamic structure

It emerges from the survey of the current situation that dynamic models of stock do exist but that they tend to neglect the dynamics of flow (Harris and Wilson, 1978, Allen and Sanglier, 1979-A, Wilson and Clarke, 1979, Allen and Sanglier, 1981-A, Wilson, 1981-C, Lombardo and Rabino, 1983-A, Clarke and Wilson, 1985, Wilson, in this book). Vice-versa: there are dynamic models of flows but these tend to neglect the dynamics of stock (Leonardi and Campisi, 1981, Weidlich and Haag, 1983, de Palma and Lefèvre in this book, Leonardi, in this book, Weibull, 1984-A). The modelling of the interaction between the dynamics of stock and the dynamics of flows is less satisfactory, even though some interesting attempts have been made in some sectors (see Snickars, 1978). It appears that from the point of view of application, the main effort needs to be concentrated on the development of theories and models which deal dynamically with both stock and flows for certain urban subsystems (eg. the residential subsystem) and for the urban system as a whole. It also seems necessary to intensify efforts on the construction of models which take into account the dynamics of the transport infrastructure. There are no models of the dynamics of transport in stock-flow interactions, though they receive a brief mention in Wilson (1983).

A further subject which should not be overlooked in this context is the analysis of the relationship between system dynamics and innovation in the underlying technological structure. This is an involved problem which includes the question of the diffusion of information (Ralston, 1983), competition between alternative technologies (Sonis, 1983) and the role of technological research in the productive apparatus (Nijkamp, 1983).

From the methodological point of view, one fundamental aspect which needs to be developed is the analysis of non-linearities (especially the phenomena of synergetics). A further aspect is the analysis of stochastic components (see de Palma and Lefèvre for the implications in dynamic analysis and Smith for the implications on the analysis of individual behaviour, both in this book).

A future research programme should include the following phases: (i) a detailed examination of the theoretical structure of models, particularly those concerning the interaction between the various subsystems and between stock and flows; (ii) the preparation of the statistical methods and computational tools necessary for empirical testing and implementation of the models; and (iii) a comparison of applications of models in different urban systems.

The evaluation and testing of performance

It emerges from the review of the present state-of-the-art that there are well developed techniques of evaluation and optimisation for static equilibrium systems (Coelho and Williams, 1978, Wilson et al, 1981, Beaumont, 1984, Colorni, in this book, Voogd, 1984). For dynamic systems the situation is satisfactory for aggregated economic systems but inadequate for spatially disaggregated systems (although an attempt to apply optimising and dynamic control methods to spatially disaggregated models has been made by Fujita, 1978).

From the methodological point of view, it should be noted that the problem of controlling a dynamic system is qualitatively different from the problem of optimisation of a static system in that it involves the use of optimisation techniques (such as dynamic programming and optimum control) but also poses problems of structural stability, adaptability and self-regulation. The following tasks therefore need to be undertaken: (i) a more complete analysis of the use of dynamic optimisation techniques; (ii) an introduction of adaptive and self-regulating mechanisms in location-transport systems; and (iii) the finding of suitable mechanisms and tools for the control of structural changes.

The research programme should be divided into the following phases: (i) a detailed examination of the problems delineated above as they relate to location-transport systems; (ii) the development of suitable techniques for simulating the control mechanisms for dynamic systems, in particular for simulating the performance of adaptive and self-regulation mechanisms.

The relationship between individual and collective behaviour

From the review of the current situation, it emerges that the various microscopic theories (most of the work of Beckmann and Papageorgiou, including Beckmann's contribution to this book and Papageorgiou, 1985), and macroscopic theories (most of the work of Wilson and Sheppard, including their contributions to this book) regarding the behaviour of the actors in the urban system are well represented. There is not, however, an equally thorough treatment of the interactions between the two levels, although de Palma and Lefèvre, Leonardi and Smith have recently carried out work on this, as can be seen in this book.

From the methodological point of view, there is a need to examine: (i) the sensitivity of the behaviour of a macro-level system to different hypotheses concerning micro-level behaviour; (ii) the effects on micro-level behaviour of constraints and interactions at macro-level; and (iii) the role of the time dimension in micro-level behaviour (processes of adaptive learning).

As far as future research is concerned, the following are necessary: (i) a detailed analysis of the theories relating to the methodological point of view (particularly the first point); and (ii) empirical testing of the theories relating to the methodological point of view (particularly the second point).

Part Two

ECONOMIC APPROACHES

Chapter 3

THE ECONOMIC ACTIVITY EQUILIBRIUM APPROACH IN LOCATION THEORY

M.J. Beckmann

3.1 Introduction: general characteristics

The Economic Activity Equilibrium (EAE) approach in location theory is as old as neoclassical economics. It begins with von Thünen (1826) and continues through Loria (1880), Launhardt (1885), Weber (1909), and Palander (1935) to Lösch (1940) and Hoover (1948). The 1950s saw the introduction of Linear Programming and Nonlinear Programming Models by Koopmans (1949), Beckmann (1952) and others. The programming approach proved to be eminently suitable for modelling spatial relationships, in particular interlocal commodity flows. In fact transportation and location are considered as complementary aspects of the same phenomena: the spatial realization of a market economy. The interaction of transportation and location is the subject of Section 3.2.

Although the EAE-approach addresses a market situation, it is applicable also to the study of locational planning in a planned economy. The object of analysis is then not market equilibrium but efficiency in the spatial allocation of resources. All prices must then be interpreted as shadow prices or dual variables rather than as competitive market prices. The programming approach is discussed in Section 3.5.1.

Within its self-imposed limits, the EAE-approach represents the most ambitious attempt to integrate location theory into the neoclassical framework of micro-economics. The logical structure of micro-economics dictates to a large extent also the structure of the EAE-approach. In particular, analysis of single markets (Sections 3.3 and 3.4) must be carried out before that of multiple markets (Section 3.5) and partial equilibrium analysis (Sections 3.4 and 3.5) precedes general equilibrium analysis (Section 3.6). Moreover, short run problems must be considered before long run problems (Sections 3.6 and 3.7).

A second structural principle is introduced by the way in which space manifests itself. In the simplest case space is homogeneous and enters economic relationships only in the form of distance. The principal way in which economic relationships are then affected by space is through transportation cost: location theory becomes the economics of distance. However, space may also be the carrier of resources. The uneven distribution of localized resources imposes its own laws on spatial economic relationships. These give rise to such matters as resources versus market orientation (Section 3.2.3) and to long distance trade as contrasted to the local relationships between centre and surrounding market or supply area (Section 3.2.4).

While benefiting from the results of neoclassical economics, the EAE-approach also suffers from its limitations, in particular those emerging from indivisibilities (3.7.3) and externalities (Section 3.7.2). It does not deny a validity of other approaches, such as political and sociological ones, but it focuses on a purely economic explanation of spatial relationships.

3.2 Transportation and Location

Although transportation and location must be considered complementary activities, the two fields of transportation economics and of location theory constitute separate disciplines with their own methodology. Broadly speaking, transportation economists while paying lip service to the fact that transportation demand depends on locational decisions in the long run, tend in actual fact to ignore this phenomenon or to deal with it in the most perfunctory manner. In the short run the interaction between transportation and location is well known and reasonably well understood. This is discussed in the present section.

3.2.1 Transportation implies location

Suppose that shipments x_{ik} of a commodity from locations i to locations k, i, k = 1, ..., n are known. Then net exports (positive for exports, negative for imports) x_i at the locations are also known. This is in fact no more than a bookkeeping relationship:

$$x_i = \sum_k (x_{ik} - x_{ki}) \tag{3.1}$$

Net exports are further divided into

local production z_i - local consumption c_i

thus

$$z_i = c_i + \sum_k (x_{ik} - x_{ki}) \tag{3.2}$$

In this way the location of production or more generally the locational distribution of the production levels z_i, is determined by the observed transportation and consumption activities.

In principle n locations i can give rise to $\frac{n(n-1)}{2}$ flow variables x_{ik} between them. It follows that the inverse problem: determining flows x_{ik} from the observed locational distribution of production z_i and consumption c_i cannot possess such a simple solution.

3.2.2 How to infer transportation from location

The classical problem from which the Entropy School (Murchland, 1966, Wilson, 1970-A) has taken off is this: to infer the home to work trips x_{ik} from the observed generation of work trips in home locations a_i and the observed termination of work trips in work locations b_i. The accounting equations

$$\sum_k x_{ik} = a_i \tag{3.3}$$

$$\sum_i x_{ik} = b_k \tag{3.4}$$

are variants of equation (3.1). Even the entropy approach requires one additional constraint and a basic assumption. The constraint considers the total miles (or km) travelled

$$\sum_{ik} r_{ik} x_{ik} = c \tag{3.5}$$

where r_{ik} is distance.

The fundamental assumption is the Principle of Maximum Likelihood. The logarithm of the likelihood function is approximated by the entropy function and the result is the well known gravity formula with "exponential resistance" effect

$$x_{ik} = \lambda_i \mu_k e^{-\gamma r_{ik}} \tag{3.6}$$

(Murchland, 1966, 1969, Wilson, 1970-A).

It will be illuminating to see how the economic activity approach treats the same problem.

If all houses were uniform and all tastes were equal, and

the housing market is competitive, then the solution would be the one which minimizes total transportation cost. The transportation problem of linear programming would be the proper vehicle for solving this allocation problem. It may be considered the answer under perfect planning.

However, these assumptions are by no means realistic. The economic activity approach proceeds in a different way, focusing on the individual decision maker, who has found a job and looks for a home. (This is realistic in the US context.) The decision maker seeks to maximize utility. The differences between households of tastes and perception in regard to housing quality give rise to a random component ε_i in the utility function for living at i and commuting to k

$$\varepsilon_i - \alpha r_{ik}$$

The notion of a random utility function is instrumental in making operational the neoclassical idea of "rational", ie maximizing behaviour. (On the notion of random utility, cf Quandt (1968), Beckmann and Golob (1971), Golob and Beckmann (1971), Domencich and McFadden (1975), McFadden (1976), and Leonardi (1982-A).)

In one version of this approach the search for a home location stops when a satisfying level of utility is achieved

$$\varepsilon_i - \alpha r_{ik} \geq u_o$$

The probability of this

$$pr(\varepsilon_i < \alpha r_{ik} + u_o)$$

can be calculated once the probability distribution is specified. Suppose it is the normal distribution (Thurstone, 1927) and that we approximate it by a logistic function (Nash, 1979)

$$\mathrm{pr}(\varepsilon_i > \alpha r_{ik} + u_o) \simeq \frac{1}{1 + e^{\frac{\beta}{\sigma}[u_o - \mu_i + \alpha r_{ik}]}} \qquad (3.7)$$

where β is a suitable constant $\beta \simeq 1.6$, μ_i is the expected value and σ is the standard deviation of ε_i. Notice that this probability may be interpreted as a trip frequency. The actual number of trips is then proportional to this probability times the work trips terminating in k

$$x_{ik} = \frac{b_k}{1 + e^{\frac{\beta}{\sigma}(u_o - \mu_i + \alpha r_{ik})}}$$

For large r_{ik} the second term in the denominator dominates so that

$$x_{ik} \simeq a_i b_k e^{-\gamma r_{ik}} \qquad (3.8)$$

where

$$a_i = e^{\frac{\beta}{\sigma}(\mu_i - u_o)}$$

$$\gamma = \frac{\alpha\beta}{\sigma}$$

The gravity law appears here not as a rabbit drawn out of the Maximum Likelihood hat into which dubious assumptions of "equally likely" events have been dropped (Wilson, 1967) but as the outcome of individual decisions. The random utility terms affecting these decisions are a reflection both of the variability of tastes among individuals and of our ignorance regarding the specific preferences of particular individuals (cf also Harris, 1964-B).

In the EAE-approach nothing short of a behavioural analysis can be satisfactory. For instance: assumptions along the lines of Reilly's Law (Reilly, 1931) do not constitute a scientific explanation. Reilly's Law states:

$$\frac{x_{ki}}{x_{ji}} = \left(\frac{r_{ij}}{r_{ik}} \right)^2 \tag{3.9}$$

where x_{ki} are sales by a firm at location k to a household at location i.

While Reilly's Law is a special case of the gravity law with "resistance" proportional to the square of distance, the following modification of Reilly's Law (Beckmann, 1968) generates the gravity law with exponential distance effect

$$\frac{x_{ki}}{x_{ji}} = f(r_{ij} - r_{ik}) \tag{3.10}$$

The classical gravity formula, and the theory of spatial interaction based on this (Zipf, 1941, Stewart, 1947), sometimes called "social physics", involves not an exponential but a power law of distance. It was first shown by Niedercorn and Bechdoldt (1969) that such power laws may be derived from utility maximizing behaviour when the utility function is also in terms of certain power functions of trip frequencies.

It has become customary to associate the term gravity law with any relationship for spatial interaction, in which the influences of origin, destination and intervening distance may be separated in a multiplicative way

$$x_{ik} = a_i b_k f(r_{ik}) \tag{3.11}$$

Equation (3.11) has the attraction of great simplicity, but it is hardly ever valid exactly. This may be seen from the fact that a great number of assumptions are needed for its derivation from behavioural postulates.

A general gravity law may in fact be obtained as follows. Consider a household at i allocating its income y_i to various trips x_{ik} and to general consumption c_i. The utility function is

$$u = u(c_i, x_{i1}, x_{i2}, .. x_{in})$$

Assume the utility function to be separable

$$u = u_o(c_i) + \sum_k u_k(x_{ik})$$

Suppose that in addition to trip frequencies x_{ik} a second variable is involved, which is not controlled by the household, the attraction a_k of destination k and assume that the u_k are homogeneous in the two variables, a standard assumption in neoclassical economics. In fact let each utility term be linear homogeneous

$$u_k = a_k \psi\left(\frac{x_{ik}}{a_k} \right)$$

If r_{ik} denotes cost of transportation from i to k (or economic distance) the amount of income that can be spent on consumption equals

$$c_i = y_i - \sum_k r_{ik} x_{ik}$$

The household seeks a maximum of

$$\max_{x_{ik}} a_o \psi\left(\frac{y_i - \sum_k r_{ik} x_{ik}}{a_o} \right) + \sum_k a_k \psi\left(\frac{x_{ik}}{a_k} \right)$$

With concave ψ the necessary and sufficient conditions are

$$0 = -r_{ik} \psi'\left(\frac{y_i - \sum_k r_{ik} x_{ik}}{a_o} \right) + \psi'\left(\frac{x_{ik}}{a_k} \right) \qquad (3.12)$$

Write $h = [\psi']^{-1}$ for the inverse function of ψ' which is a decreasing function. The solution of (3.12) states the number of trips per household in location i

$$x_{ik} = a_k . h(r_{ik} . \psi' (\frac{c_i}{a_o}))$$

Now assume that c_i is independent of location i so that $\psi' (\frac{c_i}{a_o})$ is a constant. Multiplying by the number of households N_i at location i one has the total number of trips from i to k

$$x_{ik} = N_i a_k . f(r_{ik}) \tag{3.13}$$

where

$$f(r_{ik}) = h(r_{ik} \psi' (\frac{c_i}{a_o}))$$

In the special case of power function ψ, ψ', too, is a power function and ψ' separates naturally into two factors depending on location i and transportation cost r_{ik} respectively. No assumption of constant consumption $c_i = c$ is then required.

Granted the special assumptions needed to derive (3.13), in principle it is possible to obtain any mathematical form for $f(r_{ik})$, provided f is a decreasing function, that is, interaction decreases with distance. This means that a utility function can be found to generate any observed empirical law of interaction over distance. In fact both the exponential and the power law fail to explain the well-known observation that at short distances, distance does not affect interaction materially; this means that $f'(0) \simeq 0$. On the other hand an interaction law of type (3.7) has a small derivative $f'(0)$ provided $\frac{u_o - \mu_i}{\sigma}$ is large.

Interaction or market share laws of type (3.9) and (3.10) may however be derived from a behavioural model along similar lines as follows. A customer at location i wants to decide whether to buy from a supplier at location j or location k.

While the goods may be identical, the reliability, service availability, credit terms etc of the two suppliers may be differently perceived. The utility of buying from source $m = j,k$ is ε_m. From this must be subtracted the disutility of the money expenditure on transportation r_{ik}, assumed to be linear $-\alpha r_{ik}$. The probability that a buyer at i buys from j rather than k equals

$$pr(\varepsilon_j - \alpha r_{ij} > \varepsilon_k - \alpha r_{ik})$$

or

$$pr(\varepsilon_k - \varepsilon_j < \alpha[r_{ik} - r_{ij}])$$

Assuming once more a normal distribution for $\varepsilon_k - \varepsilon_j$, approximated by a logistic function, the probability of buying from j or j's market share at i assumes the form

$$\frac{x_{ji}}{x_{ji} + x_{ki}} = \frac{1}{1 + \frac{a_k}{a_j} e^{\gamma(r_{ik} - r_{ji})}}$$

from which

$$\frac{x_{ji}}{x_{ki}} = \frac{a_j e^{-\gamma r_{ij}}}{a_k e^{-\gamma r_{ik}}} \qquad (3.14)$$

and this is a relationship of type (3.10).

3.2.3 Resource versus market orientation

So far we have considered heterogeneous goods sold to consumers. In the case of homogeneous commodities such as industrial raw materials or standardized products, the relationships between location and transportation become amenable to a straightforward analysis in terms of costs. Perhaps the most famous case in traditional location theory concerns the "orientation" of production locations at transportation cost. When does processing of a raw material found in localized resources deposits take place at the point of extraction, and what at the point of consumption?

When processing costs (labour costs) are the same at all locations this is essentially a question of a transportation cost of the product compared to transportation cost of the raw material. In order to minimize total costs one must then minimize transportation cost. Activities which are weight reducing should then be located at the resource deposit; on the other hand activities which preserve weight but increase bulk should be located at or near points of consumption.

When product and raw material are equally transportable, the industry may be attracted to locations of cheap labour, provided these lie along the route between resource deposits and points of consumption.

Given the locations of raw material supply and of product consumption, both the locations of the producing industry and the resulting transportation activities may be determined simply as a result of cost minimization, enforced by competitive markets or by a cost minimizing monopolist.

More interesting theoretical problems arise when several resource deposits are available. Cost minimizations suggests that the nearest source should always be utilized. In the short run, however, capacity limitations may interfere. The market will then respond by raising the price of the materials at favourable locations close to points of consumption until equilibrium of supply and demand is achieved. This operation of competitive markets can now be understood more clearly by means of Linear Programming.

Let resource deposit $i = 1, \ldots, m$ have capacities c_i, and let demand at consumption locations j (assumed as given independent of price) be d_j, $j = 1, \ldots, n$. Since a competitive market results in a Pareto optimum, it must imply minimum total transportation costs

$$\text{Min} \sum_{ij} r_{ij} x_{ij}$$

incurred in moving the product (or material) from locations i of availability to locations j of demand

$$\sum_j x_{ij} \leqq c_i$$
$$\sum_i x_{ij} \geqq d_j \tag{3.15}$$

This is a standard transportation problem of Linear Programming. It is feasible provided

$$\sum_j d_j \leqq \sum_i c_i \tag{3.16}$$

that is provided total production capacity is adequate to meet aggregate demand.

If this LP is feasible, it also has an optimum. Koopmans (1949) discovered the following efficiency conditions which are necessary and sufficient for an optimal solution

$$x_{ik} \left\{ \begin{matrix} = \\ \geqq \end{matrix} \right\} 0 \iff \lambda_k - \lambda_i \left\{ \begin{matrix} \leqq \\ = \\ \geqq \end{matrix} \right\} r_{ik} \tag{3.17}$$

The "dual" variables λ_j are shadow prices or efficiency prices. In a market framework they are competitive equilibrium prices. Condition (3.17) states that a system of commodity flows x_{ik} is optimal if and only if the price gain from arbitrage between locations i and k just covers the cost of transportation. Positive profits are ruled out and negative profits indicate that the transaction should not take place. The dual LP is

$$\text{Max } (\sum_j d_j \lambda_j - \sum_i c_i \lambda_i) \tag{3.18}$$

subject to

$$\lambda_j - \lambda_i \leq r_{ij}$$

The profits from trade are to be maximized subject to a constraint on the allowable price spread. From this dual it may be seen that a reduction in transportation cost necessarily tightens the constraints and reduces the maximum, hence lowers the transportation cost minimum.

3.2.4 Market and supply areas

In the long run there are no capacity limitations. However, cost differences may exist in the production of a commodity.

The long run allocation problem corresponding to the short run LP is discussed in Section 3.4.1 below which considers spatial market equilibrium. A special case has long been of interest in location theory and this is the case of constant but not uniform unit cost of production, which gives rise to given competitive prices at the various production locations. In this case the sales to consumers and the transportation activities are once more determined only by costs. More precisely it is the direction of transportation, not its volume that is determined by costs.

Interaction between buyers and sellers can now be described in terms of market and supply areas. To each location is associated an "optimal source" such that the sum of mill price and transportation cost is minimized. In this way the entire plane is divided into mutually exclusive and exhaustive market areas. When transportation costs are proportional or convex functions of distance, these market areas necessarily contain the source as an interior point. In particular when mill prices are equal, buyers will purchase from the nearest supplier. Even when mill prices differ a firm will be the exclusive seller in its market area and have no sales at all in other firm's market area: market share drops abruptly from one to zero at the boundary of a market area.

This concept seems inappropriate to deal with falling market shares in the case of heterogeneous products. We may consider, however, the following generalized concept: at each location one firm is dominant in the sense of having the largest market share. (With two firms this means a market share $>\frac{1}{2}$). Except for boundary locations (of measure zero) each location is then assigned to one and only one supplier. The market areas so defined divide the entire region into mutually exclusive and non-overlapping point sets, each set containing one and only one supplier. In this way the concept of market area can be retained and operationalized for overlapping sales territories in the case of the suppliers of heterogeneous goods.

The same applies to the concept of supply areas in regard to dominant buyers. Thus labour supply areas or commuter zones may be defined as those territories surrounding various cities in which a given city has the dominant market share among all.

3.2.5 Locational shifts

Market areas may exist in which the supplier is not located near the centre. It may be asked what is the proper definition of centre and when is a location at the centre optimal?

This question is most easily answered in a one-dimensional context or in a two-dimensional region when locations are restricted to vertices in a square grid. Consider a two-dimensional region with locations of demand and supply restricted to vertices in a square grid. Under uniform delivered pricing each customer's demand is given and equal. Assume that we have a monopoly. What is the optimal location of our plant? A moment's reflection will show that it is the median with respect to customer locations along the North-South axis as well as along the East-West axis. We can illustrate this result by considering the weights that must be moved in the four directions of the grid. At the optimal location the weights must be in equilibrium (Figure 3.1).

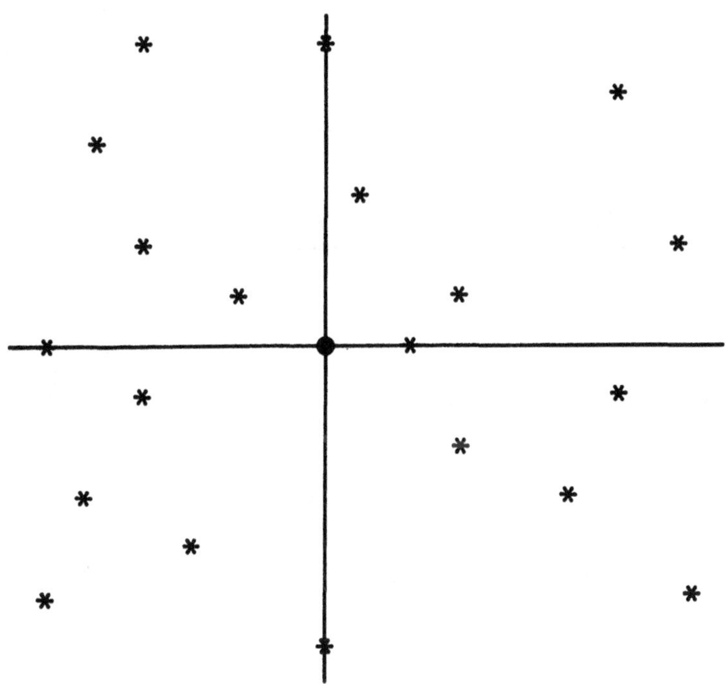

Figure 3.1: Median location

It may be slightly more surprising that the same median location is still optimal under mill pricing, provided the demand function is linear. (When customer locations are symmetric or occur at uniform density, the principle of the median holds for non-linear demand functions as well.)

It is well-known that under duopoly and when demand is inelastic, the two firms will also gravitate to the median. This is the famous Hotelling Paradox. In one-dimension, equilibrium solutions of the Hotelling type exist for even numbers of firms: clusters of 2 are formed at the centres of segments of lengths $\frac{2D}{n}$ when D is the length of the market, and n (even) is the number of firms involved. In two-dimensions Hotelling equilibria exist when n is divisible by 4 (Figure 3.2).

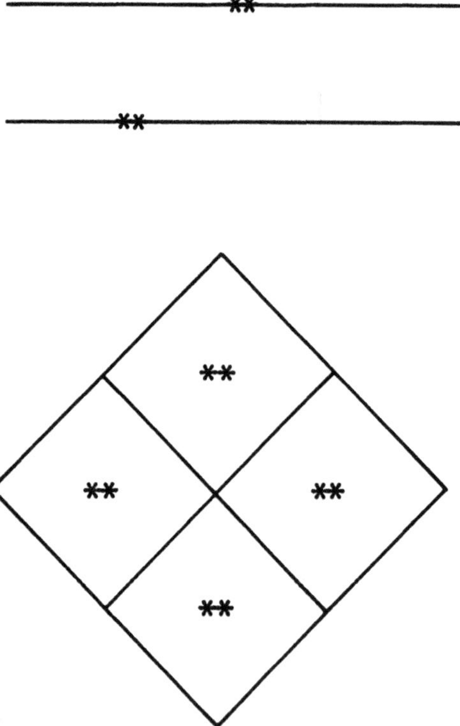

Figure 3.2: Hotelling equilibrium points

3.3 Pricing

The EAE approach considers not only production and transportation, but also the pricing decision as an economic activity. Such pricing decisions are inescapable under spatial monopoly, the situation that arises when there are well-defined market areas served by single suppliers. In Section 3.3.1 we discuss alternative pricing strategies and their economic implications for the case usually considered in location theory: that of linear demand functions. In Section 3.3.2 we turn to competitive pricing in a spatial (Greenhut and Ohta, 1975) context.

3.3.1 Spatial price policy: monopoly

We assume constant unit costs of production and constant cost of transportations per unit commodity and unit distance. By means of a linear transformation and a suitable choice of units we can achieve the following simplifications: transportation costs equals distance r, production cost is zero, and quantity demanded is:

$$q(r) = 1 - p(r) \tag{3.19}$$

Three types of price policy are usually considered:

mill pricing	$p(r) = p_m + r$
uniform delivered pricing	$p(r) = p_u$
and discriminatory pricing	$p(r)$

Let the density of consumers at distance r be $\rho(r)$ and let the market radius R be given. Profits under the three pricing strategies are then as follows:

mill pricing $$p_m \int_0^R (1 - p_m - r)\rho(r)dr \qquad (3.20)$$

uniform pricing $$(1 - p_u) \int_0^R (p_u - r)\rho(r)dr \qquad (3.21)$$

discriminatory pricing $$\int_0^R [(p_d(r) - r)][1 - p_d(r)]\rho(r)dr \qquad (3.22)$$

Now (3.20) is identical with (3.21) when we set

$$p_u = 1 - p_m \qquad (3.23)$$

It follows that the two policies are equally profitable.

Taking the derivative of (3.20) with respect to p_m and setting it equal to zero yields

$$\int_0^R (1 - 2p_m - r)\rho(r)dr = 0$$

from which

$$p_m = \frac{1}{2} - \bar{r} \qquad (3.24)$$

where

$$\bar{r} = \frac{\int r\rho dr}{\int \rho dr} \qquad (3.25)$$

is average distance of customers from the supplier. Similarly one shows that

$$p_u = \frac{1}{2} + \bar{r} \qquad (3.26)$$

The optimal price under perfect discrimination is

$$p_d = \frac{1}{2} + \frac{r}{2} \qquad (3.27)$$

and this policy is more profitable (Figure 3.3).

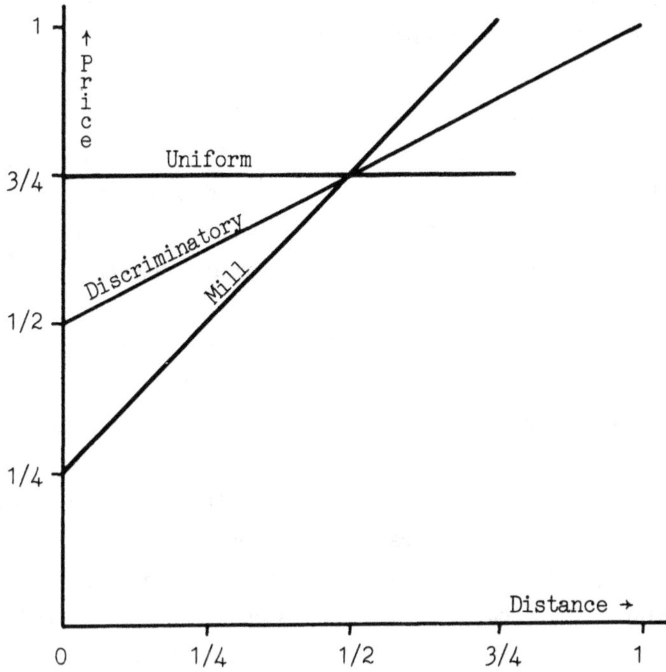

Figure 3.3: Comparison of pricing systems

The following results are readily derived (Beckmann, 1976-C). Output and average price per customer are the same under all three strategies. But welfare is largest under mill pricing and smallest under uniform pricing. In particular transportation demand is largest under uniform pricing. This important conclusion is not restricted to the linear case.

Consider a non-linear demand function f. If we assume that the uniform price lies above the mill price by approximately the amount of average transportation cost, as was the case for linear demand functions then

$$T_{mill} = \int rf(p+r)\rho(r)dr < \int rf(p+\overline{r})dr = T_{uniform} \qquad (3.28)$$

and this inequality remains valid even when price deviates somewhat from this rule. For in the left integral large values of r are associated with low values of the demand function f considered as a weight function. It agrees with economic intuition that transportation should be used more sparingly when customers have to pay for it directly.

It may also be shown that for convex demand functions mill pricing is more profitable and for concave demand functions the uniform pricing is more profitable (Stevens and Rydell, 1966).

All these statements apply for a given restrictive market radius R. When this radius is unrestricted, then under discriminatory pricing deliveries are made to the maximal distance of one, compared to a shorter but equal range under mill pricing and uniform pricing. The welfare gain from this service to distant consumers can outweigh the welfare loss in the range of common distances: but this is a question of the spatial distribution of customers and cannot be stated categorically (Holahan, 1975, Holahan and Schuler, 1977).

3.3.2 Perfect competition

When an industry is dispersed each firm has its own market area and this even when sales of different firms overlap (cf Section 3.2.5).

In its own market area a firm enjoys some monopoly power. How can this fact be reconciled with perfect competition, the foundation of neoclassical economic analysis? What are the minimum requirements for the organization of spatial markets in order that they may be considered competitive in all essential respects?

First: prices must be uniform. Clearly prices that depend on location and reflect monopoly power are inconsistent with competitive equilibrium in a market which by necessity entails a single price. In particular this implies the strategy of uniform delivered prices (rather than mill or discriminatory pricing).

Second: firms must be price takers. We rule out Bertrand-Edgeworth oligopoly of price cutting where firms try to invade other firms' market areas in order to increase sales. The gains must be perceived as only temporary and not worth the risk of retaliation.

Third: free entry. As long as profits are made, new firms will squeeze in until price falls to a level where profits are wiped out and no space remains for additional firms to break even at those prices.

This condition does not fully determine the number and spacing of firms, rather it describes only a range for spacing, having open gaps as long as they are smaller than the market areas needed by one firm to survive. It is tempting to add as a fourth requirement, one that Lösch has first introduced as the maximization of independent economic existences.

Fourth: the number of firms consistent with the first three requirements is maximized. But this condition merely serves to ensure that as far as possible every consumer is supplied. Even then the resulting market areas will be circular and contiguous leaving 9.3% of the region without supply.

Postulates one to four imply that price = minimum average cost including the cost of delivery. Only through internalizing the transportation cost through uniform delivered pricing is this result achieved and are spatial markets made to conform with markets in neoclassical economic theory.

Do the welfare theoretic consequences of uniform pricing other than the minimum cost argument support this interpretation of uniform prices as approximations to competitive prices? Only up to a point. For linear demand curves, profits are equal under uniform and mill pricing (Beckmann, 1976-C). But consumers' plus producers' surplus is larger for mill pricing. The differences are not large, however, and the result cannot be established for non-linear demand functions. On the other hand uniform pricing with overlapping market territories increases the number of potential competitors and is thus more conducive to bringing about competition.

3.3.2.1 Local markets

The standard model of location theory assumes that costs consist of a fixed cost F and proportional costs c of production (Beckmann, 1968). (This represents increasing returns to scale.) We consider uniform pricing. A representative firm supplies a market of radius R occupied by consumers living at density $\rho(r)$ and having demand functions $f(p)$. The firm's profits are

$$G = G(R) = \int_0^R f(p)(p - c - kr)\rho(r)dr - F \qquad (3.29)$$

Since the firm is a price taker, its only decision variable is R, the maximal distance of delivery or the radius of its market area.

Maximization of (3.29) with respect to R yields the condition

$$p - c - kR = 0$$

or

$$R = \frac{p - c}{k} \qquad (3.30)$$

The radius of delivery increases linearly with the product price p, decreases linearly with unit production cost c and is inversely proportional to unit transportation cost k.

In the short run this is the only decision to be taken by a competitive firm. In the long run profits must be considered.

As long as these are positive, additional firms are attracted. With overlapping market areas the effect is to reduce ρ. The resulting excess supply lowers p. Suppose that in final equilibrium market areas are contiguous rather than overlapping. Then p is determined so as to yield zero profits under the optimal decision rule (3.30) of a competitive firm. We study the resulting equilibrium conditions.

Substitute (3.30) in (3.29) to obtain

$$G = f(p)[(p-c) \int_0^{\frac{p-c}{k}} \rho(r)dr - k \int_0^{\frac{p-c}{k}} r\rho(r)dr] - F \qquad (3.31)$$

The profit function G is negative for p = c and is assumed to have a positive maximum $G(p_1) > 0$. Therefore a positive root p_o of

$$G(p_o) = 0 \qquad (3.32)$$

must exist. Consider the smallest such root. It occurs where

$$G'(p_o) > 0 \qquad (3.33)$$

(This is economically intuitive: raising the market price p increases the profit of existing firms as long as the market price lies below the monopoly price p_1.)

We consider next how the long run equilibrium price p_o depends on the problem data. Implicit differentiation of (3.31) yields

$$\text{sign}\,\frac{\partial p_o}{\partial F} = -\,\text{sign}\,\frac{G_F}{G_p} = -\,\text{sign}\,(-1) = + \qquad (3.34)$$

$$\text{sign}\,\frac{\partial p_o}{\partial c} = \text{sign}\,\frac{G_c}{G_p} = -\,\text{sign}\,f(p) = + \qquad (3.35)$$

$$\text{sign}\,\frac{\partial p_o}{\partial k} = -\,\text{sign}\,\frac{G_k}{G_p} = + \qquad (3.36)$$

$$\text{sign} \frac{\partial p_o}{\partial \rho} = - \text{ sign} \frac{G_\rho}{G_p} = - \tag{3.37}$$

In principle equations (3.34) - (3.37) predict how prices vary between regions as a result of differences in exogeneous variables such as transportation cost, proportional production cost, fixed cost and most importantly the density of demand.

3.3.2.2 Export markets

The determination of price is an entirely different problem when production involves localized resources or other inputs whose prices can vary significantly between locations. It is then that classical supply and demand analysis can be applied with modifications due to LP that are fully in our power to implement.

Consider the exporter of a product at i from local resources. He must choose the most lucrative among his potential markets k. Let market prices p_k be competitive, and let the exporter be a price taker. Subject to a capacity limit c_i he then chooses to ship quantities x_{ik} to various destinations k

$$\sum_k x_{ik} \leq c_i \tag{3.38}$$

Given the market prices p_k and transportation costs r_{ik} the profits to be maximized are

$$\sum_k (p_k - r_{ik}) x_{ik} \tag{3.39}$$

Maximizing (3.38) subject to (3.37) implies:

$$\underset{x_{ik}:\sum_k x_{ik} \leq c_i}{\text{Max}} \sum_k (p_k - r_{ik}) x_{ik} = c_i \underset{k}{\text{Max}} (p_r - r_{ik}) \tag{3.40}$$

For each supplier there exists an optimal export market k. Conversely each market location k possesses its own set of supply points, its supply area. Once more an interesting situation arises when the capacity of markets is limited: at most q_k can be sold by this supplier in market k without spoiling prices. This is a slight weakening of the concept of a competitive price. Now the exporter must allocate his shipments x_{ik} so as to maximize the same objective function (3.39) subject to (3.38) and to the additional constraints.

$$\sum_i x_{ik} \leq q_k \tag{3.41}$$

The solution is to supply markets in decreasing order of lucrativity $p_k - r_{ik}$ up to the allowable limits q_k and to the capacity limit c_i.

Consider now the set of all suppliers and assume that supply and demand curves are not rigid (ie vertical lines) as assumed before but elastic. We then have the classical economic problem of equilibrating supply and demand - in a spatial context. This is the subject of Section 3.4.

3.3.3 Remarks on spatial oligopoly

Oligopoly problems are too manifold and too diffuse to be considered within the limits of this paper (cf Philips and Thisse, 1982). Suffice it to say that the competitive model discussed above in 3.3.2 may be reinterpreted with slight modifications as an equilibrium model under monopolistic competition. This is in fact the way proposed by Palander (1935) and executed by Lösch (1940) of studying spatial market equilibrium. It is the preferred way of dealing with "non-cooperative" oligopoly strategies in a spatial context. The firms behaving as monopolistic competitors may also be viewed as Cournot oligopolists, each confronted with 6 neighbours.

Cooperative oligopolistic strategies may also be briefly referred to. They either allocate exclusive territories and thus institute spatial monopolies or fix prices as under the famous "Pittsburgh Plus" system (Beckmann, 1968, Greenhut and Ohta, 1976). Once these prices are given, firms become price takers and must decide how much and where to sell, a problem considered in 3.3.2 above.

3.4 Spatial Market Equilibrium: single commodity

The invention of Linear Programming allowed the economic activity and equilibrium approach to come into its own. In 1950 T.C. Koopmans obtained a grant from the newly founded RAND Corporation to develop Linear Programming approaches to "Efficient Allocation of Resources" in transportation and location. His team included at various times: Debreu, Herstein and McGuire, Winsten and Beckmann. Interestingly enough, the limits of LP were soon reached and the more important publications by the Cowles Commission team all focused on certain Non-Linear Programs (Beckmann, McGuire and Winsten, 1956, Koopmans and Beckmann, 1957).

3.4.1 Discrete market

The prototype of a price equilibrium model for a discrete set of spatially separated markets is the standard transportation model of LP and its variants: the trans-shipment model and the network transportation model. This was briefly examined in 3.2.3.

We consider now the NLP that is generated when supply and/ or demand depend on price. It is reasonable to assume that supply s_i and demand d_i in location i should depend on the local price p_i only.

$$s_i = s_i(p_i) \qquad s_i' \geq 0 \tag{3.42}$$

$$d_i = d_i(p_i) \qquad d_i' < 0 \tag{3.43}$$

In equilibrium, local excess demand must be covered by net imports and local excess supply must be exported. Now the exports from i are

$$\sum_j (x_{ij} - x_{ji})$$

and this must equal excess demand

$$\sum_j (x_{ij} - x_{ji}) = s_i - d_i \tag{3.44}$$

Since only excess supply or excess demand are needed in equation (3.44) we introduce

$$q_i(p_i) = d_i(p_i) - s_i(p_i) \tag{3.45}$$

excess demand and observe

$$q_i' < 0 \tag{3.46}$$

One equilibrium condition for spatial markets is therefore

$$\sum_j (x_{ij} - x_{ji}) + q_i(p_i) = 0 \tag{3.47}$$

Now consider the inverse function of $q_i(p_i)$

$$p_i = p_i(q_i) \tag{3.48}$$

and introduce the consumers' and producers' surplus integral

$$\int_o^{q_i} p_i(q)dq \tag{3.49}$$

In mathematical economics it is shown that competitive market equilibrium achieves a maximum of producers' plus consumers' surplus

$$\text{Max} \sum_i \int_o^{q_i} p_i(q)dq - \sum_{ij} r_{ij}x_{ij} \tag{3.50}$$

Observe that we have deducted transportation costs from the producers' surplus.

Substituting for q_i from (3.47)

$$\underset{x_{ij} \geqq o}{\text{Max}} \sum_i \int_o^{\sum_j x_{ji} - x_{ij}} p_i(q)dq - \sum_{ij} r_{ij}x_{ij} \tag{3.51}$$

Solution of (3.51) yields (3.47) and

$$x_{ij} \{\geqq\} o \iff p_j(q_j) - p_i(q_i) \{\leqq\} r_{ij} \tag{3.52}$$

Equations (3.47) and (3.52) are the complete statement of the conditions for spatial market equilibrium under competitive conditions. For strictly decreasing excess demand functions the solution is in fact unique. The maximum problem (3.51) has also a dual, obtained through integration by parts

$$\sum_i \int p_i dq - \sum_{ij} r_{ij}x_{ij} = \sum_i p_i q_i - \int q_i dp - \sum_{ij} r_{ij}x_{ij}$$

$$= \sum_i p_i \sum_j (x_{ji} - x_{ij}) - \int q_i dp - \sum_{ij} r_{ij}x_{ij}$$

$$(3.51) = \underset{p_j - p_i \leqq r_{ij}}{\text{Min}} \sum_i \int_{p_i}^{\infty} q_i d_p \tag{3.53}$$

This dual shows how interlocal price differences must fall when transportation cost decreases. Statement (3.51) or

(3.53) of the maximum problem are equivalent to the equilibrium conditions and may be used to carry out comparative statics (Samuelson, 1952).

Models of this type have been used to study agricultural markets in the US, the coal market in the US (Henderson, 1958) and the cement market in India.

3.4.2 Continuous markets

Perhaps the finest flowering of the EAE mode of approach is the continuous flow model. In the NLP model of spatial market equilibrium space does not occur explicitly. The continuous flow model on the other hand focuses directly on the map of trade flows and the map of "isotimes" or isoprices lines.

In equation (3.47) the location index i is replaced by a two-dimensional coordinate vector $x' = (x_1, x_2)$, excess demand is replaced by excess demand per unit area or "excess demand density" $q(x)$. Similarly the shipments x_{ij} are replaced by shipment densities whose spatial manifestation becomes a flow vector field. Denote this by

$$\phi(x) = \begin{bmatrix} \phi_1(x) \\ \phi_2(x) \end{bmatrix} \tag{3.54}$$

The direction of ϕ is that of flows passing through x and the strength $|\phi|$ of the flow field measures the amount of flow passing in a normal direction through a unit cross section.

The commodity balance equation (3.47) assumes the form of a "divergence law"

$$\frac{\partial \phi_1}{\partial x_1} + \frac{\partial \phi_2}{\partial x_2} + q(x) = 0 \tag{3.55}$$

This is also written

$$\text{div } \phi + q = 0 \tag{3.56}$$

where div is the divergence operator

$$\left(\frac{\partial}{\partial x_1}, \frac{\partial}{\partial x_2}\right)$$

What is the continuous equivalent of the profitability (or efficiency) condition (3.52)? The economic statement is that arbitrage is unprofitable and will just cover costs in the case of actual shipments. Let $D_\alpha p$ denote the directional derivative in the direction α and let $k = k(x)$ be transportation costs per unit commodity and unit distance assumed to be a function of location but independent of direction (isotropic).

$$D_\alpha p \leqq k$$

$$D_\phi p = k \qquad \text{if } \phi \neq 0.$$

This may be stated more elegantly. Recalling that the gradient of a function p(x) is the direction of its steepest ascent then

$$|\text{grad } p| \leqq k \tag{3.57}$$

and

$$\text{grad } p = k \frac{\phi}{|\phi|} \qquad \text{whenever } \phi \neq 0.$$

If the flow field fills out the entire region A, equations (3.56) and (3.57) apply throughout A. They must be supplemented by suitable boundary conditions. In the simplest case of a self-sufficient region one has

$$\phi_n = 0 \qquad \text{on } \partial A \tag{3.58}$$

where n is the direction of the outward normal to the boundary.

In our statement of the spatial equilibrium problem

excess demand was given independent of price. A spatial equilibrium exists if and only if aggregate excess demand vanishes

$$\iint q \, dx_1 dx_2 = 0 \tag{3.59}$$

This is necessary because by the Gauss integral theorem

$$\int_{\partial A} \phi_n ds = \iint_A \operatorname{div} \phi \, dx_1 dx_2 \tag{3.60}$$

Now the left-hand side of (3.60) vanishes by the boundary condition (3.58) and so must the right-hand side. Substitution of (3.56) yields (3.59).

That this condition is sufficient follows from the fact that the following minimum problem is then bounded and feasible. Its optimal solution represents the flow field uniquely determined by (3.56), (3.57) and (3.58).

$$\underset{(\phi)}{\text{Min}} \iint k|\phi| \, dx_1 dx_2$$

subject to (3.56), (3.58).

The most important aspect of these flow fields for spatial equilibrium theory is that the potential function, the price $p(x)$, must have a maximum or minimum in a closed bounded region A. The most interesting case is when the maximum and/or minimum is an interior point. A maximum then represents the centre of a market area, a minimum that of a supply area. When all flows at the boundary point inward or all point outward, at least one of these must exist; but possibly both types or combinations of several may coexist. Thus market or supply areas emerge even when there is no predetermined centre, simply as a matter of efficiency in spatial trading.

Equation (3.57) shows that the flow field intersects the iso-times or potential lines orthogonally. In fact the flow field determines the price lines uniquely and the price level up to a common additive constant. The price lines determines the flow field uniquely.

So far excess demand was considered as given, independent of price. Let now

$$q = q(x,p(x)) \qquad \frac{\partial q}{\partial p} < 0 \tag{3.61}$$

Then the equations (3.56) remains valid with $q(x,p)$ substituted for $q(x)$. The equivalent maximum problem has the form

$$\text{Max} \iint u(\text{div}\ \phi) - k|\phi| dx_1 dx_2 \tag{3.62}$$

where the utility function $u(q)$ is a consumers' surplus integral

$$u(q) = \int_0^q p(s)ds \tag{3.63}$$

and $p(q)$ is the inverse function of $q(p)$. It exists since q was monotone decreasing by (3.61).

The spatial market equilibrium model (3.56), (3.57), (3.58) is the starting point of a theory which develops the spatial and consumption activities in a continuous representation of space (Beckmann, 1952, Puu, 1977, Beckmann and Puu, 1982). As a first example we mention the possibility that production is limited by the local carrying capacity of the soil

$$z \leq c(x) \tag{3.64}$$

and involves unit costs $h = h(x)$.

A given consumption program $q = q(x)$ is then realized in a competitive market economy such that a Pareto optimum is achieved. This implies minimization of costs.

$$\text{Min} \iint hz + k|\phi| dx_1 dx_2 \qquad (3.65)$$

subject to

$$\text{div}\ \phi + q - z = 0 \qquad \text{in A} \qquad (3.66)$$

and subject to (3.58) and (3.64).

The market price $p = p(x)$ must once more satisfy (3.57). Condition (3.56) is replaced by (3.66). Moreover the market price p induces land rents $r = r(x)$ such that

$$p \left\{\begin{smallmatrix}\leq\\=\end{smallmatrix}\right\} h + r \quad \text{accordingly as} \quad z \left\{\begin{smallmatrix}=\\>\end{smallmatrix}\right\} 0 \qquad (3.67)$$

No restriction is imposed on the gradient of rent since land is immobile.

The continuous flow approach is more fully developed in Puu (1979-B) and Beckmann and Puu (1982).

3.5 Spatial Market Equilibrium: multiple commodities

The characteristic case is the von Thünen problem: how land is allocated to competing products when market location and market prices are given. We state this famous problem first as a market equilibrium problem for multiple commodities and subsequently as a general equilibrium problem (Section 3.6.1).

3.5.1 Programming model

It will be useful to restate the von Thünen problem in terms of neoclassical production functions (Beckmann, 1972-A). Let z_k be the output per hectare of product k; ℓ_k, the labour input per hectare into product k; $z_k = f_k(\ell_k)$, the production function for product k; x_k, the proportion of land allocated to the production of k; c the available land per unit area;

p_k, the price of product k in the city market; h_k the transportation cost per unit of commodity k and unit distance; w, the wage rate.

The land owner seeks to maximize profits

$$\sum_k (p_k - h_k r) f_k(\ell_k) x_k - w \sum_k x_k \ell_k \qquad (3.68)$$

subject to the constraint on land availability

$$\sum_k x_k \leq c \qquad (3.69)$$

In von Thünen's formulation the production functions f_k are generated by fixed coefficients: labour input ℓ_k is proportional to output z_k

$$\ell_k = a_k z_k \qquad (3.70)$$

The allocation problem becomes a parametric linear program

$$\underset{x_k(r)}{\text{Max}} \sum_{k=1}^{n} (p_k - h_k r) x_k - w a_k x_k \qquad (3.71)$$

subject to

$$\sum_{k=1}^{n} x_k \leq 1 \qquad (3.72)$$

However, the assumption of fixed input coefficients is not essential as we shall show below.

The principal result of model (3.71), (3.72) is stated in the efficiency conditions of this LP

$$\hat{x} \left\{ \begin{matrix} = \\ \geq \end{matrix} \right\} o \Longleftrightarrow p_k - h_k r - w a_k \left\{ \begin{matrix} < \\ = \end{matrix} \right\} \lambda \qquad (3.73)$$

where λ is the dual variable associated with (3.72). Statement

(3.73) may be rewritten

$$\lambda = \underset{k}{\mathrm{Max}}\ [p_k - h_k r - a_k w] \tag{3.74}$$

Here $\lambda = \lambda(r)$ appears as land rent. Its value equals the profit from one unit of land achieved by using the most profitable activity k. At short distances profitability depends on p_k alone. As distance from the market is increased activities with smaller p_k but lower transportation costs h_k become optimal. (Activities with lower p_k and higher h_k are dominated and will not be chosen.) The most interesting conclusion is that agricultural land use is specialized in zones, which under proportional transportation costs assume the shape of circular rings, the famous von Thünen rings.

Now consider the NLP (3.68), (3.69) in which production is described by neoclassical production functions. The efficiency conditions (Kuhn-Tucker conditions) are now

$$0 = \frac{\partial L}{\partial \ell_k} = [(p_k - h_k r)\,\frac{\partial f_k(\hat{\ell}_k)}{\partial \ell_k} - w]x_k \tag{3.75}$$

Let $\hat{f}_k = f_k(\hat{\ell}_k)$ be the optimal output intensity of product k if it is produced at distance r. Rewriting (3.75)

$$(p_k - h_k r)\,\frac{\partial f_k(\hat{\ell}_k)}{\partial \ell_k} = w \tag{3.76}$$

The location of production is once more described by a condition similar to (3.73)

$$x_k \left\{\begin{matrix} = \\ \geq \end{matrix}\right\} 0 \iff (p_k - h_k r)\,\hat{f}_k - w\hat{\ell}_k \left\{\begin{matrix} < \\ = \end{matrix}\right\} \lambda \tag{3.77}$$

where once more

$$\lambda = \underset{k}{\mathrm{Max}}\ (p_k - h_k r)\,\hat{f}_k - w\hat{\ell}_k \tag{3.78}$$

$= \lambda(r) =$ rent at distance r.

Even when this maximum in (3.78) is realized by several activities k (a hairline case) only one activity need be chosen to achieve profit maximization. We have the <u>Specialization Theorem</u>: when production has constant returns to scale, the optimal land use is achieved through specialization: each location produces only one commodity.

From the continuity of expressions in (3.77) it may be seen that locations for producing a commodity k occupy contiguous extended areas.

This is a generalization of von Thünen rings which occurs when (1) soil and climate are dependent on location; (2) markets are not concentrated in a single location but are dispersed and may even be continuously distributed.

Incidentally the intensity of land use within a given zone is no longer constant when the production function does not involve fixed coefficients. Within a given zone the labour intensity ℓ_k and hence the output intensity z_k decrease with distance from the market.

For implicit differentiation of (3.76) yields

$$\frac{d\hat{\ell}_k}{dr} = - \frac{h_k f'_k}{(p_k - h_k r) f''_k} > 0 \tag{3.79}$$

since $f' > 0, f'' < 0$, for neoclassical production functions are monotone increasing and concave.

3.5.2 Network equilibrium

A type of spatial equilibrium familiar to everybody but widely misunderstood in its structure and consequences is the equilibrium of traffic in a network. Suppose that every day during the morning rush hour q_i^k trips are started from origin locations i to destination locations k. In order to get there certain links ij in the network must be passed and the amount of traffic on ij with destination k is denoted by x_{ij}^k. These basic flows x_{ij}^k observe the conservation law

$$\sum_j x_{ij}^k + \sum_j x_{ji}^k = q_i^k \qquad i \neq k \tag{3.80}$$

This says that departing traffic equals arrived traffic plus generated traffic.

At destination k one has instead

$$\sum_j x_{ji}^k = \sum_{i \neq k} q_i^k$$

but this equation is redundant and need not be stated in the program.

If sufficient capacity is available, then everybody seeks the shortest route independently of anybody else and private cost minimization achieves total or social cost minimization.

In the presence of capacity restrictions this is no longer true. The interesting case is that where capacities are not rigid but give rise to a travel time - flow relationship such that with increasing flow travel time rises.

$$t_{ij} = f_{ij}(x_{ij}) \qquad f' > 0 \quad f'' > 0 \tag{3.81}$$

where

$$x_{ij} = \sum_k x_{ij}^k \tag{3.82}$$

Empirical measurements suggest a relationship of the type

$$f_{ij} = t_{ij} + b_{ij}x_{ij}^4$$

An efficient transportation program is one which achieves

$$\min_{x_{ij}^k \geq 0} \sum_{ij} f_{ij}(x_{ij})x_{ij}$$

subject to (3.80) and (3.82).

Consider the Lagrangean function

$$L = -\sum_{ij} f_{ij}(x_{ij})x_{ij} + \sum_i \lambda_i^k [q_i^k + \sum_j (x_{ji}^k - x_{ij}^k)]$$

The efficiency conditions for a minimum are

$$x_{ij}^k \left\{\begin{matrix} = \\ \geq \end{matrix}\right\} 0 \iff f_{ij} + x_{ij}f'_{ij} - \lambda_i^k + \lambda_j^k \left\{\begin{matrix} \leq \\ = \end{matrix}\right\} 0 \qquad (3.83)$$

This efficiency condition may be rewritten as follows:

$$\lambda_i^k = \min_j [d_{ij} + \lambda_j^k] \qquad \lambda_k^k = 0 \qquad (3.84)$$

with

$$d_{ij} = f_{ij} + x_{ij}f'_{ij} \qquad (3.85)$$

Equation (3.84) states the "principle of optimality" for shortest paths where d_{ij} is the length of link ij. A shortest path from i to k must select a next destination j such that the cost of getting to j plus the cost of the remaining trip is minimal.

The efficiency conditions state that each traveller should choose the shortest paths with the length of links calculated on the basis of marginal cost $f_{ij} + x_{ij}f'_{ij}$.

The second term measures the contribution that one unit of traffic makes to the congestion delay experienced by all traffic. The first term is the cost experienced by the traveller himself.

Now the actual traffic equilibrium is one where individuals find shortest paths based not on d_{ij} but on f_{ij}. The absence of a "congestion toll" $x_{ij}f_{ij}$ prevents the traffic equilibrium from being optimal. It gives an artificial incentive to using congested facilities since the effect of participation on others is ignored. The inefficiency experienced daily in the use of urban road systems has its root in the violation of efficiency conditions (3.84) and (3.85) (Beckmann, McGuire and Winsten, 1956).

A considerable literature has grown up on the pros and cons of "road pricing" as well as on the art and science of traffic forecasting by means of traffic equilibrium models (Smeed, 1964, Florian and Nguyen, 1976-B). The equilibrium models are all variants of the basic equation system

$$\sum_j (x_{ij}^k - x_{ij}^k) = q_i^k \qquad (3.86)$$

(the sum to be extended over all j for which links ij or ji exist in the network) and

$$\lambda_i^k = \min_j [f_{ij}(\sum_j x_{ij}^k) + \lambda_j^k] \qquad (3.87)$$

Incidentally the maximum problem associated with equations (3.80) and (3.87) is

$$\text{Min} \sum_{ij} \int_o^{\sum_k x_{ik}} t_{ij}(x)dx$$

subject to (3.86) whose solution does not constitute a welfare maximum.

3.5.3 Clustering

Consider an economy extended along a line. Suppose there are two independent economic activities occurring at distances of m and h kilometres respectively where m and h are integers. Then clusters of both activities are possible at distances (m,h) where (m,h) denotes the least common multiple.

Joint location offers the following advantages: (a) a larger market for each product; (b) a larger labour market; (c) economies of joint facilities: transportation, repair, marketing, advertising finance; (d) economies of joint social overheads: schools, hospitals, police.

When several activities occur at integer distances, clusters are possible in which any combination of 2, 3, ... n activities occur. These considerations can be extended immediately to location in two dimensions at the vertices of a rectangular grid. Now large clusters will tend to absorb nearby smaller ones, for the smaller ones can reap the benefits of joint location by joining the larger ones. This tendency to the formation of larger clusters and elimination of smaller ones is reinforced when the various activities interact through supply and demand relationships: the product of one activity becoming input into another activity.

These interdependencies give rise to an externality effect in regard to the internal locational structure of a cluster. This is usually described in terms of a quadratic assignment problem (cf Section 3.7.1).

3.6 General Equilibrium

3.6.1 von Thünen system

To close the von Thünen model so as to render it a spatial system in general equilibrium, assume that labour is perfectly mobile and express all prices in wage units. Then wage $w = 1$. The only other factor of production is land. Only one agricultural product and one industrial product are considered. We wish to determine p_o, the price of the agricultural product in the city market and p_1, the price of industrial commodity in the city market.

The agricultural product is transported to the city by means of agricultural labour (as in von Thünen's original book). Per unit commodity and unit distance an amount k of labour is required. The price of the agricultural good at distance r is then

$$p_o(r) = p_o - kr \tag{3.88}$$

The industrial good is transported free of charge on the return journey. (Its bulk and weight are small relative to the agricultural product.) Thus

$$p_1(r) = p_1 \tag{3.89}$$

Production of the industrial good is described by a Cobb-Douglas Function

$$z_1 = b_1 L_1^{\alpha} \tag{3.90}$$

The output of the agricultural product per unit of land at distance r is also described by a Cobb-Douglas Function

$$z_o = b_o(r) \ell_o^{\alpha} \tag{3.91}$$

where ℓ_o is labour employed per unit of land. The total amount of labour N is given and fully employed.

$$N = L_1 + \int_o^R 2\Pi r \, \ell_o(r) dr + K \tag{3.92}$$

Here K is the labour force employed in transportation. The maximal distance from which products are sent to the city market is given by

$$p_o(R) = 0 = p_o - KR$$

or

$$R = \frac{p_o}{K} \tag{3.93}$$

Urban and rural households are assumed to have the same tastes. For simplicity we choose a logarithmic utility function

$$u = a_o \log q_o + a_1 \log q_1 \qquad a_o + a_1 = 1 \tag{3.94}$$

where q_o is the quantity consumed of the agricultural product and q_1 is the quantity consumed of the industrial product. For a household with income y, the budget constraint is

$$q_o(p_o - kr) + q_1 p_1 = y \tag{3.95}$$

For urban households $r = 0$.

Prices p_o, p_1 will now be derived by equating aggregate supply and demand.

Maximizing utility (3.94) subject to the budget constraint (3.95) yields the demand functions for agricultural product

$$q_o = \frac{a_o}{p_o - kr} y \tag{3.96}$$

The agricultural supply is determined by profit maximization

$$\text{Max}(p_o - kr) b_o(r) \ell_o^{\alpha} - \ell_o$$

The outputs are

$$z_o = b_o^{\frac{1}{1-\alpha}} [\alpha(p_o - kr)]^{\frac{\alpha}{1-\alpha}} \tag{3.97}$$

and they are produced by a labour input/land

$$\ell_o = [\alpha b_o(p_o - kr)]^{\frac{1}{1-\alpha}} \tag{3.98}$$

Assume that all land is farmed by owners. The income of farmers per unit of land is then

$$y = z_o(p_o - kr) \tag{3.99}$$

Substitute this in the demand function (3.96) to obtain net supply per unit of land

$$z_o - q_o\ell_o = (1 - a_o)z_o = a_1 z_o = a_1 b_o^{\frac{1}{1-\alpha}}[\alpha(p_o - kr)]^{\frac{\alpha}{1-\alpha}} \tag{3.100}$$

From this the consumption of the transportation workers must be subtracted. Let the amount of agricultural product finally transported to the city from distance r be $z_o^o(r)$. Then

$$z_o^o(r) = a_1 z_o - k z_o^o$$

from which

$$z_o^o = \frac{a_1}{1 + k} z_o$$

$$z_o^o = \frac{a_1}{1 + k} b_o^{\frac{1}{1-\alpha}}[\alpha(p_o - kr)]^{\frac{\alpha}{1-\alpha}} \tag{3.101}$$

The supply of the agricultural product in the city is therefore

$$z_o = \int_o^R 2\Pi r \; z_o^o(r)dr$$

$$z_o = \frac{2\Pi a_1}{1 + k} \alpha^{\frac{\alpha}{1-\alpha}} \int_o^{\frac{p_o}{k}} b_o(r)^{\frac{1}{1-\alpha}}.r[p_o - kr]^{\frac{\alpha}{1-\alpha}}dr \tag{3.102}$$

Now the per capita demand for the agricultural product in the city is

$$\frac{a_o}{p_o}$$

using (3.96) and $w = 1$. Aggregate demand in the city for the agricultural product is therefore

$$L_1 \frac{a_o}{p_o}$$

Here

$$L_1 = N - K - L_o \tag{3.103}$$

and

$$K = \int_o^R kr.2\Pi r\; z_o^o dr$$

$$K = \frac{2\Pi k a_1}{1 + k} \alpha^{\frac{\alpha}{1-\alpha}} \int_o^{\frac{p_o}{k}} b_o(r)^{\frac{1}{1-\alpha}} r^2 [p_o - kr]^{\frac{\alpha}{1-\alpha}} dr \tag{3.104}$$

Notice also that

$$L_o = \int_o^R 2\Pi r \ell(r) dr = 2\Pi\alpha^{\frac{1}{1-\alpha}} \int_o^{\frac{p_o}{k}} [b_o(p_o - kr)]^{\frac{\alpha}{1-\alpha}} r\, dr \tag{3.105}$$

Combining equations (3.103), (3.104) and (3.105) p_o is determined.

Similarly the price of the industrial good is determined by equating supply and demand. The net output of the industrial sector is, using arguments analogous to (3.99)

$$z_1 = a_o b_1 L_1^{\alpha} \tag{3.106}$$

Aggregate expenditure on the industrial good by the agricultural and transportation sectors becomes

$$p_o z_o^o$$

Equating supply and demand

$$p_o z_o^o = p_1 z_1 = p_1 a_o b_1 L_1^{\alpha} \qquad (3.107)$$

In this way general equilibrium in a von Thünen system may be determined. A detailed discussion of its comparative statics exceeds the limits of this paper (cf Vernon, 1972).

3.6.2 The monocentric city

The classical land use model in the urban context is based, as is the von Thünen model, on a single centre as the focus of all trade and all manufacturing activities (Alonso, 1964-A, Muth, 1969). In principle several rings of specialized land use could be considered along the lines of Park and Burgess (1921), the founders of the Chicago school of urban sociology. But it is customary to consider residential land use as a homogeneous economic activity. The distinct building types are replaced by a smooth production function for housing which describes the quantity of housing space per unit of land as a function of the amount of capital invested per unit of land area.

We consider the problem of housing a given population N which settles around a "Central Business District" (CBD), where all employment and trade is located. The radius of the CBD may be finite, but distances within the CBD are neglected. Households are assumed to have the same income (a typical middle class town) and the same preferences. When different income classes are introduced this gives rise once more to a system of von Thünen rings.

The location problem is that of locating a "representative household". The equilibrium conditions state that representative households will live everywhere in a ring between the CBD (assumed to be a circle) and an outer radius (assumed given or determined endogeneously by the condition that urban rents at the city boundary must equal agricultural rents where the latter are assumed to be given).

Consider a household of income y. Its utility function is consolidated to contain only two goods: housing and "general consumption". The price of the general consumption good is standardized at unity, the price of housing p per square metre. Commuting costs and other urban travel costs to the centre are assumed proportional to distance r from the CBD, = kr. A household of income y living at distance r and occupying s square metres of housing has available for general consumption an amount

$$y = ps - kr;$$

its utility

$$u(y - ps - kr, s)$$

depends on two decisions: how much space to occupy and how far to live from the CBD.

Rather than work with general utility functions it is operational to specify the utilities in a way, so as to obtain rough agreement with observed facts. One possible choice is

$$u = a_o \log(y - ps - kr) + a_1 \log s \tag{3.108}$$

A household's choice of the amount of housing space, ie the demand for housing, is then obtained by maximizing (3.108) with respect to s

$$0 = \frac{-pa_o}{y - ps - kr} + \frac{a_1}{s}$$

from which

$$q = \frac{a_1}{a_o - a_1} \frac{y - kr}{p} \tag{3.109}$$

That the demand for housing has approximately unit elasticity for demand and unit income elasticity as stated in (3.108) is a widely accepted fact in the US.

Substituting (3.109) in (3.108) determines the level of the utility that is achieved by an optimal choice of the amount of housing, as a function of distance from the CBD

$$u_o = (a_o + a_1)\log[\frac{a_o}{a_o + a_1}(y - kr)] - a_1 \log p \tag{3.110}$$

If households are willing to live at all distances from the CBD within a range $r_o \leqq r \leqq R$ then the achieved utility must be the same throughout this region.

This means that u is a constant, ie independent of r. Of course it does depend on income y, but y itself is held constant here. Equation (3.110) can now be solved for p. It turns out that p is a function only of distance r as follows

$$p(r) = e^{-\frac{u_o}{a_1}} . [\frac{a_o}{a_o + a_1}(y - kr)]^{\frac{a_o + a_1}{a_1}} \tag{3.111}$$

$$p(r) = c_o . [y - kr]^{1 + \frac{a_o}{a_1}} \tag{3.112}$$

Equation (3.112) is the rent bid function which describes the demand side of the urban market.

In order to determine residential density, the supply of housing must be introduced. Assume that the supply function has constant price elasticity. (This may be derived formally from a Cobb-Douglas production function for housing in terms of land and capital.)

$$h = h_o p^b \qquad b > 1 \tag{3.113}$$

The number of households per unit of housing equals

$$\frac{1}{s} = \frac{a_o + a_1}{a_1} \cdot \frac{p}{y - kr} \qquad \text{from (3.109)} \qquad (3.114)$$

The number of households per unit of land area is then the algebraic product of (3.113) and (3.114). Denote this population density by m(r).

$$m(r) = \frac{h}{s} = \frac{a_o + a_1}{a_1} \frac{p^{1+b}}{y - kr}$$

$$m(r) = c_1.(y - kr)^{(1 + \frac{a_o}{a_1})(1 + b) - 1}$$

or

$$m(r) = c_1(y - kr)^{\eta} \qquad (3.115)$$

where

$$\eta = (1 + \frac{a_o}{a_1})(1 + b) - 1 > 1$$

The constant c_1 is determined by equating the total number N of households with the integral of density over the residential area.

$$N = \int_{r_o}^{R} 2\Pi r\ m(r)dr \qquad (3.116)$$

Upon substituting (3.115) in (3.116) c_1 is determined. The utility level u_o is then also determined from (3.112) and (3.114)

$$c_1 = (\frac{a_1}{a_o + a_1})^{\eta}.e^{-\frac{u_o}{a_1}(1 + b)} \qquad (3.117)$$

When not R but p(R) is given, the agricultural rent at the city boundary, the integral in (3.116) must be transformed

$$N = \int_{p(R)}^{p(r_o)} 2\Pi r(p) m(r(p)) \frac{dr}{dp} \, dp$$

where p(r) is given in (3.112).

Since commuting cost kr is usually a small part of total household income y, an approximation may be used in (3.115). Rewrite (3.115)

$$m(r) = c_1 y^{\eta} [1 - \frac{kr}{y}]^{\eta}$$

Observe that

$$1 - \frac{kr}{y} \simeq e^{-\frac{kr}{y}}$$

Thus

$$m(r) \simeq c_2 e^{-\frac{\eta k}{y} r} \qquad (3.118)$$

An exponential density law for urban residential land use has been observed in many cities, first by Clark (1951).

Formula (3.118) suggests that the exponent in this density function is not a universal constant, but depends on commuting cost k relative to income y, on the elasticity of the housing supply, and on the preference for general consumption to that for housing $\frac{a_o}{a_1}$.

This model of residential locational choice in a monocentric city is an important stepping stone towards the theory of urban economics and indirectly for city planning and city architecture.

3.7 Conclusion: problems and prospects

The objective of the EAE-approach in Location Theory has been to achieve the fullest possible integration of location theory into neoclassical micro-economics. In this way, the powerful instruments of neoclassical economic theory can be utilized in the analysis of locational problems. On the other hand, location theory itself can offer some help in solving such tricky questions of neoclassical economics as the existence of an optimum size of the firm or the reconciliation of increasing returns to scale in production with market equilibrium.

To a remarkable extent this objective has been accomplished. There remain however, some formidable difficulties, which unfortunately are not of a mathematical nature but a conceptual one. They are essentially generated by the presence of indivisibilities and externalities and give rise to the question: how well spatial markets can ever be approximated by the competitive model of neoclassical economics. Secondly, and even more seriously they raise the spectre of non-existence of equilibrium as in the so-called quadratic assignment problem (Koopmans and Beckmann, 1957).

3.7.1 Quadratic assignment problem

To illustrate non-existence of spatial equilibrium consider the following four firms and locations. Part of the output of each firm is used as input by another firm. In particular suppose that

firm 1 supplies firm 2
firm 2 supplies firm 3
firm 3 supplies firm 4
firm 4 supplies firm 1.

Let the four locations consist of two pairs of adjacent locations (Figure 3.4). Initially the firms are located as follows:

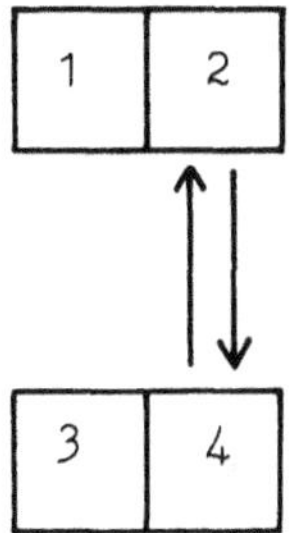

Figure 3.4: Quadratic assignment: non-equilibrium - 1

Now firms 2 and 4 can both gain by exchanging locations: firm 2 is closer to its customer 3 and firm 4 is closer to its customer 1 (we assume that the producer pays transportation costs). The result of the exchange is (Figure 3.5):

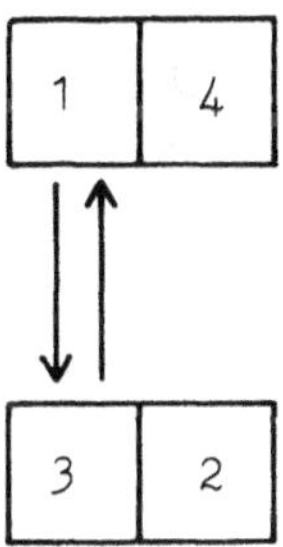

Figure 3.5: Quadratic assignment: non-equilibrium - 2

Now firms 3 and 1 have an incentive to exchange locations. The reader may show that 4 and 2 will want to exchange locations again and after that 1 and 3 once more, whereupon the original locational assignment has been reached once more.

In this way firms will be induced to rotate and no equilibrium exists. More complicated examples may be constructed to avoid obvious objections. The point remains: under the quadratic assignment problem when trade relationships among firms create "externalities", there exist situations where land rents fail to achieve and maintain spatial equilibrium in the location of firms.

How serious are these cases? What can be done about them in real life?

The situation described presumes a shortage of locations for firms wishing to locate close together. In a CBD one can often ignore distances between locations, so that within that limited zone all locations become (to a first approximation) equally good and the assignment problem disappears.

Another way of handling this type of externality is vertical integration: plants between which a great deal of trade takes place tend to be owned by the same firm.

Finally high moving costs will act to prevent the circular movements described above.

The quadratic assignment problems may thus be no more than an anomaly, a theoretical possibility that does not materialize. It points, however, to the limitations of the EAE approach, whose very foundation is the notion of equilibrium. It can not be denied that a spatial market equilibrium need not always exist.

3.7.2 Externalities

Externalities have cropped up in other areas of applied micro-economics, notably in environmental economics. Spill-over effects have a spatial dimension. They cause problems for the economy and for economic analysis because the agents (decision makers) responsible for generating the effects are not the agents who suffer or pay for the damage of these effects. An example of this situation was described in 3.5.2 network equilibrium. The externality involved is the delay imposed on other traffic by each vehicle joining a congested traffic stream. The presence of externalities does not prevent an equilibrium, but it makes the equilibrium non-optimal.

Economists have long been aware of the need to control individual decisions in such situations by imposing a charge for external damages on those responsible for these damages. In this way their inadequate cost calculations are corrected. In the network equilibrium case these charges would be "congestion tolls" to be levied on all users of congested roads.

Although in the case of network congestion devices exist that make this technically feasible, this is not always true in other cases of spill-over and damaging neighbourhood effects. More thought should be given to "second best" solutions that have the virtue of technical and/or political feasibility. Location theory, too, should be developed to support this effort by a closer study of the spatial side of externalities: neighbourhood effects, spill-over, diffusion (Beckmann, 1968, Muth, 1969).

3.7.3 Indivisibilities

Another way to look at the Quadratic Assignment Problem is to focus on the indivisibility of the plants that must be assigned to locations. In regard to locations there is usually perfect divisibility: there is no apparent limit to how much economic activity can be squeezed into the space that may be constructed on a given amount of land area.

Indivisibilities show up in many contexts. Most important perhaps is the presence of a fixed cost in production by a plant or (more subtly) the existence of increasing returns to scale in production.

In Operations Research approaches to locational problems indivisibilities show up as integer or zero-one restrictions on the variable z_{ik}: plant i is located in location k. The combination of such integer variables with continuous flow variables gives rise to the so-called location-allocation problem (Cooper, 1963, Erlenkotter, 1978).

Mathematical methods exist for computing approximate solutions to this problem with reasonable effort. But these solutions do not yield any insight that is of general interest to students of location theory. The EAE-approach based on neoclassical "marginalism" does not consider a combinatorial type of allocation problem that occurs when, say, m plants are to be placed in m among n possible locations. This fundamental barrier can be surmounted only in those situations where the spatial embedding is homogeneous. The optimal location pattern will then be a regular point lattice, and these can be studied once more by means of marginal analysis (Lösch, 1940, Mills and Lav, 1964, Beckmann, 1972-A, Eaton and Lipsey, 1976, 1977, 1978, Leonardi, 1978).

A concentrated attack on efficient allocation of indivisible resources has been made by Scarf (1981). It would be interesting to see whether his efficiency conditions can be applied to and interpreted in a spatial context.

3.7.4 Imperfect rationality

The EAE-approach like neoclassical economics assumes that decision makers act rationally. As consumers they maximize (expected) utility, as job searchers they maximize real income, as producers they maximize profits.

It is well known that these high aspirations are not always achieved in real life. To make economics more realistic and relevant, limitations must be accepted and incorporated on the degree of perfection with which, say, utility maximization is achieved. One way is that suggested by Simon (1955): to assume satisficing rather than maximizing behaviour. An example of this was the search for a residence (cf 3.2.2).

Another limitation on the applicability of simple economic models works in the same direction. When studying a "representative household" an implicit or explicit assumption is made that this household's tastes are the same as those of any other household. Such uniformity of preferences is another non-realistic feature that should be eliminated from an operational theory.

The most promising development of economic ideas intended to cope with both imperfect rationality and the diversity of tastes is the notion of "random utility", that is of stochastic components in the utility functions. We have sketched the application of this concept in an effort to explain cross hauling and the interpenetration of spatial markets in Section 3.2.4. These phenomena are clearly inconsistent with perfect rationality but may yield to analysis when random components in preferences are recognized.

Another way of coping with this type of behaviour is to assume a value of total transportation costs that lies above the minimum that can be achieved with perfect rationality, and to trace the behavioural implications of this by making plausible assumptions about what is "equally likely". That is the entropy approach mentioned above (cf 3.2.2) (Murchland, 1966, Wilson, 1970-A).

3.7.5 Dynamics

The EAE-approach as presented is a static one. Equilibrium is the key concept. This does not rule out that different equilibria may be compared that arise under different data constellations. In fact, such Comparative Statics is the very meat of an equilibrium approach. The EAE-approach has not been used, however, to study the processes by which equilibrium is reached (or not reached).

Spatial markets in disequilibrium presumably present such

problems of complexity that one has resorted instead to simulation rather than analysis.

A complicating feature is the presence of oligopoly which allows much greater strategic freedom to the participants than would be possible under the iron discipline of competitive markets (Eaton and Lipsey, 1978, Philips and Thisse, 1982).

3.7.6 Promising directions of future research

Has the EAE-approach reached its limits? The attentive reader will see at once that this is not so.

3.7.6.1 Extension of theory

Location theory as developed in the EAE-approach has cultivated certain conventions in standard models that look unnecessarily restrictive. In any case they are more special than they need be and would be in non-spatial micro-economic theory. These include:

linearity of demand functions
linearity of cost functions.

There is also a standard way of treating transportation cost which is not quite adequate for describing shopping behaviour under today's conditions: costs of transportation are assumed proportional to weight and distance. There are many challenges here to bring location theory up to a level of sophistication in its economic assumptions that compares to contemporary neoclassical economics generally (Scarf, 1981).

3.7.6.2 Random utility models

If the EAE-approach is to flourish in competition with the entropy school it must continue and strengthen the random utility mode of studying individual behaviour. There is great promise here to obtain a better understanding of the behavioural foundations of observed macroscopic laws in spatial interaction. The situation is not altogether different from that in 19th century thermo-dynamics: a real understanding of macro-phenomena is possible only on the basis of a microscopic theory (Leonardi, 1982-A).

3.7.6.3 Dynamics

No serious attempt has been made by practitioners of the EAE-approach in the past to develop simple, but operational, models that show the dynamics of spatial relationships in non-equilibrium situations. Dynamics as such is not inconsistent with an approach oriented at equilibrium. For the position relative to an equilibrium will be an important force in shaping the economic processes that occur outside of equilibrium (Lösch, 1940).

The three problem areas sketched here should be studied together, for there is a possibility of mutual benefits. They are all within the proper limits of an EAE mode of approach. By comparison the problems of spill-over and of indivisibility seem much less tractable and promising. A dissipation of research effort over too many areas should be avoided.

Chapter 4

THE CHOICE-THEORETIC APPROACH: POPULATION MOBILITY AS AN EXAMPLE

G. Leonardi

4.1 Introduction and State-of-the-art

The aim of this chapter is to develop a unified framework to model urban phenomena by embedding an explicit choice-theoretical approach into a dynamic context. More precisely, the type of phenomena addressed in the chapter can be given the general heading of *mobility processes*, that is processes where a (usually large) set of human actors change state over time, according to some evaluation and choice behaviour. The different states occupied by the actors, in the systems of our concern, are geographically distinct, so that a change in state implies a change in the geographical location where some activities are performed. The criteria for evaluation and choice are both exogenous, that is depending on some local features of the different states, and endogenous, that is depending on the interactions among different actors. Typical examples of such mobility systems are:

(i) *the residential mobility system*, where the actors are households, the states are the dwellings in each location, the changes of states are the changes of residence. The evaluation and choice process leading to the decision to move to a new dwelling is based on criteria like the availability of vacant dwellings (which is always limited), the accessibility to shops, services and other urban facilities used by the households on a daily basis, the distance from the place of work, the price of the dwelling. The endogenous factors in this choice process are the vacant housing stock and the prices, which are both dependent on the interaction and competition of all the households for the use of a limited resource.

(ii) *the joint residential-labour mobility system*, where the process described in (i) is interlinked with the process of changing job locations. If the households (or some members of the households) are also workers, the states of the system are now the pairs of dwellings and workplaces in each location, and the changes of state are both changes of residence and changes of workplace. The criteria guiding the choices are the same as before, plus the availability of new jobs and the wages offered.

Other examples of urban systems exhibiting a similar structure can be imagined, like the daily adjustments of shopping trip patterns, the choice of schools, or the route choices in a transport network. This chapter will limit itself to the above mentioned ones, and while (i) will be developed with richer details, (ii) will be outlined and proposed as a topic for future research.

This difference in depth should not be interpreted as a difference in terms of importance. Indeed the joint residential-labour mobility process is considered as the most interesting and promising direction for future developments, since it captures explicitly in dynamic terms the interactions between the two main components of urban land use, housing and workplaces, and a major source of urban transport problems, the commuting trips.

One more reason to concentrate on the above mentioned examples is the similarity in their speed. Both residential and labour mobility are medium term processes, typically undergoing changes (at the individual choice level) every several years, and their trajectories are observable over a reasonably long time span. Faster processes, like shopping trips or route choice, work at a much faster time scale (usually a few hours, or days), and their influence on the slower mobility process can be reasonably described by their steady state (for example, an accessibility indicator for shopping trips, or an equilibrium travel time for the transport network). On the other hand, processes like changes in the housing stock level (by new constructions or demolitions) or changes in the number of job opportunities (due to new investments for capacity expansion or to industrial relocation) have a much slower time scale than the mobility processes, and a time span suitable to observe the transient behaviour of residential or labour mobility is negligible to observe changes in the housing stock and the industrial capital investments. The above statement needs caution, since it is no longer true around critical points of the system dynamics, where, for instance, changes in the stock levels might induce instability and bifurcations in the mobility processes. This problem will be explored by means of comparative statics for some simple examples in a later section, and it needs for sure a deep theoretical investigation in future research.

While the idea of combining together choice theory and dynamic mobility processes seems a natural one, surprisingly enough attempts in this direction are fairly recent. Until a decade ago, disaggregate choice models and dynamic mobility models proceeded along two distinct, non-interacting paths, one ignoring the time dimension of choice behaviour, the other ignoring the choice-theoretical explanation of state changes. In spite of this, powerful analytical tools have been developed in both fields, which make it easier (although not trivial) to try a marriage now.

As for the disaggregate choice theory, among many different approaches the best developed one (and the one used in this paper) is based on *random utility theory*. This approach had its first comprehensive development in the work of Manski (1973), although its roots can be traced back to the work of older choice theorists, like Luce (1959). It has found a wide range of applications in urban modelling, mostly in transport demand analysis, and reference can be made to Ben-Akiva (1974), Domencich and McFadden (1975), Williams (1977-A), McFadden (1978), and Smith (1982-A). The idea behind random utility theory is quite attractive to urban modellers, since uncertainty in the preferences guiding the choice behaviour is explicitly introduced. It has been criticised for some lack of generality, however, due to some seemingly restrictive assumptions which are needed in order to obtain operational forms for the choice models, like the well-known *Logit* one. In some recent work Leonardi (1982-A, 1982-B) has tried to weaken some of these tight assumptions, by means of arguments based on the asymptotic properties of extremes of random variables. An independent strand of research, which derives Logit-type models from assumptions other than those of random utility theory is the *Cost efficiency theory* proposed by Smith (1983-A) (chapter in this volume). It should also be mentioned that another very popular source of Logit-type models is the *Entropy maximizing principle*, borrowed from statistical mechanics and extended to urban modelling by Wilson (1970-A, 1974). It is at least comfortable for applications that so many different theoretical justifications lead basically to the same model structure.

As for the dynamic mobility models, their early roots can perhaps be traced back to the models of migration of animal populations developed in mathematical ecology. An account of such models can be found in Bartlett (1960), and more recent advances are given by Fife (1979). The main idea behind such ecological models, that is using the theory of stochastic multistate processes to model state transitions of living populations, has been extended to social processes in the work of Bartholomew (1973), a fundamental reference for every subsequent work. The same idea of a multistate process framework has been exploited by Rogers (1975) in the field of demography and migrations. Unlike their ecological predecessors, where non-linear interactions often appear, most of the models considered both in Bartholomew and in Rogers are shaped on the structure of *a time-homogeneous Markov process*, that is, essentially a linear system. Several attempts to cope with non-linear interaction effects followed the two above mentioned pioneering works, among them notably that of Ledent (1978), Sheppard (1983-E), and Weidlich and Haag (1983). The recent book by Weidlich and Haag is interesting and relevant for this paper in many respects, since, although no explicit choice-behavioural assumption is considered by the two authors, the general form they suggest for the (non-linear) transition rates of their dynamic equations is consistent with a Logit model, and indeed very similar to the one derived in later sections of this work.

Coming now to the attempts to introduce choice-behavioural assumptions explicitly in a dynamic framework, it should be repeated again that they are very recent. An exception should be made for simulation models. Indeed many micro-simulation models of such processes as the housing market have been produced in the last twenty years, where disaggregate behaviour of households and other actors has been carefully modelled. However, this paper is concerned with *analytic* approaches (at least as a starting point), therefore this literature will not be reviewed. One of the main efforts in the analytic direction is due to de Palma and his co-workers, namely de Palma (1981), de Palma and Ben-Akiva (1981), de Palma and Lefèvre (1983). The most interesting feature of the approach developed by de Palma and others is that all the main ingredients of a truly integrated dynamic mobility model are considered, namely the *accounting framework* (a Kolmogoroff-type set of dynamic equations), the *choice-behavioural assumptions* for the transition rates (random-utility type models), the *interaction between individual choice behaviour and collective state variables* (like diffusion of information and competition due to shortage of resources).

Similar in spirit, although independently developed, is the work of Weibull (1984-A) which specifically develops for the housing market the important theme of non-linear shortage signals affecting household choice behaviour. The interesting feature of Weibull's work is that unconventional, non pure-market signals are considered, such as queues and waiting times in a rationed housing system. It is worth mentioning that the specific application worked out by Weibull for the housing market is part of his more general research inspired by his collaboration with the Hungarian economist J. Kornai on shortage economies (Kornai, 1980); a general theoretical framework to such market systems is found in Weibull (1984-B).

Closely related to the work of de Palma (and bearing similarities with the work of Weibull) is the work of Leonardi and Campisi (1981) and Leonardi (1983). This approach, which has an ancestor in Bertuglia and Leonardi (1979), introduces a new feature in the mobility process, apparently not considered in previous work: the dynamics of household evaluation and formation of expected utilities. The attempt is to try and model the evaluation process not as a pointwise signal, just due to the current state of the system and its capacity tensions, but as the outcome of the expectations the households have on the future benefits they will gain (or lose) by taking decisions to move. This approach, still at an exploratory stage, is precisely the one developed in the rest of the chapter.

4.2 Mobility in a Limited Capacity Environment: a general structure

Before more specific models and theoretical underpinnings are developed, it will be useful to state in bare-bone terms the essential features of the mobility processes considered in this chapter. Such bare-bones will require very general, intuitive assumptions only, which can be considered, in a sense, as widely acceptable, being mostly related to the way the accounting framework is built.

Consider a total population of size T, made up of individuals who can occupy different states labelled 1, ..., m. Each individual is assumed to have a *residential behaviour and a moving behaviour*, in the sense that a typical history of his life will be a sequence of stays in some states alternated to moves from one state to the other. Moreover, each state j is supposed to have a finite capacity Q_j, j = 1, ..., m, such that not more than Q_j individuals can be in state j at the same time. In order for such a system to exist, it is of course required that:

$$T \leq \sum_{j=1}^{m} Q_j$$

If one wants to model the dynamic behaviour of such a system in deterministic terms, one is led to a very simple set of differential equations. Define $P_j(t)$ as the population size in state j at time t, $\dot{P}_j(t)$ as the time derivative of $P_j(t)$, and r_{ij} as the rate of flow from i to j (that is, r_{ij} is defined in such a way that the number of moves from i to j in a small time interval, given that a population $P_i(t)$ occupies state i at the beginning of that interval, is $P_i(t)r_{ij}\Delta$), and assume that both T and Q_j, j = 1, ..., m are constant. Then the balance of inflows and outflows for each state is ensured by the following accounting equations:

$$\dot{P}_j(t) = \sum_{i=1}^{m} P_i(t) r_{ij} - P_j(t) \sum_{i=1}^{m} r_{ji}, \quad j = 1, \ldots, m \qquad (4.1)$$

A conservation property holds for equations (4.1) since:

$$\sum_{j=1}^{m} \dot{P}_j(t) = \sum_{i=1}^{m} P_i(t) \sum_{j=1}^{m} r_{ij} - \sum_{j=1}^{m} P_j(t) \sum_{i=1}^{m} r_{ji} = 0$$

So far, nothing has been assumed on the structure of the rates r_{ij}, so that equations (4.1) are fairly general. Let this structure now be specified a bit further. The r_{ij} will be assumed to depend on four main factors, listed below:

(i) a general *intensity parameter* λ, scaling the speed of the moving process;

(ii) an *origin-destination specific factor*, expressed as a friction coefficient:

$$f_{ij}, \; 0 \leq f_{ij} \leq 1, \; i,j = 1, \ldots, m$$

and summarizing all those exogenous bilateral effects (like distance, lack of information, moving cost and so on) which might reduce (or increase) the likelihood of moving between each pair of states i,j;

(iii) a *state-specific attractiveness factor*, measuring the benefits (or disbenefits) an individual expects from starting a stay in a given state. Such attractiveness factors, which might in general vary over time, will be denoted as

$$V_j(t), \; j = 1, \ldots, m$$

and a non-negative increasing function G(x) is assumed to exist, such that the flow rate from state i to state j is proportional to:

$$G[V_j(t) - V_i(t)], \; i,j = 1, \ldots, m$$

ie, it is increasing with the difference in attractiveness between the destination state and the origin state;

(iv) a *limited capacity factor*, simply measured by the quantity:

$$Q_j - P_j(t), \; j = 1, \ldots, m$$

that is, the currently unused capacity (available for new movers) in state j.

Combining all the factors above in a multiplicative way, one gets for r_{ij} the general form:

$$r_{ij} = \lambda f_{ij} G[V_j(t) - V_i(t)][Q_j - P_j(t)] \tag{4.2}$$

Equation (4.2) is very general, in the sense that many different specific behavioural assumptions could fit its form. For instance, the parameter λ might reflect at the aggregate level many different microscopic phenomena, like the intensity by which individuals are exposed to diffusion of information about available capacity, or the intensity by which a decision to explore the possibility of moving is taken. The f_{ij} coefficients might be thought of as general distance-decay terms, reflecting the fact that interaction (that is, moving between two states) is usually less likely between states which are in some sense "far apart" (distance needs not being a geographical one, as already mentioned).

The limited capacity factor does not really need comments, since it is a quite familiar one in most interaction models of this sort; it can be looked at as a generalized logistic type effect, inhibiting the mobility because of scarce capacity. The term depending on attractiveness factors needs perhaps a few more words. While it can be widely accepted that the relative gain in attractiveness is taken into account by movers, it would be desirable to specify what the $V_j(t)$ are made from or, which is the same, whether they are exogenously given or rather endogenously determined in the interaction process.

The point of view of this paper is that the second case is the appropriate one to consider. Otherwise stated, the $V_j(t)$ can be considered in general as measures of the evaluation of benefits an individual associates with each state j, $j = 1, \ldots, m$, and clearly such evaluations have no reason to be exogenous, depending on the state of the system, the competition among movers for limited space and, more important, the way movers evaluate the effect of their current moves on their foreseeable future.

The above discussion leads to the following consideration: while equations (4.1) and (4.2) represent together an acceptable general accounting model for the dynamics of stocks (the $P_j(t)$) and flows (the r_{ij} as given by (4.2), nothing is a priori known about the dynamics of state-specific evaluations (the $V_j(t)$). Equations (4.1) and (4.2) do not need many behavioural assumptions in order to be derived; but no sensible dynamic equations can be conjectured for the evaluation process, unless some explicit microeconomic assumptions are introduced.

4.3 Time-nested Random-utility Theory: the basic structure

In order to provide the general interaction model outlined in Section 4.2 with some economic underpinnings, resort to a random-utility approach will be made. While the main results of static random-utility based choice models can be considered as known (reference can be made to Manski, 1973, Domencich and McFadden, 1975, Williams, 1977-A, Ben-Akiva and Lerman, 1979, for its standard disaggregate treatment, and to Leonardi, 1982-A and 1982-B, for its more general asymptotic extreme value treatment; further results on the mathematical structure of random utility models are found in Leonardi, 1981-C, and Smith, 1982-A) its use in a dynamic context needs some new theoretical effort. Although the idea of using random-utility choice models to derive flow rates in a set of equations like (4.1) is not quite new, with almost no exception the dynamic nature of the evaluation process has been ignored. In de Palma and Ben-Akiva (1981), for instance, equations similar to (4.1) and (4.2) are derived, but only for the case of exogenously given, time-independent V_j.

The main aim of this section is to introduce a new way of looking at the dynamics of the evaluation process, relating them to an explicit micro-economic phenomenon, the formation of *expectations-over future*. This approach, called here *time-nested random-utility theory*, has been proposed in Leonardi and Campisi (1981), and further developed in Leonardi (1983).

The idea behind the approach is very simple and is clarified by the following example. Suppose an individual is subject to a mobility process of the type discussed in Section 4.2. Assume he behaves in such a way as to maximize the utility of his choices, and define $h_i(t)$ as the gain per unit time due to staying in state i, i = 1, ..., m; v_{ij} as the utility associated with the action of moving from state i to state j, i,j = 1, ..., m; in most applications, v_{ij} will typically have a negative sign and be interpreted as the cost of moving between states i and j; $V_i(t)$ as the expected utility an individual gets from an unbounded-horizon process starting in state i at time t, i = 1, ..., m; α as the time-discount parameter in estimating future benefits; since continuous time is considered here, this means each individual is assumed to discount future according to an exponential decay function with parameter α; and F(x) as the probability distribution for the random-utility term each individual will add to its evaluations.

One needs a further assumption on the state of the

knowledge each individual has at any given time. Consistently with equation (4.2), it will be assumed here that, in a small time interval Δ starting at time t, the amount of available alternatives considered for evaluation is:

$$\lambda[Q_j - P_j(t)]\Delta$$

Using the terms defined above, a set of recurrence equations for the $V_i(t-\Delta)$ and $V_i(t)$ is obtained (see Leonardi, 1983):

$$V_i(t-\Delta) = h_i(t)\Delta + (1 - \alpha\Delta)E \max\{V_i(t) + \tilde{\theta}_i, \max_{(j)}[v_{ij} + V_j(t) + \tilde{\theta}_j]\} \tag{4.3}$$

where the symbol $\max_{(j)}$ denotes maximization over all available alternatives in state j and over all states j = 1, ..., m, the symbol $\tilde{\theta}_j$ denotes a random variable with distribution function F(x), the symbol E denotes taking expectation with respect to the sequence of random variables $\{\tilde{\theta}\}$.

In order to derive differential equations from (4.3), additional assumptions on the distribution F(x) are needed. A frequently used one is (Manski, 1973, Domencich and McFadden, 1975):

$$F(x) = \exp(-e^{-\beta x}),\ \beta < 0 \tag{4.4}$$

Recent work by Leonardi (1982-A, 1982-B) has shown that, under mild conditions, the same results derived by using the tight assumption (4.4) can be obtained as well from a much broader family of distributions for which the following requirement is met:

$$\lim_{x\to\infty} \frac{F'(x)}{1 - F(x)} = \beta,\ \beta > 0 \tag{4.5}$$

No matter whether assumption (4.4) or (4.5) is preferred, both yield when applied to (4.4) (Leonardi, 1983):

$$\alpha V_i(t) - \dot{V}_i(t) = h_i(t) + \frac{\lambda}{\beta}\sum_{j=1}^{m}[Q_j - P_j(t)]e^{\beta v_{ij}}e^{\beta[V_j(t)-V_i(t)]} \qquad (4.6)$$

where $\dot{V}_i(t)$ denotes the time derivative of $V_i(t)$ (equations (4.6) are, of course, obtained by letting $\Delta \to 0$ in equations (4.3)).

Equations (4.6) thus give an answer to the question asked at the end of Section 4.2, they provide a dynamic model for the value formation process, explicitly stated in terms of the parameters and state-variables of the stock-flow process. In order to derive the flow rates consistent with equations (4.6) one can observe that both assumptions (4.4) and (4.5) imply a multinomial logit model with dispersion parameter β and alternatives:

(i) staying in the place currently occupied in state i; there is just one such alternative* and its utility (besides the random term) is $V_i(t)$;

(ii) moving to a new place in some state $j = 1, \ldots, m$; for each j there are $\lambda[Q_j - P_j(t)]\Delta$ alternatives available and each of them has utility (besides the random term) $v_{ij} + V_j(t)$.

Therefore, if one defines $P_{ij}(t,\Delta)$ as the probability that an individual in state i at time t makes a move towards state j within a small time interval Δ, then the standard

---

* Staying in the currently occupied place in i *is different* in this model from moving to another place available in state i.

multinomial logit formula yields

$$P_{ij}(t,\Delta) = \frac{\Delta\lambda[Q_j - P_j(t)]e^{\beta[v_{ij}+V_j(t)]}}{\Delta\lambda \sum_{j=1}^{m} [Q_j - P_j(t)]e^{\beta[v_{ij}+V_j(t)]} + e^{\beta V_i(t)}}$$

and one gets for $r_{ij}(t)$:

$$r_{ij}(t) = \lim_{\Delta \to 0} \frac{P_{ij}(t,\Delta)}{\Delta} = \lambda[Q_j - P_j(t)]e^{\beta[v_{ij}+V_j(t)-V_i(t)]} \tag{4.7}$$

Comparison of equations (4.7) with equations (4.2) shows that they are identical, if one defines:

$$f_{ij} = e^{\beta v_{ij}}$$

$$G(x) = e^{\beta x}$$

Substitution of result (4.7) into equations (4.6) yields for the value formation process the more concise expression:

$$\alpha V_j(t) - \dot{V}_i(t) = h_i(t) + \frac{1}{\beta} \sum_j r_{ij}(t) \tag{4.8}$$

showing that the rate of change in expected utilities can be split into two terms: (i) a *local* contribution $h_i(t)$, unspecified as yet; and (ii) an *interaction* contribution $\frac{1}{\beta} \sum_j r_{ij}(t)$, proportional to the total rate of outflow from a place in state i. While the interaction term is now well specified in terms of the physical parameters and state variables of the system, the local term is still a black box. In the next section new assumptions will be introduced which will clarify the nature of this term.

4.4 A Random-utility Price-formation Mechanism

So far just one type of actor has been considered in the general mobility process, namely the individuals consuming the capacity offered in the system and making moves among different states. Now let a new type of actor be introduced, and assume a standard market mechanism is at work: suppliers charge prices for the use of the offered capacity, and they set them so as to maximize their revenues. However, the total capacities Q_j, $j = 1, \ldots, m$ are held constant, so that no investments in capacity expansion are made by suppliers.

Since suppliers are maximizing revenues, the price for each unit of capacity in each state, in each small time interval Δ, will be adjusted so as to reach the maximum level which does not discourage the highest bidding consumer from paying for it. Due to the random nature of consumers' behaviour, the highest bids will also be random variables, for which the distribution and expected value will be determined. In order to simplify notation, time dependency will not be indicated explicitly any more from now on, but it is understood that it is still there.

If there were no prices, an individual currently in state i would move to state j if a place were available there, which is better than any other alternative (including the currently used one). In other words, he would move if

$$v_{ij} + V_j + \vartheta_j - \max[V_i + \theta_i, \max_{(k)}(v_{ik} + V_k + \vartheta_k)] \geq 0 \tag{4.9}$$

If a price were charged in j, higher than the left-hand side of (4.9), then the individual from i would not find the place in j attractive any more, and he would consider other choices or stay in the current state. The maximum price level beyond which no individual in the system would consider a place in j as a convenient choice is therefore

$$\max_{(i)}\{v_{ij}+V_j+\vartheta_j-\max[V_i+\vartheta_i,\ \max_{(k)}(v_{ik}+V_k+\vartheta_k)]\} \tag{4.10}$$

where $\max_{(i)}$ indicates maximization both over every P_i in state i and over every i = 1, ..., m. From the usual assumptions on the distribution of the random terms it is easily derived that the random variables:

$$v_{ij} + V_i + \vartheta_j$$

have distribution

$$R_{ij}(x) = \exp(-A_{ij}e^{-\beta x}) \tag{4.11}$$

where

$$A_{ij} = \lambda\Delta e^{\beta(v_{ij}+V_j)} \tag{4.12}$$

while the random variables:

$$\max[V_i + \vartheta_i,\ \max(v_{ik}+V_k+\vartheta_k)]$$

have distribution

$$S_i(x) = \exp(-B_i e^{-\beta x}) \tag{4.13}$$

where

$$B_i = e^{\beta V_i} + \lambda\Delta \sum_{k=1}^{m} e^{\beta(v_{ik} + V_k)} \tag{4.14}$$

Both (4.11) and (4.13) are therefore of the Gumbel type. The distribution of the *difference* between the two variables (that is, of the term within curly brackets in (4.10)) is given by:

$$D_{ij}(x) = \int_{-\infty}^{\infty} R_{ij}(x+y) dS_i(y)$$

$$= \int_{-\infty}^{\infty} \beta B_i \exp[-A_{ij} e^{-\beta(x+y)}] \exp(-B_i e^{-\beta y}) e^{-\beta y} dy$$

$$= \frac{B_i}{B_i + A_{ij} e^{-\beta x}} = \frac{1}{1 + \frac{A_{ij}}{B_i} e^{-\beta x}} \tag{4.15}$$

a logistic distribution. Using definitions (4.12) and (4.14) and neglecting higher order terms in Δ, (4.15) becomes approximately:

$$D_{ij}(x) = \frac{1}{1 + \lambda \Delta f_{ij} e^{\beta(V_j - V_i)} e^{-\beta x}}$$

$$\sim \exp[-\lambda \Delta f_{ij} e^{\beta(V_j - V_i)} e^{-\beta x}] \tag{4.16}$$

again a Gumbel-type distribution. Finally, the distribution for the random quantity defined in (4.10) is:

$$H_j(x) = \sum_{i=1}^{m} D_{ij}^{P_i}(x) = \exp[-e^{-\beta x} \lambda \Delta \sum_{i=1}^{m} P_i f_{ij} e^{\beta(V_j - V_i)}]$$

$$\sim 1 - \lambda \Delta \psi_j e^{-\beta x} \tag{4.17}$$

having defined:

$$\psi_j = \sum_{i=1}^{m} P_i f_{ij} e^{\beta(V_j - V_i)} \tag{4.18}$$

Now the price in state j will be set equal to the random variable with distribution $H_j(x)$, if it is greater than 0. If this condition is not met, it means that even the highest bidding consumer will never choose to move to state j, no bargaining with the supplier will take place, and no price adjustment will be made. Therefore the average price set in state j at time t, as adjusted during the time interval $(t, t+\Delta)$, is given by:

$$\int_0^\infty x dH_j(x) = \lambda\beta\Delta\psi_j\int_0^\infty xe^{-\beta x}dx = \frac{\lambda}{\beta}\psi_j\Delta \qquad (4.19)$$

If one compares equation (4.18) with equation (4.7) one can write

$$\lambda\psi_j = \frac{\sum_{i=1}^{m} P_i r_{ij}}{Q_j - P_j}$$

therefore, from (4.19) the unit price in j is:

$$\frac{1}{\beta}\frac{\sum_{i=1}^{m} P_i r_{ij}}{Q_j - P_i} \qquad (4.20)$$

The numerator in expression (4.20) is the total in-flow of individuals to state j per unit time, while the denominator is the available capacity in j. The rather lengthy mathematics of this section has thus proved a very simple and intuitive result: average prices are proportional to the ratio between attracted consumers and available capacity, the proportionality factor being $1/\beta$.

The local term in equation (4.8), h_i, can now be re-defined as:

$$h_i = a_i - \frac{\lambda}{\beta}\psi_i \qquad (4.21)$$

where a_i is a residual local utility term, depending on specific features of state i other than prices. This term, which might or might not be time-dependent, can now be considered as exogenously given.

In analogy with definition (4.18), one can define the quantity:

$$\phi_i = \sum_{j=1}^{m} f_{ij}(Q_j - P_j)e^{\beta(V_j - V_i)} \tag{4.22}$$

Equation (4.8) can finally be rewritten in the form:

$$\alpha V_i - \dot{V}_i = a_i + \frac{\lambda}{\beta}(\phi_i - \psi_i) \tag{4.23}$$

4.5 An Application to Housing Mobility

Before going further with theoretical developments, it is useful at this stage to abandon the loose generality of the terminology used so far and cast the model structure in the more concrete terms of the housing mobility problem. The variables will be redefined as follows. T is the total population living in an area (births, deaths, migrations to and from the rest of the world are for the time being neglected). i,j label different zones of the area, 1,2, ..., m; more generally, the subscripts might label submarkets defined also by non-spatial qualitative features, but introducing further disaggregation at this stage would not really change the basic structure of the model. $P_i(t)$ is the number of people living (occupying a dwelling) in zone i at time t; further disaggregations of the population into different types, as well as their clustering into households of different sizes, are ignored for the time being. $v_{ij} = -(c + t_{ij})$ is the total cost of moving from i to j (changed in sign), split into the sum of a fixed cost for moving, c, and a travel cost from i to j, t_{ij}. $V_i(t)$ is the expected utility for someone who has just occupied a dwelling in zone i at time t. β is the random-utility dispersion parameter, $\beta \geq 0$. α is the discount rate over future, $\alpha \geq 0$. λ is the intensity parameter measuring the rate of knowledge of the available housing stock; λ is defined in such a way that $\lambda\Delta$ is the probability that one person gets informed about one free dwelling in a small time interval Δ, either by search, or by advertisement, or both (the two mechanisms make no difference in the model structure considered here). $a_i(t)$ is an exogenously given indicator of the attractiveness of zone i due to accessibility to places of destination of daily trips; other features of i might be introduced, like quality of the dwelling and of the neighbourhood, but this would not change the structure of the model considered here. Q_j is the housing stock (number of dwellings) in zone j; consistent with the assumptions made on the population, each dwelling is assumed to be occupied by no more than one person.

Other derived definitions are as follows: $Q_j - P_j(t)$ is the available housing stock in zone j at time t, that is, the number of vacant dwellings. $f_{ij} = e^{-\beta(c+t_{ij})}$ is the exponential decay factor for moving cost and travel cost. $r_{ij} = \lambda f_{ij}[Q_j - P_j(t)]e^{\beta[V_j(t)-V_i(t)]}$ is the flow rate between zones i and j,

$$\phi_i(t) = \sum_{j=1}^{m} f_{ij}[Q_j - P_j(t)]e^{\beta[V_j(t)-V_i(t)]}$$

is the accessibility to vacant dwellings from zone i; the reason why the sum above is called accessibility is the evident similarity between it and the way accessibility is defined in geography and regional science (Hansen, 1959, Ben-Akiva and Lerman, 1979). The new feature here, as compared to the simple accessibility as considered, for instance, by Hansen, is the exponential term containing the difference between expected utilities at the destination and at the origin.

$$\psi_j = \sum_{i=1}^{m} P_i(t) f_{ij} e^{\beta[V_j(t)-V_i(t)]}$$

is the population potential in zone j; the term used is motivated by reasons similar to those given for accessibility: apart from the utility difference term, the analogy with the concept of population potential, as developed in social physics of Stewart and Zipf (see Isard, 1960, for a short account), is evident.

For simplicity, it will also be assumed that the housing market is purely private and dwellings are for rent only. The housing mobility process defined above will then behave according to the dynamic equations (4.1) for population sizes and (4.23) for expected utilities, while the rents will be given by:

$$\frac{\lambda}{\beta}\psi_j \tag{4.24}$$

in accordance with equation (4.19). It is useful to note that equations (4.23) might be written in an alternative way, more meaningful in some cases, which involves the expected utilities expressed in their discounted value at time 0, rather than in their current value, as it has been tacitly assumed in Section 4.3. Let the following definition be introduced: $\mu_j(t) = e^{-\alpha t}V_j(t)$ is the discounted value of the expected utility in zone j at time t (evaluated in units at time 0). Then the following equality obviously holds:

$$-\mu_j(t) = e^{-\alpha t}[\alpha V_j(t) - \dot{V}_j(t)] \tag{4.25}$$

Therefore, by multiplying both sides of (4.23) by $e^{-\alpha t}$ and substituting from (4.25), one gets:

$$-\dot{\mu}_i = e^{-\alpha t}[a_i + \frac{\lambda}{\beta}(\phi_i - \psi_i)] \tag{4.26}$$

In either equations (4.23) or (4.26) and in (4.24) it is also useful to note that the definitions of accessibility and potential allow to rephrase the main features of the utility and rent formation mechanisms in somewhat more appealing terms. Equations (4.23), or (4.26), show that the endogenous contribution to the rate of change in utility is due to the difference between accessibility and potential, while (4.24) says that rents are proportional to potentials.

As a closing remark to this section, it is worth observing that the introduction of a process for expectations over the future, based on the time-nested random-utility theory outlined in Section 4.3, is particularly appropriate for residential mobility. Many previous attempts to build explicit choice-model representations of transition rates in mobility models for human populations (for instance, inter-regional migration rates), suffer from an over-weighting of moving and travelling costs, with respect to costs and benefits incurred at the destination. What is often not realized is that the cost of the travel to move is paid once and for all, while rents are paid over a long period of time. A mechanism which properly discounts and sums in a consistent way such inhomogeneous quantities is therefore needed, and it is felt that the method proposed in Section 4.3 is an appropriate one to do the job.

4.6 An Optimal-control Representation

The results of this section are based on Leonardi (1983), and they can be summarized in non-technical terms by the following statements: (i) When the expected utilities are determined by equations (4.23), or (4.26), the trajectories of the population sizes, as determined by equations (4.1), are the optimal trajectories of a control problem. (ii) The discounted expected utilities, as given by equations (4.26), are the dual variables for this control problem. (iii) The goal function of the control problem is an entropy function.

The most important consequence of the residential mobility process being embedded by an optimal control problem lies in statement (ii), which states the duality between the physical and observable space of flows and population sizes (equations (4.1)) and the micro-economic space of values (equations (4.23) or (4.26)).

Changing values, expressed in terms of expected utilities, are the driving force of the mobility process, since they affect the flow rates. On the other hand, values themselves are affected by the physical process, since they depend on rents, which are determined by the matching between flows and stocks.

Statement (iii) is also interesting, although not surprising. It extends, in a sense, to the dynamic case the well-known Entropy maximizing method widely used to derive static spatial interaction models (Wilson, 1970-A, 1974). The reason for not being too surprised by this result is that the structure of the choice models used in this paper (logit models) is known to be consistent with the Entropy maximizing method.

The results will now be stated more formally. Define the function:

$$\begin{aligned} F(r,P) = & \sum_{i=1}^{m} P_i a_i - \sum_{i=1}^{m} P_i \sum_{i=1}^{m} \{ r_{ij}(c + t_{ij}) \\ & - \frac{1}{\beta} \log [\lambda(Q_j - P_j)]\} \\ & + \frac{1}{\beta} \sum_{i=1}^{m} P_i \sum_{j=1}^{m} r_{ij}(1 - \log r_{ij}) \end{aligned} \tag{4.27}$$

where $r = \{r_{ij}:i,j = 1, \ldots, m\}$ is the matrix of flow rates; and $P = \{P_i:i, \ldots, m\}$ is the vector of population sizes. The function defined by (4.27) is essentially an entropy function in the flow rates, to which some linear terms are added. It is therefore quite similar to those used to derive most static spatial interaction models.

Now let the following optimal control problem be considered:

$$\max_{r} \int_0^\infty e^{-\alpha t} F(r,P)dt \tag{4.28}$$

subject to

$$\dot{P}_j = \sum_{i=1}^{m} P_i r_{ij} - P_j \sum_{i=1}^{m} r_{ji}, \; j = 1, \ldots, m \tag{4.29}$$

In the terminology of optimal control theory, the flow rates r_{ij} are the control variables and the population size P_j are the state variables. The functional defined by (4.28) is the objective function, which has to be maximized by finding an appropriate trajectory for the flows r_{ij}. The objective function is nothing but the discounted integral, over an unbounded time horizon, of the function defined by (4.27). Equations (4.29) are the transformation equations, stating the dynamic laws (in this case simple accounting relationships) for the rates of change of the state variables as functions of themselves and the control variables.

In order to find a solution to problem (4.28) - (4.29), the classic Pontryiagin Maximum Principle will be used (see Hadley and Kempf, 1971, for instance). What the principle states is that, if the following Hamiltonian function (analogous to the Lagrangian function in standard mathematical programming) is defined:

$$H(r,P,\mu) = e^{-\alpha t} F(r,P) + \sum_j \dot{P}_j \mu_j \tag{4.30}$$

where μ_j are the dual variables (analogous to standard Lagrange multipliers) for the constraints (4.29) (caution: the μ_j are functions of time), and then for an optimal trajectory the following conditions must be satisfied:

$$\partial H/\partial r_{ij} = 0, \; i,j = 1, \ldots, m \tag{4.31}$$

$$- \dot{\mu}_i = \partial H/\partial P_i, \; i = 1, \ldots, m \tag{4.32}$$

Substituting from (4.29), the Hamiltonian (4.30) can be rewritten as:

$$H(r,P,\mu) = e^{-\alpha t}F(r,P) + \sum_{i=1}^{m} P_i \sum_{j=1}^{m} r_{ij}(\mu_j - \mu_i) \tag{4.33}$$

Using (4.27), the derivatives of the Hamiltonian with respect to the flow rates are:

$$\begin{aligned}\frac{\partial H}{\partial r_{ij}} &= e^{-\alpha t}P_i\{\tfrac{1}{\beta}\log[\lambda(Q_j - P_j)] - (c + t_{ij})\} \\ &\quad - e^{-\alpha t}\frac{P_i}{\beta}\log r_{ij} + P_i(\mu_j - \mu_i)\end{aligned} \tag{4.34}$$

and setting them equal to zero, according to conditions (4.31), yields for the flow rates:

$$r_{ij} = \lambda(Q_j - P_j)e^{-\beta(c + t_{ij})}e^{\beta e^{\alpha t}(\mu_j - \mu_i)} \tag{4.35}$$

By defining:

$$f_{ij} = e^{-\beta(c + t_{ij})}$$

$$V_j = e^{\alpha t}\mu_j$$

equations (4.35) become:

$$r_{ij} = \lambda(Q_j - P_j)f_{ij}e^{\beta(V_j - V_i)}; \quad i,j = 1, \ldots, m \tag{4.36}$$

As for the derivatives of the Hamiltonian with respect to the population sizes, they are:

$$\frac{\partial H}{\partial P_i} = e^{-\alpha t}a_i - e^{-\alpha t}\sum_{j=1}^{m} r_{ij}\{(c + t_{ij}) - \tfrac{1}{\beta}\log[\lambda(Q_j - P_j)]\}$$

$$- \frac{e^{-\alpha t}}{\beta}\left[\sum_{j=1}^{m} P_j r_{ji}/(Q_i - P_i)\right] + \frac{e^{-\alpha t}}{\beta}\sum_{j=1}^{m} r_{ij}(1 - \log r_{ij})$$

$$+ \sum_{j=1}^{m} r_{ij}(\mu_j - \mu_i) = e^{-\alpha t}\sum_{j=1}^{m} r_{ij}\{\frac{1}{\beta}\log[\lambda(Q_j - P_j)$$

$$- (c + t_{ij})] - \frac{1}{\beta}\log r_{ij} + (\mu_j - \mu_i)\} + e^{-\alpha t}a_i$$

$$+ \frac{e^{-\alpha t}}{\beta}\sum_{j=1}^{m} r_{ij} - \frac{e^{-\alpha t}}{\beta}\sum_{j=1}^{m}\frac{P_j r_{ji}}{Q_i - P_i} \qquad (4.37)$$

But the vanishing of derivatives (4.34), because of condition (4.31) implies the whole expression within curly brackets is zero. Moreover, substituting from (4.36) and defining

$$\psi_i = \sum_{j=1}^{m} P_j f_{ji} e^{\beta(V_i - V_j)}$$

$$\phi_i = \sum_{j=1}^{m} (Q_j - P_j) f_{ij} e^{\beta(V_j - V_i)}$$

one gets:

$$\sum_{j=1}^{m} P_j \frac{r_{ij}}{Q_i - P_i} = \lambda \sum_{j=1}^{m} P_j f_{ji} e^{\beta(V_i - V_j)} = \lambda\psi_i$$

$$\sum_{j=1}^{m} r_{ij} = \lambda \sum_{j=1}^{m} (Q_j - P_j) f_{ij} e^{\beta(V_j - V_i)} = \lambda\phi_i$$

Taking all the above considerations into account, (4.37) becomes:

$$\frac{\partial H}{\partial P_i} = e^{-\alpha t}[a_i + \frac{1}{\beta}(\phi_i - \psi_i)] \qquad (4.38)$$

Replacing result (4.38) in the right-hand side of condition (4.32) yields for the dual variables the differential equations:

$$-\dot{\mu}_i = e^{-\alpha t}[a_i + \frac{\lambda}{\beta}(\phi_i - \psi_i)], \; i = 1, \ldots, m \tag{4.39}$$

Again defining

$$V_i = e^{\alpha t}\mu_i$$

it follows that:

$$\mu_i = e^{-\alpha t}V_i$$

$$-\dot{\mu}_i = e^{-\alpha t}[\alpha V_i - \dot{V}_i]$$

hence equations (4.39) can also be written in terms of the dual variables expressed in current values as:

$$\alpha V_i - \dot{V}_i = a_i + \frac{\lambda}{\beta}(\phi_i - \psi_i), \; i = 1, \ldots, m \tag{4.40}$$

The proof of the embedding property of problem (4.28) - (4.29) is thus completed. Equations (4.39) and (4.40) are clearly identical to equations (4.26) and (4.23) respectively; the terms ϕ_i and ψ_i defined in this section are identical to accessibilities and potentials defined in Section 4.5, and the dual variables u_i and V_i are identifiable with the expected utilities, respectively in the discounted and undiscounted version.

The existence of an optimal control representation for the mobility process is important, since it allows to map the problems of analysing the trajectories of population sizes and expected values (existence, uniqueness, stability and so on) into problems which can be analysed with the tools of optimization theory (like multiplicity of solutions, concavity and so on). This mapping is not worked out in this paper, but it should constitute one of the main theoretical efforts in future research work.

A warning is needed as a concluding remark. The existence of an optimal control formulation *does not mean at all* that some "decision maker" is controlling the mobility process in a planned way. Problem (4.28) - (4.29) simply happens to be there, as an alternative representation of the *purely descriptive* model of Section 4.5.

4.7 A Joint Model for Residential and Labour Mobility

A more general model structure will now be outlined, where both changes in residence and in work-place can occur and commuting costs are introduced explicitly. Some simplifying assumptions will be used. As for the housing stock, work-places are differentiated by zone only, with no further sectoral disaggregation.

Moreover, the whole population is supposed to be made up of workers, and unemployment is not allowed. A further simplification will be introduced by dropping moving costs from the model. This is not very unrealistic for housing mobility, since it has been observed already that they are in general negligible compared with other costs and benefits associated with the use of a dwelling. It is even more realistic for labour mobility, since no real cost is paid for changing job.

Some new definitions are needed. $P_{ij}(t)$ is the number of people living in zone i and working in zone j at time t. W_k is the number of job opportunities available in zone k, assumed constant, and such that $\sum_k W_k \geq \sum_{ij} P_{ij}(t)$. c_{ij} is the cost per unit time of commuting between zone i and zone j. $r_{ij,k}(t)$ is the flow rate for residential changes made by people living in zone i and working in zone j at time t, and moving to zone k in the time interval $(t,t+\Delta)$. $s_{ij,k}(t)$ is the flow rate for workplace changes made by people living in zone j at time t, and moving to a new job in zone k in the time interval $(t,t+\Delta)$. λ is an intensity parameter for housing search (defined as before in Section 4.5). θ is an intensity parameter for job search (playing for labour mobility the same role of λ for housing mobility). a is an exogenous utility gain for unit time; it replaces the previously defined a_i (the dependence on the zone has been dropped for simplicity); it will also be assumed that $a \geq 0$. $V_{ij}(t)$ is the expected utility for an individual living in zone i and working in zone j at time t.

The dynamics of the process are quite similar to those of the simple housing mobility model of Section 4.5. At each time instant, two types of choices are now possible, changing residence and changing job (it is also possible to change nothing, of course).

Excluding the joint occurrence of both types of events (such a joint event would give rise to a higher order term in Δ, therefore negligible in building the differential equations), vacant dwellings and vacant jobs altogether can be considered as a set of exclusive choices. Arguing as in Sections 4.2 to 4.5 (the detailed derivation needs not be repeated here) the following differential equations are obtained for the population sizes and for the expected utilities (time dependency notation has been dropped for simplicity):

$$\dot{P}_{ij} = \sum_{k=1}^{m} (P_{kj}r_{kj,i}+P_{ik}s_{ik,j}) - P_{ij}\sum_{k=1}^{m} (r_{ij,k}+s_{ij,k}) \quad (4.41)$$

$$\alpha V_{ij} - \dot{V}_{ij} = a - c_{ij} + \frac{\lambda}{\beta}(\phi_{ij}-\psi_i) + \frac{\theta}{\beta}(\Omega_{ij}-\Gamma_j) \quad (4.42)$$

where

$$\Phi_{ij} = \sum_{k=1}^{m} (Q_k - \sum_{j=1}^{m} P_{kj}) e^{\beta(V_{kj}-V_{ij})}$$

is the accessibility to the vacant housing stock for people living in zone i and working in zone j.

$$\Omega_{ij} = \sum_{k=1}^{m} (W_k - \sum_{i=1}^{m} P_{ik}) e^{\beta(V_{ik}-V_{ij})}$$

is the accessibility to vacant work-places for people living in zone i and working in zone j.

$$\Psi_i = \sum_{kj} P_{kj} e^{\beta(V_{ij}-V_{kj})}$$

is the population potential in zone i for the housing market.

$$\Gamma_j = \sum_{ki} P_{ik} e^{\beta(V_{ij}-V_{ik})}$$

is the population potential in zone j for the labour market.

$$r_{ij,k} = \lambda(Q_k - \sum_{j=1}^{m} P_{kj}) e^{\beta(V_{kj}-V_{ij})}$$

are the flow rates for residential mobility.

$$s_{ij,k} = \lambda(W_k - \sum_{i=1}^{m} P_{ik}) e^{\beta(V_{ik}-V_{ij})}$$

are the flow rates for labour mobility. While equations (4.41) are a straightforward generalization of equations (4.1), and need no further discussion, equations (4.42) seem rather different from equations (4.23). First of all, the commuting cost C_{ij} appears explicitly, thus introducing the relationship among housing, work-places and transport in a dynamic framework. Moreover, accessibilities have two subscripts (for place of residence and place of work) while potentials have one subscript (for the place of residence in the case of the housing market potential, for the place of work in the case of the labour potential). Having two subscripts for accessibilities is not surprising in this model. The potentials have one subscript since they measure the competition for housing or for labour in a specific zone, and not for a specific type of individual.

Finally, there are some problems now in giving an economic interpretation to the term

$$\frac{\theta}{\beta}\Gamma_j \qquad (4.43)$$

By analogy with the interpretation given for

$$\frac{\lambda}{\beta}\psi_i$$

in Section 4.4, (4.43) should be a price of some sort. But this does not seem sensible, since workers do not pay a price for working.

On the other hand, the combined term:

$$a - \frac{\theta}{\beta}\Gamma_j \qquad (4.44)$$

could be interpreted as the wage level in zone j. When the population potential (that is, the competition among searchers for new jobs) increases, (4.44) decreases, in accordance with intuition. A more sound interpretation of (4.44) needs further investigation. For the moment, it will be accepted as a measure of an externality due to competition for limited job opportunities.

An optimal control embedding problem can also be constructed, in the style of Section 4.6. In analogy with (4.27), the following entropy function can be defined:

$$F(r,s,P) = \sum_{i=1}^{m} \sum_{j=1}^{m} P_i(a - c_{ij})$$

$$+ \frac{1}{\beta}\sum_{i=1}^{m} \sum_{j=1}^{m} P_{ij} \sum_{k=1}^{m} r_{ij,k} \log[\lambda(Q_{jk} - \sum_{j=1}^{m} P_{kj})]$$

$$+ \frac{1}{\beta}\sum_{i=1}^{m} \sum_{j=1}^{m} P_{ij} \sum_{k=1}^{m} s_{ij,k} \log[\theta(W_k - \sum_{j=1}^{m} P_{jk})]$$

$$+ \frac{1}{\beta}\sum_{i=1}^{m} \sum_{j=1}^{m} P_{ij} \sum_{k=1}^{m} r_{ij,k}(1 - \log r_{ij,k})$$

$$+ \frac{1}{\beta}\sum_{i=1}^{m} \sum_{j=1}^{m} P_{ij} \sum_{k=1}^{m} s_{ij,k}(1 - \log s_{ij,k}) \quad (4.45)$$

The associated optimal control problem is:

$$\max_{r,s} \int_0^{\infty} e^{-\alpha t} F(r,s,P)dt$$

subject to the transformation equations (4.41). By using the Pontryiagin maximum principle, as in Section 4.6, it can be easily shown that equations (4.41) and (4.42) satisfy indeed the optimality conditions, and the expected utilities V_{ij} are the dual variables.

Although the model outlined here is still lacking some realistic features, the method it suggests might have interesting future developments, and be applied to interacting activities other than housing and work-places. The model of this section represents a transition from modelling the dynamics of population counts in zones to modelling the dynamics of the entire origin-destination flow matrix. In the future, the model could be expanded, by breaking down work-places into sectors, introducing schools, retail activities and so on. This, of course, would require also introducing an explicit household structure in the population, and this problem is under study.

4.8 Some Equilibrium Considerations

Since the model of Section 4.7 describes the dynamics of commuting trips, a natural question to be asked is to what extent the steady-state solution is related to the known static trip distribution models.

In order to explore this problem, let it be assumed that $\lambda = 0$, which means residential mobility disappears and only labour mobility goes on. The total population sizes in each zone will be $P_i = \sum_j P_{ij}$ where P_i are given constants. Equations (4.41) reduce to:

$$\dot{P}_{ij} = \sum_{k=1}^{m} P_{ik} s_{ik,j} - P_{ij} \sum_{k=1}^{m} s_{ij,k}$$

and replacing the flow rates by their explicit form they become after rearranging:

$$\dot{P}_{ij} = (W_j \sum_{i=1}^{m} P_{ij}) e^{\beta V_{ij}} \sum_{k=1}^{m} P_{ik} e^{-\beta V_{ik}}$$

$$- P_{ij} e^{-\beta V_{ij}} \sum_{k=1}^{m} (W_k - \sum_{i=1}^{m} P_{ik}) e^{\beta V_{ik}} \qquad (4.46)$$

If a steady-state exists, then it must be:

$$\lim_{t \to \infty} \dot{P}_{ij} = 0$$

Setting the right-hand side of (4.46) equal to zero produces a set of equations which do not seem easily solvable. However, a simple observation will reveal the structure of the equilibrium solution. It is claimed that such a solution will satisfy the simpler equations:

$$(W_j - \sum_{i=1}^{m} P_{ij}) e^{\beta V_{ij}} = K_i P_{ij} e^{-\beta V_{ij}} \qquad (4.47)$$

where K_i are some constants of proportionality (to be determined later). The validity of equation (4.47) is readily verified by direct substitution in the right-hand side of (4.46), which yields:

$$\dot{P}_{ij} = K_i P_{ij} e^{-\beta V_{ij}} \sum_{k=1}^{m} P_{ik} e^{-\beta V_{ik}} - K_i P_{ij} e^{-\beta V_{ij}} \sum_{k=1}^{m} P_{ik} e^{-\beta V_{ik}} = 0 \tag{4.48}$$

Therefore, a solution to (4.47) causes derivatives (4.46) to vanish and is an equilibrium solution. From (4.47) one gets:

$$P_{ij} = A_i (W_j - \sum_{i=1}^{m} P_{ij}) e^{2\beta V_{ij}}$$

where

$$A_i = 1/K_i$$

The constants A_i can be determined from the constraint

$$\sum_j P_{ij} = P_i$$

and easy calculations yield finally:

$$P_{ij} = P_i \frac{(W_j - \sum_{i=1}^{m} P_{ij}) e^{2\beta V_{ij}}}{\sum_{j=1}^{m} (W_j - \sum_{i=1}^{m} P_{ij}) e^{2\beta V_{ij}}} \tag{4.49}$$

Result (4.49) is reassuring. It looks indeed like a standard travel demand model with a saturation effect built in the attractiveness factors. In this respect, it is identical with the congestion sensitive travel demand model proposed by Leonardi (1981-A, 1981-B). But a closer look at the exponential term reveals some unusual features. First, the exponent is multiplied by two. Second, and more important, the variable determining the interaction effect is not the travel cost, but the expected utility for the pair of origin-destination zones. Although this is very sensible, both in the light of the model structure which produced it and in terms of a sound micro-economic interpretation, it has many non-trivial implications which make model (4.49) "different" from a standard travel demand model based on travel costs.

By setting $\lambda = 0$ and assuming that

$$\lim_{t \to \infty} \dot{V}_{ij} = 0$$

one gets from equations (4.42):

$$V_{ij} = -\frac{c_{ij}}{\alpha} + \frac{1}{\alpha}[(a - \frac{\theta}{\beta}\Gamma_j) + \frac{\theta}{\beta}\Omega_{ij}] \qquad (4.50)$$

Therefore, when the steady state is reached, V_{ij} has a term depending on travel cost, a term which, according to the interpretation given to (4.44), is the salary level offered for jobs in zone j, and finally a term which is the accessibility to new job opportunities for people living in i and working in j. While the first and the second term are not really new, the third one introduced a seldom considered effect. Loosely speaking, it might be called an "ambition" term, measuring the expectations the worker has on future improvements in his welfare and promotions in his career. From the practical point of view, it is important to note that this term depends both on the origin and the destination, like a travel cost, and in general it has no reasons to be symmetric. This means that a model like (4.49) could produce significantly different flow estimates from those obtained by its standard counterpart, where the "ambition" effect is not included.

Whether this new structure might help improving the understanding of the frequently observed deviations of actual flow from the model-generated ones, is an exciting field of empirical investigation for future research.

As an aside, it might be noted that the equilibrium solution to the simple residential mobility model of Section 4.4 has the same structure as (4.49). Arguing as for equation (4.45), one can easily show that the steady state solution for equations (4.1) is:

$$P_j = T \frac{(Q_j - P_j)e^{2\beta V_j}}{\sum_j (Q_j - P_j)e^{2\beta V_j}} \tag{4.51}$$

and this result is quite similar to (4.49).

Coming now to the more general case when both λ and θ are positive, it can be easily shown that condition (4.47) can be generalized in the following equations:

$$P_{ij}e^{-\beta V_{ij}} = A_i \overline{W}_j e^{\beta V_{ij}} = B_j \overline{Q}_i e^{\beta V_{ij}} \tag{4.52}$$

where

$$\overline{W}_j = W_j - \sum_{i=1}^{m} P_{ij}$$

$$\overline{Q}_i = Q_i - \sum_{i=1}^{m} P_{ij}$$

and A_i and B_j are some constants of proportionality. A solution to (4.52) causes the vanishing of derivatives (4.41) (this can be verified by direct substitution), and is therefore an equilibrium point. From (4.52) one obtains:

$$P_{ij} = A_i \overline{W}_j e^{\beta V_{ij}} = B_j \overline{Q}_i e^{2\beta V_{ij}}$$

and defining

$$P_i = \sum_{j=1}^{m} P_{ij}, \quad T_j = \sum_{i=1}^{m} P_{ij}$$

two alternative representations are obtained:

$$P_{ij} = P_i \frac{\overline{W}_i e^{2\beta V_{ij}}}{\sum_{j=1}^{m} \overline{W}_j e^{2\beta V_{ij}}} \tag{4.53}$$

$$P_{ij} = T_j \frac{\overline{Q}_i e^{2\beta V_{ij}}}{\sum_{i=1}^{m} Q_i e^{2\beta V_{ij}}} \tag{4.54}$$

Equation (4.53) is identical to (4.49). Equation (4.54) is the attraction-constrained counterpart of (4.53). The steady-state utility V_{ij} is now slightly different from (4.50). Letting $\dot{V}_{ij} = 0$ in equation (4.42) and rearranging one gets:

$$V_{ij} = -\frac{C_{ij}}{\alpha} + \frac{1}{\alpha}[(a - \frac{\theta}{\beta}\Gamma_j) - \frac{\lambda}{\beta}\psi_i + \frac{1}{\beta}(\lambda\phi_{ij} + \theta\Omega_{ij})] \tag{4.55}$$

The really new term in equation (4.55) is ϕ_{ij}, the accessibility to the housing stock (the term in ψ_i cancels out in (4.53)). The same comments made before for Ω_{ij} now apply to the term $(\lambda\phi_{ij} + \theta\Omega_{ij})$, which takes into account all the expectations of people, both on housing and on work changes.

4.9 Anticipation Versus Past Memory

Instead of going on introducing additional complications, a step backwards will now be made and an alternative approach to build dynamic equations for the expected utilities will be introduced.

The approach used so far is *anticipatory*, in the sense that the future trajectory of the system determines the current evaluation. This appears clearly in the way the recurrence equations (4.3) are built. Except for the expectation operator, equations (4.3) have the same structure of a dynamic programming problem. In principle, they must be solved by *backward induction*, starting from the end of the process and going back to the current time. Even after randomness and uncertainty are introduced, this way of evaluating alternatives still remains a formidable task, and it is perhaps questionable as a behavioural assumption.

As an alternative to the anticipatory assumption, let now a very simple memory effect be introduced. It will be assumed that the actor does not try at all to conjecture on the future trajectory of the system, but rather *updates* his past experience. Let the symbols be defined as in Section 4.3, and consider the relationship among the values of V_i, the expected utility in state i, at times $t, t+\Delta$.

Assume an actor in state i updates V_i at time $t+\Delta$ by adding the following two components: (i) the gain $h_i(t+\Delta)\Delta \sim h_i(t)\Delta$ in the interval $(t+\Delta,\ t+2\Delta)$; and (ii) the expected utility (taking possible moves into account at time $t+2\Delta$).

However, he is assumed *not to know* $V_i(t+2\Delta)$; his most recent memory is of the value of V_i *just before* time $t+\Delta$, that is, he remembers $V_i(t)$. He then tries to find the value of the best alternative, whose expected utility is given by:

$$E\,\max\{V_i(t) + \vartheta_i,\ \max_{(j)}[v_{ij} + V_j(t) + \vartheta_j]\} \qquad (4.56)$$

an expression which is identical to the second term on the right-hand side of equation (4.3), except for the discount factor.

Discounting must be introduced in this case as well. But it will also be assumed that the actor is aware he has used knowledge dated Δ time units back, therefore he inflates the expected utility given by (4.56), in order to express it in values at time $t+\Delta$. If α_1 is the inflation rate and α_2 is the discount rate, expression (4.56) will be multiplied by:

$$(1 + \alpha_1\Delta)(1 - \alpha_2\Delta) \sim 1 - (\alpha_2 - \alpha_1)\Delta = 1 - \alpha\Delta$$

having defined $\alpha = (\alpha_2 - \alpha_1)$. Once this is done, an equation quite similar to (4.3) is obtained, but for $V_i(t+\Delta)$, rather than $V_i(t-\Delta)$:

$$V_i(t+\Delta) = h_i(t)\Delta + (1 - \alpha\Delta)E \max\{V_i(t) + \vartheta_i,$$

$$\max_{(j)}[v_{ij} + V_j(t) + \vartheta_j]\} \qquad (4.57)$$

Arguing as for equation (4.3), taking the limit of (4.57) for $\Delta \to 0$ yields the following differential equations:

$$\alpha V_i + \dot{V}_i = h_i + \frac{\lambda}{\beta}\sum_{j=1}^{m}(Q_j - P_j)f_{ij}e^{\beta(V_j - V_i)} \qquad (4.58)$$

In spite of the different behavioural assumptions used to derive them, equations (4.58) look very much like equations (4.6). The only formal difference is a reversal of the time direction: $\dot{V}_i$ appears with a plus, rather than a minus sign. This might imply in general a completely different dynamic behaviour, although it is evident that equations (4.6) and (4.58) have the same equilibrium points. Another important difference is the way α is defined. Being the difference between two non-negative quantities (the discount and the inflation rate), α can now take any real values, including negative ones. This also has implications on the quality of the dynamic behaviour, as the next section will show.

4.10 Stability, Waves and Bifurcations

Although a general analysis of the structure of equilibrium points of the dynamics systems considered so far is difficult to perform, some insight in the problem is given by considering a simple example. With reference to the pure residential mobility model, suppose a system of just two zones is given, with no local differentiation both in utility a_i and in housing stock Q_i.

Define T as the total population; Q as the total housing stock, it is understood that the stock in each zone is Q/2; P as the population living in the first zone; T-P is, therefore, the population living in the second zone; x as the difference between the expected utility in the first zone and that in the second zone; in the two-zones case this variable is enough to describe the evaluation and choice process. By appropriate substitutions and rearrangements on equations (4.1) and (4.23), one ends up with the following system:

$$\alpha x - \dot{x} = F(x,P) \tag{4.59}$$

$$\dot{P} = G(x,P) \tag{4.60}$$

where

$$F(x,P) = \frac{\lambda}{\beta}\{[\frac{Q}{2} + (T-2P)](1-fe^{\beta x}) - [\frac{Q}{2} - (T-2P)](1-fe^{-\beta x})\} \tag{4.61}$$

$$G(x,P) = \lambda(T-P)(\frac{Q}{2} - P)fe^{\beta x} - \lambda P(\frac{Q}{2} - T+P)fe^{-\beta x} \tag{4.62}$$

and $f = e^{-\beta C}$ is a decreasing function of the distance (or travel cost) C between the two zones.

In a similar way, for a memory-based system as discussed in Section 4.9, one obtains the equations:

$$\alpha x + \dot{x} = F(x,P) \tag{4.63}$$

$$\dot{P} = G(x,P) \tag{4.64}$$

An important question to be asked is to what extent and in which way the structure of the equilibrium point of systems (4.59) to (4.60) and (4.63) to (4.64) depends on some parameters (like α), as well as on the distance C and the housing stock Q. These are indeed the two main interlinks between the housing mobility system and the physical structure of the settlement.

First of all, it is clear from intuitive considerations that both systems above have the equilibrium solution:

$$P = \frac{T}{2}, \; x = 0 \tag{4.65}$$

since the two zones have no intrinsic relative advantages. The Taylor-expansion approximation of F(x,P) and G(x,P) around (0,T/2) yields:

$$\overline{F}(x,P) = -\lambda f Q.x + \frac{4\lambda}{\beta}(1-f).(P - \frac{T}{2})$$

$$\overline{G}(x,P) = \lambda\beta f \frac{T}{2}(Q-T).x - \lambda f Q.(P - \frac{T}{2})$$

Therefore the behaviour of the equilibrium point (4.65) can be deduced (for small perturbations) by analysing the linear system:

$$\dot{x} = \alpha x - \overline{F}(x,P)$$

$$\dot{P} = \overline{G}(x,P)$$

for the anticipatory case, and the linear system:

$$\dot{x} = \overline{F}(x,P) - \alpha x$$

$$\dot{P} = \overline{G}(u,P)$$

for the past memory case.

For the anticipatory case, the coefficient matrix is:

$$\begin{bmatrix} \alpha+\lambda fQ & , -\frac{4\lambda}{\beta}(1-f) \\ \lambda\beta f\frac{T}{2}(Q-T), & -\lambda fQ \end{bmatrix}$$

and its eigenvalues y_1, y_2 are the roots of the equation:

$$y^2 - \alpha y - A = 0 \tag{4.66}$$

where $A = \lambda f[Q(\alpha+\lambda f) + 4(1-f)\,\frac{T}{2}\,(Q-T)]$.

Since by assumption $\alpha > 0$ and $Q > T$ ($f \leq 1$ by definition), it is true that $A > 0$.

The two roots of (4.66) are:

$$y_1 = \frac{1}{2}(\alpha + \sqrt{\alpha^2 + 4A}) > 0$$

$$y_2 = \frac{1}{2}(\alpha - \sqrt{\alpha^2 + 4A}) < 0$$

Therefore, within the above assumptions for the parameters, this system is structurally very stable, but the equilibrium point is an unstable one: a *saddle point* (since the eigenvalues are both real and always opposite in sign). This means that *no* trajectory in the (x,P) plane, except two (the two apposite branches of one separatrix) will converge to the equilibrium. This is a consequence of the anticipatory assumption and of the optimal control embedding property. The implicit optimization behind the system makes it a rigid one, which is stable only if the "optimal" path is followed. This unrealistic rigidity is one more reason to replace the anticipatory assumption with the past memory one.

For the past memory case, the coefficient matrix is:

$$\begin{bmatrix} -(\lambda fQ+\alpha) & , -\frac{4\lambda}{\beta}(1-f) \\ \lambda\beta f \frac{T}{2}(Q-T), & -\lambda fQ \end{bmatrix}$$

and its eigenvalues are the roots of the equation:

$$y^2 + (\alpha+2\lambda fQ)y + \lambda f[\lambda fQ^2 + 2\lambda T(Q-T)(1-f) + \alpha Q] = 0 \quad (4.67)$$

Some calculations yield:

$$y_1 = \frac{1}{2}[-(\alpha+2\lambda fQ) + \sqrt{\alpha^2 - 8\lambda^2 T(Q-T)f(1-f)}]$$

$$y_2 = \frac{1}{2}[-(\alpha+2\lambda fQ) - \sqrt{\alpha^2 - 8\lambda^2 T(Q-T)f(1-f)}]$$

When the eigenvalues are real and $\alpha > 0$, one has:

$$y_1 < -\lambda fQ < 0$$

$$y_2 < 0$$

and the equilibrium point is a *stable node*, ie every trajectory ends in it.

When $\alpha > 0$ but the eigenvalues are complex, damped oscillations are produced and the equilibrium point becomes a *stable focus*, ie the trajectories are spirals converging to it.

In order to analyse how the oscillatory behaviour depends on the stock level and the distance between the two zones, define:

$Y = Q - T$, the *total* vacant stock.

Then the solution of the inequality:

$$\alpha^2 \leq 8\lambda^2 TYe^{-\beta C}(1-e^{-\beta C})$$

(which is the condition for having complex eigenvalues) can be plotted on the (C,Y) plane, as in Figure 4.1.

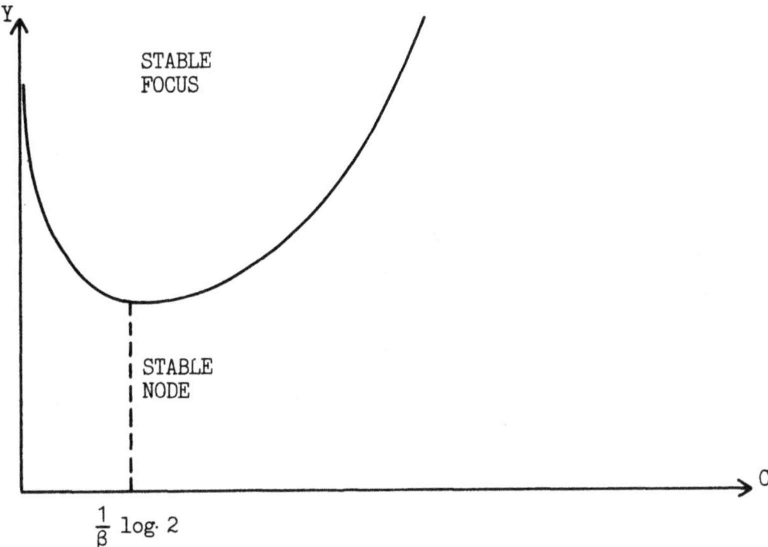

Figure 4.1: Changes in the equilibrium as a function of the distance between the zones, C, and the vacant stock Y. First case: $\alpha > 0$

It is seen from Figure 4.1 that increasing the excess capacity Y beyond a certain threshold produces oscillations. The threshold depends on the distance between the zones, and for $C < \frac{1}{\beta}\log 2$ it is decreasing while for $C > \frac{1}{\beta}\log 2$ it is increasing. It is important to notice that for C = 0 there can be no oscillations, and the eigenvalues become:

$$y_1 = -\lambda Q < 0$$

$$y_2 = -(\alpha+\lambda Q) < 0$$

corresponding to a stable node.

This means that distance is mainly responsible for waves to appear. It is also interesting to see how the damping speed and the wave length depend on Y. The damping factor is

$$\alpha + 2\lambda f(T+Y)$$

therefore increasing Y will also fasten the damping process. However, if Y is small compared to T, the damping speed will not be affected significantly.

The wave length is

$$\frac{\pi}{\sqrt{8\lambda^2 TYf(1-f) - \alpha^2}}$$

and it is decreasing with Y. Therefore in general low excess capacity levels produce long waves fading out slowly, while high excess capacity produces short waves fading out rapidly.

The situation becomes more complex when $\alpha < 0$. The changes in the type of equilibrium, plotted on the (C,Y) plane, appear as in Figure 4.2.

The positive orthant of the (C,Y) plane is divided into five regions, corresponding to five different types of equilibrium points. The region of the saddle points is the region where the inequality:

$$y_1 y_2 < 0$$

holds, ie where the eigenvalues are apposite in sign. From elementary algebra it is known that the value of the produce $y_1 y_2$ is equal to the constant term in equation (4.67), hence the inequality defining the saddle point region is:

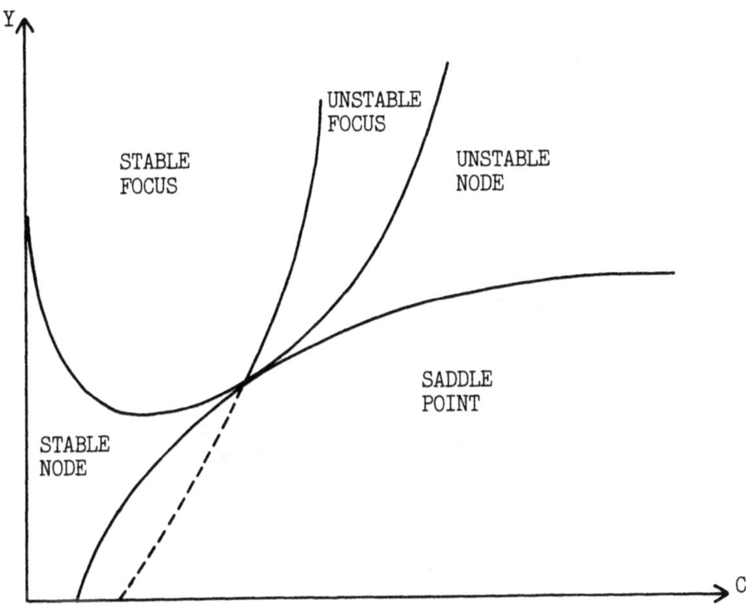

Figure 4.2: Changes in the equilibrium as a function of the distance between the zones, C, and the vacant stock Y. Second case: $\alpha < 0$

$$\lambda f(T+Y)^2 + 2\lambda TY(1-f) + \alpha(T+Y) < 0 \tag{4.68}$$

where $f = e^{-\beta C}$.

Outside the saddle point region, the eigenvalues are either of the same sign or complex conjugate. In order to have stability, one needs either real negative eigenvalues or complex conjugate eigenvalues with negative real part. Outside of the saddle point region, these conditions are equivalent to the single inequality:

$$y_1 + y_2 < 0$$

and since it is known from algebra that the sum of the eigen-values is equal to the coefficient of the first order term in equation (4.67), changed in sign, the stable region is defined by the two inequalities:

$$\alpha + 2\lambda f(T+Y) > 0 \tag{4.69}$$

$$\lambda f(T+Y)^2 + 2\lambda TY(1-f) + \alpha(T+Y) > 0 \tag{4.70}$$

These boundaries determine the union of the regions *"stable focus"* and *"stable node"* in Figure 4.2. The region of complex eigenvalues, ie of focuses (both stable and unstable) is defined by the inequality:

$$\alpha^2 < 8\lambda^2 TYf(1-f) \tag{4.71}$$

as for the case considered in Figure 4.1. The intersection of inequality (4.71) with inequality (4.69) determines the region *"stable focus"* of Figure 4.2, and, as a difference, also the region *"unstable focus"*. What is left is either a region of unstable nodes (upper right of Figure 4.2) or a region of stable nodes (lower left of Figure 4.2).

One thus can see that, even for the simple two-zones example, a wide variety of qualitatively different solutions exist, and a simple external control action, like changing the total stock level, might lead to very different results, ranging from stability to oscillations and instability. In the more general case, the situation will be even more complex. Therefore it is important to work out more general theoretical results on the topics considered in this section. This is suggested as an item for a future research agenda.

4.11 Concluding Remarks and Comments for Future Research

Many topics for future research have been already mentioned here and there in the paper, and they will not be repeated here. This section will abstract from the many technical details and improvements one could introduce in the models, and try to identify some theoretical issues and applied developments of a more general nature.

Two fundamental theoretical issues, mostly pertaining to the model structure, are proposed as directions for investigation in the near future.

The first one is the role of *spatial and temporal frictions* in determining the qualitative features of the dynamic behaviour. There is an intrinsic analogy between the two types of frictions, since both introduce a *lagged structure* in the mobility system. While the temporal frictions determine the way in which the state of the system at a given time interacts with the state of the system at different times (usually in the past), the spatial frictions determine the way in which a process taking place at a given location in space interacts with processes taking place at other locations.

A typical example of the former is the discount effect characterizing all the value formation processes considered in this paper. A typical example of the latter is the friction-of-distance factor introduced in the flow rates, as well as the commuting cost introduced in the combined residential-labour mobility model.

It is known in general systems theory that lagged structures are the main causes of instability and oscillations, and this seems to find a confirmation in the analysis of the simple example carried out in Section 4.10. More specifically, what the analysis of Section 4.10 seems to suggest is that the discount parameter is mainly responsible for the stability or instability, depending on its sign (when it is negative, it is more properly called an *inflation parameter*), while the friction of distance is mainly responsible for oscillations and waves to appear. Whether this result carries over to more general systems is hard to say, but a plausible conjecture is that, while the friction of distance is likely to be a source of oscillations anyway, the discount (or inflation) mechanism *can also be a source of oscillations*, besides the role it plays in stability. The reason why this does not happen with the example considered in Section 4.10 is because a very special time-lag structure has been assumed. This can be seen by analysing the structure of the following differential equation:

$$\dot{V} + \alpha V = h \tag{4.72}$$

It is easily seen that all the differential equations for the expected values considered in the paper have this general form. Equation (4.72) is equivalent to the integral equation:

$$V(t) = \int_0^t e^{-\alpha(t-\tau)} h[V(\tau),\tau]d\tau \tag{4.73}$$

which is a special case of the general convolution equation:

$$V(t) = \int_0^t \Omega(t-\tau) h[V(\tau),\tau]d\tau \tag{4.74}$$

where the convolution kernel $\Omega(t)$ might be any non-negative real function. The nature of the solution to (4.74) in general depends crucially on the eigenvalues of the kernel Ω. In the specific case (4.73), $\Omega = \exp(-\alpha t)$, there is just one real eigenvalue, α, which cannot therefore produce oscillations. In the more general case, other forms of Ω might admit complex eigenvalues, thus contributing to produce waves in the system.

In future theoretical investigations, alternative forms

for the time-lag kernel Ω must therefore be explored, and their effect on the quality of the solution, jointly with the distance friction, must be assessed. This should lead to some general results concerning the nature of equilibria and the existence of waves and periodic solutions.

The second theoretical issue is the problem of modelling the dynamics of the housing stock, and the interactions between them and the mobility process. The problem is not so much one of modelling skill (a sensible macroeconomic model for housing stock dynamics is not very hard to build). It rather raises another general system theoretical question, related to the *different speeds* of the two processes. While household mobility is a relatively fast process, changes in the housing stock are relatively very slow. One might therefore conjecture that such decisions as to invest in new buildings, or to demolish old ones, are just influenced by the steady state of the household mobility process, and not by its transient behaviour. This makes some sense in many cases, provided the system is working in a range where stability of the mobility process is assured.

However, the analysis of Section 4.10 has shown that changes in the housing stock level might be the very reason why the mobility process becomes unstable. In such cases, it is not quite clear what the mobility process will do, whether it will undergo an explosion or approach some limit cycle (the linear approximation analysis of Section 4.10 is not enough to answer this question). In either case, the notion of steady-state in the narrow sense loses meaning and the two processes, stock change and household mobility, will interact in some non-trivial way, not necessarily moving towards any equilibrium.

Since the control (either direct or indirect) of the housing stock trajectory is one the main policy instruments used to intervene in the housing system, the knowledge of the interactions between the two processes and their behaviour around the critical points is very important. This topic should therefore be given a high priority in a future research agenda.

Coming now to the applied developments, one can say in general that they are mostly related to gathering empirical evidence for the main theoretical underpinnings of the proposed model structure.

The thesis of this chapter is that the evaluation and choice process and the mobility process are two interacting processes which cannot be treated separately. While the accounting equations for the expected population sizes have a rather standard structure, the dynamic equations for the expected utilities are quite new and unexplored as yet.

The empirical testing should therefore be done mostly on the nature and the form of the value formation mechanism. This will require *working on historical housing mobility data* from many different urban areas. It will also require some new technical effort in *developing suitable methods for hypothesis testing and parameter estimation.*

A second set of applied developments has mainly to do with making the proposed models ready to work in a simulation model, both for *theoretical sensitivity analysis and for policy impact analysis and evaluation.*

This task can be foreseen to require the following steps:

(i) *Preparing a discrete time version* of the dynamic equations, and an overall recursive solution algorithm. A discrete time version is felt necessary to generate numerical solutions easily. However, it is not a trivial task: discretizing time does not mean simply replacing derivatives with finite differences, which would lead to inconsistent difference equations. It rather means reformulating the accounting equations, the evaluation process and the choice models in discrete terms (ie, without taking the limiting form for $\Delta\to 0$). This in general produces a model structure which looks quite different from the continuous version, although it tends to it in the limit. The way of building a discrete-time mobility model directly has been outlined in Leonardi and Campisi (1981) and the same general approach can be used for future developments.

(ii) *Carrying out policy-impact experiments* mainly in relation to the effects of introducing different controls on *rents and the rent formation mechanism*, of introducing various changes in the *housing stock level and distribution*, as well as in the *work places*, and of changing the *transport network* (ie changing transport costs, travel times and so on). In a first stage, exploratory experiments should be done in a sensitivity-analysis style, in order to assess the quality of the response of the model to different external shocks. In a second stage, comparative experiments on actual data from real urban areas should be performed, both for testing purposes (that is, trying to reproduce past trajectories and observed consequences of past policies) and for forecasting purposes.

(iii) *Developing a suitable set of indicators*, to evaluate in a compact way the performance of the system and monitor the impact of different policies. From the household welfare point of view, this should not be difficult to do, since household expected utilities, which are a consistent measure of their welfare, appear already explicitly in the proposed framework as state variables. An overall indicator of household welfare can therefore be built with sound economic foundations. Additional new effort will be required to build indicators for other features of the performance of the system, measuring the capacity tensions and the shortages (although the endogenous prices are already such an indicator) and monitoring the nearness of the system to critical points (eg thresholds in the housing stock beyond which the household mobility process becomes unstable).

As a concluding remark, it is perhaps worth saying that, although it has not been repeated explicitly, it is understood that all the above theoretical and applied developments should make reference mainly to the combined *housing-labour mobility model* outlined in Section 4.7. It is felt that this is the model framework in which the interaction between the land-use structure (in terms of housing and work places) and the transport system (in terms of commuting cost) is best captured in its dynamics.

Chapter 5

A MARXIAN MODEL OF THE GEOGRAPHY OF PRODUCTION AND TRANSPORTATION IN URBAN AND REGIONAL SYSTEMS

E. Sheppard

5.1 Introduction

The purpose of this chapter is to summarize recent research that attempts to construct a descriptive model of the geography of those multi-sectoral production, transportation and trading patterns that develop as a result of private entrepreneurial behaviour in a capitalist society. I shall attempt to introduce two bodies of literature. The first constructs an analytical Marxian model describing production and social relations in capitalist society; a constructive alternative to neo-classical models (Section 5.2). This draws on original research, notably by English and Italian economists (Joan Robinson, Ian Steedman, Luigi Pasinetti, Piero Garegnani, Luigi Spaventa and Piero Sraffa), developing multi-sectoral production models which avoid the logical contradictions of neo-classical analysis. This foundation was subsequently broadened into a Marxian framework by Morishima, Nuti, Roemer, Abraham-Frois and Berrebi. The second body of literature attempts to develop a unified approach to the geography of spatial configurations as the result of spatial interaction patterns. This is based on potential theory in all its various forms as developed in physics, differential geometry, and probability theory (Section 5.3).

Following a brief description of these two bodies of

knowledge, an attempt will be made to bring them together in describing patterns of pricing, labour values, and production in a capitalist space economy. This draws on a small but fast developing body of literature, to which I have also contributed, that seems to provide a promising way of analytically representing a Marxian political economic theory of the geography of production. By way of an introduction to the approach taken, I shall briefly outline what is meant by a Marxian approach, and what is conceived of in the term "geography of production".

A Marxian approach is to be distinguished from a Marxist approach. The latter refers to political economic analysis that attempts as closely as possible to use the methodology and categories of Karl Marx; notably dialectical reasoning, value theory, class analysis, and historical materialism (Castells, 1973). By contrast, what I refer to as a Marxian approach has more limited aims. In certain ways it represents concepts that were analysed in detail by Karl Marx. These include:

1. a model of production relations that essentially is based on the transformation problem of Marx;
2. a model of wages and profits that does not deduce these as technological parameters based on factor supplies, but rather as the result of past historical and social developments;
3. a broad division of society into classes (workers, capitalists and landlords) as a starting point, deducing that the interests of these groups are fundamentally in conflict;
4. a treatment of macro-social relations as not simply the aggregate of individual decisions but rather a reflection of the type of social systems analysed; and
5. an explicit recognition of the political and social elements in economic production relations.

However, as presented here the Marxian approach is restricted to considering those elements of the above that can be represented in an analytical model, which is clearly much narrower in conception than the range of topics covered by Marx (1967).

Despite these limitations, however, some Marxist concepts can be deduced and analysed in a spatial context; concepts that do not appear in conventional location theory. In this sense some elements of a spatial version of Marx's economic theory can be represented. These include:

1. The exploitation of labour as a necessary prerequisite to profit-making by capitalists.
2. The geography of class conflicts between interests representing capital and labour.
3. The apparent inevitability of crises in the process of capital intervention, justifying Marxist interpretations of state intervention.
4. Unequal exchange in the sense of Emmanuel (1972).
5. Absolute and class monopoly land rents in addition to differential (Ricardian) rent.
6. The role of circulation time in the marketing of commodities as a barrier to capital accumulation.

It is not by any means claimed that a Marxist spatial economic theory is proposed here; only a few limited results have been attained, and it is yet to be proven that progress towards such a theory is possible from this starting point. However, a constructive alternative to the neo-classical school does seem to emerge.

The concept "geography of production" refers to a description of the locations (points, zones, cities or regions) occupied for the production of goods of different types; a description of the prices and labour values of these goods at the various locations; a description of the trading patterns and balances of payments experienced at each location; and a description of the geography of economic growth and capital accumulation. It is of interest to note that transportation is just one sector in this multi-sectoral space economy, albeit a sector whose services are available everywhere. The price of transportation is endogenously determined at each location and influences patterns of trade and thus production and geographical specialization. No full spatial equilibrium will be described here, but many of the elements of such an equilibrium will be presented (Section 5.5). Potential theory will be used to give simultaneously a geographical interpretation (based on accessibility and location principles) as well as an economic interpretation of the geography of production (Section 5.4). This is done in the firm belief that the geographical and economic approaches represent complementary interpretations of the identical phenomenon. Thus, for example, investment behaviour is the dual of location theory; choice of trading partners is a form of technological choice, and economic values may be interpreted as spatial accessibilities.

It will be shown that whereas the geography of value systems seems to be inherently stable, that of production quantities is inherently unstable (Section 5.7). This raises serious doubts as to the ability of the market system to resolve crises. Finally an accounting mechanism spatially disaggregating the macro-economic accounts will be presented (Section 5.6), and extensions to include the institutional structure of corporations as well as fixed capital are described (Section 5.8).

5.2 A Neo-Marxian Paradigm: background

5.2.1 Introduction

Since the late 1950s a group of British and Italian economists have been steadily developing an analytical theory of economic production and accumulation that contains elements of Marxist, Keynesian, and Ricardian thinking and is fundamentally opposed in spirit to the neo-classical paradigm. In order to demonstrate that this represents a significant advance over neo-classical theory it will be necessary to briefly retrace these developments.

5.2.2 Aggregate neo-classical production theory

Stripped to its bare essentials, neo-classical theory states that in region i:

$$Y_{it} = f(L_{it}, K_{it}, t) \tag{5.1}$$

where Y_{it} is the income in i, f(.) is an aggregate production function, L_{it} and K_{it} are the local supply of labour and capital, and t is time (often explicitly introduced as a surrogate for technical change). Equation (5.1) is typically a function that is first order homogeneous in L_{it} and K_{it}; demonstrating constant returns to scale. This highly aggregate and thus elegant model, as is well known, predicts: a stable dynamic equilibrium for regional growth; an equalization across space in wages and profits (at least to the extent allowed by the spatial costs of factor mobility); and wage and profit rates that equal the marginal productivities ($\partial Y/\partial K$ and $\partial Y/\partial L$) of these factors (Richardson, 1973-A). As a consequence wages and profits are purported to represent the contribution of labour and capital to economic production (Ferguson, 1969). Since this depends on the technology as represented in f(.), income distribution is seen as a technical issue; the most appropriate division of net output between workers and capital owners is not a political question, but rather is solved efficiently and automatically in a perfectly competitive space-economy.

Any aggregate model is a deliberate simplification of reality, and the aggregate neo-classical theory of production is no exception. The utility of an aggregate model, however, is greatly limited if it is not consistent with more disaggregate formulations. A major achievement of the analytical paradigm to be described here has been to demonstrate that neo-classical theory is inconsistent in two senses. First, the internal logic is partly inconsistent. Second, those conclusions of the aggregate model which were described above are all contradicted when a more disaggregate version of the economy is analysed.

5.2.3 The "capital controversies"

Robinson (1953-54) pointed out a circularity of reasoning in the aggregate neo-classical model. The notion of "capital" is in fact a compilation of all non-labour inputs to production. In order to measure how much capital exists, each of these non-labour inputs must be added to the others, an operation only possible if a common measure of value exists. In neo-classical analysis that common denominator of all capital goods is the rate of return, and this must therefore be known in order to calculate the quantity of capital in supply in a region. However, to calculate the rate of profit it is necessary to know the quantity of capital available, since the profit rate equals the marginal productivity of capital, itself a function of the quantity of capital. This results in a circular process of reasoning hopelessly confounding the quantity of capital with its value.

A natural alternative to avoid this problem is to abandon a single capital good model and take a multi-commodity approach; determining prices separately for each good. This was explored by neo-classical economists, but perhaps the most penetrating insights from such an analysis are due to Sraffa (1960). His model of multi-commodity price determination is:

$$\underline{p}' = \underline{p}'A^*(1+r) + w.\underline{\ell}' \qquad (5.2)$$

where $\underline{p}' = [p_1, \ldots, p_n]$; $A^* = \{a_{mn}\}$, $\underline{\ell}' = [\ell_1, \ldots, \ell_n]$. p_n is the price of good n, ℓ_n is the hours of direct labour needed to produce a unit of n, a_{mn} is the input-output coefficient representing the requirements of capital good m in producing a unit of n, w is the hourly wage rate and r is the rate of profit. Here a competitive economy is assumed in the sense that wages are equalized, and profit rates in all sectors are equal. Thus in sector n:

$$p_n = (1+r) \sum_{m=1}^{K} a_{mn} p_m + w.\ell_n \tag{5.3}$$

where {K} is the set of capital goods.

One interesting aspect of this model can be seen by expressing the wage in real terms:

$$w = \sum_{c=1}^{C} b_c p_c / T \tag{5.4}$$

where b_c is the daily consumption of good c by a worker and his/her dependants, {C} is the set of wage goods, and T is the length of the workday in hours. The vector $\underline{b}' = [b_1, \ldots, b_C]$ is a consumption bundle that is socially and historically determined. Defining $a_{mn} = b_m \ell_n / T$ for all $m \varepsilon \{C\}$, and assuming that wages are paid out at the start of a production period (see Section 5.4.2), equation (5.3) becomes (Sraffa, 1960, Pasinetti, 1977-A, Morishima, 1973):

$$\underline{p}' = \underline{p}' A(1+r) \tag{5.5}$$

where A is an augmented input-output matrix, incorporating wage good inputs to production as a measure of labour requirements.

But equation (5.5) is simply the celebrated "transformation problem" of Karl Marx (1967, Volume 3), corrected so that the value of each good as an input equals its value as an output (a correction that Marx recognized as necessary but was unable to incorporate (Lipietz, 1982)). Analysis of this equation has shown that Marx's published solution to the transformation problem is inconsistent (ie labour values are not directly translatable into money prices) unless r equals zero or each good is produced with identical inputs (all columns of A are identical; an equal organic composition of capital. See Sweezy, 1946, Steedman, 1977). This substantiates a long-standing criticism of Marx's pricing system that has led to a rejection of this approach by neo-classical economists (Samuelson, 1971). It is, however, possible to conclude that a multi-commodity approach allows certain aspects of Marxist economic theory also to be studied.

Sraffa (1960) demonstrated that a multi-commodity approach also reveals internal inconsistencies in the neo-classical account. Contrary to theorems of neo-classical aggregate production theory, in a multi-commodity model the rate of profit does not equal the marginal productivity of capital (Pasinetti, 1962). This can be demonstrated by counter-example even in a two-commodity economy (Harcourt, 1972). As a result, there is no equation to determine the rate of profit. In terms of equation (5.2), there are more unknowns (p, w and r) than equations, suggesting that the technical conditions of production are not sufficient to determine the distribution of income even if one price is fixed. This is true even when prices are normalized in some way, such as by setting one price arbitrarily equal to one. In Marxist terms (equation (5.4)), the basic wage $\underline{b}$ must be given by social, cultural and historical factors rather than by technical requirements. Furthermore, and because of this, the physical availability of, and intensity in the use of capital goods are not inversely related to the rate of profit. Given two separate technologies for producing the N goods of an economy, represented by two input-output matrices A_1 and A_2, it has been demonstrated (cf Garegnani, 1970) that it is possible for the more capital intensive technology to be more profitable when the rate of profit is *high*, and the more labour intensive technology to be more profitable when the profit rate is low (and the wage rate high); a "perverse" switch of technologies from the neo-classical standpoint. Indeed, "reswitching" can also occur in the sense that the capital intensive technology is more profitable with high *and* low rates of profit, with the other technology being more profitable at intermediate profit rates. After an extensive debate, these criticisms were accepted by neo-classical economists: "... we must accept nature as she is ... it is quite possible to encounter switch points in which lower profit rates are associated with lower steady-state capital-output ratios" (Samuelson, 1966, p. 579).

Ironically, it can be shown that the neo-classical aggregate theory is only correct if the rate of profit is zero or each good is produced with identical inputs. In other words, the criticism applied by neo-classical economists to Marx's solution of the transformation problem is equally true for the neo-classical account. Just as some Marxists have attempted to ignore or assume away the basis for this criticism, so some neo-classical capital theorists have ignored the problem by assuming that the economy is "regular"; ie that the input-output coefficients are such that perverse switches do not occur. For then the neo-classical model can be happily pursued even in a multi-commodity context with the price of each good given by its marginal productivity (Burmeister, 1980). This is, of course, an unsatisfactory solution, whether applied by Marxists or neo-classicists. Indeed the very terminology of "perverse" switches and "regular" economies implies that in some sense received neo-classical theory represents the intuitively correct account of reality, rather than being an outcome of the sociology of economic thought (Harcourt, 1972).

5.2.4 Implications for spatial economic theory

As yet, there exists no full analysis of the effect of these conclusions on conventional wisdom in regional science and economic geography. However, analysis of a model such as equation (5.2) or equation (5.4) has led to conclusions that certainly challenge conventional thinking. For further criticisms see Smolka (1980).

First, if factor prices at a location are no longer inversely related to the local physical abundance of those factors, as is postulated by marginal productivity pricing, then even if capital and labour were to flow smoothly to locations of highest return this need not lead to equalized regional growth rates in equation (5.1). Indeed, if capital rich regions have higher profit rates the opposite would occur. This can no longer be ruled out, given the inconsistency of the neo-classical account.

Similar problems arise with the other mechanism that supposedly eliminates geographical differences in economic prosperity; specialization and trade. The Hecksher-Ohlin theory of trade, that regions will specialize in producing goods for which the factor requirements most closely match local factor availabilities is again no longer necessarily true. It may be more appropriate to specialize in labour intensive goods in a capital intensive region and *vice versa* (Steedman, 1979-A). Choice of specialization depends on local price ratios, but since (see Section 5.5.2) prices depend on trading patterns this leads to some very difficult questions as to whether specialization that seems to be profitable *a priori* is in fact beneficial (Barnes, 1982-B).

Finally, arguments about the determinants of factor prices can be extended to the case of land rent (Steedman and Metcalfe, 1972). In comparing two technologies for the production of a set of agricultural goods in a von Thünen economy with a single market, a spatial extension of one aspect of reswitching, Barnes and Sheppard (1984) have shown:

(a) When transport costs increase, it is possible that the technical combination requiring a more intensive use of transport resources may be more profitable.

(b) If the distance between producers and consumers is increased the technical combination requiring a more intensive use of transportation may be more profitable. This implies that conditions may exist where the profitability of specialization and trade within a space economy is positively related to the cost of transportation.

(c) Reswitching (one technique being superior at two very different levels of transportation cost) is also possible.

(d) Total differential rent paid in the economy may decrease or increase as transport costs increase, depending on the relative profitability of the techniques available, and on the wage and profit rates. Thus rent is not simply a measure of the scarcity of land; it also depends on the social relations determining wage rates.

The above analysis discusses comparisons of two spatial economies in equilibrium; the profitability of shifts from one technique to the other by an economy are not discussed. A related but less studied issue is the existence of similar results within a single space-economy. Schweizer (1978), Schweizer and Varaiya (1976, 1977), Hartwick (1976) and Scott (1979) demonstrate that differential rent, and the intensity of land use, need not decrease with distance from the market, and that one land use may appear at several different distance ranges away from the market. A further area of research has not yet been explored: the degree to which perverse switches can occur at one location in a space economy when it is not isolated but interacts with other locations. This is a necessary step if a full analysis of the applicability of the capital controversy to spatial economic theory is to be completed. Without this full analysis, the importance of the phenomena described above is difficult to evaluate. However, since these types of results do occur, and contradict the naive application of neo-classical theory to spatial economies, it is at least reasonable to conclude that a more consistent alternative cannot reduce economic production to a homogeneous capital good, but should incorporate the complexity of the multi-commodity case.

5.3 Potential Theory: the generation of spatial configurations

5.3.1 Introduction

The geographical element of social science theory consists of two components; a theory of spatial interdependencies, and a theory of the effect of these interdependencies on the spatial configurations of social science phenomena (Sheppard, 1979-A). This section describes a methodology for calculating the latter element, in spatial equilibrium and applicable in discrete and continuous space, for deterministic and stochastic theories.

Define u_j as the potential at location j; the impact observed at j is a result of spatial interactions. Assume that the impact of each location i on j is additive:

$$u_j = \sum_i u_{ij} \qquad (5.6)$$

where u_{ij} is the total impact at j of flows emanating from i. Equation (5.6) states that the potential at j is thus the sum of the effects of potential fields emanating from all origins.

5.3.2 Continuous space

Assume the existence of (not necessarily continuous) distributions m(x,y) and a(x,y) representing the interaction generating variable and interaction attracting variable at location (x,y). Define a flow vector at (x,y):

$$\underline{f}(x,y) = \underline{f}(a,m,x,y) \qquad (5.7)$$

This flow vector is the sum of flows through point (x,y) from all locations in the system which generate interaction. For simplicity consider a finite number of such point sources. Then

$$\underline{f}(x_j,y_j) = \sum_i \underline{f}(m_i,a_j,d_{ij}) \tag{5.8}$$

where $m_i = m(x_i,y_i)$, $a_j = a(x_j,y_j)$ and $d_{ij} = [(x_i-x_j)^2 + (y_i-y_j)^2]^{\frac{1}{2}}$. The potential u(x,y) depends on the flow vectors. Indeed, a theorem of vector analysis states that all vector fields that are conservative are gradients of a potential field, in which case the following holds:

$$\underline{f}(x,y) = \text{grad } u(x,y) \tag{5.9}$$

or (using $\underline{p}$ and $\underline{q}$ to represent the basis vectors in the x and y directions):

$$\underline{f}(x,y) = \frac{\partial u}{\partial x}\cdot\underline{p}\ \frac{\partial u}{\partial y}\cdot\underline{q} \tag{5.10}$$

A vector field $\underline{f}$ is conservative if (Sheppard, 1979-A):

$$\frac{\partial}{\partial x}\frac{\partial \underline{f}}{\partial y} = \frac{\partial}{\partial y}\frac{\partial \underline{f}}{\partial x} \tag{5.11}$$

Assume that the interaction model generating the flow vector is separable (Sheppard, 1976) in the sense that:

$$\underline{f}(x_j,y_j) = \sum_i g(m_i,a_j)\underline{h}(d_{ij}) \tag{5.12}$$

Then, employing the relation between a conservative vector field and its potential field, if (5.11) holds, then:

$$u(x_j,y_j) = \pm\sum_i(\int \underline{f}_{ij} d\underline{r}) \tag{5.13}$$

where $\underline{f}_{ij} = \underline{f}(m_i, a_j, d_{ij})$. Thus, by equations (5.10), (5.12):

$$u(x_j, y_j) = \pm\sum_i(\int \underline{f}_{ij}^{\bar{x}} d\bar{x} + \int \underline{f}_{ij}^{\bar{y}} d\bar{y}) = \pm\sum_i [g_{ij}(\int \underline{h}_{ij}^{\bar{x}} d\bar{x} + \int \underline{h}_{ij}^{\bar{y}} d\bar{y})] \tag{5.14}$$

Here, $\underline{f}_{ij}^{\bar{x}}$ and $\underline{f}_{ij}^{\bar{y}}$ are the elements of the vector $\underline{f}_{ij}$ in the x and y directions:

$$\underline{f}_{ij} = \underline{f}_{ij}^{\bar{x}} \cdot \underline{p} + \underline{f}_{ij}^{\bar{y}} \cdot \underline{q} \tag{5.15}$$

$g_{ij} = g(m_i, a_j)$, $\bar{x} = |x_i - x_j|$ and $\bar{y} = |y_i - y_j|$.

By Stokes' theorem, the vector field $\underline{f}$ is conservative if curl $\underline{f} = 0$. Given the definitions of $\underline{f}_{ij}$ and g_{ij}, if the curl of $\underline{h}_{ij}$ is zero this is sufficient to guarantee that $\underline{f}$ is conservative. A conservative vector field is irrotational; the potential difference between two points is independent of the path taken and thus a potential surface can be defined. The condition of conservativeness is nothing more than the application in vector analysis of the integrability condition of integral calculus.

5.3.3 Some examples

It is possible to show that all of the spatial interaction models commonly used in geography are conservative. This is true of gravity models (Sheppard, 1979-A) and intervening opportunities models of both the Stouffer and Schneider type (Sheppard, 1980-A). Thus for all of these cases a potential field in continuous space may be defined. Some examples are listed here (for derivation, see Kellogg, 1929, Sternberg and Smith, 1946, Sheppard, 1979-A).

$$\underline{f}_{ij} = m_i a_j d_{ij}^{-\beta}, \text{ then } u(x_j,y_j) = a_j \sum_i m_i d_{ij}^{\beta-1} \ (n>1) \qquad (5.16)$$

$$\underline{f}_{ij} = m_i a_j d_{ij}^{-1}, \text{ then } u(x_j,y_j) = a_j \sum_i m_i \ln d_{ij} \qquad (5.17)$$

$$\underline{f}_{ij} = \frac{m_i a_j e^{-\beta d_{ij}}}{\sum_k a_k e^{-\beta d_{ik}}}, \text{ then } u(x_j,y_j) = \frac{1}{\beta} \sum_i m_i \ln \sum_j a_j e^{-\beta d_{ij}} \qquad (5.18)$$

For intervening opportunities models a general solution for u(x,y) has yet to be derived (Sheppard, 1980-A). The potential field may be interpreted as a measure of the total interaction terminating at location (x,y), or the total influence of all locations on point (x,y).

Of the three cases outlined above the first two have the distinct disadvantage that the potential field cannot be defined at locations i which are sources of interaction, unless some convention is adopted for defining d_{ij}. The third case does not possess this disadvantage and is defined everywhere in the plane. Note also that only the second case satisfies Laplace's equation in two dimensions. In this case only, is the potential at each point equal to the simple average of potentials at surrounding points.

5.3.4 A stochastic interpretation: potentials in discrete space

Consider the simplest stochastic interaction model: a random walk in two dimensions. It is known that this is the discrete equivalent of two-dimensional Brownian motion (Einstein, 1906, Wiener, 1923), and possesses the following potential function:

$$u_{ij} = 2G \ln d_{ij} \qquad (5.19)$$

where G is a constant. This in turn is equivalent to equation (5.17), if a(x,y) and m(x,y) are uniform surfaces, and thus it can be concluded that a stochastic random walk and the deterministic interaction model

$$\underline{f}_{ij} = G/d_{ij} \tag{5.20}$$

have the same potential function.

Rewriting the two-dimensional random walk as a Markov process with a denumerable transition matrix P, it can be shown that (Kemeny, Snell and Knapp, 1966, Dynkin and Yushkevich, 1969, Spitzer, 1964):

$$u_{ij} = \lim_{n\to\infty} \sum_{k=0}^{n} (p_{oo}^{(k)} - p_{ij}^{(k)}) = ZG \ln d_{ij} \tag{5.21}$$

Here $p_{ij}^{(k)}$ is the probability that state j is reached at the k-th step by a random walk starting in i, and $p_{oo}^{(k)}$ is the probability that a state is returned to at the k-th step. Re-expressed in matrices:

$$G = \sum_{k=0}^{\infty} (\mathrm{diag}(P^k).E - P^k) \tag{5.22}$$

where G is a potential operator for a transient Markov process; $\mathrm{diag}(P^k)$ is a diagonal matrix containing the diagonal of P^k; and E is a matrix of ones.

A two-dimensional random walk is a recurrent Markov process. For a transient process (Kemeny, Snell and Knapp, 1966, Seneta, 1981):

$$G = \sum_{k=0}^{\infty} P^k = [I-P]^{-1} \tag{5.23}$$

G represents a potential operator since it may be applied to any initial probability distribution a_j among states to derive an associated potential distribution, u_j.

Further results will be given only for transient processes, since they are applicable to the neo-Marxian model of this paper. If the states of a Markov process represent locations in space, and if P is a matrix of spatial interaction probabilities in equilibrium, then the following results hold for a denumerably infinite transition matrix in which all states are transient (Seneta, 1981):

(i) A potential vector is a non-negative vector $\underline{u} = G\underline{m}$ where $\underline{m}$ is an element-wise finite non-negative vector.

(ii) If $\underline{u} = G\underline{m} < \infty$ then (a) there is a unique transformation between $\underline{m}$ and $\underline{u}$, and (b) any potential vector $\underline{u}$ is super-regular: $P.\underline{u} \leq u$.

(iii) If $\lim_{n\to\infty} P^n\underline{u} = 0$ then a necessary and sufficient condition for $\underline{u}$ to be a finite potential vector is that $\underline{u}$ be super-regular.

(iv) It is true for any super-regular vector that $\underline{u} = \underline{r}+\underline{g}$ where $\underline{r}$ is a regular vector (equal to $P^{\infty}.\underline{u}$), and $\underline{g}$ is a potential vector (equal to $G(\underline{u}-P\underline{u})$). The decomposition is unique.

(v) If $\underline{h}$ is a super-regular vector and $\underline{u}$ a finite potential vector, then (a) $c = \min(\underline{u},\underline{h})$ is also a potential, and (b) there exists a non-decreasing sequence of finite potentials converging element-wise to $\underline{h}$.

Although these results assume a denumerably infinite number of states, when space is aggregated into fewer regions the corresponding analysis for a finite number of locations may be regarded as an approximation to the infinite case. However, in this finite case boundary effects on the edge of the study area are likely to influence the internal distribution of potentials.

The potential u_j may be interpreted as the expected number of times that state j is visited, given the interaction matrix and the probability distribution, a_j, specifying where the process may start. Since all possible sequences of states, appropriately weighted, are considered then the stochastic nature of the interpretation is sufficient to guarantee that the potentials are conservative. An expectation over all paths is taken when calculating potentials, making the potential difference between two points independent of the path followed. The advantage of the matrix specification of potentials is that no particular model of interaction is necessary. For any matrix of (stationary) interaction probabilities a potential distribution may be derived.

5.3.5 Deterministic potentials in discrete space

Consider a set of locations i connected by distances c_{ij}. Let the interaction between i and j be given by the differentiable function:

$$I_{ij} = m_i f_{ij}(\underline{a}, C) \tag{5.24}$$

where $\underline{a}$ is the vector $\{a_i\}$ and C is the matrix $\{c_{ij}\}$. Assume m_i, the trips generated at i, is independent of m_j for $i \neq j$. Then potential theory describes the impact of interactions as follows:

$$u_j = \sum_i u_{ij} \tag{5.25}$$

where

$$du_{ij} = \sum_{k,\ell} (\partial u_{ij}/\partial c_{k\ell}) dc_{k\ell} \tag{5.26}$$

Equation (5.26) may be readily solved if the integrability conditions:

$$\partial(\partial u_{ij}/\partial c_{k\ell})/\partial c_{mn} = \partial(\partial u_{ij}/\partial c_{mn})/\partial c_{k\ell} \tag{5.27}$$

are satisfied, for all pairs k,ℓ and m,n. In short, the Hessian matrix of u_{ij} must be symmetric. If $u_{ij} = m_i \cdot g_{ij}(\underline{a}, D)$, where

$g_{ij}(.)$ is the potential operator, then

$$u_j = \sum_i m_i . g_{ij}(.) \tag{5.28}$$

which is the deterministic equivalent of the definition of potentials given by point (i) of the previous section.

Leonardi (1982-A, 1982-B) has shown, following Williams (1977-A) that if:

$$I_{ij} = m_i a_j \frac{e^{-\beta c_{ij}}}{\sum_k a_k e^{-\beta c_{ik}}} \tag{5.29}$$

then

$$I_{ik} = \partial u_{ij} / \partial c_{ik} \tag{5.30}$$

and

$$u_{ij} = \sum_{k,\ell} \int I_{ij} dc_{k\ell} \tag{5.31}$$

$$u_{ij} = \frac{1}{\beta} m_i \ln \sum_j a_j e^{-\beta c_{ij}} \tag{5.32}$$

The integrability conditions (5.27) are satisfied, and u_{ij} is a potential function, associated with the interaction model (5.29), that exists in a space of arbitrary geometry, and is defined by equation (5.26). By contrast, the integrability conditions guaranteeing the existence of potential models (5.16) and (5.17) are only satisfied in Euclidean space. Comparison of equations (5.13) and (5.18) with equations (5.31) and (5.32) illustrates that potential theory provides a theory of spatial configurations that is equivalent in discrete and continuous space.

As a second example consider the following spatially autoregressive formulation describing a spatial multiplier:

$$\underline{u} = F.\underline{u} + \underline{m} \tag{5.33}$$

where F is the matrix $\{f_{ij}(\underline{a},C)\}$. If the non-negative matrix F has all eigenvalues less than one in absolute value:

$$\underline{u} = (I-F)^{-1}\underline{m} \tag{5.34}$$

$$= G.\underline{m} \tag{5.35}$$

where G is the matrix $\{g_{ij}(\underline{a},C)\}$. For example, the transfer function of a stationary spatially autocorrelated process is equal to the potential function associated with the partial autocorrelation function in space (Sheppard, 1976). Comparing (5.35) with the definition of potentials for a transient Markov process, it can be seen that potential theory provides a theory of spatial configurations for deterministic and stochastic specifications.

5.3.6 Maximal representations of spatial interaction

Theoretical models describing the geography of a fully efficient trading pattern in spatial equilibrium are typically formulated as the solution to some mathematical optimization. Specifications range in complexity from the classic transportation problem to the more sophisticated models stimulated by Takayama and Judge (1964), and exist for both discrete and continuous space specifications (Beckmann, 1952, 1953, Puu, 1979-B, 1982-A, 1982-B, 1982-D). Sheppard and Curry (1982) have noted that for such models a potential function also exists and is given by the dual variables, or rents and market prices, of the optimal solution. In continuous space this equivalence is directly exploited by Beckmann and Puu. In discrete space models the earliest literature (Koopmans and Reiter, 1951, Kantorovich, 1965) directly refers to the dual variables as potentials, no doubt due to the fact that electrical analogue model solutions to such problems derive the dual variables from potential theory (cf Enke, 1951, Sheppard and Curry, 1982).

Although the conditions under which the dual variables of such maximal representations are mathematically equivalent to the theory of potentials as described above have not yet been derived, the evidence is impressive. Thus it seems already possible to argue that potential theory is indeed a unified method of describing the generation of spatial configurations from spatial interactions. This approach applies both to maximal representations as well as to descriptive theories of spatial interaction (Sheppard and Curry, 1982, see also Section 5.5 below), to discrete and continuous space representations, and to deterministic and stochastic theories. In all cases, the space potentials describe the aggregate effect of direct and indirect interactions between locations, or their accessibility to one another (Sheppard, 1979-A, 1979-B).

5.4 The Basic Model

5.4.1 Main features

The previous two sections have summarized some recent developments in economics and in the theory of spatial configurations. As yet, both bodies of literature, although voluminous in their own right, have seen only limited application to spatial patterns of production and transportation. Thus much of what follows will draw on work that is not yet widely available. I shall, however, attempt to demonstrate that a coherent framework of considerable potential can be developed.

Consider the spatial distribution of private production in a competitive capitalist economy. It will be assumed initially that capitalist society has the following features. There exist (at least) two types of individual: those who own few capital resources and must trade their labour for commodities (workers), and those who own significant non-labour resources and purchase labour to convert these resources into marketable commodities (capitalists). It is argued (Sheppard, 1983-B) that this is more realistic than the social relations assumed in Walrasian equilibrium theory (Walsh and Gram, 1980, Weintraub, 1979). This assertion has been analytically supported by Roemer's (1982) demonstration that the existence of a labour market, an incontrovertible fact in capitalist economies, and the existence of private ownership imply such a class division. Furthermore, we shall initially assume that capitalist production is competitive in the sense that capital is shifted between economic sectors until the rate of profit is equalized everywhere. However, the rate of profit is not reduced to a minimal level since consumer sovereignty does not rule consumption. Rather, consumer behaviour represents choice bounded by: the income distribution between capitalists and workers, biological necessities, cultural and social norms, and the range of goods made available by capitalist production (Pasinetti, 1981). Spatial elements of consumer behaviour are also similarly constrained (Burnett, 1980, Sheppard, 1980-A). It is in this sense that we assume a daily consumption bundle $\underline{b}$ which is given by cultural, social and historical considerations and represents the real wage. Assuming such a bundle does not imply a complete absence of consumer choice, $\underline{b}$ may equally be regarded as an optimal choice within the constraints specified, with little effect on the theory (Roemer, 1981). Finally, it is assumed that the economy is productive; it is capable of reproducing itself. This is a necessary condition for the mode of production to be viable.

Consider a set of locations $\{i,j \varepsilon J\}$ and a distribution of production of goods m,n $\{m,n \varepsilon N\}$ given by the vector $\underline{x} = \{x_j^n\}$. One of these goods, good t, is transportation services which are also regarded as a produced commodity. It will be assumed that transportation services are available everywhere. Define the matrix $A = \{a_{ij}^{mn}\}$ as the inter-regional input-output matrix showing the quantity of m shipped from i to produce a unit of n in j. Note $a_{ij}^{mn} > 0$ if $x_i^m, x_j^n > 0$. If $\underline{b}$ is the consumption bundle, b_{ij}^c is the quantity of wage good c, consumed per day by workers in j, that is shipped from i. These coefficients reflect the spatial shopping behaviour of consumers as well as retail marketing strategies. Define a_i^{mn} as the amount of m required per unit of good n produced at location i. It then follows that (Sheppard, 1983-B):

$$a_j^{mn} = \sum_i a_{ij}^{mn};\ b_n = \sum_i b_{ij}^n,\ \forall j \tag{5.36}$$

Under the assumption that the economy is productive (Morishima, 1973, Abraham-Frois and Berrebi, 1979):

$$\sum_{jn}\sum a_{ij}^{mn} \leq 1\ \forall i,m \tag{5.37}$$

with the inequality holding in at least one case. This expresses the notion that output must exceed requirements.

The terms a_i^{mn} and b_n refer to the inputs socially necessary to produce goods and reproduce the labour-force, where the term "socially necessary" means that these reflect the dominant technology and consumption behaviour in the economy. It is not assumed that all producers of n in i, or all consumers, utilize exactly this quantity of input, but rather that these coefficients represent that behaviour which is influential in setting prices (Fine, 1979). Alternatively, a_i^{mn} and b_n may be interpreted as the mean quantity of inputs used; the expectation of an input requirement that varies stochastically.

The process of production and exchange will initially be examined as a spatial equilibrium pattern. In the strictly static case, the matrix A does not represent a linear technology with no substitution between inputs (Sraffa, 1960), since it can equally well be interpreted as the optimal technology chosen from a convex production set (Roemer, 1981). The inter-regional input-output matrix A has elements as follows:

$$a_{ij}^{mn} = \begin{cases} a_{ij}^{mn} & m\varepsilon\{K\}\ m\neq t \\ b_{ij}^{m}\ell_n/T & m\varepsilon\{c\} \\ \sum\limits_{m\neq t} a_{ij}^{mn}\tau_{ij}^{m} & m=t \end{cases} \qquad (5.38)$$

where τ_{ij}^{m} is the quantity of transportation services necessary to ship a unit of m from i to j. It is assumed that A is indecomposable; the economy cannot be divided into completely autonomous sub-sections. On the basis of this, three circuits can be described in the space-economy which parallel the circulation of money, labour values and use values theorized by Marx (1967, Volume 2; see also Desai, 1979).

5.4.2 The three circuits of capital

Prices are given as the cost of inputs incremented by the rate of profit:

$$p_j^n = (1+r) \sum_{i,m} a_{ij}^{mn} p_i^m \qquad (5.39)$$

From the definitions of equation (5.38), the price at the factory gate is the sum of non-labour inputs, plus wages expressed as the cost of the real wage, plus transportation costs. In matrix form:

$$\underline{p}' = (1+r).\underline{p}'A \qquad (5.40)$$

where $\underline{p}' = \{p_i^m\}$ is the vector of spatial prices in a competitive economy. A is an indecomposable non-negative matrix. Therefore by the Perron-Frobenius theorems there is a unique non-negative solution to (5.40), given by the largest eigenvalue $\lambda = (1+r)^{-1}$ and the associated left-hand eigenvector of A. Because the economy is productive (equation (5.37)), λ is less than one and the rate of profit r is positive. Because A is indecomposable, $\underline{p}$ is positive (Morishima, 1973, Pasinetti, 1977-B).

From Section 5.3.4, it can be shown that $\underline{p}$ is a vector of potentials. This is true because by equations (5.37) and (5.40), $\underline{p}$ is a super-regular vector, and $A^{\infty} = 0$. Therefore

$$\underline{p}' = \underline{m}'G \qquad (5.41)$$

where $G = [I-A]^{-1}$. Indeed, since $\underline{p}'$ is an eigenvector of A

$$\lambda_m^k \underline{p}' = \underline{p}'A^k \qquad (5.42)$$

Further, since $0 < \lambda_m < 1$,

$$\sum_{k=0}^{\infty} \lambda_m^k \underline{p}' = \frac{1}{1-\lambda_m} . \underline{p}' = \sum_{k=0}^{\infty} \underline{p}'A^k = \underline{p}'.[I-A]^{-1} \qquad (5.43)$$

Therefore in the potential equation (5.41):

$$\underline{p}' = \underline{m}'G = \frac{r}{1+r} . \underline{p}'.G \qquad (5.44)$$

Equations (5.40) and (5.44) provide two equivalent interpretations of spatial pricing for all goods in a competitive capitalist economy. The two give rise to identical relative prices. Thus to say that prices are set in an inter-dependent economy at a level such that the rate of profit is equal for all capitalists (equation (5.40)), is the same as saying that in a completely interdependent capitalist space economy prices represent that (unique) spatial distribution of monetary value which is not altered by the spatial circulation of money as expressed through commodity trade (equation (5.44)). This represents a unique insight into the parallels between economic and geographic theorizing.

Two further points are worth noting. The selection of equation system (5.5) from Section 5.2, rather than system (5.2) involves not only expressing the wage in real terms, but also assuming that a rate of profit is made on wage payments as well as on payments for capital goods. This means that either the wage is paid at the start of a production period, with the profit made on wage payments representing the return that capitalists make for taking this money out of circulation, or it means that wages are paid at the end of the production period but that the money reserved for wage payments is invested elsewhere in the meantime. Profits are paid as the return on capitalists loaning their money for production purposes; thus the fact that production takes time and that this must be compensated for by paying profits, is a key to the analysis (Roemer, 1981). In this light the multiplier $r/(1+r)$, in equation (5.44), converting initial to final prices, is simply an expression of the creation of monetary value that occurs through the time taken for the spatial circulation of commodities. This expresses the increment in value due to circulation which Marx (1967, Volume 2) expressed as M-C...P...C'-M'. Here M and C are the quantity of money and capital goods before production, P is the process of production, and M',C' are the incremented values of M and C at the end of the production and circulation process (see also Mandel, 1962). In equation (5.44), however, an important assumption becomes explicit. It is assumed that the time for production and circulation, ie the time lag between investing capital and realizing its return, is the same for all goods circulated on all routes. However, especially when long distances are involved, circulation time may vary significantly on different routes. Marx (1967,

Volume 2) discussed at some length the complications that this introduces, and Steedman (1977) has suggested a way of allowing for this in analytical treatments.

The second circuit is that of labour values. Although Marx defined labour values in several ways, in static equilibrium these all reduce to the same analytical form (Morishima, 1973, Zalai, 1981):

$$\lambda_j^n = \sum_i \sum_{m\varepsilon\{K\}} a_{ij}^{mn}.\lambda_i^m + \sum_i \sum_{m\varepsilon\{K\}} a_{ij}^{mn}\tau_{ij}^m\lambda_i^t + \ell_j^n, \forall n\varepsilon\{N\}, j\varepsilon\{J\} \quad (5.45)$$

Here the labour value, λ_j^n, of good n produced at j is the sum of the labour value of capital inputs, the labour value of transportation necessary to assemble capital inputs, and the hours of direct labour, ℓ_j^n, involved. In matrix form

$$\underline{\Lambda}' = \underline{\Lambda}'.A^* + \underline{L}' \quad (5.46)$$

where $\underline{\Lambda}' = \{\Lambda_j^n\}$, $\underline{L}' = \{\ell_j^n\}$, and A* is an input-output matrix with all wage good inputs eliminated. Thus

$$\underline{\Lambda}' = \underline{L}'[I-A^*]^{-1} = \underline{L}'.G^* \quad (5.47)$$

where $G^* = [I-A^*]^{-1}$.

From equation (5.46), $\underline{\Lambda}$ is super-regular, and from equation (5.47) it is clear that the spatial distribution of labour values is a distribution of potentials expressing the final spatial distribution of labour as a result of production and circulation.

It follows from the above that the rate of exploitation of labour at each location, e_i, may be calculated (Morishima, 1973):

$$e_i = (1-v_i)/v_i \quad (5.48)$$

where v_i, the labour value of the real wage, is (Sheppard, 1983-B):

$$v_i = \sum_j \sum_{m\varepsilon\{c\}} b^m_{ji}[\lambda^m_j + \tau^m_{ji}\lambda^t_j]/T \qquad (5.49)$$

It can be shown that even if the real wage is identical everywhere, v_i and thus e_i will vary with location. Thus if trade patterns show any distance-decay effect, v_i is a weighted average of local labour values of consumption and transportation services. It can be further shown that, in equilibrium

$$r \leq \frac{\bar{e}}{\hat{K}} \qquad (5.50)$$

where $\bar{e}$, the mean rate of exploitation, is:

$$\bar{e} = \sum_{i,m} \ell^m_i x^m_i (1-v_i) / \sum_{i,m} \ell^m_i x^m_i v_i \qquad (5.51)$$

and $\hat{K}$ is the aggregate organic composition:

$$\hat{K} = \sum_{j,n} \sum_{i,m\varepsilon\{K\}} \Lambda^m_i a^{mn}_{ij} x^n_j / \sum\sum_{im} \ell^m_i x^m_i v_i \qquad (5.52)$$

Finally, at all times

$$r < \underset{i}{\text{Max}}\ e_i \qquad (5.53)$$

For details see Sheppard (1983-B). These results represent a spatial generalization of the Fundamental Marxian Theorem (Okishio, 1963, Morishima and Seton, 1961). A competitive capitalist economy can make a positive profit only if at least one region experiences positive exploitation of labour in a Marxist sense. Marxist exploitation is thus a sine qua non of capitalism.

Another unique feature of the paradigm is that it gives insight into the social conflicts underlying spatial economic change (see Sheppard, 1983-C). From the Perron-Frobenius theorems, $\partial r/\partial b^n_{ij} < 0$ and $\partial r/\partial T > 0$. Thus there is a conflict over the division of the surplus of economic production between workers seeking to increase their wage and capitalists seeking to augment their profits. As argued above, this conflict is resolved in the political sphere of a class struggle, since wages and profits are not fully determined within the realm of production (cf Marx, 1967, Mandel, 1962). In this sense the economic model can provide no complete picture of socioeconomic change. These conflicts have, of course, a spatial dimension. Unequal rates of exploitation, at a fixed real wage, in space imply that workers in some places are better served by capitalist production than in other places. This provides some theoretical support for the notion that the interests of a group may be closer aligned to those of other classes in the same location, than with those of the same class elsewhere. This supposed paradox has caused considerable conflict in Marxist social theory (Bettelheim, 1972, Emmanuel, 1972, Appendix II, Castells, 1978, Urry, 1981, for further implications, see Sheppard, 1983-C).

The final circuit is that of quantities, or use values. Since a physical surplus is continually being produced, this circuit is by nature dynamic. However, a static spatial distribution of relative production exists (Morishima, 1973, Sheppard, 1983-D) that satisfies conditions of dynamic equilibrium. Dynamic equilibrium exists when all sectors in all locations grow at the same rate:

$$\underline{x}_{t+1} = (1+g)\underline{x}_t \tag{5.54}$$

and production in time period t equals demand at time t+1:

$$A.\underline{x}_{t+1} = \underline{x}_t \tag{5.55}$$

Combining equations (5.54) and (5.55):

$$\underline{x}^* = (1+g).A.\underline{x}^* \tag{5.56}$$

where $\underline{x}^*$ is a vector of relative production levels; the geography of production that allows crisis-free accumulation. Given a non-negative and irreducible matrix A, it can be deduced that g equals r and $\underline{x}^*$ is the right-hand eigenvector of A associated with its largest eigenvalue. It also follows that:

$$\underline{x}^* = [I-A]^{-1}.\ \frac{g}{1+g}\ \underline{x}^* \tag{5.57}$$

This potential theoretic version of (5.56) shows that $\underline{x}^*$ may be interpreted as that configuration of production which is not altered as a result of the physical circulation of commodities, but is merely augmented everywhere by the fraction (1+g)/g. This is, of course, exactly what the economic conditions of equilibrium mean in geographical terms. The stability of this model of accumulation is also of interest, and will be examined in Section 5.7.

5.5 Spatial Equilibrium

5.5.1 Introduction

The basic model described above could be interpreted as being in a state of spatial equilibrium. However, this would strictly speaking be incorrect, since the results given above hold for any matrix A. In other words it would seem that any interaction pattern could be incorporated in A and would represent a spatial equilibrium. Spatial equilibrium, however, requires not only that spatial configurations are in equilibrium with respect to interaction patterns, but also vice versa. Flows and structures are interdependent (Sheppard, 1979-B).

5.5.2 Trading equilibria

Assume that the pattern of spatial specialization is known; it is known in which locations each good is produced, and the technology of production, a_{i}^{mn}, is also known. Thus for each location it is known how much of each good must be purchased, but the locations from which it is purchased may be freely chosen. Postulate the following choice model:

$$a_{ij}^{mn} = a_{j}^{mn}.e^{-\beta q_{ij}^{m}}/\sum_{K} e^{-\beta q_{ik}^{m}}, \ \forall m \neq t \tag{5.58}$$

where q_{ij}^{m} is the delivered price of unit of m in location j, given it is produced in i:

$$q_{ij}^{m} = p_{i}^{m} + \tau_{ij}^{m} p_{i}^{t} \tag{5.59}$$

Equation (5.58) seems quite general for choice models (Leonardi, 1982-A); and without any precise specification of the choice process, β may be regarded as an index of the efficiency of the trading system. As β tends to infinity, a completely efficient trading system would be imposed, with purchases solely from the cheapest seller, no crosshauling, and a potential gradient of prices that strictly determines the direction of flow of commodities (Evans, 1973, Senior and Wilson, 1974-B, Williams, 1977-A, Sheppard, 1983-D, Sheppard and Curry, 1982). Finite (positive) values of β allow inefficiencies of trade for whatever reason, with the only stipulation being that the level of inefficiency is geographically uniform. When β equals zero trade patterns are random and independent of prices. A spatial equilibrium of trading requires that equations (5.40), (5.58) and (5.59) hold simultaneously. This jointly determines spatial pricing patterns and the trading components of the matrix A, and may be regarded as a trading equilibrium.

This trading equilibrium may be regarded as a non-linear characteristic equation of the following form:

$$\underline{p}' = (1+r).\underline{p}'.A(\underline{p}) \qquad (5.60)$$

where the matrix function $A(\underline{p})$ is given by equations (5.58) and (5.59). As yet, no analytical solution to (5.60) has been derived. In a number of dynamic simulations, however, where a_{ij}^{mn} in (5.58) at time T is calculated based on prices set at time T-1, a unique stable solution has always been found such that for a given $\{a_i^{mn}\}$ and β, a single price vector and matrix A are converged on from widely varying initial trading patterns. Furthermore, the patterns of spatial pricing respond systematically to such variables as the efficiency of the trading system (cf Curry, 1983), the difficulty of transportation, and the length of the working day (for details, see Sheppard, 1983-D).

5.5.3 Spatial specialization

The trading equilibrium described above also cannot be regarded as a full spatial equilibrium since the spatial pattern of specialization is given exogenously. Indeed, the equalization of profit rates implies a trivial location theory; all locations and thus all location patterns of activities are equally attractive. Clearly this is unsatisfactory; in this sense the immediate generalization of the economic paradigm does not describe real features of a space economy. This problem has not been discussed in the literature, but some brief proposals can be made (see also Sheppard, 1983-C).

5.5.3.1 The economic literature

Given the inconsistency of the Hecksher-Ohlin model, specialization based on local factor abundance is not a satisfactory solution in a multi-commodity model (Steedman and Metcalfe, 1977, Metcalfe and Steedman, 1973). Extensive work (see the collection edited by Steedman, 1979-A) has established, however, that a comparative advantage principle still exists. Each location can increase its rate of profit if it specializes in a good for which the local price, relative to the local production price for other goods, is lower than the "world" price of this good measured relatively to the "world" price of other goods. In the spirit of Ricardo, however, this result is generally true only when profit rates are not then subsequently equalized; ie when no rule for fixing the international trading ratio is given. If it is assumed that profit rates are subsequently equalized, then it is still possible for specialization to be profitable (Gibson, 1980), but only for a restricted set of cases (Barnes, 1982-B). Such results may also be obtained for growing economies, although in these cases comparative advantage need not imply a gain from trade (Steedman, 1979-B, Metcalfe and Steedman, 1974).

5.5.3.2 A spatial application

The application of this principle to spatial production patterns can be given in a von Thünen world. Assume market prices in a central city to be given; the equivalent of the "world prices" discussed above. Assume further that each good is centrally marketed, that production costs are uniform, and that there is no interdependent production. If producers choose to produce at each location that product which maximizes the rate of profit to be made there, then it may be shown that the crop with the lower relative price is specialized in. Consider a von Thünen model with two crops. At distance s from the market:

$$p_A^* = (1+r_A(s)).[p_A + t_A(s)] \tag{5.61}$$

$$p_B^* = (1+r_B(s)).[p_B + t_B(s)] \tag{5.62}$$

where p_n^* is the (exogenous) market price for good n, p_n is the production cost of good n, $t_n(s)$ is the transport cost of good n over distance s, and $r_n(s)$ is the rate of profit made on good n at distance s. In equations (5.61) - (5.62) the term in square brackets is the production cost including shipment. It follows that:

$$1 + r_A(s) > 1 + r_B(s) \tag{5.63}$$

if, and only if:

$$p_A^*/[p_A+t_A(s)] > p_B^*/[p_B+t_B(s)] \tag{5.64}$$

In words, at distance s, good A is more profitable if and only if the effective production cost of good A, relative to that of good B at distance s, is less than the market price of A relative to B. In this simple model, then, local "prices" determine spatial specialization. Systematic patterns of specialization will occur as long as:

$$p_n + t_n(s) = k_n(s) \quad \forall n \tag{5.65}$$

is not independent of location, and

$$k_m(s) \neq k_n(s) \quad \forall s,n,m \tag{5.66}$$

Barnes (1982-B) has noted that this particular model of specialization, based strictly on the economic literature, is very hard to generalize to spatial economies. In the above case these problems can be easily seen. First, the market prices are exogenous, and not derived from trading patterns (or equation (5.60)). Second, trading patterns are also exogenous and do not depend on prices; a result that only is valid in the case of a single market (cf equation (5.58)).

However, two features of this simple model seem broadly applicable. First, the necessary conditions for specialization seem quite general. Puu (1982-B) derives the same result for a model with endogenous trade patterns, and it should be applicable for generalizations of system (5.61) - (5.62) where production is interdependent, and the price of transportation is made endogenous (as in Barnes and Sheppard, 1984). The second general issue is that the pattern of specialization determined by (5.63), even in this simple model, will lead to different specialization patterns to the conventional von Thünen model. In the latter, good A is specialised in at distance s if:

$$(1+r_A(s)).[p_A+t_A(s)].y_A > (1+r_B(s))[p_B+t_B(s)]y_B \qquad (5.67)$$

where y_n is the number of units of n produced per hectare; the intensity of land use. In (5.67), the land use yielding the greater total rent is selected, whereas in (5.63) the land use with the greatest rate of profit is selected. The two rules are only equivalent if $y_m = y_n$ for all m,n. When this is not the case, it is perfectly feasible that the sequence of land use zones deduced from (5.67) can be the opposite of that deduced from (5.63).

This conclusion has profound implications. The calculation of capitalist entrepreneurs is essentially a dynamic one, and involves maximizing the return on capital invested;

implying a choice of specialization based on (5.63). The calculation of landlords, however, involves maximizing rent per acre as defined by (5.67). Thus the geographical pattern of specialization will depend on the institutional structure of land tenure. When land is owned by one social class, and production is carried on by another, then this would be sufficient for the traditional von Thünen model to apply. This in turn suggests that the specialization principle due to Steedman and Metcalfe is entirely inapplicable. If, on the other hand, the land is owned by capitalist entrepreneurs who wish to determine the most profitable land use, then the rule defined in equation (5.63) is relevant. This problem has been almost entirely ignored in the location theoretic literature, where maximization of aggregate profit has been typically identified as in the interests of capitalists (cf Stevens, 1961). An important conflict of interest between social classes has thus been neglected.

5.5.3.3 Towards a more satisfactory solution

Barnes (1982-B) has noted that the rule of specialization exploited above can be inconsistent, because it regards the derivation of trading patterns as a result of the decision to specialize as a trivial aspect that does not affect pricing patterns. As indicated in Section 5.5.2 this is evidently false. On the other hand, the model of Section 5.5.2 is unsatisfactory as it does not allow for spatial variations in the profitability of production. This latter occurs because there is no tendency to uniform pricing in individual market places. Thus the f.o.b. price of good m as delivered in region j will vary, depending on the region of origin of the good, in such a way that profits are everywhere equalized. This is a problem caused by the naive application of the neo-Marxian economic paradigm to spatial problems. One interpretation of the neo-Marxian paradigm is that it assumes no substitutability between the outputs of different sectors (but see Pasinetti, 1977-B). However, good m as delivered in j from i is obviously perfectly substitutable for good m as delivered in j from k, and some convergence in the respective f.o.b. prices is to be expected.

The process of equalization of delivered prices for a good sold in a particular location itself can reflect a decline in demand for shipments from more expensive sources. It is not to be expected that complete convergence will occur to a uniform delivered price, q_j^n:

$$q_{ij}^n \neq q_j^n \quad \forall i \tag{5.68}$$

This is because of inefficiency in spatial markets as well as in trading patterns. Thus, a decline in demand for more expensive sources, which affects trading patterns, could achieve convergence in a manner not solely captured by β (equation (5.58)).

A second type of solution is to assert that the effective selling price in region j is given by the maximum delivered price:

$$q_j^n = \underset{i}{\text{Max}} \{q_{ij}^n\} \tag{5.69}$$

This implies a uniform delivered price in region j, which strictly speaking is only to be expected in a region of very small size. However, under the assumption (5.69), a pattern of trade and pricing could in principle be derived, given the requirements for good n as an input to production in region i. The differentials between q_{kj}^n and q_j^n represent excess profits leading to spatial variations in the profit rate (Harvey, 1982). Such variations can exist in spatial equilibrium because of the institutional feature of private land ownership under capitalism.

Thus either landlords can extract differential rents, or the private ownership of land by capitalists can lead to a maintenance of unequal profits, since landownership can prevent capital flowing between locations to equalize profit rates. As noted in the previous section, the difference between these last two strategies is crucial, because different patterns of specialization can be expected. In either event, spatial monopoly rents can also be expected due to the geography of production (Sheppard and Curry, 1982).

A full solution to this problem, determining simultaneously pricing and trading patterns endogenously under the condition of a convergence of delivered prices, has not been solved. This represents an important area for future research.

5.5.3.4 The distribution of income

The spatial equilibrium principles derived above represent attempts to solve this problem entirely within the sphere of economic production. However, as noted in Section 5.2, one of the principal elements of the neo-Marxian approach is that economic production patterns depend on the distribution of income between wages and profits. The assumption made previously of a fixed real wage defines a distribution of income that is constant in real terms across space. If this distribution changes over time for historical reasons, then the spatial equilibrium will also change. This is because prices and the profit rate depend on the wage. As a result, even with no change in technology of production $\{a_j^{mn}\}$, the equilibrium trading patterns, production patterns and patterns of spatial specialization will all be altered. In this sense the geography of production and trade depends on the social relations, the state of the struggle between workers and capitalists.

However, given that the distribution of income depends on social relations, and given that different regions display different levels of economic development, it is to be expected that social relations will not be identical between regions. At the regional level this is clear; regions such as the north-east United States, midland England, and northern Italy, which have long histories of industrial production, experience higher levels of unionized employment and wages than elsewhere in these countries. Indeed this high labour cost has contributed to current economic problems in such regions as capital is reinvested elsewhere (cf Bluestone and Harrison, 1980). Such differences also occur at more local geographical scales. Scott (1980, 1982) has, for example, confirmed speculations that such differences also exist within metropolitan areas in the United States, namely between central city and suburban locations.

Analytically, this factor may be allowed for by specifying a different real wage vector $\underline{b}_i$ for each region i. If it is assumed that the rate of profit is equalized interregionally, the model as described here may be readily computed to determine the effect of differential wage vectors on spatial equilibrium solutions. The model may be further generalized by imposing interregional barriers to the reinvestment of capital. This will then lead to interregional differences in profitability. Whether this last generalization is necessary in order to account for the observed disinvestment of capital from high wage regions can only be determined when the model is placed in a dynamic context. Certainly, rates of interest do differ by one or two percentage points between regions of the United States. It is highly unlikely that such differences exist at the intraregional scale, but at this scale there do exist "high risk" areas where financial capital refuses to invest, such as inner-city locations in the United States.

5.5.4 Residential activities

Since the basic structure of this model parallels that of an input-output model, it is relatively straightforward to introduce the location of residences (cf Macgill, 1977-B). Webber (1981-A) has developed an initial version of such a model. The major implication of such an extension is that it would permit a discussion of intraurban spatial interdependencies. This section merely sketches out a few basic elements of such an extension; no satisfactory formulation has yet been completed.

Assume that the price of a unit of housing of type h in location i is given by:

$$p_i^h = (1+r) \sum_{i,m} a_{ji}^{mh} p_j^m \tag{5.70}$$

The real wage of a worker living in housing of type h at j is given by $\underline{b}_j^h$, where

$$\underline{b}_j^h = \{\underline{b},\ b^h,\ \tau_{jk}^w\} \tag{5.71}$$

Here b^h is the number of units of housing of type h necessary to support a family, and τ_{jk}^w is the transportation consumed in commuting to work at location k. The money value of this wage, for a worker working at location k is:

$$w_{jk}^h = w_j + p_j^h b^h + p_i^t . \tau_{jk}^w \tag{5.72}$$

Equation (5.72) would suggest that wages at location k are not equal for all workers. A more reasonable assumption would be that wages are set at a level that reflects the local history of the struggle between capital and labour; say at a value $\overline{w}_k$. This wage level would then place a constraint on housing and residential locations that are available to workers at k. The

following conditions would then hold:
1. If $w^h_{jk} > \bar{w}_k$, no workers at k can live in housing of type h in location j;
2. If $w^h_{jk} < \bar{w}_k$, then workers at k living in housing of type h at location j make a surplus money wage. This will be paid as differential land rent. The mean rent $\bar{\psi}^h_j$, is given as:

$$\bar{\psi}^h_j = [\sum_k(\bar{w}_k - w^h_{jk})m^h_{jk}/\sum_k m^h_{jk}].[y_h/b^h] \tag{5.73}$$

where m^h_{jk} is the number of workers in housing type h and j who work at k, and y_h is the density of housing type h per hectare.

5.5.5 Land rent

Sections 5.5.3 and 5.5.4 have sketched out how differential land rent can occur in a capitalist space economy as a result of differential locational advantage for production and residential activities. Scott (1976) has developed in detail patterns of differential rent in a von Thünen economy with interdependent production between agricultural producers, based on the specialization principle of equation (5.67). Barnes (1982-A) has extended this approach to consider multiple commodity non-agricultural production in a market centre with a single agricultural good produced in the hinterland, based on the work of Kurz (1978). Huriot (1981) and Barnes and Sheppard (1984) have proceeded further in relating differential rents to wages and profits.

To briefly summarize, the following results can be obtained:
1. Rents are subtracted from the economic surplus, that is otherwise divided between wages and profits (Steedman and Metcalfe, 1972, Huriot, 1981, Barnes and Sheppard, 1984).
2. There is no natural definition of the marginal plot of land; that plot where no differential rent is paid. The

marginal plot of land is a function of the wage and profit rates (Barnes, 1982-A). This suggests the hypothesis that the most remote plot of land in a von Thünen landscape need not be the marginal plot of land.

3. Rents depend on the technology of production; the intensity of land use and the level of rents need not decline with distance from the market (Scott, 1976).

4. Differential rent of both types analysed by Marx (1967, Volume 3), based on land fertility and technique of production, may be integrated (Barnes, 1982-A).

5. The overall levels of differential rent are not necessarily positively related at the physical scarcity of land (Barnes and Sheppard, 1984).

In addition to differential rent, however, Marx postulates two other categories of land rent; monopoly rent (or class monopoly rent; cf Harvey, 1973-B, Walker, 1974, Bruegel, 1975, Ive, 1975), and absolute rent. Class monopoly rent refers to a minimal rent that is charged on even marginal land, due to the monopoly on ownership of land possessed by the landowning class. The size of this rent would depend on the social power that this class has developed historically, and is thus determined by factors that lie outside the system of production. This is perfectly consistent with the conception of the determination of profits and wages in the neo-Marxian approach. Note that the level of class monopoly rent need not be related to the scarcity of land.

Formally, the price determination equations become:

$$\underline{p}' = (1+r).\underline{p}'A + [\underline{\psi}' + k.\underline{i}'].(Y)^{-1} \qquad (5.74)$$

where $\underline{\psi}'$ is the vector of differential rents for each land use at each location, k is a scalar representing the level of class monopoly rent per hectare, and (Y) is a diagonal matrix containing the intensity of production per hectare for each good at each location.

Absolute rent is a Marxist category that refers to relationships between labour values and prices. The application of labour values in economic analysis is currently the subject of bitter debate (Steedman, 1977, Hodgson, 1980–81, Lippi, 1979, Elson, 1979, Steedman and Sweezy, 1981). Rather than repeating that debate here, I shall simply indicate how absolute rent as conceived by Marx could be calculated. Consider a comparison of the price vector with the vector of labour values, adjusted so that the sum of prices equals the sum of labour values:

$$\underline{p}^{*\prime} = (1+r)\underline{p}^{*\prime}A \tag{5.75}$$

$$\underline{p}^{*\prime}\underline{i} = \underline{\Lambda}'.\underline{i} = \underline{L}'(I-A^*)^{-1}.\underline{i} \tag{5.76}$$

where $p^{*\prime}$ is the price vector normalized by the constraint (5.76) instead of the usual constraint $p_1^1 = 1$.

Absolute rent is made by landlords owning property where the production price given by equations (5.75), (5.76) is less than the labour value of production there:

$$p_i^n < \lambda_i^n$$

If labour values represent the exchange value of goods in a non-capitalist system, where investment is not redirected between sectors to equalize the rate of profit, then in places where $\lambda_i^n > p_i^n$, relative prices would fall as a result of such equalization. Marx (1967, Volume 3) postulated that in these cases landlords could use their monopoly over the land to erect barriers to investment flows in these sectors, forcing the price of production to remain equal to the labour value.

This may be expressed formally as a generalization of equation (5.74):

$$\underline{p}^{*\prime} = (1+r)\underline{p}^{*\prime}.A + (\underline{\psi}' + k.\underline{i}').(Y)^{-1} + \underline{\alpha}' \qquad (5.77)$$

$$\underline{p}^{*\prime}.\underline{i} = \underline{L}'(I-A^{*}).\underline{i} = \underline{\Lambda}'\underline{i} \qquad (5.78)$$

$$\underline{\alpha}' = \mathrm{Max}(\underline{0}', \underline{\Lambda}' - \underline{p}^{*\prime}) \qquad (5.79)$$

where $\underline{0}$ is a vector of zeros. Marx postulated further that absolute rent would occur if and only if the capital to output ratio for a producer was below the average for the economy. This was based on comparing the inputs to production for an essentially single capital good economy. In the case of multiple capital goods, the capital/labour composition of the inputs to these inputs must be considered. Tracing this infinite series backwards, Marx's postulate may not be true in this more complex system.

Note that the discussion of land rent here has incorporated the same error as was observed in Sections 5.5.3.1 and 5.5.3.2. The geography of a specialization and trade as represented by A is postulated a priori and is not affected by rents. A full spatial equilibrium solution would have to incorporate the effect of rents on A, following the suggestions in Sections 5.5.2 and 5.5.2.3 above.

5.6 Spatial Accounting

5.6.1 Basic accounting

In the closed spatial economic system being modelled, certain macroeconomic accounting relations are always satisfied. In particular, the following are true:

$$Y^{*} = Y + W + \Pi \qquad (5.80)$$

where Y^{*} is total income, and Y is the money value of capital good inputs necessary to reproduce production at current levels. The remaining net income or monetary surplus is made up from wages (W) and profits (Π). Secondly (Marx, 1967):

$$V^* = C + V + S \tag{5.81}$$

where V^* is the labour value of production, C is the labour value of capital good inputs (constant capital), V is the labour value of labour inputs (variable capital), and S is the labour value of the uncompensated labour (surplus value).

Equation (5.80) may be rewritten (Sheppard, 1983-C) as:

$$(1+r).\underline{p}'.A.\underline{x} = \underline{p}'.A^*.\underline{x} + \underline{p}'.B.\underline{x} + r.\underline{p}'.A.\underline{x} \tag{5.82}$$

where (cf equation (5.46)) $B = A - A^*$; the matrix of wage good inputs. Similarly, equation (5.81) becomes:

$$\underline{\Lambda}'.\underline{x} = \underline{\Lambda}'.A^*.\underline{x} + \underline{\Lambda}'.B.\underline{x} + \underline{\Lambda}'.B.(E).\underline{x} \tag{5.83}$$

where (E) is a diagonal matrix with the rate of exploitation e_i for each region i in those diagonal entries referring to production in that region. e_i is given by equation (5.48).

In equations (5.82) and (5.83), the vector $\underline{x}$ refers to production levels and may be any non-negative vector. p' and $\underline{\Lambda}'$ are the vectors of values calculated from A by equations (5.40) and (5.47). For any observed production levels relations (5.82) and (5.83) hold; they represent general accounting relations. Note that monetary surplus is calculated on all inputs whereas surplus value is accumulated solely from uncompensated labour. This accounts mathematically for the difference between the two value systems.

Both equations (5.82) and (5.83) may be further disaggregated spatially. The following matrix notation is introduced. An interregional flow matrix H may be partitioned into a series of submatrices H_{ij} of the same dimension. H_{ij} is defined as the matrix H, but with all entries that do not refer to a flow from region i to region j set equal to zero. Thus:

$$H = \sum_{ij}\sum H_{ij} \qquad (5.84)$$

On the basis of this notation, the money flowing from region i to region j, y^*_{ij}, equals the money value of goods from region j sold in region i:

$$y^*_{ij} = (1+r).\underline{p}'.A_{ji}.\underline{x} \qquad (5.85)$$

Indeed:

$$y^*_{ij} = y_{ij} + w_{ij} + \pi_{ij} \qquad (5.86)$$

where π_{ij} is the profit flowing from i to j based on sales of products from j in region i; y_{ij} is the fraction of the money flow needed to reproduce capital good inputs for this production, and w_{ij} is the fraction of the money flow needed to pay labour for this production:

$$\pi_{ij} = r.\underline{p}'A_{ji}.\underline{x} \qquad (5.87)$$

$$w_{ij} = \underline{p}'.B_{ji}.\underline{x} \qquad (5.88)$$

$$y_{ij} = \underline{p}'.A^*_{ji}.\underline{x} \qquad (5.89)$$

The monetary balance of trade for region i is:

$$\bar{y}_j = \sum_i(y_{ij} - y_{ji}) \qquad (5.90)$$

Similarly in the sphere of labour values, with obvious notation:

$$v^*_{ij} = c_{ij} + v_{ij} + s_{ij} \quad (5.91)$$

$$c_{ij} = \underline{\Lambda}'.A^*_{ij}\underline{x} \quad (5.92)$$

$$v_{ij} = \underline{\Lambda}'.B_{ij}\underline{x} \quad (5.93)$$

$$s_{ij} = \underline{\Lambda}'.B_{ij}.(E).\underline{x} \quad (5.94)$$

$$v^*_{ij} = \underline{\Lambda}'[A_{ij} + B_{ij}(E)]\underline{x} \quad (5.95)$$

In contradistinction to the monetary accounting, equations (5.91) - (5.95) are interpreted as the labour value of products flowing from region i to region j.

The utility of such an accounting framework is threefold. First, it allows the construction of spatial flow matrices of values in the economic system. Second, it allows the identification of certain important elements and their geographical distribution; especially profits and surplus value which are the source of capital accumulation. Third, labour value and money value flows may be compared, allowing a comparison of traditional Marxist with other economic theories.

5.6.2 Unequal exchange

Emmanuel (1972) postulated a Marxist theory of trade and unequal exchange which has become a much-discussed explanation of underdevelopment through trade at the international scale. More recently, other authors have suggested that the same concepts may be applicable inter-regionally (Lovering, 1978, Liossatos, 1980-A, 1980-B, 1981). Emmanuel showed that when trade between two nations with different wage levels is such that in monetary terms trade is balanced, the country with the lower wage level exports more labour value than it imports thus experiencing a trade deficit in labour value terms. He then argued that this loss of resources by low wage Third World countries implied that free trade contributed to continued under-development.

A careful examination of Emmanuel's model shows that unequal wage levels essentially is equivalent to unequal rates of exploitation (Barnes, 1982-B). Using Barnes' (1982-B) definition of unequal exchange between two regions as occurring when:

$$y^*_{ij}/y^*_{ji} \neq v^*_{ij}/V^*_{ji} \tag{5.96}$$

it is clear from equations (5.85) and (5.95) that the inequality in (5.96) generally holds. A broader definition would be that:

$$\sum_i y^*_{ij}/\sum_i y^*_{ji} \neq \sum_i v^*_{ij}/\sum_i v^*_{ji} \tag{5.97}$$

which is also generally true. Thus it can be concluded that unequal exchange is a general feature of spatial economic systems.

A second source of unequal exchange is when the labour force is heterogeneous, and inter-regional differences in wages occur as a result of variations in the proportions of more and less skilled labour. Liossatos (1982) has analysed this case, showing that indeed unequal exchange does result. Whether unequal exchange is an important source of regional differences in development rates is a controversial question (cf Gibson, 1980, Barnes, 1982-B). That issue, however, is beyond the scope of this chapter.

Emmanuel's analysis depends on the difference between labour and monetary values. One of the distinctive features of traditional Marxist analysis is that economic relations are often theorized in terms of labour values (Sheppard, 1983-C). An interesting side issue is the level of correspondence between the price vector and the labour value vector. If the two were closely correlated, then analyses carried out in the value sphere would also apply in the price sphere. One of the principles of Marxist economic thought is that the two spheres are very different. Indeed, it is argued that relations in the price circuit can disguise fundamental social forces revealed in the labour value circuit. However, there is some reason to believe that in practice the price and labour value circuits may be quite closely related.

Comparing equations (5.40) and (5.47), two differences emerge. First, in (5.47) the wage good inputs are removed. Second, the functional form on the right hand side is different in each case. Examining this second difference alone, by substituting A for A* in equation (5.47), it can be argued that despite the difference in functional form under plausible conditions both calculation methods lead to almost the identical vector. Consider the following three points, assuming that above substitution of A for A* has been performed.

1. If $[I-A]^{-1} \propto \underline{d}.\underline{w}'$, where $\underline{d}$ is an arbitrary vector and $\underline{w}'$ is the left hand eigenvector associated with the largest eigenvalue of A, then $\underline{p}' = \underline{\Lambda}'$. This follows because $\Lambda = \underline{L}'.\underline{d}.\underline{w}' \equiv k.w' \propto \underline{p}'$ since $\underline{p}' \propto \underline{w}'$ by equation (5.40).

2. If A is singular, with second largest eigenvalue equal to zero, $A^k = \lambda_m^k.\underline{v}.\underline{w}'$ for all $k > n-1$, where n is the dimension of A, λ_m is the largest eigenvalue, and $\underline{v}$ is the associated left hand eigenvector (Seneta, 1981). Since $[I-A]^{-1} = \sum_{k=0}^{\infty} A^k$, it follows that $[I-A]^{-1} = \sum_{k=0}^{n-1} A^k + [\sum_{k=n}^{\infty} r^k].\underline{vw}'$. Thus, particularly if λ_m is close to one, the relation under point 1 above may be closely approximated.

3. If A has an eigenvalue equal to one Adj $[I-A] \propto k.\underline{v}.\underline{w}'$ (Seneta, 1981). But $[I-A]^{-1} = \text{Adj}(I-A)/|I-A|$. Thus when A has an eigenvalue very close to one, then $[I-A]^{-1}$ will be approximately proportional to $\underline{v}.\underline{w}'$.

Observed spatial interaction matrices, of which A is an example, often are nearly singular. Further, the principal eigenvalue of A will be typically slightly less than one, since the economic surplus produced in capitalist economies (and thus the rate of profit) is not a very large proportion of total production. Thus, it is to be expected that empirical examples of A may have characteristics approaching both of those described under 2 and 3 above. This may well imply that condition 1 is quite closely approximated in practice. When the above argument is valid, the difference between $\underline{\Lambda}'$ and $\underline{p}'$ reduces to the difference between A and A*. Thus the degree of deviation between labour values and prices depends on the pattern of consumption of wage goods and on geographical variations in their price. There may also exist conditions when these differences are small, and $\underline{\Lambda}' \simeq \underline{p}'$. One should not conclude from this, however, that Marxist theory may be reduced to that of other paradigms, since the opposite conclusion is equally valid. Clearly some empirical calculations of $\underline{p}'$ and $\underline{\Lambda}'$ would provide instructive information.

5.7 Capital Accumulation Dynamics

5.7.1 Introduction

Section 5.5 examined the spatial equilibrium of the two value circuits for the space economy. In this case, although no complete analysis was presented the spatial equilibrium seems to be stable with respect to changes in the trading patterns for given production methods (Section 5.5.3.3 and Sheppard, 1983-D) and with respect to choice of technology (Sheppard, 1983-C). One implication to be drawn from this is that, at least with respect to the value spheres, the matrix A stabilizes over time in the absence of fundamental changes such as the introduction of new production methods.

However, spatial equilibrium in the circuit of production quantities and capital accumulation presents a strikingly different picture. The conditions of dynamic equilibrium (equations (5.54) and (5.55)) guarantee smooth accumulation over time. If condition (5.54) is satisfied, then reinvestment of all profits is possible, since each industry grows at the same rate (g) at which capital in that industry accumulates. This is sufficient to avoid a realization crisis, which would occur when produced goods are not sold, and profits on investments are not realized. If condition (5.55) is satisfied, then supplies match demands and a disproportionality crisis is avoided (cf Harris, 1978, Roemer, 1981). In this closed system, if dynamic accumulation does not occur in a pattern described by equation (5.56) then both types of crisis will result. The existence of disproportionality crisis leads in turn to a realization crisis. A key question is the stability of the dynamic equilibrium ray defined by (5.56) under local disturbances about $\underline{x}^*$. It may be easily shown that the equilibrium is unstable.

Rewriting equation (5.55):

$$\underline{x}_t = A^{-1} \cdot \underline{x}_t - 1 \qquad (5.98)$$

the eigenvalues of A^{-1} all exceed one, guaranteeing instability. This has profound implications. Hahn (1966) had already shown in a neo-classical multi-commodity model that a similar instability exists. He concluded that this represents "the golden nail in the coffin of capitalism" (Shell, 1973, p. 208), since it implies that the private action of entrepreneurs cannot lead to stable accumulation; in a growth context that 'hidden hand' of Adam Smith simply does not operate. In the Marxian model here the problem is even deeper. In the neo-classical multi-commodity model a vector of prices can be found that if held to through central planning would maintain equilibrium (Burmeister,

1980). In the Marxian construction prices and quantities are not directly related, so such a price vector does not exist. A more fundamental form of government intervention is thus necessary.

The behaviour of (5.98) out of equilibrium is difficult to directly analyse due to the interdependencies between sectors. Through a mathematical transformation, however, it is possible to perceive the forces underlying accumulation (Goodwin, 1976, Sheppard, 1983-D). If M is the matrix of left hand eigenvectors of A,

$$M.A.M^{-1} = Q \tag{5.99}$$

where Q is a diagonal matrix containing the eigenvalues of A. Then (5.98) becomes:

$$\underline{x}_t^e = Q^{-1}.\underline{x}_{t-1}^e \tag{5.100}$$

where $\underline{x}^e = M.\underline{x}$ is a vector of independent production configurations. But from (5.54):

$$\underline{x}_t^e = \lambda_m^{-1}.\underline{x}_{t-1}^e \tag{5.101}$$

In all cases where $\underline{x}_{t-1}$ does not equal $\underline{x}^*$, (5.100) and (5.101) are not identical. In these cases the production configuration may be partitioned into those where $q_i^{-1} < \lambda_m^{-1}$, and those where $q_i^{-1} > \lambda_m^{-1}$; q_i being the i-th diagonal entry of Q. In the former case, the rate of growth necessary to avoid a disproportionality crisis is greater than that achievable if all profits are reinvested. Here a tendency to underaccumulation exists in that sufficient profits cannot be made. Conversely in the other configurations overaccumulation exists in that a reinvestment of profits leads to excessive supplies.

It can then be concluded that any disturbance from

equilibrium is self-reinforcing. Attempts to counter this instability founder through a combination of supply and demand imbalance (disproportionality crisis), together with realization crises that follow any success in clearing the market. In this context it is clear that government intervention in the capitalist space economy is a necessary prerequisite for avoiding accumulation crises. Further, government intervention must take the form of measures to protect or subsidize the profitability of private investment. Marxist theories of state action maintain that the state must do more than efficiently provide public goods. The state must go further and invest to subsidize capitalist accumulation on the one hand, and compensate for social inequalities created as a result of such subsidies on the other hand, in order to avoid economic or political crises (Offe, 1972, Clark and Dear, 1981). This is perfectly consistent with the economic analysis presented here, and opens up some interesting directions of research into the links between spatial capitalist development, state planning and state action due to geographical differences in accumulation dynamics (cf Scott, 1980).

5.7.2 Avoiding accumulation crises

The crises described above are based on the assumption of a constant matrix A over time. However, when capitalists face accumulation crises they will take actions that modify A. Thus the question remaining is whether actions by individual capitalists that lead to changes in A can induce a stability into accumulation dynamics that is not otherwise there. This question has barely been treated at all. Five possibilities do, however, exist (cf Sheppard, 1983-C):

(a) *Exporting the crisis*. By changing interactions with other areas outside the region of study, crises can be alleviated by exporting surplus and importing goods in shortage. This strongly parallels the Marxist notion of imperialism (Barratt-Brown, 1974).

(b) *Changing trade patterns.* To a degree, crises may be alleviated by changing the sources of supply and the marketing locations in favour of those that increase profits. However, it has been shown (Section 5.5.2, Sheppard, 1983-D) that this leads to a stable matrix A, which in turn implies unstable capital accumulation dynamics.

(c) *Altering the labour process.* A typical response to falling profits is to attempt to reduce the cost of labour either directly by introducing more severe working conditions and reducing the wage, or indirectly by rationalizing the work process. All such changes reduce the size of some elements in A, which by the Perron-Frobenius theorem will increase the common rate of profit. Thus conflicts between labour and capital, and the dynamics of the non-economic determinants of wages in regions, are a concomitant of the geography of accumulation crises.

(d) *Changing the techniques of production.* Introduction of process or product innovations may avoid crises by reducing the requirements of goods in shortage, or by reducing production of goods no longer in demand. Although there is much discussion of this issue by economists, a large part of it is based on single capital good macroeconomic models which provide little insight into the multicommodity case. Discussion of multicommodity models is typically only a comparative static comparison of different (unstable) technological mixes (Harcourt, 1972). The few cases of a dynamic analysis, of which the best are represented by Spaventa (1973) and Pasinetti (1981), are purely planning models and do not attempt to describe how capitalists will change the production process or the degree to which this induces stability into accumulation dynamics. Thus this is largely an unexplored area.

(e) *Direct alterations in the geography of production.*

Accumulation crises will occur to different degrees in different areas. In response to this, investments will flow in and out of locations leading to changes in the production vector $\underline{x}_t$, and even in the geography of specialization. Obviously such changes in $\underline{x}_t$ may push the geography of production toward the equilibrium configuration. Sheppard (1983-C) has tentatively suggested some investment rules, but this issue (which amounts to a descriptive dynamic theory of location) is also unexplored.

5.7.3 Analysing the growth ray

Within economics a very extensive literature exists analysing the growth ray defined by equation (5.56). Thus Spaventa (1970) has shown that growth and consumption levels in the context of equilibrated capital accumulation are the mirror image of profits and wages in the static price equilibrium. Further analyses include Abraham-Frois and Berrebi (1979) and Pasinetti (1981). Another broad avenue of research is on the growth ray as a path for maximizing economic growth using such concepts as the turnpike theorem (Burmeister, 1980). All of this research could be easily adapted into the spatial context. However, unless it can be shown that some stability exists around the growth ray, it is not a useful concept for any explanation of the capitalist space economy. Thus this research will not be further pursued here.

5.8 Extensions

5.8.1 Corporate power

It is well known that the geography of production, and all of its concomitants such as transportation patterns, is strongly influenced currently by the institutional structure of large corporations (Herman, 1981). This is a topic that conventional location theory has not been able to discuss at all easily, reflecting the difficulties of introducing monopolistic competition into macroeconomic theory. In this case the neo-Marxian approach has a distinct advantage; spatial pricing and investment rules can be introduced that reflect, and influence, the geography of corporate ownership. This opens the possibility of moving beyond descriptive and loose explanatory studies of corporate organization (Thrift, 1981, Westaway, 1974) to some more sophisticated analyses.

Sheppard (1983-A) has investigated this issue at some depth; just a brief summary is given here. Consider a description of the geography of corporate power, defined by a J by J matrix C with entries c_{ij} representing the number of jobs in region j controlled by corporations headquartered in region i. Postulate that the rate of profit in a region depends on the degree of corporate power headquartered there (a spatial interpretation of the monopoly power hypothesis of Kalecki, 1938):

$$r_i = f(c_{i.}, r) \tag{5.102}$$

where $c_{i.} = \sum_j c_{ij}$ and r is the general rate of profit. Then the model of price determination (equation (5.40)) is generalized as follows:

$$\underline{p}' = \underline{p}'.(R).A \tag{5.103}$$

where (R) is a diagonal matrix with entries $1+r_i$ for all production sectors in region i. Equation (5.103) is soluble given C and a definition of the function in (5.102).

The profits controlled by each region, Π_i^c, equal the profits made in that region, plus the profits made elsewhere but controlled from this region:

$$\Pi_i^c = (\sum_j \Pi_{ji}).\gamma_{ii} + \sum_k \gamma_{ik}.\sum_j \Pi_{jk} \tag{5.104}$$

where Π_{ij} is given from a matrix of profit flows defined (cf equation (5.87)) by:

$$\Pi_{ji} = \underline{p}'.[(R)-I]A_{ij}\underline{x} \tag{5.105}$$

In equation (5.104) $\gamma_{ik} = c_{ik}/c_{.k}$, the proportion of plants in region k owned in region i.

Profits thus accumulate to regions in a manner that reflects the corporate power centred there. However, one cannot conclude with Pred (1976) that the prosperity of such regions depends directly on their corporate power, since the profits spent on maintaining and extending corporate headquarters is a very small proportion of total expenditures. To make statements about the effects of corporate power on the geography of capital accumulation, a model of direct corporate investment must be introduced. Sheppard (1983-A) has proposed a simple model based on the notions of Hymer (1976, 1979):

$$R_{ij} = \Pi_i^c[\alpha.(Y_j/\sum_k Y_k) + \beta(r_j/\sum_k r_k) + \delta(c_{ij}/\sum_k c_{ik})] \tag{5.106}$$

where R_{ij} is the profit controlled by region i that is invested in region j, and $Y_j = \sum_i Y_{ji}$ is the total value of economic activity produced in region j. In equation (5.106) the first term reflects portfolio investment that occurs through the capital market where interest rates are approximately equal everywhere. Thus this investment follows largely the level of economic activity. The second term refers to that part of direct investment that is directed to regions on the basis of the local profitability of corporate investment there. The third term refers to direct investment in locations where branch plants already exist. α,β,δ are parameters reflecting the importance of the three types of investment. Equations (5.102) - (5.106) may be written in the form of a dynamic model of capital accumulation in a capitalist space economy, with the addition of an extra expression accounting for changes in C as a function of investment patterns (Sheppard, 1983-A). The special case of a space economy without multilocational corporations is defined by representing C as a diagonal matrix; this may always be compared to the corporate case.

5.8.2 Fixed capital

The implicit assumption has been made that all capital good inputs are completely used up during the production period in each industry. In reality of course this is not the case; fixed capital of varying durability is in operation in different industries. Perhaps the most striking example of this is land as fixed capital. It may be shown that fixed capital can be easily introduced by generalizing the neo-Marxian model into a Von Neumann model (Morishima and Catephores, 1978, Abraham-Frois and Berrebi, 1979, Von Neumann, 1945). Sheppard (1983-C) has outlined some of the problems to be addressed in a spatial version of this approach. Quadrio Curzio (1980) indicates how differential land rents can be derived from such an approach, treating land as fixed capital.

5.9 Conclusions

The purpose of this chapter has been to present a constructive alternative to neo-classical macro-scale spatial economic theory. Contradictions in neo-classical theory were shown to be removed by formulating the space economy as an interrelated production system of heterogeneous goods, rather than a separable series of production functions consuming homogeneous factors. The resulting framework contradicts neo-classical theory in a number of crucial deductions, and necessarily reintroduces into analytical regional science a series of concepts from Marx's economic theory that have been neglected.

One principal achievement of the chapter has been to show that a spatial equilibrium of production can be constructed where, given the production technologies applied at each location, the real wage, and some specified level of inefficiency in spatial markets, trading behaviour and the patterns of spatial pricing are consistent with one another. In addition it was demonstrated that the spatial prices, as well as a dual system of spatial labour values, can be represented by potential theory. In that a potential theory provides a mathematical statement of the geography of impacts of spatial interdependencies, this last result may not be surprising. It does, however, provide a rigorous dual interpretation of value systems as being indices of spatial accessibility as well as of economic attributes. Further, it was shown that the spatial separation of production points implies that economic rules for geographical specialization and trade are inadequate, in that specialization in response to observed prices changes the trading system which will alter prices.

A key question in the above analysis is the relation between individual actions of autonomous entrepreneurs, and the aggregate patterns of production and pricing that represent some profit maximizing equilibrium for capitalist production in space. Dynamic simulations have shown that the pricing-trading equilibrium is stable. However, it is as yet unknown whether individual actions can also guarantee an optimal, or even satisfactory, geographical pattern of specialization.

Other conclusions from this framework relate the results to Marx's economic theory. Thus, in the sphere of labour values, at least one region must have an exploited labour force (where the labour value of the hourly wage is less than that of one hour of labour) if the economy as a whole is to make a money profit. Further, a conflict of interest between capitalists, workers and landlords is shown to exist, a conflict albeit modified by location in that the degree of exploitation of labour varies from place to place. Finally, and perhaps most importantly, the division of the economic surplus between these three groups is partly exogenously determined, but itself is a determinant of prices, trading patterns and location patterns. Thus the geography of production depends on those political and social forces that influence the distribution of income.

Given an optimal geographical pattern of production, a unique set of relative quantities can be determined specifying the levels of production necessary to maintain equal growth rates and market clearance. This also has a potential theoretical interpretation. In general this dynamic equilibrium is highly unstable in the absence of fundamental adjustments by entrepreneurs, or state intervention. Possible adjustments are suggested, but as yet their effects on the stability of spatial capital accumulation are unknown. Resolution of this issue once again involves a consideration of the link between individual responses and aggregate outcomes.

The paper also shows that this space economy is consistent both with Keynesian accounting in the price sphere, and Marxist accounting in the labour value sphere. These accounts may be spatially disaggregated to examine flows of profits, or trade balances in the price and labour value spheres. Finally, extensions to include corporate ownership, and fixed capital together with joint production, are indicated.

Future research involves at least three major initiatives. First, at the theoretical level there are a number of unresolved issues about the ability of individual entrepreneurs to act in a way that optimizes their collective welfare. At issue here is the ability of the "hidden hand" of the market to guide the space economy. The nature of the optimal geography of production, its achievability by individual actions, and the dynamic stability of capital accumulation in the face of adjustments in the production process by entrepreneurs, are all issues of this kind. These can only be resolved by theoretical research and simulation experiments designed to elucidate the relation between individual actions and aggregate outcomes.

Second, the framework must be adapted to be applicable in particular contexts. Of special importance is application in the urban context. Here, five issues that must be included are: a housing sector, commuting by workers, land rents, spatial externalities, and road congestion. Such adaptations pose no particular problems, with the possible exception of spatial externalities. Division of a city into zones, specification of a set of prices outside the city, and identification of housing, commuting and congestion as important elements in this application should suffice to construct an initial model.

Third, the doubt cast by this approach on the ability of market competition to resolve economic crises, and the explicit recognition of social conflicts made possible in this approach, allow for a more critical discussion of the role of planning.

In addition to the usual technical issues of identifying and executing optimal plans, two further issues can be discussed. First, if the market mechanism is indeed inherently crises-ridden, then the necessity of planning, as a permanent and fundamental force rather than an occasional tool to eliminate market imperfections, is supported. Second, the impact of planning on the conflicting social groups may be identified and used to evaluate the goals of the planning process. Thus, for instance, planning an efficient, profit maximizing spatial system will tend to minimize wages and increase the social and political power of capitalists; a result that would cast doubt on the belief that planning is a socially progressive activity (Scott, 1980, Broadbent, 1977,

Glickmann, 1981).

It is in casting doubt on conventional (neo-classical) wisdom about the social desirability of markets, together with the corollaries of rejecting that position, that this alternative has potential; quite apart from its usefulness in explaining observed spatial structures. In removing inconsistencies, a theory results that allows for a questioning of the status quo which is not existent in the neo-classical approach.

Part Three

OPERATIONAL RESEARCH

Chapter 6

OPTIMIZATION TECHNIQUES IN LOCATIONAL MODELLING

A. Colorni

6.1 Introduction

We intend to examine the following decision problem, which we refer to as a location problem: the choice of a set of points, conventionally named plants, selected from a finite or infinite number of candidate points, with the aim of minimizing one (or more) objective function(s) in relation to the costs associated with the spatial distribution of the selected points and the distance of these from another set of points conventionally named customers. The definition is intentionally restrictive. We will examine the problem from a quantitative point of view, using mathematical models of optimization. We shall be looking mainly at the location of single-sector facilities, both private (such as the location of industrial plants) and public (the location of public services and facilities).

The operational research approach adopted here means that only certain aspects of location phenomena are examined. This is because optimization models are strongly conditioned by the classic concept of rationality, ie the existence of one or more decision-makers who act in accordance with coherent and optimal rules of behaviour. (Only recently have some aspects of "irrationality" been introduced.) They are also affected by the marginalist theories of economics (eg the economic interpretation of linear programming and duality theory) and finally the fact that optimization models neglect or only marginally touch on aspects such as planning regulations, location incentives/disincentives, data analysis, technology, other aspects connected with transport, economic analysis, environmental impact and so on. There are, obviously, other aspects of the location problem, many of which are discussed elsewhere in this book. I limit myself here to examining the operational research approach and in particular mathematical models of optimization. Let us now examine, through a few examples, some characteristics of this approach.

Example 1

A firm distributes its products from a central plant to several peripheral sales departments. For this purpose it wants to locate some trans-shipment plants (warehouses) which receive the products from the central plant and supply the sales departments, minimizing total costs connected with production, fluctuation of demand (and therefore quantities of goods stored), transport and distribution. This is a problem with one decision-maker (the firm) which governs both the choice of location of the warehouses and that of supply (ie the problem of location as well as that of resource storing). Moreover the objective function is quite easy to quantify: it reduces to balancing transport costs and the construction/management costs of the trans-shipment plants.

Example 2

A certain number of terminals are connected to each other by a network. In each terminal is stored a number of different files, which we want to be available to create a number of data-bases in some (unknown) nodes of the network. Here too there is a single decision-maker. His objective function is expressed by minimizing a sum of costs relating to transmission channels and utilization time, taking into consideration the state of the network.

Example 3

The main purpose of an emergency service is to arrive at the place of the call as soon as possible. We want to decide where to locate a certain (fixed) number of emergency stations on the basis of a forecast of calls. The criterion for the planner in this case must be the maximum time of reply to a call and he must therefore formulate an objective function that minimizes this time (ie that uses the result corresponding to the worst case).

Example 4

Some social groups (each with its own weight) contribute to the taking of a decision that involves the choice of two continuous decision variables x_1 and x_2. The representation of the choices of each group in the space of variables (ie in this case in the x_1-x_2 plane) produces a set of "heavy" points, while the search for a compromise solution is equivalent to the location of the median of the point system.

What unifies these cases? (a) The presence of a spatial decision problem; (b) the representation of the problem through a certain number of variables and constraints; (c) the formulation of one or more choice criteria (objectives); (d) the deterministic or stochastic knowledge of problem data and decision effects. In other words they all involve mathematical decision models in operations research. It is the intention in this chapter to offer a systematic examination of the many models designed for use in location problems. It is also an opportunity to define the relevant hypotheses and their relevance to different kinds of problem, to evaluate and compare the complexity and the data structure of the different models and to speculate about possible future developments.

We shall firstly, however, make a few introductory remarks

on the approach adopted. First, in the survey and analysis an attempt will be made to classify the various existing models, methods and algorithms. Like all classifications it is obviously open to criticism but nevertheless serves a useful didactic function. Secondly, as the problem is being considered from the operational research point of view the following aspects will be examined: (i) the use of optimization techniques, especially mathematical programming and combinatorial optimization; (ii) the examination of complex decision structures through multi-objective and multi-level programming; (iii) the comparison of algorithms and the study of their efficiency; (iv) the examination of computer codes and their computational complexity.

Thirdly, we turn to mathematical models which are essentially to be considered in this context as instruments of decision support. This will be the case if the problem (i) has the relevant dimension and/or complexity; (ii) has a particular structure; (iii) needs a sensitivity analysis. Fourthly, the survey is based on articles from the main international journals (see Section 6.6) and recent books, with direct reference, however, only to the most important ones. Fifthly, the examination of problems will also be focused on location (ie zoning, scheduling, etc) and defined in relation to the principal fields where location models are used.

Three periods can be distinguished in the history of location models: (i) problem formulation (from Weber until the 1940s); (ii) use of models in the industrial sector (1950s and 1960s); (iii) development of models in the public sector (1970s). In the first period the computational instruments were completely inadequate in relation to the problems. The development of a theory was mainly based on geometric and analytic results in continuous space, with contributions also from other fields (Kuhn, 1973). Among the important names were Cavalieri, Fermat and Steiner. The second period is characterized by the parallel development of computers and discrete mathematics. The problem therefore began to be formulated through graphs (which represent the transport network and its characteristics), 0-1 programming (which expresses the decision problem relative to point location) and conditions that take account of technological aspects (Zimmermann and Sovereign, 1974). The third and more recent period, is characterized by increasing numbers of applications to the public sector. The problem of introducing efficiency indicators other than pure cost arose and the range of techniques widened with the formulation of multi-objective programs and models that take into account the not-perfect rationality of the customer (see the special issue of *Sistemi Urbani*, 1981). When these studies are evaluated in a historical perspective, an over-emphasis on costs connected with transport clearly emerges. These costs, in fact are becoming less and less important, at least in private industry (though this is probably less true in the public sector) because the people who pay construction costs and transportation costs are often different.

The rest of the chapter is organized as follows. In Section 6.2, connections between the location problem and other problems of planning and management processes are stressed. In Section 6.3, the characteristics of the location problem and the parameters and the structure of the associated models are examined. In Section 6.4, the more usual techniques are briefly described. In Section 6.5, a survey of the standard models is carried out. In Section 6.6, some possible trends are identified. Conclusions are drawn in the last Section (6.7).

6.2 The Location Problem in the Context of Planning and Management Problems

In the previous section we defined a location problem as being normally inserted in a planning and management decision process.

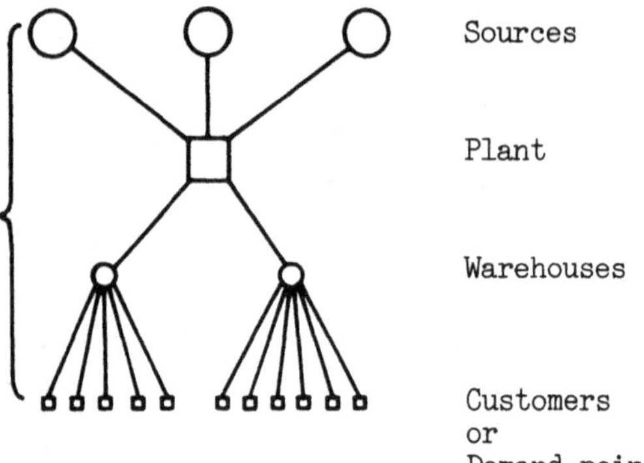

Figure 6.1: The location system

A diagram, taken from Eilon, Watson-Gandy and Christophides (1971) and reproduced as Figure 6.1, can be used to represent the problems of such a process. In this representation of a logistic system a few source-points, a plant, a few warehouses and finally the customers (or demand points) are indicated. Connections between the nodes of this graph are not orientated because, depending on the problem, it is possible to follow either direction. Typically, in a problem of industrial production, the process moves from the sources (where material is located) to the plant (where transformations are carried out) to the intermediate warehouses and finally to the final demand (the customers). In a public facility location problem such as solid waste collection, the process goes from demand points to (possible) intermediate collection points and finally to the disposal plant. In contrast, for development and traffic problems in urban areas, movements are in both directions, linking résidence zones as sources and places of work as points of demand.

There are two kinds of costs for this kind of system, those associated with the nodes and those associated with the arcs of the graph: (i) costs connected with plants and/or warehouses (in some cases also customers and sources), which represent construction costs, maintenance, management, and so on: they have wide temporal horizons, from years to months; and (ii) costs connected with transport and/or local distribution, which depend on quantities transported, the origin and destination of the trip, the kind of transport, and so on. They normally have a restricted temporal horizon, of the order of months or weeks. There are also revenues which generally have these same attributes.

The location problem involves determining the number and the sites of plants and warehouses in a given region. Industrial plants will tend to locate in positions which take into account both material sources and sales markets. Public facilities however will be located in positions which focus on demand points. Emergency services, on the other hand, are not located on the basis of transport and plant costs, because the quality of this service is not connected to its costs but to the promptness of intervention. Environmental protection, particularly water pollution, involves plant location which obeys different rules again, connected with demand points (ie polluting discharges) as well as the laws of nature.

Problems connected with location are strategic (before location) and tactical-operational (after location). Problems in the first category include the analysis of the region and the analysis of the decision structure (in particular the coordination among decision-makers at different levels). The second category includes problems of space distribution (routing), time distribution (scheduling), and also others (for instance traffic control). We now list some of them briefly, stressing their connections with location problems.

The analysis of the characteristics of the region is very important for at least two reasons. First, customers of plants and facilities are generally distributed continuously, though it is often necessary to represent them through a finite number of nodes, each provided with a few easily quantifiable characteristics. This step, normally called zoning, generally implies the use of binary programming and/or graph theory models (cf Garfinkel and Nemhauser, 1972). Secondly, the transport network, which connects customers with possible location points (if they are finite in number) must be examined in order to select the routes, aggregate the data and, more important, determine the set of best routes (for instance the minimum cost paths) from the various nodes of the network. This last problem, classic in graph theory, can be solved by very efficient combinatorial optimization algorithms (Gallo and Pallottino, 1982).

The examination and coordination of the decision structure is necessary because very often, especially in the case of public facilities, location problems require choices that involve decision-makers of different levels and competence. For instance, the problem of the location of measurement stations in a large river basin which will involve river authorities, local boards, public boards for hydroelectric energy production, private industries, agricultural unions and so on. Coordination among the various components of the system requires the use of decentralized and multi-objective, multi-level models (Haimes, 1977).

A different group of problems concerns space distribution or routing. This is a set of operational problems of more limited importance, although often very complex, which arise when plants have already been located. The problem is to organize the paths in an area so as to satisfy a constant or periodic demand and minimize transport and plant management costs. These problems are solved with combinatorial optimization methods, generally heuristic methods, because of the considerable dimensions involved and presence of constraints (Bodin et al, 1981).

Problems of scheduling concern organization and involve shift working, shift rotation and the size of facility necessary to meet a known demand and time variable. In this problem, which is very important in public facilities, the aspects which require closest attention are not transport and/or plant management costs but manpower costs (in other words the cost of the teams that carry out the service), which will be related to the number of people and the time employed which can amount to 80% of total costs. In this case too, mathematical programming techniques (particularly linear programming) can solve the problem efficiently (Bodin, 1973, Bodin et al, 1981).

Let us now go back to actual location problems. There is a remarkable difference between those in the private sector, and those in the public sector (ReVelle, Marks and Liebman, 1970). In the private sector, the most important problem is the location of industrial plants and the following two conditions generally apply: (a_1) there is only one decision-maker, responsible for location choices and also, in some cases, allocation choices of plant to customers (ie the transport model); (a_2) some clear indicators exist making it possible to quantify the objectives; for instance costs to be minimized, profits or market shares to be maximized and incentives to be achieved (Bartezzaghi, 1979). There is in addition a series of location factors of considerable importance which cannot be expressed directly in terms of cost. We will briefly come back to them at the conclusion of this section.

In the public sector the most important problem is the location of facilities and the following conditions generally apply: (b_1) there is an articulate decision structure, which includes one or more public decision-makers and the set of customers. Normally the public authority and the customers operate at different stages of the process, one at the plant-location stage, the other in the management-allocation stage (Eilon, Watson-Gandy and Christofides, 1971). (b_2) the behaviour of customers (also because of their number) cannot be precisely defined and is not always rational; this is partly taken into consideration by introducing stochastic terms in the model (Wilson et al, 1981, Coelho, 1983). (b_3) it is not always possible to define precisely indicators that express the efficiency of the various solutions; sometimes they are even conflicting. This problem is faced by using some "surrogates" of public utility or making recourse to aggregation mechanisms or multi-objective programming (Nijkamp, 1977, Haimes, 1977).

In addition, in the public sector, location problems have different characteristics according to the context in which they are applied; it is possible to single out the following kinds of problems (Colorni, 1982): (i) location with the creation of districts; (ii) location with scheduling and/or routing; (iii) location and dynamic process·simulation; (iv) location conditioned by constraints; (v) location with many non-rational decision-makers; (vi) location of emergency services. Despite the fact that this is an arbitrary classification, it allows us to stress some of the differences between the various problems, which we shall now try to specify.

Location with districts is typical of education, social or medical facilities. Here location is faced as a strategic problem in the context of analysis and zoning of the region. Sometimes the problem is solved with mathematical programming methods, but more often with "ad hoc" procedures which take account of the geographical-administrative conditions of the area. Some methods for application in this field have been developed at the International Institute for Applied Systems Analysis (IIASA), other studies include Benito-Alonso and Devaux (1981), Bertuglia, Leonardi and Tadei (1981), Helly (1975), Greenberg (1978), Sisson (ed) (1974).

There are a number of applications of location with scheduling or routing in public facilities such as solid waste collection, mail distribution, road cleaning, etc. Location becomes a typical problem faced in the management context, often it is a matter of locating temporary intermediate plants or even mobile facilities. One of the main research centres is Maryland University, but other studies have been published in this field (Sisson (ed), 1974, Marks, 1976, Beltrami, 1977, Bodin et al, 1981).

Location and dynamic process simulation is typical of environmental problems (and particularly pollution and water management). Here location is generally not relative to places but rather to the numbers and optimal sizes of plant. The particular nature of the product dealt with, water, (seen from a quantitative and/or qualitative point of view) makes it necessary to incorporate dynamic aspects into the model. For this reason models must be obtained with the aid of simulation combined with optimization algorithms. Works on location are embedded in a more general context (Louks, Stedinger and Haith, 1981, Rinaldi et al, 1979, Greenberg, 1978).

Location 'conditioned by constraints' is illustrated by forecasting and control of atmospheric phenomena, energy production and distribution and, generally, in the location of obnoxious activities. In these cases plant location is not based on costs, but rather on motives of political interest or technical needs. This means that it turns out to be constraint-determined rather than determined by objectives. It must be noted, however, that when the problem is formulated with an optimization model, the objective function shows remarkable analogies with one of the objective functions relative to emergency service location (the criterion of the worst case, see later). Some work done by the research group of Johns Hopkins University is pertinent to the location of energy plants and obnoxious facilities and activities (Cohon et al, 1980, Cohon et al, 1982), others concern location of atmospheric pollution networks and similar facilities (Fortak, 1982).

In the fifth type of problem, location with non-rational decision-makers (which is typical of transportation problems) the location of infrastructure must take into account some specific characteristics. First, the territorial scale (generally very wide) and the difficulties of finding and analysing the data, and secondly the very great number of decision-makers (the customers), whose behaviour is often non-rational and has characteristics which are difficult to quantify. The main studies come from the Wilson school (along with articles in journals such as *Transportation Science* and *Transportation Research* (Wilson et al, 1981, Bertuglia and Leonardi, 1982, Helly, 1975).

Emergency facility location involves services such as fire stations, emergency hospital services and police. Location generally must take account of two factors, costs and intervention time, which cannot always be aggregated into a single objective function. There are basically two approaches. One is to consider one of the factors as a constraint and the other as objective function, the second one is to use multi-objective programming. The principal studies come from the American school, in particular M.I.T. (Handler and Mirchandani, 1979, Larson and Odoni, 1981, Beltrami, 1977, Beltrami, 1979, Revelle, Cohon, Shobrys, 1981).

In considering decision structures, we can distinguish the following criteria for formulating the objective function: (i) efficiency (min-sum), ie where the function to be minimized is a weighted sum of terms that takes into account all customers to be satisfied (ie the median case); (ii) worst case (min-max), ie where the function to be minimized takes account of the customer in the least favourable conditions (the one to whom the maximum time or cost of intervention corresponds). In this second case, for instance for emergency service location problems, it is practically a matter of "covering" the region under examination with a number of points (stations), in order to satisfy one of these two situations: (ii1) given p stations, locate them so as to minimize the intervention time δ_{max} in the most unfavourable case; (ii2) given the intervention time δ beyond which intervention is no longer efficient locate the minimum number of stations p_{min} necessary to respond to each call efficiently.

The criterion of the worst case connects this problem with the combinatorial optimization problem known as "set covering", for which several methods of solution exist (Salkin, 1975) - many of which are heuristic. This is due to the remarkable dimension of the problem and to the fact that in some cases (eg for ambulances) location must be periodically redefined. We shall return to this in Section 6.5.2.2.

Before concluding this section we shall briefly examine the decision process involved in location problems, looking firstly at the main location factors, and then at the conditions under which the decision process takes place. We present this analysis, based on Bartezzaghi, Colorni, Palermo (1976) and Zimmermann and Sovereign (1974) in order to provide a basis for the section on the evaluation of models made in Section 6.5.

Location is a decision process with a long time horizon for which it is necessary to examine a large number of factors and evaluate the consequences of the possible decisions. The main location factors are listed in Table 6.1. The role they play is different in the private sector (the location of the firm) from the public sector (location of services). Some of them are quite easily represented with the aid of a mathematical model, others far less. Cost factors usually enter into the objective function; other factors into the constraints. The relevance of location factors depends on the kind of service and its characteristics. It can vary according to the step in the decision process. In fact the complexity of the location process is such that it is generally represented as a series of decision steps, ie the choice of the location area, then

Table 6.1: Main location factors

Factors connected with costs:	transportation costs
	distribution of the labour force
	location of supply sources
	incentives and/or taxation systems
Factors connected to demand:	market areas
	spatial distribution of demand
	distribution network
Territorial factors:	external facilities
	availability of finance in the areas
	energy supply
	land availability, etc
Extra-economic factors:	political, social, cultural characteristics
	institutional conditions and constraints

the choice of the place in this area and finally the choice of the specific point. In each of these steps certain factors may prevail depending on the kind of facility to be located. For instance, transport costs and market area location prevail for the choice of the location area, availability of work and external economies for the choice of the place, infrastructures and natural factors for the choice of the final point.

In relation to the conditions in which the location process is carried out, attempts have been made to define the schemes of logic and interpretation underlying the location process (in the private sector in particular). In such schemes the influence of the different location factors on choice and the context in which the decision is taken are examined. It is possible to distinguish three categories of location problem: (A1) constrained by one or more factors; (A2) determined by one prevailing factor; (A3) conditioned by many different factors.

It is possible to have five kinds of decision environment: (B1) adaptation to existing environment (choices are taken within the limits of external, non-modifiable political and economic data); (B2) dependent on exogenous parameters (choices are conditioned by the behaviour of other decision-makers); (B3) interdependent (choices are conditioned by and condition other decision processes); (B4) independent and controllable (choices can influence other processes); (B5) planned (decisions implement plans for the entire area development).

Combining these two classifications (Bartezzaghi, 1979), it is possible to obtain a typology of situations suitable for estimating the significance of models, shown in Table 6.2.

	(B1)	(B2)	(B3)	(B4)	(B5)
(A1)			■	■	■
(A2)	X	X			
(A3)	X				

Table 6.2: Location factors and the decision environment (boxes with a square indicate combinations to be logically excluded, boxes with a cross indicate combinations for which, in present conditions, the use of models is more meaningful, the remaining boxes indicate situations of partial use of models)

Some evaluations and hypotheses can be explored. For line (A1), recourse to location models is not possible in certain cases; nevertheless, if the location area were constrained, use of a model for the choice of a location point may be meaningful (with a suitable specification of location factors at this level of analysis). Model use is at present especially useful for line (A2), in particular for cases in which "traditional" location factors, such as transportation costs, labour force and market areas are relevant. Model development, with the removal of limiting hypotheses and the possibility of solving more complex models, makes it possible to deal with the situation of line (A3) and to consider more complicated location factors (such as externalities) using where necessary prior analyses to determine convenient cost functions and constraint systems.

Column (B1) represents the most typical cases of application of mathematical programming models; in such cases parameters (product, prices and demand, cost and availability of factors, etc) are determined exogenously. In column (B2) the case where location is conditioned by single factors is meaningful. In column (B3) the limitations of present models (which assume all aspects that should be considered endogenous to be exogenous) are highlighted. These models can be used in simulation, assuming different values of parameters. In column (B4), and especially in (B5), we find more general models, relating to the location of economic activities, developed within the limits of spatial economies and regional planning methods.

In the following sections several types of mathematical model used for tackling location problems will be examined. Their use is directly related to their accuracy in representing the actual decision process. The use of such models requires, generally, a relatively exact quantification of the various aspects of the problem and is not of course the only way of resolving it. There are other approaches that allow a less formal analysis and an examination of more qualitative aspects.

6.3 Analysis of the Problem

The production of papers on location models has been and still is very prolific though there are signs of a slowing down. It is therefore necessary to have at our disposal criteria for the interpretation of existing material. This will be attempted in the present section, distinguishing between the examination of a few fundamental typological variables and parameters on the one hand and the model structure on the other. The contents of this section have been taken, in part, from a previous work of the author (Bartezzaghi, Colorni and Palermo, 1976).

6.3.1 The fundamental parameters for classification

The main parameters which form the basis of a classification are presented in Table 6.3. More detail is available in Bartezzaghi, Colorni and Palermo (1976) and Coelho (1983).

Parameters (a)-(d) describe the problem, parameters (e)-(j) the model; (e)-(g) the objective function and (h)-(j) the constraints.

Case (a1), in which location may be in any point of the relevant territory, historically corresponds to the earliest models. A recent survey is given in Hansen and Thisse (1983). We shall look at this type and the relative metrics problem in Section 6.5.2.1. Although this case may seem the most general, it has been progressively abandoned in favour of discrete models (a2) because the use of graphs makes it possible to express with greater precision distances, times and road conditions corresponding to the existing transport network and because discrete models take account more easily of particular geographical, administrative and market constraints that a priori limit the possible location points. In the discrete case the distance between two points is given by the minimum path on the graph representing the transport network.

Table 6.3: Main parameters for a classification of location problems

(a) Space: (a1) continuous (a11) rectilinear metrics
(a12) euclidean metrics
(a13) other kinds of metrics
(a2) discrete

(b) Time: (b1) static model
(b2) dynamic model (multi-periodical)

(c) Sector: (c1) private
(c2) public
(c21) ordinary services
(c22) emergency services

(d) Production: (d1) mono-sectorial
(d2) multi-sectorial
(d21) without interdependencies
(d22) with interdependencies

(e) Objective function: (e1) efficiency criterion
(e2) worst case criterion
(e3) multi-objective programming

(f) Nature of cost functions: (f1) connected to production
(f2) connected to distribution
(f21) long distance transportation
(f22) local distribution

(g) Form of cost functions: (g1) linear
(g2) linear with fixed charge
(g3) concave (or piecewise linear)

(h) Demand: (h1) fixed (h11) divisible
(h12) indivisible
(h2) elastic (h21) known
(h22) stochastic

(i) Capacity: (i1) unlimited
(i2) limited (i21) fixed
(i22) variable

(j) Number of plants: (j1) fixed
(j2) to be determined

Case (b1) is more common than (b2), which is treated as a multi-periodic problem (ie with decisions taken at different times) rather than a real dynamic problem (with state variables that take account of previous decisions) (Erlenkotter, 1981, Van Roy and Erlenkotter, 1982).

(c1) and (c2), with the further subdivisions of the latter (and the conditions given by emergency services), have already been discussed in the previous section and therefore will not be commented on further.

Most existing applications are of type (d1). It should be noted that case (d21) in practice belongs to (d1), except that it has a greater number of variables. The situation is different in case (d22), however: meaningful contributions are unusual because of the modelling and computational difficulties (Scherer et al, 1975).

The distinction between the various kinds of objective functions (e), already explained in the previous section, is treated in detail by Coelho (1983), ReVelle (1982) and Nijkamp and Rietveld (1980) and will be examined in Section 6.5.2.

Cases (f) and (g) both refer to costs appearing in the objective function; the distinction of case (f), also dealt with in Eilon, Watson-Gandy and Christofides (1971), relates to the nature of costs (not always all present in the various location problems that we shall refer to), while (g) refers to their form; case (g1) expresses the hypothesis of constant efficiency; case (g2) (a component of fixed cost independent of the production level) and case (g3) (in which a piecewise linear function, with the use of separable programming, normally approximates a concave function) express the more realistic hypothesis of economies of scale. The cost functions are shown in Figure 6.2.

Classifications (h), (i) and (j) refer to the problem constraints. Case (h11) is the most common. A few articles have been recently devoted to case (h2) (such as Sheppard,

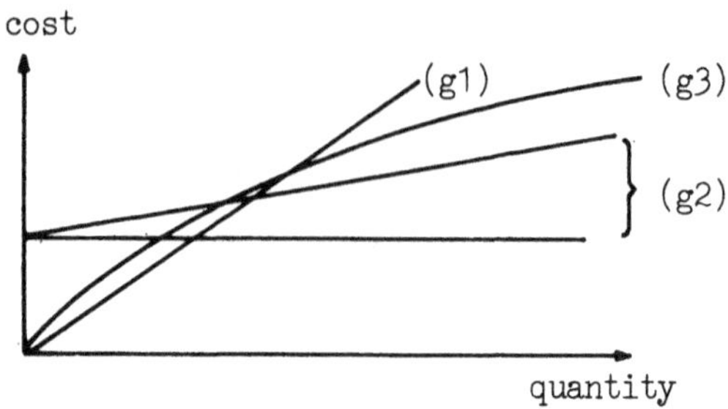

Figure 6.2: The main forms of cost functions

1981-A).

Parameter (i) generally expresses the set of constraints imposed by production technology on the good or service to be located. Case (i1) makes condition (h12), of demand indivisibility, practically meaningless - in fact each customer may be supplied for the entire amount of his demand from the more favourable plant. Case (i22) normally requires a discrete capacity variation, having a finite number of possible values.

Parameter (j) is very important for solution methodologies. Case (j1) assumes spatially undifferentiated plant costs (and therefore only the number of plants to be located counts): in cases where it is not realistic, condition (j2) is substituted with a budget constraint.

Some important aspects deriving from the combination of different objective functions and constraints will be illustrated in the following section. Here it is opportune to stress the main typologies of location problems in broad terms.

A first typology is obtained by combining parameters (c) (sector) and (e) (objective function). The situation is presented in Table 6.4.

Objective function \ Sector	Private	Public
efficiency	plant and warehouses 1	ordinary 4
worst case	obnoxious plants 2	emergency services 5
multi-objectives	quantity vs risk 3	quantity vs quality 6

Table 6.4: A typology of location problems

In the table, indications of the main application appear next to each case (ReVelle, Marks and Liebman, 1970). The six models, however, are not equally meaningful: cases 2 and 3 in fact are rarely found in literature, whereas cases 1 and 4 frequently occur. In case 1 the public authority sometimes operates to influence industrial location in the private sector through laws (ie problem constraints) and/or incentives (ie components of the objective function).

A second more solution-oriented typology is obtained by joining parameters (a) (space), (j) (number of plants) and (i) (capacity), in particular (i1) and (i21). Figure 6.3 shows an "abstract" representation of various models resulting from it.

In this case, too, certain nodes of the graph are more meaningful than others: for instance, combinations 000 and 111 are among the more frequently studied (as will be seen in detail in Section 6.5). Also note that combinations with j=0 and i=1 may be meaningless if the number of plants and capacities are too low, while combinations with j=1 and i=0 have meaning as optimization problems only for certain cost functions (for instance, with linear plant costs the obvious

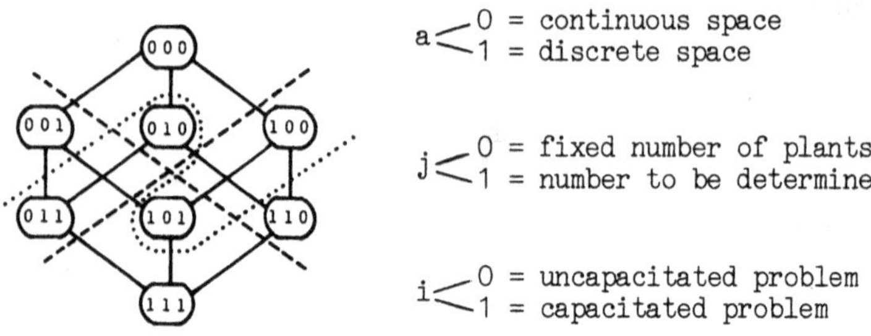

Figure 6.3: Representation (with binary variables) of a typology of location problems (a, j, i)

solution is always the opening of all possible plants; with high fixed costs, the solution is always the opening of only one plant).

6.3.2 The model structure

The models we are examining are mathematical programming decision models, therefore one (or more) objective functions and a set of constraints always appear. We have already discussed the objective function in detail above. We shall add only two points here. First, the three formulations (e) are expressed mathematically by minimizing functions

(e1) $f(x)$ = cost sum

(e2) $f(x)$ = max distance

(e3) $$\underline{\underline{f}}(x) = \begin{vmatrix} f_1(x) \\ \vdots \\ f_k(x) \end{vmatrix}$$

Secondly, the costs which enter the objective function (e1) act differently. In fact, (i) costs (f1) connected with plant construction/management "push" towards centralized solutions in order to take advantage of economies of scale; (ii) costs (f2) connected with distribution (in particular costs (f21) of long distance transportation) "push" towards decentralized solutions, in order to favour customers by reducing transportation costs; and (iii) in addition there are costs independent of location and transportation which are not included in the optimization process although they are part of the problem (and they may be considered as a constant term).

The main constraints can be classified into the following seven groups.

(1) Demand satisfaction: this is a set of constraints (one for each customer) always present in private sector production/ distribution problems as well as in public facility planning/ management problems.

(2) Technological constraints: these are conditions which reflect the way plants or facilities to be located are operated; the most common are capacity constraints, but sometimes inter-dependency conditions exist as well in the case of more than one product (see Section 6.3.1).

(3) Number of plants: this constraint usually appears in decentralized facility location problems (warehouses, trans-shipments); generally the number of plants is fixed according to organizational or territorial considerations.

(4) Budget constraint: this is a condition which is usually determined on the basis of economic investment analysis and fixes the capital available for the construction of new plants.

(5) Demand indivisibility: this is a set of constraints (one for each customer) which means that each customer can be supplied from only one plant or facility; typical examples are educational or medical facilities because they are organized on a district basis.

(6) Transportation capacity: this is a particular set of conditions which apply when the location and organization which apply when the location and organization of the distribution network are dealt with together. Such constraints may require the examination of combinatorial optimization problems.
(7) Assignment and "side constraints" (Spielberg, 1969): these include conditions whch preclude or impose supply from certain sources and/or distribution to certain customers, conditions of mutual exclusion and connected selection of some alternatives. They usually result from accessibility, cost or service planning restrictions.
This list is not of course exhaustive. Other more specific constraints, relating to particular cases may exist.

It is now possible to combine the main objective functions with the main constraints, in order to show some effects deriving from the structure of the models.

This has been done in Table 6.5.

We shall examine the table by column, but first, we should stress a few general points. (a) A constraint of demand satisfaction is always present. (b) Constraints (3) on the number of plants and (4) on the budget are in fact alternatives; the presence of both may make the problem infeasible. (c) Constraint (5) of demand indivisibility is restrictive only in the presence of constraint (2) of capacity; where this is not the case it is automatically satisfied. (d) Capacity constraint (2) may be inconsistent with constraints (3) or (4) which limit the number of plants to be constructed. (e) Certain conditions, especially conditions (6) and (7), are not more characterstic of one kind of objective function than another; their presence merely increases the computational difficulty.

The first column corresponds to the use of the efficiency criterion in the case of cost functions with constant yields. The capacity constraint may or may not be present (in the case of spatially indifferentiated costs it is meaningless since

Constraints \ Objective function	min-sum (1)	min-sum (2)	min-max	multi-objectives
1 demand	X	X	X	X
2 capacity	(X)	X		(X)
3 number	X	(X)	X	(X)
4 budget	(X)			
5 indivisibility			X	
6 transportation				
7 assignment			X	(X)

(1) constant yields (linear costs)
(2) increasing yields (fixed charge or concave costs)

Table 6.5: Structure of location models (objective functions vs main constraints)

many small plants are equivalent to a big one); condition (3) almost always exists (if not, the presence of transportation costs would lead to the opening of all possible plants) while conditions (5), (6), (7) do not characterize the problem.

The second column expresses the efficiency criterion in the case of functions with increasing yields. Constraint (3) regarding the number of plants, acts in accordance with the objective function (by limiting the proliferation of small plants) while constraint (4) is, in fact, superfluous.

Constraint (2) is often present since otherwise where there are high plant costs the final solution would be the establishment of a single big plant in order to take advantage of the economies of scale; constraints (5), (6), (7) do not characterize the problem.

The third column corresponds to the use of the worst case criterion. Normally the number of plants is fixed; assignment conditions may often be given (ie the exclusion of certain configurations). Demand indivisibility (which almost always exists, since these problems are closely connected with zoning problems) is satisfied by the absence of capacity constraints.

Lastly, the fourth column shows the presence of different conflicting criteria. Conditions (2) (capacity) and (3) (number of plants) may or may not be present: these two constraints are in conflict because whereas constraint (2), more connected with quantitative aspects, tends to result in a proliferation of plants, constraint (3), more connected with qualitative aspects, tends to reduce the number of plants. In addition assignment conditions, connected to the worst case criterion, may be present.

In conclusion, it is possible, with the simplification that such operations require, to show some typical formulations of location problems, by expressing their objective function and constraints in a limited number of combinations. This will be done in Section 6.5. This does not mean, of course, that more specific cases and complex formulations cannot occur.

6.4 Techniques for Solving Location Problems

It is intended in this section to give a brief review of the main methods used for solving location problems. The reader is therefore assumed to have a basic knowledge of mathematical programming and combinatorial optimization techniques. This section precedes Section 6.5 (the survey of location models) because it seems to the author more useful to have some idea of the solution algorithms, before looking at the different kinds of models in more detail.

A location problem of p plants on a network which includes n customers, each considered as a candidate point for location, has $\binom{n}{p}$ possible solutions. If n is a fairly large number (say about one hundred) and p is small, this value is very high. This fact poses two problems: (i) the critical dimensions of the algorithms; and (ii) the use of heuristic methods in the solution. The location problem is, as a rule*, an NP-complete decision problem (Garey and Johnson, 1979); the definition of this kind of problem, typical of combinatorial optimization, has been given by Karp (1972) as follows. A decision problem π belongs to the class of NP-complete problems if: (1) $\pi \in$ NP, ie the problem π may be solved in polynomial time by a non-deterministric algorithm; and (2) π' is equivalent to π for all problems $\pi' \in$ NP, ie a transformation in polynomial time that reduces π' to π exists.

Essentially a combinatorial optimization problem of this kind cannot be solved, at least with our present knowledge, in polynomial time, ie in a time measured by a polynomial function of the problem dimension**. This means that critical dimensions, ie those beyond which solution time becomes explosive,

---

* This statement is not always valid: for instance, if the graph is a tree and the problem is the p-median one (see Section 6.5.2.2), it is not true.

** In Garey and Johnson (1979) a table comparing functions that express the algorithm's computational complexity is shown: it can be seen that, if for instance the problem dimension is n=60, algorithms of polynomial complexity such as $O(n^5)$ solve it in 13 minutes, while algorithms of exponential complexity such as $O(2^n)$ would employ 366 centuries of computer time (algorithms of factorial complexity such as $O(n!)$ would require even longer).

are relatively low. This fact makes it necessary to use heuristic methods in many cases and to be satisfied with a good solution (not the optimal one) provided that the time is reasonable. In fact, in the location literature, a number of heuristic methods have been proposed.

The main techniques for solving location problems have been summarized in Table 6.6.

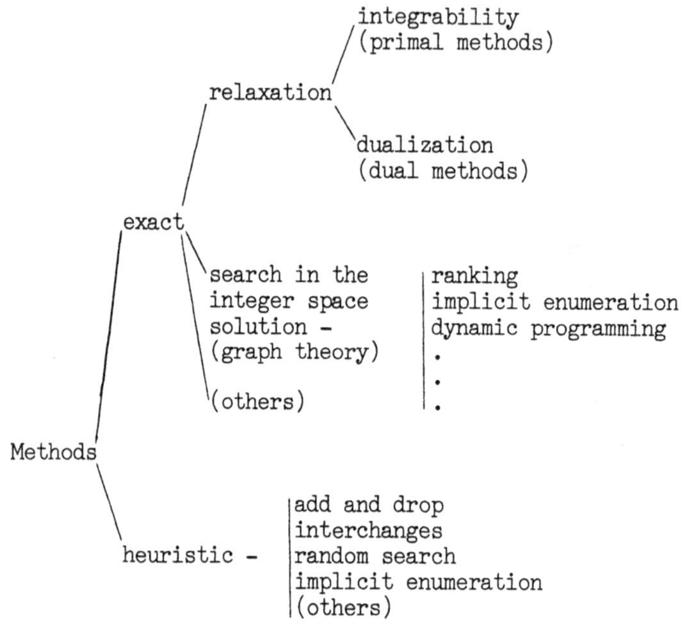

Table 6.6: Methods for resolving location problems

Many of the exact methods make use of relaxation methods which reformulate the problem in order to obtain a more easily solved problem - care being taken to ensure that the solution of the associated problem is also valid for the original problem. A first group of such algorithms relaxes, ie ignores, integrability conditions for some variables obtaining a linear (and in some cases non-linear) programming problem. A classic example of this procedure is the method of Efroymson and Ray (1966) for solving the problem that will be examined in Section 6.5.3, ie a case with linear transport costs, fixed charge plant costs and without capacity constraints. The structure is typical of the branch-and-bound methods. The main advantage of these methods is that the relaxation of integrability conditions makes it possible to obtain problems for which very powerful and quick algorithms exist (for instance simplex or transportation algorithms).

A second group of relaxation algorithms is based on dualization procedures and the use of the Lagrangian function: the problem is reformulated by inserting some constraints, each multiplied by the relevant coefficient (called a multiplier or dual variable) in the objective function. A very efficient example of this procedure is given by Erlenkotter (1978). There are two main advantages. One is the possibility of solving a series of simpler problems instead of a single complex one and the second is the possibility of separating the parts of the problem that interact using dualized constraints: see, Nijkamp and Rietveld (1980) and Haimes (1977), for multi-objective and multi-level programming.

A different approach is the search in space for the integer solution. This is possible because there are always some discrete variables which therefore have only a finite number of values. This means that the problem can be formulated in terms of combinatorial optimization by studying its characteristics in the space of solutions (which are finite). There are a few variants to this approach and a few different methods. One of them involves examining solutions through a ranking procedure which arranges them according to an appropriate criterion (Murty, 1968, Gray, 1971, Bartezzaghi, Colorni and Palermo, 1981). In particular, Bartezzaghi, Colorni and Palermo (1981) present a search algorithm that solves the problem Section 6.5.4 (transportation and plant costs, capacity constraints) by ranking the fixed plant costs and generating solutions "adjacent" to those already examined in a search tree; a test based on an over-estimate of the costs makes it possible to stop the algorithm, examining only a limited number of the possible solutions.

The main advantage of search methods in the integer solution space is that at any time during the process we have an admissible solution to the problem (which does not occur with relaxation methods). The quality of the solution will depend on the depth of the search. Very often, therefore, such methods give rise to simpler and faster heuristic-type procedures based on similar ideas.

Heuristic methods have been numerous in the solution of location problems since the beginning of the 1960s. One of the first and most famous was the method of Kuehn and Hamburger (1963) for the capacitated problem with fixed charges. All the methods appear to be a little different from each other and to have been built "ad hoc" to suit each individual problem. It is nevertheless possible to distinguish some general types.

"Add and drop" methods begin with an initial feasible solution, ie from a set of open plants, and perturb this solution by adding or dropping plants. In practice we pass from a vector of 0 and 1 (corresponding to the state of the plants) to an adjacent one in binary variable space, then to another and so on, improving the objective function each time. When an additional improvement is impossible, the algorithm stops and the last solution obtained is assumed final. Algorithms of this kind are strongly influenced by the starting values. Some begin with the maximum number of plants open, others do the opposite (beginning with no open plants); and others start from the intermediate situations. They are used for discrete problems with concave plant costs or with fixed charges. Two classic examples of this procedure are found in Kuehn and Hamburger (1963), Manne (1964).

Another group of heuristic methods, which we shall call inter-exchange methods, is based on the difference between the location phase and the process of allocation of the customers to the plant. Firstly an initial feasible solution is determined; the next step is to optimally allocate the customers to the open plants: this step (allocation) brings about a subdivision of the territory into zones, each gravitating to one plant; on the basis of such subdivisions a new solution is calculated, followed by a new allocation step and so on. The algorithm ends when the allocation step does not modify the zone subdivision of the previous iteration. These methods also depend on starting values. They have been used in the solution of problems with a fixed number of plants, both in continuous and in discrete space. Some well known examples are presented by Maranzana (1964) and Miehle (1958).

Another group of heuristic methods using random search techniques which has, like all stochastic optimization methods, been developed recently, deserves to be included. The fundamental idea is to examine a certain number of solutions drawn at random from the set of admissible solutions, obtaining information helpful to the subsequent search (ie the exploration of new solutions obtained at random). It is necessary, of course, to establish an upper limit to the number of draws and to use search methods that allow concentration on the most promising zones (clustering methods). Algorithms of this kind are less dependent on starting values and may, theoretically, be used for any kind of location problem (continuous or discrete, capacitated or otherwise, with or without a fixed number of plants). In some cases, indicators of the closeness of the solution to the optimal solution exist. An example of this kind is given in Camerini, Colorni and Maffioli (1983).

Both exact and heuristic algorithms are, to a greater or lesser degree, conditioned by the data on which they are based. This concerns not only the quantity of data (ie the dimension of the problem) but also its structure. Certain algorithms, with problems of the same dimension work better if transportation costs prevail, others plant costs, some for uniform data values, others for diversified data values, and so on. This aspect is too often ignored in the analysis of solution methods.

Clearly the question of data structure and its implications differs from the question of computational complexity mentioned at the beginning of this section (although it is complementary). In the examination of the complexity of an algorithm the important thing is its behaviour in the worst case, while in the examination of data structure its behaviour in the typical case is important. We shall come back to this in the following section.

6.5 Location Models

In this section, we describe the most important location models, grouping them in classes of increasing complexity: that is, according to the complexity of the situations represented and the difficulty involved in solving them. The description is based on the main algorithms involved and any possible computational aspects. First, a general framework will be presented (Section 6.5.1), then each of the five classes into which the models have been divided will be analysed (Sections 6.5.2 - 6.5.6).

6.5.1 A general framework

A classification according to the structure of the location model, devised by Bartezzaghi, Colorni and Palermo (1976) for the private sector, is extended here to the public sector. This division consists of five levels. At the first level transport costs, assumed as linear, are the determinant location factors; plant costs do not exist or they are spatially undifferentiated (with a fixed number of plants). The second level introduces non-linear yields or "economic indivisibilities" which remove the hypothesis of spatially undifferentiated plant costs. There are two types of factor in the objective function one (linear) connected to transport costs, the other (with economies of scale) connected to plant costs. At the third level, technological constraints, which remove the hypothesis that production is perfectly flexible, are introduced - the main one being capacity. There are two further levels relating to the greater complexity arising when we deal with public sector (cf Section 6.2). In this case, rational behaviour of customers cannot always be assumed and comparison between the various alternatives must take account of criteria other than pure cost. So we can define a fourth level which includes random utility terms in the objective function, removing the hypothesis of perfect rationality within the system (due to the presence of many single decision-makers). The model, which is the same as the previous one as far as the constraints are concerned but which constrains stochastic terms in the objective function, is then reduced to a deterministic program. Lastly, the fifth level includes problems whose formulation and solution is carried out with the aid of multi-objective programming. This corresponds to the removal of the hypothesis of perfect substitution between objectives of a different nature.

These five main levels can obviously be subdivided because of the presence of further constraints (Section 6.3.2) and because of possible combinations of the fundamental parameters (Section 6.3.1). Nevertheless this basic classification seems to be valid and corresponds, in addition, to the historical development of modelling in this field. It is represented diagrammatically in Table 6.7. Each level is described in the following sections.

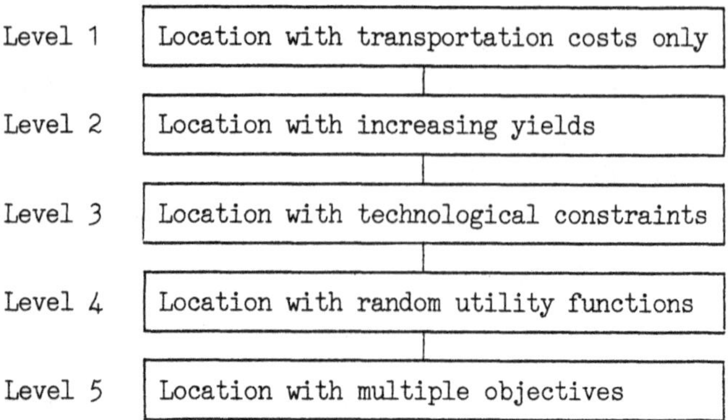

Table 6.7: Levels of increasing complexity in the location problem

In order to facilitate matters, we shall define here all the variables and indices that will appear later:

n = number of customers,

j = location of a generic customer ($j = i, \ldots, n$),

m = number of possible location points,

p = number of plants to be located (fixed),

i = location of a plant ($i = 1, \ldots, m$, or $i = 1, \ldots, p$), or also $i = 1, \ldots, n$ if plants can be located near the n customers),

(x_j, y_j) = coordinates of customer j in continuous space,

(X_i, Y_i) = coordinates of plant i in continuous space,

$d_{ij}(t_{ij})$ = minimum distance (time) between plant i and customers j. (If the problem is described with a graph, the distance between two points is given by the minimum path between the nodes.)

$a_{ij}(e_{ij})$ = element of a Boolean matrix of incidence (covering) between plants and customers (equal to 1 if connection between plant i and customer j is possible, 0 if not),

c_{ij} = unit transportation cost between plant i and customer j,

x_{ij} = quantity transported between plant i and customer j,

f_i = cost function (possibly constant) relative to construction and/or management of plant i,

π_i = decision variable relative to plant i (it is equal to 1 if the plant is open, 0 vice versa),

δ_{ij} = Boolean variable matching plants and customers (it is equal to 1 if customer j is served from open plant i, 0 vice versa),

q_i = capacity of plant i,

w_j = demand of customer j.

The problems that will be dealt with in the following involve different levels of use of models. It is therefore useful to summarize the most important aspects of them. A system of evaluation that will be applied to all the problems dealt with is given below. This evaluation is made on the basis of four parameters: (a) algorithms, ie presence of both exact and heuristic methods of solution; (b) computer codes, ie documentation of the existence of programs (specific or derived from general optimization programs); (c) theory, ie presence of well-established theoretical results and/or a body of theory relating to the problem; (d) computational complexity, ie the theoretical properties of algorithms and comparison of their performance. The order of these four parameters corresponds (historically and conceptually) to the development of knowledge in this field. Further comments on qualitative aspects are made in Section 6.6.

6.5.2 Location with transportation costs only

This is the simplest case, since the following hypotheses are assumed: (a) unique preference indicator given by costs; (b) perfect rationality of the decision-maker; (c) absence of technological constraints; (d) absence of plant costs (or indifference to location). Hypotheses (c) and (d) together mean that a fixed number of plants must be located for the problem to have meaning. If not (with p free), the solution that minimizes transportation costs would be the location of a separate plant for each customer.

There are, for this kind of problem, several examples of application both in the public and private sector, as well as several exact and heuristic solution methods. The main surveys in the field are by Handler and Mirchandani (1979), Eilon, Watson-Gandy and Christofides (1971), Hansen and Thisse (1983), Coelho (1983), Halpern and Maimon (1982). The fundamental parameters that define the problem are (see Figure 6.3) space (continuous or discrete) and the objective function (efficiency criterion or "worst case" criterion) and in addition, for public sector problems, type of service required (or obnoxious, which involve negative externalities). We will examine separately the two cases identified by the space parameter.

6.5.2.1 The continuous case

The formulation, mainly taken from Hansen and Thisse (1983) and Eilon, Watson-Gandy and Christofides (1971), is the following. In the space R^2, a norm $||.||$ which allows us to calculate the distance d_{ij} between two points i and j of the space, is defined. It is assumed that

$$d_{ij} = ||i-j|| = [|X_i-x_j|^h + |Y_i-y_j|^h]^{1/h} \qquad (6.1)$$

which determines, with different values of h, the main ways of defining the distance. In fact:

(i) if $h = 1$, we obtain the so-called 'rectilinear' metrics (typical of American cities);

(ii) if $h = 2$, we obtain the classic Euclidean metrics (distance defined "as the crow flies", typical of isotropic space);

(iii) if $h = \infty$, we obtain the so-called 'infinite' metrics (frequently used with the worst case criterion) in which the value of the distance between two points is given by greatest differences between coordinates.

In Figure 6.4, the behaviour of the three different metrics, which is analysed in detail in the bibliographical references quoted in Hansen and Thisse (1983), is represented diagrammatically.

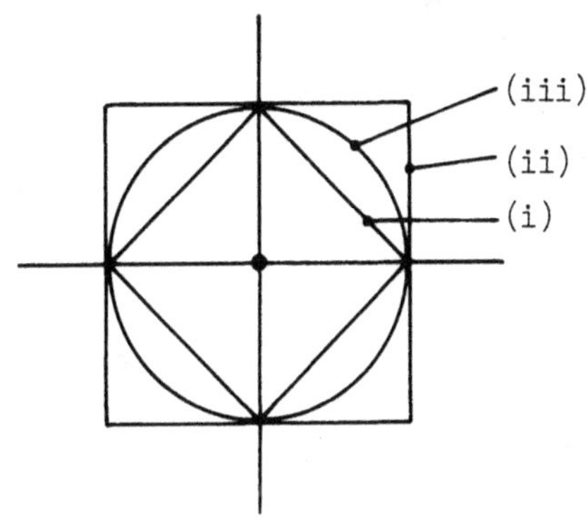

Figure 6.4: The set of points equidistant from the central point, (i) in rectilinear metrics, (ii) in Euclidean metrics, (iii) in infinite metrics

Cost functions are only connected with transportation and increase continuously with the plant-customer distance if the activity or facility to be located is required, and decrease if it is obnoxious. The most frequent cases are linear functions in which the cost for customer j, should he make use of plant i, is:

$$C_j = w_j c_{ij} d_{ij} \tag{6.2}$$

with a positive or negative sign according to whether the kind of service is required or obnoxious.

The objective function determines the two following formulations (valid in the case of required services).

The Weber problem corresponds to the use of the efficiency criterion (ie minimization of the sum of distances to be covered). In the case of linear costs its formulation is (Eilon, Watson-Gandy and Christofides, 1971):

$$\min\left[\sum_{1}^{p}{}_{i}\sum_{1}^{n}{}_{j} w_j c_{ij} d_{ij} \delta_{ij}\right] \tag{6.3}$$

$$\left.\begin{array}{l}\delta_{ij} = 0 \\ \delta_{lj} = 1\end{array}\right\} (\forall i \neq l;\ l : \min_i d_{ij})(j = 1, \ldots, n) \tag{6.4}$$

$$d_{ij} \text{ defined by (6.1) } (\forall i,j) \tag{6.5}$$

while in the general case in (6.3) the relevant increasing cost functions will appear.

The worst case problem corresponds to the use of the worst case criterion (ie minimization of the maximum distance to be covered). Still in the hypothesis of linear costs its formulation is (Hansen and Thisse, 1983):

$$\min\left[\max_{i = 1, \ldots, p;\ j = 1, \ldots, n} w_j c_{ij} d_{ij} \delta_{ij}\right] \tag{6.6}$$

$$\left.\begin{array}{l}\delta_{ij} = 0 \\ \delta_{lj} = 1\end{array}\right\} (\forall i \neq l;\ l : \min_i d_{ij})(j = 1, \ldots, n) \tag{6.7}$$

$$d_{ij} \text{ defined by (6.1) } (\forall j) \tag{6.8}$$

Of course in the case of obnoxious facilities cost functions will have the opposite sign and consequently the following will be obtained (in the hypothesis of linear costs):

$$\max[\sum_{1}^{p}{}_{i}\sum_{1}^{n}{}_{j} w_j c_{ij} d_{ij} \delta_{ij}] \qquad (6.9)$$

$$\max[\min_{i = 1, \ldots, p;\ j = 1, \ldots, n} w_j c_{ij} d_{ij} \delta_{ij}] \qquad (6.10)$$

for Weber and worst case problems respectively.

Boolean variables δ_{ij} express the matching among plants and customers ($\delta_{ij} = 1$ means that customer j is served by plant i). If p=1 they are useless, because the problem will be expressed only in terms of the variables X and Y (plant coordinates) which appear in (6.1) and define distances d_j (j = 1, ..., n) to the various customers. The presence of variables δ_{ij}, where p>1, complicates things considerably. Nevertheless the assumption of unlimited capacity, typical of this kind of problem, allows us to determine the value of δ_{ij}. In fact, supposing that each plant is able to satisfy any demand, customer j will certainly make use of the nearest plant; this fact is expressed by conditions (6.4), or by (6.7) (which are exactly the same), one for each customer.

Problem (6.3) - (6.5) (and (6.9)) is the most well-known: it even dates back to Cavalieri and Fermat (see Kuhn, 1973, for a historical review) before being made known in the classical formulation given by Weber in 1909 for the case with p=1 and η=3. Problem (6.6) - (6.8) (and (6.9)) deals with equity criteria in the protection of customers and is frequently used, for instance, in the location of emergency services. A bibliography of both (and their versions for obnoxious facilities) is given in Hansen and Thisse (1983).

The theory of this kind of problem has been much developed since Weber's (1909) formulation. An early theoretical contribution concerned determination of the set of efficient solutions, ie the points of R^2 not dominated by other points, without taking account of transport costs or of customer demand.

It contains an optimal solution that depends on cost c_{ij} and demand w_j. Other results relate to the definition of the constrained case (ie in which some areas of R^2 are not feasible). The definition of the concept of visibility which contributes to the determination of the efficient solutions for such cases is found in Goldman (1971). Finally, other theoretical results regard the determination of the optimal solution for certain functions. We shall now examine solution algorithms, distinguishing the two problems (6.3) - (6.5) and (6.6) - (6.8).

For the Weber problem the main results can be summarized as follows. In the case of rectilinear metrics, Chalmet, Francis and Kohen (1981) proposed an algorithm, whose computational complexity is O(n log n), for the determination of the set of efficient solutions. For the calculation of the optimal solution, the commonest approach is the interchange method, as defined in Section 6.4. This is exact, ie it provides the optimal solution if p=1, whereas it is heuristic if p>1. A demonstration of this point is given by Eilon, Watson-Gandy and Christofides (1971). Colorni et al (1979) show in detail a similar algorithm with a computer code based on a proposal by Miehle (1958). The flowchart of this algorithm is shown in Figure 6.5.

Other exact methods are based on branch-and-bound techniques involving successive divisions of the plane (Hansen and Thisse, 1983) and on Lagrangian relaxation techniques (Schaefer and Hurter, 1974).

For the worst case problem the main results can be summarized as follows. In the case of Euclidean metrics, Shamos and Hoey (1975) describe an algorithm of complexity O(n log n) for the exact solution of the problem with p=1 and $w_j=1$, $\forall_j$. This algorithm divides the plane into a maximum of n areas: each area A_j (j = 1, ..., n) contains the points that are farther from customer j than from any other customers; subsequently the algorithm determines the optimal solution by

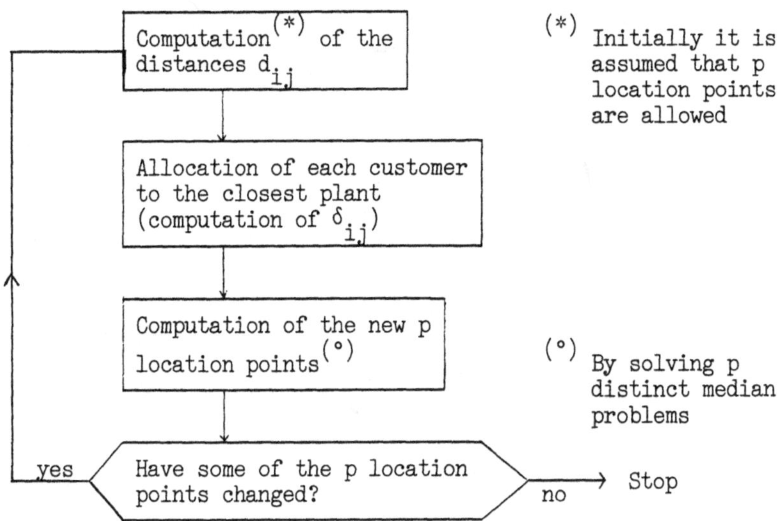

Figure 6.5: The Miehle heuristic method for the location of p points (Weber problem)

examining the set of the intersections of the straight lines dividing the region.

In the case of location of obnoxious facilities the partition of the plane is carried out so that each area A_j contains the points closer to customer j than to any other and the optimal solution is found at the intersection of the straight lines dividing the region into the n areas or at the intersection of such lines with the boundary of the region itself. Figure 6.6 shows an example of n=5. The optimal solutions are point A for the first case and point B for the second case.

Other methods, both exact and heuristic, relating to the case with demand $w_j \neq 1$ and any value of p, are commonly based on geometric considerations. Drezner and Wesolowsky (1980) proposed an "add" type iterative procedure which solves the problem starting with the 3 farthest customers from the centre of gravity and subsequently introducing the others into the computation, if necessary. Such algorithms also have polynomial

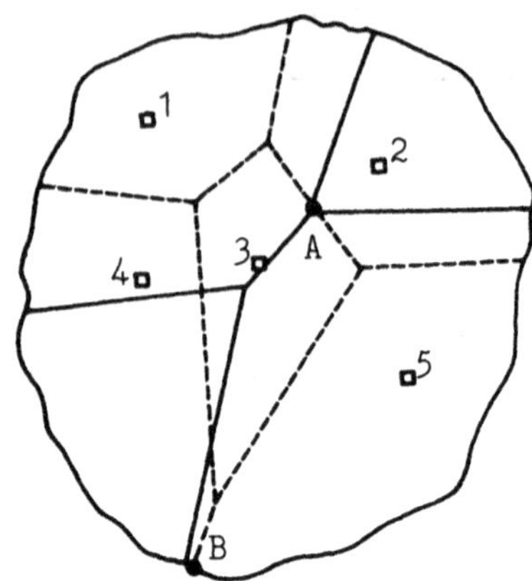

Figure 6.6: Partition into areas for the solution of the worst case problem, using the Shamos-Hoey method, for $n=5$, $p=1$, $w_j=1$ ($j = 1, \ldots, n$)

———: boundaries of the 4 areas containing the points farther from customer j than from any other (case of required service)

------: boundaries of the 5 areas containing the points closer to customer j than to any other (case of obnoxious service)

complexity greater than n (Hansen and Thisse, 1983).

6.5.2.2 The discrete case

The formulation, mainly derived from Handler and Mirchandani (1979) and Garey and Johnson (1979), is the following. A graph $G = (N,A)$ of n nodes linked by arcs a is given, with w_j values associated with the nodes (representing the customer demand) and d_{ij} values associated with the pairs of nodes (representing the minimum distances or times). The matrix $D = \{d_{ij}\}$ of the optimal distances between all the pairs of nodes of a graph can be obtained by solving a classic problem of combinatorial optimization with polynomial complexity of $O(n^3)$. A recent review of the main algorithms relating to this problem can be found in Gallo and Pallottino (1982). The cost functions, which represent the transport costs, show a continuous increase with increasing distance. Only the case of required facilities or services, which is the most common, will be illustrated here. The case of obnoxious facilities can be derived utilizing procedures similar to those used for the continuous problem previously illustrated.

The most frequent case is that involving linear functions in which the cost for a customer j utilizing the plant i, is given by (6.2). It is often assumed that the unit costs c_{ij} in (6.2) are constant and therefore independent of i and j, which allows us to ignore them in the problem formulation. Also in this case there are two main formulations, corresponding to the use of either the efficiency criterion or the worst case criterion.

The p-median problem, which is analogous to the continuous Weber problem, can be formulated as follows in the linear case ($c_{ij} = 1, \forall i,j$):

$$\min\left[\sum_{1}^{n}{}_{i}\sum_{1}^{n}{}_{j} w_j d_{ij} \delta_{ij}\right] \tag{6.11}$$

$$\sum_{1}^{n}{}_{i} \delta_{ij} = 1 \quad (j = 1, \ldots, n) \tag{6.12}$$

$$\sum_{1}^{n}{}_{i} \delta_{ii} = p \tag{6.13}$$

$$\sum_{1}^{n}{}_{j} \delta_{ij} \leq n\delta_{ii} \quad (i = 1, \ldots, n) \tag{6.14}$$

$$\delta_{ij} = 0,1 \quad (\forall i,j) \tag{6.15}$$

where the objective function (6.11) gives the (linear) transport costs, the n equations (6.12) require that each customer be allocated to a plant, the condition (6.13) requires that the open plants number exactly p, the inequalities (6.14) mean that all the variables d_{ij} of the i-th row must be zero when $\delta_{ii} = 0$, while they are non-influent when $\delta_{ii} = 1$.

Formulation (6.11) - (6.15) of the problem assumes that the candidate nodes for location are the n nodes corresponding to the customers (ie that $d_{ii} = 0$ and δ_{ii} becomes the location variable relating to the choice of node i). Under the hypothesis that there are m candidate nodes which belong to a different set the summations over index i and the meanings of d_{ij} (d_{ii} can be > 0) and δ_{ij} must be changed. A formulation for this case is shown by Cornuejols, Fisher and Nemhauser (1977) who make use of the location variables π_i (i = 1, ..., m) with the conditions

$$\sum_{1}^{m} {}_i \pi_i = p \tag{6.16}$$

$$\delta_{ij} \leq \pi_i \quad (i = 1, \ldots, m;\ j = 1, \ldots, n) \tag{6.17}$$

in place of (6.13) and (6.14) and with $\pi_i = 0,1$ (i = 1, ..., m).

The p-centre problem, which is analogous to the worst case continuous problem, can be formulated as follows in case of linear costs ($c_{ij} = 1, \forall i,j$):

$$\min[\max_{i = 1, \ldots, n;\ j = 1, \ldots, n} w_j d_{ij} \delta_{ij}] \tag{6.18}$$

$$\sum_{1}^{n} {}_i \delta_{ij} = 1 \quad (j = 1, \ldots, n) \tag{6.19}$$

$$\sum_{1}^{n} {}_i \delta_{ii} = p \tag{6.20}$$

$$\sum_{1}^{n} {}_i \delta_{ij} \leq n\delta_{ii} \quad (i = 1, \ldots, n) \tag{6.21}$$

$$\delta_{ij} = 0,1 \quad (\forall i,j) \tag{6.22}$$

to which the same observations made in connection with the

p-median problem, when the candidate points do not coincide with the n customers, apply. The objective function (6.18) is of interest not only in the case of emergency services, but also in the location of schools, bus stops, libraries and other public services, where the maximum distance from the population served is the primary concern.

Figure 6.7 shows a graph with $n = 5$ ($w_j = 1$, for $j = 1, \ldots, 5$) in which the problems of p-medians and p-centres are solved for $p = 2$. As well as the graph indicating the direct distances, the incidence matrix $A = \{a_{ij}\}$ and the minimum distance matrix $\underset{\sim}{D}_x = \{d_{ij}\}$ are also shown. As the graph is directed and the matrix $\underset{\sim}{D}_x$ is not symmetrical, the solutions will be different in the two cases of plant location, ie with transport from the plant to the customer or from the customer to the plant. The figure shows the solution of the problems for the first case.

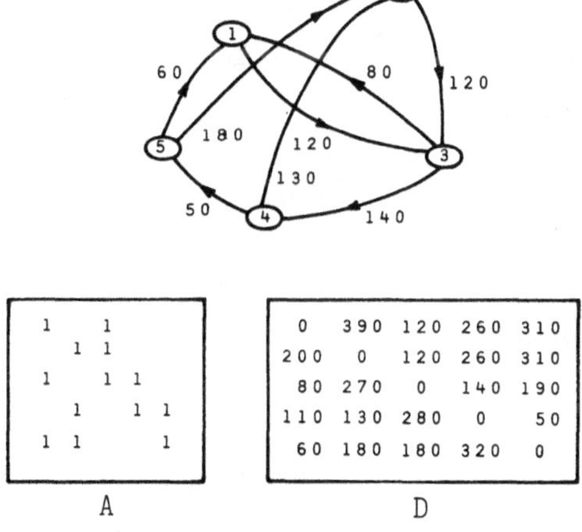

<u>Figure 6.7</u>: Solutions to the problems ($p = 2$)

- of p-medians (nodes 3 and 4, with an objective function of 260)
- of p-centres (nodes 2 and 4, with an objective function of 120)

In the p-median problem, the optimal value obtained for the objective function (260 in the example) represents the total cost of transport from the plants to the customers: obviously, by dividing this value by the number n, the average cost per customer is obtained (52 in the example). This can be compared with the value of the objective function in the p-centre problem (120 in the example).

The formulation of this type of discrete problem and the main theoretical results, obtained by Hakimi (1964, 1965) are more recent than the analogous continuous problems. Basically Hakimi demonstrated two facts connected with the most general formulation of the problem, which envisages the possibility of location not only in the nodes but also along the arcs of the graph, namely: (i) the optimal solution to the p-median problem is the same, whether location takes place only in the nodes or along the arcs, and it always corresponds to a location in p nodes (this allows us to assert that the solution to problem (6.11) - (6.15) holds also in the general case); (ii) the optimal solution to the p-centre problem is different in the case represented by equations (6.18) - (6.22), corresponding to a location in the nodes only, from the general case where the p points can also be chosen along the arcs.

With respect to the problem of p-centres, as we are concerned in the present study mainly with the case of location in the nodes, we shall briefy mention the general case which Handler and Mirchandani (1979) deal with in far greater detail. The basic problem formulation is therefore (6.18) - (6.22). Figure 6.8 gives an example of the Hakimi results for a case with $p=1$ and $n=2$, $w_1=2$ and $w_2=18$, $d_{12}=d_{21}=100$.

It is also to be noted that using a suitable reformulation (Krarup and Pruzan, 1981), a p-median problem can be reduced to a p-centre problem and vice versa, so that an algorithm which can solve one can solve also the other.

Let us now examine the solution algorithms, keeping the

1 —— 100 ——•— 2 A	1-median (in the nodes) : node 2 (200) 1-median (general) : node 2 (200)
(Point A is at a distance 10 from node 2)	1-centre (in the nodes) : node 2 (200) 1-centre (general) : point A (180)

Figure 6.8: Results in the case of location in the nodes and in the general case

two types of problems (6.11) - (6.15) and (6.18) - (6.22) distinct. We do this because of their different nature and the different results obtained (Hakimi's theorems) as well as on the grounds that problem (6.18) - (6.22), as will be shown later, is closely connected with a well known "inverse" problem. In both cases the problem is NP-complete (Garey and Johnson, 1979), and therefore the use of exact, non-polynomial methods may be impossible for medium-to-large problems.

The p-median problem is mainly solved (see scheme in Section 6.4) through: (a) the search method in integer solution space; (b) branch-and-bound methods; (c) constraint dualization methods; or (d) heuristic methods. The first are the easiest, though not very efficient. Hakimi (1965) had already proposed a method for the enumeration of all the configurations. This method, however, involves the examination of $\binom{n}{p}$ combinations, which may be prohibitive. If the graph is a non-oriented tree, the polynomial methods proposed by Goldman (1971) and again Hakimi (Kariv and Hakimi, 1979) can be considered: these methods, having a complexity of $O(n^2p^3)$, are based on a theoretical result by Goldman.

The branch-and-bound methods (also called primal methods) have the characteristic of relaxing the integrability conditions (6.15). The condition $\delta_{ij} = 0,1$ with i=j can be correctly replaced by $\delta_{ij} \geq 0$ under the assumption of unlimited capacity, whilst it is effectively relaxed for δ_{ii} and replaced by $0 \leq \delta_{ii} \leq 1$. The branch tree is explored by defining at any node the sets of the open, closed and free plants; the branch operation being carried out on the last of these. The basic articles on the subject are by Jarvinen, Rajala and Sinervo (1972) and Cornuejols, Fisher and Nemhauser (1977).

The dualization methods reformulate the problem by transferring some constraints (usually the constraints (6.12) and/or (6.13)) into the Lagrangian multiplier. This allows us to obtain a set of n sub-problems interconnected through the dual variables (constraint multipliers) which are easier to solve separately. The most notable examples of this procedure are shown by Erlenkotter (1978), Christofides and Beasley (1982), and Cornuejols, Fisher and Nemhauser (1977) where the branch-and-bound and the duality methods are combined with very effective results.

Finally, we examine the main heuristic methods which are very frequently used in the p-median problem. Maranzana (1964) proposed an interchange method, which is analogous in the discrete case of the Niehle method for the continuous case (see Figure 6.5): p nodes are selected, every customer is allocated to the closest plant, a partition of the graph nodes into p subsets is induced, for each subset the median is calculated obtaining other p nodes and the procedure is repeated until the locations are changed. Kuehn and Hamburger (1963), Teitz and Bart (1968) describe some "add" or "add and drop" methods, based on the replacement of one of the p location nodes by another node which is more favourable and has not yet been selected. Jarvinen, Rajala and Sinervo (1972) report a heuristic method based on a branch-and-bound technique.

In general the size of the problems which can be handled by the above algorithms is limited. Using the exact methods, problems with several dozen plants and customers can be handled, while the heuristic methods can handle one or two hundred customers and ten or twenty plants. These figures are derived from Cornuejols, Fisher and Nemhauser (1977), which is probably the best work published in recent years on this subject.

The p-centre problem, exhaustively dealt with by Handler and Mirchandani (1979) and Larson and Odoni (1981), is usually tackled using graph theory technique, ie by search techniques in integer solution space. Let us start by examining the location problem for p=1. If the problem simply involves the location of nodes (location of the centre of a graph), it can be easily solved by inspecting a matrix obtained through multiplication of each element of the rows (columns) of the matrix $\underline{\underline{D}}$ by the weight w_j of each customer and by subsequently selecting the node corresponding to the row (column) where the value of the maximum element is lowest. In the example shown in Figure 6.7 where all weights are unitary, the centre of the graph is at node 4 if the service is from the plant to the customer and at node 1 if it is from the customer to the plant.

On the other hand, if the problem is general (location of the point representing the absolute centre of the graph), Handler and Mirchandani (1979) illustrate a method based on the results by Hakimi (1964) and utilizing these results calculate the so-called local centres of the arcs: the point solving the problem is the best of all the local centres. By applying a theorem of Odoni (Larson and Odoni, 1981) we can obtain a test which greatly reduces the number of arcs on which the local centre calculation is based. Figure 6.9 shows the calculation of local centres and optimal solution for a case where n=3, w_j=1 with j=1,2,3 (and, naturally, p=1).

It should be noted that, when the graph is a tree we can apply a remarkably simple algorithm devised by Handler which will solve the problem of both location in the nodes and in the general case. The algorithm consists of the three following steps: (1) take any vertex i of the graph, find the terminal node (which has degree 1, ie it has only one incident arc) at the greatest distance from i (let this node be h); (2) find the

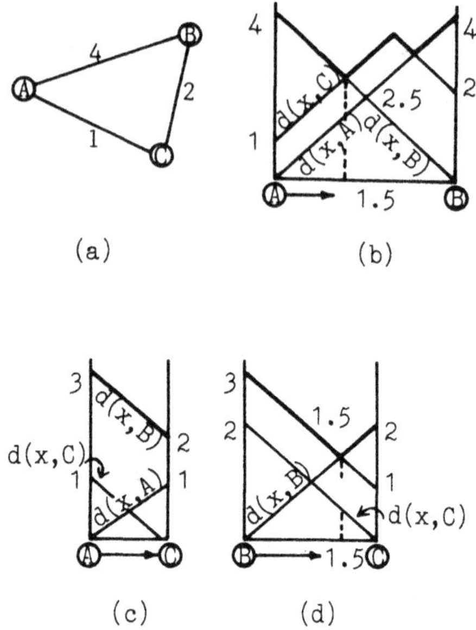

Figure 6.9: Graphic solution to the location problem of the absolute centre in a graph:

(a) the graph (n=3) and the direct distances;
(b) the broken line representing the maximum distance from the nodes which allows us to find the local centre on the arc (A,B), ie the point at a distance 1.5 from A and a maximum distance of 2.5;
(c) the same for the local centre of the arc (A,C), ie the point C with a maximum distance of 2;
(d) the same for the local centre on the arc (B,C), ie the point having a distance 1.5 from B with a maximum distance of 1.5.

The solution corresponds to the local centre on the arc (B,C) and the value of the objective function is 1.5.

terminal node at the greatest distance from h (let this node be k); (3) point x, corresponding to the absolute centre of the graph, is the midpoint between h and k, while the node corresponding to the centre of the graph is the node closest to point x. The algorithm complexity is O(n) (Handler, 1979).

The case p>1 will be considered only briefly as it has been described in detail by Halpern and Maimon (1982), and Handler and Mirchandani (1979), who make a comparison between existing algorithms, many of which were devised by Minieka (1970) and Handler (1979). Basically, two types of approach have been utilized: (a) decomposition of the initial problem into p sub-problems through a graph partition and the subsequent solution of p (related) sub-problems of centre determination; (b) iterative use of set-covering techniques, which will be dealt with later on. Exact algorithms with their heuristic version, whose efficiency allows handling of medium-size problems exist: Garfinkel, Neebel and Rao (1977) show some results for graphs containing up to 60 nodes and one or two hundred arcs.

The problem of p-centres, for location in the nodes only, is closely connected with another classic problem of combinatorial optimization, the so-called set-covering problem: one of its formulations, the one most specifically connected with the p-centre problem, is as follows:

$$\min\left(\sum_{1}^{n}{}_{i}\delta_{ii}\right) \tag{6.23}$$

$$\sum_{1}^{n}{}_{i}e_{ij}\delta_{ij} = 1 \quad (j = 1, \ldots, n) \tag{6.24}$$

$$\sum_{1}^{n}{}_{i}\delta_{ij} \leq n\delta_{ii} \quad (i = 1, \ldots, n) \tag{6.25}$$

$$\delta_{ij} = 0,1 \quad (\forall i,j) \tag{6.26}$$

$$e_{ij} = \begin{cases} 1 \text{ if } d_{ij} \leq \tau \\ 0 \text{ otherwise} \end{cases} \quad (\forall i,j) \tag{6.27}$$

where τ is a parameter denoting the maximum cost (or distance or time) which can be afforded by customers j, that is, the cost beyond which the service provided by the facility to be located is no longer effective. In the case of emergency services, for instance, τ denotes the maximum response time.

In practice, the problem involves "covering" the nodes of the graph on the basis of the arcs identified by the matrix $\underline{\underline{E}} = \{e_{ij}\}$, while minimizing the number of nodes required by this operation. (Problem (6.23) - (6.27) can be seen as a kind of "inverse" of problem (6.18) - (6.22), as the objective function of the latter determines the values e_{ij} in (6.27), while condition (6.20) of the p-centre problem becomes the objective function of the set-covering problem.)

Figure 6.10 shows an undirected graph (with unit weights in the nodes) together with the matrix $\underline{\underline{D}}$ of minimum distances and two examples of matrix $\underline{\underline{E}}$ corresponding to two different values of the parameter τ.

The set-covering problem has many applications apart from location and represents a classic problem of operations research. Its solution is sought through: (a) integer programming methods (particularly Boolean programming); or (b) search tree methods, and branch-and-bound techniques. A review of the algorithms, with an appraisal of their computational complexity, can be found in Salkin (1975) and Garey and Johnson (1979).

We shall now complete the discussion of the location problem of p plants in the discrete case with a brief mention of some generalizations of the models examined. The first of these relates to the possibility of considering the two types of objectives, namely minimization of the sum of transportation costs (average cost) and minimization of the maximum cost, together. An example is the location of school services, where it is important to take into consideration both the average and the maximum distance. This problem is only referred to briefly here and will be given more detailed treatment in Section 6.5.6 in connection with the case of multiple objectives.

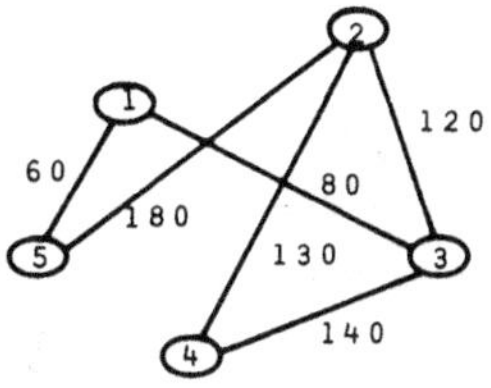

0	200	80	220	60
200	0	120	130	180
80	120	0	140	140
220	130	140	0	280
60	180	140	280	0

D

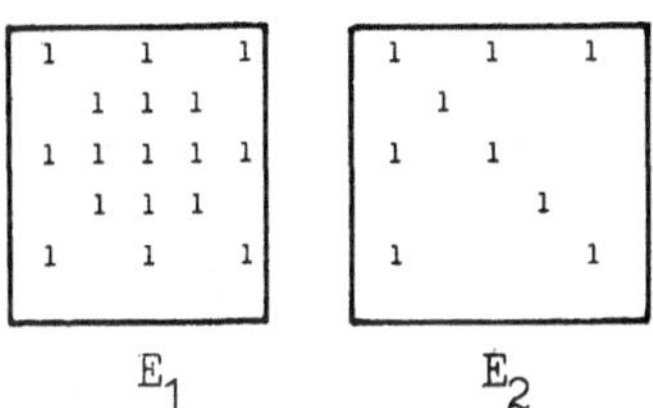

1		1		1
	1	1	1	
1	1	1	1	1
	1	1	1	
1		1		1

E_1

1		1		1
	1			
1		1		
			1	
1				1

E_2

Figure 6.10: A set covering problem. Solutions for

(1) $\tau = 150$ (matrix $\underline{\underline{E}}_1$): $\sum_1^n {}_i \delta_{ii} = 1$ (node 3)

(2) $\tau = 100$ (matrix $\underline{\underline{E}}_2$): $\sum_1^n {}_i \delta_{ii} = 3$ (nodes 1,2,4)

The second generalization relates to the possibility of considering the dynamic problem, ie the location of p-plants in time and/or the possibility of their periodic reallocation. This problem can be of considerable interest whenever the reciprocal relations between the transportation costs are subject to changes in time. It is reduced in fact to a problem with a greater number of decision-making variables. Some results of this approach are given by Wesolowsky and Truscott (1975).

The third generalization relates to the possibility of considering certain stochastic aspects of the problem, particularly the existence of stochastic graphs (ie graphs in which times or distances are subject to change, or locations are mobile and can be reallocated in time) and the existence of facilities that are not available for part of the time, so requiring possible assistance from other facilities to respond to the customer requests (a typical example is given by the emergency services in the case of many close-spaced incoming calls). Problems of this kind are dealt with in Berman and Odoni (1982) and in some contributions by Beltrami, for instance Beltrami (1979).

6.5.2.3 Characteristics of the location problem with transportation costs only

Since the problem has been dealt with in some detail and a number of different cases looked at we shall now summarize its fundamental aspects using the evaluation scheme outlined in Section 6.5.1.

Algorithms: there are many algorithms available; exact and heuristic, for continuous or discrete problems based on the efficiency criterion as well as on the worst case criterion. These algorithms cover practically the whole spectrum of methodologies (see Section 6.4).

Codes: almost all algorithms, except the early ones proposed at the beginning of the sixties, are well documented in terms of both computer codes and computational results with regard to a number of standard problems.

Theory: this is the commonest case dealt with by location theory and in some cases theory has preceded or assisted in the development of a solution.

Complexity: also from this point of view there are well-established results on the complexity of the discrete case (polynomial if the graph is a tree, NP-complete for the general problem) and the evaluation of the main heuristic algorithms.

6.5.3 Location with transport and plant costs (increasing yields)

This section describes the second level formulation of the location problem. The assumption that the plant costs are absent (or unimportant to location) is dropped, while the other assumptions are maintained, namely: (a) costs representing the unique preference indicator; (b) complete rationality of the decision-maker; and (c) absence of technological constraints. In the structure of the problem, the presence of costs with increasing yields acts as a limiting factor on the number of plants to be located, thus making the presence of the constraints on the number of plants superfluous or even inadmissible (though this does not apply if the plant costs are linear). The absence of technological constraints, especially on plant capacity, makes the structure relatively simple (similar to the case dealt with in Section 6.5.2) and means it can be assumed that each customer utilizes the plant closest to him, which greatly aids computation. The problem is referred to as 'uncapacitated' to emphasize this property.

The fundamental parameters which define the problem are: (i) the objective function, expressed according to the efficiency criterion; and (ii) discrete space. There are, therefore, fewer problems involved than in Section 6.5.2. This is due to the higher complexity of the objective function, which must consider and balance two effects, namely the effect of transportation costs which pushes towards decentralized solutions (many small plants in the vicinity of customers) and the effect of the plant costs which pushes towards centralized solutions (few large plants with economies of scale).

A subdivision can be made (see point (g) of Section 6.3.1) based on the cost functions relating to the plants, which can be: (g1) linear; (g2) linear with fixed charge; or (g3) concave with piecewise-linear. We shall disregard the first type of function, which has little significance, to concentrate on the other two.

There are many reports of single applications of these methods in both the public and private sector. A selected bibliography has been compiled by Francis and Goldstein (1974) and a review of more recent works is given by Coelho (1983). Other review papers include ReVelle, Marks and Liebman (1970) and Bartezzaghi (1979) but there are very few books or comprehensive treatments of the subject.

The formulation of the uncapacitated location problem with fixed charge (case (g2)), by Efroymson and Ray (1966), is as follows:

$$\min\left[\sum_{1}^{m}{}_{i}\sum_{1}^{n}{}_{j}c_{ij}x_{ij} + \sum_{1}^{m}{}_{i}f_{i}\pi_{i}\right] \tag{6.28}$$

$$\sum_{1}^{m}{}_{i}x_{ij} = 1 \quad (j = 1, \ldots, n) \tag{6.29}$$

$$\sum_{1}^{n}{}_{j}x_{ij} \leq n\pi_{i} \quad (i = 1, \ldots, m) \tag{6.30}$$

$$x_{ij} \geq 0 \quad (\forall i,j) \tag{6.31}$$

$$\pi_{i} = 0,1 \quad (\forall i) \tag{6.32}$$

where the variables x_{ij} represent the fraction of demand of customer j satisfied by plant i and the cost c_{ij} is obtained through the knowledge of minimum distance d_{ij} and demand w_j (for instance, it is $c_{ij} = kd_{ij}w_j$).

Early contributions to this problem were made by Kuehn and Hamburger (1963) and Manne (1964) and involved the formulation of the problem and the implementation of heuristic add-and-drop algorithms, followed by proposals of exact algorithms based on branch-and-bound methods. The theoretical results are scanty, apart from the general ones on integer programming of which problem (6.28) - (6.32) represents a special case.

One of the most useful results, especially for the branch-and-bound type algorithms, is a property of the Boolean location variables π_i demonstrated by Efroymson and Ray (1966). If the integrability conditions (6.32) for the variables y_i are relaxed and replaced by

$$0 \leqq \pi_i \leqq 1 \quad (i = 1, \ldots, m) \tag{6.33}$$

the program (6.28) - (6.33) becomes linear. Efroymson and Ray have demonstrated that the optimal solution for this program must satisfy (6.30) with the equality sign: this enables the a priori elimination of the variable π_i and the solution of the problem in the variables x_{ij} by "inspection" only, ie by simply examining the problem data (in this case its objective function) leaving a set of n uncoupled problems, one for each user. Of course, this operation must be carried out at each node of the branch tree, with respect to the free variables π_i*.

---

* Each node of the tree has some y_i variables fixed at the value 0, some variables fixed at the value 1 and others free (ie capable of assuming values between 0 and 1).

Another theoretical property of the problem (McKeown, 1975) derives from the fact that, both in the form (g2) with fixed charges and in the form (g3) with concave costs, we have a mathematical program with a concave objective function and constraints linear in the variables x_{ij}. This allows us to assert that the optimal solution to the problem is found at one of the extreme points of the region of feasible solutions in the space of the variables x_{ij} (ie that in practice the optimal solution is that where $x_{ij} = 0$ or 1, $\forall i,j$). This is obviously in accordance with the assumption that each customer utilizes only one plant. This fact can be exploited to transform the problem into a combinatorial one, by examining only the integer solutions. Other properties used in algorithms are of a more general type, for instance those based on Lagrangian relaxation used by Swain (1974).

The main approaches to the exact solution of the uncapacitated problem with fixed charge are: (a) methods of constraint relaxation; or (b) methods of search in the integer variable space. The branch-and-bound algorithms of Efroymson and Ray (1966), Spielberg (1969) and Khumavala (1972) belong to the first group. These algorithms often differ only in the rules of selection of the branch variables and many of them are based on the above properties. The Lagrangian relaxation algorithms of Swain (1974) and Erlenkotter (1978) also belong to the first type. These algorithms reformulate the problem using information obtainable from the dual problem. In the second type are the algorithms that, taking advantage of the second property described above, make use of procedures of implicit enumeration and/or ranking of integer solutions. Examples are given by Gray (1971), McKeown (1975), Bartezzaghi, Colorni and Palermo (1981).

Numerous heuristic methods are also available. In the initial formulation by Kuehn and Hamburger (1963) there is mention of one of the most frequently used in which one plant is opened at a time. Other variants of the add-and-drop techniques are the methods suggested by Manne (1964) and Walker (1976). Another group of such algorithms is based on the extension of the solution methods for the p-median problem to the case where fixed plant costs must also be considered. An example is given by Hochbaum (1982). Recently the application of random search and global optimization methods has opened a promising new approach (Camerini, Colorni and Maffioli, 1983).

The dimension of the problems which can be handled is of the same order of magnitude as the p-median and p-centre problems. The exact methods can cope with cases with $m = 100$ and $n = 200$, while the heuristic methods can handle slightly larger numbers. These figures can be obtained directly from the papers cited, which also generally give times and information on the computer codes. An exact algorithm based on duality methods has been published recently (Van Roy and Erlenkotter, 1982), for tackling the dynamic, uncapacitated problem. Its results in handling problems with a high number of variables (due to the multiplicative effect of the dynamic structure) are remarkable: $m = 25$, $n = 50$, both to be multiplied by 10, the number of periods. One of the heuristic methods proposed very recently (Hochbaum, 1982) is accompanied by a detailed calculation of the computational complexity, which is $0\ (n^2m)$.

We complete the examination of the problem with fixed charges by briefly mentioning some generalizations of the models. The first relates to the dynamic case: the paper by Van Roy and Erlenkotter (1982) mentioned earlier is the foremost example. The second relates to the case where a certain number of intermediate plants can also be located, see ReVelle, Marks and Liebman (1970). Other possible generalizations will be examined in connection with the capacitated case, for which they are more significant.

The formulation of the location problem with concave costs (case (g3)), taken from Feldman, Lehrer and Ray (1966), is as follows:

$$\min\left[\sum_{1}^{m}{}_{i}\sum_{1}^{n}{}_{j}c_{ij}x_{ij} + \sum_{1}^{m}{}_{i}f_{i}(\pi_{i})\right] \tag{6.34}$$

$$\sum_{1}^{m}{}_{i}x_{ij} = w_{j} \quad (j = 1, \ldots, n) \tag{6.35}$$

$$\sum_{1}^{n}{}_{j}x_{ij} = \pi_{i} \quad (i = 1, \ldots, m) \tag{6.36}$$

$$x_{ij} \geqq 0 \quad (\forall i,j) \tag{6.37}$$

$$\pi_{i} \geqq 0 \quad (\forall i) \tag{6.38}$$

where the variables x_{ij} represent the request of customer j satisfied by plant i (not, as in problem (6.28) - (6.32), the demand fractions) and the variables π_i represent the plant dimensions.

The problem with concave costs was initially formulated by Feldman, Lehrer and Ray (1966) as an extension of the problem proposed by Kuehn and Hamburger and by Manne. In this case too the solution method was heuristic. The theoretical results here are connected with the fact that this is a problem of separable programming (ie consisting of a set of linear constraints with an objective function represented by a sum of non-linear terms $f_i(\pi_i)$, each being a function of one variable only). In this case, a reformulation is possible, in which the functions $f_i(\pi_i)$ are replaced by piecewise-linear functions: this permits a linearization of the problem, though at the cost of an increased number of variables.

The main approach to the solution of the problem with concave costs is therefore linearization together with branch-and-bound methods for the search in variable space of the reformulated problem. The commonest algorithm along these lines is that in Soland (1974), which is applicable, with few modifications, both in the uncapacitated and capacitated cases. The heuristic methods are of the add-and-drop type. The one proposed by Feldman, Lehrer and Ray (1966) starts with an inspection of the configuration with all plants open and then closes one plant at a time. The dimension of the problems considered are $m = 25$ and $n = 50$, in the case of exact solution (Soland), and the same as the Kuehn-Hamburger standard problem in the case of heuristic methods. The generalizations, which are more theoretical than practical, are once more the same as in the case with fixed charges.

It is now possible to summarize the major aspects of the location problem with transportation and plant costs (uncapacitated case) using the evaluation scheme presented in Section 6.5.1.

Algorithms: the many available algorithms, both exact and heuristic, cover a wide spectrum of methodologies (see Section 6.4).

Codes: practically all of the algorithms proposed are well documented in terms of computer codes and results calculated for a certain number of sample problems (not infrequently the problem involved is the same, as in the case proposed by Kuehn and Hamburger, which makes it possible to compare the various programs).

Theory: this is not particularly developed and in any case is not specific, as it mainly follows the general methodologies of integer programming (for example, the relaxation methods).

Complexity: this has not been thoroughly considered, except in some very recent papers (for example Hochbaum, 1892); we are dealing in any case with an NP-complete problem.

6.5.4 Location with technological constraints

This section deals with the third level formulation of the location problem. The assumption that technological constraints are absent is dropped, while the other assumptions are maintained, namely: (a) costs representing the unique preference indicator; and (b) complete rationality of the decision-maker. The structure of the problem includes a series of additional constraints (see Section 6.3.2) which will be described later and which result in a better correspondence of the problem with reality, even though in some cases the solution becomes more complicated. Of these constraints, referred to here as "technological", one in particular has the property of radically modifying the problem structure: the plant capacity constraint, which invalidates the property (used up to this point) that each customer is served by the closest plant (ie that the demand is indivisible).

In the case we are considering here, a solution of the problem involves two distinct steps: (i) location of plants; and (ii) allocation of the customers to the plants. Step (ii) involves solving a transportation problem (if the relative costs are linear) and must be repeated, at least in theory, for each location, ie each time step (i) is carried out. The problem complexity and the solution speed basically depend on the number of times step (ii) is repeated (though this number can be significantly reduced with respect to the theoretical requirement), rather than on the behaviour of the algorithm during the search for solutions. The effect of other constraints, which is more marginal, will be discussed when examining the generalizations of the problem. This problem is often referred to as the capacitated problem to emphasize this characteristic.

The fundamental parameters defining the problem (see Table 6.3 and Figure 6.3) are: (i) the objective function, expressed according to the efficiency criterion (and, generally, for plant costs of linear type with fixed charges); and (ii) discrete space. The number of plants to be opened is obviously determined by the ratio of the transportation costs to plant costs and by plant capacity. The location step and the allocation step are controlled by the same decision-maker.

A review of studies covering this kind of problem is provided by Francis and Goldstein (1974), ReVelle, Marks and Liebman (1970), Salkin (1975, Chapter 12) for the private sector and Coelho (1983) for the public sector. There have been major applications in the private sector, also in cases of multi-sectorial production (with possible production interdependence) and/or multi-period production.

The classic formulation of the capacitated problem, if other technological constraints are disregarded and for the case of linear costs with fixed charge, is as follows:

$$\min\Big[\sum_{i=1}^{m}\sum_{j=1}^{n} c_{ij}x_{ij} + \sum_{i=1}^{m} f_i\pi_i\Big] \tag{6.39}$$

$$\sum_{i=1}^{m} x_{ij} = 1_j \quad (j = 1, \ldots, n) \tag{6.40}$$

$$\sum_{j=1}^{n} x_{ij} \leq q_i\pi_i \quad (i = 1, \ldots, m) \tag{6.41}$$

$$x_{ij} \geq 0 \quad (\forall i,j) \tag{6.42}$$

$$\pi_i = 0 \quad (\forall i) \tag{6.43}$$

The earliest contributions to the solution of this problem are by Sa (1969): the problem originated as an extension of the uncapacitated case and the same theoretical structure used for linear integer programming was applied (see Section 6.5.3). The main approaches to the exact solution of the problem are: (a) branch-and-bound methods; and (b) search methods in integer variable space. In the first group are, among others, the algorithms proposed by Sa (1969), Soland (1974) (who applies them also to the uncapacitated case with concave costs), Akinc and Khumavala (1977) who provide some efficient selection criteria for the nodes and variables in the branch operations,

Geoffrion and McBride (1978) who couple the branch-and-bound technique with theoretical results derived from Lagrangian relaxation and by Ross and Soland (1977) who reformulate the problem in terms of assignment. Among the search methods in the integer variable space is the ranking algorithm proposed by Bartezzaghi, Colorni and Palermo (1981). The majority of heuristic methods belong to the add-and-drop type (Sa, 1969, Kuehn and Hamburger, 1963, Feldman, Lehrer and Ray, 1966), but some methods of global optimization are now being worked on.

The dimension of the problems which can be handled does not depend so much on the number of candidate plants (m) and customers (n) as on the number of transportation problems actually solved with respect to the theoretical ones. The latter depends in turn on the structure of the data and in particular on the ratio of fixed costs to variable costs, the uniformity of their values and on capacity values. A study of this aspect has been made by Bartezzaghi, Colorni and Palermo (1976, 1981). The order of magnitude is a few dozen for m (15 to 25) and slightly higher for n (40 to 50). These details are given in the papers quoted, together with information on computer codes.

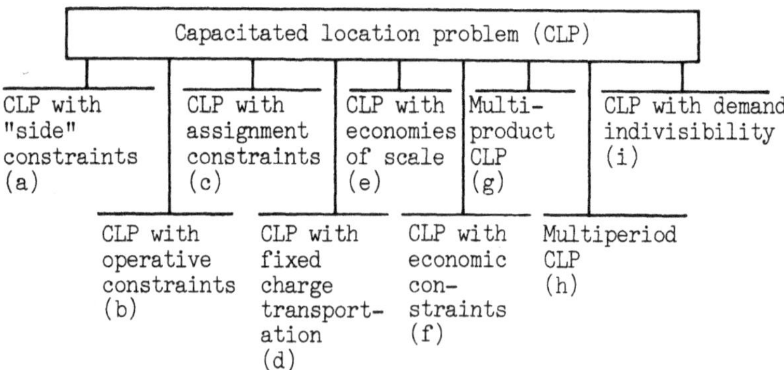

Figure 6.11: Possible generalizations of the capacitated location problem

Some possible developments and generalizations of the capacitated location problem proposed by Bartezzaghi, Colorni, Palermo (1976) are shown in Figure 6.11, and relate to the constraint classification of Section 6.3.2. Some of the categories in Figure 6.11 are self-explanatory, others have already been examined in Section 6.3.2 and the remainder will be commented on here. Prior to any comment, however, it should be pointed out that in the majority of the cases, these constraints can be expressed by linear conditions of the type

$$Ax + By = b \qquad (6.44)$$

which should be added to problem (6.39) - (6.43) (Coehlo, 1983). Here A and B are matrices and b is a vector of suitable dimension, so that conditions (6.44) do not destroy the linearity of the system of constraints. This is not true, for instance, for cases (d) and (e) of Figure 6.11 (but the non-linear variations relate to the objective function).

Let us now comment on some of the above cases. The location problem in the case of a multi-product company has been examined, among others, by Warszawski (1974), by means of an algorithm with implicit enumeration of the solutions. The problem, with linear constraints owing to the assumption of absence of induced effects among the various productions, is essentially expressed through an increase in the number of variables.

The multi-period location problem introduces a recursive aspect into time and/or space. (In some cases, in fact, the choices take place at different stages corresponding to different territorial levels of the problem, for instance production plants, intermediate plants, warehouses, final demand.) Some dynamic problems are looked at by Erlenkotter (1981) in a review of heuristic methods and also by Warszawski (1974) and a number of space-recursive situations are examined by Nagelhout and Thompson (1981) and by Moore and ReVelle (1982).

Finally, there are several papers dealing with transportation problems with fixed charges, ie the case where the transportation costs c_{ij} are non-linear, but are of the type shown as curve (g2) in Figure 6.2. Among others, we cite Murty (1968) and Gray (1971), which are important as they were among the first to supply efficient rules for the search in the integer solution-space, and also Kennington and Unger (1976), who make use of branch-and-bound methods complemented by "ad hoc" techniques.

We finally summarize the most important aspects of the location problem with technological constraints (capacitated case), using the evaluation scheme of Section 6.5.1.

Algorithms: these are quite numerous (though not as numerous as for the uncapacitated case) and are both exact and heuristic; predominantly a branch-and-bound methodology is used, with a number of specific variants for the different generalizations of the problem.

Codes: the various algorithms proposed give information on the computer codes; the comparative evaluation of the computational results is, however, rather poor and there is no analysis of results in terms of data structure (costs, capacity, etc), which would be highly desirable for this type of problem.

Theory: the few theoretical contributions to this subject are non-specific; no particular attention is given, for instance, to the allocation steps, ie to the transportation problem, which, being repetitive and utilizing quite similar data, could be approached and solved in a more structured way within the overall problem.

Complexity: this has not been studied at all, either for exact algorithms (also because it depends on the number of transportation problems actually solved) or for heuristic algorithms.

6.5.5 Rationality and non-rationality of customers (entropic models)

This section describes the fourth level formulation of the location problem. The assumption of complete rationality of decision-makers is dropped, while the first assumption is maintained: costs representing the unique preference indicator. This problem structure is characteristic of public facilities location (see the relevant comment under Section 6.2, point (b)). The problem involves a decision-maker who must take into account the fact that customers do not always behave, or do not all behave, in a rational way (ie minimizing certain indicators that express the service cost in a generalized sense). This situation, which is typical of the public sector, means that the decision-maker controls the location step, but does not control the allocation of customers to the plants (Coelho, 1983): this produces a flow between customers and plants, which does not obey the criterion of cost minimization but also may well be determined by other factors. This produces a certain degree of scattering of the flow with respect to the minimum cost solution. This concept is expressed through the notions of random utility and/or consumer surplus (Wilson et al, 1981) and involves a modification of the objective function to take into account the effect of non-complete rationality. In practice, this means that the objective function includes, besides the terms of real cost described in the previous sections, a term of generalized cost (or benefit) which represents the random utility.

Apart from this, the complexity of the problem will depend on the factors previously discussed. There are normally constraints of demand satisfaction and plant or service capacity even though the latter are usually interpreted (due to their derivation from transportation simulation models and in particular the gravity models) as conditions affecting the total flow from the origins (plants or customers) to the destination (and vice versa).

The fundamental parameters defining the problem are: (i) the objective function expressed according to the efficiency criterion, ie as a minimization (maximization) of a sum of cost (benefit) terms; and (ii) discrete space, which allows us to express "a priori" the cost of a trip between i and j. Other parameters are less useful for this problem.

The applications, as already mentioned, are almost entirely related to the location of public services. A recent review of problems and solution techniques has been made by Wilson (Wilson et al, 1981) who is undoubtedly the most well-known exponent of this type of approach on which he has been working since the late sixties. Other reviews are by Leonardi (1978, 1981-A), Coelho (1983) and Palermo (1981).

The formulation of the location problem with maximization of the consumer surplus (rather than simply cost minimization), based on the model of Bertuglia and Leonardi (1982) with some formal modifications to make it consistent with our previous notation, is as follows:

$$\max(\eta.\omega(x_{ij}) - \sum_{1}^{m}{}_{i}\sum_{1}^{n}{}_{j} c_{ij}x_{ij} - \sum_{1}^{m}{}_{i} f_i\pi_i) \qquad (6.45)$$

$$\sum_{1}^{m}{}_{i} x_{ij} = w_j \quad (j = 1, \ldots, n) \qquad (6.46)$$

$$\sum_{1}^{n}{}_{j} x_{ij} \leq q_i\pi_i \quad (i = 1, \ldots, m) \qquad (6.47)$$

$$x_{ij} \geq 0 \quad (\forall i,j) \qquad (6.48)$$

$$\pi_i = 0,1 \quad (\forall i) \qquad (6.49)$$

where the plants are the origins of the flows and the customers are the destinations. (It is assumed that $\sum_{1}^{m}{}_{i} q_i\pi_i \geq \sum_{1}^{n}{}_{j} w_j$, a condition which can easily be changed into an equality by the addition of a fictitious customer with a demand equal to the difference between the left and the right side terms.) The term $\omega(x_{ij})$ represents a measure of scattering of the flows and η is a scale factor which renders the terms of (6.45) homogeneous. The utility function, $\omega(x_{ij})$ minus the costs of location and transportation which produce the flows $\{x_{ij}\}$, must be maximized.

As a measure of the scattering we assume here an entropy function

$$\omega(x_{ij}) = N!/\Pi_i\Pi_j x_{ij}! \tag{6.50}$$

where $N = \sum_1^m{}_i\sum_1^n{}_j x_{ij}$ represents the totality of the flows, and we choose to maximize the logarithm of function (6.50) by substituting for $\eta.\omega(x_{ij})$ the value

$$\mu.\log\omega(x_{ij}) = -\mu.\log\Pi_i\Pi_j x_{ij}! + K$$

$$= -\mu.\Sigma_i\Sigma_j\log x_{ij}! + K \simeq -\mu.\Sigma_i\Sigma_j x_{ij}.(\log x_{ij} - 1) + K$$

where the last (approximate) equality is obtained by applying the Stirling formula, K is a constant representing log N! which can be neglected in the maximization and μ is a parameter connected with the cost of scattering. Usually the parameter μ is assumed to be equal to $1/\beta$, where β is the coefficient of the exponential function measuring the space "friction" between i and j in the entropic model (Coelho, 1983). The objective function of problem (6.45) - (6.49) therefore becomes

$$\min[\frac{1}{\beta}\sum_1^m{}_i\sum_1^n{}_j x_{ij}.(\log x_{ij} - 1) + \sum_1^m{}_i\sum_1^n{}_j c_{ij}x_{ij} + \sum_1^m{}_i f_i\pi_i] \tag{6.51}$$

and so as $\beta\to\infty$, the overall model is the same once again as model (6.39) - (6.43) of the capacitated problem.

Parameter β consequently becomes a dispersion factor for the whole group of customers: for increasing values of β, the "friction" due to distance is felt with increasing discomfort by the customers and the resulting distribution of the flows is less scattered. Under conditions of complete rationality, ie for $\beta \to \infty$, the discomfort due to distance is maximum and the group of customers is allocated so as to minimize the total transportation cost for a given number of plants. Model (6.45) - (6.49) is more like the usual kind of the entropic models, so called because the flows obtained by these models are those which maximize the entropy of the system for a given value of the scattering factor β. For a fuller discussion of entropic models the reader should refer to Wilson et al (1981) or to Wilson's chapter in this book. The same holds for the numerous theoretical contributions to the subject.

The approaches used to solve problem (6.45) - (6.49), in general involve the use of mathematical programming conditions (Lagrange and Kuhn-Tucker theorems) and in particular the Lagrange relaxation techniques. This results, however, in the following limitations: (a) The use of the analytical conditions generally means that the variables must be continuous and differentiable (even though this is not always necessary): this imposes some limits to the use of the entropic models when binary variables are present (see, for instance, the reformulation of the Efroymson and Ray problem by Bertuglia and Leonardi (1982), which involves elimination of the location variables π_i). (b) The result obtained by the application of analytical conditions is a system of equalities and inequalities which are not always easy to solve (beyond the recurrent case where the solution is an exponential) and numerical methods must often be resorted to. (c) The non-utilization of iterative methods prevents a comparison of the algorithms, their complexity, their performance and so on. The consequences of the above is that, in fact, there are no computational results for standard problems and therefore it is not possible to define the dimension of the problems that can be handled with any accuracy.

The major generalizations of problem (6.45) - (6.49), are as follows. The first relates to the case where the random component of the objective function is intrinsic not only to customer behaviour, but also to the network behaviour. In Section 6.5.2, in connection with the p-median or p-centre problems, we have already referred to the case of stochastic graphs (Berman and Odoni, 1982). A further example, given by Ermoliev and Leonardi (1981), takes into consideration stochastic aspects of demand and network. The second involves introducing a whole series of technological constraints into the problem: see the comments in the last part of Section 6.5.4 and Figure 6.11. A further generalization (Mayhew and Leonardi, 1982) consists of formally considering different criteria, ie programming with multiple objectives which will be seen in Section 6.5.6.

We can now summarize the major aspects of the location problem with cost fucntions and random utility (the entropic model).

Algorithms: these are not numerous and cover a very narrow spectrum (use of the Lagrangian and Kuhn-Tucker conditions); heuristic algorithms and general comparisons of the various methods are lacking.

Codes: are in general lacking, at least in published documentation; there are also few computational results on standard problems.

Theory: is very wide, even though not directly addressed to location problems (but usually transportation problems or problems connected with behavioural theories).

Complexity: has not been dealt with at all.

6.5.6 Multiple objectives

This section deals with the fifth (and last) level of formulation for the location problem. Here even the first assumption, ie the existence of only one preference indicator, is dropped. The problem structure (typical of the public sector) is determined by the "complex" decisional system (see Section 6.2) which may include one or more decision-makers and/or the totality of the customers. These decision-makers have different objectives, which cannot always be aggregated into one single objective function, even using scale factors, as they are partially or totally in conflict with one another. In addition to this, it is necessary to express the efficiency of the various solutions through certain indicators (risk, comfort, etc) which is not always easy to define as they are qualitative and cannot be directly compared with other quantitative indicators. This situation has stimulated the study, in recent years, of the development of the decision problem in the presence of multiple objectives and, in general, with a complex decision structure. Among these studies, some are specifically oriented towards environment and territory problems (Nijkamp, 1977, Haimes, 1977), as well as location problems (ReVelle, Cohon and Shobrys, 1981).

There are basically two fundamental parameters: (i) space; and (ii) the set of objective functions. As regards the space parameter, there are articles concerning continuous problems (Nijkamp and Spronk, 1981, Wendell and McKelvey, 1981) and discrete problems (ReVelle, Cohon and Shobrys, 1981, Moore and ReVelle, 1982). As regards the set of objective functions, we refer back to Section 6.5.2 where mention was made of the cases where two objectives must coexist. In fact, there are often two objective functions, one of a more quantitative type, usually relating to facility costs (eg the efficiency criterion in 6.5.2), the other of a more qualitative type, usually relating to the service quality levels (eg the worst case criterion in 6.5.2).

Applications are more and more frequently found in the public sector, although less so in the private sector, for the location of both required and obnoxious facilities. An exhaustive review of the various problems and the different types of objectives to be considered can be found among the various works by ReVelle (eg 1982).

As an example of a multi-objective problem, let us consider the following case: (i) discrete space; (ii) presence of linear transportation costs only; (iii) plants with no capacity constraints; (iv) complete rationality of the decision structure; (v) multiple objectives. In practice this example represents a generalization of the case dealt with in 6.5.2. Let the objectives be the following: (a) minimization of the average distance for servicing all customers from p plants; (b) minimization of the maximum distance for servicing all customers from p plants; (c) maximization of the customer demand served by p plants within a fixed distance; (d) minimization of the plants necessary for servicing all the customers within a fixed distance. In place of the distance d_{ij} the transportation times t_{ij} are often used, for instance in the case of emergency services. This, from a formal point of view, changes nothing in the formulation which follows. Let

$$e_{ij} = e_{ij}(\tau) = \begin{cases} 1 \text{ if } d_{ij} \leqq \tau \\ 0 \text{ if not} \end{cases} \qquad (6.52)$$

by the element of an incidence matrix E depending on the value of parameter τ: in (6.52)

$$e_{ij} = 1 \ (\forall i,j) \quad \text{for } \tau \rightarrow \infty$$
$$e_{ij} = 0 \ (i \neq j) \quad \text{for } \tau \rightarrow 0$$

In addition, let

$$\varepsilon_j = 0,1 \ (\forall j)$$

be a binary variable which has the value 1 if customer j is served, the value 0 if he is not.

The formulation of the problem is as follows:

$$\min Z \tag{6.53}$$

subject to

$$\sum_{1}^{n} {}_i e_{ij}\delta_{ij} \geq \varepsilon_j \quad (j = 1, \ldots, n) \tag{6.54}$$

$$\sum_{1}^{n} {}_j \delta_{ij} \leq n\delta_{ii} \quad (i = 1, \ldots, n) \tag{6.55}$$

$$\sum_{1}^{n} {}_i \delta_{ii} \leq p \tag{6.56}$$

$$\delta_{ij} = 0,1, \ \varepsilon_j = 0,1 \ (\forall i,j) \tag{6.57}$$

There are four cases:

case (i): $\tau \to \infty, \ \varepsilon_j = 1 \ (\forall j)$

$$Z = [\frac{1}{n} \sum_{1}^{n} {}_i \sum_{1}^{n} {}_j w_j d_{ij} \delta_{ij}]$$

case (ii): $\tau \to \infty, \ \varepsilon_j = 1 \ (\forall j)$

$$Z = [\max_{i,j} w_j d_{ij} \delta_{ij}]$$

case (iii): $\tau = \bar{\tau}, \ \varepsilon_j = 0,1$ (decisional variable)

$$Z = -[\sum_{1}^{n} {}_j w_j \delta_j]$$

case (iv): $\tau = \bar{\tau}$, $\varepsilon_j = 1$ ($\forall j$), $p = n$

$$Z = [\sum_{1}^{n} \delta_{ii}]$$

Case (i) represents the p-median problem, case (ii) the p-centre problem (limited to the nodes), case (iii), the so-called max-covering problem, and case (iv) the set-covering problem. Conditions (6.54) imply that each customer must be served (or may be served, in case (iii), if $\varepsilon_j = 1$) by at least one plant. Conditions (6.55) mean that no customer is served by plant i if this is not open. Inequality (6.56) establishes a maximum limit to the number of plants that can be opened.

Formulation (6.53) - (6.57) includes four different problems, whose objectives may be (partially) conflicting or not directly comparable. Case (iv) by itself may even represent quite different problems depending on the meaning attributed to the weight w_j. For instance, in the case of protection by emergency services, the "value" to be protected in node j may represent population, property and private goods, areas and public goods present in the node and so on, giving rise to different objectives.

How can these problems be handled? Let us consider the problem formulated as follows

$$\min f(x) \tag{6.58}$$

$$\text{s.t. } x \varepsilon X \tag{6.59}$$

where f(x) is a vector of functions $f_1(x)$, $f_2(x)$, ..., $f_n(x)$.

One of the major theoretical contributions to the treatment of mathematical programming with multiple objectives (and therefore to the case of location) is by Kuhn and Tucker (1951). It provides two distinct methods, the weight method and the constraint method, to determine the set of Pareto-optimal solutions in the objective function space. This set consists of the solution x* (ie that satisfy conditions (6.59)) and for which there exist no other feasible solutions x such that

$$f_h(x) \leqq f_h(x^*) \quad (h = 1, \ldots, \ell) \tag{6.60}$$

where inequality (6.60) is strictly verified for at least one h. In other words this is the set of the compromise solutions among the various objectives.

It is not possible here to examine the theoretical aspects and the methodological implications of multi-objective programming. The reader should refer to the work of Nijkamp (1977) for a more detailed examination of the problems dealt with here. It is worth adding that as in many cases problem (6.53) - (6.57) is discrete, the set of Pareto solutions is also a discrete set (ie a set consisting of a finite number of points). This provides a number of advantages from the operative point of view. A series of examples of the determination of the Pareto set for problems corresponding to (6.53) - (6.57) are given by ReVelle, Cohon and Shobrys (1981). The same paper describes a method for comparing the various objectives, based on the fact that the problem is discrete.

The exact methods usually involve the determination of the Pareto set, providing the complete set of final Pareto solutions (weight or constraint methods) or a sub-set (goal programming), while many heuristic methods[‡] are also available which usually provide only one final solution (ie a compromise point among the various objectives). The dimensions of the problems handled are those indicated in the previous sections, as the

[‡] In this case we mean by heuristic methods those methods that do not express the characteristics of the various objective functions analytically, but provide a description in quality and/or dominance terms (Nijkamp, 1977, Palermo, 1981).

presence of more than one objective does not alter the complexity of the problem, but at most introduces a multiplicative factor into the execution time. Applications of these techniques have been made by Benito-Alonso and Devaux (1981) for infants' schools, Cohon et al (1982) for nuclear fuel plants, Mayhew and Leonardi (1982) for hospital systems, ReVelle, Cohon and Shobrys (1981) for emergency services.

The generalizations of the multi-objective problem may affect the type of model, making the system of constraints (plant budget, capacitated case, etc) more complex, or the type of concept, by adopting a more complex decision structure (multi-level systems, theory and games, etc): at present, both types are almost exclusively theoretical.

We can again summarize the major aspects of the multi-objective location problem.

Algorithms: there are many which have originated as a derivation from the corresponding single-objective case; but few have been developed specifically for multi-objective programming.

Codes: are very few in number and are cited for some applications with reference to the few computational results.

Theory: this is the general theory of multi-objective mathematical programming, with some additional contributions deriving from the discrete nature of the location problem.

Complexity: has only been considered as an extension of the corresponding single-objective cases.

6.6 A Summary

In this section we summarize the most important applications of mathematical models to location problems. We also identify some possible directions for future research in this area. This overall appraisal is based on papers published in the major international journals covering theoretical aspects (operations research, mathematical programming, graph theory and combinatorial optimization) and practical aspects (management, territory planning, transportation): *Operations Research*, *European Journal of Operational Research*, *Ricerca Operativa*, *Mathematical Programming*, *Networks*, *Discrete Mathematics*, *Management Science*, *Environment and Planning*, *Sistemi Urbani*, *Transportation Science*. A number of other articles and books published recently also contain relevant material. These have not been listed in full; an interpretative approach was adopted and only the most important have been cited.

Over the past twenty or thirty years there has been an impressive amount of research dedicated to location problems. With reference to the five levels of complexity distinguished in Section 6.5 we find that they also represent a chronological development: while in recent years there have been fewer studies involving the lower levels, more have been dedicated to problems of higher complexity. In other words, there have been increasing attempts to make the representation of the problem more realistic by removing the most restrictive assumptions and exploiting the theoretical and computational possibilities made available by the development of more advanced techniques.

Our evaluation is based on the examination of the different parameters introduced in Section 6.5.1 - algorithms (exact and heuristic), computer codes, theory, and computational complexity. They represent the main steps which the modelling procedure usually follows. First of all some solution algorithms are proposed, mostly developed "ad hoc"; this is followed by a comparison of the algorithms, through the creation of computer codes and an examination of some test problems and their solution times. When a certain number of solution techniques have been established there is a theoretical elaboration and organization of the existing algorithms and results in terms of general methodologies; finally a comparison is made between classes of problems (and solution techniques) according to their computational complexity.

A combined examination of different levels of location problem and elaboration steps is shown in Table 6.8. This table lends itself to a number of observations. The contributions are differentiated into low, medium and high levels of development. This is obviously a highly simplified summary of the results of Section 6.5, but makes it possible to identify three different areas of development.

The first area corresponds to the high development level: it includes all the aspects of the problem with costs of transportation only and some of the aspects of the uncapacitated problem. The main features are: a well established and generalized body of research; a large number of applications; and that relevant software is readily available.

The second area corresponds to a medium development level: it includes the remaining aspects of the uncapacitated problem, almost all the aspects of the capacitated problem and the theoretical aspects of the random utility problem. The main features are: a generalized and still developing body of research; fewer applications; and software is available to individual researchers.

The third area corresponds to a low development level at present: includes the last two types of problem (random utility and multiple objectives), and one aspect of the capacitated problem. Features are an advanced body of research; a very few applications; and limited availability of software.

Table 6.8(b) aggregates the column indicators into one and gives an idea of the level of development of the five types of location problem examined in Section 6.5. Possible ways of filling the gaps indicated by Table 6.8 could be through: generalized applications to actual cases; diffusion of these methodologies through university education; and the development of new research areas. We discuss each in turn.

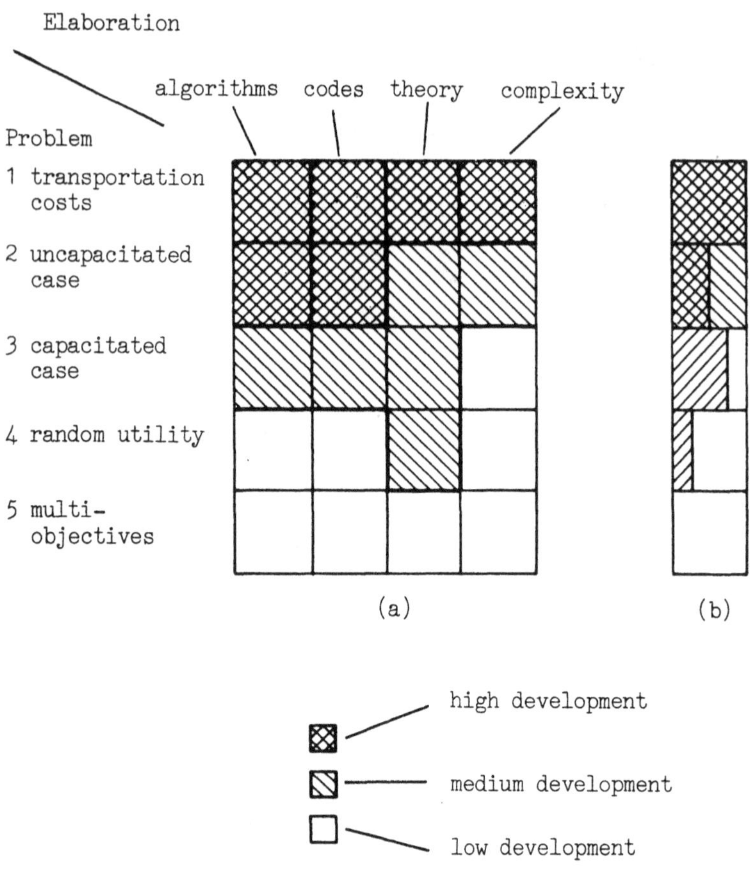

Table 6.8: Classification of models used in location problems

The possible applications of the methodologies described in this work, long since available for levels 1, 2 and 3, are now being extended to levels 4 (Bertuglia, Leonardi and Tadei, 1981) and 5 (Cohon et al, 1980). Applications of this kind, still isolated at present, are likely to represent an interesting development in the future, also in connection with the use of integrated models (for example location-transportation models).

The possible educational diffusion of these methodologies

is reflected in a correspondence between the above three areas and three different university educational levels - undergraduate, graduate and research. This could be shown in more detail through an analysis of the programs of the courses in the United States and the United Kingdom, though this is beyond the scope of the present work.

Finally, in relation to new research areas, it seems obvious that the third area identified in Table 6.8 is on the whole the most promising, though original contributions cannot be excluded also for the other two areas. We can argue that modelling methods in general have two forms of application: (a) as a formalization of theoretical problems; and (b) as an operational support to decisions regarding actual problems. In the case of the location models, the first is becoming predominant, whereas it would be more desirable if the two aspects were more balanced. Conversely, it would also be useful if alongside the continuous search for new algorithms, some attempt was made to create a modelling theory of location (in addition to the relatively few approaches which already exist). Finally, we should conclude by reminding ourselves that the modelling approach is not the only possible one and in many cases it may not be the best: there are others, less formalized or more attentive to the qualitative aspects of the problem, which should not be disregarded.

Part Four

INTERACTION AND PROBABILISTIC TRANSITION APPROACHES

Chapter 7

TRANSPORT, LOCATION AND SPATIAL SYSTEMS: PLANNING WITH SPATIAL INTERACTION MODELS

A.G. Wilson

7.1 Introduction

Spatial interaction concepts lie at the heart of much urban and regional modelling. Indeed, a system of models can be developed to cover most of the major subsystems, with each transport or location component constructed on the basis of the appropriate spatial interaction element and linked with other relevant factors. Such a model system was described, for example, in Wilson (1974). The purpose of this chapter is to report the state-of-the-art which has been reached nearly ten years since that book was written, to present current research problems and to examine the way in which currently available models can be used in planning. Comparisons with other approaches to urban modelling are made briefly.

In Section 7.2 below, we outline a framework which contains the main submodels of an urban and regional model system and we sketch in broad terms the planning uses of such a system. The heart of the chapter is Section 7.3. There, the basic submodels are reviewed in successive subsections. In most cases, there are recent advances to report on research on the main spatial interaction submodels themselves. In the cases of the retail model and the residential location model it is now also possible to add supply side models of housing and retail supply. This makes it possible to explore the stability of systems and the variety of spatial forms which may occur in the future. These extensions involve the methods of dynamical systems theory, and these methods also allow us to offer major extensions in the field of industrial location. It remains important to consider the effects of interdependence and this is done, with various possible methods, in the last subsection of Section 7.3. In Section 7.4 we briefly compare the spatial-interaction system with other possible approaches. Planning problems in relation to urban models are reviewed together with the range of applications in Section 7.5. A number of recommendations on model system design and implementation are made in Section 7.6.

7.2 The Model System and Planning Applications

7.2.1 The model system

The main elements of a model system are shown in Figure 7.1. This shows that it is useful to distinguish regional, urban and intra-urban scales. In this paper, we concentrate mainly on the urban scale though we briefly examine models which are appropriate for representing the demographic and economic backcloths early in Section 7.3. We will see in Section 7.3 that when the main subsystem variables are defined, they form sets of accounting variables which both form a useful basis for the study of urban problems (which we pursue in Section 7.5) and also provides the linkages between the different submodels.

Figure 7.1 enables us to structure the argument of Section 7.3. In subsections 7.3.2 and 7.3.3 we look briefly at the demographic and economic backcloths respectively. We then discuss in turn the major subsystems relating to services, residential location and industrial location. In the first two of these cases, we tackle the questions implied by the left and

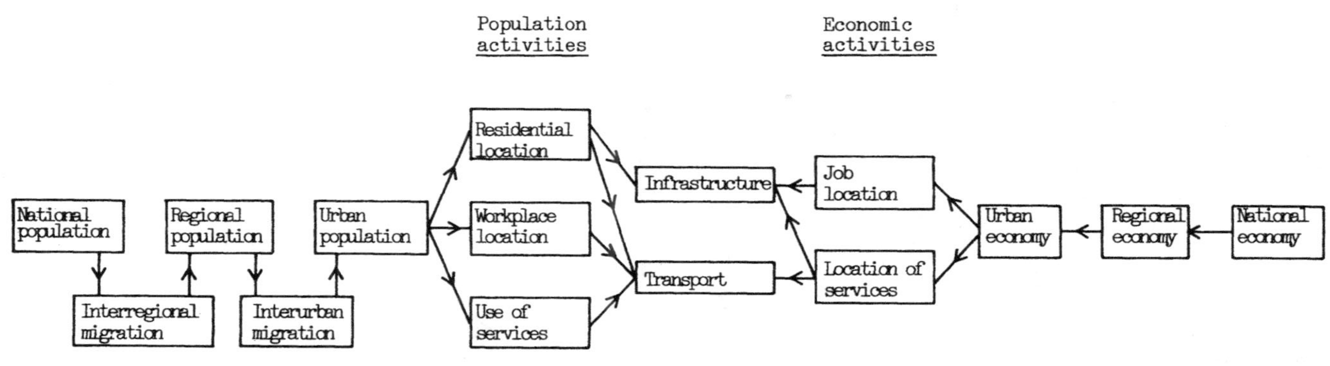

Figure 7.1: The main elements of an urban and regional model system

right hand sides of Figure 7.1 within the same subsection. That is, we first present a model of consumers' behaviour and then, in the light of this, of suppliers' behaviour. In the industrial location case, the problem is one of the producers only, though the output includes the job opportunities available to the population. One of the most striking features of Figure 7.1 is that it clearly shows how transport flows are functions of the locational properties within other subsystems. We tackle transport models in this light in the penultimate major subsection of Section 7.3. Finally, we have always stressed that many important effects arise from the interdependence of the various subsystems, and different methods of constructing integrated models are therefore considered in the last subsection.

7.2.2 Planning applications

Many of the submodels can, of course, be used on their own in tackling planning problems - with everything else taken as a given backcloth. It is always important to remember though that the effects of interdependence may be important, and the elucidation of the degree of that importance is a continuing research task.

Another major task in the exploration of the role of models in planning is the specification of 'controllable' variables. These will vary in different countries and at different times (for example, with the policies of different governments where more or less may be left to the free market or to planning respectively).

The traditional mode of use of urban models has been conditional forecasting of the impact of plans. A setting of values of controllable variables (which will usually represent aspects of public expenditure or regulation) constitutes a plan, and these variables constitute exogenous inputs for a model run. The outputs can then be used to construct various indicators of the impact of the plans.

In some circumstances, this remains an appropriate use of the models. But recent discoveries involving the supply side models using catastrophe theory and bifurcation theory have two consequences in relation to the use of models in planning. First, great caution must be exercised in using the models for forecasting; and secondly, new kinds of uses concerned with the analysis of stability and resilience emerge. We consider each, briefly in turn. The two effects are related. They stem from the existence of multiple equilibrium solutions arising from the presence of non-linearities and a high degree of interdependence. This means that at any time there are alternative equilibrium solutions available and that, through time, there are many alternative paths of development and evolution. These situations are complicated by the fact that when parameters (or other exo-genous variables) change smoothly, there is the possibility of jumps in the equilibrium state. It is the combination of these kinds of effects which makes forecasting intrinsically difficult: historical 'accidents', for example, could have a major effect on the development path adopted by a system. But the other side of the coin is a new use for models in planning: it is possible in principle to identify regions of parameter space associated with a particular (possibly 'type of') equilibrium solution and hence to assess the stability and resilience of that situation. Another possibility is to seek, from this basis, a shift in a parameter which will create a desired structural change.

We will reassess the usefulness of the models in applications in Section 7.5 when we have completed our review of the models themselves.

7.3 A Review of Models and Theory

7.3.1 Introduction

This chapter is restricted to the set of urban models and submodels based on 'spatial interaction' ideas. What are these ideas? At a general level, it is a recognition that many aspects of urban structure, activities and change build on spatial interaction and so it must be a central feature of any models which are constructed. At a more specific level, there is a set of models which make up the spatial interaction 'family'. There is a lot of experience with the basic family of models (cf Wilson, 1971-A, 1974) and many developments and extensions of it.

Spatial interaction models have a long history, the details of which need not concern us here. Most early manifestations were in the form of 'gravity' models and were based on some kind of Newtonian analogy. We start from the development of entropy-maximising models from the late 1960s (Wilson, 1967, 1970-A). The utility of this approach is not so much the particular derivation - though that still has something to be said for it! - but that it clarified the structure of a *family* of spatial interaction models which was determined by a priori knowledge of hypotheses about the row and column sums of the interaction matrix. This generated a basic family of four models: (i) unconstrained; (ii) production-constrained; (iii) attraction-constrained; and (iv) production-attraction- (or, doubly-) constrained.

The family could be extended through the development of hybrid models - for example, in which row sums were 'known' for some zones but not others, perhaps through planning controls - and through disaggregation. (See Cordey-Hayes and Wilson, 1971 and Wilson, 1971-A, for a discussion of the details of these ideas.)

It was clear from an early date that singly-constrained models would function as *location* models: the elements of the interaction matrix can be summed along the rows or columns which are unconstrained and the resulting vector is a set of locational properties such as the revenue attracted to shopping centres or the residential population of a particular area. It is this property, given that many locational phenomena are strongly related to interactions, which enables spatial interaction modelling to form a foundation for so many submodels. But also, we should emphasise, as we will see, that the interaction element in a submodel can be one factor among many - and not even necessarily the most important one.

The spatial interaction models are not, of course, universally applicable. It can be argued (Wilson, 1981-B, following Weaver, 1958) that they are applicable to systems of disorganised complexity. Such systems have large numbers of elements which interact only weakly, and this allows statistical averaging methods to be used. Entropy-maximising methods are examples of these, though there are alternative derivations. This means, for urban models, that they are most applicable to population activities (or to the aggregate models - the demographic and economic backcloths). When we look at economic activities, and in particular the supply side and economic locational behaviour, we have to seek new methods. It turns out that this can be increasingly achieved using methods of bifurcation theory. This is now possible and can be integrated with spatial interaction models which represent consumers' behaviour. This is one of the major kinds of advance to be reported in this chapter.

One further general point needs to be noted: once the general ideas of spatial interaction modelling have been understood, the major part of the research in a particular context is in moulding the abstract model to the particular case. Appropriate forms of disaggregation have to be developed for example; and much attention has to be paid to the forms of attractiveness factor used, particularly when the models are being used in singly-constrained form as location models.

We outline the use of spatial interaction models in three main contexts below. We begin with service sector models and explain the development of ideas in some detail (Section 7.3.4). This is convenient because they are the most extensively used *location* models, and the presentation of ideas forms a basis for the other major sectors. The next is residential location, about which there is some experience (7.3.5); the third is industrial location (7.3.6), about which there are new ideas but relatively little operational knowledge. In Section 7.3.7 we consider transport, which is important in its own right but also provides a key link for the study of land use-transport interdependence. Finally, we examine the role of spatial interaction models in integrated model frameworks and show how the Lowry model can be extended to include dynamic supply-side submodels.

All of these models need, however, in some form or other, demographic and economic backcloths and so a preliminary task is to describe briefly the models which are available for these purposes and we do this in Sections 7.3.2 and 7.3.3 respectively.

7.3.2 The demographic backcloth

The demand for housing, labour supply and the demand for services in a region all arise, at least in part, from the demography of the region. Planners, therefore, need an understanding of that demography and models are available to provide the basis for this. Since the form of these models is not central to the theme of this chapter, we restrict ourselves to mentioning the main models available and noting the kind of information they provide.

The usual subdivisions of the population in demographic models are age and sex. The models can be run almost separately for each sex (except, of course, that male births are generated by the female population), but there is a variety of models according to how age is treated. The most useful basis as a backcloth for urban modelling is usually taken as discrete age groups in a framework in which time moves discretely. (The alternatives are exact age groups - which lead to life-table models, combined with either discrete or continuous time; or discrete age-groups and continuous time.)

The main (matrix) form of the current type of model was established by Leslie (1945). He showed how to project forward a vector of population by age (restricting ourselves to one sex from now on) by multiplying by a matrix of appropriate rates. This was extended by Rogers (1966) to the multi-region case, thus adding 'region' to 'age and sex'. The output of such a model is therefore the array $P_i^r(t)$, the population in region i at time t who are in age group r (and for a particular sex). There were some weaknesses in practice in these formulations because of the difficulties of measuring the rates properly from available data. These were resolved, and some new concepts added, by the accounting framework and models of Rees and Wilson (1977).

We can proceed, therefore, with the assumption that arrays like $P_i^r(t)$ are available to us. The latest versions of the models are described in Rogers (1980) and Rees (1980) and suitable computer programmes can be easily obtained. But one final issue needs to be raised: what is a region? In this context, it is usually taken as relatively large: as what would constitute the whole area of an urban (modelling-based) study. In such a case, the demographic model, operating in the context of migration to and from other such regions, does indeed provide the demographic backcloth to an urban study. (Spatial interaction concepts can be used for the migration submodels - as in Stillwell, 1978, Rees and Stillwell, 1982.) But it is possible to apply the concepts to smaller areas within cities and that is occasionally useful. One such example is in King (1974), for a small area within Leeds. However, when the areas become very small, like the zones of an urban study, then the problem of inter-area migration becomes one of intra-urban residential location and is treated under the latter heading - as in Section 7.3.5 below.

7.3.3 The economic backcloth

As we can model the population of a region as a whole by age and sex, so also can we model economic activity by sector. The usual way of achieving this is by use of the input-output model in one of its various forms. This can be done for a single region - which is the most common case - with imports and exports treated exogenously, or as part of a multi-regional system.

The most common applications of input-output modelling are at the *national* scale. Regional applications are harder because of data problems: there is no measurement of the flow of goods and services across regional boundaries. The models can only be built, therefore, if large and expensive surveys are carried out. Many studies are therefore forced into the simpler economic base methods as a not-very-adequate alternative.

The classic study of a metropolitan input-output model was provided by Artle's (1959) work on Stockholm. More commonly, more attention has been paid to non-survey methods for constructing input-output models which usually involve modifying some known input-output coefficients - say national ones. A survey of such methods is offered by Morrison and Smith (1974), Hewings (1977) and Round (1978). Examples of model building are offered by Burdekin (1978), Smith and Morrison (1974) or Smith and Leigh (1977).

7.3.4 The use of services, and service supply

7.3.4.1 Introduction

The service sector is a major component of modern economics and this will be reflected in 'economic backcloth' models. Most services are supplied to the population from facilities which do not coincide with their residential location; and some services are supplied to firms and other organisations. A fundamental problem of locational analysis and planning is therefore to understand the spatial system of service supply and its relationship to the distribution of population and other sources of demand. This understanding is built up in two stages: (i) how consumers behave in relation to a given set of facilities; (ii) how a particular spatial system of facility-supply develops. The first of these is obviously a spatial interaction modelling task and the second will be influenced by the results of that.

Two basic types of service facility can be distinguished. First, those services where consumer choice is sovereign; and secondly, those where the consumer is allocated to a facility by some state organisation. An example of the first is retailing; of the second, the allocation of houses to stations for fire fighting and protection. Some services may fall into one or other of these categories in different countries. The school system will usually be a public system falling (to a large extent, but perhaps with limited choice) into the second category; but it may be a private system and fall into the first in some countries.

Most work has been done on consumer behaviour in retailing systems and we use this as our first example below - though the models are described in such a way that they can easily be applied to any other service of the same type as we make clear at an early stage. In subsection 7.3.4.2, we describe the basic model of consumer behaviour giving special emphasis to the kinds of indicators which can be generated by the model which are potentially useful for planning purposes. Supply-side models are described in subsection 7.3.4.3. The models are potentially most useful when they are disaggregated and we show a variety of ways of adding more detail in subsection 7.3.4.4. The problem is that, in practice, it is difficult to add all desirable disaggregations simultaneously. We then turn to the second kind of service system and review different kinds of location-allocation model (subsection 7.3.4.5).

It is useful to conclude this introduction by referring to a factorial analysis by McCarthy (1980) which generated a summary of the features of retailing systems which seemed to be of importance to consumers. We would seek to incorporate these factors into any models. They were: (i) generalised trip convenience; (ii) generalised trip comfort; (iii) generalised trip safety; (iv) generalised shopping area attraction; (v) generalised shopping area mobility. The first three of these obviously relate to elements of the associated transport system; the last two, to aspects of 'attractiveness', as we shall see. This seems to emphasise the importance of the transport system in determining the nature of the spatial structures of retail and service facilities which evolve. Service trips also form a substantial component of overall flows in a transport model.

7.3.4.2 The basic (aggregate) spatial interaction model for service systems

The most commonly used spatial interaction model takes the following form:

$$S_{ij} = A_i e_i P_i f(W_j) g(c_{ij}) \tag{7.1}$$

where

$$A_i = 1/\sum_k f(W_k)g(c_{ik}) \qquad (7.2)$$

to ensure that

$$\sum_j S_{ij} = e_i P_i \qquad (7.3)$$

S_{ij} is the flow from residents in i to facilities in j (which we take to be shops for illustrative purposes at this stage); e_i is the per capita demand by residents of i; P_i, the population of i; W_j, a measure of attractiveness of j; c_{ij} the generalised cost of travel from i to j. f and g are functions whose forms are to be explored theoretically and confirmed empirically. For *illustrative purposes*, we will take f to be a power function and g to be negative exponential so the model becomes

$$S_{ij} = A_i e_i P_i W_j^{\alpha} e^{-\beta c_{ij}} \qquad (7.4)$$

with

$$A_i = 1/\sum_k W_k^{\alpha} e^{-\beta c_{ik}} \qquad (7.5)$$

where α and β are parameters. Models of this kind were first used by Huff (1964), Harris (1964-A) and Lakshmanan and Hansen (1965) and much experience has now been gained. The particular distance function arises because the model, in this form, can be seen as an entropy-maximising model (Wilson, 1967). And the model can be recognised as an example of the production-constrained variety of a family of spatial interaction models (Cordey Hayes and Wilson, 1971, Wilson, 1971-A). The most common use of the model involves calibrating the model against a set of interaction data to find α and β; and then taking a set of W_j's - say as a trial 'plan', and testing the impact of these by running the model with them as inputs. This is facilitated by the common assumption that attractiveness - McCarthy's last two factors - can be measured, approximately, by size of facilities in j.

There are practical difficulties: different zoning systems can be used for i-zones and j-zones; how should they be chosen? But conceptually, there are no serious problems and so we will postpone a review of practice until the end of the section.

The impact of a trial 'plan' is measured by the flow matrix $\{S_{ij}\}$. But this also allows the following quantities to be calculated:

$$D_j = \sum_i S_{ij} \tag{7.6}$$

These are the revenues attracted to zone j (or the demands allocated to j from various i's). These, of course, are *locational* variables and this shows that the interaction model, when singly-constrained, predicts important locational characteristics too. This can be taken as the first of a number of *indicators* generated by the model which are useful for both analytical and planning purposes. We incorporate this, therefore, in the list of such outputs which now follows.

(i) The S_{ij}'s are measured as cash flows. By making assumptions about (and carrying out empirical investigations on) trip frequency, these can be converted to trip counts and used as a contribution to the transport model.

(ii) $\{D_j\}$, as noted above, is a measure of revenues attracted to each of the j's. Note that

$$D_j = \sum_i \frac{e_i P_i W_j^{\alpha} e^{-\beta c_{ij}}}{\sum_k W_k^{\alpha} e^{-\beta c_{ik}}} \tag{7.7}$$

An approximate version of (7.7) is

$$Y_j = k\sum_i e_i P_i e^{-\beta c_{ij}} \tag{7.8}$$

(for a suitable constant, k) and this is often taken as the *population potential* at j - a rough estimate of potential market. However, it is better to use the exact form (7.7).

(iii) A feature of spatial interaction models is that consumers do not necessarily go to the nearest facility. (This is because of market imperfection, lack of information, differences in taste not explicitly represented in the model - or whatever.) In the $\beta\to\infty$ limit, they do; otherwise, the smaller β, the less this is the case. Thus *market areas* overlap. But it is still possible to define market areas in this overlapping sense. For any j, a plot of S_{ij}'s (and an examination of $S_{ij}/\sum_j S_{ij}$, the proportion attracted from i, for a set of i's) gives a suitable indicator.

(iv) The A_i term in (7.4), given in (7.5), is interesting and provides the basis of three different indicators which we take in turn. A_i itself can be taken as a measure of the *competition* of shopping centres in the neighbourhood of i. It will be smaller if there is more competition and the trade from i will be more shared out.

(v) The inverse of A_i, however, is more directly useful:

$$X_i = 1/A_i = \sum_k W_k^{\alpha} e^{-\beta c_{ik}} \tag{7.9}$$

This can then be interpreted as a measure of the *accessibility* of residents of i to shopping centres. It should be emphasised that this is but one measure of a concept which is at best intuitively defined. But it is useful in many planning contexts and this particular measure, through the parameters α and β, is rooted in observed behaviour. An important feature of this particular indicator is that each term in the sum is made up from two components - the W_j^{α} factor which means that, other things being equal, bigger facilities contribute more; and the $e^{-\beta c_{ij}}$ which is the more familiar element of accessibility, measuring the effect of 'nearness'. The nature of these different elements will be better understood after our discussion of costs and benefits, next.

(vi) The third use of A_i relates to cost and benefit measures. First, we approach this in an intuitive way. The term

$$W_j^{\alpha} e^{-\beta c_{ij}} \tag{7.10}$$

in the model equations can be written, after some obvious manipulation as

$$e^{\beta(\frac{\alpha}{\beta} \log W_j - c_{ij})} \tag{7.11}$$

We can understand c_{ij} as a direct measure of the disutility of travel and so (7.11) suggests that $\alpha/\beta \log W_j$ is, correspondingly, a measure of the benefits of facility size. This will be a useful concept for later use and is already reflected in the measure of accessibility defined above.

It is also useful to be more formal about cost and benefit measurement. If either W_j's or c_{ij}'s are changed, there is a change in consumer surplus - indicated for a transport cost change in Figure 7.2. Williams (1977-B) has shown that an exact measure of change in consumer surplus, written ΔC.S., can be written in terms of A_j's as:

$$\Delta C.S. = \frac{1}{\beta} \Delta \log \sum_j W_j^{\alpha} e^{-\beta c_{ij}} \tag{7.12}$$

(vii) Finally, we note an indicator which is useful in its own right but is also useful as the foundation for much later dynamical analysis. We might call it *supply-demand imbalance*.

If D_j is the revenue attracted to a size-W_j facility at j, then if k_j is the unit cost of supply that facility

$$D_j - k_jW_j \tag{7.13}$$

is a measure of profit (if positive) or loss (if negative).

This completes our review of the main model concepts at the aggregate level for a static model. The next step is to investigate dynamics with this model (7.3.4.3 below) before looking at all the ideas introduced in the context of disaggregated models (7.3.4.4).

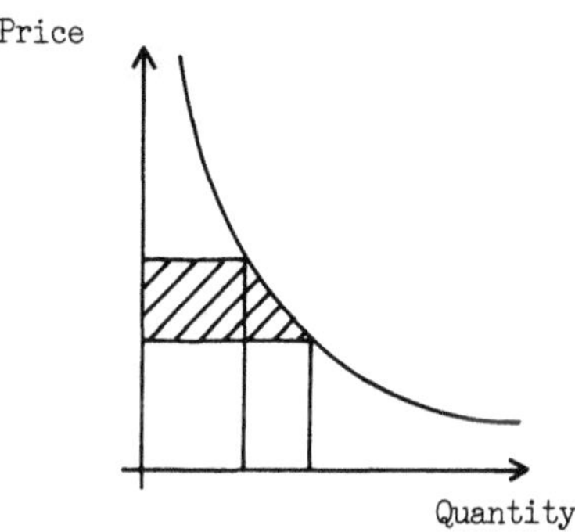

Figure 7.2: Change in consumers' surplus

7.3.4.3 Dynamics and planning

We noted earlier that the standard use of the model outlined has been to assess the impact of a 'plan' specified as a set of W_j's, written $\{W_j\}$. More recently, following work by Harris and Wilson (1978), Wilson and Clarke (1979) and Wilson (1981-A), it has been possible to add hypotheses about the behaviour of suppliers and in the resulting analyses to investigate the equilibrium patterns which can be *predicted* for $\{W_j\}$ together with an analysis of stability at the zonal and pattern level; and to predict the behaviour of the system over time either on a comparative-static basis or from states of disequilibrium.

This does not necessarily contradict the earlier approach to planning. It can be seen as adding a new analytical power and as offering a new contribution to planning methodology. For example, it is now possible to analyse the 'nearness-to-equilibrium' of a trial $\{W_j\}$ as the stability of facilities in particular zones, and this is obviously valuable. More radically, it may offer planners the opportunity to make relatively small adjustments to the system in the knowledge that the system itself will then generate bigger changes in some desired direction. The other side of the coin is that these new insights do show that there are inherent difficulties in making the traditional conditional forecasts with this type of model. We will elaborate on all these ideas about the relationship of dynamical analyses to planning after outlining the main concepts involved.

The key to dynamical analysis is provided by (7.13) above which we noted as measuring profit or loss at j. This immediately suggests that a suitable hypothesis for change in W_j can be written

$$\frac{dW_j}{dt} = \dot{W}_j = \varepsilon(D_j - k_j W_j) \tag{7.14}$$

for some suitable constant ε. More generally, we can add a factor W_j^n which simply changes the shape of the rate of growth near to $W_j = 0$:

$$\dot{W}_j = \varepsilon(D_j - k_j W_j)W_j^n \tag{7.15}$$

In either case, an equilibrium state is reached when

$$D_j = k_j W_j \tag{7.16}$$

Note that in each of (7.14), (7.15) and (7.16), the equations hold for each j, and that, through the D_j terms, all the W_k's,

$k \neq j$, appear in each j equation. So we have to consider the differential equations and the equilibrium condition as sets of interlinked simultaneous equations.

The ε-parameter measures the strength of response of suppliers, instantaneously, to profit or loss. In many cases, such responses will not be instantaneous. If we define a unit time period (an 'accounting year' say?) which is the basis of a response, then the differential equations should be converted to difference equations. For example, if we take $n = 1$ in (7.15), then W_j grows logistically near to $W_j = 0$. The equation is

$$\dot{W}_j = \varepsilon(D_j - k_j W_j)W_j \tag{7.17}$$

Assuming a unit time period and adding time subscripts, this can be written in difference equation form as

$$W_{jt+1} - W_{jt} = \varepsilon(D_{jt} - k_j W_{jt})W_{jt} \tag{7.18}$$

or, with some rearrangement, as

$$W_{jt+1} = (1 + \varepsilon D_j)W_{jt} - \varepsilon k_j W_{jt}^2 \tag{7.19}$$

To complete our preliminary presentation, we note that D_j was written explicitly (repeating (7.7) for convenience) as

$$D_j = \sum_i \frac{e_i P_i W_j^\alpha e^{-\beta c_{ij}}}{\sum_k W_k^\alpha e^{-\beta c_{ik}}} \tag{7.20}$$

This enables us to see that, taking (7.16) and (7.17) as examples, the interdependent differential equations and equilibrium conditions are

$$\dot{W}_j = \varepsilon \left[\sum_i \frac{e_i P_i W_j^{\alpha} e^{-\beta c_{ij}}}{\sum_k W_k^{\alpha} e^{-\beta c_{ik}}} - k_j W_j \right] W_j \tag{7.21}$$

and

$$\sum_i \frac{e_i P_i W_j^{\alpha} e^{-\beta c_{ij}}}{\sum_k W_k^{\alpha} e^{-\beta c_{ik}}} = k_j W_j \tag{7.22}$$

and such equations form the raw material of our subsequent analyses.

There are two striking features of equations (7.21) and (7.22): first, they are highly nonlinear, mainly through the A_i terms - representing competition; and secondly, again through the A_i terms, they are highly interdependent. Both features mean that when we try to seek equilibrium solutions to the equations (7.22), there will usually be many (stable) solutions. Further, and most interestingly, when parameters change slowly and smoothly, there is the possibility of jumps in the pattern - in effect from one stable equilibrium solution to another when the first one 'disappears'. These discrete jumps occur, in some cases, in a comparative static analysis when all parameters are expected to change smoothly. In the cases where the system is in disequilibrium, it turns out that another kind of bifurcation can occur: if ε is too large, then oscillations or worse can set in. The system can be sent into disequilibrium by exogenous (possibly planned) changes, or by small (random) fluctuations. Even small fluctuations can lead to fundamental changes in the path of system development - in effect, choosing one of a very large number of possible paths from among the alternative equilibrium states for each set of parameter values. It is these features which makes any kind of forecasting of variables like $\{W_j\}$ intrinsically difficult.

Fortunately, we can get more insight into the nature of zonal and pattern stability and change. Denote the left hand side of (7.22), the revenue, as a function of W_j as $D_j(W_j)$ and the right hand side, the costs, as $C_j(W_j)$. The insights are then gained by plotting D_j against W_j and C_j against W_j and seeking equilibria at the intersections of the two curves. The main situations which can arise at the zonal scale are shown in Figure 7.3 for $\alpha < 1$, $\alpha = 1$ and $\alpha > 1$ respectively. Stable intersection (which can be checked by looking at the sign of $\dot{W}_j$ in (7.21)) are marked with a circle, unstable intersections with a cross. We concentrate for the time being on the more interesting $\alpha > 1$ case.

The crucial distinction is between zones in which development is possible (DP) and those in which it is not (NDP). But note that when there is a transition from one such state to the other it involves a *jump* from 0 to a non-zero W_j or vice versa. Note also that in the DP case, development is possible but not *necessary* as $W_j = 0$ remains a stable solution. It is the existence of possible zeros among the DP-zones which generates the multiplicity of alternative patterns: typically, the number of patterns will be of the order $\prod_{p=1}^{n-1} {}^{n}C_{p}$ where n is the number of DP-zones and we consider the various ways of selecting combinations of zeros. We should also, of course, emphasise that these results apply for $\alpha > 1$ and $\alpha = 1$ is obviously itself a critical value.

The insights into the mechanisms of change can only be gained easily at the zonal level. It is clear that, for a zone in the NDP state, if costs decrease or revenue increases, then a stable intersection becomes more likely. Similarly we can say that if α decreases or β increases, the revenue curve moves 'upwards' in such a way that a stable intersection becomes more likely and hence a jump to the DP state. A corollary of this observation is that for lower α and higher

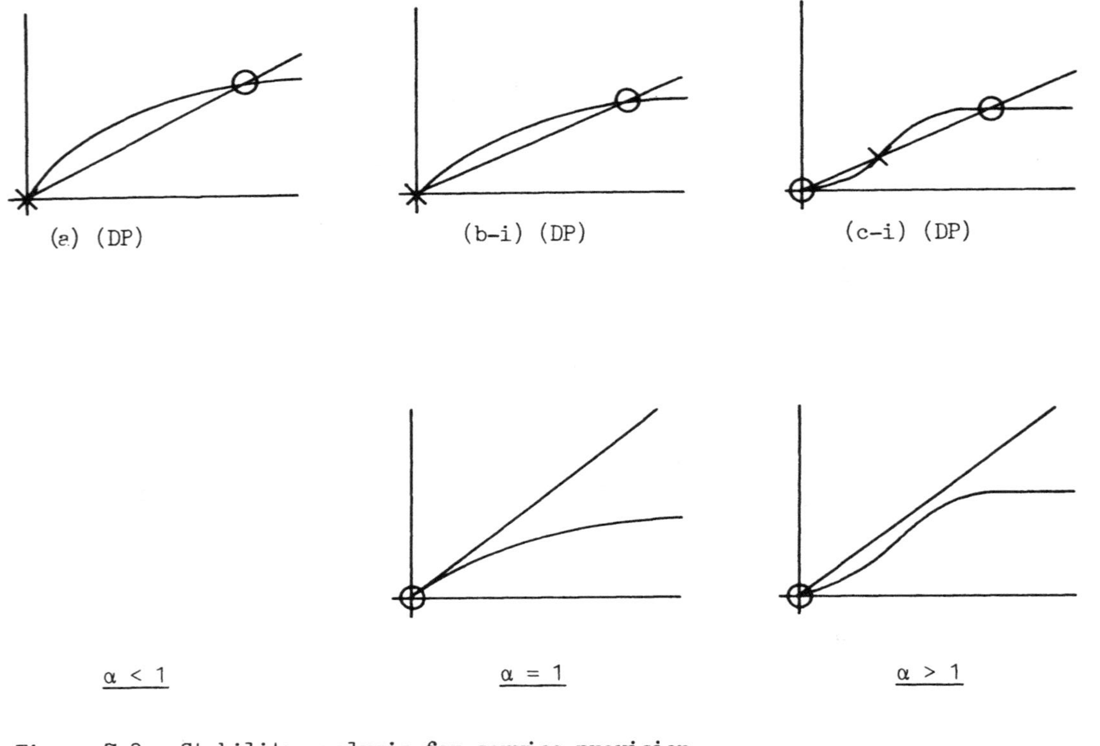

Figure 7.3: Stability analysis for service provision

β we expect patterns with greater numbers of non-zero W_j zones and vice versa. This is confirmed by results such as those shown in Figure 7.4 - from Clarke and Wilson (1983). Thus we can proceed from zonal insights to infer something about pattern. One problem in making this transition is that while it is possible to do so in general terms it is more difficult to do so in practice because of a hard theoretical problem discussed in detail by Wilson and Clarke (1979). The analysis for each zone which produces figures like 7.4 depends on the assumption that, in relation to j, all other W_k's, $k \neq j$, are fixed. That is, the analysis for one zone depends on the *pattern* in all other zones. And yet it is the addition of W_j to the list $\{W_k\}$, $k \neq j$, which produces the overall pattern. The insights gained are valuable overall, but we also have to recognise that there are many remaining research problems even in the analysis of equilibrium patterns.

In the case of the full dynamical system, not necessarily in equilibrium, the new bifurcations arise in relation to the ε-parameter in equations (7.19) or (7.21). The 'logistic' difference equation system (7.19) provides an interesting illustration. A result of May (1976) can be used to show that if

$$1 + \varepsilon D_{jt} > 2 \tag{7.23}$$

then oscillations (or a jump to zero for W_{jt}) will occur. This obviously depends on the value of ε in relation to typical magnitudes of D_{jt}. Some zonal plots which illustrate this and are self-explanatory (taken from Clarke and Wilson, 1983) are presented as Figure 7.5. Three cases are clearly visible: (i) steady growth to equilibrium; (ii) different kinds of oscillations; and (iii) jumps to zero.

We conclude this subsection by summarising and extending the implications for planning with models which the results as

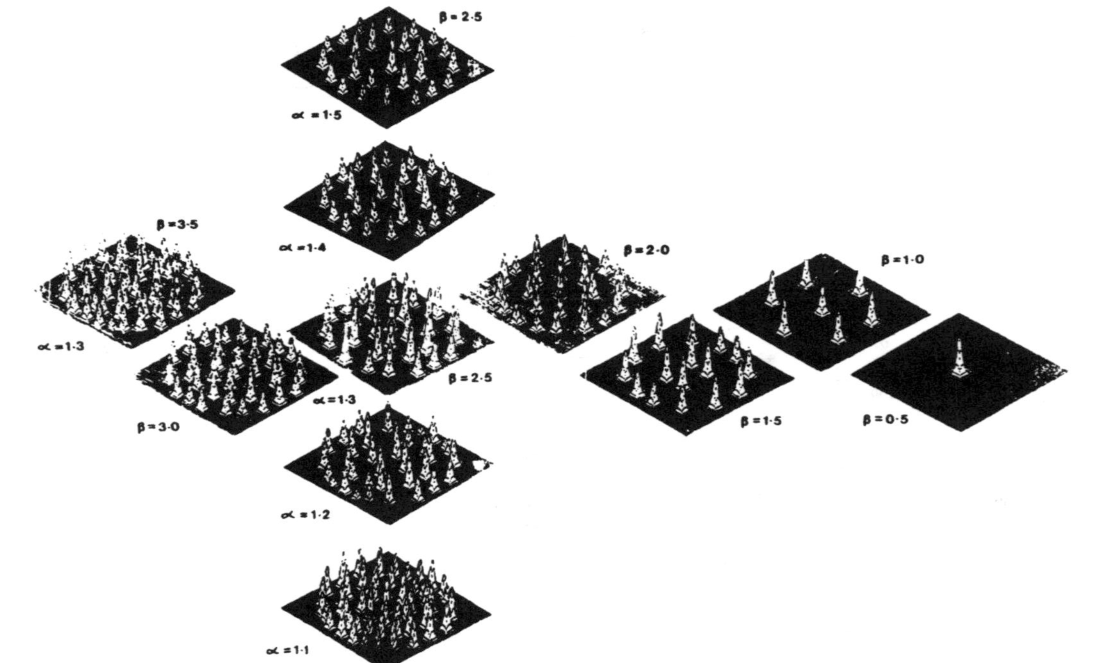

Figure 7.4: Equilibrium pattern of retail facilities for various alpha and beta values (729 zone symmetric spatial system)

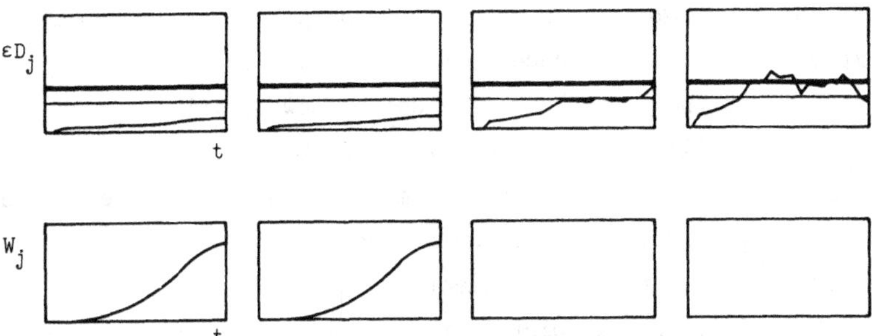

(a) Zone 251, varying epsilon

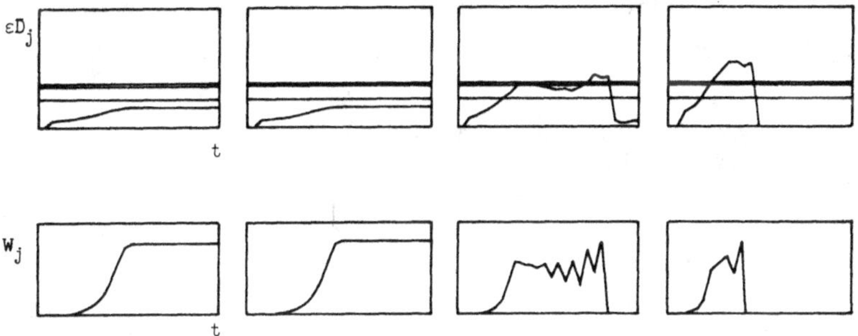

(b) Zone 259, varying epsilon

Figure 7.5: Dynamic modelling: zone service facilities against time

dynamics show. First, to recap: the traditional mode of model use for conditional forecasting may now be seen as problematic - there are likely to be many more alternative paths of evolution and development than can be picked up in a conventional comparative-static sequence. It is possible to test the stability at the zonal level (by seeing how 'near' each zone is to criticality) and to some extent in terms of patterns - in the latter case by running the model a number of times, each time adding random fluctuations to the W_j's to see to what extent different paths are selected.

This is a useful point in the argument at which to note that, in this case, the equilibrium solution of (7.22), which is in practice obtained iteratively, can also be written as a mathematical programme in a number of alternative ways. One programme we might consider is to find the $\{W_j\}$ to maximise benefits measured by $(\alpha/\beta \log W_j - c_{ij})$ in (7.10) subject to spatial interaction model consumer behaviour and an overall constraint on W_j's. This can be written

$$\underset{\{S_{ij}, W_j\}}{\text{Max}} \; Z = \sum_{ij} S_{ij}\left(\frac{\alpha}{\beta} \log W_j - c_{ij}\right) \tag{7.24}$$

subject to

$$S_{ij} = \frac{e_i P_i W_j^{\alpha} e^{-\beta c_{ij}}}{\sum_k W_k^{\alpha} e^{-\beta c_{ik}}} \tag{7.25}$$

and

$$\sum_j W_j = W \tag{7.26}$$

This last constraint is necessary to avoid an infinite supply of retail floorspace.

This programme is difficult to handle in practice because of the nonlinearities in the constraints - there are algorithms which handle nonlinear objective functions and linear constraints and so we need to recast it in such an (equivalent) form. This can be achieved by recognising that (7.25) itself derives from a mathematical programme - the entropy maximising basis - and it is possible to combine this with the above planning problem using an embedding theorem (Coelho and Wilson, 1977, Coelho, Williams and Wilson, 1978) to form the following:

$$\max_{\{S_{ij}, W_j\}} Z = -\Sigma S_{ij} \log S_{ij} + \Sigma S_{ij}\left(\frac{\alpha}{\beta} \log W_j - c_{ij}\right) \tag{7.27}$$

subject to

$$\sum_j S_{ij} = e_i P_i \tag{7.28}$$

and

$$\sum_j W_j = W \tag{7.29}$$

There are algorithms available to solve this problem (see Coelho and Wilson, 1976, for an example). Remarkably the problems (7.22), (7.24) - (7.26) and (7.27) - (7.29) are all equivalent - 'remarkably' because the iterative scheme was based on a hypothesis about suppliers' behaviour while the mathematical programming formulations were based on the maximisation of consumer benefits. The equivalence arises because the supply-equilibrium condition, $D_j = k_j W_j$, drops out of (7.27) - (7.29) as an optimisation condition (provided k_j is taken as α/γ where γ is the Lagrangian multiplier associated with (7.29)).

From a planning point of view, this interpretation means that the $\{W_j\}$-equilibrium pattern is at least a useful starting point in a sketch-planning procedure. Two additional comments are useful: first, the model can easily be run in an incremental mode, calculating W_{jt+1} at each step but with the condition $W_{jt+1} > W_{jt}$; or possibly to allow reductions in a 'stepped' way. Secondly, the results of a plan obtained in this way - incrementally or otherwise - can be related to the list of model outputs listed in the previous subsection. For example, although a particular $\{W_j\}$-pattern may represent an overall optimum, it may be desirable, for example, to improve accessibilities for particular small (locational) groups.

The more exciting possibility for planning arises from the nature of bifurcation phenomena: for a small and smooth change in a parameter or variable near its critical value, there can be a sudden and dramatic change in structure. If these phenomena can be clearly identified and their existence established, then this knowledge has useful implications for planners in two ways. First, negatively, if a system is about to jump or is in danger of jumping to an undesirable state, then action can be taken to prevent parameters reaching a critical value. Secondly, positively, it may be possible to guide the system to a desirable state by making relatively small changes (say in investment or regulations) which would take parameters through the appropriate critical values. There are difficulties, however, in immediately making this last kind of idea operational. It involves calibrating models in such a way that we can convince ourselves that we have an empirical as well as a (possible) theoretical understanding of structural change.

7.3.4.4 Towards more realistic disaggregated models

So far, the whole discussion has been presented in terms of the aggregate model. This is obviously hopelessly unrealistic in practice and so the next step is to disaggregate. In this section, we begin by presenting a model which has all (or most!) potentially desirable features. This is likely to involve too many indices for most practical purposes, but it does provide a foundation for the discussion of more approximate operational models. (And there is also the possibility of proceeding on the highly-disaggregated basis using micro-simulation techniques.)

The obvious (and one less obvious) elements of disaggregation are: (i) type of good or service g; (ii) type of facility at which g is available, h; (iii) person type, W_j; and (iv) mode of transport, k. The main array of spatial interaction variables could then be written $\{S_{ij}^{ghwk}\}$. The only definition which needs elaboration here (if only because its appearance in the literature is recent - see Wilson, 1982) is that of facility type. Consider the simple retailing example shown in Table 7.1. There we see shop types hierarchically ordered according to the range of goods they sell. But in modern retail structures, this kind of hierarchy is becoming more complicated. There may, for example, be rapid development of out-of-town facilities, isolated and specialising in a single-type of good such as furniture. This representation here enables us to represent such phenomena and to see how the facilities of different h-types might develop in competition with each other and with different locational structures.

<u>Table 7.1</u>: An example of goods types related to shop types

Goods type (g)	Shop type (h)			
g.	h.			
1. Food	1.	5 (small supermarket) (covers 1–2)		
2. Hardware	2.		6 (large supermarket) (covers 1–3)	
3. Clothes	3.			7 (department store) (covers 1–4)
4. Jewellery	4.			

The aggregate model equations (7.4) and (7.5) can now easily be modified to

$$S_{ij}^{ghwk} = A_i^{gw} e_i^{gw} P_i^w \hat{W}_j^{ghw} e^{-\beta^{gw} c_{ij}^k} \tag{7.30}$$

where

$$A_i^{gw} = 1/ \sum_{jhk} \hat{W}_j^{ghw} e^{-\beta^{gw} c_{ij}^k} \tag{7.31}$$

to ensure that

$$\sum_{jhk} S_{ij}^{ghwk} = e_i^{gw} P_i^w \tag{7.32}$$

The definitions of the variables and parameters are mostly obvious extensions of those in the aggregate model. The more complex concept in this context is the attractiveness term $\hat{W}_j^{ghw}$. The ^ has been added so that it can be made a function of the facility size variables W_j^g, and to distinguish it from those variables. New elements of interdependence arise in relation to this term. It will typically, for example, depend on $W_j^{g'}$'s for g' ≠ g. For example, it will be an advantage to a g-outlet if other g''s are available nearby for multi-purpose trips, and the benefits of this to consumers need to be represented in the attractiveness function. The next step is to see what form this function could take. One suggestion, to fix ideas, is taken from Wilson (1982):

$$W_j^{ghw} = (\sum_{j,g'>g} W_j^{g'h})^{\alpha_1^w} (W_j^{gh})^{\alpha_2^w} e^{-\gamma^w p_j^k} \tag{7.33}$$

where W_j^{gh} is the floorspace devoted to selling (or supplying) good (or service) g in our h-type facility at j.

The first factor on the right hand side of (7.33), $(\sum_{h,g'>g} W_j^{g'h})^{\alpha_1^w}$ represents the availability of the same or higher order goods. (It is reported in Clarke and Wilson, 1985, that sensible results are a consequence of this assumption, while if the 'other' goods are restricted to higher orders only, then the spatial structure of the top order dominates the spatial pattern at all lower levels.) The range of the summation is not entirely clear and is not intended to be algebraic: the details would have to be worked out in relation to g and h definitions in particular circumstances.

The second factor, $(W_j^{gh})^{\alpha_2^w}$ simply represents availability of floorspace for g in h at j. Each of these factors is raised to a power which may vary with person type group (which will probably be 'income group'). Thus α_1^w and α_2^w between them do the job of α in the aggregate model - though it is α_2^w which still has to exceed 1 for bifurcation effects to occur - see Wilson (1981-A). The third factor is common to all (g,w) combinations at j: p_j^k is the terminal cost for mode k at j. It might be a parking charge for car users or an (average) additional walking time for public transport users. $e^{-\gamma^w p_j^k}$ therefore measures the effect of these, the intensity of which is also taken as a function of income through the γ^w parameter. It is obviously a straightforward matter to add further factors to this kind of attractiveness function if necessary.

The rest of the argument can proceed as for the aggregate model. We sketch briefly, in turn, the use of the model in generating equilibrium patterns, the analysis of stability via differential or difference equations and the possibility of modelling a disaggregated system which is not in equilibrium. There is one further preliminary though: that is to disaggregate supply side costs. In the aggregate case, we assumed that costs could be represented by $k_j W_j$ with k_j as a unit cost, and the unit as floorspace. It is potentially more effective to distinguish, as inputs to facility supply, at least land, floorspace, labour and capital. Let x_k^{gh} be the kth such component of cost for the g-part of an h-facility. Then let γ_{jk}^{gh} be the corresponding unit cost at j - to allow for spatial variation. To fix ideas, take the set of definitions in Table 7.1.

These definitions form the basis for greater realism but create an immediate difficulty. In the aggregate case, the equilibrium conditions and dynamical analyses were carried out in terms of floorspace, W_j. The corresponding term here, W_j^{gh}, is now simply one among a number and so we appear to need a set of equations for each. And yet we know that the quantities of various inputs will be related through a production function. This allows us to have realism but to revert to one set of variables measuring 'size'. This can be done by defining y_j^{gh} to be the *level of activity* of (g,h) in j and then to assume that each input is a function of this. Formally

$$x_{jk}^{gh} = x_{jk}^{gh}(y_j^{gh}) \tag{7.34}$$

where we have now added a j-subscript to the input term. Total supply side cost is now

$$C_j^{gh} = \sum_k \gamma_{jk}^{gh}(x_{jk}^{gh})x_{jk}^{gh}(y_j^{gh}) \tag{7.35}$$

where we have also shown the unit costs γ_{jk}^{gh} to be functions of x_{jk}^{gh} to allow for scale economies or diseconomies; and, of course, through (7.34), these unit costs are functions of activity levels*.

We are now in a position to state for the disaggregated model the equations which provided the foundations of our

---

* Of course, we should also consider as a research task the development of a more general model in which the unit costs were functions of other activity levels and costs - eg. the land rent components which will be partly determined by the competition for land for different uses.

analysis for the aggregate model. The revenue equation is

$$D_j^{gh} = \sum_{iwk} S_{ij}^{ghwk} \tag{7.36}$$

The differential equations (or corresponding difference equations) can be written in terms of the activity level variables as

$$\dot{y}_j^{gh} = \varepsilon^{gh}\left[D_j^{gh} - \sum_k \gamma_{jk}^{gh}(x_{jk}^{gh})x_{jk}^{gh}(y_{jk}^{gh})\right] \tag{7.37}$$

with equilibrium conditions

$$D_j^{gh} = C_j^{gh} = \sum_k \gamma_{jk}^{gh}\left[x_{jk}^{gh}(y_j^{gh})\right]x_{jk}^{gh}(y_j^{gh}) \tag{7.38}$$

These equations are a rich basis for the study of equilibrium patterns and modes of evolution of service systems. It is not now as straightforward to apply the Harris and Wilson (1978) kind of analysis because there are new (and as yet unspecified) nonlinear functions, particularly on the supply side. What we can be sure of, however, is that any results will be rich in bifurcation phenomena, since the only conditions for these to occur are the presence of nonlinearities and interdependencies which are represented here in abundance.

It is intuitively clear that this system can generate a great variety of patterns. The detailed possibilities need to be worked out through numerical experiments and empirical work. Four observations about possible phenomena, however, will be a useful conclusion to this section. First, one kind of result from the aggregate model will carry over. If α_2^{ghw} and β^{gw} are, respectively larger or smaller, then there will be a smaller number of larger (g,h) facilities. Secondly, the larger α_1^w, the greater will be the consumer-drive to spatial agglomeration. Thirdly, notwithstanding the previous point, if some unit costs are very cheap, say at some ex-urban location, then a larger (isolated) g-h facility may develop at such locations. Fourthly, if the unit costs include elements representing scale and agglomeration economies, then there will be a supply-side drive towards spatial agglomeration. The evident pattern in many city regions at the present time is a mixture of all these kinds of phenomena and it should be possible to use a model of this kind to represent them all, and their inter-dependencies, simultaneously.

It is necessary to conclude this section on a note of caution. Although the disaggregated models presented are very rich, it would be very difficult to handle them in practice with so many indices. The transport model superscript k is not usually used; to some extent, in a service model, its effects are picked up by the w-index and the β^w parameter. It may also be possible in some cases to drop the w-disaggregation and to rely on the spatial variation of $\{e_i\}$ to build a certain amount of social structure into the model - e_i representing greater expenditure from 'richer' areas when appropriate. It may also be difficult to persist with the (g,h) categorisation. The alternatives are to use goods, g, irrespective of the type of outlet; or to form a composite index, say g again, from both g and h categories. Typically, therefore, the array to be used would be $\{S_{ij}^g\}$ or $\{S_{ij}^{gw}\}$; and it is straightforward to make the appropriate adjustments to the argument presented above.

7.3.4.5 Other service sector approaches: the location-allocation models

There is an extensive class of models known as location-allocation models at least some of which need to be included in the modellers' repertoire. These have been seen as mainly applicable to the *location* of public facilities and the *allocation* of users to these facilities. The allocation mechanism usually took the simple form of using the *nearest* facility. The objective, therefore, in a location-allocation model is to minimise supplier's costs and at the same time to minimise user's travel time. There is a trade-off involved here - the *efficiency-equity* problem. The supplier's tendency is to locate a smaller number of larger facilities at the cheapest (for the supplier) of locations; the user 'needs' a larger number of dispersed facilities to reduce travel costs.

Relatively recently (and for an excellent review, see Leonardi, 1981-B) the framework of location-allocation modelling has been expanded, particularly to include user behaviour which is represented by a spatial interaction submodel to replace the hypothesis of travel to the nearest centre. This is particularly appropriate for what Leonardi calls *user-attracting systems*, where the user determines the allocation, as distinct from *delivery systems* where the public authority determines the allocation. A good example of the latter is the delivery of emergency services such as fire, ambulance and so on. To complicate matters, some services - such as education or health - are often mixed: some user choice but some public authority allocation.

In the most general terms, a location-allocation model can be formulated as follows:

$$\max_{\{\text{location, allocation}\}} Z = \lambda(\text{user benefits}) - (\text{supplier costs}) \quad (7.39)$$

subject to

$$\text{constraints} = 0 \quad (7.40)$$

Leonardi's argument is that user benefits are often not measured in money terms and so need to be weighted by a parameter like λ. λ can also be taken to reflect the relative importance of user benefits and suppliers' costs in the overall optimisation. If λ is large, the former dominate; and vice versa. The constraints specify, implicitly, other elements of models of supplier and user behaviour.

The objective function (7.39) can be written, without loss of generality, as

$$\underset{\{\text{locations} \atop \text{allocations}\}}{\text{Max}} \quad Z = (\text{user benefits}) - \frac{1}{\lambda}\,(\text{suppliers' costs}) \tag{7.41}$$

Leonardi then makes the suggestion that suppliers will not usually be minimising costs as such but spending for greatest efficiency up to some budget constraint B. $1/\lambda$ can then be considered as a Lagrangian multiplier and the problem reformulated as

$$\underset{\{\text{locations,} \atop \text{allocations}\}}{\text{Max}} \quad Z = \text{user benefits} \tag{7.42}$$

subject to

$$\text{constraints} = 0 \tag{7.43}$$

$$\text{suppliers' costs} < B. \tag{7.44}$$

We henceforth consider models only of the form (7.42) - (7.44). There is a rich variety of such models. It is worth beginning a survey of some of these by observing that the retail model considered earlier in this section can be fitted into such a framework. For a convenient comparison, let us take the aggregate model which can be written in the form

$$\underset{\{S_{ij}, W_j\}}{\text{Max}} \; Z = -\sum_{ij} S_{ij} \log S_{ij} + \sum_{ij} S_{ij}\left(\frac{\alpha}{\beta} \log W_j - c_{ij}\right) \tag{7.45}$$

subject to

$$\sum_j S_{ij} = e_i P_i \quad (7.46)$$

$$\sum_j W_j = W \quad (7.47)$$

Leonardi notes that the objective function (7.45), following Neuburger (1971-A), can be taken as a measure of consumers' surplus and so constitutes user benefits. Alternatively, as we saw, $\alpha/\beta \log W_j$ can be taken as unit 'size' benefits and c_{ij}, of course, as travel costs. The entropy term, $-\sum_{ij} S_{ij} \log S_{ij}$, can then be considered as added to represent dispersion and to ensure that user behaviour is described by a spatial interaction model. (7.46) is then a constraint saying the demand should be satisfied while (7.47) can now be seen as equivalent to the budget constraint with the same unit costs at each location.

We can use this as a framework to see how this model differs from some of the more usual location-allocation models. We begin with two general observations and then look at some examples. First, the location-allocation models in the literature seem, from the user benefit side, always to concern themselves with minimising travel costs and do not include a size benefit term. This is perfectly appropriate, of course, for some types of facility, but not for others. Secondly, if it is assumed that the costs of supplying facilities at j include a fixed element, say b_j in $a_j W_j + b_j$, then this introduces a combinatorial element into the problem and makes it considerably more difficult as we will see - and yet it is obviously realistic in some instances and so has to be coped with. We should perhaps also remark that it is possible to formulate the location side of the problem in continuous space (as in the classic Weber triangle problem in industrial location which can be seen as a special case of this general formulation). However, here we will stick to the discrete zone formulation which is mathematically more convenient and which is always adequate provided there is a sufficiently fine-scale zone system for possible facility locations. We can now proceed to review some examples.

The main alternative to (7.45) - (7.47) can be written

$$\underset{\{S_{ij},W_j\}}{\text{Max}} \; Z = -\frac{\alpha}{\beta}\sum_{ij} S_{ij} \log S_{ij} - \sum_{ij} S_{ij} c_{ij} \tag{7.48}$$

subject to

$$\sum_j S_{ij} = e_i P_i \tag{7.49}$$

$$\sum_j S_{ij} < W_j \tag{7.50}$$

$$\sum_j a_j W_j < B \tag{7.51}$$

$$W_j > 0 \tag{7.52}$$

In this case, as noted earlier, there are no size benefits in the objective function and the locational costs, a_j, vary with j. Also (7.50) is imposed on a capacity restraint.

The W_j-optimality condition for the problem (7.45) - (7.47) can be written

$$W_j = k\sum_i S_{ij} \tag{7.53}$$

for suitable k. This means as Leonardi notes, that capacity (W_j) is allocated in proportion to demand, ($\sum_i S_{ij}$). This will continue to be so - that is, there will be proportionate changes to all W_j's - if W, the 'budget' in this problem, is reduced. In the alternative model, (7.48) - (7.52), however, if B is reduced, there will be a tendency to concentrate facilities where a_j's are cheaper and the resulting pattern could be quite different.

In the alternative model given above, there were no fixed

costs and so no combinatorial selection problem. If the supply costs are $a_jW_j + b_j$, then the problem must be rewritten in the following way with L as the set of facility locations (a subset of all j's) to be selected as part of the optimisation problem:

$$\underset{\{S_{ij},W_j,L\}}{\text{Max}} \quad Z = -\frac{\alpha}{\beta} \sum_{ij\varepsilon L} S_{ij} \log S_{ij} - \sum_{ij\varepsilon L} S_{ij}c_{ij} \tag{7.54}$$

subject to

$$\sum_{j\varepsilon L} S_{ij} = e_iP_i \tag{7.55}$$

$$\sum_i S_{ij} < W_j \tag{7.56}$$

$$\sum_{j\varepsilon L} (a_jW_j + b_j) < B \tag{7.57}$$

Finally, note that if we let $\beta \to \infty$, the entropy term is knocked out of the objective function. This has the effect of sending users to the nearest centre and so is suitable for delivery systems. This programme can be written

$$\underset{\{S_{ij},W_j,L\}}{\text{Max}} \quad Z = - \sum_{ij\varepsilon L} S_{ij}c_{ij} \tag{7.58}$$

subject to the constraints (7.55) - (7.57).

7.3.5 Residential location and housing

7.3.5.1 Introduction: a historical review

In one sense, residential location and housing models have similar structures to the retail use and supply models of the previous section. In each case, consumers choose facilities (houses, shops) in relation to access from a fixed point (jobs, residences) and suppliers meet demand making normal profits. In the residential case however, disaggregation is vital:

different types of households seek different types of houses in different locations, and suppliers respond to these patterns of demand. However, the similarities are close enough that a briefer treatment can be offered of residential location and housing models. In this introductory subsection, we sketch the history of the development of these models, mainly restricting ourselves to those built on spatial-interaction model principles or which are related in some way.

The starting point is the kind of aggregate model used by Lowry (1964). This allocated workers to residential areas around jobs purely on a gravity-like 'distance' basis - in effect using an unconstrained spatial interaction model with a unit (i.e. no) attractiveness factor. Wilson (1969-A) showed how, formally, to represent such aggregate models in singly-constrained form with an attractiveness factor, and also how to extend this to hybrid forms - partially singly-constrained and partially doubly-constrained, the residential end constraints in the latter occurring when there was an upper bound fixed as a matter of planning policy.

All this becomes more interesting when the model is disaggregated (Wilson, 1970-B). An array $\{T_{ij}^{kw}\}$ is computed where T_{ij}^{kw} is the number of type-w residents of zone i in type-k housing who work in zone j. w is usually taken as income group, and in this formulation, the income is seen as being derived from the job. There is an implicit assumption of one worker per household, but this can be relaxed without any difficulty. The full theoretical and empirical development of this model is described in Senior and Wilson (1974-A).

All of this spatial interaction model work was preceded by an economic analysis of residential location culminating in the work of Alonso (1960, 1964-A). These were continuous-space models typical of what was later seen as a precursor of the 'new urban economics' school of modelling (Richardson, 1977-B) but there was one productive discrete zone representation of it: the Herbert and Stevens (1960) model. This assumes that preferences for housing can be represented in the form of bid rents (less journey to work costs) which are then maximised subject to constraints on availability of housing stock and land availability. The outcomes - the allocation of people to stock - are determined by a linear programme. It was then shown that the Herbert-Stevens model is a special case of the disaggregated spatial interaction model (Senior and Wilson, 1974-A). This uses the principle mentioned earlier through which an entropy term can be used to create 'dispersion' within certain kinds of economic model. In the residential location case, this explained why the spatial interaction model was more effective in empirical work but conversely suggested that different forms of attractiveness function could be used. Some of these ideas are introduced in the disaggregated model which is presented below.

Most of the models mentioned above are concerned with residential allocation of households to a given housing stock; or they make simple assumptions, as in the Lowry model, that supply of housing follows demand. An exception was the Bay Area simulation model described by Robinson, Wolfe and Barringer (1965). Housing was represented explicitly in their model and 'aged'. They then estimated how much different kinds of people would be prepared to pay for different kinds of housing and then new housing supply was that which produced the highest yield for developers. There was relatively little spatial detail in their model, however, and such methods have not been pursued much since until the more recent micro-simulation models of Clarke, Keys and Williams (1981).

7.3.5.2 A general disaggregated model

We have to decide at the outset whether a disaggregated model should be unconstrained, singly-constrained or doubly-constrained. Since we are going to combine it with a supply-side model, there is no case for the last of these. There is a case for an unconstrained model which would remove the usual explicit dependence on the relationship to workplaces. This would take the form

$$T_{ij}^{kw} = \frac{TW_{ij}^{kw}}{\sum\limits_{ikw} W_{ij}^{kw}} \tag{7.59}$$

where T is the total number of people to be allocated and $\{W_{ij}^{kw}\}$ is an array of suitable attractiveness factors. The corresponding singly-constrained model is

$$T_{ij}^{kw} = B_j^w W_{ij}^{kw} E_j^w \tag{7.60}$$

where

$$B_j^w = 1/\sum_{ik} W_{ij}^{kw} \tag{7.61}$$

to ensure that

$$\sum_{ik} T_{ij}^{kw} = E_j^w \tag{7.62}$$

In this case, E_j^w is the number of type w jobs at j and $\{W_{ij}^{kw}\}$ the array of attractiveness factors. The usual travel impedance term will be considered to be part of the W_{ij}^{kw} terms, and this is one of the reasons why a j-subscript has been added, making this version different in that respect from the usual singly-constrained model, though the account can easily be modified to accommodate the unconstrained version*.

The major task ahead is the specification of the attractiveness factors W_{ij}^{kw}. We can write a typical one formally as a mixture of general (as-yet-unspecified) terms and specific factors which have proved useful in earlier versions of disaggregated models.

* We proceed below with the simply-constrained model.

Thus:

$$W_{ij}^{kw} = (X_{1i}^{k})^{\alpha_1^w}(X_{2i}^{k})^{\alpha_2^w} \ldots H_i^k E^{-\beta^w c_{ij}} \times e^{-\mu^w\left[p_i^k - q^w(I^w - c'_{ij})^{\alpha}\right]^2} \tag{7.63}$$

Housing supply $\{H_i^k\}$ is explicitly represented as is the travel impedance term, $e^{-\beta^w c_{ij}}$. The last factor appeared in the first disaggregated model (Wilson, 1970-B) to match housing expenditure and house price for particular household types (w-income groups). p_i^k is the price of a type k house in i; q^w, the average proportion of income spent on housing by a type-w household *after* journey-to-work money costs (c'_{ij} - a component of generalised costs, c_{ij}) have been deducted. $X_{\ell i}^k$ is then the ℓth component of other factors within the overall attractiveness term. X_{1i}^k, for example, might represent accessibility to retail facilities; X_{2i}^{kw}, affinity (or disaffinity) to live in the same zone as other social groups - and, n.b., a w superscript has to be added here; and so on. A very 'rich' model can be developed.

The only modification for the unconstrained model would involve taking one of the $X_{\ell i}^k$ terms to represent 'accessibility to jobs'.

7.3.5.3 Dynamics and planning

We begin by noting that the residential location model can be used in a straightforward way for planning purposes in exactly the same way as the service model. That is, a trial array, $\{H_i^k\}$, forming a plan could be input to the model and households would then be allocated to the housing stock. Various indicators could be developed to measure the advantages or disadvantages of a particular plan. The way this was done would depend to an extent on the way the w- and k-groups were defined, particularly the latter. For example, k could itself be a list which included size, quality and tenure group.

It is also possible, however, to apply the argument about methods for dynamical analysis to housing, though it turns out to be somewhat more complicated than the services' case for two reasons: first, there is 'inertia' in the housing stock - it is not likely to be run down or demolished as rapidly as unprofitable retail facilities might be; and secondly, housing consumes land on a much bigger scale than service facilities. The first of these complications means that there are two kinds of bifurcations to worry about: first, the social mixes of population occupying certain types of stock in certain places; secondly, and more analogously to the service case, jumps in the provision of housing stock itself*. The second complication means that ideally, a land-use accounting mechanism has to be built into the dynamic model and we outline one way (of many possible ways) of doing this.

We start by developing a costs model for housing development. Suppose there are two kinds of costs - for building, $\gamma^{(1)k}$ - which can be assumed independent of i, and for land, $\rho_i^k\gamma_i^{(2)}$, where ρ_i^k is the average plot size of a type k house in i and $\gamma_i^{(2)}$ is the unit cost of land. The latter can be assumed to be independent of k because unit costs will be equalised across different uses by the workings of the land market. Thus, if C_i^k is the total cost of a type k house in i, then

$$C_i^k = (\gamma^{(1)k} + \rho^k\gamma_i^{(2)})H_i^k \tag{7.64}$$

Total revenue (assuming all costs and revenues can be put on the same, say annual, basis), is

$$D_i^k = \sum_{jw} T_{ij}^{kw} p_i^k \tag{7.65}$$

---

* These can be seen as fast dynamics and slow dynamics respectively.

and thus the equilibrium condition is

$$D_i^k = C_i^k \tag{7.66}$$

We need to specify explicitly a land-use accounting mechanism, and we do this here through the land price $\gamma_i^{(2)}$. Let L_i^{res} be the total land area in zone i available for housing, then, approximately because ρ_i^k is an average

$$L_{it}^{newres} = L_i^{res} - \sum_i \rho_i^k H_{it}^k \tag{7.67}$$

will be the amount of land available for new development after time t. We can then make $\gamma_i^{(2)}$ a function of this (among other things, like accessibility) land availability:

$$\gamma_{it}^2 = \gamma_{it}^2 (L_{it}^{newres}, \ldots) \tag{7.68}$$

and we can specify the shape of this function so that the price shoots up rapidly when L_{it}^{newres} becomes small. We can then take H_i^k as the set of variables which form the basis of dynamical equations, and the above argument suggests that we should work with difference equations. The analogue of (7.19) becomes

$$H_{it+1}^k - H_{it}^k = \varepsilon \left[D_{it}^k p_i^k - (\gamma^{(1)k} + \rho^k \gamma_{it}^{(2)} (L_{it}^{newres} H_{it}^k)) \right] \times H_{it}^k \tag{7.69}$$

or

$$H_{it+1}^k = (1+\varepsilon D_{it}^k p_i^k) H_{it}^k - \varepsilon (\gamma^{(1)k} + \rho^k \gamma_{it}^{(1)} (L_{it}^{newres})) H_{it}^{k2} \tag{7.70}$$

with the additionally imposed condition to represent inertia that

$$H^k_{it+1} > H^k_{it} \tag{7.71}$$

One of the residential location models - (7.59) or (7.60) - with a time subscript added and with D^k_i calculated from (7.65) can then be coupled with (7.70) - (7.71) to provide a rich and interesting dynamic model.

In this model, the prices p^k_i are assumed to be given exogenously. A possible development is to model these as a function of, say, house size, residential density, proportions of people in different w-classes, and so on. Then, as the population grew (or declined) and the pattern of allocation to the existing stock changed, then this could be reflected in corresponding p^k_i - price changes. This would increase the 'richness' of the model still further.

This model could be used by planners to predict the stability of, and likely changes of direction in, any particular given situation; and for predicting the likely modes of evolution of the system. It is more likely, however, that some of the variables are more directly controllable, particularly if k included a tenure subdivision and one tenure group represented public sector housing. Land-use zoning regulations could then be interpreted as controlling L^{newres}_i directly, and such constraints could easily be incorporated into the model directly. Or, direct controls could be imposed on some of the H^k_i's - either as demolitions (slum clearance) or as public sector building. As in the retail case, adjustments could also be sought which took into account the fact that some parameters were near to critical values.

7.3.6 Industrial location

7.3.6.1 Introduction

We have considered the service and residential sectors before the industrial sector because they are probably intrinsically simpler. In those cases, it is possible to use statistical averaging methods of some kind or other to represent the behaviour of consumers or house-occupiers; but even there, we had to turn to new methods of dynamical systems theory to represent the supply side. This turns out to give us the clue for making progress with industrial location submodels, but there are new difficulties because of the greater complexities involved. This means that it is difficult, in this case, to offer operational models - more a glimpse of a research frontier.

For urban modelling purposes, we need a comprehensive approach and much traditional theory is of little help in this respect. Weber, for example, shows how a single firm would locate given a known pattern of inputs and outputs (and the locations of all these). Since, in a real problem, many of the input and output sources will be other firms, and we need to know their behaviour too, this is not helpful. Other approaches have focused on the identification of market areas of firms at *given* locations, but again this is not what we are looking for (cf Palander, 1935, Hoover, 1937, Christaller, 1933, Lösch, 1940). A third approach involves modelling competition directly, building on Hotelling's (1929) famous 'ice-cream man on a linear beach' example (cf Williams and Senior, 1977-B, Eaton and Lipsey, 1975). This could be considered to culminate in game-theoretic approaches, as in Isard et al (1969). The problem with all these approaches is that they involve relatively small numbers of firms and so, again, do not provide the basis for comprehensive modelling.

Further progress in building a comprehensive industrial location model involves three steps: first, a systematic identification of all the factors involved with associated theories of behaviour; secondly, an adequate method for representing these, which copes with aggregation and incorporates an explicit representation of spatial structure; and thirdly, the deployment of suitable methods for model building - which turn out to be mathematical programming (for static models) and dynamical systems theory. We discuss these topics in turn in three subsections: first on the system and its representation (7.3.6.2); secondly on mathematical programming models (7.3.6.3) and thirdly, on dynamic models (7.3.6.4). Some concluding comments, including comparisons with a traditional spatial interaction approach, are made in the final subsection (7.3.6.5).

7.3.6.2 The elements of industrial systems

The main elements are firms (or other such organisations) and their linkages - their inputs and outputs. We begin, therefore, by listing typical inputs and outputs for each firm but noting that we will be able to aggregate firms of the same type in each of a system of spatial zones and the concepts developed for firms by location can then be applied to sectors by zone.

The main inputs are: (a) raw materials; (b) utilities; (c) government services; (d) goods and services from other firms; (e) transport services; (f) labour; (g) capital; and (h) land. The main outputs are: (a) goods and services to markets; (b) non-marketable products, like trained skilled-labour. A key element in the description of the processes will be the *production function* of a firm, which will show what can be produced for any combination of inputs. We will also set about calculating the total costs of, and revenues deriving from, a particular location, and then we can take profit maximisation (or whatever) as the basis of a location theory.

We can now be more specific about the way this subsystem can be described. Let r, s, v be used to label firms, m and g types of raw materials or goods or services; i and j locations. We are assuming implicitly, as usual, here a discrete zoning system. Then the inputs of a firm s can be taken as the array $\{x_{ij}^{rsm}\}$, where x_{ij}^{rsm} is the flow of inputs of type m from r in i to s in j. The outputs can similarly be characterised by y_{jk}^{svg}, the flows of goods or services, g, from s in j to v in k. Assumptions have to be made about prices and transport costs[‡]. If we assume that all pricing is fob (freight on board) and that purchasers pay transport costs, then the unit costs of m-inputs at j from i can be taken as $p_i^m + c_{ij}^m$, where p_i^m is the unit fob price at i and c_{ij}^m is the unit (i,j) - transport cost for m (which may be taken as a transport rate multiplied by distance). Then total input costs for firm s at j are

$$C_j^s = \sum_{irm} x_{ij}^{rsm}(p_i^m + c_{ij}^m) \tag{7.72}$$

and total revenue is

$$D_j^s = \sum_{vkg} y_{jk}^{svg} p_j^g \tag{7.73}$$

If we use an asterisk replacing an index to denote summation, then the *production function* of s at j is

$$y_{j*}^{s*g}(\{x_{*j}^{*sm}\}) \tag{7.74}$$

shown here as a function of all its inputs. Note that throughout these definitions, m should range over all the inputs linked earlier, including labour and capital for example.

We can now proceed in two stages: first, an examination

---

‡ Again, for present purposes, we assume the main prices to be given exogenously; but we note that a future research task is to integrate this approach with others, such as the modelling of inter-regional trade, within which more of the prices become endogenous.

of a static mathematical programming model (7.3.6.3) and secondly, we look at dynamic models (7.3.6.4).

7.3.6.3 Mathematical programming approaches

Suppose now r, s, v ... are sectors in zones, i, j, k ... . Then the natural way to seek to build a comprehensive model of structure at a particular time is by mathematical programming. For example, if we wished to maximise overall profits, the programme would be

$$\max_{\{x_{ij}^{rsm}, y_{jk}^{svg}\}} Z = \sum_{js} (D_j^s - C_j^s) \tag{7.75}$$

with C_j^s and D_j^s given in (7.72) and (7.73) respectively. It will usually be appropriate to specify constraints on the $\underline{x}$ and $\underline{y}$ arrays. There are many different ways in which this can be done, and a correspondingly great variety of models can be generated. One example, which can be recast in this format, is the model of Paelink and Nijkamp (1975) who were in turn building on work of Beckmann and Marshak (1955). It is also possible to combine these with input-output analysis. There is one thread of work here which began with the paper by Cripps, Macgill and Wilson (1974) which has been taken considerably further by Macgill (1977-A, 1977-B).

None of these models, however, is effectively operational and so their design for an urban model package remains a matter for further research. It may well be that, for the present, the kinds of assumptions used in the past about 'basic employment being given' have to be continued - though possibly refined with insights to be gained from the kinds of models described here and, more especially, in the next subsection to which we now proceed.

7.3.6.4 Dynamic models

The general arrays $\{x_{ij}^{rsm}\}$ and $\{y_{jk}^{svg}\}$ and the cost and revenue equations (7.72) and (7.73), provide the basis for building a dynamic model. The key set of variables to attempt to predict in a dynamic model is the array $\{y_{j*}^{s*g}\}$ where an asterisk replacing an index denotes summation. Since this is disaggregated to g, we can do the same for costs and revenues:

$$C_j^{sg} = \sum_{irm} \hat{a}^{mg} x_{ij}^{rsm}(p_i^m + c_{ij}^m) \tag{7.76}$$

where $\hat{a}^{mg}$ is the amount of m used in the production of g in s at j and

$$D_j^{sg} = \sum_{vk} y_{jk}^{srg} p_j^g \tag{7.77}$$

Suppose now we separate the spatial interaction elements from those representing production as such. Let q_{ij}^{rsm} be the proportion of m-materials used by s in j which came from r in i; let $\hat{q}_{jk}^{svg}$ be the corresponding set of proportions which connect g produced in s at j to markets v at k. Then

$$x_{ij}^{rsm} = q_{ij}^{rsm}.a^{mg}.y_{j*}^{s*g} \tag{7.78}$$

where a^{mg} is the amount of m needed to produce a unit of g (and is thus more like a standard input-output coefficient, which $\hat{a}^{mg}$, defined earlier, is not) and

$$y_{jk}^{svg} = y_{j*}^{s*g}.\hat{q}_{jk}^{svg} \tag{7.79}$$

The arrays $\underline{q}$ and $\hat{\underline{q}}$ can be estimated using usual spatial interaction model principles. The cost and revenue equations can now be rewritten as

$$C_j^{sg} = \sum_{irm} q_{ij}^{rsm} a^{mg} y_{j*}^{s*g} \tag{7.80}$$

and

$$D_j^{sg} = \sum_{vk} y_{j*}^{s*g} \hat{q}_{jk}^{svg} \tag{7.81}$$

A now-standard line of reasoning on the construction of dynamic models suggests the following differential equations (or corresponding difference equations):

$$\dot{y}_{j*}^{s*g} = \varepsilon^{sg}(D_j^{sg} - C_j^{sg}) \tag{7.82}$$

which can be written explicitly, using (7.80) and (7.81) as

$$\dot{y}_{j*}^{s*g} = \varepsilon^{sg}\left(\sum_{vk} \hat{q}_{jk}^{svg} - \sum_{irm} q_{ij}^{rms} a^{mg}\right) y_{j*}^{s*g} \tag{7.83}$$

where we take y_{j*}^{s*g} out on the right hand side as a common factor.

The interest will now follow with the detailed specification of q_{jk}^{srg} and $\hat{q}_{ij}^{rsm}$. Also, nonlinearities could be introduced into (7.78) and (7.83) by making the a^{mg}'s function of activity levels for example to incorporate economies of scale. There will also be a high level of interdependence because of the way the $\hat{\underline{q}}$ and $\underline{q}$ arrays will represent the competition of firms in different sectors both for raw materials and other inputs (such as labour - which is to be taken as one of the r's which will be related to residential areas at the j-end). The interest will arise from specifying the detailed difference of inputs, outputs and production functions. Most of this remains a research task yet to be carried out.

It is also worth emphasising that we found in the case of retail location, and are currently finding in the case of residential location and housing, that it is only through numerical experimentation (and ultimately realistic empirical work) that a good understanding of the range of forms which can be generated by the models can be achieved. Our work with industrial location has not yet reached this stage. This is the next step, therefore. It is necessary to define sectors and a spatial level of resolution which reflects the decentralisation processes which have been occurring and the inter-regional (ultimately multinational) economies in which these processes are embedded. We can then investigate the extent to which the models as represented above can reproduce the kinds of patterns and changing structures which are observable.

Once this stage has been reached, then further research questions will have to be considered. Are the scale-economies mechanism and the fob transport costs mechanism adequate to reproduce agglomeration? We will also need to consider the problem of changing technologies and substitution and the way these are represented in the input-output coefficients. The latter is particularly difficult to handle (for example when services bought externally are internalised, or vice versa).

7.3.6.5 Concluding comments

We have seen that, in principle, models of industrial location systems can be built using the same kinds of ideas as used for retail supply (cf Section 7.3.4). However, the greater complexities of the industrial system means that effective operational models have not yet been developed and it was suggested earlier that it may be better in the short run to specify industrial location (and rents) exogenously. Some authors, however, have sought simpler modelling methods. For example Putman and Ducca (1978-C) use a model of the following form:

$$E_{jt+1} = \lambda \sum_i P_i \frac{W_j f(c_{ij})}{\sum_k W_k f(c_{ik})} + (1 - \lambda) E_{jt} \qquad (7.84)$$

λ is a parameter. If λ is near to zero, then E_{jt+1} is dominated by E_{jt}. It is modified by what is, in effect, a spatial interaction term of the type used in the retail model. Interestingly this model can be written in the form

$$E_{jt+1} - E_{jt} = \lambda\left[\sum_i P_i \frac{W_j f(c_{ij})}{\sum_k W_k f(c_{ik})} - E_{jt}\right] \quad (7.85)$$

which is rather like the retail model equation (7.19) with the parameter λ playing the role of ε in the retail model. There will thus be a critical value of λ above which divergence or oscillation could set in.

On the whole, however, we have to await the results of further research in this field.

7.3.7 Transport

7.3.7.1 Introduction: transport models in a broad planning context

There has always been a potential problem in relating transport models to spatial-interaction-based location models. The latter, as we have seen in the preceding sections, do produce estimates of trips for different purposes from each zone to any other zone: service trips and, in the residential location model, the journey to work. Yet for transport planning purposes, these estimates have usually not been regarded as good enough. More accurate predictions can be made with specially-designed transport models. In this section, we describe the latter, but we begin in this introduction by discussing the relationship between the different kinds of models.

In an ideal world, the predictions made of the journey to work in a residential location model and in a transport model would be the same. In fact, the focus of each model is somewhat different. The aim of the transport modeller is to predict flows on links, and to reflect congestion, accurately. The residential location modeller is using the interaction element as one among many (the others being terms representing housing quality, social class of neighbours, and so on) to incorporate a relatively rough notion of accessibility to work (and indeed to services) in the model. He is happy to accept approximations like 'one worker per household' which would not be good enough in a transport model. The transport modeller is aiming, therefore, to produce an accurate picture of trip patterns at an instant in time; the location modeller to incorporate rougher measures of accessibility. In the latter case, a crucial array in the models is that of transport generalised costs, $\{c_{ij}\}$. We will say more later about the constitution of these. But this represents perhaps the main link between the two sets of models. If $\{c_{ij}\}$ is obtained in the transport model, then it should include decent estimates of the weightings of different components and a good representation of congestion. All this will be important in location models.

Another element of the difference between the two approaches is the time-scale of users' response to change (cf networks, nodal levels of service) in a transport system is likely to be rapid; locational structures change more slowly. This is another reason why the models can reasonably be different in relation to what they produce: again, we observe that the transport model is an instantaneous picture while the interaction parts of a locational model can be seen more as representing an average over a period of time.

The users of the different models have very different objectives and a review of these takes us very near to one of the main goals of this paper: the exploration of the relationship between transport provision and land use. Transport facilities consist of modal networks and service facilities on them - the latter being the planning of routes and frequencies on the public part of the system. There are complications because one of the public systems - buses - shares the road system with the private car and interacts through congestion levels (although this interaction can be minimised - with other consequences - through the use of bus-only lanes as one of the design options). The transport planner, therefore, is concerned with the design of these networks and service levels. The objectives of such a process were originally taken to be mainly concerned with the relief of congestion - and this remains a priority in many engineer-based transport planning organisations. This can be achieved, in transport policy terms either by the building of new roads or by diverting some car traffic to public transport either by imposing penalties on car users (say through parking charges) or by improving public transport service levels. A prime objective of a transport planner, therefore, is to use models to predict the extent to which congestion is relieved by a new 'plan' of some kind.

Such traditional attitudes beg a number of questions. Is 'relief of congestion' the best measure? Is the most effective method for relieving congestion through the instruments of *transport* policy? An obvious alternative is the rearrangement of land uses in some better way. There have been a number of responses to these questions. First, economists have attempted to improve the measurement of the benefits of transport changes through the idea of consumers' surplus, an important element of which is made up of savings in travellers' time. These measures can be incorporated in the full framework of cost-benefit analysis. But this still takes, implicitly, transport as the prime good. If we assume that transport is a secondary good whose purpose is to allow the consumer to undertake other activities, then the prime focus should become those other activities - and these constitute the subject matter of location models. It may then be that measures of 'accessibility provision' for different groups, are more powerful than either congestion relief or even, in its present form, consumers' surplus.

A major conclusion of this analysis is that transport planning and locational-structure planning should be carried out simultaneously. Congestion, which can only be effectively calculated in a detailed transport model, will be an important element, through the c_{ij}'s, in locational models*. The arrangement of land uses will in any case affect congestion levels. And most importantly of all, the design of transport facilities *together with* land use structures should be related to the prime objective of maximising people's choice of their activities - maximising various accessibilities. This is far from straightforward. An important question, for example, is: how are different components of accessibility to be weighted relative to each other?

With these preliminary remarks, we can now proceed to an account of the structure of typical transport models.

7.3.7.2 A typical transport model

In the interaction component of locational models, we have focused on what we will now call trip distribution: in the retail model, for example, who goes *where* from particular origins. That is, how are trips distributed from particular origins? In the residential location model: how are trips distributed from work-places to residential locations? In the transport model, four stages are needed to achieve the appropriate level of detail. These are responses to the

---

* It should be borne in mind, however, that lags will almost certainly be involved: new c_{ij}'s will affect transport flows before they change residential location patterns.

questions: whether to make a trip, where, by what mode and by what route? The four submodels therefore have the names: trip generation, trip distribution, modal choice and assignment - the latter referring to 'assignment of trips to modal networks'. A crucial feature of such models is this: the distribution model (and possibly even the generation model, as we will see) needs the generalised cost array $\{c_{ij}\}$ as an input. But this can only be effectively estimated after trip assignment, taking congestion into account. The model therefore has an iterative structure as shown in Figure 7.6. This is one distinctive contribution which the transport model has to offer over and above locational models and why, preferably, the $\{c_{ij}\}$ for the latter should come from the former. Note also that the concept of a trip generation model helps to relate the different interaction predictions of transport and locational models in another way. In a residential location model, for example, there is one work trip per household per day. But, on average, this may not be one; some people may travel to work twice a day; some may not travel fives times per week. The trip generation model, for the journey to work, attempts to estimate such averages more precisely. For the location model, such precision in a direct sense does not matter; but it does matter for the estimation of congestion, and therefore it matters indirectly for the location model.

We now present a typical disaggregated transport model. Let T_{ij}^{knp} be the number of trips from i to j by persons of type n by mode k for purpose p. The arrays to be predicted by the trip generation submodel are O_i^{np}, the number of trip predictions (or origins) for purpose-p trips at i by type n people and D_j^p, the corresponding number of p-destinations (or attractions) - and note that this is not split by n: different person types are assumed to compete for the same attractions. We let c_{ij}^k be the generalised cost of travelling from i to j by mode k, and to fix ideas we assume that this is made up of

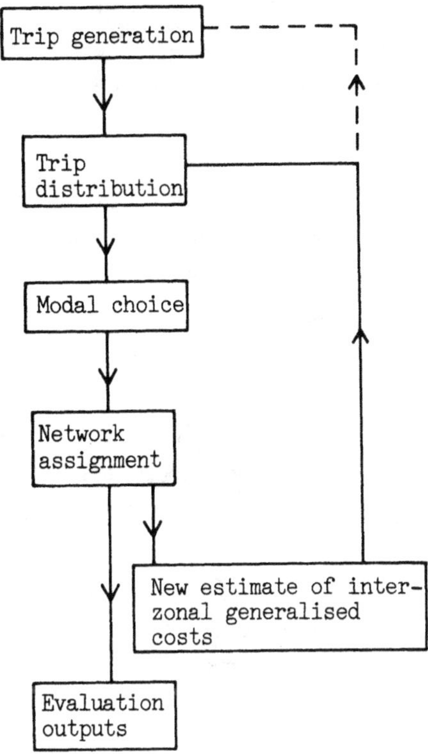

(--- added if there is an accessibility-dependent trip generation submodel)

Figure 7.6: Main elements of a transport model

a money cost, γ_{ij}^{k} and a time cost t_{ij}^{k} combined as

$$c_{ij}^{k} = \gamma_{ij}^{k} + \mu t_{ij}^{k} \tag{7.86}$$

where μ is the value of time. We might expect this to differ by person type and so introduce an n to give

$$c_{ij}^{kn} = \gamma_{ij}^{k} + \mu^{n} t_{ij}^{k} \tag{7.87}$$

It is more customary to use (7.86), however, and to pick up n-variation in the other parameters, as we will see later.

With these preliminary definitions, we now construct each submodel in turn.

(i) Trip generation

The n-category is usually taken as referring to car-ownership (or more accurately, availability) or non-car-ownership. At the trip generation level, a more detailed categorisation than this is needed. We use an index list, h = (w, n, f, ...) where w denotes income group, n car-ownership level, and f is an index of family structure and size (following Wootton and Pick, 1967). Other categories could be added as appropriate. One common form of trip generation model is known as category analysis. In effect, it is assumed that there are reasonably stable averages for trip rates within an h-category. Thus, if a^{hp} is such a rate for purpose p and P_i^h is the number of people in category h in i, then $a^{hp}P_i^h$ is the number of trips for purpose p generated by h-people in i. If we denote by $\gamma(n)$ the set of h categories which make up n, then,

$$O_i^{np} = \sum_{h\epsilon\gamma(n)} a^{hp}P_i^h \tag{7.88}$$

Trip attractions are worked out on a similar basis, but with rates against E_j^ℓ which is the ℓth category of economic activity in j. Then if $b^{\ell p}$ is the trip attraction rate

$$D_j^p = \sum_\ell b^{\ell p}E_j^\ell \tag{7.89}$$

Note that, for most p's, one of the ℓ's would represent population, since residences attract trips. Here, and in the rest of this presentation, we assume that all trips are home-based (as indeed most are). It is relatively simple and straightforward to extend the model for non-home-based trips.

Note also that it is in the trip generation submodel that the transport model has its own explicit links with location models through the arrays $\{P_i^h\}$ and $\{E_j^o\}$ which appear as exogenous variables here.

The model in this form often suffices reasonably well. There is one obvious weakness: the predictions are inelastic; there is no change in numbers of trips if there is a change in the level of transport service. This problem has not yet been satisfactorily resolved. The kind of thing which is needed is an accessibility factor of the form

$$O_i^{np} = \left(\frac{X_i^{np}}{X_i^{npo}} \right)^{\phi} O_i^{npo} \tag{7.90}$$

where the additional superscript 'o' denotes a base year and X_i^{np} is accessibility for type n people for purpose p from i, measured as

$$X_i^{np} = \sum_j D_j^p e^{-\beta^n c_{ij}} \tag{7.91}$$

Then, if either D_j^p or c_{ij} changes (or, indeed, β^n) then O_i^{np} will change through X_i^{np} in (7.90). The parameters ϕ will measure the significance of the effect.

(ii) Trip distribution

A 'conventional' trip distribution model would be doubly-constrained and would take the form

$$T_{ij}^{*np} = A_i^{np} B_j^p O_i^{np} D_j^p e^{-\beta^{np} c_{ij}^n} \tag{7.92}$$

where c_{ij}^n is a *composite cost*. The balancing factors A_i^{np} and B_j^p are calculated as

$$A_i^{np} = \sum_j B_j^p D_j^p e^{-\beta^{np} c_{ij}^n} \tag{7.93}$$

and

$$B_j^p = \sum_{in} A_i^{np} O_i^{np} e^{-\beta^{np} c_{ij}^n} \qquad (7.94)$$

to ensure that

$$\sum_j T_{ij}^{*np} = O_i^{np} \qquad (7.95)$$

and

$$\sum_{in} T_{ij}^{*np} = D_j^p \qquad (7.96)$$

Note that at this stage we have replaced the modal choice superscript, k, by our asterisk to denote summation.

The composite cost is worked out from

$$e^{-\beta^{np} c_{ij}^n} = \sum_{k\varepsilon\gamma^m(n)} e^{-\beta^{np} c_{ij}^k} \qquad (7.97)$$

where the c_{ij}^k's are modal costs. $\gamma^m(n)$ is the set of modes, k, available to type n-people. The composite cost for a person type is an exponentially-weighted average of modal costs - and it is the latter which are produced as a by-product of the assignment procedure, as we will see shortly.

(iii) Modal choice

A suitable modal choice model is

$$T_{ij}^{knp} = T_{ij}^{*np} \frac{e^{-\lambda^{np} c_{ik}^k}}{\sum_{k\varepsilon\gamma(n)} e^{-\lambda^{np} c_{ij}^k}} \qquad (7.98)$$

If λ^{np} can be taken to be the same as β^{np} (though, unfortunately, there is little reason why it should be), the equations (7.92), (7.97) and (7.98) show that we can have a composite distribution-modal choice model of the form

$$T_{ij}^{knp} = A_i^{np} B_j^p O_i^{np} D_j^p e^{-\beta^{np} c_{ik}^k} \tag{7.99}$$

(iv) Assignment

There are many possible assignment submodels. Here, we will use the simplest possible idea to illustrate the kinds of concepts involved and then show how it can be extended. For each model, a network has to be defined consisting of nodes and links. A link is defined by the nodes at either end, as (ℓ,m) say. Some of the nodes can be considered to coincide with the centres of origin and destination zones, i and j. A route is a connected set of nodes from an origin to a destination, and we can define R_{ij}^k to be the set of nodes forming the minimum cost path from i to j by mode k. Then if $\gamma_{\ell m}$ is the cost of travel on link (ℓ,m) and it can be expressed as

$$\gamma_{\ell m} = \gamma_{\ell m}^{money} + \lambda t_{\ell m} \tag{7.100}$$

for an average value of time λ (cf equation (7.86)). Then, in the road case

$$t_{\ell m} = t_{\ell m}(x_{\ell m}) \tag{7.101}$$

where $x_{\ell m}$ is the flow of vehicles on link (ℓ,m). As the flow increases (once it is above a certain threshold) then so does the time because of congestion. Some typical functional forms are shown in Figure 7.7. Congestion costs (through time) will affect bus travel as well as car - though in both cases it may be necessary to distinguish peak and off-peak trips, something we have not done here explicitly. Nodal link costs on other public transport nodes can be specified exogenously. Origin-destination modal costs can then be obtained as

$$c_{ij}^k = \sum_{(\ell,m)\varepsilon R_{ij}^k} \gamma_{\ell m}^k \tag{7.102}$$

(a)

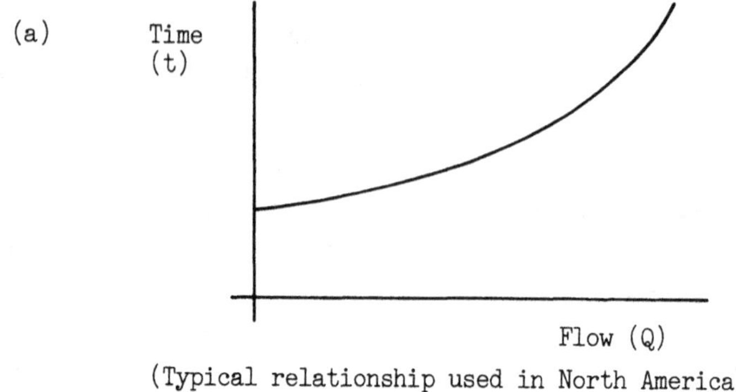

(Typical relationship used in North America)

(b)

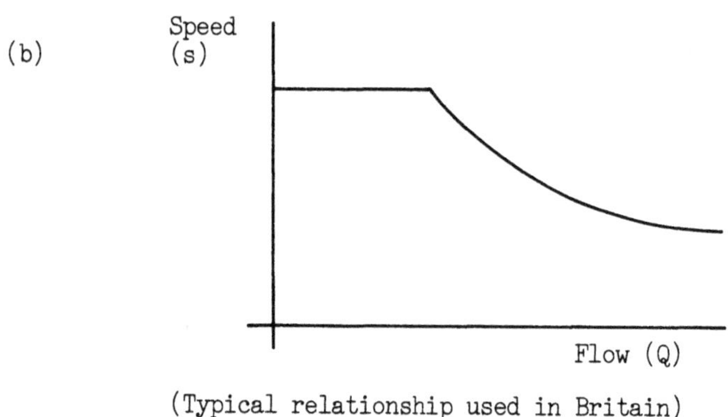

(Typical relationship used in Britain)

Figure 7.7: Time-flow and speed-flow relationships

We are now at the heart of the iterative problem: the c_{ij}^k's are functions of link costs; these in turn, for some modes, are functions of link flows. The link flows are functions of origin-destination flows. Indeed

$$x_{\ell m} = \sum_{\substack{kpn \\ (i,j)\varepsilon(R_{\ell m}^k)^{-1}}} T_{ij}^{knp} \qquad (7.103)$$

where $(R_{\ell m}^k)^{-1}$ is the set of origins and destinations for which the link (ℓ,m) is on the minimum cost path. (This is another way of arranging the information contained in the sets R_{ij}^k, ranging over i and j and, as the notation indicates, is a kind of inverse.) But, to complete the circle, the origin-destination modal flows, T_{ij}^{knp}, are functions of the c_{ij}^k's.

The solution procedure for the model as a whole can now be stated as follows. Start with guessed $\{c_{ij}^k\}$ - perhaps using existing survey values. Calculate $\{T_{ij}^{knp}\}$ from the distribution and modal choice models. Enter the assignment routine and work out best paths. Assign flows to these to obtain $x_{\ell m}$ from (7.103). Then adjust the travel time component of link costs using (7.101) and compute new $\gamma_{\ell m}$'s. There is then a choice. *Either*, proceed with an inner iteration, and reassign T_{ij}^{knp} within the assignment model, and continue this until network equilibrium is achieved. *Or*, assume that this will be looked after in the outer iteration. (*Or*, a mixture of these.) At the end of the assignment model run, new c_{ij}^k's are available which can then be used for a new iteration of the whole model either beginning with trip generation (if an elastic model is being used) or with trip distribution (if not).

We have already noted that there are more elaborate forms of assignment model. For example, as with other aspects of urban and regional modelling, it is found in practice that drivers do not always allocate themselves to the 'best' routes.

We therefore need to find a way of allocating them to 'second best' and 'third best' routes and so on. It is then possible to have modal costs as an exponentially-weighted average of route costs. The allocation to other routes can be made either by a procedure analogous to that used for modal choice; or, for example, by storing the results of each 'inner' iteration and averaging them; or, by using an incremental assignment procedure. It is also possible to use the integrated distribution-assignment mathematical programming procedure of Evans (1976) now that suitable algorithms have been developed (as in Florian, 1977).

7.3.8 Integrated models and approaches

7.3.8.1 Introduction

So far, we have only considered interdependence within major sectors - competition for different types of housing by different groups in the residential location model, the elements involving several goods in the attractiveness function for one good in a retail model, and so on. It is obvious from the variable definitions - since some arrays which are exogenous in one model are endogenous in another - that there are potentially strong interdependencies between models. For example, the service models are dependent on the spatial distribution of population predicted by residential location models; the residential location models relate to employment distribution (which include service jobs); and so on. All sectors compete for the same land, and so land-use accounting is likely to be a particularly significant component of a comprehensive integrated model. It is also within such a framework that we can best consider the fundamental problem of transport-land-use interdependence. This is a feedback which obviously operates in both directions.

The most well-known set of comprehensive models based on spatial-interaction principles are those developed from the Lowry (1964) model. There have been many variants, mostly involving improvements to the basic interaction models which inevitably form the core: residential location and the service sector models. These developments are along the lines described in the preceding subsections. The most recent (still 'potential') addition is the incorporation of the supply-side submodels for housing and service facilities. We begin this section, therefore, with a presentation of such an up-to-date Lowry-type model (subsection 7.3.8.2). We present a dynamic version in subsection 7.3.8.3. There are accounts elsewhere of the developments which have lead up to this point and so we do not need to go into detail here (cf Wilson, 1971-B, Goldner, 1971, Batty, 1976, 1978 for example).

Within the comprehensive approach, there is also the possibility of partial integration. An example of this is to take the best model of congestion assignment (following the work of Evans, 1976, Florian, 1977, Boyce and Southworth, 1979) and to integrate this with the residential location model.

It is obviously important to have measures of congestion included in the $\{c_{ij}\}$ arrays used in location models; whether it is necessary to go to such lengths - which would involve full coding of the underpinning networks - is yet to be established. We do not, therefore, pursue this kind of integration any further here. We simply note the important point that the best and most detailed features of any submodels could be included in a comprehensive model. The art is to know which ones of these to select because they have a major bearing on results which arise from interdependencies between the submodels.

We do, however, briefly consider one other set of methods and ideas about comprehensive model building which, for different reasons, may affect the design of comprehensive models in the future. That is micro-simulation and we consider it here mainly as a method of computation when we have arrays involving large numbers of indices (subsection 7.3.8.4). There are also a number of approaches which focus in different ways on the patterns of human activity. These range from economic analyses where consumption is seen as an activity with goods and time as inputs, via games to 'time geography'. See, for example, Becker (1965), Isard et al (1969) and Hagerstrand (1970). However, a discussion of these methods takes us beyond the scope of this paper and they remain largely at the research level.

7.3.8.2 An extended 'Lowry' model

The Lowry (1964) model can be considered to proceed in the following steps (in the order given in Wilson, 1974):

- (i) Calculate total employment
- (ii) Calculate land available from housing
- (iii) (a) Residential location
  - (b) Housing supply
- (iv) (a) Service facility usage
  - (b) Service facility supply
  - (c) Service facility land use
  - (d) Service facility employment.

Steps (iii)(b) and (iv)(b) are the main additions here to those of a conventional (extended) Lowry model. The submodels for steps (iii) and (iv) can largely be taken from those presented in subsections 7.3.5 and 7.3.4 respectively. It remains customary to assume that basic employment is given because of the relative inadequacy of comprehensive models of industrial location though the alternatives of Putman (1978) and Coelho and Williams (1978) mentioned in subsection 7.3.6 could possibly be incorporated. We do not do so here.

We begin with a static model.

(i) Total employment

Suppose the basic employment distribution $\{E_j^B\}$ is given; and let y^{Bw} be the proportion of basic sector jobs of w-type. Let E_j^{gh} be the number of jobs in (g,h) service facilities - goods or service type, g, facility type h - and let y^{ghw} be the proportion of type w. Then the number of type w jobs in j, which is the distribution we need for the residential location model, is

$$E_j^w = y^{Bw}E_j^B + \sum_{gh} y^{ghw}E_j^{gh} \tag{7.104}$$

(ii) Land available for housing

Let L_i be total land area in zone i; L_i^{res}, land available for residences; L_i^U, unusable land; L_i^B, basic sector land; and L_i^s, service sector land. Assume other sectors have priority over housing - that is, that they can outbid. Then

$$L_i^{res} = L_i - L_i^U - L_i^B - L_i^s \tag{7.105}$$

(iii) (a) Residential location

We can take the residential location model from (7.60) and (7.61), with one notational change: we replace W_i^{kw} by V_i^{kw} to distinguish clearly residential attractiveness from retail attractiveness. So,

$$T_{ij}^{kw} = B_j^w V_i^{kw} E_j^w \tag{7.106}$$

and

$$B_j^w = 1/\sum_{ik} V_i^{kw} \tag{7.107}$$

with

$$V_i^{kw} = \prod_{\ell}(X_{\ell i}^k)^{\alpha_\ell^w} H_i^k . e^{-\beta^w c_{ij}} . e^{-\mu^w [p_i^k - q^w(I^w - c_{ij})]^2} \tag{7.108}$$

from (7.63).

(iii) (b) Housing supply

The equilibrium condition to be solved for housing supply $\{H_i^k\}$ is, from (7.65)

$$D_i^k p_i^k = [\gamma^{(1)k} + \rho^k \gamma_i^{(2)}(L_i^{res})]H_i^k \tag{7.109}$$

where

$$D_i^k = \sum_{jw} T_{ij}^{kw} \tag{7.110}$$

and the other variables are defined in relation to equation (7.69). The residential land-use mechanism operates through the land cost term $\gamma_i^{(2)}(L_i^{res})$, and this will be less satisfactory in this static form than in the dynamic form of Section 7.3.5. A modification may be needed here, therefore, if the model is to be run in static form. For example, $\gamma_i^{(2)}$, the land price, could be taken as an approximate form and related to distance from the city centre. We will also proceed shortly to specify a version of the whole model in dynamic form.

(iv) (a) Service facility usage

Let us use equations (7.30) and (7.31), but without the k-disaggregation. Thus

$$S_{ij}^{ghw} = A_i^{gw} e_i^{gw} P_i^w \hat{W}_j^{ghw} e^{-\beta^{gw} c_{ij}} \tag{7.111}$$

where

$$A_i^{gw} = \sum_{jh} \hat{W}_j^{ghw} e^{-\beta^{gw} c_{ij}} \tag{7.112}$$

P_i^w can now be considered to be obtained from the residential location model, and this becomes one of the main linkages:

$$P_i^w = \sum_{jk} T_{ij}^{kw} \tag{7.113}$$

The attractiveness term, $\hat{W}_j^{ghw}$ is taken from (7.33) as

$$\hat{W}_j^{ghw} = \Big(\sum_{h,g'>g} W_j^{g'h}\Big)^{\alpha_1^w} (W_j^{gh})^{\alpha_2^w} e^{-\gamma^w p_j} \tag{7.114}$$

(iv) (b) Service facility supply

The equilibrium condition is taken from (7.38) as

$$D_j^{gh} = \sum_{\ell} \gamma_j^{gh} [x_{j\ell}^{gh}(y_{j\ell}^{gh})] x_{j\ell}^{gh}(y_{j\ell}^{gh}) \tag{7.115}$$

to be solved in terms of activity levels $\{y_j^{gh}\}$. D_j^{gh} is, of course, given by

$$D_j^{gh} = \sum_{iw} S_{ij}^{ghw} \tag{7.116}$$

Floorspace is related to activity levels by

$$W_j^{gh} = \chi^{gh} y_j^{gh} \tag{7.117}$$

if a linear relationship is assumed, for suitable constants, χ^{gh}; but a more general functional relationship could easily be inserted here to allow for, say, scale economies.

(iv) (c) Service facility land use

Land use can also be taken as proportional to the

activity level: say

$$L_j^s = \sum_{gh} \xi^{gh} y_j^{gh} \tag{7.118}$$

for suitable constants ξ^{gh}.

(iv) (d) Service employment

Finally, service employment can be calculated in a similar way:

$$E_j^{gh} = \xi^{gh} y_j^{gh} \tag{7.119}$$

The whole equation system can now be solved iteratively. Initially, in (7.104) above, we would have $E_j^{gh} = 0$ and $L_i^{res} = L_i - L_i^U - L_i^B$; a quick check shows that the remaining quantities are all calculated on each cycle through the iteration.

Lowry always insisted that the iterations in his model were the mathematical means of solving *static* model equations and were not to be interpreted as representing urban growth. With explicit supply side models added and difference equations (7.37) and (7.70) available, it is now, however, possible to consider a dynamic version and so we do this next.

7.3.8.3 A 'dynamic extended' Lowry model

The model just presented is essentially an equilibrium model. We can use the methods of earlier subsections to add dynamic supply-side models and also to decide what is 'driving' the model through time. Changes in basic sector jobs, E_{jt}^B, would be given and estimates would have to be made of parameter change over time. This would range from changes in y^{Bw} and y^{ghw} - which would effectively represent the increase or, now, decrease, in incomes by changing the numbers in each w group, through changing e_i^{ghw} values, to parameters like α_k^w and β^w. Assuming that at least reasonable estimates of all these can be made (and it is difficult to achieve more than this at present – there are hard research problems here), then we can proceed to specify the dynamic model.

(i) Total employment. (7.104) with time subscripts added.

(ii) Land available for housing. (7.105) with time subscripts added. But also with a constraint like

$$L_{it+1}^{res} = \lambda^I L_{it}^{res} \tag{7.120}$$

(where λ^I is an inertial parameter between 0 and 1), and the calculation of currently available residential land as

$$L_{it+1}^{curr\ res} = L_{it+1}^{res} - \sum_k \rho^k H_i^k \tag{7.121}$$

In other words, land currently available for residential use is total such land available less that actually used.

(iii) (a) Residential location. Equations (7.106) – (7.108) with time subscripts added.

(iii) (b) Housing supply. We can now replace the equilibrium condition (7.109) by the difference equation (7.70), but where we use $L_{it+1}^{curr\ res}$ rather than L_{it+1}^{newres}. It then becomes

$$H_{it+1}^k = (1 + \varepsilon D_{it}^k p_i^k) H_{it}^k - \varepsilon[\gamma^{(1)k} + \rho^k \gamma_{it}^{(1)}(L_{it}^{curr\ res})] H_{it}^k \tag{7.122}$$

with H_{it+1}^k being adjusted so that the following constraint is satisfied:

$$H_{it+1}^k > H_{it}^k \tag{7.123}$$

(This assumption could be modified to allow for a relatively slow rate of demolition or even conversion; or, as we will see when we discuss 'planning' uses, such adjustments could be made exogenously in the model as part of the planning process.)

(iv) (a) Service facility usage. Equations (7.111) - (7.112) with time subscripts added.

(iv) (b) Service facility supply. The equilibrium condition (7.115) is replaced by a difference equation version of (7.37). This could be written, with the same kinds of adjustments made in the housing supply model above, as

$$y^{gh}_{jt+1} = (1 + \varepsilon^{gh}D^{gh}_{j})y^{gh}_{jt} - \varepsilon^{gh}[\sum_{\ell}\gamma^{gh}_{j\ell}(x^{gh}_{j\ell}(y^{gh}_{j}))x^{gh}_{j\ell}(y^{gh}_{j})] \tag{7.124}$$

(iv) (c) Service facility land use. Equation (7.118) with time subscripts added.

(iv) (d) Service employment. Equation (7.119) with time subscripts added.

If the system is run in this form, the housing and service sectors will, typically, not actually achieve equilibrium, though its development path will be governed by 'underlying' (possibly 'near') equilibria at each time step. This may be realistic. On the other hand, if the time step length is relatively long, there may be an argument that the system is in equilibrium in each interval. In this case, the static model should be run with a series of time subscripts on each variable in each equation together with a set of assumptions about exogenously specified change of variables and parameters where appropriate.

This model could be used in a planning context in exactly the same way as the residential and service sector models whose uses we described in Sections 7.3.4 and 7.3.5. The same set of variables can be taken as 'controlled' and the same range of experiments conducted: to test stability and likely changes of direction; predicting likely modes of system evolution; adjusting directly controllable variables like demolitions (slum clearance) or the location of major facilities and exploring the impacts; or seeking to make small adjustments which inhibit or encourage bigger changes because some parameters are near to critical values. In addition, because the distribution of basic employment, E_j^B, determines much of the structure, it is possible to experiment with alternative *planned* E_j^B-distributions and to assess their impact on system structure.

Is the development of an integrated model of this kind worth it? At least it provides an accounting framework which links variables which have to be taken as exogenous in a particular submodel (and more of this later). It means in particular that when there are subsystem bifurcations, the consequences of these will be immediately transmitted to other submodels - and these may in turn cause other bifurcations. This argument could be extended if it was possible to bring industrial location models within the framework or to incorporate input-output relations to replace the economic-base model as described by Macgill (1977-B).

7.3.8.4 Micro-simulation

We have seen in a number of instances that we are driven to define arrays with large numbers of subscripts and superscripts - for example the S_{ij}^{ghwk} of a disaggregated retail model. In general terms, consider an array $T_{i_1 i_2 i_3 \ldots i_N}$ and let $a_1, a_2 \ldots, a_N$ be the number of values which can be taken by indices $i_1, i_2 \ldots, i_N$. Then the array has $\prod_{k=1}^{N} a_k$ cells, and this number increases geometrically as N increases. In the case of a fully disaggregated retail model, if there are 100 zones (i,j), 10 types of goods (g), 5 types of facilities (h), 3 person types (w) and 2 modes (k), the S_{ij}^{ghwk} array will have 3,000,000 cells. An alternative representation involves listing a sample of the population of the study, and the characteristics of each. Say, for the sake of illustration, it was possible to take a sample of 10,000 people from a total population of 1,000,000; and that we gave each in the sample a number (as a 'name' and 6 characteristics (g,h,w,k,i,j)). Then the number of elements of information to store would be 70,000, and this is much less than 3,000,000. In some circumstances, therefore, it is worth using this direct representation simply for computational reasons. For each individual in the sample, the characteristics are obtained via the model arrays (or whatever) converted into probability distributions and a random number generation to select from the distribution, and the method is thus called a micro-simulation method. (There would be little to be gained, of course, if the whole array had to be stored in each case as the basis of this procedure, but in most cases, elements can be recomputed as necessary.)

The end-product of such a simulation is a hypothetical sample population whose characteristics are in accord with all known information represented as probability distributions. Formally, if x_k^r is the kth characteristic of the rth individual we can write

$$x_k^r = x_k^r[P_k(x_k^r \mid \ldots), R_k^r, \underline{\Gamma}] \tag{7.125}$$

where P_k is the conditional probability distribution which is the basis for calculating x_k^r, R_k^r is a random number and $\underline{\Gamma}$ is a set of constraints (cf Wilson and Pownall, 1976). The $\underline{\Gamma}$-constraints are additional inter-relationships - for example budget constraints - which can be imposed during the simulation. If this is done, then the model can incorporate dimensions of interdependence over and above those implied by the hypothesised probability distributions.

An even more important use of micro-simulation procedures arises in dynamic modelling. Suppose account-based differential (or difference) equations are taken as the basis of a dynamic model:

$$\frac{dN_i}{dt} = \sum_k (a_{ki}N_k - a_{ik}N_i) \tag{7.126}$$

or

$$N_{it+1} - N_{it} = \sum_k (a_{ki}N_k - a_{ik}N_i) \tag{7.127}$$

where the N_i's are numbers in state i at a time and the array $\{a_{ik}\}$ represents transition probabilities. Each of i and k, the state labels, can be index lists. If, pursuing our earlier example, the state is described by (g,h,w,k,i,j), then $\{N_i\}$ has (in that case) 3,000,000 elements. The transition array $\{a_{ik}\}$ thus has 9×10^{12} elements! But the progression of the system through time can be handled by micro-simulation methods which can thus be seen as numerical ways of solving sets of equations like (7.126) or (7.127) over time. See Clarke, Keys and Williams (1981) for a full account.

7.4 Comparisons With Other Approaches

7.4.1 Some basic dimensions of model design

Now that the various submodels which can be derived on the basis of spatial-interaction concepts have been reviewed, it is appropriate to step back and to see how they fit into a broader picture and to relate them to alternative methodologies. We begin by referring to some basic dimensions of model design which provide a framework for the choices faced by the modeller and hence a basis for comparison. Then, in Section 7.4.2 we make some comparisons with alternative formulations and finally in Section 7.4.3, we summarise the basis of the spatial-interaction methodology in the light of this analysis.

It can be argued (cf Wilson, 1981-B) that there are six basic dimensions of choice faced by the modeller:

(i) entitation - enumerating the basic components of the system of interest;

(ii) scale - what level of resolution should be adopted?

(iii) spatial representation - the treatment of space in a *continuous* way, so that exact locations of activities can be determined (or precise boundaries, for example to demarcate land uses) or in a *discrete* way with a zoning system which provides the basis for (a coarser) spatial resolution;

(iv) partial versus comprehensive: do we consider the location of the *marginal* activity - say a firm or a household - given the rest of the system as an environment, or do we consider all activities simultaneously, thus reflecting competitive processes and so on?

(v) what theory and methods do we use for the static analysis of structure and form?

(vi) what theory and methods do we use for the dynamic analysis of evolution and change?

We can illustrate the meaning of these ideas by explaining alternative modelling strategies in the light of the framework they provide.

7.4.2 Alternative methodologies

The first four dimensions in the analysis of the previous sections are of a somewhat different character to the last two. They determine the way we look at the system of interest for analytical purposes; the last two relate to detailed specification of theories and methods. The first point to make, therefore about the comparison of alternatives, is that differences can arise because of these choices even though the real 'theoretical' basis may be the same. For example, continuous space economic models and discrete space economic models look very different, but are still underpinned by the usual assumption of economic theory.

Any differences which arise here, particularly with regard to the second and fourth, can be very important. Continuous space models, for example, are much more likely than discrete zone models to necessitate restrictive assumptions - such as 'all employment at the centre of the city' - in order to make the mathematics practicable. Similarly, the more partial the model, the easier its mathematical basis is likely to be.

It is with respect to the last two dimensions (though perhaps in this case 'entitation' should also be included) that the main differences in theoretical stance emerge. The main alternatives to spatial interaction modelling are based on economic assumptions (see Richardson,1977-B, for a review) or a behavioural kind of activity analysis as mentioned in Section 7.3.8.1 above. Different models may also result from different assumptions about planning, either in terms of more or less controllable variables or by shifting the focus of the study.

It is always tempting to seek a 'behavioural' basis and often right to do so. However, it does not follow that assumptions which have this kind of appeal - such as those of the neo-classical theory of consumers' behaviour, or the theory of the firm, are, *because of that appeal*, true. Indeed, it is likely that the underpinning theory of spatial interaction modelling, applicable at a coarser scale, is less restrictive (as well as easier to handle) and will in many cases offer better approximations. And, as we will see in the next section, spatial interaction models can be seen as having a 'better' theoretical basis than is often realised.

One of the striking features of alternative approaches is that in many cases - once the aggregation problem is solved for those with a micro-behavioural base - the mathematical form of the models is identical or similar. However, this is not necessarily as comforting as it might seem, since in some such cases - eg between entropy maximising models and random utility models - the interpretation of the parameters is fundamentally different and this is important for forecasting. See Macgill and Wilson (1979) and Wilson and Macgill (1979) for a review of these matters in more detail.

7.4.3 Spatial interaction modelling in the context of alternative approaches

In the terms of the previous section, spatial interaction models are based on discrete zone systems at a meso scale of resolution and a comprehensive view. The entropy-maximising method is neutral with respect to underlying behavioural assumptions. However, it is also possible to interpret the entropy term as adding a realistic degree of dispersion to optimising behaviour - based on the maximisation of locational benefits and the minimisation of transport costs (cf Senior and Wilson, 1974-A), and this is a very general procedure for extending models based on such assumptions.

Such (say 'economic') models can be freed from their most restrictive assumptions (noted above) if they are based on discrete zone concepts. It was in this way that Herbert and Stevens (1960) were able to operationalise Alonso's (1960, 1964-A) continuous space model. This is because mathematical programming techniques can then be used to solve the aggregation problem. We are now arguing, however, that it is usually appropriate to add an entropy term to the objective function of such models to add a realistic degree of dispersion. Senior and Wilson (1974-A) did this to complete the Alonso to Herbert and Stevens progression. Wilson (1981-B) includes a more general account of the implications of this method.

The important recent step has been the addition of dynamic supply-side models to the 'consumer-side' of spatial interaction modelling. This provides a broad basis and, as we saw in Section 7.3 above, a substantial foundation for work in urban modelling. In this case, economic assumptions are used directly with dispersion, though it is interesting to note that Popkov (1980) and others have used entropy-dispersion terms in this context also.

7.5 Planning Problems and the Application of Models

7.5.1 Urban problems 1 - the backcloth

In the last 30 years, there has been rapid economic development, demographic growth, rising per capita income, rising car ownership, better housing, and improved services, both public and private. The effect of these processes on Western cities has been decentralisation usually accompanied by increasing social polarisation. The problems which result, from an urban planning point of view, are the problems of the new spatial structures which have evolved from these processes and these problems should be stated in terms of the various categories of people involved: the poor left in the inner cities, the poor accessibility of many suburban residents (either without cars or with one car used by the one male worker of the family) and so on. A particular feature of urban spatial structure overall is the tendency to provide service facilities in larger units. This is often advantageous as users of schools, hospitals, health centres, shopping centres and whatever, gain the benefits of size: higher standards, variety of choice, lower prices, and so on. However, this has to be set against the increased costs of travel and this is the basis for serious problems for many - for example the poor, the young and the old who do not have cars.

It is possible to approach these problems in a systematic way. For an individual, we might argue that important characteristics which provide a basis for describing urban problems are: (i) residential location, i; (ii) workplace location, j; (iii) income of associated household, w; (iv) car ownership, n. All of these relate directly to the models introduced earlier. We might also add (v) age, r; (vi) ethnic group, e, and (vii) sex, f. Then T_{ij}^{wnref} is the number of people in a particular category. Note that, already, we have more indices than can comfortably be coped with - so either we have to take a series of coarser views, say to look at $\{T_{ij}^{wn}\}$, $\{T_{i}^{wnr}\}$ and so on; or, alternatively to use a micro-simulation model as a basis.

This procedure, even as a sequence of coarse views, provides a systematic basis for identifying problems. To illustrate the idea, consider the simple definitions of categories implied by Table 7.2.

i = (1 inner city
(2 suburban (public housing)
(3 suburban (private housing)

j = (1 inner city
(2 suburban
(3 unemployed

w = (1 poor
(2 middle
(3 rich

n = (0 cars
(1 or more cars

Table 7.2: Categories for urban problem analysis

These coarse definitions generate 54 T_{ij}^{wn} categories. It is interesting, then, to describe the typical urban problems for each of these. For example, T_{12}^{10} is the population of poor people without a car, living in the inner city and working in the suburbs. Their problems are mainly of poor quality housing, the difficulties of out-commuting and the lack of an adequate income to begin to resolve the problems directly. T_{31}^{31} represent a well-off group, resident in the suburbs, working in the city centre, owning one or more cars. Their 'problems' are likely to be restricted to facing traffic congestion as they commute to work.

7.5.2 Urban problems 2 - more recent trends

The kind of analysis of problems proposed in the previous section has been appropriate for thirty years or more; and still is. But there are newer trends of recent years which change the picture. The most important new features are: (i) the increase in energy prices since 1973 which, in the long run, is likely to continue; (ii) economic recession and increasing unemployment; (iii) declines in levels of public-expenditure; (iv) declining birth rates. In many cases, these trends have exacerbated problems previously identified - such as the consequence of decentralisation and social polarisation in terms of the concentration of problems in inner city areas.

7.5.3 Models and urban problems

It has been argued in the two preceding sections that urban problems should be seen as the problems of the people (in different categories) of a city or region and that these problems can be seen as arising out of two sets of trends: the economic development and growth of the last 30 years followed by energy-led recession of the last 10 years. At an aggregate level, these trends are the backcloths of urban change and are largely represented as the exogenous parameters of the models we have described. The models can thus be used to predict the nature and scale of decentralisation, changing patterns of service facilities and so on and can be used to generate indicators of the impact of these trends on people in cities and regions. In this sense, they provide the basis for an *analysis* of urban problems. It may also be possible to predict the scale of future problems by projecting the exogenous variables and using the models for forecasting. Problems can be articulated in terms of sets of indicators - and one such set was specified in detail for retail models in Section 7.3.4 above.

Models have a more direct connection to *planning* in relation to urban problems when they are used to predict the consequences of (again through lists of indicators) the settings of what are seen to be the controllable variables in particular situations. Indeed, models may also provide an aid to *design* if they can be embedded within a suitable optimising procedure and an overall mathematical programme. Ideally, these kinds of uses of models in planning should be within the framework of an interactive computing system so that a planner could explore the consequences of alternative strategies at a computer terminal.

This mode of use of models is essentially *conditional* forecasting, the 'conditions' being the settings of the planned variables and projections of exogenous parameters. But we have also seen that if the forecasting is for the longer term, there are dangers in this - indeed it may be almost impossible except in the broadest possible terms - because of bifurcation effects. But, as we saw, there are then new possibilities: models can be used to investigate the *stability* of spatial structures and plans can be made to maintain stability or to *encourage structural change* in some desired direction.

7.5.4 Concluding comments: the range of applications of models - past and prospective

There have been an enormous number of model applications in planning and it is beyond the scope of this paper to review them all in detail (though quite a number are referred to in the references in the bibliography. Typically, however, best possible practise has not been achieved. The models used have often been too simple and perhaps not appropriate for the planning problems being tackled. What is usually needed is a good degree of disaggregation (and if necessary the use of micro-simulation methods as a base of calculation) and a wide ranging list of indicators related to planning problems and objectives. These two elements of strategy would force planners to focus on the details of problems of finely-categorised social groups. This has been most nearly achieved in the transport-planning field and could perhaps now be extended to residential location and housing and the use of services. There are longer run prospects for industrial location and other aspects of the supply side as we will see in the discussion of priorities in model development and research in the next section.

7.6 Recommendations on Model Design, Research and Implementation

7.6.1 A basic model system

It is worthwhile to develop a model system on a modular basis. The principles involved in building the different models are similar. The retail, residential location and transport models all derive from the basic family of spatial interaction models, though they are disaggregated in different ways. This means that different computer programmes have to be written in each case, but once the first one has been written, the others are relatively easy. Similarly, the supply-side models are different in detail but the same principles can be used to build models for retail facilities and for housing - though some modifications would be needed when these are used in a planning context to enable some or all of the variables concerned to be fixed exogenously.

In the case of the transport model, it should also be added that the spatial interaction part of the model - representing trip distribution and modal choice - has to be sandwiched between trip generation and assignment submodels, usually within an iterative framework. The various elements of the transport model are the ones which are most likely to be easily available from elsewhere - though it is worth emphasising that, in general, it is usually better if an in-house team can develop its own computer programmes.

Finally, we can note that, given that all the submodels are available, it is relatively straightforward to assemble them (at whatever is judged to be the appropriate, usually coarser, level of resolution) into an integrated model.

The shape of an overall model system is shown in Figure 7.8. The model system and its inputs and outputs has a central role of course, but three other elements are emphasised also: firstly, the management of data; secondly, the concept of an information system; and thirdly, the development of appropriate interactive routines. The information system contains both data and model outputs and should be arranged in terms of sets of accounts (like $\{T_{ij}^{kwn\ldots}\}$, or micro-simulation model arrays). The interactive routines enable the analyst and planner to 'interrogate' the information system and to organise new model runs.

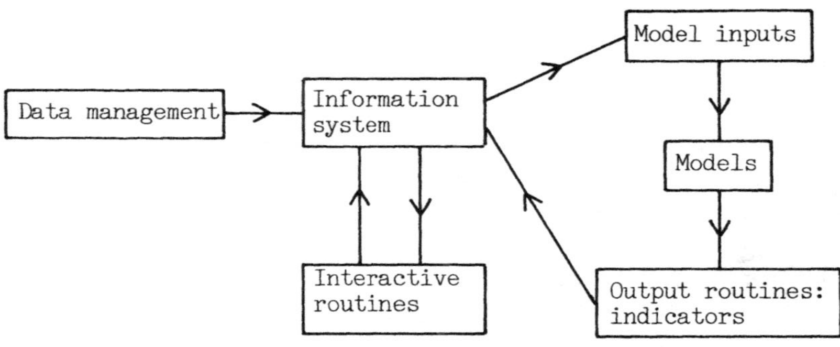

Figure 7.8 : Elements of model-based analysis

7.6.2 Research and development tasks

Three kinds of tasks have been identified implicitly in the course of this chapter: (i) the development and extension of existing models; (ii) the development of new models; and (iii) the development of planning techniques which build on discoveries in bifurcation theory and urban and regional modelling. We discuss each of these briefly in turn.

(i) Developments of existing models

There has been relatively little experience in many cases of empirical work with models at useful (disaggregated) levels of detail. A prime concern, therefore, must be to build up such experience. A number of examples will illustrate the point. Retail models need to be developed based on 'shop types' as well as a 'type of good' classification. Indeed, this comment can be broadened to draw attention to the need for more work on other service sectors, and this may lead to new types of models. Residential location models need to be tested with a much wider range of attractiveness factors. It would be useful to explore whether the complex representation of phenomena such as congestion in transport models should be directly built into location models.

Important recent additions have been the retail and residential supply-side models. Little experience has been gained with these except with idealised systems and an urgent task is to rectify this. It is also interesting to note that these supply-side submodels can be added to the Lowry model, as we saw in Section 7.3.8.

The addition of supply-side models in the context of bifurcation theory leaves a major research problem. Our understanding of bifurcation is based on *zonal* analyses - development possible (DP) or not (NDP). We also need to understand *pattern* bifurcations, and relatively little progress has been made as yet with this task.

(ii) The development of new models

In Section 7.3.4 above, we outlined principles for building industrial location models, but there is almost no experience with this kind of model. This is therefore one major item on the agenda for the development of new models. Another is the supply-side dynamics of the transport model. This involves problems which are more complex than those of the basic location models, partly because of transport-land-use interaction and in part because of the complexities of networks per se. This is an example of a topic which has not really been touched.

(iii) Developments in planning technique

Conditional forecasting will remain useful for short-run planning. Otherwise, we have continually emphasised in this paper the need for a shift from impact analyses (in the longer run) to analyses of stability and resilience and the exploration of desirable directions of change in the light of such analyses. In practice, this is likely to involve a lot of effort in the development of new techniques, the foundation of which will be the embedding of dynamical analyses in an interactive framework.

In all these approaches, there is one basic need for development and research: for each submodel or planning area of concern, to construct an adequate and comprehensive set of indicators as a matter of routine. We attempted to begin this process for the retail model above (in Section 7.3.4), but it can be further extended and developed. A part of this process will be recognising that the information system has an effective *accounting* basis of the type sketched in Section 7.6.1 above. These steps would help to couple modelling and planning in the context of urban problems and would form the foundations of a *best practice* approach to planning methods.

7.6.3 Concluding comments

It is typically the situation that models are not employed effectively in planning: 'best possible practice' is not achieved. The reasons for this are many and varied. Different disciplines have been involved in model development and their contribution to planning has not always been well coordinated. Planners have not usually been receptive - at least in part because they do not have suitable skills which enable them to absorb the new methods. But above all, perhaps, urban and regional science is a young field. Research in the field has been exciting and has progressed rapidly in the last twenty years. With the application of new methods of dynamic modelling, the excitement should continue. But this research effort needs to be matched by a greater amount of *development* effort, often needing teams of people. Governments have not yet organised themselves effectively to produce this. This is why the proposals of Sections 7.6.1 and 7.6.2 above are made up of *both* development and research arms. What is needed is the will to implement them on a substantial scale.

Chapter Eight

A COST-EFFICIENCY THEORY OF DISPERSED NETWORK EQUILIBRIUM

T.E. Smith

8.1 Introduction

The purpose of this paper is to unite two current approaches to the modelling of dispersed spatial interaction behaviour - namely the entropy-smoothing approach (Erlander, 1977, 1980, Boyce et al, 1981, 1983) and the cost-efficiency approach (Smith, 1978-A, 1983-A). At first glance, these approaches appear to be quite different. For entropy-smoothing is deterministic in nature and treats spatial interactions as continuous flows, while cost-efficiency is probabilistic in nature and treats spatial interactions as discrete events. But further reflection suggests that both approaches are quite similar in spirit. For in each approach, spatial actors are essentially regarded as cost-minimizers who, in the presence of other behavioural factors, tend to exhibit some deviation from pure cost-minimizing travel behaviour. Hence, in spite of their formal differences, both approaches stem from a common view of spatial interaction behaviour.

With this in mind, our central result is to show that this similarity goes much deeper. In particular, we establish a Correspondence Theorem (Theorem 1 below) which shows that the class of dispersed flow patterns obtained from entropy-smoothing techniques can be derived within the theoretical framework of the cost-efficiency principle, and, indeed, correspond to the most probable cost-efficient interaction flows consistent with any given (large) levels of trip activity. This Correspondence Theorem serves not only to clarify the precise relation between these two approaches, but also shows how they effectively complement one another. On the one hand, entropy-smoothing programming models have been strongly criticized on theoretical grounds as being no more than ad hoc computational procedures. Hence, the Correspondence Theorem now provides a clear theoretical interpretation for the solutions to these models, and shows that in the presence of cost-efficient behaviour, such flow patterns are indeed the most likely ones to be observed. On the other hand, while the cost-efficiency principle is conceptually intuitive and quite compelling from a theoretical viewpoint, it suffers from severe computational limitations. Hence, the Correspondence Theorem also shows that for large levels of trip activity, entropy-smoothing programs provide an efficient computational procedure for approximating the flow patterns predicted by this theory.

To establish these results, we begin in the next section with a general development of entropy-smoothing models which includes both the 'entropy-constrained' and 'entropy-maximizing' models. In particular, we formulate a class of dispersed network equilibrium models (DNE-models), and show that both entropy-constrained and entropy-maximizing programs amount to different ways of computing dispersed network equilibria. In Section 8.3 we then review the basic elements of the cost-efficiency view of spatial interaction behaviour, and define the most probable flow patterns within this theory. These two lines of development are synthesized in Section 8.4, where the fundamental Correspondence Theorem between most probable flow patterns and dispersed network equilibria is established. Given this correspondence, we next show in Section 8.5 that for large levels of trip activity (and for almost all travel cost structures of interest), these dispersed network equilibrium flow patterns are in fact overwhelmingly more probable than any other patterns. Hence they do indeed constitute the uniquely most prominent candidates for representing cost-efficient spatial interaction behaviour. In the light of these theoretical results, we then take up the important practical question of calibrating DNE-models in Section 8.6. In particular, both maximum-entropy and maximum-likelihood techniques are developed for estimating the fundamental 'cost-sensitivity' parameter of these models. Finally, a number of possible extensions of these results are outlined in Section 8.7, including both structural extensions of DNE-models, and behavioural extensions of the theory itself.

8.2 Dispersed Network Equilibria

To motivate the basic notion of network equilibrium, we begin by considering the problem of modelling morning rush-hour traffic behaviour within a large metropolitan area. Here one can assume for simplicity that all drivers are commuters, and hence that the origin and destination of each journey-to-work trip is fixed. Thus the only relevant decision for each driver is the choice of a specific route to work. More formally, if I and J denote the relevant sets of origins and destinations, respectively, then the decision problem for each commuter from $i \varepsilon I$ to $j \varepsilon J$ is the choice of a route r from the relevant set R_{ij} of feasible routes from i to j. The question of interest is thus to model the pattern of traffic resulting from the combined decisions of all such commuters.

8.2.1 Continuous network equilibrium

The simplest approach to modelling the decision process for individual commuters is to assume that each commuter seeks to minimize his own travel time, or more generally, his route cost to work, and has perfect information regarding the nature of such costs. In this context, it is natural to expect that the only traffic patterns which can long persist are those in which every commuter is currently choosing a minimum-cost route, given the route choices of all other commuters. Hence, in such 'equilibrium' patterns, the travel costs on all routes used between each location pair i and j must be the same, and no other routes in R_{ij} can have lower costs. To state these conditions more precisely, let f_{ijr} denote the traffic flow on each route $r \epsilon R_{ij}$, and let the vector $f = (f_{ijr})$ denote the resulting flow pattern on the network. Now if these quantities are treated as continuous variables, and if the corresponding travel costs $c_{ijr}(f)$ on each route $r \epsilon R_{ij}$ are taken to be continuous functions of these flow patterns f, then it is always meaningful to speak of flows which actually equate travel costs on two or more routes in R_{ij}. Hence in this context, we now define $f^* = (f^*_{ijr})$ to be a (continuous) network equilibrium flow pattern if and only if f* satisfies the following two conditions for all origins $i \epsilon I$, destinations $j \epsilon J$, and routes $r, s \epsilon R_{ij}$:

$$(f^*_{ijr} > 0,\ f^*_{ijs} > 0) \Rightarrow\ c_{ijr}(f^*) = c_{ijs}(f^*) \qquad (8.1)$$

$$(f^*_{ijr} > 0,\ f^*_{ijs} = 0) \Rightarrow\ c_{ijr}(f^*) \leq c_{ijs}(f^*) \qquad (8.2)$$

To determine flow patterns which can actually satisfy these equilibrium conditions, we need more explicit information about the nature of travel costs $c_{ijr}(f)$. The simplest approach here is to treat the underlying road network as a set of connected links $\ell \epsilon L$, and to characterize each relevant route $r \epsilon R_{ij}$ as a connected (nonrepeating) sequence of links $r = (\ell_1, \ldots, \ell_n)$ from i to j. Next, if we set $\delta^\ell_{ijr} = 1$ when route $r \epsilon R_{ij}$ contains link ℓ and set $\delta^\ell_{ijr} = 0$ otherwise, then for any traffic flow pattern $f = (f_{ijr})$ the total link flow

f_ℓ on ℓ is given by

$$f_\ell = \sum_{ijr} \delta^\ell_{ijr} f_{ijr}, \quad \ell \varepsilon L \tag{8.3}$$

Finally, if for each traffic flow pattern f the travel cost on each link ℓ is representable by a continuous link cost function c_ℓ which is increasing in f_ℓ, and if the associated route cost function c_{ijr} are simply the sum of their link costs, then the travel cost $c_{ijr}(f)$ on each route $r\varepsilon R_{ij}$ under flow pattern f is expressible as

$$c_{ijr}(f) = \sum_\ell \delta^\ell_{ijr} c_\ell(f_\ell), \quad r\varepsilon R_{ij} \tag{8.4}$$

Within this explicit travel cost framework, Beckmann, McGuire, Winsten (1956) showed that there always exists a network equilibrium flow pattern satisfying (8.1), (8.2), (8.4). More importantly, they showed that the link flows for such equilibria are always unique, and can be computed as the solutions of an explicit convex programming problem. To formulate this program, we now let N_{ij} denote the number of commuters from i to j, and define the feasible flow set F of all non-negative flow patterns consistent with these totals by:

$$F = \{f = (f_{ijr}) \geq 0 \mid \sum_{r\varepsilon R_{ij}} f_{ijr} = N_{ij}, \forall (ij)\} \tag{8.5}$$

If we then define the following (convex differentiable) cumulative flow-cost function C over the (compact convex) set F by:

$$C(f) = \sum_{\ell \varepsilon L} \int_0^{f_\ell} c_\ell(x)dx, \quad f\varepsilon F \tag{8.6}$$

then Beckmann (1955) showed that the network equilibrium $f^*\varepsilon F$ defined by (8.1), (8.2), (8.4) is given by the solution to the following convex program (P)*:

$$\text{min: } C(F), \text{ subject to: } f \varepsilon F \tag{8.7}$$

This celebrated result is widely regarded to be the cornerstone of modern network equilibrium analysis**.

8.2.2 Introduction of dispersion

While such network equilibria do serve to indicate the general tendencies of actual rush-hour traffic patterns, an examination of conditions (8.1) and (8.2) shows that the patterns predicted by this simple theory tend to be too extreme. In particular,

---

* Such equilibria are generally unique only with respect to their link flows. To be precise, if for each flow pattern $f \varepsilon F$ we let $f_L = (f_\ell | \ell \varepsilon L)$ denote the associated link flow pattern, then since (8.6) is a strictly convex function of f_L, it follows that (8.7) yields a unique link flow solution f_L^*. Hence, letting the matrix of linkpath relations be denoted by $\Delta = (\delta_{kjr}^\ell)$, and writing the equation system (8.3) in vector form as $f_L = \Delta f$, it follows from Beckmann's results that the set of network equilibria satisfying (8.1), (8.2), (8.4) is given by $F^* = \{f \varepsilon F \,|\Delta f = f_L^*\}$. We then take f^* to be any representative element of F^*. See, also, footnote** on page 435).

** This basic result has of course been considerably generalized in recent years. In particular, the introduction of nonlinear complementarity and variational inequality techniques have allowed much more general models of route costs $c_{ijr}(f)$ to be introduced. Such extensions will be considered briefly in Section 8.7.1 below.

all routes utilized between i and j must have exactly the same route costs, and more importantly, all routes with higher costs (no matter how slight) are never used. From a behavioural viewpoint it is clear that such conditions are overly simplistic. For example, many route-choice decisions are based on a combination factor other than pure cost considerations (such as stopping for a bite to eat on the way to work, and so on). Moreover, even those commuters who are solely concerned with travel time seldom have precise information about prevailing traffic conditions. Hence, from a modelling viewpoint, the question arises as to how we might incorporate this myriad of additional behavioural factors in a way which more accurately reflects actual traffic flows.

One approach is suggested by further consideration of Beckmann's programming formulation of the problem. In particular, if the system objective function C(f) in (8.7) is taken to reflect pure cost-minimizing behaviour on the part of commuters, then one may ask how this objective function might be modified to include a term reflecting the host of 'all other factors' influencing travel behaviour. If one has explicit information about the distribution of such factors as travel preferences and cost information among the commuting population, then one could in principle incorporate this information directly into the objective function of (8.7). (Indeed, the random utility framework proposed by Sheffi and Daganzo 1977, 1980, among others, is designed precisely with this end in mind. Such possibilities will be considered in the concluding section of this paper.) But in the absence of such explicit information, one may still ask whether it is possible to modify the objective function in (8.7) in a manner which at least 'smooths' the network equilibrium flow pattern f* in some reasonable way.

While there is apparently little in the way of behavioural theory here, it has nonetheless been recognized that certain information-theoretical techniques seem to yield plausible results. In particular, the classical (Shannon) entropy function H defined for all flow patterns $f = (f_{ijr}) \varepsilon F$ by*

$$H(f) = - \sum_{ijr} f_{ijr} \ln(f_{ijr}) \tag{8.8}$$

has proved to be a remarkably useful smoothing device. More specifically, if for any positive weight θ, we now subtract the term $\frac{1}{\theta}H(f)$ from (8.6) then the program P in (8.7) can be embedded with the following larger class of convex programs (P_θ):

$$\text{min: } C(f) - \frac{1}{\theta}H(f), \text{ subject to: } f \varepsilon F \tag{8.9}$$

It is evident from the form of this new objective function (together with the differentiability and strict concavity of H) that each program P_θ yields a unique solution f^θ in F, defined by the first-order conditions of the following Lagrangian function:

$$L(f,\theta,\{\lambda_{ij}\}) = C(f) - \frac{1}{\theta}H(f) - \sum_{ij} \lambda_{ij}[\sum_r f_{ijr} - N_{ij}] \tag{8.10}$$

To see the form of the resulting solution, observe from (8.4) and (8.6) that each component flow f^θ_{ijr} must satisfy

$$0 = \left.\frac{\partial L}{\partial f_{ijr}}\right|_{f^\theta_{ijr}} = [\sum_\ell \delta^\ell_{ijr} c_\ell(f^\theta_\ell)] + \frac{1}{\theta}[1 + \ln(f^\theta_{ijr})] - \lambda_{ij}$$

$$\Rightarrow \ln(f^\theta_{ijr}) = (\theta\lambda_{ij} - 1) - \theta c_{ijr}(f^\theta)$$

---

* Note that since total flows are constant for all $f \varepsilon F$, this definition of entropy is essentially equivalent to the usual probabilistic form, and is notationally more convenient for our purposes.

$$\Rightarrow f^{\theta}_{ijr} = A_{ij} \exp[-\theta c_{ijr}(f^{\theta})],\ A_{ij} = \exp(\theta\lambda_{ij} - 1) \quad (8.11)$$

Thus, employing the equality constraints in (8.5) we may conclude that each A_{ij} is of the form $A_{ij}=N_{ij}(\sum_r \exp[-\theta c_{ijr}(f^{\theta})])^{-1}$, and hence that

$$f^{\theta}_{ijr} = N_{ij} \frac{\exp[-\theta c_{ijr}(f^{\theta})]}{\sum_{s\varepsilon R_{ij}} \exp[-\theta c_{ijs}(f^{\theta})]},\ r\varepsilon R_{ij},\ ij\varepsilon I\mathrm{x}J \quad (8.12)$$

Equation (8.12) characterizes f^{θ} as the fixed point of a continuous transformation from F into itself, which can be obtained by standard iterative techniques*. The essential features of these flow patterns are that each component flow f^{θ}_{ijr} is always positive, and is a decreasing function of its corresponding flow cost $c_{ijr}(f^{\theta})$. Moreover, it should be clear from the continuity of the objective function in the parameter θ that $f^{\theta} \to f^*$ as $\theta \to \infty$ (ie, as $\frac{1}{\theta} \to 0$)**. Hence, for large values of θ, these patterns

---

* See Boyce et al (1981, 1983) for further examples of such solutions and computational procedures. In addition, see Chon (1982) for a recent empirical application of this technique.

** While this convergence statement is intuitively clear, it requires further explanation since the network equilibrium f^* itself is not unique. To give this statement more precise meaning, observe that since the set of network equilibria F^* defined in footnote* on page 432 is a compact convex subset of F, the entropy function H (which is strictly concave on all of F) must achieve a unique maximum in F^*. Moreover, if this unique maximum-entropy pattern $f^*\varepsilon F^*$ is taken to be the representative network equilibrium in F^*, then f^{θ} does indeed converge to f^* as $\theta \to \infty$. To see this, observe simply that by definition each f^{θ} maximizes H over the set $\{f\varepsilon F \,|\, C(f) \le C(f^{\theta})\}$. Hence, it follows at once from (8.7) that the limit of this sequence must maximize H over the set of global minima for the function C in F, which is precisely the definition of f^*.

do indeed represent a plausible 'smoothing' of the network equilibrium flow pattern f^*. (This will also be shown graphically in Figure 8.1 below.)

This entropy-smoothing technique can be given a certain degree of motivation within the present context as follows. Suppose we begin by considering the opposite extreme case from pure cost-minimizing behaviour in which travel costs are regarded as insignificant (or are at least outweighed by a host of other considerations for commuters). If alternative routes are no longer distinguishable on the basis of travel costs, and if no other distinguishing features predominate, then one might expect route-choice behaviour to be 'maximally dispersed' in the sense that no route between a given origin-destination pair is chosen more frequently than any other route. More formally, if n_{ij} denotes the number of routes in R_{ij}, then for any given numbers of commuters (N_{ij}), this maximally dispersed travel behaviour corresponds to the uniform flow pattern $f^u = (f^u_{ijr})$ in F, where

$$f^u_{ijr} = \frac{1}{n_{ij}} N_{ij}, \quad r \varepsilon R_{ij} \tag{8.13}$$

Hence, if one is to model this opposite extreme case by a system-wide objective function paralleling the cumulative flow-cost function of Beckmann, then it is natural to seek a (strictly convex differentiable) function which achieves its unique minimum over each feasible flow set F at the corresponding uniform flow pattern $f^u \varepsilon F$. With this end in mind, one may readily verify that the convex program

$$\min: -H(f), \text{ subject to: } f \varepsilon F \tag{8.14}$$

defined by the negative entropy function exhibits precisely these properties. Hence the family of programs (P_θ) comprising all weighted combinations of these objective functions can be

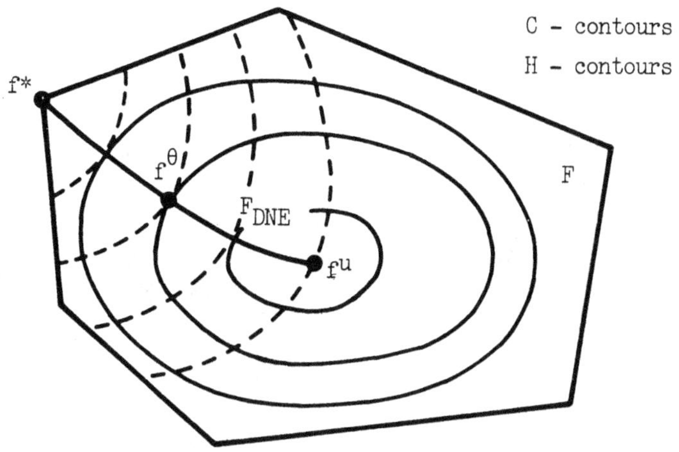

Figure 8.1: Locus of dispersed network equilibria

viewed as describing all 'intermediate cases' between pure cost-minimizing behaviour and maximally dispersed behaviour. From this viewpoint, it is natural to regard each of the resulting flow patterns f^{θ} as a dispersed network equilibrium. More formally, we now designate the class of programs $\{P_{\theta}|0 < \theta < \infty\}$ as dispersed network equilibrium models (DNE-models) and designate the associated family of solutions $F_{DNE} = \{f^{\theta} \varepsilon F|0 < \theta < \infty\}$ as the dispersed network equilibria in F, where higher values of θ denote lower levels of dispersion.

This class of dispersed network equilibria F_{DNE} can be depicted graphically in terms of Figure 8.1, where the contours of the cumulative flow-cost function (C) and the entropy function (H) are plotted over a two-dimensional version of the feasible flow set F (which is typically a convex polyhedron in higher dimensional space). The function C (shown in dotted line) achieves its minimum at the network equilibrium pattern

f^*, and the function H (shown in solid lines) achieves its maximum (ie -H achieves its minimum) at the uniform pattern f^u in F. Hence the family F_{DNE} of dispersed network equilibria (with typical element f^θ) is precisely the locus of tangencies between these two functions, extending from f^* to f^u.

This graphical depiction of dispersed network equilibria also helps to clarify their 'smoothing' properties. In particular, the presence of zero flows (on all routes with non-minimal route costs) in the network equilibrium flow pattern f^* means that f^* will typically lie on the boundary of F (indicating that some of the non-negativity constraints on feasible flows are binding for f^*). On the other hand, the uniform flow pattern f^u must lie at the centre of F, in the sense that all flows between each origin-destination pair are equal and positive. Hence the essential effect of introducing dispersion is to 'pull' the solution toward the interior of F, thereby smoothing the extreme flow levels exhibited by the network equilibrium f^*.

8.2.3 Equivalent formulations of dispersed network equilibria

Programming models of the type described by the DNE-models in (8.9) date back at least as far as the work of Evans (1976) on the combined distribution and assignment problem. But while this formulation has the conceptual advantage of making explicit the tradeoff between cost considerations (C) and all other travel considerations (H), its solution requires a prior specification of the crucial tradeoff parameter θ in the objective function. (We shall return to this point in Section 8.6 below.) However, Figure 8.1 shows that there are several (mathematically) equivalent formulations of (8.9) which do not require the prior specification of θ.

As a first possibility, observe that if one prespecifies some maximal level of cumulative flow-costs, say C_θ, and

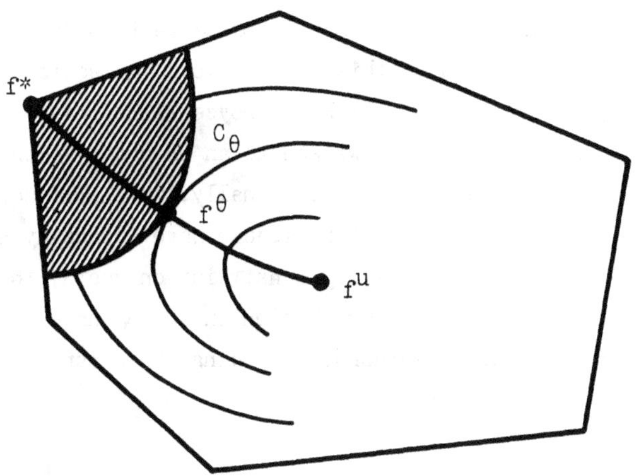

Figure 8.2: Equivalent EM-program

maximizes H over the new constraint set $F(C_\theta) = \{f \varepsilon F | C(f) \leq C_\theta\}$, as shown in Figure 8.2 then the resulting entropy-maximizing model (EM-model) given by

$$\text{max: } H(f), \text{ subject to: } f \varepsilon F(C_\theta) \qquad (8.15)$$

is seen to yield a solution which is precisely the dispersed network equilibrium f^θ in Figure 8.1. Hence, if one is able to prespecify the level of cumulative flow-cost C_θ associated with an unobserved dispersed network equilibrium f^θ, then this flow pattern can be obtained without knowing the value of θ. Indeed, the corresponding value of θ is now computable as the associated Lagrange multiplier for the cost constraint defined by the constraint set $F(C_\theta)$. This type of programming formulation, which amounts to finding the most dispersed patterns consistent with given 'suboptimal' levels of system costs, has been most clearly articulated by Senior and Wilson (1974-B) in the context of residential location behaviour. However, the theoretical roots of this procedure are to be found in the original work of Wilson (1967) on most-probable trip distributions. (We shall return to this seminal work in Section 8.2.4 below.) More recently, Fisk and Boyce (1982) have extended the original model of Wilson to an EM-model which explicitly treats congestion costs. Finally, we should note that while the above examples of EM-models have typically been formulated in terms of an equality constraint on costs, the advantages of the inequality formulation in (8.15) have been recognized by a number of authors, including Choukroun (1975).

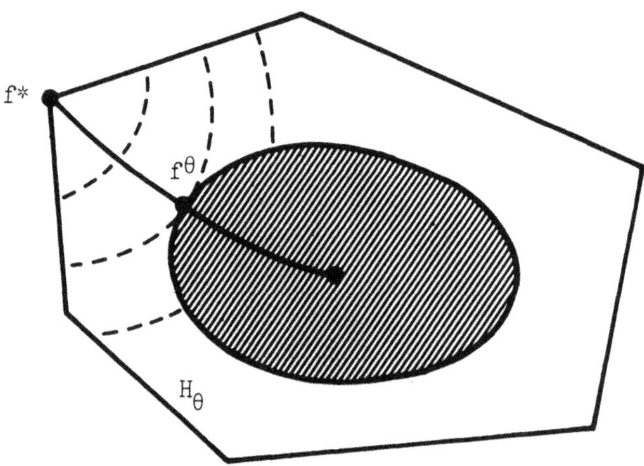

Figure 8.3: Equivalent EC-program

As a second possibility, observe that if one prespecifies some minimal level of entropy, say H_θ, and minimizes C over the new constraint set $F(H_\nu) = \{f \varepsilon F | H(p) \geq H_\theta\}$ as shown in Figure 8.3 then it is again clear from Figure 8.1 that the resulting entropy-constrained model (EC-model) given by

$$\text{min: } C(f), \text{ subject to } f \varepsilon F(H_\theta) \tag{8.16}$$

yields the same dispersed network equilibrium solution f^θ. Hence, if the entropy level H_θ associated with an unobserved equilibrium pattern f^θ can be prespecified, then this pattern can again be computed by (8.16) and the associated value of θ can be obtained as the Lagrange multiplier for the entropy constraint defined by the constraint set $F(H_\theta)$. This alternative programming formulation, which amounts to finding the least costly pattern consistent with some level of system dispersion, was first proposed by Erlander (1977, 1980). More recently, such EC-models have been explored in depth and extended in a number of directions by Boyce et al (1981, 1983).

8.2.4 The need for a behavioural theory

While dispersed network equilibria are readily computable by the above techniques, and are seen to exhibit some intuitive appeal, the heuristic motivation given in Section 8.2.2 above fails to provide any solid theoretical foundation for this approach. In particular, all the arguments used to motivate the entropy function here work equally well for a host of alternative functions. Indeed, if one interprets negative entropy as a measure of (Kullback) distance from the uniform flow pattern f^u in F, then it becomes clear that any number of other standard distance measures work equally well. For example, the simple Euclidean distance function $D(f) = ||f-f^u||$ shares all the essential convexity and differentiability properties of $-H(f)$, and of course achieves its global minimum at f^u. Hence, if one replaces the H-contours in Figure 8.1 by concentric circles about f^u, it is immediately clear that the resulting locus of tangencies [defined by the corresponding minimum values of $C(f) + \frac{1}{\theta}D(f)$] share all the same qualitative features of the dispersed network equilibria in F_{DNE} - even though the specific flow patterns for each level of θ can differ considerably from those in F_{DNE}.* Hence, it should be clear that a stronger theoretical interpretation of dispersed network equilibria is required in order to distinguish this family from its many potential competitors.

Along these lines, a number of attempts have been made to interpret entropy directly as a 'macro behavioural' quantity. For example, Erlander (1977) has suggested that entropy might be interpreted as a measure of the degree of 'accessibility' between spatially separated behaving units. Alternatively, Boyce and Jansen (1980) view entropy as reflecting the level of 'spatial interaction' inherent in a given flow pattern. But while such interpretations are often very suggestive, they fail to distinguish between entropy and the many other smoothing functions which could equally well be given such interpretations.

A more powerful theoretical interpretation is suggested by the original entropy-maximizing formulation of Wilson (1967) in the context of inter-zonal trip frequencies. In particular, Wilson showed (by a standard argument from classical statistical mechanics) that if all micro configurations of individual trips consistent with any given origin-destination totals and travel-cost total are assumed to be equally likely, then the most probable frequency distribution of inter-zonal trips (for large levels of trip activity) is approximated by the maximum-entropy frequency distribution. Hence at all sufficiently large levels of such macro trip activity, the most probable states of the system are those with maximum entropy. This result (which is developed in more detail in Section 8.5.2 below) shows that the entropy function can be strongly distinguished from all possible

---

* Other distance functions which are even closer to Shannon entropy in their qualitative behaviour include the family of 'Renyi entropies' developed, for example, in Aczél and Daroczy (1975, Chapter 5).

competitors on theoretical grounds which are entirely independent of any 'smoothing' considerations whatsoever.

But in spite of the theoretical appeal of this result, the actual structure of the Wilson model implicitly ignores much of the travel behaviour which we are presently concerned with. First, this model assumes that travel costs are constant, and hence independent of traffic levels. Thus, all interaction effects among commuters are assumed away, and all questions of route choice are reduced to a triviality. Second, this model treats total travel costs as fixed, and hence ignores the influence of travel costs on travel behaviour. (This absence of cost-sensitivity considerations in the model is reflected by a resulting indeterminancy in the sign of the crucial 'cost-sensitivity' parameter θ, as discussed in detail by Choukroun, 1975 and Smith, 1978-A.) While such simplistic assumptions may well be appropriate for modelling long-run averages of relative trip frequencies between aggregated zones within a city, they cannot begin to capture the types of short-run behaviour implicit in morning rush-hour traffic, for example.

In view of these behavioural limitations, it would appear at first glance that this type of long-run model has little bearing on the present problem. However, we shall show that in spite of these limitations, the basic result of the Wilson model continues to hold in a much more general setting. In particular, the characterization of maximum-entropy flow patterns as most probable states of the system is capable of far reaching generalization. Within the present context of travel behaviour, this generalization is made possible by reformulating the problem in terms of a 'cost-efficiency' theory of travel behaviour. This theory, which is essentially probabilistic in nature, will allow the question of 'most probable states' to be formulated in a meaningful way.

8.3 The Cost-efficiency Theory of Travel Behaviour

To motivate the essential elements of this theory, let us return to the problem of modelling rush-hour traffic. In the present approach, we shall begin by constructing a very detailed picture of such traffic patterns in the following way. On any given morning, each commuter from i to j chooses some route $r \varepsilon R_{ij}$. Hence, each individual trip in the system must correspond to some element in the set $R = \bigcup_{ij} R_{ij}$ of all such routes. Now if exactly n trips occur on a given morning, then the resulting trip pattern t can be represented as a list of n trip choices from R, ie $t = (r_1, \ldots, r_n) \varepsilon R^n$. Hence, the set of all feasible trip patterns is given by $S = \bigcup_n R^n$, where n is assumed to be bounded by some large finite value (say by the total population in the system). This enormous (finite) set T thus contains all possible micro descriptions of trip patterns which could conceivably occur on any given morning.

Now most of the trip patterns in S will be highly improbable (to say the least). But nevertheless, a large number of such patterns may be quite possible on any given morning. Hence, the basic idea of the present approach is to describe such trip behaviour in terms of some (unknown) probability distribution P over S, in which patterns t with higher values of P(t) are by definition the more probable ones to occur on any given morning. In this context, the present theory of travel behaviour will essentially amount to a theory about which patterns in S are more likely to occur.

As with the dispersed network equilibrium models above, the central hypothesis implicit in this theory is that cost-minimizing considerations are the major (but not the only) ingredient in travel behaviour. In the case of morning rush-hour traffic, for example, it is implicitly assumed that most travellers are commuters who are anxious to get to work on time. Hence, to motivate the behavioural assumptions of the theory, it is natural to begin with the 'bench mark' case of pure cost-minimizing behaviour (in a manner which completely parallels the development in Section 8.2 above).

8.3.1 Pure cost-minimizing behaviour

Within the present setting, let us again consider the route-choice decision for a traveller entering the network at i destined for j, and ask what his choice might be if he were a pure cost-minimizer (with perfect information and unlimited computational capacity). Under these conditions, one may imagine the mental calculation he might make in determining the cheapest (quickest) route from i to j. First, if the current trips on the network are denoted by $(r_1, \ldots, r_n)$, then in a manner identical to Section 8.2, one may compute the current route cost which this traveller would incur if he were to choose a given route $r \varepsilon R_{ij}$. In particular, if the resulting trip pattern is designated by $t = (r_1, \ldots, r_n, r)$, and if f^t_{ijr} denotes the (integer valued) flow on route $r \varepsilon R_{ij}$ generated by pattern t, then the corresponding (integer valued) flow on each link ℓ is given, in a manner identical to (8.3) by

$$f^t_\ell = \sum_{ijr} \delta^\ell_{ijr} f^t_{ijr} \tag{8.17}$$

Hence, the route cost $c(r|t)$ which he would incur on route $r \varepsilon R_{ij}$ under the given traffic conditions is given by

$$c(r|t) = c(r|r_1, \ldots, r_n, r) = \sum_\ell \delta^\ell_{ijr} c_\ell (f^t_\ell) \tag{8.18}$$

The resulting cost minimization problem for this traveller is thus to find that route $r \varepsilon R_{ij}$ which minimizes (8.18).

Next, suppose we consider a sequence of n pure cost-minimizers entering the network one at a time. The relevant decision problem for traveller 1 is to minimize $c(r_1|r_1)$ over his possible route choices r_1. Similarly, the problem for traveller 2 is to minimize $c(r_2|r_1,r_2)$ over his relevant set of route choices r_2, and so on. Hence, if we now define the cumulative user-cost function $C(t)$ over each feasible pattern of route choices $t = (r_1, \ldots, r_n)$ in S by

$$C(t) = C(r_1, \ldots, r_n) = \sum_{k=1}^{n} c(r_k|r_1, \ldots, r_k) \tag{8.19}$$

then it is clear that each entering traveller k seeks to minimize his own increment $c(r_k|r_1, \ldots, r_k)$ to this cumulative user-cost function. Hence, under conditions of pure cost-minimizing behaviour, one might well expect to observe trip patterns t with minimal levels of cumulative user-costs $C(t)$. This intuition is confirmed by the results in Smith (1983-A) where it is shown that such minimum cost patterns do indeed correspond to user-equilibria for pure cost-minimizers.

8.3.2 Discrete network equilibria

To make this notion of user-equilibrium precise, we begin in a manner paralleling the continuous case in Section 8.2.1 by considering the set of commuters (and other trip makers) travelling during a given rush-hour period. If N_{ij} again denotes the (integer valued) number of trips between each origin i and destination j, then we now designate the vector $N = (N_{ij})$ as the relevant trip-activity profile for that period, and let $M = \sum_{ij} N_{ij}$ denote the total number of trips in profile N. For this collection of M travellers, we next consider the possible trip patterns in S which might actually be realized. In particular, if for each trip pattern $t \varepsilon S$ we let

$$N_{ij}^{t} = \sum_{r \varepsilon R_{ij}} f_{ijr}^{t} \tag{8.20}$$

denote the number of trips in t going from i to j, and let $N^t = (N^t_{ij})$ denote the corresponding trip-activity profile for t, then the set of trip patterns in S which give rise to each profile N is defined by

$$S_N = \{t\varepsilon S | N^t = N\} \tag{8.21}$$

Now if all M travellers are pure cost-minimizers, then as in Section 8.2.1 we may identify an 'equilibrium' trip pattern in S_N to be one in which all travellers are currently choosing minimum-cost routes, given the route choices of the others. More formally, if for any trip pattern $t = (r_1, \ldots, r_m)\varepsilon L_N$ and any traveller k we let i_k and j_k denote his origin and destination, respectively, and let $t_k(r_1, \ldots r_{k-1}, r_{k+1}, \ldots r_m)$ denote the route choices of all travellers other than k, then in terms of the travel cost increments in (8.18) we now say that a trip pattern $t^* = (r^*_1, \ldots, r^*_m)$ is a user-equilibrium in S_N if and only if for all travellers k = 1, ..., M and routes $r\varepsilon R$,

$$r\varepsilon R_{i_k, j_k} \Rightarrow c(r^*_k | t^*_k, r^*_k) \leq c(r | t^*_k, r) \tag{8.22}$$

In other words, t* is a user-equilibrium if and only if no traveller has an alternative route choice which he prefers to his current choice in t*.

In terms of this definition, it is shown in Smith (1983-A, Theorem 3.5) that for any given trip-activity profile N, the trip patterns $t^*\varepsilon S_N$ with minimum cumulative user-cost $C(S^*)$ are always user-equilibria for these activity levels. More generally if we now designate a pair of trip patterns $t, t'\varepsilon S$ to be activity-equivalent if and only if $N^t = N^{t'}$, then those trip patterns $t^*\varepsilon S$ with minimum cumulative user-costs among all activity-equivalent trip patterns in S are always user-equilibria.

This result not only shows that such equilibria must always exist (by the finiteness of S), but also suggests a strong parallel between the discrete and continuous cases. For in each case, the desired equilibria are obtainable by minimizing an appropriate system cost function. This parallel may be sharpened even further by observing that for each trip pattern $t\varepsilon S$ we may identify a corresponding flow pattern $f^t = (f^t_{ijr})$, with integer valued components f^t_{ijr} given by (8.17). Moreover, an inspection of (8.17) to (8.19) shows that cumulative user-cost for each trip pattern t is expressible solely as a function of its corresponding flow pattern f^t. In particular, if for any given trip-activity profile N we now let

$$F_N = \{f^t | t\varepsilon T_N\} \tag{8.23}$$

denote the (discrete) feasible flow set for activity levels N, and define the following (discrete) cumulative flow-cost function C_N on F_N by

$$C_N(f) = \sum_\ell [\sum_{k=1}^{f_\ell} c_\ell(k)], \; f\varepsilon F_N \tag{8.24}$$

then it is shown in Smith (1983-A, Lemma 3.7) that for all $t\varepsilon T_N$,

$$C(t) = C_N(f^t) \tag{8.25}$$

Hence, the full extent of the parallel between the discrete and continuous cases is now clear. For a comparison of (8.6) and (8.25) shows that the cumulative flow-costs in (8.6) are precisely the continuous analogue of those in (8.25). One immediate consequence of this relationship is to provide an interesting behavioural interpretation of Beckmann's system cost function C in the continuous case. For if one views each additional commuter on route $r\varepsilon R_{ij}$ as an infinitesimal increment to the continuous flow f_{ijr}, then it is clear from (8.4) and (8.6) that the cost he incurs on entering the network is precisely the derivative of C with respect to flow f_{ijr}. This means that if all commuters are pure cost-minimizers, then each seeks to minimize the derivative (rate of increase) of the function C at his point of entropy. Hence, as in the discrete case, we may expect to observe minimum total values of C - which leads us directly to programming problem P in (8.7).

Moreover, this parallel between discrete and continuous flow costs may be extended to the notion of network equilibria by observing from (8.20) that if we minimize the function C_N over the finite set F_N of feasible flows, then the resulting minimum-cost patterns f* must correspond to 'equilibrium flows' in the sense each trip pattern t* with $f^{t*} = f^*$ is necessarily a user-equilibrium. Hence, in a manner paralleling the continuous case, it is natural to designate each such minimum-cost pattern f* as a (discrete) network equilibrium flow pattern.

Thus we may conclude that there is a complete correspondence between the discrete and continuous cases with respect to pure cost-minimizing behaviour, as shown in Figure 8.4 below.

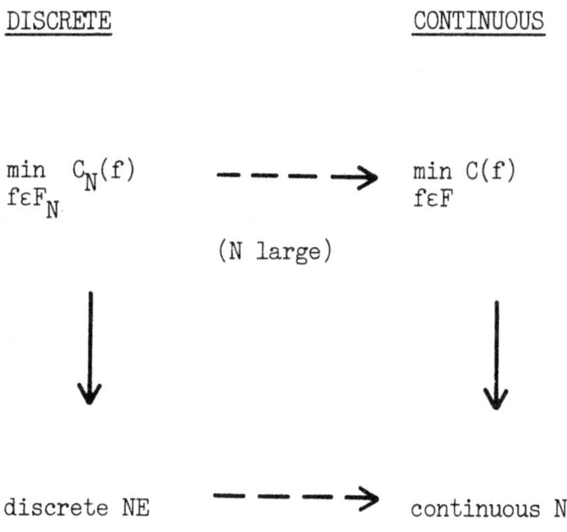

Figure 8.4: Correspondence for pure cost-minimizing case

In the discrete case, minimization of (discrete) cumulative flow-costs yields a discrete network equilibrium (discrete NE), and in the continuous case, minimization of (continuous) cumulative flow-costs yields a continuous network equlibrium (continuous NE). Moreover, for large levels of trip activity, both the cumulative flow-costs and network equilibria for the discrete case are well approximated by their continuous analogues.

8.3.3 Pattern probability distributions

With the above relationships in mind, our ultimate objective is to show that this correspondence between the discrete and continuous cases can indeed be extended to the full range of dispersed network equilibria. To do so, we now return to our original question of which trip patterns in *S* are more likely to occur during a given rush-hour period. As mentioned in the introductory remarks to this section, this question can be given precise meaning by treating such patterns as realizations from some underlying probability distribution P on T - which we now designate as a pattern probability distribution.

To learn something about this distribution, suppose that we were actually able to observe the trip patterns $t_1, \ldots, t_n$ occurring during a series of morning rush-hour periods. If these patterns are taken to be a sequence of random samples from P, then the frequencies of observed patterns should eventually give us a good picture of this distribution - and hence a good picture of travel behaviour during morning rush hour. [There is an implicit assumption here that both the network structure and individual travel behaviour remain sufficiently stable to allow such sampling to be meaningful. For example, if one were to observe travel behaviour during periods of temporary road repairs, then the resulting short-term disruptions in travel behaviour (including both fluctuations in realized travel costs and day-to-day learning effects by drivers) would render such sampling assumptions meaningless. Hence, from a conceptual viewpoint, our notion of a 'sample sequence' here is probably best viewed as a series of virtual samples from the hypothetical population of behaviour patterns under 'normal rush-hour traffic conditions'.] In particular, if the mean level of observed cumulative user-costs is taken to reflect typical cost levels on each morning, then the results of Section 8.3.2 suggest that these mean cost levels should eventually give us a good picture of the cost-minimizing tendencies in this travel behaviour. For example, if typical cost levels $C(t_i)$ for trip patterns t_i are very close to their minimum levels (among all activity-equivalent patterns), then the resulting travel patterns must be very close to equilibrium. Hence one may reasonably infer that cost-minimizing tendencies are dominant in this population. More generally, if cost-minimization is at least a strong component of this behaviour, then from among all activity-equivalent sequences of trip patterns, one may expect to observe sequences with lower rather than higher mean cost levels. This is the essence of the cost-efficiency principle which we now formalize.

8.3.4 Cost-efficiency principle

To formulate this principle in a precise way, we begin by letting $T = (t_1, \ldots, t_n)$ denote a typical trip-pattern sequence, and recalling that if such sequences are random samples from a pattern probability distribution P, then for any given sample size n, the probability of observing T is given by the pattern-sequence probability

$$P(T) = P(t_1)P(t_2) \ldots P(t_n) \tag{8.26}$$

Next, if $N^T = (N^{t_1}, \ldots, N^{t_n})$ denotes the activity-profile sequence associated with T, then two pattern sequences T and T' are activity-equivalent if and only if $N^T = N^{T'}$ (ie if and only if their individual trip patterns are activity-equivalent). In this context, if we now designate the mean cost for sequence T to be

$$\overline{C}(T) = \frac{1}{n}\sum_{i=1}^{n} C(t_i) \qquad (8.27)$$

then the desired principle may be stated formally as follows:

> COST-EFFICIENCY PRINCIPLE. A pattern probability distribution P is said to satisfy the cost-efficiency principle if and only if for all activity-equivalent trip pattern sequences T and T',
>
> $$\overline{C}(T) \leq \overline{C}(T') \rightarrow P(T) \geq P(T') \qquad (8.28)$$

This principle, which essentially postulates an inverse relationship between the mean cost levels of trip pattern sequences and their relative likelihood of occurring, forms the cost hypothesis of the present cost-efficiency theory of spatial interaction behaviour.

8.3.5 Exponential pattern probability distributions

The central consequence of this theory is that all pattern probability distributions satisfying the cost-efficiency principle must be negative exponential in form. In particular, the pattern probability for each trip pattern t must have the explicit form of (8.29). [This result is a direct corollary of Theorem 3.2 in Smith (1983-A). In particular, if $n = \{N^t | t \in S\}$ denotes the set of all trip-activity profiles for trip patterns in S, then the map $\Phi:\{1\}\times N \times S \rightarrow \{0,1\}$ defined for all $N \in N$ and $t \in S$ by $\Phi_{(1,N)}(t) = 1$ if $N^t = N$ and $\Phi_{(1,N)}(t) = 0$ otherwise, is a (cost-independent) partition scheme on T. Hence, in a manner completely paralleling Theorem 3.3 together with expression (3.58) in Smith (1983-A) it follows that P_θ is of the form (8.29) in the text. Finally we should note that Theorem 3.2 in Smith (1983-A) assumes that P_θ is continuous in travel costs, this prior assumption turns out to be unnecessary, as is shown in Erlander and Smith (1983).]

$$P_\theta(t) = w(N^t)\exp[-\theta C(t)],\ t \in S \tag{8.29}$$

where w is some positive weight function of trip-activity profiles, and where θ is a non-negative cost-sensitivity parameter. The resulting probability distribution P_θ is designated as an exponential pattern probability distribution. We subscript this distribution by θ to indicate that within each class of activity-equivalent trip pattern S_N in S, the conditional distribution

$$P_\theta(t|N) = \frac{\exp[-\theta C(t)]}{\sum_{t' \in S_N} \exp[-\theta C(t')]},\ t \in S_N \tag{8.30}$$

is completely determined by the cost-sensitivity parameter θ alone. The most immediate consequence of this fact is that within each activity-equivalence class S_N, these conditional probabilities are monotone decreasing functions of cumulative user-costs (except for the degenerate case of $\theta = 0$). Hence, we may conclude from the results of Section 8.3.2 above that: For all cost-efficient travel behaviour, the most probable trip patterns at each level of travel activity are always user-equilibria.

Hence the theory reflects our intuition that user-equilibria should continue to be the single most prominent mode of behaviour in populations of cost-sensitive trip makers. Moreover, the increasing dependence of route costs on traffic volumes shows that as congestion levels go up, the distribution P_θ in (8.29) becomes very 'peaked' at its modal value. Hence the theory again confirms the intuition that tendencies toward pure cost-minimizing behaviour should become overwhelming during periods of highest congestion. (For further discussion of these points, see Smith, 1983-A.)

8.4 Most Probable Flow Patterns: the Correspondence Theorem

Given the above characterization of pattern probability distributions for cost-efficient travel behaviour, we are now in a position to study the associated probability distribution over cost-efficient flow patterns. For since each flow pattern f is determined by some underlying trip pattern t, it follows that flow pattern probabilities $P_\theta(f)$ can be computed from their associated trip pattern probabilities $P_\theta(t)$. These flow probabilities will in turn lead us to the main result of this paper - namely that for large trip-activity levels, the most probable flow patterns consistent with cost-efficiency correspond to the dispersed network equilibria defined in Section 8.2.1 above. More formally, our objective in this section is to establish the following Correspondence Theorem:

Theorem 1. (Correspondence Theorem) For large levels of cost-efficient spatial interaction activity, the most probable flow patterns consistent with this activity always correspond to dispersed network equilibria.

To establish this result, we begin by deriving an explicit form for such flow pattern probabilities. First, if for any given trip-activity profile N and feasible flow pattern $f \epsilon F_N$ we let $S_N(f) = \{t \epsilon S_N | f^t = f\}$ denote the subset of trip patterns consistent with flow pattern f, then by (8.29)

$$P_\theta(f) = \sum_{t \epsilon S_N(f)} P_\theta(t) = \sum_{t \epsilon S_N(f)} w(N^t)\exp[-\theta C(t)] \qquad (8.31)$$

Next, recall from (8.25) that cumulative user-costs depend only on flows, and hence that $C(t) = C_N(f)$ for all $t \epsilon S_N(f)$. Moreover since $N^t = N$ for all such t, it follows that (8.31) reduces to:

$$P_\theta(f) = w(N)\exp[-\theta C_N(f)](\#S_N(f)) \qquad (8.32)$$

where $\#S_N(f)$ denotes the cardinality of the set $S_N(f)$. But recalling that $M = \sum_{ij} N_{ij}$ denotes the total number of trips in profile N, it also follows that for each flow pattern $f = (f_{ijr}) \epsilon F_N$, the number of elements in $S_N(f)$ is simply the number of ways of choosing M trips with exactly f_{ijr} trips on each route, and hence is given by the multinomial coefficient:

$$S_N(f) = \frac{M!}{\prod_{ijr}(f_{ijr})!} \qquad (8.33)$$

Finally, combining (8.32) and (8.33) we obtain the following exact expression for each flow pattern probability:

$$P_\theta(f) = \frac{M!}{\prod_{ijr}(f_{ijr})!} w(N)\exp[-\theta C_N(f)] \qquad (8.34)$$

Hence, to obtain the most probable flow pattern in F_N, we must maximize (8.34) over the set F_N. But the positivity of $P_\theta(f)$ allows us to write (8.34) in natural log form as:

$$\ln P_\theta(f) = \ln[M!w(N)] - \theta C_N(f) - \sum_{ijr} \ln(f_{ijr}!) \qquad (8.35)$$

Now if we henceforth restrict our attention to positive values of θ (ie if we ignore the degenerate case $\theta = 0$), then (8.35) may be rewritten as

$$\ln P_\theta(f) = (\ln[M!w(N)] - M) - \theta[C_N(f) - \frac{1}{\theta}(M - \sum_{ijr} \ln(f_{ijr}!))] \qquad (8.36)$$

But, in this form, it may be observed from the positivity of θ and the constancy of the first term in (8.36) that $\ln P_\theta(f)$ is maximized precisely when the last bracket in (8.36) is minimized. Hence, by setting

$$H_N(f) = M - \sum_{ijr} \ln(f_{ijr}!),\ f \varepsilon F_N \tag{8.37}$$

we may conclude that the most probable flow pattern in F_N is given by the solution to the following minimization problem:

$$\min:\ C_N(f) - \frac{1}{\theta}H_N(f),\ \text{subject to } f \varepsilon F_N \tag{8.38}$$

A quick comparison of (8.38) with the programming problem P in (8.9) shows that our goal is now in sight. For if it can be shown that for large trip-activity levels $N = (N_{ij})$ we can replace C_N, H_N, and F_N by C, H, and F, respectively, then the solutions of (8.38) and (8.9) must be the same - and the Correspondence Theorem will be established.

To see that such approximations are valid, observe first that F_N consists precisely of the integer valued flow patterns in F. Hence F is clearly the natural continuous approximation of F_N for large N*. Similarly, as was pointed out in Section

---

* In fact, F is the smallest convex set containing F_N (ie the convex hull of F_N) and represents the best possible convex approximation to F_N in this sense. Moreover, if one formulates the problem in terms of flow distributions $p = \frac{1}{M}f$ (as in Section 8.5 below), then the corresponding set of discrete flow distributions P_N for flows in F_N actually converges to a dense subset of the flow distribution set P for F. Hence the notion of a continuous approximation can be made quite sharp in terms of this distributional framework.

8.3.2, the cumulative flow-cost function C in (8.6) is the natural continuous approximation of its discrete version C_N in (8.24)*. Hence the only real question here concerns the replacement of H_N by H. But for these functions, a quick comparison of (8.37) and (8.8) suggests that an application of Stirling's approximation should yield the desired result. To see that this is indeed the case, we first isolate the role of H_N in (8.38) by decomposing this minimization problem into two stages as follows: Let $C(F_N) = \{C_N(f) | f \varepsilon F_N\}$ denote the set of cumulative flow-cost levels associated with flow patterns in F_N, and for each cost level $C \varepsilon C(F_N)$ let $F_N(C) = \{f \varepsilon F_N | C_N(f) = C\}$ denote the subset of flow patterns consistent with that cost level. Then by construction, the sets $F_N(C)$ partition F_N into a family of nonempty disjoint subsets. Hence the minimization problem in (8.38) can be solved by first solving the corresponding minimization problem within each subset $F_n(C)$, and then choosing the best of these solutions. More formally, if we now observe that the value of cumulative flow-costs is constant within each of these subproblems, then this decomposition of (8.38) can be expressed as follows:

$$\begin{aligned}\min_{f \varepsilon F_N} [C_N(f) - \tfrac{1}{\theta} H_N(f)] &= \min_{C \varepsilon C(F_N)} \{ \min_{f \varepsilon F_N(C)} [C_N(f) - \tfrac{1}{\theta} H_N(f)]\} \\ &= \min_{C \varepsilon C(F_N)} \{C + \min_{f \varepsilon F_N(C)} [- \tfrac{1}{\theta} H_N(f)]\} \\ &= \min_{C \varepsilon C(F_N)} \{C - \tfrac{1}{\theta}[\max_{f \varepsilon F_N(C)} H_N(f)]\} \qquad (8.39)\end{aligned}$$

---

* More precisely, (8.24) consists of the classical 'upper sums' for each (Riemann) integral in (8.6). Hence, for large profile values $N = (N_{ij})$ it is clear that $C_N(f) \approx C(f)$ holds for each flow pattern $f \varepsilon F_N$.

Hence, to solve (8.38) we may begin by solving each maximization problem on the right hand side of (8.39), namely:

$$\max: H_N(f), \text{ subject to: } f \varepsilon F_N(C) \tag{8.40}$$

But each of these maximization problems is seen to be a direct generalization of the original 'maximum entropy' problem formulated by Wilson (1967). Thus, his use of Stirling's approximation is easily seen to hold here as well. For if the number of trips N_{ij} between each relevant origin-destination pair are assumed to be large, then it is clear from (8.37) that the maximum value of $H_N(f)$ must lie among the flow patterns in $F_N(C)$ for which all flow components f_{ijr} are large (ie are as equal as possible). Hence, the classical Stirling approximation

$$\ln(F_{ijr}!) \approx f_{ijr}\ln(f_{ijr}) - f_{ijr}, \; r \varepsilon R_{ij} \tag{8.41}$$

must hold in some neighbourhood of the solution to (8.40). Finally, recalling the definition of entropy H in (8.8) together with the definition of $M = \sum_{ij} N_{ij} = \sum_{ijr} f_{ijr}$, it follows that

$$\begin{aligned} H_N(f) &\approx M - \sum_{ijr} [f_{ijr}\ln(f_{ijr}) - f_{ijr}] \\ &= -\sum_{ijr} f_{ijr}\ln(f_{ijr}) + (M - \sum_{ijr} f_{ijr}) = H(f) \end{aligned} \tag{8.42}$$

must also hold in this neighbourhood, and hence that (8.39) can be rewritten as

$$\begin{aligned} \min_{f\varepsilon F_N} [C_N(f) - \tfrac{1}{\theta}H_N(f)] &= \min_{C\varepsilon C(F_N)} [C - \frac{1}{\theta} \max_{f\varepsilon F_N(C)} H_N(f)] \\ &\approx \min_{C\varepsilon C(F_N)} [C - \frac{1}{\theta} \max_{f\varepsilon F_N(C)} H(f)] \end{aligned}$$

$$= \min_{f \varepsilon F_N} [C_N(f) - \tfrac{1}{\theta}H(f)]$$

$$\simeq \min_{f \varepsilon F} [C(f) - \tfrac{1}{\theta}H(f)] \qquad (8.43)$$

Thus we may conclude that the solutions to (8.38) are indeed approximated by the solutions to (8.9) for large trip activity levels N, and the Correspondence Theorem is established.

8.5 Probability Dominance of Dispersed Network Equilibria

Having established the Correspondence Theorem, there remains one important theoretical question to be addressed - namely how probable are dispersed network equilibria? For even though these patterns are always the most probable ones, it is theoretically possible that they are not 'significantly' more probable than other patterns. Hence, if we are to adopt dispersed network equilibria as the unique representatives of cost-efficient spatial interaction behaviour, it is important to establish conditions under which they are in fact overwhelmingly more probable than any other alternatives.

In his original 1967 paper, Wilson showed that for the case of constant travel costs, the maximum-entropy flow pattern corresponds to a strong 'peak' in the flow pattern probability distribution. This argument (which involved an analysis of the derivatives of the probability distribution in the neighbourhood of the maximum) was sharpened by Jaynes (1968) who showed that for large sample sizes the ratio of probability of the maximum-entropy pattern to that of any other pattern becomes infinitely large. With this in mind, our main objective in this section is to extend the argument of Jaynes to the more complex case of congestion-dependent travel costs. [For the case of constant travel costs, one can strengthen the argument of Jaynes by showing that all probability mass eventually concentrates in arbitrarily small neighbourhoods of the maximum-entropy pattern.

Indeed, one may actually compute lower bounds on the magnitude of this probability for specified neighbourhood sizes. Further details are given in Smith (1981).]

When such congestion effects are introduced, the simple limiting argument employed by Jaynes does not hold without further assumptions. The main difficulty here is that the cumulative flow-cost term C(f) in the objective function of (8.9) eventually overwhelms the entropy term $-\frac{1}{\theta}H(f)$, regardless of the value of $\theta > 0$. Hence one cannot make general statements without further assumptions about the limiting behaviour of the cumulative flow-cost function C. To analyse this problem in a formal way, we begin in the next section by reparameterizing flow patterns in terms of their associated flow distributions (together with the scale factor corresponding to total trip activity). This normalization allows us to treat 'large' flow patterns in terms of a single parameter - namely total trip activity. In addition, this formulation will highlight the fundamental role of average flow costs in the analysis to follow. Within this distributional framework, we start by considering the simple case of constant travel costs studied by Wilson (1967). For this case we show that, even when multiple route choices are introduced, the original argument of Jaynes (1968) goes through intact. Next, to motivate our general results for congested networks, we consider the important special case of 'polynomial' flow costs. This case not only illustrates the general results to follow, but also includes most of the congestion cost functions actually used in practice. The analysis of this case reveals that the corresponding dispersed network equilibria do indeed become overwhelmingly more probable than any other patterns, and eventually converge to the network equilibrium pattern. Hence, for very large trip-activity levels, the results for flow patterns look very much the same as those for their corresponding trip patterns as developed in Section 8.3.2 above - namely that under conditions of cost-efficiency, the only flow patterns which have any significant likelihood of occurring are those very close to network equilibrium. Finally, in Section 8.5.3 these results are extended to a more general class of 'regularly-increasing' flow-cost structures which cover almost all cases of practical interest.

8.5.1 Reparameterization of flow patterns

In order to analyse large flow patterns in a systematic way, it is convenient to normalize flow patterns $f = (f_{ijr})$ as follows. If $M = \sum_{ijr} f_{ijr}$ denotes the total trip activity of f (as in Section 8.4 above), and if $p_{ijr} = f_{ijr}/M$ denotes the relative flow on route $r \varepsilon R_{ij}$ in f, then each pattern f defines a unique flow distribution $p = (p_{ijr})$ which is related to f by $f = pM$. Similarly, if for all origin-destination pairs (ij) we let $p_{ij} = \sum_r p_{ijr}$ denote the corresponding relative trip-activity levels, then the associated feasible flow distribution set P is defined by

$$P = \{p = (p_{ijr}) | p_{ij} = \sum_r p_{ijr}, \forall (ij)\} \qquad (8.44)$$

In this context, we can now investigate the relative probabilities among large flow patterns by holding relative trip-activity levels fixed, and allowing total trip activity M to become large. In particular, each relevant trip-activity profile $(N_{ij}) = (p_{ij}M)$ is now parameterized by the scalar M, so that we may express the corresponding feasible flow set for each activity level M as $F_M = \{f = pM | p \varepsilon P\}$. Hence, for any exponential pattern probability distribution P_θ in (8.29) we can now define corresponding flow pattern probabilities $P_\theta(pM)$ over the (integer valued) patterns in F_M, and for each pair of flow distributions $p, q \varepsilon P$ can study the behaviour of the relative flow probabilities $P_\theta(pM)/P_\theta(qM)$ as M becomes large. In this context, we now say that p is overwhelmingly more probable than q for large M if and only if:

$$\lim_{M\to\infty} \frac{P_\theta(pM)}{P_\theta(qM)} = \infty \tag{8.45}$$

To analyse these ratios for large M, it is convenient to take natural logs and employ the approximations in Section 8.4 above as follows. First, recall that since the relevant trip-activity profiles $N = (N_{ij}) = (p_{ij}M)$ are parameterized solely in terms of M, it follows that the associated cumulative flow-cost $C_N(f)$ for each flow $f \varepsilon F_N$ is expressible solely as a function of p and M, and may be rewritten as $C_N(f) \equiv C_M(p)$. Similarly, $H_N(f)$ in (8.37) may be written as $H_N(f) \equiv H_M(p)$. In these terms, it follows from (8.35) to (8.37) that

$$\begin{aligned} \ln\left[\frac{P_\theta(pM)}{P_\theta(qM)}\right] &= \ln P_\theta(pM) - \ln P_\theta(qM) \\ &= [H_M(p) - \theta C_M(p)] - [H_M(q) - \theta C_M(q)] \\ &= [H_M(p) - H_M(q)] + \theta[C_M(q) - C_M(p)] \end{aligned} \tag{8.46}$$

Moreover, from (8.42) it follows that for large M,

$$H_M(p) \approx H(pM) = MH(p) - M\ln(M) \tag{8.47}$$

so that

$$\ln\left[\frac{P_\theta(pM)}{P_\theta(qM)}\right] \approx M[H(p) - H(q)] + \theta[C_M(q) - C_M(p)] \tag{8.48}$$

Finally, if we designate

$$\overline{C}_M(p) = \frac{1}{M}C_M(p) \tag{8.49}$$

as the average cumulative flow-cost for pattern pM, then by

exponentiating both sides of (8.46) it follows that the relative flow probabilities of pM and qM for large M are approximated by:

$$\frac{P_\theta(pM)}{P_\theta(qM)} \approx \exp\{M([H(p) - H(q)] + \theta[\overline{C}_M(q) - \overline{C}_M(p)])\} \quad (8.50)$$

In this form, the limit in expression (8.45) is seen to depend entirely on the difference between the average cumulative flow-costs of qM and pM, respectively. The behaviour of these average cost differences will thus play a central role in the analysis to follow.

8.5.2 Constant flow costs

To illustrate the nature of this behaviour, it is instructive to begin with the simple case of constant flow costs first studied by Wilson (1967). In our terminology, this means that the underlying link cost functions are assumed to be positive constants, say $c_\ell(f_\ell) = c_\ell > 0$ for each $f_\ell \geq 0$ and $\ell \varepsilon L$. (In addition, Wilson's formulation assumes that there is a constant route cost between each origin-destination pair, which in our terms amounts to assuming that each route set R_{ij} contains only a single link $\ell = (i,j)$.) Hence, if for each flow distribution $p = (p_{ijr}) \varepsilon P$ we now define $p_\ell = \sum_{ijr} \delta^\ell_{ijr} p_{ijr}$ as in (8.3) then it follows from (8.24) and (8.49) that for all $p \varepsilon P$

$$\overline{C}_M(p) = \frac{1}{M}\sum_\ell \left(\sum_{k=1}^{p_\ell M} c_\ell\right) = \frac{1}{M}\sum_\ell (p_\ell M c_\ell) = \sum_\ell p_\ell c_\ell \quad (8.51)$$

So for this case, $\overline{C}_M(p)$ is independent of M, and we may write $\overline{C}_M(p) = \overline{C}(p)$. Thus, setting

$$Z_\theta(p) = \overline{C}(p) - \frac{1}{\theta}H(p), \; p \varepsilon P \quad (8.52)$$

we see that (8.50) reduces to

$$\frac{P_\theta(pM)}{P_\theta(qM)} \approx \exp\{\theta M[Z_\theta(q) - Z_\theta(p)]\} \tag{8.53}$$

The results for this case are now clear. For since Z_θ is independent of M, it follows at once from (8.53) that $P_\theta(pM)/P_\theta(qM) \to \infty$ if and only if $Z_\theta(p) < Z_\theta(q)$. Moreover, since for large M,

$$\begin{aligned} MZ_\theta(p) + \frac{1}{\theta}M\ln(M) &= M\overline{C}(p) - \frac{1}{\theta}[MH(p) - M\ln(M)] \\ &= C_M(p) - \frac{1}{\theta}H_M(p) \\ &\approx C(pM) - \frac{1}{\theta}H(pM) \end{aligned} \tag{8.54}$$

implies that the objective function in (8.9) is asymptotically monotone in Z_θ, we may conclude that the solution to (8.9) yields a flow distribution which is eventually overwhelmingly more probable than any other flow distribution in P. Hence, if we now designate all cost-efficient travel behaviour characterized by the specific cost-sensitivity parameter value θ as θ-efficient trip activity, and denote the associated dispersed network equilibrium flow pattern for each trip activity level M by $f_M^\theta = p_M^\theta M$, then the results for this case maybe summarized as follows:

Theorem 2. (Constant Flow Costs) For large levels of θ-efficient trip activity M on networks with constant flow costs, the dispersed network distribution $p_M^\theta \varepsilon P$ is overwhelmingly more probable than any other distribution in P.

With this result in mind, we turn now to the more difficult case of congestion-dependent flow costs. Here it should be clear from (8.50) above that we must make some assumptions about the behaviour of average cumulative flow-costs $\overline{C}_M(p)$.

To motivate the type of assumptions which appear to be most reasonable here, it is instructive to begin with the important special case of polynomial flow costs - which includes most link cost functions actually used in practice. (For a typical application, see for example Chon, 1982, Section 3.2.)

8.5.3 Polynomial flow costs

We now designate c_ℓ to be a polynomial link cost function if and only if for some $n \geq 3$ there exist non-negative constants $c_{\ell 1}, \ldots, c_{\ell n}$ with $c_{\ell n} > 0$ such that for all $f_\ell = 0$,

$$c_\ell(f_\ell) = \sum_{k=1}^{n} c_{\ell k} f_\ell^{k-1} \tag{8.55}$$

(The requirements that $n \geq 3$ and $c_{\ell n} > 0$ ensure that the corresponding marginal congestion costs are everywhere increasing.) For such link cost functions we see from (8.6) that the associated cumulative flow-costs for each pattern $pM \varepsilon F_M$ are of the form:

$$\begin{aligned} C(pM) &= \sum_\ell \int_o^{p_\ell M} [\sum_k c_{\ell k} x^{k-1}]dx \\ &= \sum_\ell [\sum_{k=1}^{n} \frac{1}{k} c_{\ell k}(p_\ell M)^k] \\ &= \sum_{k=1}^{n} M^k [\frac{1}{k} \sum_\ell c_{\ell k} p_\ell^k] \\ &= \sum_{k=1}^{n} M^k \phi_k(p) \end{aligned} \tag{8.56}$$

where $\phi_k(p) = \frac{1}{k} \sum_\ell c_{\ell k} p_\ell^k$, $k = 1, \ldots, n$. Hence it follows from (8.49) that

$$M^{1-n} \overline{C}_M(p) = M^{-n} C(pM) = \sum_{k=1}^{n} M^{k-n} \phi_k(p) \tag{8.57}$$

But since $M^{k-n} \to 0$ for all $k < n$, we see that for large M,

$$\overline{C}_M(p) \approx M^{n-1}\phi_n(p) \tag{8.58}$$

Moreover, since $n \geq 3$, it follows from (8.50) that

$$\lim_{M\to\infty}(M^{1-n}\ln\left[\frac{P_\theta(pM)}{P_\theta(qM)}\right]) = \theta[\phi_n(q) - \phi_n(p)] \tag{8.59}$$

and hence that for large M,

$$\frac{P_\theta(pM)}{P_\theta(qM)} \approx \exp\{\theta M^{n-1}[\phi_n(q) - \phi_n(p)]\} \tag{8.60}$$

Finally, comparing (8.60) with (8.53) we see that in a manner paralleling the constant-cost case, $P_\theta(pM)/P_\theta(qM) \to \infty$ if and only if $\phi_n(p) < \phi_n(q)$. Moreover, since $M^{1-n}[H(p) - \ln(M)] \to 0$, it follows from (8.57) that

$$M^{-n}[C(pM) - \tfrac{1}{\theta}H(pM)] = M^{1-n}\overline{C}_M(p) - \tfrac{1}{\theta}M^{1-n}[H(p) - \ln(M)]$$

$$\Rightarrow \lim_{M\to\infty} M^{-n}[C(pM) - \tfrac{1}{\theta}H(pM)] = \lim_{M\to\infty} M^{1-n}\overline{C}_M(p) = \phi_n(p)$$

$$\Rightarrow C(pM) - \tfrac{1}{\theta}H(pM) \approx M^n\phi_n(p) \tag{8.61}$$

Hence, the objective function in (8.9) is seen to be asymptotically monotone in ϕ_n, so that the solution to (8.9) is again overwhelmingly more probable than any other flow distribution in P for large M.

However, there is an important difference between this case and the constant-cost case above. For now the limiting objective function ϕ_n is actually independent of θ as well. This means that all dispersed network equilibria p_M^θ must converge to the same limit $p^*\varepsilon P$ given by the unique solution of the convex program:

$$\underline{\min}: \phi_n(p) = \frac{1}{n}\sum_\ell c_{\ell n}p_\ell^n, \text{ subject to: } p\varepsilon P \tag{8.62}$$

Moreover, since (8.58) implies that ϕ_n is simply the monotone limit of cumulative flow-costs C, this unique distribution p* is also the limit of the network equlibrium distributions p^*_M obtained from the solutions $f^*_M = p^*_M M \varepsilon F_M$ to (8.7) for each M. Hence, for the case of polynomial flow costs, we may summarize the above results as follows*:

Theorem 3. (Polynomial Flow Cost) For large levels of θ-efficient trip activity M on networks with polynomial flow costs, the families of network equilibria (p^*_M) and dispersed network equilibria (p^θ_M) both converge to the same overwhelmingly most probable limit distribution $p^* \varepsilon P$ given by the unique solution to (8.62).

8.5.4 Regularly-increasing flow costs

To extend this result for polynomial flow costs to more general flow-cost structures, we begin by observing from (8.58) that the two most important structural features of the polynomial case can be summarized as follows. First, the (continuous, strictly convex) ordering defined over P for each M by average costs $\overline{C}_M$ eventually converges to a (continuous, strictly convex) limit ordering on P defined by the function ϕ_n. Second, each strict inequality $\phi_n(p) < \phi_n(q)$ in this limit ordering implies divergence of the corresponding average cost difference ie $\overline{C}_M(q) - \overline{C}_M(p) \to \infty$. These properties turn out to be the key ingredients in establishing Theorem 3 above. Hence our objective in this section is to construct a more general class of 'regularly-increasing' flow-cost structures which also exhibit these properties.

---

* The careful reader will have noticed that the above argument is not completely rigorous. However, Theorem 3 is easily seen to be a special case of Theorem 4 below, and a rigorous proof of this more general result is given in the Appendix to this chapter.

To begin with, recall from the polynomial case that if $\phi_n(p) < \phi_n(q)$ holds for any p and q, then the convergence of the cumulative flow-cost ordering to this limit order implies that p must eventually 'dominate' q with respect to cumulative flow-costs in the sense that $C(pM) < C(qM)$ must hold for all sufficiently large trip activity levels M. This cost-dominance property thus reflects the behaviour of the limit order ϕ_n. With this in mind, we can capture the effects of such a limit order by extending this notion of cost-dominance to more general flow-cost structures as follows. For any cumulative flow-cost function C and flow distributions $p,q \varepsilon P$, we now say that p cost-dominates q with respect to C, and write $p \underset{c}{<} q$, if and only if there exists a sufficiently large trip activity level M_{pq} such that $C(pM) < C(qM)$ holds for all $M \geq M_{pq}$. On the other hand, if p fails to dominate q in this sense, then we write $q \underset{\bar{c}}{\leq} p$. In terms of this cost-dominance relation, we can now define the desired class of flow-cost structures as follows:

DEFINITION. A cumulative flow-cost function C is said to be regularly increasing if and only if C satisfies the following three conditions for all distinct flow distributions $p,q \varepsilon P$ and all sequences of flow distributions (p_n), (q_n) and trip activity levels (M_n) with $p_n \to p$, $q_n \to q$, and $M_n \to \infty$:

C1. (Continuity) $[C(p_n M_n) \leq C(q_n M_n); \forall n] \Rightarrow p \underset{\bar{c}}{\leq} q$

C2. (Convexity) $[p \underset{\bar{c}}{\leq} q,\ q \underset{\bar{c}}{\leq} p] \Rightarrow (\tfrac{1}{2}p + \tfrac{1}{2}q) \underset{c}{<} p$

C3. (Divergence) $p \underset{c}{<} q \Rightarrow \bar{C}_{M_n}(q_n) - \bar{C}_{M_n}(p_n) \to \infty$

The Continuity and Convexity conditions (C1, C2) are designed to guarantee that the cost-dominance relation $\underset{c}{<}$ generates an ordering over P which essentially plays the role of the limit ordering induced by ϕ_n in the polynomial case. Moreover, the

Divergence condition (C3) implies that this ordering must generate probability-dominance relations of the form (8.45). Hence, one may expect these flow-cost structures to exhibit all the essential features of the polynomial case. That this is indeed the case is shown in the Appendix to this paper, where the following generalization of Theorem 3 above is established:

Theorem 4. (Regularly-Increasing Flow Costs) For large levels of θ-efficient trip activity M on networks with regularly-increasing flow costs, the families of network equilibria (p_M^*) *and dispersed network equilibria* (p_M^θ) *both converge to the same overwhelmingly most probable distribution in P.*

8.6 Operationalizing Dispersed Network Equilibrium Models

Having established a theoretical foundation for DNE-models of spatial interaction behaviour, we turn finally to the important question of operationalizing these models. In particular, recall from the discussion in Section 8.2.3 above that DNE-models provide us with no direct way of estimating the crucial cost-sensitivity parameter θ. Hence, to apply these models to actual situations, it is essential to develop practical procedures for estimating θ. To do so, it is important to observe first that from a practical viewpoint, the size and complexity of actual transportation networks generally prohibit the complete observation of traffic flow patterns. Hence, estimates of θ must necessarily be based on partial information about such flows. Moreover, the estimation problem for DNE-models is further complicated by the fact that the basic flow variables (f_{ijr}) of these models are path flows, which involve explicit information about route-choice decisions for individual travellers. Such data is generally only obtainable by direct home-interview surveys, and hence is (at best) limited to small samples from the relevant population of trip makers.

With this in mind, we begin in Section 8.6.1 below by developing one procedure for estimating θ which does not require any information about explicit path flows. In particular, this procedure utilizes only link flow data (f_ℓ) which can be obtained directly from link traffic counts on the network. However, it should be clear from the behavioural theory developed above that, when home-interview survey data is available (even for only small selected samples from the relevant population), this data is extremely valuable in illuminating actual travel behaviour. Hence it is imperative to develop estimation procedures which can make the best possible use of this information. With this in mind, we develop a class of maximum-likelihood procedures for estimating θ in Section 8.6.2 below which focus explicitly on this type of route-choice information. Finally, we employ this estimation procedure to construct a simple test of the cost-efficiency theory itself in Section 8.6.3.

8.6.1 A maximum-entropy estimation procedure

Recall from the discussion in Section 8.2.3 that an alternative to estimating θ directly is to reparameterize the problem in terms of some fixed exogenous level of entropy H_θ or cumulative flow-costs C_θ, and then to determine θ as the corresponding Lagrange multiplier in the associated EC-program or EM-program respectively. Hence, if a prevailing level of entropy H^o or cumulative flow-cost C^o can be estimated, then θ can be determined on the basis of this estimate. In the present context, however, it is clear from (8.8) that entropy levels $H(f)$ depend directly on the path flows (f_{ijr}), and in fact are no easier to estimate than is the unobserved flow pattern itself. But fortunately, this is not the case for cumulative flow-costs

$C(f)$. For as is clear from (8.6) this cost quantity depends only on the associated link flows (f_ℓ) and hence can in principle be estimated by link traffic counts on the network. In particular, Fisk and Boyce (1982) have recently developed a stratified-sampling procedure for doing so. Hence the procedure proposed by Fisk and Boyce provides an operational method for estimating θ without knowledge of path flows.

To utilize this procedure specifically within the present context, let us suppose that for some given metropolitan area, data is obtained on both link flows (f_ℓ^o) and origin-destination trip totals (N_{ij}^o) for morning rush-hour traffic during some sampling period. If we assume that these trip totals approximate the prevailing trip-activity profile $N^o = (N_{ij}^o)$ during the given sampling period, and assume that commuting behaviour is both cost-efficient and (reasonably) constant over that period, then the unobserved trip pattern t^o which generated this data can be treated as a realization from a conditional pattern-probability distribution $P_\theta(t|N^o)$ of the form (8.30). Hence, under these conditions, it follows from the results of Sections 8.4 and 8.5 above that for large trip activity levels (N_{ij}^o), the prevailing level of cumulative flow-costs should approximate the level C_θ associated with the (overwhelmingly) most probable flow pattern f^θ in F_{N^o}. In other words, if C^o denotes the cumulative flow-cost level estimated by the procedure of Fisk and Boyce (1982) from the link flow data (f_ℓ^o), then it is reasonable to postulate that $C_\theta \simeq C^o$. Under these conditions, it follows from (8.40) that f^θ is given approximately by the solution of the following sub-problem:

$$\max: H_{N^o}(f), \text{ subject to: } f \varepsilon F_{N^o}(C^o) \qquad (8.63)$$

Hence by employing the large-flow approximations in Section 8.4, we obtain the following smoothed version of (8.63), where F^o denotes the smoothing (ie convex hull) of F_{N^o}:

$$\max: H(f), \text{ subject to: } f \varepsilon F^o, \ C(f) = C^o \tag{8.64}$$

Finally, observe that since $f^\theta \varepsilon F^o_{DNE}$ implies $C_\theta < C(f^u)$ for all $\theta > 0$, it follows (from Figure 8.1) that within this cost range, the programming problem in (8.64) with an equality constraint is equivalent to the following EM-program with an inequality constraint:

$$\max: H(f), \text{ subject to: } f \varepsilon F^o(C^o) \tag{8.65}$$

Hence, the most probable flow pattern f^θ consistent with the estimated cost level $C_\theta \simeq C^o$ is given by the solution to (8.65) and the corresponding estimate of θ is given by the Lagrange multiplier for the cost constraint in this EM-program*.

8.6.2 A maximum-likelihood estimation procedure

It should be clear from the development of the cost-efficiency theory in Section 8.3 above that (within the present context of modelling rush-hour traffic flows) this theory focuses entirely on the nature of route-choice behaviour by trip makers. Hence, any direct information which can be obtained about this choice behaviour (through home-interview surveys, questionnaires, etc) should play an important role in calibrating DNE-models. With this in mind, our present objective is to develop a maximum-likelihood procedure for estimating θ which directly incorporates such information.

---

* This computational procedure completely parallels the procedure proposed by Fisk and Boyce (1982) for estimating the β-coefficient in the exponential travel demand function of Erlander (1977) when 'demand entropy' levels are not observable.

To begin with, let us suppose that (as in Section 8.6.1) estimates of prevailing traffic-flow totals $N^o = (N^o_{ij})$ during morning rush hour are available for a given sampling period. If we again postulate that commuting behaviour is cost-efficient, then the overwhelmingly most probable flow pattern during this period must be well approximated by the dispersed network equilibrium $f^\theta \varepsilon F_{N^o}$ for the relevant cost-sensitivity parameter θ of this population of commuters. To obtain further information about actual route-choice behaviour within this population, let us suppose that a series of home-interviews has been conducted (say a one percent sample of this population), and that information on both route choices and travel times to work has been obtained. If for simplicity we take these travel times to represent the relevant costs for each commuter, and if we let $(ijr)_k$ and c^k_{ijr} denote the respective route choice and route cost for the kth commuter (with residence at i and work place at j), then this home-interview survey yields the following data set $\{(ijr)_k, c^k_{ijr} | k=1,\ldots,n\}$.

Given this survey data, our objective is to construct a maximum-likelihood estimation procedure for θ. Basically, our approach will be to construct an explicit probability model of the possible route choices for this random sample of n commuters, given an observed set of relevant control data. This control data of course includes the given trip-activity profile $N^o = (N^o_{ij})$. In addition, this data includes the structural parameters of the particular sampling scheme employed in the home-interview survey. For our purposes it suffices to assume that these home interviews are drawn from an implicit probability distribution $P^o = (P^o_i)$ over residential zones $i \varepsilon I$, and that commuters from each zone have some chance of being interviewed, ie that each P^o_i is positive. Finally, this control data includes both the relevant route choice sets and prevailing route costs which are observed in this survey. More precisely, if n_{ijr} denotes the number of commuters interviewed at i who work at j and select route r to work, then we now designate

$$R^o_{ij} = \{r | n_{ijr} > 0\} \tag{8.66}$$

as the observed route set between i and j, and for each $r \varepsilon R^o_{ij}$ we take the average cost reported by those commuters using route (ijr) to be the observed route cost*

$$c^o_{ijr} = \frac{1}{n_{ijr}} \sum_{k=1}^{n_{ijr}} c^k_{ijr}, \; r \varepsilon R^o_{ij} \tag{8.67}$$

Hence, the relevant control data set D^o for this estimation problem is given by

$$D^o = \{N^o, P^o, (R^o_{ij}), (c^o_{ijr})\} \tag{8.68}$$

In terms of this control data, the unobserved dispersed network equilibrium $f^\theta \varepsilon F_{N^o}$ can now be characterized as follows. If the observed route costs c^o_{ijr} are taken to approximate the most probable route costs, ie if we assume that

$$c_{ijr}(f^\theta) \simeq c^o_{ijr} \tag{8.69}$$

holds for all i,j, and $r \varepsilon R^o_{ij}$, then by (8.12) the corresponding dispersed network equilibrium must satisfy

$$f^\theta_{ijr} = N^o_{ij} \frac{\exp(-\theta c^o_{ijr})}{\sum_{s \varepsilon R^o_{ij}} \exp(-\theta c^o_{ijs})} \tag{8.70}$$

---

* Alternatively, one may employ link traffic-count data to obtain estimates of prevailing route costs c_{ijr}. However, from a behavioural viewpoint, the actual travel times perceived by commuters yields a more meaningful cost estimate when such data are available.

In this context, the desired likelihood function for θ may now be constructed as follows. If $P_\theta(ijr|D^o)$ denotes the probability that a randomly sampled commuter (under survey-sampling scheme P^o and prevailing flow pattern f^θ) will choose trip (ijr), then the likelihood of θ given sample frequencies (n_{ijr}) and control data D^o is given by

$$L[\theta|(n_{ijr}), D^o] = \pi_{ijr} P_\theta(ijr|D^o)^{n_{ijr}} \quad (8.71)$$

To express this likelihood function in explicit form, we now decompose the probability $P_\theta(ijr|D^o)$ into the following product of conditional probabilities:

$$P_\theta(ijr|D^o) = P_\theta(i|D^o)P_\theta(j|i,D^o)P_\theta(r|i,j,D^o) \quad (8.72)$$

Each of these probabilities can in turn be specified as follows. First, the probability $P_\theta(i|D^o)$ that any randomly sampled commuter will reside in zone i is given by the sample-survey scheme P^o in D^o, ie

$$P_\theta(i|D^o) = P_i^o, \; i\varepsilon I \quad (8.73)$$

Second, the probability $P_\theta(j|i,D^o)$ that a randomly sampled commuter from i works at j must be proportional to the commuting flows between i and j. Hence, these probabilities are given by the trip-activity profile N^o in D^o as follows:

$$P_\theta(j|i,D^o) = \frac{N_{ij}^o}{\sum_k N_{ik}^o}, \; j\varepsilon J \quad (8.74)$$

Finally, the actual route-choice probabilities $P_\theta(r|i,j,D^o)$ for any randomly sampled commuter from i to j must be proportional to the prevailing route flows f_{ijr}^θ, so that by (8.70),

$$P_\theta(r|i,j,D^o) = \frac{f^\theta_{ijr}}{N^o_{ij}} = \frac{\exp(-\theta c^o_{ijr})}{\sum_s \exp(-\theta c^o_{ijs})}, \quad r \varepsilon R^o_{ij} \tag{8.75}$$

Hence, combining (8.71) to (8.75) we obtain the following explicit likelihood function for θ:

$$L[\theta|(n_{ijr}),D^o] = \pi_{ijr} \{P^o_i(\frac{N^o_{ij}}{\sum_k N^o_{ik}})(\frac{\exp(-\theta c^o_{ijr})}{\sum_s \exp(-\theta c^o_{ijs})})\} \tag{8.76}$$

If we transform to logs and ignore constant terms, then the desired maximum-likelihood estimate of θ is obtained by maximizing the log-likelihood function:

$$\ell[\theta|(n_{ijr}),D^o] = \sum_{ij}\{\sum_{r\varepsilon R^o_{ij}} n_{ijr} \ln\left[\frac{\exp(-\theta c^o_{ijr})}{\sum_s \exp(-\theta c^o_{ijs})}\right]\} \tag{8.77}$$

In this form, the likelihood function in (8.76) is easily seen to yield a unique maximum. Indeed, if for each route set R^o_{ij} we define the random 'cost' variable C^o_{ij} with probability distribution

$$p_\theta(c^o_{ijr}) = \text{Prob}(C^o_{ij} = c^o_{ijr}) = \frac{\exp(-\theta c^o_{ijr})}{\sum_s \exp(-\theta c^o_{ijs})} \tag{8.78}$$

and population mean $E_\theta(C^o_{ij}) = \sum_r c^o_{ijr} p_\theta(c^o_{ijr})$, then letting $\overline{C}^o_{ij} = \frac{1}{n_{ij}} \sum_r n_{ijr} c^o_{ijr}$ denote the associated sample mean with $n_{ij} = \sum_r n_{ijr}$, it may readily be verified that

$$\frac{\partial \ell}{\partial \theta} = 0 \iff \sum_{ij} n_{ij} E_\theta(C^o_{ij}) = \sum_{ij} n_{ij} \overline{C}^o_{ij} \tag{8.79}$$

Similarly, if $\text{var}_\theta(C^o_{ij})$ denotes the population variance of C^o_{ij}, then it may also be verified that

$$\frac{\partial^2 \ell}{\partial \theta^2} = - \sum_{ij} n_{ij} \mathrm{var}_\theta(C^o_{ij}) < 0 \tag{8.80}$$

Hence by (8.80) the function ℓ is strictly concave, and by (8.79) the resulting unique maximum-likelihood estimator of θ is precisely that value θ^* for which the total population mean cost $\sum_{ij} n_{ij} E_\theta(C^o_{ij})$ equals the total sample mean cost $\sum_{ij} n_{ij} \overline{C}^o_{ij}$. This value may be obtained from (8.79) by standard iterative techniques.

Several additional observations about this estimation procedure are worth making here. First of all, while we have included an explicit trip-activity profile $N^o = (N^o_{ij})$ and survey-sampling distribution $P^o = (P^o_i)$ in the control data set D^o for this estimation problem, it is clear from (8.77) that the final estimate θ^* requires no knowledge of these parameter values. However, knowledge of the trip-activity profile N^o will prove useful in testing the underlying hypothesis of cost-efficient behaviour (in Section 8.6.3 below). Moreover, the assumed positivity of the parameters P^o_i and N^o_{ij} turns out to be important for establishing consistency of the resulting estimate of θ. In particular, observe that if each R^o_{ij} is regarded as the choice set for randomly sampled commuters from i to j, then the likelihood function in (8.76) is seen to be an instance of the general likelihood function for random samples from multinomial logit choice models with choice-set probabilities

$$\mathrm{Prob}(R^o_{ij}) = P^o_i\left(\frac{N^o_{ij}}{\sum_k N^o_{ik}}\right) \tag{8.81}$$

Moreover, since these probabilities satisfy the positive conditioning and uniform conditioning properties in McFadden (1978), it follows that the resulting estimate θ^* is a consistent estimator for θ. Hence, even for a one-percent sample of commuters, the resulting sample size is generally large enough to ensure a reasonably good estimate of the true value of θ under the hypothesis of cost-efficient behaviour.

8.6.3 Testing the cost-efficiency hypothesis

Finally, it is important to observe that this estimation procedure also yields a simple test of the cost-efficiency hypothesis itself. For all the calculations here have been based on the assumption that the prevailing flow pattern f^{θ} satisfies (8.12) for some value of $\theta > 0$. Hence, if we are given an explicit trip-activity profile N^{o} together with estimates of actual travel-time functions c_{ℓ} on each link ℓ, then the maximum-likelihood estimate θ^* above can be employed in (8.12) to solve for the unobserved dispersed network equilibrium $f^{\theta^*} \varepsilon F^{o}$. Moreover, if the resulting flow pattern f^{θ^*} is consistent with our observed control data, then in particular, it follows from (8.69) that the computed flow costs on each route (ijr) should be well approximated by the sample estimates c^{o}_{ijr}, ie that

$$c_{ijr}(f^{\theta^*}) \simeq c^{o}_{ijr} \tag{8.82}$$

should hold for all i,j, and $r \varepsilon R^{o}_{ij}$. Hence, assuming that the estimated travel-time functions c_{ℓ} and trip-activity levels N^{o}_{ij} are reasonably accurate, condition (8.82) in principle provides a test of the cost-efficiency hypothesis itself.

8.7 Extensions and Directions for Further Research

It should be clear from the results developed above that the Correspondence Theorem opens up many avenues for further research. Hence it is appropriate to touch on a few of the more salient possibilities here. We turn first in Section

8.7.1 below to a consideration of possible structural extensions of the present modelling framework, and then take up the question in Section 8.7.2 of extending the behavioural theory itself.

8.7.1 Structural extensions

The Correspondence Theorem has been developed here under the assumption of fixed travel demands for a single transportation mode on a network with separable link cost functions. Such structural assumptions not only simplified the presentation, but also served to motivate the basic theory in terms of its single most compelling example - namely route-choice behaviour during periods of significant traffic congestion. However, it should be clear that the fundamental theory itself does not depend on any of these structural assumptions. First of all, one may of course consider many travel modes (such as cars, buses, and trucks) which interact in terms of the joint congestion effects they create for one another. In particular, the present theory is directly extendable to the class of multimodal dispersed network equilibria derived in terms of entropy-constrained models by Boyce et al (1981, 1983). Such an extension requires the introduction of multiple user-cost functions into the cost-efficiency principle of Section 8.3.4 above. Generalizations of this type are developed in a paper by Erlander and Smith (1983).

Turning next to the assumption of fixed travel demands, the present theory is readily extendable to cases involving other types of macro constraints. For example, if only origin and/or destination totals of trip activity are observed, then the present theory is again directly extendable to this case. Indeed, the cost-efficiency theory in Smith (1983-A) was developed for precisely this case. Hence, if the constraint set in (8.9) is replaced by an alternative set of origin and/or destination constraints, then an appropriate notion of dispersed network equilibria can again be defined as the solution to this new problem. In particular, the results of Sections 8.4 and 8.5 above again imply that the resulting patterns (given in this case by the iterative solution of a system of Lagrangian 'balance equations') are again overwhelmingly most probable for large levels of cost-efficient travel activity. Other extensions of fixed travel demands will be considered in Section 8.7.2 below.

Turning finally to the assumption of separable link costs, it should again be clear that the basic behavioural theory is in no way dependent on this assumption. However, the programming formulation of dispersed network equilibria is very dependent on this assumption. Indeed, if interactions between link cost functions are introduced (such as 'head-on traffic' effects between opposite lanes and 'stop light' effects at intersections between links), then it is well known that no programming formulation may be possible at all. The argument here is usually stated in terms of the dependence of the integrals in (8.6) on the 'path of integration'. But in view of the discrete formulation of cumulative user-costs in Section 8.3.1 above, one may now gain deeper insight into this problem. In particular, the structural effect of introducing such interactions is to create explicit order-dependencies in the resulting cumulative user-cost function $C(t) = C(r_1, \ldots, r_n)$. For since the costs incurred by each driver entering the system now depend not only on current traffic in his lane, but also in the 'head-on' lane (together with all 'intersecting' links), it is clear that the value of $C(r_1, \ldots, r_n)$ depends critically on the order in which trips $(r_1, \ldots, r_n)$ enter the system. This discrete micro-behavioural view now only clarifies the true nature of the 'integrability' problem in the continuous case, but also suggests one possible resolution. For while the total value of $C(r_1, \ldots, r_n)$ is order-dependent, each individual increment $c(r_k|r_1, \ldots, r_k)$ in (8.19) is seen to be locally order-independent in the sense that the costs incurred by each driver k entering the system under current traffic conditions $t^k = (r_1, \ldots, r_{k-1}, r_k)$ depends only on the corresponding flow pattern f^{t^k}, and not on the order in which these previous trips entered the system. Hence, if one applies the cost-efficiency principle to these individual cost increments (and focuses on the possible 'steady-state' flows which can emerge from such a process), then it is possible to extend the present theory to the case of link-interdependent flow costs. This extension will be developed in a subsequent paper.

8.7.2 Behavioural extensions

The cost-efficiency principle developed here has focused exclusively on route-choice behaviour. Hence, the resulting pattern probability models in (8.29) are only uniquely specified in terms of their associated conditional distributions in (8.30) for each given level of trip activity. With this in mind, it is of interest to ask what additional behavioural assumptions can be employed to yield a full specification of the pattern probability distribution.

One approach here is to extend the present cost-efficiency principle beyond the class of activity-equivalent sequences of trip patterns. In particular, recall that one of our basic underlying assumptions in Section 8.3.3 was that travel behaviour remain sufficiently constant over time to allow pattern sequences $T = (t_1, \ldots, t_n)$ to be treated as random samples from the same underlying probability distribution. This constancy assumption also formed the implicit basis for our choice of mean costs $\overline{C}(T)$ to represent typical daily flow costs in the system of interest. More generally, it is well known that under these sampling conditions, a wide range of population behaviour is representable by system averages.

With this in mind, it is of interest to consider modelling trip activity levels themselves in terms of system averages. Hence, if we now denote the mean activity profile for each trip pattern sequence $T = (t_1, \ldots, t_n)$ by

$$\bar{N}^T = \frac{1}{n} \sum_{i=1}^{n} N^{t_i} \tag{8.83}$$

then one may consider cost-efficiency comparisons among pattern sequences T and T' which are mean activity equivalent in the sense that $\bar{N}^T = \bar{N}^{T'}$. If the cost-efficiency principle in (8.28) continues to hold for all such pattern sequences, then in a manner analogous to Smith (1983-A) we designate the resulting travel behaviour as strongly cost-efficient.

In a subsequent paper (Smith, 1983-B), it is shown that this strengthening of the cost-efficiency theory leads in the present case to a class of pattern probability distributions with the following separable exponential form:

$$P_{\theta,\alpha}(t) = \lambda\left(\prod_{ij} \alpha_{ij}^{N_{ij}^t}\right) \exp[-\theta C(t)], \quad t \in S \tag{8.84}$$

Hence, the unspecified weight function $w(N^t)$ in (8.29) is now seen to have the following explicit (log linear) form:

$$w(N^t) = \lambda \prod_{ij} \alpha_{ij}^{N_{ij}^t} \tag{8.85}$$

This implies that the pattern probability distributions in (8.29) now correspond to a fully specified finite-parameter family of distributions $P_{\theta,\alpha}$ with cost-sensitivity parameter θ and positive weight vector $\alpha = (\alpha_{ij})$. This class of distributions will be studied in detail in Smith (1983-B).

Finally, we note that full specifications of pattern probability distributions can also be achieved by combining cost-efficiency with other theories of travel behaviour. In particular, the definition of trip-activity profiles N^t

suggests that the unspecified weight function $w(N^t)$ in (8.29) may be interpreted as an implicit travel demand function. From this point of view, the formal consequence of the strong cost-efficiency principle above is to imply a log linear form for these implicit travel demands (which may be equivalently viewed as a multinomial distribution of stochastic travel demands, as is shown in Smith (1983-B)). Moreover, this interpretation suggests that if additional travel demand information is available, then this information may be employed together with cost-efficiency to complete the model in (8.29). For example, the many random-utility models of travel demand currently in use form natural candidates for such combined models. Models of this type exhibit a strong resemblance to the 'stochastic equilibrium' models proposed by Sheffi and Daganzo (1977, 1980). The relationships among these models will be explored further in subsequent papers.

8.7.3 Applicational extensions

A final area of extensions relates to the wider range of possible applications of the cost-efficiency theory. We shall briefly outline two possible areas of application which appear to be particularly promising.

Spatial Price Equilibria in Market Networks

It has recently been recognized that the classical models of spatial price equilibria originally introduced by Samuelson (1952) and later extended by Takayama and Judge (1964, 1971) can be generalized to include congestion effects in commodity flow networks. The most recent extensions in this direction include the work of Florian and Los (1982) and Friesz et al (1983). The basic idea is to combine the classical market equilibrium conditions for commodity prices with the Wardrop network equilibrium conditions for commodity flows, and thereby to determine simultaneously a set of equlibrium commodity prices at each market together with equilibrium commodity flows between markets.

In this context, it should be clear that the same types of dispersion phenomena developed above for traffic flows are perfectly meaningful for commodity flows. For example, the hidden costs of re-routing freight (together with the myriad of existing freight regulations) can lead to apparently non-optimal routing of commodity flows. Hence, in many cases it may be quite appropriate to model such flows in terms of cost-efficient behaviour, and thereby seek to determine the most probable cost-efficient patterns of commodity flows.

In addition, it has long been recognized that actual price dispersion between spatially separated markets tends to include many effects other than simple shipment costs between markets. Hence it is also meaningful to model such price dispersion in terms of efficiency concepts. Indeed, one may attempt to combine the dispersion effects in both commodity prices and flows by postulating that price-flow patterns consistent with higher average profit levels in the system are at least as probable as those with lower levels. The representational consequences of such a 'profit-efficiency' principle will be explored in a subsequent paper.

Transportation and Land-use Equilibria

A second area of possible application of the cost-efficiency theory relates to the current efforts by many researchers to model the interaction effects between transportation and land-use patterns. By way of illustration, it is of interest to consider the simple class of (Lowry-type) equilibrium models formulated by Wilson (1976-C) and extended by Harris and Wilson (1978) among others. These models are designed to study the spatial interaction effects between residential and retail land-use patterns. Here the underlying urban transportation network, which is characterized by fixed travel costs between locations, plays a fundamental role in determining the basic (gravity-type) spatial market demands for each retailer. However, it is clear that at the intra-urban scale for which these models are intended, traffic congestion effects can play a major role in determining shopping patterns. Hence it is of real interest to extend these models to include the effects of congested networks. Such efforts have yet to be made even for the simple case of Wardropian equilibrium. Hence the further extension of these models to more realistic dispersed network equilibria is quite speculative at this stage. Nevertheless, it is clear that the same basic behavioural principles should apply here as well.

APPENDIX: Probability Dominance for Regularly-increasing Flow Costs

The objective of this Appendix is to establish Theorem 4 in the text. To do so, we begin with a number of preliminary observations. First, observe that since the set of flow distributions P is by construction a compact metric space (with Euclidean metric), the class of infinite sequences (p_n) on P possesses certain special properties. To state these properties formally we require the notion of an 'accumulation point'. An element $p \varepsilon P$ is said to be an accumulation point of a given sequence (p_n) on P if there exists a subsequence (p_{n_k}) of (p_n) with $p_{n_k} \rightarrow p$. If $A(p_n)$ denotes the set of all accumulation points for (p_n), then the following properties of sequences in P are well known:

LEMMA 1. For all sequences (p_n) on P and all elements $p \varepsilon P$,

$$A(p_n) \neq \emptyset \tag{8.86}$$

$$\lim_{n\to\infty} p_n = p \iff A(p_n) = \{p\} \tag{8.87}$$

Next, recall from the definition of average cumulative user-costs $\overline{C}_M(p) = \frac{1}{M}C(pM)$ together with the programming formulation of network equilibria in (8.7) that the sequence (p_M^*) on P satisfying

$$\overline{C}_M(p_M^*) = \min\{\overline{C}_M(p) \mid p\varepsilon P\} \tag{8.88}$$

for all positive integers M is uniquely defined, and corresponds precisely to the sequence of network equilibria for each trip activity level M. Similarly, since

$$C(pM) - \frac{1}{\theta}H(pM) = C(pM) - \frac{1}{\theta}[MH(p) - M\ln(M)]$$

$$= M[\overline{C}_M(p) - \frac{1}{\theta}H(p)] + \frac{1}{\theta}M\ln(M) \tag{8.89}$$

implies that the objective function in (8.9) is monotone increasing in $\overline{C}_M(p) - \frac{1}{\theta}H(p)$ for each positive M and θ, it follows that the sequence (p_M^θ) on P satisfying

$$\overline{C}_M(p_M^\theta) - \frac{1}{\theta}H(p_M^\theta) = \min\{\overline{C}_M(p) - \frac{1}{\theta}H(p) \mid p\varepsilon P\} \tag{8.90}$$

is also uniquely defined, and corresponds to the sequence of (θ-efficient) dispersed network equilibria for each trip activity level M. In terms of these definitions, we can now establish the following fundamental properties of regularly-increasing flow costs:

LEMMA 2. For any regularly-increasing cumulative flow-cost function C, there exists a unique $p^*\varepsilon P$ satisfying the following two conditions for all $p\varepsilon P$ and $\theta > 0$,

$$p \neq p^* \Rightarrow p^* \underset{C}{<} p \tag{8.91}$$

$$\lim_{M\to\infty} p_M^* = p^* = \lim_{M\to\infty} p_M^\theta \tag{8.92}$$

Proof: By property (8.86) of Lemma 1, there must exist some $p^*\varepsilon A(p_M^*)$. Hence our first objective is to show that p^* is unique, ie that

$$A(p_M^*) = \{p^*\} \tag{8.93}$$

To do so, we first show that no such p^* can be cost-dominated by any other flow distribution in P, ie that for all $q\varepsilon P$,

$$p^*\varepsilon A(p_M^*) \Rightarrow p^* \underset{C}{\lesseqgtr} q \tag{8.94}$$

To see this, observe first that $p^*\varepsilon A(p_M^*)$ implies the existence of a subsequence $(p_{M_n}^*)$ with $p_{M_n}^* \to p^*$. Hence, if we set $(p_n) = (p_{M_n}^*)$ and for any $q\varepsilon P$ define the constant sequence $(q_n = q)$, then (8.88) implies that $\overline{C}_{M_n}(p_n) \leq \overline{C}_{M_n}(q_n)$ for all n, and hence that $C(p_nM_n) \leq C(q_nM_n)$ for all n. Thus, the continuity property (C1) of regularly-increasing C together with $p_n \to p^*$ and $q_n \to q$ allows us to conclude that $p^* \underset{C}{\lesseqgtr} q$, and hence that (8.94) holds. Next we employ (8.94) to show that p^* actually satisfies (8.91). For if not, then there exists some $p\varepsilon P-\{p^*\}$ with $p \underset{C}{\lesseqgtr} p^*$. But since (8.94) implies that $p^* \underset{C}{\lesseqgtr} p$ also holds, it follows from the convexity property (C2) of regularly-increasing C that $q \underset{C}{<} p^*$ must hold with $q = \frac{1}{2}(p^*+p)\varepsilon P$. Hence the existence of such a p leads to a contradiction of (8.94) and we may conclude that p^* must satisfy (8.91). Moreover, this in turn implies that (8.93) must hold. For if there were another $q^*\varepsilon A(p_M^*)$, then the above argument would imply that both $p^* \underset{C}{<} q^*$ and $q^* \underset{C}{<} p^*$ hold - which contradicts the obvious asymmetry of the relation $\underset{C}{<}$. Hence p^* is unique, and we may conclude from property (8.87) of Lemma 1 that the first equality in (8.92) must hold.

To complete the proof, it thus remains to establish the

second equality in (8.92) for any choice of positive θ. To do so, observe again from (8.87) of Lemma 1 that this is equivalent to showing that $A(p_M^\theta) = \{p^*\}$. Moreover, since $A(p_M^\theta) \neq \emptyset$ by property (8.86) of Lemma 1, it suffices to show that p^* is the only possible accumulation point of (p_M^θ), ie that

$$p^\theta \varepsilon A(p_M^\theta) \Rightarrow p^\theta = p^* \tag{8.95}$$

To establish (8.95) let us suppose to the contrary that there exists some element $p^\theta \varepsilon A(p_M^\theta) - \{p^*\}$. Then $p^\theta \varepsilon A(p_M^\theta)$ implies the existence of a sub-sequence $(p_{M_n}^\theta)$ of (p_M^θ) with $p_{M_n}^\theta \to p^\theta$. Hence it follows from (8.91) together with the divergence property (C3) of regularly-increasing C that by setting $(p_n) = (p_{M_n}^\theta)$ and $(q_n = p^*)$ we must have

$$p^\theta \neq p^* \Rightarrow p^* \underset{c}{<} p^\theta$$

$$\Rightarrow \overline{C}_{M_n}(p_{M_n}^\theta) - \overline{C}_{M_n}(p^*) \to \infty \tag{8.96}$$

On the other hand, if we set $H^* = \max\{H(p)|p\varepsilon P\} < \infty$, then it follows from (8.90) that for all n,

$$\overline{C}_{M_n}(p_{M_n}^\theta) - \frac{1}{\theta}H(p_{M_n}^\theta) \leq \overline{C}_{M_n}(p^*) - \frac{1}{\theta}H(p^*)$$

$$\overline{C}_{M_n}(p_{M_n}^\theta) - \overline{C}_{M_n}(p^*) \leq \frac{1}{\theta}[H(p_{M_n}^\theta) - H(p^*)]$$

$$\leq \frac{1}{\theta}[H^* - H(p^*)] < \infty \tag{8.97}$$

But since this contradicts (8.96) we may conclude that no such p^θ exists, and the result is established. End of Proof.

In terms of these results, the proof of Theorem 4 is now immediate:

Theorem 4. (Regularly-Increasing Flow Costs) For large levels of θ-efficient trip activity M on networks with *regularly-increasing flow costs, the families of network equilibria* (p_M^*) *and dispersed network equilibria* (p_M^θ) *both converge to the same overwhelmingly most probable distribution in P.*

Proof: By expression (8.92) in Lemma 2 above, both (p_M^*) and (p_M^θ) share the same limit distribution $p^* \varepsilon P$. Moreover, the cost-dominance of p^* in expression (8.91) of Lemma 2 together with expression (8.50) in the text implies that if we set $(p_M = p^*)$ and $(q_M = q)$ for any $q \neq p^*$, then we may conclude from the divergence property (C3) of regularly-increasing C that:

$$p^* \underset{c}{<} q \Rightarrow \overline{C}_M(q) - \overline{C}_M(p^*) \to \infty$$

$$\Rightarrow \exp\{M([H(p^*) - H(q)] + \theta[\overline{C}_M(q) - \overline{C}_M(p^*)])\} \to \infty$$

$$\Rightarrow P_\theta(p^*M)/P_\theta(qM) \to \infty \qquad (8.98)$$

Hence p^* is overwhelmingly more probable than any other distribution $q \varepsilon P$ for large M, and the result is established. End of Proof.

Chapter Nine

THE THEORY OF DETERMINISTIC AND STOCHASTIC COMPARTMENTAL MODELS AND ITS APPLICATIONS

A. de Palma and Cl. Lefèvre

9.1 Introduction

The economical and social systems whose behaviour depends on the aggregation of a large number of individual decisions are naturally embedded in a statistical description which tries to find laws or regulations which do not appear when looking at the units of the system considered separately. Mathematical models are used more and more frequently to study such social systems, and have given rise to a large literature. Two different points of view are considered: on the one hand, the normative approach examines socio-economical systems in relation to value (normative) criteria selected a priori*. On the other hand, the descriptive approach explains the evolution of such systems on the basis of the behaviour of their units.

In this chapter, we will focus only on the descriptive approach and we will present the principal mathematical tools used. The techniques involved are specific to the description of systems in terms of processes: indeed, in this case, no variational principle, characteristic of the normative approach, seems to apply. The models currently used can be subdivided in two classes: the deterministic models in terms of differential

---

* For a recent bibliography on this subject, see the review paper by Fujita (1983).

or difference equations, and the stochastic models in terms of Markov processes or chains. More recently, quasi-deterministic models in terms of differential or difference stochastic equations have been developed. In this paper, we will present these three general approaches and we will discuss in particular their hypotheses, their applicability and their mutual connections. The models will be discussed in the spatio-temporal context specific to regional sciences, and will be principally illustrated in the fields of transportation and residential location. We have also thought that it is interesting to mention similar studies in the fields of chemistry and biology.

9.2 The Compartmental Models

A compartmental model is concerned with the description of a system subdivided into a finite number of subsystems called compartments between which the fundamental units of the system move. The purpose of this model is to describe the temporal evolution of the state of the system which is defined as the number of units in the different compartments. We will first justify the relevance of this model in social and biochemical sciences (9.2.1). Then, we will present its mathematical characteristics and the different modelling methods (9.2.2).

9.2.1 An overview of the applications of these models

Very often in social sciences, the populations of individuals are stratified in classes in relation to their socio-economical characteristics. So, for the description of the propagation of a rumour or innovation (Bass, 1969, Rogers and Shoemaker, 1971, and Urban and Hauser, 1980), the population is subdivided into strata related to economical criteria (income for example), geographical criteria (location for example) and relation to their state and attitude towards the innovation (active or passive, user or not for example). Similarly in the hierarchical population models used in enterprises for the manpower planning, the compartments of the system correspond to the different grades in the enterprises and the transitions between the compartments correspond to the promotions, arrivals or departures (Bartholomew, 1973, Vajda, 1978, and McLean, 1980). Finally, for the decision-making problems in collective systems, the individual choice behaviours are described in terms of transitions between compartments which are then interpreted as the different options available for individuals (de Palma and Lefèvre, 1983). Several studies correspond well with this formulation: in residential location (Bertuglia and Leonardi, 1979, and de Palma and Ben-Akiva, 1981), and in the fields of interregional migration (Ginsberg, 1972, and Wilson, 1974), and of transportation (de Palma et al, 1983, and Kahn, Deneubourg and de Palma, 1982).

The compartmental models are also used in chemical and biological sciences. A number of authors describe chemical systems as a set of cells which communicate between them by processes of energy and mass transportation (Malek-Mansour and Nicolis, 1975, and Nicolis and Prigogine, 1977). In biology, some systems are described in a natural way by compartmental models; this is the case, for example, when studying the reactions of the systems components after the introduction of some external entities (in pharmacology and in ecology for example). These works have given rise to important theoretical studies (Chiang, 1968, Jacquez, 1972, 1979, and Matis and Wehrly, 1979). In a rather surprising way, mathematical models in epidemiology have been developed with a point of view similar to that used in the studies of the diffusion of rumours and innovations. The objective of these models is to describe qualitatively or quantitatively the spread of an infectious disease through a population stratified in regard to the degree of susceptibility and infectivity of the individuals

(Watson, 1972, Bailey, 1975, and Spicer, 1979).

9.2.2 The different approaches

The compartmental models defined here are intrinsically dynamic because the state of the system is the consequence of the various past transitions; so, the results derived describe the transient (finite time) and stationary (infinite time) regimes of the models. Moreover, the systems considered are concerned with populations of units; so, special attention is paid to macroscopic behaviours and collective phenomena.

Two qualitatively different situations occur. In the "linear" systems, the individuals have independent behaviours and consequently, the state of the population can be deduced simply from the behaviour of their units; this situation is of application in manpower planning and very often in biology and migration models. In the opposite case, for the "nonlinear" models, the individuals have interdependent behaviours whose aggregation can give rise to qualitatively new situations (spatio-temporal structuration for example); this is true for epidemic models, kinetic models in chemistry, diffusion models in marketing and for individual choice models in collective systems. Another important distinction is between open and closed systems. Closed systems do not allow transitions of units between the system and the "external world". On the contrary, this type of transition is allowed in open systems and, as a matter of fact, has fundamental consequences because it can modify in a crucial way the evolution of the system.

Several different mathematical tools are available in compartmental analysis. The selection of a particular tool is of course induced by the physical properties of the system but also by considerations which are connected with the tractability of the techniques. An important distinction is made between the deterministic and stochastic models (Eisenfeld,

1979). The system is deterministic when its evolution can be predicted with certainty. In social sciences for instance, this is seldom true; indeed, there are often random factors which perturb the evolution of the systems, either because the systems are not completely specified, or because the behaviours of the individuals display intrinsically stochastic elements. The stochastic version is then more appropriate; unfortunately, it leads often to more complicated problems from the analytical point of view. Another distinction can be made between discrete and continuous time models. The continuous time formulation is easier to use whilst the discrete time formulation is more adequate for estimation procedures.

This chapter is divided in seven sections. In the first three sections, continuous time models are developed, and the probabilistic (9.3), deterministic (9.4), and quasi-deterministic (9.5) versions are discussed. In each of these sections, the linear and nonlinear cases are studied (Hearon, 1953); the connections between these approaches are also analysed. A similar study is made in Section 9.6 for discrete time models. In Section 9.7 we review other different approaches which can be applied to the analysis of compartmental systems. In the last section, 9.8, we discuss an example of application of compartmental analysis in the domain of residential location.

9.3 The Markovian Approach

We make here the Markov assumption which states that the individuals move from compartment to compartment with probabilities which depend on the characteristics of these compartments but not on the previously occupied compartments ("the future depends on the present but not on the past"). We consider the cases where the transition probabilities do not depend (linear case) or depend (nonlinear case) on the state of the system (that is to say, on the number of individuals in the compartments).

9.3.1 Derivation of the master equations

Let us consider a compartment model with J compartments. $X_j(t)$ will denote the number of individuals in compartment j at time t, $t \geq 0$, and x_j a possible realization of $X_j(t)$, $j = 1, \ldots, J$. Let $\underline{X}(t)$ be the J x 1 column vector $[X_1(t), \ldots, X_J(t)]'$ and $\underline{x}$ a possible realization of $\underline{X}(t)$. We define by $R_{i,j}(\underline{x},t)\Delta t + o(\Delta t)$, $1 \leq i \neq j \leq J$, the probability that during the infinitesimal time interval $(t, t+\Delta t)$, a given individual moves from compartment i to compartment j when the system is in the state $\underline{x}$ at time t. For an open system, $R_{i,0}(\underline{x},t)\Delta t + o(\Delta t)$ represents the probability that this individual leaves the compartment i to go to the external world, and $R_{0,j}(x,t)\Delta t + o(\Delta t)$ the probability of arrival of an individual from the external world into compartment j. The different transition probabilities are shown in Figure 9.1.

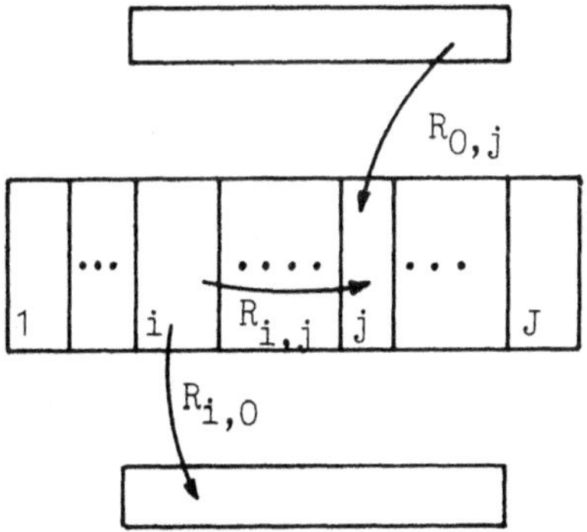

Figure 9.1: Schematic representation of a compartment model

Let $P_{\underline{x}_0,\underline{x}}(t)$ denote the probability that $\underline{X}(t) = \underline{x}$ given the initial condition $\underline{X}(0) = \underline{x}_0$. Let $\underline{e}_j = [\delta_{1,j}, \ldots, \delta_{J,j}]'$, $j = 1, \ldots J$, be an orthonormal base of R^J. The Kolmogorov forward differential equations give the temporal evolution of the probability distribution of the system's state - which accounts for the "gain" terms (transitions to the state x) and the "loss" terms (transitions from the state x) and take the form (Cox and Miller, 1965):

$$\frac{d}{dt} P_{\underline{x}_0,\underline{x}}(t) = \sum_{i=1}^{J} \sum_{\substack{j=1 \\ \neq i}}^{J} P_{\underline{x}_0,\underline{x}+\underline{e}_i-\underline{e}_j}(t).(x_i+1).R_{i,j}(\underline{x}+\underline{e}_i-\underline{e}_j,t)$$

$$+ \sum_{j=1}^{J} P_{\underline{x}_0,\underline{x}+\underline{e}_j}(t).(x_j+1).R_{j,0}(\underline{x}+\underline{e}_j,t)$$

$$+ \sum_{j=1}^{J} P_{\underline{x}_0,\underline{x}-\underline{e}_j}(t).R_{0,j}(\underline{x}-\underline{e}_j,t) - P_{\underline{x}_0,\underline{x}}(t).$$

$$\{ \sum_{i=1}^{J} \sum_{\substack{j=1 \\ \neq i}}^{J} x_i.R_{i,j}(\underline{x},t) + \sum_{j=1}^{J} x_j.R_{j,0}(\underline{x},t)$$

$$+ \sum_{j=1}^{J} R_{0,j}(\underline{x},t)\} \qquad (9.1)$$

Equations (9.1) are the master equations for the multivariate birth and death process. These equations are difficult to solve in general. Nevertheless, we show below how to obtain some information on the evolution of the system's state.

9.3.2 The linear case

In this case, the transition rates $R_{i,j}(\underline{x},t)$, $R_{0,j}(\underline{x},t)$ and $R_{j,0}(\underline{x},t)$ are supposed to be independent of the system state

$\underline{x}$; the argument $\underline{x}$ can be thus omitted.

The solution of (9.1) can be then obtained by the method of generating functions or by a more direct probabilistic argument. We recall below the main results derived by Faddy (1977), McLean (1980), and Capasso and Paveri-Fontana (1981).

9.3.2.1 The transient distribution

Let us denote by $p_{i,j}(t)$ the probability that an individual initially in compartment i is in compartment j at time t, $1 \leq i, j \leq J$, and let $\underline{P}(t)$ be the J x J matrix of the $p_{i,j}(t)$'s. The Kolmogorov forward differential equations can be written in matrix form as:

$$\frac{d}{dt}\underline{P}(t) = \underline{P}(t).\underline{R}(t) \tag{9.2}$$

where $\underline{R}(t)$ is the J x J matrix of the rates $R_{i,j}(t)$, $1 \leq i, j \leq J$, with $R_{j,j}(t)$, $1 \leq j \leq J$, defined by

$$R_{j,j}(t) = -\sum_{\substack{k=0 \\ \neq j}}^{J} R_{j,k}(t) \tag{9.3}$$

If $\underline{R}(t)$ is a constant matrix $\underline{R}$, equation (9.2) has the following solution:

$$\underline{P}(t) = \exp[\underline{R}.t] \tag{9.4}$$

In the other cases, it is more difficult to write the solution of (9.2) in a simple way.

Now, it is possible to establish rigorously the following intuitive result:

$$\underline{X}(t) = \underline{X}_1(t) + \underline{X}_2(t) \tag{9.5}$$

where $\underline{X}_1(t)$ represents the state of the system at time t if it was initially empty, and $\underline{X}_2(t)$ represents its state if there were no arrival. Let us denote by $G(\underline{\xi},t)$, $G_1(\underline{\xi},t)$ and $G_2(\underline{\xi},t)$ the generating functions of the vectors $\underline{X}(t)$, $\underline{X}_1(t)$ and $\underline{X}_2(t)$ respectively; so for example:

$$G(\underline{\xi},t) = \sum_{\underline{x}} \underline{\xi}^{\underline{x}}.P_{\underline{x}_0,\underline{x}}(t) \tag{9.6}$$

where

$$\underline{\xi}\varepsilon C^J, \quad |\xi_j| < 1, \ 1 \leq j \leq J,$$

$$\underline{\xi}^{\underline{x}} \equiv \xi_1^{x_1} \ldots \xi_J^{x_J}.$$

As the individuals do not interact, the variables $\underline{X}_1(t)$ and $\underline{X}_2(t)$ are independent so that:

$$G(\underline{\xi},t) = G_1(\underline{\xi},t).G_2(\underline{\xi},t) \tag{9.7}$$

The value of $G_1(\underline{\xi},t)$ and $G_2(\underline{\xi},t)$ must now be calculated. One can show that (Karlin and Taylor, 1981):

$$G_1(\underline{\xi},t) = \exp[(\underline{\xi}-\underline{u})'.\int_0^t P'(\tau,t).R_0(\tau)d\tau],$$

$$G_2(\underline{\xi},t) = [\underline{P}(t).(\underline{\xi}-\underline{u}) + \underline{u}]^{\underline{x}_0} \tag{9.8}$$

where $\underline{u}$ and $R_0(\tau)$ are the J x 1 column vectors $[1, \ldots, \ell]'$ and $[R_{0,1}(\tau), \ldots, R_{0,J}(\tau)]'$ respectively, $\underline{P}(t)$ is the J x J matrix solution of (2) and $\underline{P}(\tau,t)$ is the J x J matrix of the probabilities $p_{i,j}(\tau,t)$ that an individual in compartment i at time τ is in compartment j at time t (the matrix $\underline{P}(\tau,t)$ can be derived from an equation similar to (9.2)).

9.3.2.2 Mean and covariance matrix

Let $\underline{M}(t)$ be the expected state of the system at time t, that is, $\underline{M}(t) = E[\underline{X}(t)]$. It is easily shown that:

$$\frac{d}{dt}\underline{M}(t) = \underline{R}'(t).\underline{M}(t) + \underline{R}_0(t) \tag{9.9}$$

which yields:

$$\underline{M}(t) = \underline{P}'(t).\underline{x}_0 + \int_0^t \underline{P}'(\tau,t).R_0(\tau)d\tau \tag{9.10}$$

Let $\underline{C}(t)$ be the covariance matrix of $\underline{X}(t)$, that is, $\underline{C}(t) = E[\underline{X}(t).\underline{X}'(t)] - E[\underline{X}(t)].E[\underline{X}'(t)]$, and $\underline{C}^M(t)$ its modification defined by:

$$\underline{C}^M(t) = \underline{C}(t) - \text{diag}[\underline{M}(t)] \tag{9.11}$$

It can be deduced from (9.1) that:

$$\frac{d}{dt}\underline{C}^M(t) = \underline{R}'(t).\underline{C}^M(t) + \underline{C}^M(t).\underline{R}(t) \tag{9.12}$$

which gives:

$$\underline{C}^M(t) = \underline{P}'(t).\underline{C}^M(0).\underline{P}(t) \tag{9.13}$$

and thus:

$$\underline{C}(t) = \underline{C}^M(t) + \text{diag}[\underline{M}(t)] \tag{9.14}$$

We emphasize that the arrivals do not affect the evolution of $\underline{C}^M(t)$ and consequently, have no influence on the covariances between the numbers of individuals in the different compartments (but do on their variances!).

9.3.2.3 The stationary distribution

When the transition rates do not depend explicitly on time, the stationary distribution of the system's state can be derived from (9.7) and (9.8). We will consider here two particular situations of special interest.

If the compartmental model is irreducible (that is to say, all compartments intercommunicate), and if there are no arrivals and departures, then:

$$\lim_{t\to\infty} G(\xi,t) = (\underline{p}'.\underline{\xi})^{\underline{x}'_0.\underline{u}} \tag{9.15}$$

where $\underline{p}$ is a J x 1 Perron vector (see, for example, Cox and Miller, 1965) whose components are positive and of sum equal to 1. Consequently, at the stationary state, G is the generating function of a multinomial vector of exponent $\underline{x}'_0.\underline{u}$ and of parameters $\underline{p}$. It can be verified that:

$$\lim_{t\to\infty} \underline{M}(t) = (\underline{x}'_0.\underline{u}).\underline{p} \tag{9.16}$$

$$\lim_{t\to\infty} C^M(t) = (u'.C^M(0).u).\underline{p}.\underline{p}' \tag{9.17}$$

If the compartmental model is nonsingular (that is to say, det $|R| \neq 0$, which implies the existence of departures), then:

$$\lim_{t\to\infty} G(\underline{\xi},t) = \exp[(\underline{\xi}-\underline{u})'.(-\underline{R}'^{-1}.\underline{R}_0)] \tag{9.18}$$

At the stationary state, G is thus the generating function of a Poisson vector with independent components and of parameters $-R'^{-1}.R_0$. It is easily verified that:

$$\lim_{t\to\infty} \underline{M}(t) = -\underline{R}'^{-1}.\underline{R}_0 \tag{9.19}$$

$$\lim_{t \to \infty} \underline{C}^M(t) = \underline{0} \tag{9.20}$$

9.3.2.4 Applications of these models

Several authors (Gardiner et al, 1976 and Nicolis and Prigogine, 1977, for example) have tried to describe the importance of fluctuations in the chemical-physic systems and have proposed a representation of the chemical reactions in terms of Markov processes. This formulation involves equations of type (9.1). The variable $X_j(t)$ represents the number of molecules of product j, j = 1, ..., J. In the linear case considered here, $R_{i,j}$, $1 \leqq i \neq j \leqq J$, is a transition rate corresponding to a monomolecular reaction (no reactive collisions occur in the system). The arrivals correspond to chemical reactions for which the initial products are maintained constant (which implies constant arrival rates).

In pharmacology, a large number of situations can be modelled with some compartmental systems. So, various studies describe and quantify the effects that drugs may have on the different parts of the organism. The great attraction of the models based on equations of type (9.1) for the physiological systems, rests on the simple but satisfying explanation of the passage of molecules among the physiological subsystems (Matis and Hartley, 1971, and Anderson et al, 1977, for example).

In ecology, most of the models use nonlinear kinetics. Nevertheless, the linear approach has lead to valuable approximations in some specific cases, for example for the study of the response of ecosystems to the introduction of an external element (see, for example, Matis and Wehrly, 1979).

The compartmental models have been used in different fields of social sciences. Several stochastic approaches have described the interregional mobility and the intraurban movement decisions (Ginsberg, 1972, and Bartholomew, 1973).

Similar works have been made to study the problems of social mobility and manpower planning in hierarchical structures (universities and enterprises for example); we refer the reader to Coleman (1964) and McLean (1978). As pointed out by Conlisk (1976), linear models have been widely used because of the simplicity of their analysis and estimation. However, the hypothesis of independence between the individual behaviours is often restrictive, in particular for the modelling of the individual choices in the fields of residential location and transportation.

9.3.3 The nonlinear case

In this case, the transition rates $R_{i,j}(\underline{x},t)$, $R_{j,0}(\underline{x},t)$ and $R_{0,j}(\underline{x},t)$ depend explicitly on the state of the system.

The presence of the argument $\underline{x}$ in the transition rates makes equations (9.1) difficult to solve. Indeed, the method of generating functions leads no more, as in the linear case, to a simple first-order partial differential equation. Only particular models have been analysed until now. We will discuss below two examples which permit the derivation of analytical results from (9.1).

9.3.3.1 A model of choice behaviour in a collective system

Let us consider a closed population of N individuals, each individual having to select one between two choices C_1 and C_2. These could represent a transportation mode (bus and car), a product which is accepted or not, or a location (city and country) for example. The choice behaviour of the individuals in the population is described by a compartmental model, each choice corresponding to a compartment in the system. The population is closed and we will thus describe the state of the system with one variable, $X_1(t)$ for example, whose realizations are denoted by x. Let us now give the structure of the transition rates $R_{i,j}(x,t)$, $1 \leq i, j \leq 2$.

We will suppose that an individual decides to review and modify his choice through two successive steps (de Palma and Lefèvre, 1983). First, during $(t, t + \Delta t)$, he reconsiders his present choice C_i with a probability $R^{(i)}\Delta t + o(\Delta t)$; then, he selects a choice C_j with a probability $p^{(j)}(x)$ which has the following logit form:

$$p^{(j)}(x) = \exp[v^{(j)}(x)/\mu]/\{\exp[v^{(1)}(x)/\mu] + \exp[v^{(2)}(x)/\mu]\},$$

$$j = 1,2 \qquad (9.21)$$

where $v^{(1)}(x)$ and $v^{(2)}(x)$ represent the utility functions of choices C_1 and C_2 respectively, and μ is a positive parameter which expresses the degree of uncertainty in the individual's behaviour. This formula can be justified with microeconomic arguments based on the optimization rule of a random utility function associated with each choice (Domencich and McFadden, 1975). Let us emphasize that index i, characteristic of the present choice C_i, does not appear in (9.21). This implies in particular that there does not exist any transaction cost. We have discussed in two other papers the situation where such transaction costs are taken into account: see de Palma and Lefèvre (1983), and de Palma and Ben-Akiva (1981) for a particular application in residential location.

It is clear that the process $X_1(t)$ is reduced to an invariate birth and death process. The global distribution of individual choices strongly depends on the structure of the utility functions. For illustration, we will examine the cases where the utilities of each choice is a linear or logarithmic function of the number of individuals who have adopted this choice (that is, $v^{(1)}(x)$ and $v^{(2)}(x)$ are linear or logarithmic functions of x and N-x respectively).

Let us first consider the case where the utility functions are linear:

$$v^{(1)}(x) = a + bx \qquad x = 0, \ldots, N \qquad (9.22)$$
$$v^{(2)}(x) = c + d(N-x)$$

The Markov process is then irreducible so that $\lim_{t\to\infty} P_{x_0,x}(t) \equiv P_x$ exist and are independent of x_0 (Cox and Miller, 1965). We will now examine the symmetrical situation where $R^{(1)} = R^{(2)}$, $a = c$ and $b = d$ to illustrate in a simple way the importance of nonlinearities. Clearly, the stationary distribution is symmetrical. When $b = 0$ (linear case), the stationary state is a binomial distribution of exponent N and parameter 0.5 (see equation (9.15)). The values of b which are positive [negative] express a behaviour of imitation [anti-imitation]. It can be proved that if the imitation behaviour becomes sufficiently important ($b > 2\,\mu/N$), the stationary distribution passes from a unimodal to a bimodal shape: the state N/2 is no longer the mode of the distribution and even corresponds to a local minimum of the distribution; see Figure 9.2.

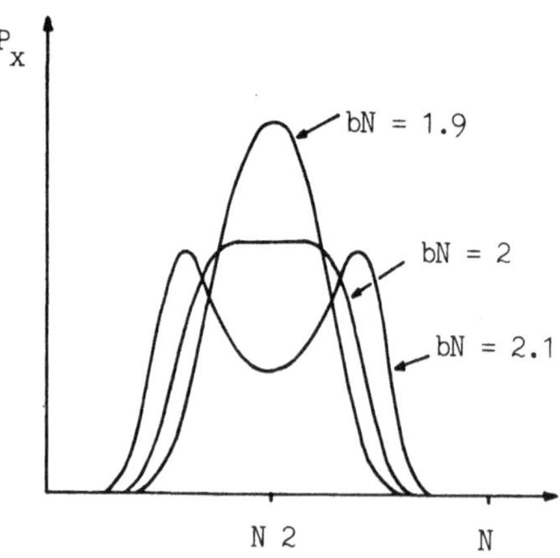

Figure 9.2: Stationary distribution in the linear case when $\mu=1$

Let us now consider the case where the utility functions are logarithmic:

$$v^{(1)}(x) = a + b \ln x \qquad x = 0, \ldots, N \qquad (9.23)$$
$$v^{(2)}(x) = c + d \ln(N-x)$$

The Markov process is then either irreducible or absorbing in relation to the sign of the coefficients b and d. For example, when b and d are positive, there exist two absorbing states 0 and N. In this case, it is quite plausible that one of these two states, 0 for example, is in fact preferable to the other N. As the absorption probabilities depend on μ, it is then natural to consider this parameter (interpreted here as the information level accessible to individuals) as a control parameter to maximize the probability of absorption in state 0. It can be proved that there exists an optimal stationary policy which consists in taking for μ the largest possible value when the choice distribution x favours C_1 to the detriment of C_2 [that is when $v^{(2)}(x) < v^{(1)}(x)$] and the smallest possible in the contrary case; see Figure 9.3.

9.3.3.2 A model for the diffusion of rumours and epidemics

The so-called general epidemic model (Bailey, 1975) describes the propagation of an epidemic or information through a population of size N. We will adopt here the presentation specific to the spread of information (Bartholomew, 1973). The system is compartmental and subdivided in two compartments. The first one corresponds to the individuals, in number x_1, who are susceptible to hear about the information, and the second one to those individuals, in number x_2, who are aware of the information and are spreading it by a word-of-mouth process. An unique transition, at a rate $R_{1,2}(\underline{x},t) \equiv \beta x_2$, is then allowed

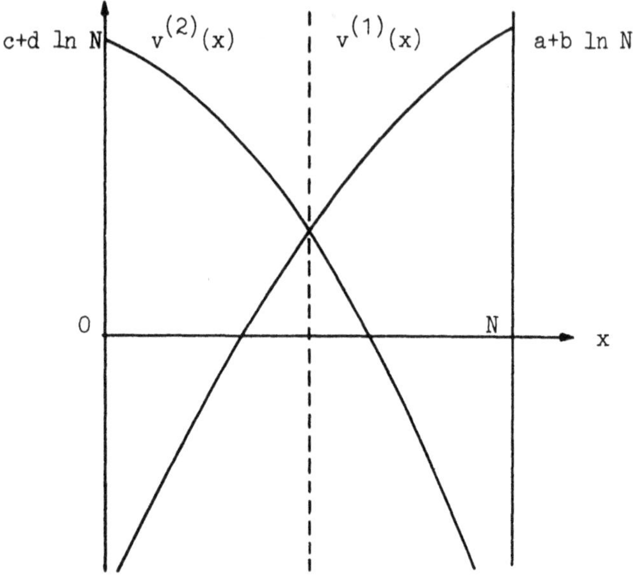

Figure 9.3: Logarithmic utility functions

within the system. Moreover, the individuals in the second compartment can stop to diffuse the information and then leave the system definitively; the associated transition has a rate $R_{2,0}(\underline{x},t) \equiv \gamma$. Of course, at time 0, we have $X_1(0) + X_2(0)=N$.

The diffusion of the information terminates when the number of individuals in the second compartment becomes null. An essential result of the model concerns the distribution of individuals who have heard about the information during the diffusion process. Intuitively, one expects the existence of a critical threshold in order that a significant number of individuals have become aware of the information. The existence of a threshold phenomenon has been established by Kendall (1956): "for $X_1(0)$ large, either $X_1(0)\ \beta/\gamma \leq 1$ and the diffusion terminates quickly, or $X_1(0)\ \beta/\gamma > 1$ and the diffusion ends rapidly with the probability $[\gamma/(X_1(0)\beta)]^{X_2(0)}$

or spreads widely with the complementary probability". More generally, one can show that a necessary condition to obtain a threshold phenomenon is the nonlinearity of the kinetics involved.

9.3.3.3 Other applications of these models

We have presented here two simple nonlinear models which lead to analytical results. In most of the real situations, the linear approach has been used for reasons of simplicity and provides an approximation, sometimes very rough, of dynamics which are intrinsically nonlinear.

In the choice problems, the attributes of the different choices depend frequently on the global distribution of the population. So, the residential location choice is affected by the population densities (Lerman, 1975, and Anas, 1980) and the choice of a transportation mode or a departure time for home-job trips depends crucially on the choices of the whole population (Ben-Akiva et al, 1980, and de Palma et al, 1983).

For the study of diffusion of information, the epidemic model presented above has been generalized in several directions to take account of the spatial nature of the process and the segmentation of the population on the basis of socio-economic criteria and awareness levels. A large number of papers in this field have been published in the *Journal of Mathematical Sociology* (see, eg, Karmeshu and Pathria, 1980).

The probabilistic aspects in nonlinear models have been found of special interest in genetics and population dynamics. In genetics, several works have tried to understand how a population of genes can be affected by the presence of mutants; we refer the reader to the many papers published in *Theoretical Population Biology*. In ecology, the stability of a set of interacting species and their extinction has been largely studied (Bartlett, 1960 and Pielou, 1977, for example). In pharmacology, some authors have pointed out the nonlinear character of the kinetics of the diffusion of drugs in living systems; until now, however, only a few modelling works have been made in this direction.

Most of the chemical reactions are not nomomolecular and then lead to nonlinear kinetics which have been described by birth and death processes. Several authors have studied the spatio-temporal behaviour of the corresponding systems and have discovered spectacular organization phenomena (Malek-Mansour and Nicolis, 1975, Nicolis and Prigogine, 1977 and Oppenheim, Shuler and Weiss, 1977).

It is worth emphasizing that from a physical point of view, the stochastic approach is more general than the deterministic one. A discussion of the domain of validity of the deterministic approach will be presented in Sections 9.4 and 9.5. Moreover, the Markovian approach is very appropriate for a proper statistical analysis of data. Unfortunately, it often involves great mathematical difficulty, and there are a number of situations where the deterministic approach provides some explicit results while the stochastic one is intractable (see Sections 9.4 and 9.8). Nevertheless, when no analytical results are available in both approaches, it is more advisable to simulate the very Markov process underlying the master equations with classical Monte Carlo methods than to simulate the differential equations of the deterministic version with some approximate methods, the modified Euler method or the Runge-Kutta method for example (see, for example, Gillespie, 1976, and Frankowicz and Gudowska-Nowak, 1982).

9.4 The Deterministic Approach

We suppose here that the state of the compartmental system is governed by a set of differential equations. As in Section 9.3 we will consider the linear and nonlinear cases. First, we will establish with a theorem due to Kurtz (1978) a connection between the Markovian and the deterministic approaches.

9.4.1 Derivation of the deterministic model

Several phenomena in biology and sociology are concerned with a large number of units and have been described by systems of differential equations. This representation, called macroscopic, presupposes that there is a clear distinction between the macroscopic variables (solutions of the differential equations) and the fluctuations inevitable in all real systems. For the compartmental model described in Section 9.3.1, the associated deterministic version is defined by the following differential equations:

$$\begin{aligned} \frac{d}{dt}x_j(t) = & \sum_{\substack{i=1\\ \neq j}}^{J} x_i(t).R_{i,j}[\underline{x}(t),t] \\ & - x_j(t).\sum_{\substack{i=1\\ \neq j}}^{J} R_{j,i}[\underline{x}(t),t] - x_j(t).R_{j,0}[\underline{x}(t),t] \\ & + R_{0,j}[\underline{x}(t),t], \quad j = 1, \ldots, J \end{aligned} \tag{9.24}$$

where $\underline{x}(t) \equiv [x_1(t), \ldots, x_J(t)]'$ is the j x 1 column vector of the state of the system at time t, and the $R_{i,j}[\underline{x},t]$'s represent the rates defined before.

In the linear case, equation (9.24) reduces to (in obvious notation):

$$\frac{d}{dt}\underline{x}(t) = \underline{R}'(t).\underline{x}(t) - \underline{R}_0(t) \tag{9.25}$$

which is equivalent to (9.9). Consequently, in the linear case, the state of the system in the deterministic version is the expected state in the Markovian version - for identical initial conditions - (Faddy, 1977).

In the nonlinear case, this result is no longer true. A

theorem due to Kurtz (1978) establishes a connection, under certain hypotheses, between the deterministic and Markovian versions. This result can be applied when the total number of individuals is important, say proportional to a large number $\bar{N}$. In addition, it supposes that the arrival rates in the system take the form $\bar{N}R_{0,j}$, and that the rates $R_{0,j}$, $R_{j,0}$ and $R_{i,j}$, $1 \leq i, j \leq J$, depend on the state of the system through the quantities $\underline{x}/\bar{N}$ (and not on the absolute frequencies $\underline{x}$). This property, called extensivity of the transition probabilities, is always satisfied in chemistry but not necessarily in social sciences. Let $\underline{Z}^{\bar{N}}(t)$ denote the density $\underline{X}(t)/\bar{N}$ and $\underline{z}(t)$ the density $\underline{x}(t)/\bar{N}$ for the stochastic and deterministic versions respectively. Kurtz has proved the following theorem: "under the hypotheses given above, if $\lim_{\bar{N}\to\infty} \underline{Z}^{\bar{N}}(0) = \underline{z}(0)$, then for every T, $0 \leq T < \infty$:

$$\lim_{\bar{N}\to\infty} \sup_{t\leq T} |\underline{Z}^{\bar{N}}(t) - \underline{z}(t)| = 0 \text{"} \quad \text{a.s.} \tag{9.26}$$

that is to say, the normalized state in the Markovian version converges almost always to the normalized state in the deterministic version. We will present in Section 9.5 the speed of convergence of the process $\underline{Z}^{\bar{N}}(t)$.

9.4.2 The linear case

9.4.2.1 Analytical results

The transient solution of the system (9.25) is:

$$\underline{x}(t) = \underline{P}'(t).\underline{x}(0) + \int_0^t \underline{P}'(\tau,t).\underline{R}_0(\tau)d\tau \tag{9.27}$$

where $\underline{P}'(t)$ and $\underline{P}'(\tau,t)$ are the matrices defined in 9.3.2.

The asymptotic behaviour ($t \to \infty$) of the system's state can be easily determined when the transition rates do not depend on time. We will consider here the two cases discussed in 9.3.2.3. In the first case:

$$\lim_{t\to\infty} \underline{x}(t) = [\underline{x}'(0).\underline{u}].\underline{p} \tag{9.28}$$

and in the second case:

$$\lim_{t\to\infty} \underline{x}(t) = -\underline{R}'^{-1}.\underline{R}_0 \tag{9.29}$$

where we have used the notation of Section 9.3.2. For general study of linear systems, we refer the reader to the paper by Hearon (1963).

9.4.2.2 Applications of these models

For chemical systems, it is well known that the nonlinearities and the openness of the system are two necessary conditions to find spatio-temporal organization. Consequently, most of the recent works have been developed for the nonlinear case.

For social and biological systems, such a property does not hold necessarily. This explains partly why linear models are still very popular in these disciplines. Moreover, the deterministic approach is used more than the stochastic one because of the simplicity of study of linear differential equations. We have seen that in fact, the analysis of the Markovian linear case is not more difficult, and consequently, in our sense, the stochastic approach should be preferred. It is worth mentioning that the linear deterministic compartmental models have been mostly applied in biology; a large number of results have been published in the journal *Mathematical Biosciences*.

9.4.3 The nonlinear case

9.4.3.1 Mathematical tools

We discuss first the system (9.24) in the autonomous case. It is convenient to rewrite the system (9.24) as:

$$\frac{d}{dt} x_j(t) = F_j[x_1(t), \ldots, x_J(t)], \; j = 1, \ldots, J \qquad (9.30)$$

In general, it is not possible to solve this system explicitly. Nevertheless, mathematical methods do exist to obtain some information on the solution. Among these methods, we mention bifurcation theory (Rabinowitz, 1977), catastrophe theory (Thom, 1972) and stability theory (Sattinger, 1973). The stationary states of (9.30), denoted by $x^* = (x_1^*, \ldots, x_J^*)'$, are defined by:

$$\frac{d}{dt} x_j(t) = 0, \; j = 1, \ldots, J \qquad (9.31)$$

and are solutions of the following algebraic system:

$$F_j(x_1^*, \ldots, x_J^*) = 0, \; j = 1, \ldots, J \qquad (9.32)$$

Bifurcation theory studies the multiplicity of the solutions of (9.32) as a function of some parameter θ of the model. A bifurcation point $[\theta_b, \underline{x}^*(\theta_b)]$ is a point such that in its neighbourhood, the multiplicity of the stationary state changes. Catastrophe theory provides a general method to classify the stationary states of (9.30) when the system admits a potential $V[\underline{x}(t)]$ defined by:

$$\frac{d}{dt} x_j(t) = - \frac{\partial}{\partial x_j} V[\underline{x}(t)], \; j = 1, \ldots, J \qquad (9.33)$$

We will discuss in more detail a general procedure to analyse the stability of the stationary states.

A stability analysis studies the behaviour of the trajectories in the neighbourhood of a stationary state. For this purpose, the solution of (9.30) at the neighbourhood of $\underline{x}^*$ is written as

$$\underline{x}(t) = \underline{x}^* + \tilde{\underline{x}}(t) \tag{9.34}$$

where $\tilde{\underline{x}}(0)$ is an initial perturbation which satisfies $|\tilde{x}_j(t)/x_j^*| << 1$, $j = 1, ..., J$. At the first order approximation, we deduce from (9.30) and (9.32) that the $\tilde{x}_j(t)$'s are solutions of the following system of linear differential equations:

$$\frac{d}{dt} \tilde{x}_j(t) = \sum_{i=1}^{J} a_{ji}.\tilde{x}_i(t), \; j = 1, ..., J \tag{9.35}$$

where:

$$a_{ji} = \frac{\partial}{\partial x_i} F_j \Big|_{\underline{x}(t)=\underline{x}^*}, \; i,j = 1, ..., J \tag{9.36}$$

This system, which is written in matrix form as $d\tilde{\underline{x}}(t)/dt=\underline{A}.\tilde{\underline{x}}(t)$, has the solution:

$$\tilde{x}_j(t) = \sum_{i=1}^{m} b_{ji}\left(\sum_{k=0}^{m_i-1} c_{jik}t^k\right)e^{\lambda_i t}, \; j = 1, ..., J \tag{9.37}$$

where the coefficients b and c are constants and the λ_i are the distinct eigenvalues of the matrix A, supposed to be m in number and of respective multiplicity m_i. These eigenvalues are complex or real numbers. The complex part induces an oscillating behaviour whilst the real part gives rise to an exponentially increasing or decreasing evolution according to its sign being positive or negative. Consequently, the stationary state $\underline{x}^*$ is asymptotically stable if all the real parts are negative (that is, if the trivial solution of (9.35) is asymptotically stable); the state $\underline{x}^*$ is unstable if there exists at least one positive real part. In addition, the state $\underline{x}^*$ is marginally stable (Lyapounov stable) if there is at least one eigenvalue whose real part is null and if all the other eigenvalues have a negative real part. We will now treat briefly the one and two variable systems; the systems with more than two variables are much more complicated and are not discussed here.

For the one variable case, the system (9.30) becomes:

$$\frac{d}{dt}\, x(t) = F[x(t)] \equiv F^{+}[x(t)] - F^{-}[x(t)] \qquad (9.38)$$

where F^{+} and F^{-} are non-negative functions. One can show easily that this system cannot have oscillating behaviour, and that between two successive stable [unstable] stationary states there exists at least [at most] one unstable [stable] stationary state.

For the two variables case, the system (9.30) becomes:

$$\frac{d}{dt}\, x_j(t) = F_j[x_1(t),\ x_2(t)],\ j = 1,2 \qquad (9.39)$$

The eigenvalues of the matrix A defined in (9.36) are solutions of the following characteristic equation:

$$\lambda^2 - T\lambda + \Delta = 0 \qquad (9.40)$$

with

$$T = a_{11} + a_{22},\ \text{and}\ \Delta = a_{11}a_{22} - a_{12}a_{21} \qquad (9.41)$$

The type of the singular point $\underline{x}^*$ is discussed in Figure 9.4 in relation to the values of T and Δ: $\underline{x}^*$ can be stable (stable node or focus), unstable (unstable node or focus), or marginally stable (centre).

A stability analysis provides some information on the behaviour in the neighbourhood of $\underline{x}^*$: it appears that very often, this information is sufficient to give a good idea of the qualitative behaviour of the system in the whole phase space. We note that this analysis can be extended to spatial

Conditions on T and Δ		Conditions on λ_1 and λ_2	Type of the stationary point	Stability of the stationary point	Trajectories in the phase space
$T^2 - 4\Delta \geq 0$	$T \neq 0$ and $\Delta > 0$	λ_1 and λ_2 are reals of the same sign	Node	T<0: stable point, monotonous evolution	x_2, x_1
				T>0: unstable point, monotonous divergence	x_2, x_1
	$T \neq 0$ and $\Delta < 0$	λ_1 and λ_2 are reals of apposite signs	Saddle point	Unstable	x_2, x_1
$T^2 - 4\Delta < 0$	$T \neq 0$	λ_1 and λ_2 are complexes with nonnull real parts	Focus	T<0: stable point, oscillating behaviour	x_2, x_1
				T>0: unstable point, oscillating behaviour	x_2, x_1
	$T = 0$ and $\Delta > 0$	λ_1 and λ_2 are complexes with null real parts	Centre	Marginally stable	x_2, x_1

Figure 9.4: Type and stability of the stationary states of the system (9.39)

systems.

9.4.3.2 A model of choice behaviour in a collective system

We reconsider the binary choice model introduced in 9.3.3.1. We suppose that the hypotheses of Kurtz's theorem are satisfied. As the model is concerned with a closed population of size N, we take $\overline{N} \equiv N$; the utilities of the choices depend thus on the state of the system through the density $z^N = x^N/N$ of the individuals who have adopted the choice C_1. For N large, the deterministic version of the Markovian model becomes (de Palma and Lefèvre, 1983):

$$\frac{d}{dt} z(t) = R^{(2)}.p^{(1)}[z(t)] - \{R^{(2)}.p^{(1)}[z(t)] + R^{(1)}.p^{(2)}[z(t)]\}.z(t) \qquad (9.42)$$

where z(t) represents the density of adopters of C_1 at time t and the $p^{(j)}[z(t)]$'s are defined in (9.21).

We begin by examining the case where the utility functions are linear. For illustration, we suppose that $R^{(1)} = R^{(2)}$. The stationary states z* are solutions of:

$$z^* = 1/\{1 + \exp[(A - B.z^*)/\mu]\} \qquad (9.43)$$

where

$$A = c + d - a, \text{ and } B = b + d \qquad (9.44)$$

Let us take c as a bifurcation parameter. Two qualitatively different solutions arise according to the sign of $B - 4\mu$; they are illustrated in Figures 9.5a and 9.5b.

A stability analysis (see 9.4.3.1) shows that the branches z^*_+ and z^*_- are stable whilst the branch z^*_0 is unstable. When

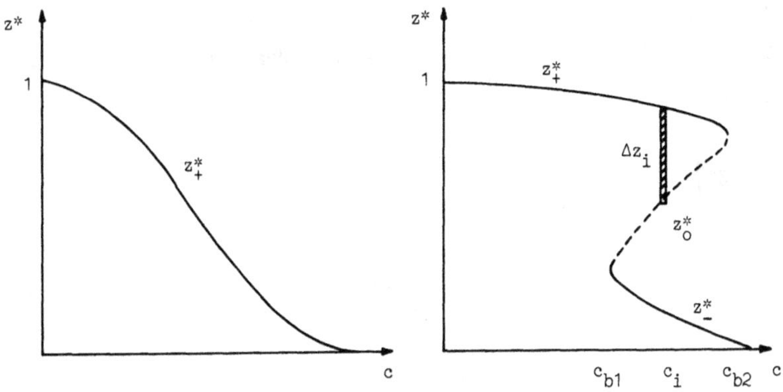

Figure 9.5a: Bifurcation diagram $z^*=z^*(c)$ when $B-4\mu<0$

Figure 9.5b: Bifurcation diagram $z^*=z^*(c)$ when $B-4\mu>0$

$B - 4\mu > 0$, which implies a sufficiently strong imitative behaviour among the individuals, the system admits two bifurcation points $[c_{b1}, z^*(c_{b1})]$ and $[c_{b2}, z^*(c_{b2})]$, and there is an hysteresis phenomenon. In Figure 9.5b, Δz_i represents, for a value of c_i $[c_{b1}, c_{b2}]$, the size of the perturbation which allows passage from the branch z^*_+ to the branch z^*_-. Let us consider the symmetrical case where $a = c$ and $b = d$. The condition $B - 4\mu > 0$ reduces thus to $b > 2\mu$ which is precisely the condition derived in the stochastic case to have a bimodal distribution (9.3.3.1) as expected, the deterministic model then has two stable stationary states.

We now examine the case where the utility functions are logarithmic. The system admits from one to four stationary states according to the values of the parameters. For example, let b and d be positive. The states $z^* = 0$ and $z^* = 1$ are then two trivial singular points. In Figure 9.6 we have considered the particular situation where $b > \mu$ and $0 < d < \mu$, and we have taken A, defined in (9.44), as a bifurcation parameter. The point $[A_b, z^*(A_b)]$ is a bifurcation point because two new solutions appear when $A > A_b$.

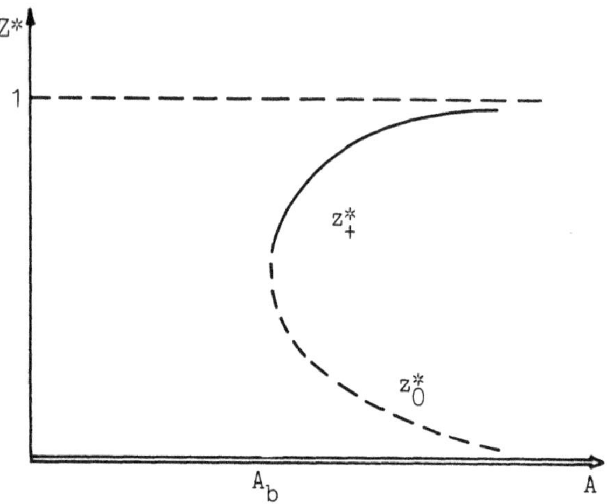

Figure 9.6: Bifurcation diagram $z^*=z^*(A)$ when $b>\mu$ and $0<d<\mu$

We recall that in the Markovian version, b and d positive imply that there are only two absorbing states 0 and 1. Consequently, the asymptotic behaviours of the deterministic and stochastic models are quite different; this result has not to be viewed as surprising because the validity of the Kurtz theorem requires that t is finite. We refer the reader to Oppenheim, Shuler and Weiss (1977), and Turner and Malek-Mansour (1978) for the study of a simple chemical system when t and N are large.

9.4.3.3 A model for the diffusion of rumours and epidemics

We reconsider the general epidemic model introduced in 9.3.3.2.

The corresponding deterministic version is defined by:

$$\frac{d}{dt} x_1(t) = - \beta x_1(t)x_2(t) \tag{9.45}$$

$$\frac{d}{dt} x_2(t) = - \beta x_1(t)x_2(t) - \gamma x_2(t) \tag{9.46}$$

with

$$x_1(0) + x_2(0) = N \tag{9.47}$$

The stationary states are characterized by $x_2^* = 0$. The solutions of equation (9.40) are:

$$\lambda_1 = 0, \text{ and } \lambda_2 = \beta x_1^* - \gamma.$$

Thus, a stationary state $(x_1^*,0)$ is marginally stable [unstable] if $x_1^* \leqq \gamma/\beta$ $[x_1^* > \gamma/\beta]$. The value $x_1^* = \gamma/\beta$ can be interpreted as a threshold: a small perturbation gives rise to an epidemic only if $x_1^* > \gamma/\beta$. Let us emphasize that this condition is similar to that derived in the Markovian model (9.3.3.2).

The deterministic version (9.45) - (9.47) assumes that the transition rate $R_{1,2} \equiv \beta x_2$ depends on the absolute frequency x_2 and not on the density z_2, so that Kurtz's theorem cannot be applied. This presentation is classical in mathematical epidemiology: indeed, the formulation in terms of density is not satisfactory because it does not permit to account for the size effect in the threshold condition.

9.4.3.4 Other applications of these models

In a large number of social systems, modelling with nonlinear differential equations is used to take account of the times of adjustment in the individual decisions and the interdependency between individual behaviours. So, in the field of residential location, friction effects have been shown by Hanushek and Quigley (1979); for urban systems, the congestion is clearly a nonlinear phenomenon. The structurization of urban systems has been studied in several works. Two main approaches can be distinguished: the "ecological" one, which describes, for example, the competition and cooperativity between different social classes, and the micro-economical one, which assumes the maximization of an individual utility function. We refer the reader to the works of Ingram, Kain and Ginn (1972), Wilson (1974), Allen and Sanglier (1978), Miyao (1979), Tomlin (1979), Weidlich and Haag (1980-B), Beaumont, Clarke and Wilson (1981-A), and de Palma and Ben-Akiva (1981). At the inter-regional scale, nonlinear dynamic models have described the migrations of individuals; see, for example, Okabe (1979). Several applications of the dynamical choice model presented in 9.4.3.2 have been done in the field of transportation (Kahn, Deneubourg and de Palma, 1981, de Palma et al, 1983, and Kahn, Deneubourg and de Palma, 1982). A number of models derived from the mathematical theory of epidemics (Waltman, 1974) have been used to describe the diffusion of an information or of a product through a population (Bartholomew, 1973, Dodson and Muller, 1978, Webber and Joseph, 1978, 1979, and Mahajan and Muller, 1979).

Bifurcation theory has been applied with success to nonlinear chemical systems in order to explain the various spatio-temporal structurizations observed experimentally; see, for example, Tyson (1976), and Erneux (1979) for a more systematic analysis. Several similar biological models have been used to study the viability of different biological structures; we mention, for example, the morphogenesis, the glycolytic oscillations and the process of cellular differentiation (Nicolis and Prigogine, 1977). In ecology, the evolution of ecosystems has been described using nonlinear mathematical tools; in particular, the study of the structural stability

(stability of the system with regard to new processes) has lead to a better understanding of the connections between stability and complexity (MacArthur, 1972, and May, 1973).

9.5 The Quasi-deterministic Approach

We have seen in (9.26) that under certain assumptions, the normalized Markovian process converges to its associated deterministic version almost surely as the population size becomes very large. Let us consider the situations where the theorem is of application. It is then natural to approximate the stochastic model by the deterministic one. However, the theorem does not give any information on the quality of this approximation over time. We are going to mention a complementary theorem of Kurtz (1978) which states that the stochastic process can be written as the sum of the deterministic process and a stochastic diffusion process. The result allows us to judge the validity of the approximation as a function of time. Moreover, it is also very useful for statistical inference because a likelihood function can then be easily constructed from the data. This theorem has been rederived recently by Lehoczky (1980) in a different context more adapted to our chapter. For this reason, we begin by presenting the Lehoczky result.

9.5.1 The theorem of Lehoczky

For simplicity, we treat here the case where the system is closed and of size N (no arrival or departure is allowed), and autonomous (the transition rates do not depend explicitly on time). We use the same notation as in 9.4.1, that is, the vectors $\underline{Z}^N(t)$ and $\underline{z}(t)$ represent the densities of individuals in the different compartments at time t for the stochastic and deterministic versions respectively.

The theorem of Lehoczky (1980) assumes that the transaction probabilities are extensive (the transition rates R_{ij}, $1 \leq i, j \leq J$, depend on the state of the system through the densities). It can be written as follows. "If as $N \to \infty$:

$$\underline{Z}^N(0) \xrightarrow{p} \underline{z}(0)$$

$$\sqrt{N}[\underline{Z}^N(0) - \underline{z}(0)] \xrightarrow{w} N[\underline{0}, \underline{\Sigma}(0)]$$

then as $N \to \infty$:

$$\underline{Z}^N(t) \xrightarrow{p} \underline{z}(t)$$
$$\sqrt{N}[\underline{Z}^N(t) - \underline{z}(t)] \xrightarrow{w} N[\underline{0}, \underline{\Sigma}(t)] \tag{9.48}$$

where $\underline{\Sigma}(0)$ is a non-negative definite covariance matrix and $\underline{\Sigma}(t)$ satisfies the following matrix equation:

$$\frac{d}{dt}\,\underline{\Sigma}(t) = \underline{G}\,[\underline{z}(t)].\underline{\Sigma}(t) + \underline{\Sigma}(t).\underline{G}'[\underline{z}(t)] + \underline{B}[\underline{z}(t)] \tag{9.49}$$

In (9.49), $\underline{G}[\underline{z}(t)]$ and $\underline{B}[\underline{z}(t)]$ are two J x J matrices whose elements g_{ij} and b_{ij}, $1 \leq i, j \leq J$, are defined respectively by:

$$g_{ij}[\underline{z}(t)] = R_{j,i}[\underline{z}(t)] + \sum_{\ell=1}^{J} z_\ell(t).\,\frac{\partial}{\partial z_j(t)}\,R_{\ell,i}[\underline{z}(t)] \tag{9.50}$$

and

$$b_{ij}[\underline{z}(t)] = \begin{cases} -z_i(t).R_{i,j}[\underline{z}(t)] - z_j(t).R_{j,i}[\underline{z}(t)], & i \neq j \\ -z_i(t).R_{i,i}[\underline{z}(t)] + \sum\limits_{\substack{\ell=1 \\ \neq i}}^{J} z_\ell(t).R_{\ell,i}[\underline{z}(t)], & i=j \end{cases} \tag{9.51}$$

Thus, for N large, the diffusion approximation yields:

$$\underline{Z}^N(t) \simeq \underline{z}(t) + \frac{1}{\sqrt{N}} N[\underline{0}, \underline{\Sigma}(t)]." \tag{9.52}$$

To establish the weak convergence of the Markov processes $\underline{K}^N(t) \equiv \sqrt{N}[\underline{Z}^N(t) - \underline{z}(t)]$, Lehoczky proves that the infinitesimal generators associated with each $\underline{K}^N(t)$ converge to a limiting generator which corresponds to a certain diffusion process $\underline{K}^\infty(t)$. This limiting process is defined by the Ito stochastic differential equation:

$$d\underline{K}^\infty(t) = \underline{G}[\underline{z}(t)].\underline{K}^\infty(t)dt + \underline{B}^{1/2}[\underline{z}(t)]d\underline{W}(t) \tag{9.53}$$

where $\{\underline{W}(t), t \geq 0\}$ is a multivariate standard Wiener process. This equation is a linear non-stationary stochastic differential equation, and as such, has been extensively studied (see for example, Arnold, 1974). In fact, the result (9.48) is a direct consequence of (9.53). Other results can be derived from (9.53), for example the covariance between $\underline{K}^\infty(t)$ and $\underline{K}^\infty(s)$, s, t ≥ 0.

9.5.2 The theorem of Kurtz

Kurtz (1978, 1981) has derived several approximation theorems which complete the result of Lehoczky and extend it to a wider class of Markov processes.

More precisely, Kurtz considers the variety of Markov processes $\underline{Z}^N(t)$ which are solutions of equations of the form:

$$\underline{Z}^N(t) = \underline{z}(0) + \sum_{\underline{\ell}} \frac{1}{N}.\underline{\ell}.Y_{\underline{\ell}}[N\int_0^t f_{\underline{\ell}}(\underline{Z}^N(s))ds] \tag{9.54}$$

where $\underline{\ell}\varepsilon Z^J$ and the $Y_{\underline{\ell}}$'s are independent Poisson processes. The associated deterministic version is defined by:

$$\underline{z}(t) = \underline{z}(0) + \int_0^t \sum_{\underline{\ell}} \underline{\ell}.f_{\underline{\ell}}(\underline{z}(s))ds \tag{9.55}$$

We note that for the compartmental system considered in this chapter, the vector $\underline{\ell}$ corresponding to the transition $i \to j$ is simply given by $\underline{e}_j - \underline{e}_i$ and the associated function $f_{\underline{\ell}}(\underline{Z}^N(t))$ is equal to $Z_i^N(t).R_{i,j}(\underline{Z}^N(t))$.

Among the many results derived by Kurtz for this class of Markov process, we mention the two following ones. "Under very general conditions, the result (9.26) remains true, that is, for every T, $0 \leq T < \infty$:

$$\lim_{N\to\infty} \sup_{t\leq T} |\underline{Z}^N(t) - \underline{z}(t)| = 0 \quad \text{a.s.} \tag{9.56}$$

Moreover, the normalized difference between the stochastic and deterministic processes can be written as:

$$\sqrt{N}\ [\underline{Z}^N(t) - \underline{z}(t)] \simeq \underline{V}(t) + O(\frac{\log\ N}{\sqrt{N}}) \tag{9.57}$$

where $\underline{V}(t)$ is the Gaussian process which satisfies:

$$\underline{V}(t) = \sum_{\underline{\ell}} \underline{\ell}.\int_o^t \sqrt{f_{\underline{\ell}}(t)(\underline{z}(s))}\ dW_{\underline{\ell}}(s) + \int_o^t [\partial \sum_{\underline{\ell}} \underline{\ell}.f_{\underline{\ell}}(\underline{z}(s))].\underline{V}(s)ds \tag{9.58}$$

Here, the $W_{\ell}(t)$'s are independent standard Wiener processes, and $\partial \sum_{\underline{\ell}} \underline{\ell}.f_{\underline{\ell}}(.)$ denotes the gradient of $\sum_{\underline{\ell}} \underline{\ell}.f_{\underline{\ell}}(.)$." It can be seen that this theorem extends the Lehoczky result given in 9.5.1.

Several applications of these approximation methods have been used in physics, chemistry and biology; see, for example, Arnold and Lefever (1981), Lehoczky and Gaver (1977). In sociology, the interest of these approximations has been shown by Lehoczky (1980) in the framework of the interactive Markov processes; see also, for example, Karmeshu and Pathria (1980), and Sikdar and Karmeshu (1982) for the use of similar approximations in the study of certain social systems. We point out, however, that the extensivity of the transition probabilities, which is a fundamental hypothesis, is not always true in social sciences.

9.6 Discrete Time Models

We are going to show briefly that the analyses presented in Sections 9.3, 9.4 and 9.5 can be extended from continuous time to discrete time compartmental models.

9.6.1 The Markovian approach

Let us reconsider a compartmental system subdivided into J classes, but assume now a discrete time scale $t = 0, 1, 2, \ldots$. The discrete time version of the Markov process presented in 9.3.1 can be constructed in the following way.

Let $\underline{X}(t) = [X_1(t), \ldots, X_J(t)]'$ denote the state of the system at time t. We suppose that individual transitions between the compartments take place according to a so-called interactive Markov chain (Conlisk, 1976). More specifically, if at time t, the state of the system is given by $\underline{x}$, then at time t + 1 the individuals of any compartment i, $1 \leq i \leq J$, make independent transition decisions, and each of them either moves to compartment j with probability $R_{i,j}(\underline{x},t)$, $1 \leq j \leq J$, or leaves the system definitively with probability $R_{i,0}(\underline{x},t)$. Next, we suppose that the number of individuals entering the system at t + 1 is a Poisson variate with parameter $\Lambda(\underline{x},t)$, and each new individual goes into the various compartments with probabilities $\tilde{R}_{0,j}(\underline{x},t)$, $1 \leq j \leq J$; we put $R_{0,j}(\underline{x},t) \equiv \Lambda(\underline{x},t)$. $\tilde{R}_{0,j}(\underline{x},t)$, $1 \leq j \leq J$. Consequently, the state $\underline{X}(t+1)$ given $\underline{X}(t) = \underline{x}$ is the sum of the (J+1) following independent random vectors: a Poisson vector with parameters $[R_{0,1}(\underline{x},t), \ldots, R_{0,J}(\underline{x},t)]$ and J multinomial vectors with exponent x_i and parameters $[R_{i,1}(\underline{x},t), \ldots, R_{i,J}(\underline{x},t)]'$ respectively. The state of the system at time t+1 is thus a random vector with a well-defined but complicated distribution.

9.6.1.1 The linear case

Let us suppose that the quantities $R_{i,j}(\underline{x},t)$, $R_{0,j}(\underline{x},t)$ and $R_{j,0}(\underline{x},t)$ are independent of $\underline{x}$.

The distribution of $\underline{X}(t)$ can be found by using an argument similar to the one adopted in 9.3.2. Let $p_{i,j}(t)$ denote the probability that an individual in compartment i at time 0 is in compartment j at time t, and $\underline{P}(t)$ the J x J matrix of these $p_{i,j}(t)$'s. Clearly

$$\underline{P}(t+1) = \underline{P}(t).\underline{R}(t) \tag{9.59}$$

where $\underline{R}(t)$ is the J x J matrix of the $R_{i,j}(t)$'s. We note that if $\underline{R}(t)$ is a constant matrix $\underline{R}$, then:

$$\underline{P}(t) = \underline{R}^t \tag{9.60}$$

By adopting the same decomposition as in (9.5), it is easily shown that the generating fucntion of $\underline{X}(t)$ can be written as in (7), with $G_2(\underline{\xi},t)$ given by (9.8) and $G_1(\underline{\xi},t)$ equal to (in obvious notations):

$$G_1(\underline{\xi},t) = \exp[(\underline{\xi}-\underline{u})'.\sum_{\tau=1}^{t} \underline{P}'(\tau,t)\underline{R}_0(\tau-1)] \tag{9.61}$$

The expectation of $\underline{X}(t)$, as well as its covariance matrix and its asymptotic behaviour, can also be derived easily. For example, $\underline{M}(t) \equiv E[\underline{X}(t)]$ is the solution of the difference equation:

$$\underline{M}(t+1) = \underline{R}'(t).\underline{M}(t) + \underline{R}_0(t) \tag{9.62}$$

For more details, we refer the reader to the papers of Pollard

(1967) and Vassiliou (1982).

9.6.1.2 The nonlinear case

The nonlinear case is much more difficult to analyse and very little work has been done until now. It seems that in the literature, such models have been considered mainly in mathematical epidemiology. However, even in this field, the discrete time models have been very little developed in comparison with the continuous time models (see, for example, Bailey's book, 1975). We present below the discrete-time version of the simple epidemic process, more often referred to in the literature as the logistic process. Although this model has been widely used in its continuous time version, to our knowledge there exists no systematic analysis of its discrete time version.

The simple epidemic model is concerned with a closed population of size N subdivided in two classes. In the application to diffusion of information, the first compartment corresponds to the individuals, in number x_1, who can hear about the information, and the second one to those individuals, in number x_2, who know the information and transmit it by a word-of-mouth process. The main difference with the general epidemic model (see 9.3.3.2) is that here no forgetting phenomenon is allowed; thus, the only possible transition is from compartment 1 to compartment 2. Let q be the probability that any given individual of compartment 1 "escapes" contact with any given individual of compartment 2 per unit time. A direct probabilistic argument shows that the probability $R_{1,2}(\underline{x},t)$ is then equal to $1 - q^{x_2}$. Now, for this particular model, the state of the system can be described with one variable, $X_2(t)$ for example. It is clear that $X_2(t)$ is simply a Markov chain with the following transition probabilities:

$$P[X_2(t+1) = x_2 + k|X_2(t) = x_2] = \binom{N-x_2}{k}.(1-q^{x_2}).q^{kx_2(N-x_2-k)}$$

$$0 \leq k \leq N-x_2 \qquad (9.63)$$

It is then possible to find an explicit formula for the transient distribution of $X_2(t)$ and the generating function of the "cost" of the diffusion process; these results are given in Lefèvre (1982).

9.6.2 The deterministic approach

The deterministic version associated with the Markov model presented above is constructed formally by putting $\underline{x}(t+1) \equiv E[\underline{X}(t+1)|\underline{X}(t)]$ and $\underline{x}(t) \equiv \underline{X}(t)$. Thus $\underline{x}(t)$ is solution of the following system of difference equations:

$$\underline{x}(t+1) = R'[\underline{x}(t),t].\underline{x}(t) + \underline{R}_0[\underline{x}(t),t] \qquad (9.64)$$

So, the deterministic version of the simple epidemic process is defined by:

$$x_2(t+1) = [N - x_2(t)].[1 - q^{x_2(t)}] + x_2(t) \qquad (9.65)$$

9.6.2.1 The linear case

In the linear case, equations (9.64) reduce to (9.62), which means that, as in the continuous time version, the state of the deterministic model is equal to the expected state of the Markovian model (for identical initial conditions).

The study of systems of linear difference equations is well known and will not be treated here.

9.6.2.2 The nonlinear case

In the nonlinear case, the system (9.64) no longer describes the temporal evolution of the expected state of the Markovian model. However, Lehoczky (1980) has proved a theorem which established, under certain conditions, a connection between the stochastic and the deterministic models. This result is similar to the theorem of Kurtz recalled in (9.26) and is not given here for reasons of brevity.

Let us consider the system (9.64) in the autonomous case. We are going to show how to extend the stability analysis presented in 9.4.3.1. For this purpose, it is convenient to denote by τ (instead of 1) the constant time interval and to rewrite (9.64) as:

$$x_j(t+\tau) = x_j(t) + F_j[x_1(t), \ldots, x_J(t)], \; j = 1, \ldots, J \tag{9.66}$$

The stationary states $\underline{x}^*$ are defined by:

$$x_j(t+\tau) = x_j(t), \; j = 1, \ldots, J \tag{9.67}$$

and are thus solutions of the algebraic system:

$$F_j(x_1^*, \ldots, x_J^*) = 0, \; j = 1, \ldots, J \tag{9.68}$$

Let us write the solution (9.66) in the neighbourhood of $\underline{x}^*$ as:

$$\underline{x}(t) = \underline{x}^* + \underline{\tilde{x}}(t) \tag{9.69}$$

where $\underline{\tilde{x}}(0)$ is the initial perturbation which is taken such that $|\tilde{x}_j(t)/x_j^*| \ll 1$. The first order approximation leads to the matrix equation:

$$\underset{\sim}{x}(t+\tau) = (\tau A + I).\underset{\sim}{x}(t) \tag{9.70}$$

where A is again defined by (9.36). It can then be deduced that the system is stable if all the eigenvalues λ_i of A satisfy the condition:

$$|\lambda_i + 1/\tau| < 1/\tau, \; i = 1, \ldots, m \tag{9.71}$$

Let us remark that when $\tau \to 0$, the system (9.66) reduces to (9.30), and the condition (9.71) becomes $|\lambda_i| < 0$, $i = 1, \ldots, m$ which is the condition of stability derived for the continuous-time model. It is also worth noting that (9.71) is in fact more stringent than $|\lambda_i| < 0$, $i = 1, \ldots, m$.

9.6.3 The quasi-deterministic approach

Lehoczky (1980) has shown how to construct a quasi-deterministic approximation for the Markov models presented in 9.6.1. This approximation is, in fact, "similar" to the one derived by Kurtz for continuous time Markov processes (see Section 9.5). Roughly, Lehoczky has proved that under certain hypotheses, the difference between the normalized stochastic system and its associated deterministic version has a normal distribution with zero expectation and specified covariance matrix.

So, for the simple epidemic model, this result can be written as follows. "Suppose that q takes the form $q \equiv \exp[-\lambda/N]$, with $\lambda > 0$ independent of N. Let $Z_2^N(t)$ and $z_2(t)$ denote the densities $X_2(t)/N$ and $x_2(t)/N$ for the stochastic and deterministic versions respectively. If as $N \to \infty$:

$$Z_2^N(0) \xrightarrow{a.s} z_2(0)$$

$$\sqrt{N}[Z_2^N(0) - z_2(0)] \xrightarrow{w} N[0, \sigma^2(0)]$$

then as $N \to \infty$:

$$Z_2^N(t) \xrightarrow{a.s} z_2(t)$$

$$\sqrt{N}[Z_2^N(t) - z_2(t)] \xrightarrow{w} N[0,\sigma^2(t)]$$

(9.72)

where $\sigma^2(0)$ is some non-negative constant and $\sigma^2(t)$ satisfies the recurrence relation:

$$\sigma^2(t+1) = c(t) + [d(t)]^2.\sigma^2(t) \tag{9.73}$$

with

$$c(t) = [1 - z_2(t)].\{1 - \exp[-\lambda z_2(t)]\}.\exp[-\lambda z_2(t)]$$

$$d(t) = \{1 + \lambda[1 - z_2(t)]\}.\exp[-\lambda z_2(t)]."$$

9.6.4 Applications of these models

The discrete time models have been applied in a wide variety of social science areas ranging from population migration and occupational mobility to brand affiliation and information diffusion.

Generally, these models describe the behaviour of a population of individuals who act independently of each other. For the deterministic case, we mention the works of Rogers (1975) and Liaw (1975) in migration theory, and Keyfitz (1977) in demography; for the stochastic case, those of Coleman (1964) in sociology, Massy, Montgomery and Morrison (1970) in marketing, Burnett (1974) in location theory, Stewman (1976) for occupational mobility studies, and Bartholomew (1973) in manpower planning.

However, the assumption that there is no interaction among

individuals is very restrictive in modelling social process, and recently nonlinear models have received an increasing attention. For the deterministic case, we mention the works of May (1973) and Cooke (1975) in population dynamics, Conlisk (1976) in sociology, Mackinnon and Rogerson (1980) in migration theory, and Wilson (1981-A) for location problems. For the stochastic case, it seems that nonlinear models have been mainly studied in epidemic theory; see, for example, Gani and Jerwood (1971), Ludwig (1975), Von Barh and Martin-Löf (1980) and Lefèvre (1982).

9.7 Some Other Different Approaches

9.7.1 Differential inclusions

To close, we present briefly some other different mathematical techniques which could be used to study the deterministic and stochastic compartmental models.

A recent theory, called differential inclusions and viability theory, enlarges the theory of differential equations and provides a framework which, although nonpredictive, is, in some sense, better adapted to social sciences. In this approach (Aubin and Cellina, 1982, 1984), the evolution of a system is no more described by a unique trajectory but by a bundle of trajectories ($dx(t)/dt \in A[x(t)]$, where A is a correspondence). Each acceptable trajectory must obey a feasible dynamic and constraints. Some regulatory mechanisms, subject to inertia, try to maintain the trajectories in the domain of viability of the system (or to modify it): if the search for a new regulatory control cannot be achieved, the trajectory disappears. This theory is beginning to be applied to explain the regulatory mechanism of prices in an economy. The authors of the theory hope to use it to study some aspects of the evolution of biological systems.

9.7.2 Chaotic systems

Lorenz (1963) introduced, in the study of atmospheric phenomena, simple difference equations exhibiting complicated dynamics. We have already remarked that sufficient nonlinearities (in fact non-differentiability) induce instabilities (see equation (9.71)). Several works have examined the analytical conditions for the existence of chaotic behaviour (see, for example, Li and Yorke, 1982). Chaotic systems are of particular interest for the modeller because in such systems simple mechanisms can induce complex behaviours. In population dynamics, difference equations of the type $x(t+1) = F[x(t)]$ have been studied by May (1976), May and Oster (1976) and Marotto (1982). In regional science, we mention the works of Wilson (1981-C) who studied the bifurcating and chaotic behaviour of some discrete time models. In economics, simple models are attempting to take account of the chaotic aspects of various economic indexes (Day, 1982); this was made until now by complex models (Forrester, 1972).

9.7.3 Boolean algebra

Several systems in engineering suggest a description in terms of 0/1 changes occurring in continuous time. These systems are sequential in the sense that the knowledge of the arrival rates is not sufficient to determine the value of the variables; some memory variables which take account of delays are then incorporated. The model reduces to a set of implicit difference equations (Florine, 1964). When the number of variables is small (<10), the temporal evolutions and the asymptotic state can be computed very easily by hand. This explains perhaps why this tool has been applied with success in genetics by Kaufmann (1969), Thomas (1973). These methods have been also used in the urban context (Boon and de Palma,

1979). Some connections between this approach and the stochastic one (in terms of master equations) have been discussed in the book by Thomas (1979).

9.7.4 Random evolutions

The compartmental systems in biology are seldom completely deterministic. For that reason, some authors (see, for example, Bécus, 1979) have tried to apply the theory of random evolutions (Griego and Hersh, 1971) to compartmental analysis. Random evolution theory is concerned with systems of differential equations which are to some extent subject to external stochastic elements. More precisely, in this formulation, the matrix of transition rates depends on an external Markov process. For linear systems, the expected time evolution can be easily computed; a two compartmental system with two modes of evolution and Poisson switching has been discussed in detail by Bécus (1979).

A similar idea has been developed by Saunders (1976) who has generalized the Markovian processes presented in Section 9.3 by supposing that the transition rates depend, in a specific way, on an exterior stochastic process.

9.7.5 Semi-Markov models

A basic hypothesis in Markov models is that the distribution of time between the transitions is exponential. Empirical evidence has shown that this hypothesis is questionable for different applications. In the semi-Markov formulation, the distribution of the duration of stay is general, and may depend on the initial as well as the final state ("pushes and pulls"). Semi-Markov models have been applied with success in different fields. In manpower planning, McLean (1980) has considered a multigrade population with semi-Markov transitions between grades. In migration, Ginsberg (1972) has used the semi-Markov approach to take account of duration of stay effects. In transportation theory, Lerman (1979) has developed and applied a semi-Markov model for the problem of trip chaining.

9.8 Application of Compartmental Models: an example

In this section we discuss in more detail an example of application of compartmental analysis in the domain of residential location.

Let us consider a system consisting of an homogeneous population of individuals who face a residential location decision problem. The system is dynamic: due to high transaction costs associated to residential move, the relocation decisions of the individuals are not instantaneous so that the system cannot be considered always at equilibrium. The system is described as a compartmental system: the compartments are homogeneous neighbourhoods in the city and correspond, for example, to the census tracts used in the surveys. The rates $R_{0,j}$ correspond here to immigration and birth, the rates $R_{i,0}$ to emigration and death, and the rates $R_{i,j}$ to the decisions to move from one neighbourhood to another neighbourhood. The system finally is nonlinear: the individual decisions are not independent in general, they interact either directly (in such a case the individual decisions depend on the location of the other individuals) or indirectly (through variables which depend on factors - on the supply side for example - whose time evolution depends on the individual location decisions). We refer the reader to de Palma and Ben-Akiva (1981) for a presentation of the first case, in a situation where the decisions to move derive from a sequence of choices based on the logit model. We will be concerned here with the second case (de Palma and Lefèvre, 1982).

For reasons of simplicity, we consider a closed population

of size N and suppose that the housing market is subdivided in only two parts, a single neighbourhood labelled i and the outside world labelled 0. Using the deterministic approach described in Section 9.4 we obtain (see equation (9.24)):

$$\frac{dx_i(t)}{dt} = [N - x_i(t)].R_{0,i}(t) - x_i(t).R_{i,0}(t) \tag{9.74}$$

where $x_i(t)$ is the population of the neighbourhood and $N-x_i(t)$ the population in the outside world. The rates $R_{0,i}(t)$ and $R_{i,0}(t)$ are assumed to derive from the same principle of utility maximization as described in 9.3.3.1; more precisely, they are defined by:

$$R_{0,i}(t) = R\,\frac{e^{v^{(i)}(t)}}{e^{v^{(i)}(t)} + e^{\theta}}$$

$$R_{i,0}(t) = R - R_{0,i}(t) \tag{9.75}$$

Here, R represents the reviewing rate of the individuals and θ the utility function of the outside world; they are supposed constant. $v^{(i)}(t)$ is the utility function of the neighbourhood and has now to be specified. Up to the present, we have considered the situations where the utility functions and more generally the transition rates depend either exogeneously on time or directly on the distribution of the individuals in the different compartments. In this application, we will suppose that the utility function $v^{(i)}(t)$ depends on a variable, the neighbourhood quality, whose evolution is a function of the state $x_i(t)$ of the system. We begin by writing $v^{(i)}(t)$ as:

$$v^{(i)}(t) = \alpha^{(i)} + q^{(i)}(t) - \beta.P^{(i)}(t) \tag{9.76}$$

where $\alpha^{(i)}$ represents the local attributes of the neighbourhood, $q^{(i)}(t)$ the housing quality, $P^{(i)}(t)$ the housing price and β a positive parameter. Moreover, we suppose that $p^{(i)}(t)$ is just equal to the attractivity of the neighbourhood, which yields:

$$p^{(i)}(t) = (\alpha^{(i)} + q^{(i)}(t) + \gamma)/(1 + \beta) \qquad (9.77)$$

where γ is the Euler constant. Thus, by (9.76) and (9.77), $v^{(i)}(t)$ depends on time through the variable $q^{(i)}(t)$. Now, housing quality deteriorates spontaneously over time, but can be improved if maintained. It is here assumed that a particular policy of maintenance expenditures has been decided for the whole neighbourhood. This policy has not been fixed exogeneously, but is a function of the current income from housing units, and therefore of the number of individuals located in the neighbourhood. This leads to the following quality deterioration equation:

$$\frac{dq^{(i)}(t)}{dt} = h[x_i(t)] - \ell q^{(i)}(t) \qquad (9.78)$$

where $\ell > 0$ is the rate of deterioration, and $h[x_i(t)]$ is the beneficial effect of the maintenance expenditures invested when $x_i(t)$ individuals are located in the neighbourhood. Thus, as announced, $q^{(i)}(t)$ depends on the state $x_i(t)$ of the system. To summarize, the system is described by the two coupled differential equations (9.74) and (9.78).

Let us examine the stationary states of this system. It is easily found that the stationary states $q^{(i)*}$ and x_i^* satisfy the relations:

$$q^{(i)*} = h(x_i^*)/\ell$$

$$N/x_i^* = 1 + \vartheta \exp\{-h(x_i^*)/[\ell(1 + \beta)]\} \qquad (9.79)$$

where

$$\vartheta = \theta \exp[(\beta\gamma - \alpha)/(1 + \beta)]$$

There, the number of stationary solutions depends on the function form of h(.). Qualitatively different situations have been discussed in de Palma and Lefèvre (1982). We shall restrict here the discussion to the following plausible maintenance policy: the maintenance expenditures increase with the number of individuals located in the neighbourhood provided that this number remains smaller than a given size $\bar{x}$; beyond this point, the investments increase less rapidly or even decrease. For illustration, we take $\ell = 1$ and define h(.) as follows.

$$1 + \vartheta\exp[-h(x_i)/(1+\beta)] = \begin{cases} a + bx_i, \text{for } x_i \in [0,\bar{x}] \\ a + b\bar{x} + c(x_i-\bar{x}), \text{ for } x_i \in [\bar{x},N] \end{cases} \tag{9.80}$$

where a, b and c are three constant parameters, with $b < 0$ and $c > b$ (c positive or not). Supplementary conditions on a, b and c guarantee the existence of three stationary states (see the paper mentioned). A stability calculation shows then that the first two stationary states are respectively a stable node and a saddle point, while the third one is a stable focus or node accordingly as c is positive or negative (see 9.4.3). This is illustrated in Figures 9.7a and 9.7b.

It is worth noting that the existence of three stationary states implies a threshold phenomenon, which could induce segregation in a system with J neighbourhoods and 2 populations.

We have presented this example to show how the classical framework of compartmental analysis can be used and extended to the study of systems whose evolution results from an inter-

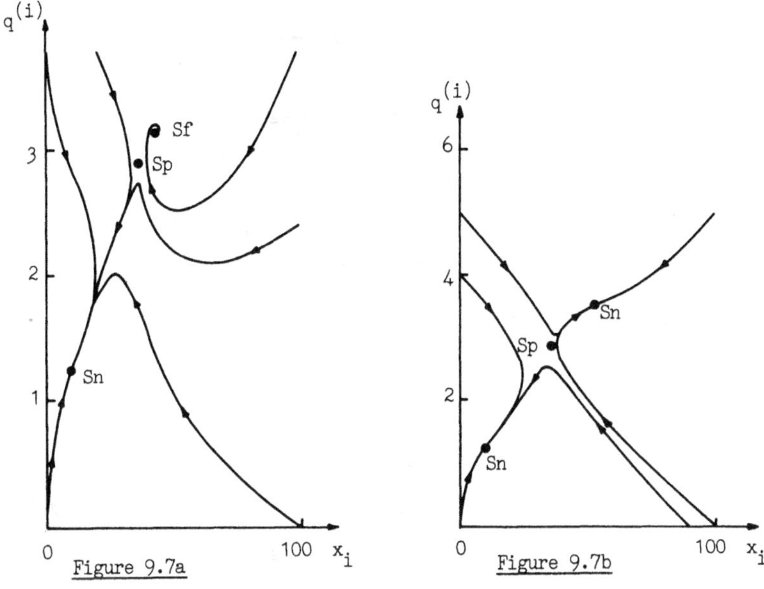

Figure 9.7: Phase space diagrams when in (9.80), a=12, b=-0.25, $\bar{x}$=40, γ=30, and c is either 0.1 (Figure 9.7a) or -1/120 (Figure 9.7b). Sn denotes a stable node, Sp a saddle point and Sf a stable focus.

action between demand and supply. This case is of particular interest in a large number of situations occurring in regional science.

Roughly, the basic model is then a classical compartmental model (see Figure 9.1), but where the transition rates depend on supply variables $p_1, \ldots, p_L$ such as prices, trip times, waiting times for example. The value of these variables results from a dynamical adjustment of the supply based on the demand, that is, on the distribution of the individuals in the different compartments (see Figure 9.8).

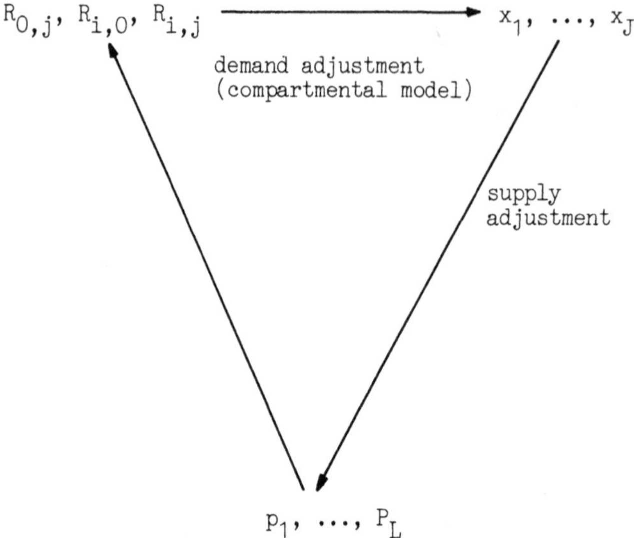

Figure 9.8: Extension of the compartmental model to describe the adjustment between supply and demand

Recently, we have applied this idea to describe the departure time choices for the home to work trip and to study the problem of peak period traffic congestion (de Palma, Ingenbleek and Lefèvre, 1983). We believe that similar extensions of compartmental analysis should be explored in order to develop a better understanding of the spatial interactions.

Part Five

METHODOLOGICAL INTEGRATION

Chapter 10

THE INTEGRATION OF ALTERNATIVE METHODOLOGICAL APPROACHES TO URBAN DEMAND MODELLING

C.S. Bertuglia, G. Leonardi, S. Occelli, G.A. Rabino, R. Tadei

10.1 Relationships Between the Different Approaches to the Modelling of Demand Behaviour

10.1.1 Introduction

The purpose of this chapter is to compare systematically the main approaches to modelling demand behaviour and to show through a series of theorems that there are many equivalences.

The most important demand models in a location-transport system are those involving consumer choice between alternatives, which are usually spatially differentiated. We are particularly interested in choice models for trip destination, for the transport mode and for a route in a network. Apart from the specific content which varies from case to case, there is a fundamental similarity in the structure of these models in that all envisage a situation of choice between a discrete set of alternatives (of destination, route or mode) and measures of distance or cost which reduce the possibility of using them. A first distinction can be made between static models of choice and dynamic models of choice. Even though in the following we concentrate exclusively on comparative analysis of static models, we should specify that the exclusion of dynamic models is only for the following reasons. First, the literature on dynamic choice models is very limited and sporadic and therefore insufficient to carry out a real comparative study. Secondly, it can be argued that dynamic choice behaviour is simply a sequence in time of locally static choices, and therefore the basic mechanism is in fact the same as that of the static models we examine here. What differentiates dynamic choice models is essentially the fact that the attributes of the alternatives (in general expressed in terms of a measure of utility) are not constant, but vary in time as a function of the interactions between individuals and also the interactions between individuals and the physical environment in which the choice is made. Typical examples of attributes which vary because of these interactions are limited capacity (for example of the housing stock or a road link), prices, and all the negative externalities deriving from competition between different individuals for the use of limited alternatives. However, while we acknowledge that the introduction of dynamics is one of the most interesting challenges for future research, we observe that this dynamic quality has more to do with the analysis of the different attributes of alternatives than with the basic mechanism that produces the evaluation and choice. This mechanism, which is locally static, is the subject of the following analysis and is the fundamental element underlying all choice models, whether static or dynamic.

A further classification can be based on the distinction between aggregated models, based on observed phenomena at the macroscopic level, and disaggregated models, based on explicit assumptions (in general micro-economic) relative to the process of individual choice. Among the former are included the models based on entropy maximising or the cost-efficiency principle. Among the latter we have the classic models of utility maximisation typical of urban economics, and those based on random utility theory. What is surprising is that such different and apparently conflicting theoretical assumptions lead to almost identical models. More precisely, we find that all the approaches which introduce effects of random dispersion on choice - ie entropy-maximising, cost-efficiency and random utility - produce, under relatively weak assumptions, the so-called multinomial logit model. In the following sections we analyse the theoretical aspect of these similarities and the relationships which make it possible to map one approach into the others.

10.1.2 Entropy-maximisation and cost-efficiency

The equivalence between the two principles has been proved in the contribution of Smith to this book, to which the reader should refer for technical details. Here we mention only the main features of the two methods and their equivalence. It should be added that Smith applies the principle to an assignment problem in a congested network, but obviously it can be extended to any problem of choice between discrete alternatives. For this reason the comparative analysis of the two principles can be based on the simplest problem of choice between discrete alternatives, which is the following.

Let us take a population of P consumers and a set of alternatives $j = 1, \ldots, n$. Associated with each alternative is a real number v_j which we can call the utility of alternative j for the population considered and which measures the attractiveness or relative advantages associated with the choice of j. In many applications v_j will consist either of a term for the cost of access to alternative j (eg cost of transport) or a term for the specific attractiveness of j (eg the dimensions of the shopping centre capacity, etc). However, from the theoretical point of view, which is what interests us here, such a distinction and disaggregation is not relevant, so we can consider a single numerical value for v_j which will be referred to as the utility of alternative j.

The way in which the entropy-maximising method as proposed

by Wilson (1970-A, 1974) deals with the problem of determining the distribution of choice between the various alternatives is well-known. Here we give a brief reminder. Supposing that all the possible configurations are equally probable (except for constraints) at the micro-level, the probability of finding a certain distribution at the aggregate level will be proportional to the number of possible configurations at the micro-level which produce the given distribution at the macro-level.

Let T_j be the number of consumers who choose alternative j. The vector $T = [T_1, \ldots, T_n]$ therefore represents the choice distribution at the aggregate level. Obviously we have the constraint:

$$\sum_{j=1}^{n} T_j = P \tag{10.1}$$

On the basis of the assumptions made above, the probability of observing the vector T is proportional to:

$$W(T) = \frac{P!}{\prod_{j=1}^{n} T_j!} \tag{10.2}$$

The additional assumption that P and T_j, $j = 1, \ldots, n$, are large allows us to use the Stirling approximation:

$$\ln T_j! \sim T_j(\ln T_j - 1) \tag{10.3}$$

(or, if necessary, one can use the Shannon measure of entropy directly). Therefore, if we want to find the most probable distribution $\underline{T} = \{T_j\}$ that is the one which maximises given $W(\underline{T})$ by

$$\ln W(T) = - \sum_j \ln T_j! + \ln P!$$

since the search for the maximum is not affected by an increasing monotonic transformation of the maximising functions.

Ignoring the constant ln P! which does not affect the location of the maximum and using the approximation (10.3) it follows that the most probable distribution T is that which maximises the function:

$$E(\underline{T}) = -\sum_j T_j(\ln T_j - 1) \tag{10.4}$$

This function is known as entropy of the distribution $\underline{T}$.

According to Wilson and in analogy with the use of this method in statistical mechanics, the search for the maximum of E(T) is subject not only to constraint (10.1) but also to a further constraint of conversation of some kind of "total energy" of the system. Wilson identifies this energy with total journey cost (or time). In the formulation used here, this is translated and generalised into the total utility of the system, that is the quantity:

$$\sum_j T_j v_j \tag{10.5}$$

From the above, it follows that the most probable distribution T is the solution to the mathematical programming problem

$$\max_T \{E(\underline{T}): \sum_{j=1}^{n} T_j = P, \sum_{j=1}^{n} T_j v_j = V\} \tag{10.6}$$

in which V is the given level of total utility. It is easily verified that the function $E(\underline{T})$ is concave, therefore problem (10.6) is a concave programming problem (being subject to linear constraints). This means that the classic Lagrange multiplier method can be used to determine the unique solution.

The Lagrange formulation corresponding to problem (10.6) is:

$$L(\underline{T},\nu,\mu) = \underline{E}(\underline{T}) - \nu(P - \sum_{j=1}^{n} T_j) - \mu(V - \sum_{j=1}^{n} T_j v_j) \tag{10.7}$$

in which ν and μ are the multipliers associated with constraints (10.1) and (10.5) respectively.

By setting the Lagrangian's derivatives with respect to each T_j to zero we obtain:

$$\ln T_j = -(\nu + \mu v_j)$$

that is:

$$T_j = ke^{-\mu v_j} \tag{10.8}$$

in which

$$k = e^{-\nu}$$

Constraint (10.1) allows us to eliminate the constant k from (10.8). In addition, without losing generality, we can define

$$\beta = -\mu$$

(in fact β is empirically always non-negative). We therefore have:

$$T_j = P \frac{e^{\beta v_j}}{\sum_j e^{\beta v_j}} \tag{10.9}$$

which is the formula of the multinomial logit model in its simplest form. The value of the function $E(\underline{T})$ associated with distribution (10.9) is given by:

$$E(\underline{T}) = -\sum_j T_j(\beta v_j + \ln P - \ln \sum_j e^{\beta v_j} - 1)$$

$$= P \ln \sum_j e^{\beta v_j} + \text{constants}$$

and as entropy is generally defined up to an additive arbitrary constant we can redefine it so that:

$$E(T) = P \ln \sum_j e^{\beta v_j} \tag{10.10}$$

The entropy-maximising principle, having been borrowed from statistical mechanics, does not have a direct macro-economic interpretation. Despite this, economic behaviour is induced in the solution (10.9), which shows a tendency for choices to be concentrated on the alternatives with higher utility.

This tendency, obtained as a result by Wilson, is used by Smith (1978-A, 1983-A) as a starting assumption for his cost efficiency principle (which, given the formulation used here, could be more appropriately renamed utility efficiency principle). Here we briefly examine how the simple problem of distribution is dealt with using this approach. We consider once again a total population P, a set of alternatives $R = \{j: j = 1, \ldots, n\}$, and a utility v_j associated with each alternative $j \varepsilon R$.

We denote with:

$$\underline{t} = (r_1, \ldots, r_P);\ r_k \varepsilon R,\ k = 1, \ldots, P$$

a choice pattern consisting of the list of alternatives chosen by the first, second, ..., n^{th} individual. For different realisations (for example, different days) we find in general different patterns $\underline{t}$.

Let $\underline{T} = (\underline{t}_1, \ldots, \underline{t}_m)$ be a sequence of realisations of different patterns and $Q(\underline{T})$ the probability of observing $\underline{T}$. It is shown by Smith (1982-B) that the form of $Q(\underline{T})$ is completely determined by the following two assumptions, which constitute the essence of the utility efficiency method.

Assumption 1 (Independence)

The terms of the sequence $\underline{T}$ are independent. From this it follows that:

$$Q(\underline{T}) = \prod_{k=1}^{m} Q(\underline{t}_k)$$

Assumption 2 (Utility efficiency principle)

Define:

$$\overline{V}(\underline{T}) = \frac{1}{m} \sum_{k=1}^{m} V(\underline{t}_k)$$

the average utility of the sequence T in which:

$$V(\underline{t}) = \sum_{j=1}^{P} v(r_j) \qquad (10.11)$$

is the cumulative utility for all P consumers in the pattern $t = (r_1, \ldots, r_p)$. If for two sequences, $\underline{T}$, $\underline{T}'$

$$\overline{V}(\underline{T}) \geq \overline{V}(\underline{T}')$$

then

$$Q(\underline{T}) \geq Q(\underline{T}')$$

Assumption 2 introduces an explicit condition of macroeconomic regularity, which is however very weak (much weaker, for example, than utility maximisation). It simply says that it is more probable to observe sequences of choice patterns with high average utility than vice versa. Smith shows that from assumptions 1 and 2 we can derive

$$Q(t) = ke^{\beta V(t)}, \quad \beta \geq 0 \qquad (10.12)$$

in which k is a normalising constant and β is a parameter.

The result (10.12) and the definition (10.11) are sufficient to show the equivalence between the utility efficiency principle and the entropy maximising principle. In fact, if we let $\underline{F} = (F_1, \ldots, F_n)$ be the vector of the distribution of the P consumers among the alternatives 1, ..., n, such that

$$\sum_{j=1}^{n} F_j = P \tag{10.13}$$

and we consider all the choice patterns t which produce the same vector F, the total number of patterns is given by

$$\frac{P!}{\prod_{j=1}^{n} F_j!} \tag{10.14}$$

In addition, they all have the same cumulative utility:

$$V(\underline{t}) = V(\underline{F}) = \sum_{j=1}^{n} F_j v_j$$

and therefore, are equally probable, with a probability given by (10.12):

$$k \exp\left(\beta \sum_{j=1}^{n} F_j v_j\right) \tag{10.15}$$

Combining (10.14) and (10.15) we find that the probability associated with a distribution F is proportional to:

$$W(\underline{F}) = \frac{P!}{\prod_{j=1}^{n} F_j!} \exp\left(\beta \sum_{j=1}^{n} F_j v_j\right) \tag{10.16}$$

and the most probable distribution $\underline{F}$ can be determined as the solution of the mathematical programming problems:

$$\max_{F} \{\ln W(\underline{F}): \sum_{j=1}^{n} F_j = P\} \tag{10.17}$$

Using as usual the assumption that the F_j are sufficiently large and Stirling's approximation

$$\ln F_j! \sim F_j(\ln F_j - 1)$$

we have

$$\ln W(F) = \ln P! + \beta \sum_{j=1}^{n} F_j v_j - \sum_{j=1}^{n} \ln F_j!$$

$$\sim - \sum_{j=1}^{n} F_j(\ln F_j - 1) + \beta \sum_{j=1}^{n} F_j v_j + \ln P!$$

Going back to (10.4) (definition of the entropy function) and ignoring the additive constants, we see that the problem (10.17) is equivalent to the problem

$$\max_{F}\{E(\underline{F}) + \beta \sum_{j=1}^{n} F_j v_j : \sum_{j=1}^{n} F_j = P\} \qquad (10.18)$$

It is evident that problem (10.18) is a Lagrangian relaxation of problem (10.6) since a constraint of the type:

$$\sum_{j=1}^{n} F_j v_j = V$$

which appears in problem (10.6) is replaced by the term

$$\beta \sum_{j=1}^{n} F_j v_j$$

added to the objective function. Therefore, if the numerical value of the parameter β used in (10.18) is the same as that of the Lagrange multipliers β relative to the second constraint of (10.6), problems (10.6) and (10.18) are completely equivalent; that is, they have the same optimal solution and the objective function has the same optimum value. From this equivalence and from (10.9) it follows that the most probable distribution F based on utility efficiency is:

$$F_j = P \frac{e^{\beta v_j}}{\sum_j e^{\beta v_j}} \tag{10.19}$$

10.1.3 Random utility theory and entropy-maximisation

In 10.1.2 the equivalence between two macroscopic principles, one from statistical mechanics (entropy maximisation) and the other macro-economic (utility efficiency) was shown. In both cases it involved principles based on relatively weak assumptions and which imposed relatively few constraints on individual behaviours. In this section we examine a theory based explicitly on microscopic assumptions, ie random utility theory, and determine under what conditions it produces results equivalent to the macroscopic theories mentioned above.

We consider once again the choice situation discussed in 10.1.2 but examine in particular the behaviour of a single individual when facing the alternatives j, $j = 1, \ldots, n$. In the aggregate approaches previously discussed we introduced a set of numerical weights v_j, called "utility" (even though neither of the two theories is strictly "utilitarian"), which measure the different relative attractiveness of the alternatives. From a traditional utility point of view, if the v_j were actually interpreted as utility functions defined by each member of the population P on the set of alternatives, and if the population were to be composed of P perfectly homogeneous members with respect to their evaluation of the alternatives (ie with the same utility function), then an individual drawn at random from the P individuals would choose the alternative k for which the utility v_k is maximum:

$$v_k = \max_j v_j \tag{10.20}$$

Assumption (10.20), which will be defined as the deterministic utility maximisation, characterises most of neo-classical urban economic models. The principle of choice of the alternative with maximum utility or minimum cost also constitutes the base of the classical theory of location of economic activities and services, from Weber's model to the assignment and location models proposed within Operational Research. (Some of the principal models of this type are described and discussed by Beckmann and Colorni in this book.) However, we know that this principle does not produce very realistic choice patterns. If the population P were really homogeneous, we would observe that the totality of choices would be concentrated on alternative k which corresponds to the maximum utility v_k, while all the other alternatives $j \neq k$ for which $v_j < v_k$, would be neglected. A way of eliminating this undesirable aspect is to assume that the population P is heterogeneous with respect to the evaluation of alternatives, that is that each individual has a different utility function. As direct observation of the utility function of each single individual is impossible, a description in deterministic terms of a disaggregated choice process with a heterogeneous population is also impossible.

The theory of random utilities, proposed by Luce (1959) and developed by Manski (1973), Domencich and McFadden (1975), Williams (1977-A) and Ben-Akiva and Lerman (1979) tackles this problem by explicitly introducing stochastic elements in the choice process. To solve the problem the theory suggests giving the following description in probability terms.

Suppose an individual chosen randomly from population P assigns to alternative j the utility

$$\tilde{u}_j = v_j + \tilde{\theta}_j \tag{10.21}$$

in which v_j are the quantities used previously, which can be interpreted as deterministic components of utility, identical for all individuals (and dependent on observable characteristics of alternative j), while $\tilde{\theta}_j$ are random variables which can be interpreted as stochastic components of utility, varying from individual to individual and independent of observable characteristics of the alternatives. A simplifying assumption often introduced is that $\{\tilde{\theta}_j\}$ is a sequence of identically distributed independent random variables, for which a probability distribution is assumed to exist:

$$F(x) = Pr\{\tilde{\theta}_j \leqq x\},\ j = 1,\ \ldots,\ n \tag{10.22}$$

Assumptions (10.20) and (10.21) make it possible to obtain closed-form expressions for the distribution of maximum utility and the choice probabilities among alternatives. First from (10.20) and (10.21) it follows that the probability distribution of total utility for alternative j is given by:

$$P_r\{\tilde{u}_j \leqq x\} = P_r\{v_j + \tilde{\theta}_j \leqq x\} = P_r\{\tilde{\theta}_j \leqq x - v_j\} = F(x - v_j) \tag{10.23}$$

Therefore defining the random variable:

$$\tilde{u} = \max_j \tilde{u}_j$$

and noting the equivalence between the two events:

$$\tilde{u} \leqq x$$

and

$$\tilde{u}_j \leqq x \text{ for all } j = 1,\ \ldots,\ n$$

it follows that:

$$H(x) = P_r\{\tilde{u} \leqq x\} = P_r\{\tilde{u}_1 \leqq x,\ \ldots,\ \tilde{u}_n \leqq x\}$$

$$= \prod_{j=1}^{n} P_r\{\tilde{u}_j \leqq x\} = \prod_{j=1}^{n} F(x - v_j) \tag{10.24}$$

The probability density h(x) associated with H(x) is:

$$h(x) = H'(x) = \sum_{j=1}^{n} F'(x - v_j) \prod_{k \neq j} F(x - v_k) \tag{10.25}$$

and the expected utility associated with the choice of an alternative with maximum total utility is:

$$V = \int_{-\infty}^{\infty} x dH(x) = \int_{-\infty}^{\infty} x h(x) dx = \int_{-\infty}^{\infty} x \sum_{j=1}^{n} F'(x - v_j) \prod_{k \neq j} F(x - v_k) dx \tag{10.26}$$

Finally, the choice probability for alternative j, that is, the probability of the event:

$$\tilde{u}_j = \max_k \tilde{u}_k$$

is given by

$$P_j = \int_{-\infty}^{\infty} F'(x - v_j) \prod_{k \neq j} F(x - v_k) dx \tag{10.27}$$

and from (10.25) it follows that:

$$\sum_{j=1}^{n} p_j = \int_{-\infty}^{\infty} h(x) dx = 1$$

If specific assumptions are introduced on the form of the distribution F(x) of the random components of utility, the equations (10.24) - (10.27) assume different explicit forms. Particular importance has been given in the theory and the applications to the assumption:

$$F(x) = \exp(-e^{-\beta x}) \tag{10.28}$$

The distribution (10.28) is known as the extreme value distribution or Gumbel's distribution. Its importance is due to the fact that it implies the multinomial logit model, obtained already in (10.9) and (10.19). This can be shown more easily by introducing the transformation:

$$\tilde{y}_j = e^{-\beta\tilde{u}_j} = e^{-\beta(\tilde{\vartheta}_j - v_j)} \tag{10.29}$$

The sequence of random variables $\{\tilde{y}_j\}$ is a non-increasing monotonic transformation of the sequence of total utilities $\{\tilde{u}_j\}$, therefore $\tilde{y}_j$ can be considered a measure of the disutility of alternative $j = 1, \ldots, n$. It is easily seen that the random variables $\tilde{y}_j$ are distributed exponentially. In fact, if we let

$$V_j = e^{\beta v_j} \tag{10.30}$$

from (10.28) we obtain

$$G_j(x) = P_r\{e^{-\beta(\tilde{\vartheta}_j + v_j)} \leq x\} = P_r\{\tilde{\vartheta}_j > -\frac{1}{\beta}\ln x - v_j\}$$

$$= 1 - F(-\frac{1}{\beta}\ln x - v_j) = 1 - e^{-V_j x} \tag{10.31}$$

Alternative j is chosen if its disutility y_j is minimum, which occurs with the probability:

$$P_j = \int_0^\infty G_j'(x) \prod_{k \neq j} [1 - G_k(x)]dx = V_j \int_0^\infty e^{-x\sum_k V_k} dx = \frac{V_j}{\sum_k V_k}$$

or, substituting from (10.30):

$$P_j = \frac{e^{\beta v_j}}{\sum_k e^{\beta v_k}} \tag{10.32}$$

Equation (10.32) is clearly identical to (10.9) and (10.19). The distribution of the random variable:

$$\tilde{y} = \min_j e^{-\beta\tilde{u}_j} = e^{-\beta\tilde{u}}$$

is given by:

$$L(x) = 1 - \prod_{j=1}^{n} [1 - G_j(x)] = 1 - e^{-\Phi x} \qquad (10.33)$$

having put

$$\Phi = \sum_j V_j = \sum_j e^{\beta v_j}$$

The mean value of $\tilde{u}$, expressed as a function of $\tilde{y}$ by the equation:

$$\tilde{u} = -\frac{1}{\beta}\ln \tilde{y}$$

is therefore given by:

$$V = E\{\tilde{u}\} = E\{-\frac{1}{\beta}\ln \tilde{y}\} = -\frac{1}{\beta}\int_0^\infty \Phi e^{-\Phi x}\ln x \, dx$$

$$= \frac{1}{\beta}\int_0^\infty (\ln \Phi - \ln y)e^{-y}dy = \frac{1}{\beta}\ln \Phi + \frac{\gamma}{\beta} \qquad (10.34)$$

in which γ is Euler's constant. It is important to note that the expected utility given by (10.34), apart from the additive constant γ/β which can be ignored, and the multiplicative $\frac{1}{\beta}$, is identical to the second term on the right-hand side of (10.10). In fact, the term

$$V = \frac{1}{\beta}\ln \Phi = \frac{1}{\beta}\ln \sum_j e^{\beta v_j}$$

is the expected utility of an optimal choice for a single individual. The expected utility aggregated for a population of P individuals is therefore:

$$PV = \frac{1}{\beta}P \ln \sum_j e^{\beta v_j} \qquad (10.35)$$

and the comparison of (10.35) with (10.10) shows that the

aggregated utility, as it is obtained from the theory of random utility under the assumption (10.28), is formally identical (except for a constant of proportionality) to the maximum value of the entropy function in the optimisation problem (10.6).

This analogy suggests a micro-economic interpretation of entropy, as well as a substantial equivalence between the theory of random utility and theory of entropy maximising (and, as a consequence, utility efficiency). There is, however, one aspect of this reasoning which at first sight seems unsatisfactory. While both entropy-maximisation and utility efficiency are principles based on very weak and not highly constraining assumptions at the level of individual behaviour, the results (10.32) and (10.35) were obtained using a very specific assumption on the heterogeneity of preferences, ie the distribution (10.28). It is not immediately evident that (10.28) has general theoretical foundations and is not simply an ad hoc assumption made for the sake of the simplicity of the calculation. In fact, it is possible to derive (10.28) as an asymptotic result from weaker assumptions, exploiting the properties of maxima of sequences of random variables. This approach, apparently ignored in the literature, that implicitly considers assumption (10.28) as necessary to the derivation of the logit model (see, for example, Domencich and McFadden, 1975), has been explored and developed in some recent papers by Leonardi (1982-A, 1982-B).

In order to clarify this argument, let us assume that the alternatives are partitioned into n homogeneous classes 1, 2, ..., j, ..., n and define v_j as the deterministic utility associated with an alternative from class j. It is assumed in addition that each individual, in order to choose, considers a sample of alternatives drawn sequentially, and so define w_j as the probability that for a given draw, the alternative is drawn from class j, $w_j \geq 0$, $\sum_{j=1}^{n} w_j = 1$.

If $F(x) = P_r\{\vartheta_j \leq x\}$ is the probability distribution for the random utilities, which for the moment we shall consider generic, it emerges that the utility distribution associated with any alternative at any draw is:

$$G(x) = \sum_j w_j F(x - v_j) \tag{10.36}$$

because of (10.23). The maximum utility distribution in a sample of N alternatives is therefore:

$$H_N(x) = G^N(x) \tag{10.37}$$

which is valid for any distribution F(x). We now introduce the following assumption concerning F(x):

$$\lim_{y\to\infty} \frac{1 - F(x+y)}{1 - F(y)} = e^{-\beta x}, \ \beta > 0 \tag{10.38}$$

It is easily verified that the property (10.38) is equivalent to:

$$\lim_{x\to\infty} \frac{F'(x)}{1 - F(x)} = \beta, \ \beta > 0 \tag{10.39}$$

(10.38) or (10.39) characterise a family of probability distributions for which the following theorem holds.

Theorem 1 (Leonardi)

Under the assumption (10.38) we have:

$$\lim_{N\to\infty} G^N(x + \frac{1}{\beta}\ln \Phi + a_N) = \exp(-e^{-\beta x}) \tag{10.40}$$

in which

$$\Phi = \sum_{j=1}^{n} w_j e^{\beta v_j} \tag{10.41}$$

and a_N is the root of the equation:

$$1 - F(a_N) = 1/N \tag{10.42}$$

Here, and with the following theorems, proofs are not given. They are available in full in Leonardi (1985).

Intuitively, Theorem 1 states that, if we can suppose that each individual considers for the choice a sufficiently large sample of alternatives of total size N the distribution of the utility associated with the best alternative is approximately:

$$H_N(x) - \exp[-\Phi e^{-\beta(x - a_N)}] \tag{10.43}$$

and the bigger N the better this approximation is. The constant a_N has only the effect of shifting the origin of the utility scale and therefore does not influence choice behaviour. Except for additive constants, the mean of the distribution (10.43) is:

$$V = \frac{1}{\beta}\ln \Phi$$

which is in agreement with (10.34).

It is important to note that Theorem 1, with its consequent results, was obtained without any specific assumptions about the form of the distribution F(x). Instead a weak property, (10.38), is assumed, which characterises a wide family of distributions. (10.38) is in fact satisfied by most of the more well-known distributions and intuitively requires that the tail of the distribution F(x) can be asymptotically approximated with an exponential. In any case, from the point of view of the constraints posed on individual behaviour, assumption (10.38) is of a level of generality which can be compared with that of the principles of entropy maximising on utility efficiency.

As a complement to Theorem 1, which establishes the asymptotic form of the utility distribution, we give an analogous result on the asymptotic form of the choice probability. Define $p_j(N)$ as the probability that an individual who has drawn a sample of size N (in the way described above) chooses an alternative of type j, j = 1, ..., n. Then the following theorem is valid.

Theorem 2 (Leonardi)

Under the same assumptions as for Theorem 1:

$$\lim_{N\to\infty} p_j(N) = \frac{w_j e^{\beta v_j}}{\sum_{j=1}^{n} w_j e^{\beta v_j}} \qquad (10.44)$$

Theorem 2 suggests a complete correspondence between random utility theory, entropy maximising and also utility efficiency theory, as implied by the equivalence proved by Smith (in this book). It should be noted that (10.44) is slightly more general than (10.9), in that each alternative is weighted differently with weights w_j. This however does not constitute a real structural difference between the two models. If we assume that the w_j are proportional to the number of alternatives of type j, that is

$$w_j = kN_j$$

in which N_j is the total number of alternatives of type j, then equation (10.9), applied to such a situation and counting the alternatives correctly, would give

$$T_j = P \frac{N_j e^{\beta v_j}}{\sum_j N_j e^{\beta v_j}} = P \frac{w_j e^{\beta v_j}}{\sum_j w_j e^{\beta v_j}}$$

It is possible to establish the following theorem.

Theorem 3 (Leonardi)

The function F(v) (expected utility) and E(y) (entropy) defined above are reciprocally conjugate in the duality induced by the Legendre transform. The two spaces placed in duality are the space of deterministic utilities v, $v \varepsilon R^n$, and the space of the choice probabilities y, $y \varepsilon S$, in which

$$S = \{x : x \varepsilon \Gamma^n, \sum_j x_j = 1\}$$

The result of Theorem 3 is valid for the behaviour of a single individual. It can, however, be extended without difficulty to the case of P individuals. In this case the choice probability will be replaced by expected flows, that is, by the distribution of the P individuals among the various alternatives, simply by multiplying P by y. We find in this way that the choice behaviour has two completely equivalent alternative representations. One representation is in the utility space, through the expected utility function F(v), corresponding to random utility theory, and the other representation is in the flows space, through the entropy function E(y) corresponding to the principle of entropy maximising.

10.1.4 Conclusions

The equivalence between the three different approaches to modelling choice behaviour with probabilistic dispersion was shown with the use of a simple model, which can be considered the basic prototype of all choice models in which individual behaviour is independent of that of other individuals. More complex cases can be imagined in which factors such as a limited number of alternatives or limited capacity or excessive congestion introduce effects of mutual disturbance, inhibition and competition among individuals. In such cases the choices are subject to further constraints and in general the utility of each alternative depends on the number of individuals who choose it. In other words, it is necessary to introduce endogenous signals of scarcity, in the form of negative externalities or prices. A comparative analysis of the different approaches to the introduction of such signals is the subject of a later section.

A final comment concerns the relationship between random utility maximising and deterministic utility maximising. It is obvious that the latter can be deduced as a limiting case of the former, when the assumption of heterogeneity of the population is dropped. More precisely, it has been shown by Evans (1973) that a model of type (10.9), (10.19) or (10.44) coincides with the deterministic choice model when the parameter β goes to infinity. As, according to the interpretation of the theory of random utilities, β is inversely proportional to the variance of the distribution (10.28), this limiting case coincides with that in which the distribution of the random utility terms degenerates into a concentration on a single value, that is, the heterogeneity of the population disappears. This can be demonstrated even without assuming a specific form for the distribution (10.28). We suppose that the distribution F(x) degenerates into a concentration on a given value a, that is:

$$F(x) = \begin{cases} 0, & x \leqq a \\ 1, & x > a \end{cases} \tag{10.45}$$

In this case, the corresponding density will be:

$$F'(x) = \delta(x - a) \tag{10.46}$$

where $\delta\,(x - a)$ is a Dirac delta lumped on the value a. Substituting (10.45) and (10.46) in (10.27) and noting that:

$$\prod_{k \neq j} F(x - v_k - a) = \begin{cases} 0, & x \leq \max_{k \neq j} (v_k + a) \\ 1, & x > \max_{k \neq j} (v_k + a) \end{cases}$$

we obtain

$$P_j = \int_{\max_{k \neq j} (v_k + a)}^{\infty} \delta(x - v_j - a)dx = \begin{cases} 1, & \text{if } v_j > \max_{k \neq j} v_k \\ 0, & \text{if } v_j < \max_{k \neq j} v_k \end{cases} \tag{10.47}$$

That is, the choice concentrates on the alternative with maximum utility, which is precisely the neo-classic principle of deterministic utility maximisation.

10.2 Mechanism of Price Formation and Spatial Differentiation in Location-Transport Systems

10.2.1 Introduction

Any system of transport and location will always involve the interaction between demand flows on the one hand and stocks of goods and services on the other. The former are mobile and subject to relatively fast changes, the latter are immobile and subject to very slow changes. This difference inevitably creates situations of disequilibrium and gives rise to self-regulating mechanisms which try to increase or reduce the demand flows depending upon whether stock is abundant or scarce. These mechanisms take the form of negative externalities, which we refer to as "prices". This concept of price includes both monetary and non-monetary prices. Housing rents for example are clearly expressed in money terms, but other important signals, such as queuing time for housing assignment (discussed by Weibull, 1984-A) often occurring in publicly regulated housing markets, can also be considered as price.

In the same way, the time taken to travel a certain distance in a congested network (as discussed by Smith in this book) is also a price. These prices do not always reflect the existence of an actual market. For this to be the case it is necessary for the stock of goods and services offered to be controlled by suppliers who will attempt in some way to make a profit from their sale. This is typically the case of rents and house prices and also retail prices in shopping centres. It is not true, however, of journey times for example which are purely physical phenomena determined by traffic flow and levels of congestion.

Although the definition of price used here is essentially dynamic, as prices are seen as a mechanism of adaptation to disequilibrium, most classic theory concerning price setting in spatial and multi-regional systems is based on situations of static equilibrium. It is clear however that a dynamic formulation constitutes the most natural future development for a spatial theory of prices.

A further important distinction concerns the assumption made about the information possessed by consumers and suppliers. In classic theory it is assumed that both parties have perfect knowledge of the market and that demand is homogeneous and non-stochastic. In certain more recent studies although demand is considered to be heterogeneous and stochastic, the supplier is still assumed to have perfect knowledge of demand (cf Anas, 1979, 1982). Leonardi in this book however makes no a priori assumption about knowledge on the part of the supplier of the relationship between price and demand. He considers prices to be generated in real time through direct bargaining between consumer and supplier.

We now analyse if and to what extent the progressive introduction of stochastic elements in the classic deterministic static approach allows us to construct a coherent general frame of reference.

10.2.2 The deterministic equilibrium model and linear programming

We consider once again a situation in which the consumer has to choose between a discrete set of alternatives. Each consumer can choose only one alternative. From the supply-side each alternative is controlled by an entrepreneur who sets the price. We define: i, j, the subscripts associated with different zones i, j = 1, ..., m; v_{ij}, the utility of an alternative in zone j for a consumer in zone i (v_{ij} may also include the cost of transport between i and j), if the alternative is offered at zero price; r_j, the price of an alternative offered in zone j. We suppose that the consumer seeks to maximise utility and that the supplier seeks to maximise profit. It is also assumed that the utility function is linear in prices. This implies that if each consumer in zone i chooses in such a way as to maximise his utility and if market prices are r_j, j = 1, ..., m, in an equilibrium situation, the utility for a consumer will be:

$$V_i = \max_j (v_{ij} - r_j), \quad i = 1, \ldots, m \qquad (10.48)$$

If (10.48) is satisfied by a particular k, we have

$$v_{ik} - r_k = V_i, \text{ if } v_{ik} - r_k = \max_j (v_{ij} - r_j)$$

or

$$r_k = v_{ik} - V_i \qquad (10.49)$$

As the suppliers maximise profit, the price will be set equal to the highest level consistent with (10.49), that is by choosing the consumer willing to pay the highest price. Hence,

$$r_j = \max_i (v_{ij} - V_i), \quad j = 1, \ldots, m \qquad (10.50)$$

Equations (10.48) and (10.50) constitute the equilibrium

conditions of the market in the classic sense of the term. These conditions, even if derived through micro-economic reasoning, are equivalent to the optimum conditions of a linear programming problem. If we consider the problem:

$$\max_{x} \{ \sum_{ij} x_{ij} v_{ij} : \sum_{j} x_{ij} = P_i, \sum_{i} x_{ij} = Q_j, x_{ij} > 0 \} \qquad (10.51)$$

in which P_i is the total number of consumers in zone i and Q_j is the total supply (number of alternatives available) in zone j, and $\sum_j Q_j = \sum_i P_i$.

The dual problem associated with (10.51) is:

$$\min_{\nu,\mu} \{ \sum_{i} P_i \nu_i + \sum_{j} Q_j \mu_j : \nu_i + \mu_j \geq v_{ij} \} \qquad (10.52)$$

in which ν_i, μ_j are the shadow prices associated with the constraints of origin and destination respectively. From the structure of the objective function and the constraints of (10.52) it follows that μ_j must satisfy the condition:

$$\mu_j = \max_{i} (v_{ij} - \nu_i), \; j = 1, \ldots, m \qquad (10.53)$$

Reasoning in the same way, ν_j must satisfy the condition:

$$\nu_i = \max_{j} (v_{ij} - \mu_j), \; i = 1, \ldots, m \qquad (10.54)$$

Comparing (10.53) with (10.54) and (10.54) with (10.48) we find that the shadow prices μ_j are identifiable with the real prices r_j while the shadow prices ν_i are identifiable with the utilities V_i.

Problem (10.51) is one of the simplest problems of linear programming (known as the "assignment problem") and can be considered as a basic prototype for a model of general equilibrium of a spatial market. When the goods exchanged are dwellings, problem (10.51) is essentially the same as the model of Herbert and Stevens (1960), which constitutes a translation into discrete space of the classic theory of housing market equilibrium (Alonso, 1964-A).

An important feature of the model expressed in (10.51) and (10.52) is its perfect consistency in neo-classic terms. The conditions (10.53) and (10.54), which as shown are equivalent to (10.48) and (10.50), imply that the "rational" behaviour of consumers and producers at the individual microscopic level (the maximisation of utility and maximisation of profit respectively) is equivalent to the rational behaviour of the system at macroscopic level. The objective function of the dual problem (10.52) can be broken down into two elements: $\sum_i P_i \nu_i$, aggregated utility for all consumers or, in other words, consumer surplus; and $\sum_j Q_j \mu_j$ aggregated profit for all producers or, in other words, producer surplus. The sum of the two components is the so-called "Total Social Benefit". The conditions (10.53) and (10.54) plus the observations made above show that individual optimum behaviour of demand and supply implies the optimisation of Total Social Benefit. This result is obtained assuming that the utility function is linear, that there is a state of general equilibrium, that demand is homogeneous and that information is perfect for consumers and producers. We now show how the result can be generalised (or changed by various degrees) by relaxing one or more of these assumptions.

10.2.3 The stochastic equilibrium model and entropy-maximisation

A first step towards generalisation is to keep all the previous assumptions, except the homogeneity of demand. We therefore suppose that consumers have different preferences and that this heterogeneity is known stochastically. As in random utility theory this can be modelled assuming that the utility of an alternative in j for a consumer in i is given by

$$v_{ij} - r_j + \tilde{\varepsilon}_{ij},$$

in which v_{ij} and r_j are defined as previously and $\tilde{\varepsilon}_{ij}$ is a random variable which reflects the heterogeneity of preference of the consumer. The variables $\{\tilde{\varepsilon}_{ij}\}$ are assumed to be independent and identically distributed with a distribution

$$P_r\{\tilde{\varepsilon}_{ij} \leq x\} = F(x)$$

As an additional hypothesis, it is also assumed that F(x) is asymptotically exponential in its right-hand tail, that is, that the following property is valid:

$$\lim_{y\to\infty} \frac{1 - F(x + y)}{1 - F(y)} = e^{-\beta x}, \; \beta > 0 \tag{10.55}$$

The equations analogous to (10.48) and (10.50) are respectively

$$V_i = \max_j \, (v_{ij} - r_j + \tilde{\varepsilon}_{ij}) \tag{10.56}$$

$$r_j = \max_i \, (v_{ij} - V_i + \tilde{\varepsilon}_{ij}) \tag{10.57}$$

Since $\tilde{\varepsilon}_{ij}$ are random variables, the utility V_i and the prices r_j are also random variables. When the number of consumers (equal to the number of alternatives) is large, the distribution of V_i and r_j and also the resulting choice model, assume a particularly simple form. In fact we have the following:

Theorem 4 (Leonardi)

Let the property (10.55) hold, and $\sum_i P_i = \sum_j Q_j = Q$ and let there be constants $\omega_j > 0$, $\sum_j \omega_j = 1$, $\alpha_i > 0$, $\sum_i \alpha_i = 1$, such that

$$Q_j = Q\omega_j, \; P_i = Q\alpha_i \tag{10.58}$$

Define also:

$$A(Q) = F^{-1}(1 - \frac{1}{Q}) \tag{10.59}$$

Then,

$$\lim_{Q\to\infty} \Pr\{V_i - A(Q) \leq x | r_j = y_j\} = \exp\{-\phi_i(y)e^{-\beta x}\} \tag{10.60}$$

$$\lim_{Q\to\infty} \Pr\{r_j - A(Q) \leq x | V_i = y_i\} = \exp\{-\psi_j(y)e^{-\beta x}\} \tag{10.61}$$

where

$$\phi_i(y) = \sum_j e^{\beta(v_{ij} - y_j)} \omega_j \tag{10.62}$$

$$\psi_j(y) = \sum_i \alpha_i . e^{\beta(v_{ij} - y_i)} \tag{10.63}$$

From the above it follows that, apart from an additive constant $A(Q)$, which simply has the effect of shifting the origin of the utility and prices and which in any case is arbitrary, both the utility distribution, which depends on prices, and the price distribution, which depends on utilities, are extreme values distributions (Galambos, 1978). Their models are respectively:

$$\nu_i = \frac{1}{\beta} \ln \phi_i(\mu) \tag{10.64}$$

$$\mu_j = \frac{1}{\beta} \ln \psi_j(\nu) \tag{10.65}$$

in which ϕ_i and ψ_i are defined from (10.62) and (10.63). The probability of a consumer choosing an alternative in j, is given, using (10.60), by the logit formula:

$$p_{ij} = \frac{e^{\beta(v_{ij} - \mu_j)} \omega_j}{\phi_i \ (\mu)} \tag{10.66}$$

Analogously, the probability that a supplier in j sells to a consumer in i, using (10.61), is given by the logit formula:

$$q_{ji} = \frac{e^{\beta(v_{ij} - \nu_i)}\alpha_i}{\psi_j(\nu)} \tag{10.67}$$

It is easy to verify that demand and supply find an equilibrium for each (i,j) pair, ie that:

$$P_i p_{ij} = Q_j q_{ji} \tag{10.68}$$

In fact, substituting (10.68) from (10.62) and (10.63) we obtain with one or two steps:

$$\frac{\psi_i}{\phi_i} = \frac{e^{\beta\mu_j}}{e^{\beta\nu_i}} \tag{10.69}$$

and this equality is obviously true because of (10.64) and (10.65).

It is also simple to show a precise relationship between (10.64) - (10.67) and a classic entropy-maximisation problem. We now present this as a theorem.

Theorem 5 (Leonardi)

The mathematical programming problem

$$\max_{x} \{ \sum_{ij} x_{ij}(v_{ij} - \frac{1}{\beta} \ln x_{ij}) : \sum_j x_{ij} = P_i, \sum_i x_{ij} = Q_j \} \tag{10.70}$$

has as primal solution

$$x_{ij} = P_i p_{ij} = Q_j q_{ji}$$

and ν_i and μ_j as dual variables.

This result has already been proved and is well known (see Wilson, 1970-A, for the derivation of this and analogous results).

The result which we are interested in here, but which is in general ignored, is the complete equivalence between the micro-economic formulation of Theorem 4 and the entropic formulation of Theorem 5.

We can show that the dual equation (10.70), up to additive constants, is given by:

$$D(\mu) = \frac{1}{\beta} \sum_i P_j \ln \phi_i(\mu) + \sum_j Q_j \mu_j = \sum_i P_i \nu_i + \sum_j Q_j \mu_j$$

a result which is essentially identical to (10.52) and can also be interpreted as the sum of consumer surplus and producer surplus.

10.2.4 Spatial differentiation of prices and utility

Given the stochastic formulation of the preceding point it is clear that prices and utilities will never be uniform as they are subject to random variations within the same zone. It is interesting to analyse whether apart from random fluctuations there are other systematic causes of the variations (or uniformity) of prices and utility and how such causes can be traced back to geographical factors. For this analysis it is sufficient to consider the modes (10.64) and (10.65). Transport can be introduced through

$$v_{ij} = - c_{ij}$$

in which c_{ij} is the cost of transport between i and j. We therefore have

$$\phi_i(\mu) = \sum_j e^{-\beta(c_{ij} + \mu_j)} \omega_j \tag{10.71}$$

$$\psi_j(\nu) = \sum_j \alpha_i e^{-\beta(c_{ij} + \nu_i)} \tag{10.72}$$

Equation (10.71) can clearly be interpreted as a measure of accessibility from i to all the alternatives. The difference between (10.71) and a classic accessibility indicator (cf for example, Hansen, 1959) is that the total access cost to j from i also contains the destination price μ_j and not only the transport cost c_{ij}. Similarly (10.72) can be interpreted as a demand potential in j from all the origins. Here too the total measure of distance contains an added term, the utility at the origin. This means that the attractiveness of j for consumers in i decreases as their utility ν_i implies in general strong competition from other alternatives, that is, a vast range of choice for consumers in i and therefore a lesser probability that they choose alternative j.

From (10.71) and (10.72), and the geographical interpretation just given, it is clear that the only case in which accessibility and potential (and therefore utility and prices) are uniform is that in which there are no differences in transport costs. In fact if:

$$c_{ij} = c, \ \forall ij$$

then

$$\phi_i(\mu) = \sum_j e^{-\beta(c + \mu_j)} \omega_j = \phi(\mu), \ \forall i$$

$$\psi_j(\nu) = \sum_i \alpha_i e^{-\beta(c + \nu_i)} = \psi(\nu), \ \forall j$$

and therefore from (10.64) and (10.65)

$$\nu_i = \frac{1}{\beta} \ln \phi(\mu) = \nu, \ \forall i$$

$$\mu_j = \frac{1}{\beta} \ln \psi(\nu) = \mu, \ \forall j$$

On the other hand, let:

$$\nu_i = \nu, \ \forall i$$

$$\mu_j = \mu, \ \forall j$$

Then, because of (10.64) and (10.65):

$$\nu = \frac{1}{\beta} \ln \sum_j e^{-\beta c_{ij}} \omega_j - \mu$$

$$\mu = \frac{1}{\beta} \ln \sum_i \alpha_i e^{-\beta c_{ij}} - \nu$$

or

$$\nu + \mu = \frac{1}{\beta} \ln \sum_j e^{-\beta c_{ij}} \omega_j$$

$$\nu + \mu = \frac{1}{\beta} \ln \sum_i \alpha_i e^{-\beta c_{ij}}$$

These equations hold only if:

$$\sum_j e^{-\beta c_{ij}} \omega_j = \sum_i \alpha_i e^{-\beta c_{ij}} \qquad (10.73)$$

In general, the equality (10.73) is true only if:

$$c_{ij} = c, \ \forall i,j.$$

10.2.5 General equilibrium with a given supply function

The cases considered up to now have been based on precise micro-economic assumptions on the behaviour of both demand and supply. In particular it is assumed that the supply-side will maximise profit subordinately to stock constraints and that this assumption is sufficient (added to that of utility maximisation for the consumer) to determine the equilibrium configuration of prices. We now look at the case in which the demand has the same behaviour as before, but the supply sets prices through a mechanism which is not necessarily, or at least not explicitly, bound to the maximisation of profits. This includes both the case of profit-maximising suppliers although with heterogeneities in information and decision rules which are unobservable at a disaggregate level, and the case where supply has no profit maximising management (and possibly no management at all).

In both cases the supply behaviour will be described not at a micro-economic level as previously, but directly at a macro-economic level postulating the existence of a set of supply functions such that $\mu_j(D)$ is the offered price for alternative j, when the demand level is D_j. In this formulation constraints on the stock of available alternatives no longer appear explicitly. In theory, an unlimited number of consumers have access to each alternative. However, the supply price acts as a negative externality, which will alter the attractiveness of the alternative as a function of the number of consumers requesting it by inhibiting or incentivating the demand. The fact that in theory the number of alternatives is unlimited and not simply very large makes the assumptions of Theorem 4 artificial, as it is not plausible to suppose that each consumer has perfect knowledge of an infinite number of trials. We can therefore replace the assumption of utility maximisation with the assumption of the choice of a "satisficing" alternative. We suppose that each consumer collects information about a sequence of alternatives, randomly drawn from those available, until he finds one with a utility which reaches a certain satisficing threshold level. This change of assumptions is more apparent than real, as we shall show, since the choice of a satisficing solution for high thresholds of utility is equivalent to utility maximisation with complete information. However in this case the formulation in terms of a satisficing choice is more natural as it introduces in a simple way the idea of a process of learning by trial and error and a rule for interrupting such a process. This result is stated rigorously in the following theorem.

Theorem 6 (Leonardi)

Let property (10.55) hold, and assume that consumers have satisficing behaviour with threshold utility y and let the prices μ_j, j = 1, ..., m be given. Then the choice probabilities p_{ij} for a consumer in i of an alternative in j satisfy the asymptotic property:

$$\lim_{y\to\infty} p_{ij} = \frac{e^{\beta(v_{ij} - \mu_j)}}{\sum_j e^{\beta(v_{ij} - \mu_j)}} \tag{10.74}$$

The result (10.74) is practically equivalent to equation (10.66), which was derived assuming utility maximisation. The equation (10.74) provides the demand function which, in equilibrium, must counter-balance supply. In fact the expected demand in j, D_j is given by:

$$D_j = \sum_i P_i \frac{e^{\beta(v_{ij} - \mu_j)}}{\sum_j e^{\beta(v_{ij} - \mu_j)}}$$

and since the supply function is known, ie the functions $\mu_j(D)$ are given, the equilibrium values for D_j and μ_i can be obtained as solutions to the set of equations

$$D_j = \sum_i P_i \frac{\exp\{\beta[v_{ij} - \mu_j(D_j)]\}}{\sum_j \exp\{\beta[v_{ij} - \mu_j(D_j)]\}}; \; j = 1, \ldots, m \tag{10.75}$$

As far as the existence and uniqueness of the solutions of (10.75) are concerned, it is interesting to note that they can be embedded in a concave programming problem which, besides ensuring the required properties, has a similar structure to that of problems (10.51) and (10.69) and shares the same economic interpretation. This result is established in the next theorem.

Theorem 7 (Leonardi)

Assume:

$$\mu'_j \geq 0, \text{ where } \mu'_j = \frac{d\mu_j}{dD_j}$$

Then the optimisation problem:

$$\max_{x,D}\{ \sum_{ij} x_{ij}(v_{ij} - \frac{1}{\beta} \ln x_{ij}) - \sum_j \int_0^{D_j} \mu_j(z)dz : \sum_j x_{ij}=P_i, \ \sum_i x_{ij}=D_j\} \tag{10.76}$$

is a concave program with the solution:

$$x_{ij} = P_i \frac{e^{\beta v_{ij} - \mu_j(D_j)}}{\sum_j e^{\beta v_{ij} - \mu_j(D_j)}} \tag{10.77}$$

in which the values D_j are determined from equation (10.75). In addition, the value of the objective function corresponding to the optimum solution is equal, except for the additive constant, to the Total Social Benefit, that is:

$$\frac{1}{\beta} \sum_i P_i \ln \sum_j e^{\beta[v_{ij} - \mu_j(D_j)]} + \sum_j\{D_j\mu_j(D_j) - \int_0^{D_j} \mu_j(z)dz\} \tag{10.78}$$

in which $\frac{1}{\beta} \sum_i P_i \ln \sum_j e^{\beta[v_{ij} - \mu_j(D_j)]}$ is the consumer surplus, and $\sum_j\{D_j\mu_j(D_j) - \int_0^{D_j} \mu_j(z)dz\}$ is the producer surplus.

What is important is that Theorem 7 is valid independently of the fact that the supply functions $\mu_j(D_j)$ are real monetary prices. For example, (10.77) is formally identical to the equilibrium model of traffic assignment (discussed in this book by Smith).

Still in the field of traffic assignment, the classic problem of Beckmann, McGuire and Winsten (1956) is included in Theorem 7 as a special case. In fact the idea of treating a negative externality (in this particular case, transport costs) as a supply function and of considering its integral as a "producer surplus" (even when real producers as such are not identifiable) can be attributed to these authors.

Other externalities which condition spatial markets can be treated in the same way. For example, the waiting time for the assignment of a dwelling in a rationed housing market, which is discussed by Weibull (1984-A), could be embedded in a problem similar to (10.76), even though this is not explicitly considered by the author.

10.2.6 General equilibrium and spatial differentiation of prices in exchange markets

So far we considered the situation in which a mobile demand consumes stock of immobile goods and services (eg residences, road network and shopping centres). We look here briefly at the opposite case in which mobile goods are exchanged between different points in space and consumed by an immobile demand. We show that this situation can be formulated in terms which exhibit a structure quite similar to that considered in the preceding cases. To this end, let us look at the Samuelson model (1952), discussed by Beckmann in this book. In its original version a single product is exchanged between the various points in space in which it is produced and consumed. If μ_j is the price paid for one unit of product in j; $q_j(\mu_j)$ is the net demand (ie demand minus production) in j, such that $q_j' < 0$; $\mu_j(q_j)$ is the inverse function of $q_j(\mu_j)$; x_{ij} is the export from i to j; r_{ij} is the unit transport cost between i and j; then, according to Samuelson the equilibrium pattern of prices and flows is determined by the solution to the concave programming problem:

$$\max_{q,x} \{\sum_j \int_0^{q_j} \mu_j(z)dz - \sum_{ij} r_{ij}x_{ij} : q_j = \sum_i (x_{ij} - x_{ji})\} \qquad (10.79)$$

The objective function of (10.79) is the Total Benefit (sum of consumer and producer surplus), minus transport costs, while the constraints are simple equations of import/export balance.

It is shown by Beckmann (in this book), that (10.79) corresponds to the dual problem:

$$\min_{\mu} \{\sum_j \int_{\mu_j}^{\infty} q_j(z)dz : \mu_j - \mu_i \leq r_{ij}\} \qquad (10.80)$$

In addition, from (10.79) or (10.80) we can derive the equilibrium conditions which have the following form:

$$\left.\begin{array}{l} \text{if } \mu_j - \mu_i < r_{ij},\ x_{ij} = 0 \\ \\ \text{if } \mu_j - \mu_i = r_{ij},\ x_{ij} \geq 0 \end{array}\right\} \qquad (10.81)$$

that is, there can be exports only when the relative advantage in terms of selling prices counterbalances the transport cost.

From the constraint of (10.80) we derive the fact (already mentioned previously) that transport costs are the main factors responsible for the local variation in prices, and that a reduction in transport costs consequently reduces such a variation. From the conditions (10.81) we can derive a rule of local specialisation which is reasonable but possibly too rigid. Indeed, supposing there are exports from i to j that is:

$$\mu_j - \mu_i = r_{ij}$$

It follows that:

$$\mu_i - \mu_j = -r_{ij} < r_{ij} \Rightarrow x_{ji} = 0$$

(assuming of course that transport costs are not negative). Hence, the exports can go in a single direction - if i exports to j, j does not export to i. This extreme tendency can be corrected by introducing a certain dispersion of flows, as was done in (10.69) and (10.76), that is, by introducing an "entropy" in the objective function. As was shown in Theorems 4 and 6 this is equivalent to the introduction of stochastic heterogeneity of preferences and choices at the micro-level. A micro-economic justification of the introduction of an entropy in problem (10.79) would be argued in the same way so will not be repeated here. The result is established in the following theorem.

Theorem 8 (Leonardi)

If $q_j' < 0$ and $\beta > 0$ the programming problem:

$$\max_{q,x} \{\sum_j \int_0^{q_j} \mu_j(z)dz - \sum_{ij} x_{ij}(r_{ij} + \frac{1}{\beta} \ln x_{ij}) : q_j = \sum_i (x_{ij} - x_{ji})\} \tag{10.82}$$

is concave and has the solution:

$$x_{ij} = e^{-1} e^{\beta[(\mu_j - \mu_i) - r_{ij}]} \tag{10.83}$$

in which μ_j are determined as the solution to the equations:

$$q_j(\mu_j) = e^{-1} \sum_i \{e^{\beta[(\mu_j - \mu_i) - r_{ij}]} - e^{\beta[(\mu_i - \mu_j)] - r_{ji}]}\} \tag{10.84}$$

In addition, (10.82) has the corresponding dual

$$\min_{\mu}\{\sum_j \int_{\mu_j}^{\infty} q_j(z)dz + \frac{e^{-1}}{\beta} \sum_{ij} e^{\beta[(\mu_j - \mu_i) - r_{ij}]}\} \tag{10.85}$$

The problem (10.85) is convex and:

$\sum_j \int_{\mu_j}^{\infty} q_j(z)dz$ is the consumer surplus and

$\frac{e^{-1}}{\beta} \sum_{ij} e^{\beta[(\mu_j - \mu_i) - r_{ij}]}$ is the producer surplus

The structure of (10.82) is formally analogous but in fact opposite to that of problem (10.76). In the latter, dispersion is introduced into consumer flows (which are taken to be mobile) and the supply function is considered given. In (10.82) dispersion is introduced in commodity flows (considered to be mobile), while consumers are taken to be immobile and the demand function given. Solution (10.83) is clearly more flexible than the classic conditions (10.81) since all flows, in all directions, are in general non-zero and we can have exports even when the relative advantage in selling prices does not counterbalance the transport cost. Export flows are nevertheless increasing with the difference:

$$(\mu_j - \mu_i) - r_{ij} = (\mu_j - r_{ij}) - \mu_i$$

which is the difference between net profit deriving from the sale of one unit of product in j, given by the price in j minus the transport cost, and the profit deriving from the same sale in i without transport cost. In general transport costs are not the sole costs responsible for local differentiation in prices. Even when we set $r_{ij} = 0$, $\forall i,j$ in (10.84), in general they will not have a solution of the type $\mu_j = \mu \forall j$, since this would imply that:

$$q_j(\mu) = 0, \ \forall j$$

and in general net demand functions are different in each j. However, in the special case when they do not vary locally, that is:

$$q_j(\mu) = q(\mu), \ \forall j$$

the price which satisfies the equation:

$$q(\mu) = 0$$

also satisfies (10.84) with $r_{ij} = 0$ and is therefore a solution of problem (10.82). In this case there is a uniform price, net demand disappears in all points (ie consumption and production are equalised locally), but this does not imply there are no exports. In fact if we set $\mu_j = \mu$ and $r_{ij} = 0$ in (10.83) we obtain

$$x_{ij} = e^{-1} > 0.$$

10.2.7 A short note on price equilibrium in multi-sector systems

The equilibrium conditions we have looked at up to now concern a single commodity and are essentially neo-classical as they can be reduced to the total benefit maximisation principle. Here we examine a case in which the neo-classical paradigm seems to lead to a paradox. A more detailed discussion of the subject is given in this book by Sheppard. We look at some simpler examples. Consider a multi-sector non-spatial system with linear technology, defined by the following input-output coefficients: a_{ij} quantity of product i used to produce j. Define further: x_j total production in sector j; μ_j price of product j; $q_j(\mu_j)$ final demand of product j. In the absence of stock accumulations, the balance equations must be:

$$x_i = \sum_j a_{ij}x_j + q_i(\mu_i) \tag{10.86}$$

that is, the production of each sector must be equal to the sum of the demand of other sectors and the final demand. Using the same reasoning as in 10.2.6 we can try to determine the level of price and quantity in equilibrium by maximising total benefit, given by:

$$\sum_i \int_0^{q_j} \mu_i(z)dz \qquad (10.87)$$

in which $\mu_i(z)$ is the inverse function of q_i, subject to the constraints (10.86).

The corresponding Lagrangian is:

$$L = \sum_i \int_0^{q_j} \mu_i(z)dz + \sum_i \gamma_i[x_i - \sum_j a_{ij}x_j - q_i] \qquad (10.88)$$

in which the γ_i are shadow prices associated with the constraints (10.86). The vanishing of derivatives of (10.88) implies that:

$$\frac{\partial L}{\partial q_i} = \mu_i(q_i) - \gamma_i = 0 \qquad (10.89)$$

$$\frac{\partial L}{\partial x_i} = \gamma_i - \sum_j \gamma_j a_{ji} = 0 \qquad (10.90)$$

Equation (10.89) implies, as before, that the shadow prices equal actual market prices. Equation (10.90) has a non-zero solution only if the input-output matrix has an eigenvalue equal to 1 (in this case the prices are the associated right eigenvector). We know, however, from economic theory (cf Sheppard, in this book) that for a real input-output matrix the maximum eigenvalue is less than 1. The only possible solution for (10.90) is therefore:

$$\gamma_i = 0, \forall i$$

which clearly makes no sense in any real system. The degenerate nature of such a solution leads us naturally to a generalisation of the constraints (10.86). We assume that there is a stock accumulation directly proportional to total demand, such that:

$$x_i = (1 + \alpha)[\sum_j a_{ij}x_j + q_i(\mu_i)] \tag{10.91}$$

in which $\alpha > 0$ is an accumulation rate (at present unknown) which is equal for all sectors. The maximisation of (10.87) subject to the constraints (10.88) gives the Lagrangian:

$$L = \sum_i \int_0^{q_j} \mu_i(z)dz + \sum_i \gamma_i[x_i - (1 + \alpha)(\sum_j a_{ij}x_j + q_i)] \tag{10.92}$$

and the conditions:

$$\frac{\partial L}{\partial q_i} = \mu_i(q_i) - (1 + \alpha)\gamma_i = 0 \tag{10.93}$$

$$\frac{\partial L}{\partial x_i} = \gamma_i - \sum_j (1 + \alpha)\gamma_j a_{ji} = 0 \tag{10.94}$$

Substituting (10.93) in (10.94) we obtain:

$$\mu_i = (1 + \alpha)\sum_j \mu_j a_{ji}$$

or in matrix form:

$$\mu = (1 + \alpha)\mu A \tag{10.95}$$

in which

$$\mu = \{\mu_i\}$$

$$A = \{a_{ij}\}$$

(10.95) clearly has the same structure as the price formation equation proposed by several Marxian economists such as Sraffa (1960), Morishima (1973) and Sheppard (in this book). The unknown α can be determined by imposing the condition that prices are non-negative. One solution, obtained previously, but of no practical interest, is that in which prices are zero everywhere. Another solution is provided by matrix analysis. We know that the only non-negative eigenvector associated with a positive matrix is that corresponding to the maximum eigenvalue. If we define:

$$\lambda = 1/(1 + \alpha)$$

equation (10.95) can be rewritten as

$$\lambda\mu = \mu A$$

where λ must be the maximum eigenvalue of A. As stated before, we know that:

$$\lambda < 1$$

and this implies that $\alpha > 0$, as required.

Equation (10.95) shows that α can be interpreted not only as a stock accumulation rate, but also as profit rate. In fact, if $\alpha = 0$, prices would be equal to production costs and as we have shown this policy would give us, in equilibrium, zero prices everywhere. What is perhaps surprising is that the result (10.95) was obtained by introducing a slight modification (ie the stock accumulation rate) in an essentially neo-classical problem, much as total benefit maximisation, a concept obviously ignored in Marxian economics.

10.3 The Technological Structure of Inter-sector Transactions and Production and Consumption Mechanisms

10.3.1 Introduction

In this section we analyse the relationships between location and transport, considering them as consequences of the technological structure underlying production, consumption and the transport of goods. In this book we find two completely opposite approaches to the problem - the neo-classical approach of Beckmann and the Marxian approach of Sheppard - and a number of other contributions which deal with the question of technological structure less explicitly, but, in treating the entropic dispersion of neo-classical equilibrium in various ways form a kind of "bridge" between the two extremes. This analysis is divided into three parts. The first covers the neo-classical approach and refers principally, as explained above, to Beckmann's work, although including mention of other authors, not necessarily from this book. The second concerns studies defined above as involving entropic dispersion. The third discusses the Marxian approach. In the concluding section we examine a number of important questions concerning technological structure not explicitly dealt with in the other chapters of this book. These questions and in particular the problems involved in the innovation process constitute an important subject for future research in each of the three approaches mentioned above (neo-classic, entropic and Marxian). Naturally in dealing with the relationship between location, transport and mechanisms of production and consumption we cannot ignore the close interrelationships between quantities (produced and consumed) and the relative prices. In this respect the analysis carried out here is closely linked to that in 10.2 which focused on the mechanisms for the formation and spatial differentiation of price.

10.3.2 The neo-classical approach

The standard theory of transport and location was developed during the 1950s with the work of authoritative economists such as Samuelson (1952) and Beckmann (1968). Paraphrasing Andersson (1983), it can be said that the neo-classical model dealing with the relationships between location, trade and transport has the following basic elements: (a) a set of goods located in a set of regions; (b) a predefined type of production technology for the above good described by a typical neo-classical production function (ie concave, continuous, and at least twice differentiable) with different values from region to region; (c) a transport system connecting each region with all the other regions with a demand proportional to the volume of goods to be transferred from one region to another and a supply defined by a typical neo-classical production function; (d) a function of total welfare (which is continuous concave and at least twice differentiable) which when optimised provides a description of the desired state of the system that is, a state of global stable equilibrium). By defining the above elements in different ways, different versions of the basic model are obtained, some of which are discussed by Beckmann in this book. For example, Samuelson gave the following formulation:

$$\max_{q,x} \left[\sum_j \int_0^{q_j} \mu_j(z)dz - \sum_{ij} r_{ij}x_{ij}\right] \tag{10.96}$$

subject to the constraint:

$$\sum_i (x_{ij} - x_{ji}) = q_i \tag{10.97}$$

where q_j is the net quantity of the good demanded in j; μ_j is the price in j of the good (function of q_j); r_{ij} is the cost of transport from i to j; x_{ij} is the flow of goods from i to j.

According to the general rule, the solution to the programming problem (10.96) with the constraint (10.97) is a solution of stable equilibrium given by the conditions:

$$x_{ij} > 0 \text{ if } p_j - p_i = r_{ij}$$
$$x_{ij} = 0 \text{ if } p_j - p_i < r_{ij} \tag{10.98}$$

The problem of location and transport can obviously be analysed in the context of continuous space as well as discrete space. Samuelson's model has an elegant continuous version formulated by Beckmann (1952). In this version the constraint (10.97) is expressed as:

$$\text{div } \Phi + q = 0 \tag{10.99}$$

which states that the divergence of the flow of goods is equal to the net quantity demanded. The maximising welfare function (10.96) becomes the following variational problem:

$$\min_{\Phi} \int_R k|\Phi| dR \tag{10.100}$$

(which k is the unit cost of transport in a given point of the region R), whose solution is:

$$k \frac{\Phi}{|\Phi|} = \text{grad } p, \text{ if } \Phi \neq 0 \tag{10.101}$$

which states that the direction of the flows is given by the gradient of a potential function p, which represents prices.

The advantage of using continuous space is that under the usual highly simplified hypotheses (of homogeneous and isotropic space) it is often possible to analyse spatial structures deriving from these models. A great deal of work has been achieved in this aspect by Puu (1979-A). We should like to mention his work on the spatial organisation of structurally stable flows. He bases his reasoning on the fact that commodity flows are defined (see (10.101)) by a potential function which means that we can apply to them structural stability considerations of the type found in catastrophe theory. On these bases, we can deduce that the flows actually observed are those which are structurally stable and not completely altered by small disturbances.

It is also shown that as far as critical points in the flow space are concerned, the most probable to occur in reality are isolated critical points (ie isolated nodes and saddles). Putting together these two observations and using theorems relating to the general properties of differential equations, Puu comes to the conclusion that the flow structure which links isolated critical points is a square grid pattern whereas the triangular grid, which would result from the spatial organisation pattern described by Christaller and Lösch, is unstable. This important result clearly deserves more detailed examination in future studies, as well as the relationship between the perturbed flows considered by Puu and the flows described by the entropic dispersion of the neo-classical optimum (which could also be viewed as disturbed flows).

10.3.3 Entropic dispersion

In 10.3.2 we referred to the production function as one of the central elements in the location of economic activities. This function links the output of one industrial sector in a given location with its input:

$$y_{j*}^{s*g} = y_{j*}^{s*g}(\{x_{*j}^{*om}\}) \tag{10.102}$$

where x_{ij}^{rsm} is the flow of goods or services of type m, used by a firm s located in j and produced by a firm r located in i; y_{jk}^{svg} is the flow of goods or services of type g, produced by a firm s located in j and used by a firm v located in k; (the star stands for summation over the indices replaced). Taking a neo-classical approach, this function must satisfy a certain set of properties. Among these properties is the existence of a defined and constant production technology which can be described by a matrix of technological coefficients. This technology can be introduced into the production function using the following kind of formula:

$$x_{ij}^{rsm} = q_{ij}^{rsm} a^{mg} y_{j*}^{s*g} \tag{10.103}$$

where a^{mg} is the quantity of good m required to produce one unit of product g; q_{ij}^{rsm} is the quantity of good m used by a firm s in j coming from another firm r in i.

The matrix a^{mg} in (10.103) contains information on the degree of interdependence of production and the matrix q_{ij}^{rsm} contains information on spatial interdependence. There is an important difference in the treatment of these two aspects. While the technological coefficient matrix is a structure which is descriptive of the process of intersectoral interactions, the matrix of spatial interdependence coefficients an optimum structure which is in certain respects unrealistic. If for example $q_{ij}^{rsm} > 0 \Rightarrow q_{ji}^{rsm} = 0$, this means that the flows are always one-directional, which is rarely the case - in reality, flows are usually two-directional. The introduction of a term of entropic dispersion in the neo-classical optimum function by Wilson (1970-A) provided a description of the structure of spatial relations more like that of intersectoral relations. The concept of entropic dispersion is also found in intersector transaction analysis. A very common method for updating input-output matrices, the RAS method of bi-proportional adjustment (Bacharach, 1970) can be considered an estimating technique using entropy-maximisation. In the same way studies of economic dominance (Lantner, 1974) can be seen as a search for the latent "optimal" structure in a given sectoral interdependence matrix.

Various theoretical justifications have been given of the

entropic structure of spatial (and sector) relations in addition to the socio-physical justification of Wilson - random utility, consumer surplus etc. Smith in this book gives a further one, that of cost-efficiency. This is particularly interesting as, more than the others, it provides a clear behavioural base to structures of entropically dispersed spatial interaction. Let us consider the objective function:

$$\min_{(T_{ij})} C(T_{ij}) - \frac{1}{\theta} H(T_{ij}) \qquad (10.104)$$

where T_{ij} are the flows, H is the flows entropy and C is the overall cost of flows. We can recognise in this function either the problem of entropy-maximising associated with a transport cost constraint or a problem of minimisation of transport costs (Beckmann) with an entropic dispersion. Smith shows that it can be derived from a principle of cost-efficiency which postulates that:

$$\overline{C} \leq \overline{C}' \Rightarrow P \geq P' \qquad (10.105)$$

that is, the average costs of two flows distributions are in inverse relation to the probabilities of the two distributions.

Given the above we can add that Wilson in his contribution to this book formulates a general model of the interrelationships between transport and location with a production function of the kind in (10.103) which is consistent with an entropic dispersion of commodity flows. Using the same symbols as above this gives:

$$\max_{\{x_{ij}^{rsm}, y_{ik}^{svg}\}} Z = \sum_{js} (D_j^s - C_j^s) \qquad (10.106)$$

which is a mathematical programming problem in which D_j^s are revenues from the output of the industrial units (s,v,j) and C_j^s the costs of the related inputs. (10.106) must of course be solved taking into account specific constraints on the matrices x_{ij}^{rsm} and y_{ik}^{svg} which also describe the production technology and the entropic structure of spatial interaction. The formulation of an operational version on (10.106) constitutes one of the most promising directions for future research. In conclusion we point out that Wilson in this book proposes a dynamic version of model (10.106), this dynamic character deriving from the disequilibrium between costs and revenue:

$$\dot{y}_{j*}^{s*g} = \varepsilon^{sg}(D_j^{sg} - C_j^{sg}) \qquad (10.107)$$

where D_j^{sg} and C_j^{sg} are respectively the revenue and cost functions (in general non-linear) of y_{j*}^{s*g}.

10.3.4 The Marxian approach

To introduce this section we shall first of all look briefly again at the mathematical programming problem (10.106). It is clear that given the general terms in which the problem is formulated we do not know whether it is convex or concave, in other words we have no idea whether the system of locations and transport considered will have one or more solutions or whether they will be stable or unstable. It should be added however that when, as suggested in 10.2.2, we make the usual neo-classical assumptions, the system will have in fact one stable solution. The question that we must ask therefore, is whether the addition of entropic dispersion in commodity flows will modify the neo-classical results. We are not able at present to come to any definite conclusions about this. There is on the one hand the result of Macgill (1977-B) which shows that an input-output model which is spatially disaggregated with entropic spatial relations has a stable equilibrium solution. On the other hand there is a notable similarity between model

(10.107) and the model of service location of Harris and Wilson (1978) which leads us to believe that for particular forms of non-linearity in spatial interaction we may have solutions of multiple or instable equilibrium or no solutions at all. It remains to be seen in this second case whether the hypotheses which lead to these non-linearities are in contrast with the neo-classical assumptions or not.

It is in this context, the discussion of the existence of equilibrium in the location transport system, that Sheppard's contribution to this book is particularly relevant. He begins with the extension to the spatialised economy (ie the location-transport system) of the criticisms which the neo-Ricardian economists, and in particular Sraffa (1960), made of Walras' general economic equilibrium.

In this way Sheppard develops a descriptive Marxian model of multi-sector activity location, the spatial structure of commodity prices and the value of labour

$$p = (1 + r)pA(p) \qquad (10.108)$$

where p is the price vector; r is the profit rate; A is the input-output matrix extended to include wages as a production input. It is a function of p; and its spatial structure is described by an entropy-gravitational type expression (where spatial interaction is a function of p; and its spatial structure is described by an entropy-gravitational type expression (where spatial interaction is a function of p and transport costs). Sheppard then shows that given the spatial structure of the production (10.108) will have an equilibrium solution, which is not, however, the neo-classical Walrasian equilibrium as previously assumed, but quite different, because it depends on a set of social factors from Marxian and Ricardian analysis (competitive capitalism, conflicting social classes, exploitation of the labour force and political power) which are considered in the production structure.

As far as the dynamic aspects of the spatial equilibrium

of Sheppard's model are concerned, given that unstable spatial structures of production may occur over time, there may also be instability in geograhical structures, ie in the locations of multi-sectoral activities and their spatial interrelations. The general conclusion is that anarchy in competitive capitalism cannot produce a market equilibrium (which is the opposite of the standard neo-classical conclusion) without government intervention.

A further point of great interest in Sheppard's chapter is that the system of pricing determined by (10.108), that is, the Marxian pricing system, is shown to be equivalent to that obtained from the consideration of "potentials" associated with the spatial interaction between economic activities:

$$p = iU \tag{10.109}$$

where i is a vector of ones; U is the matrix of potentials associated with the iterative process of goods transfer of which one step is described by the matrix A considered earlier. In other words the Marxian system of pricing is equivalent, approximately speaking, to the pricing system determined by the respective geographical accessibilities of the different activities. This result means that the geographical and economic approaches are virtually the same, which is in complete contrast with the conventional socio-economic theory (which tends to make spatial interaction depend on economic quantities) and opens up a highly promising area for future research.

10.3.5 Some remarks on technological structures

There is one aspect of the technological structure of production - innovation in technology - which at present is the subject of great interest, prompted by the stimulus of what is happening in contemporary economies. It is an aspect which has been relatively neglected in the contributions to this book. Only Sheppard's chapter considers the consequence of variations in the matrix of sectoral and spatial interdependencies (extended to consider also the labour force) and deduces from them the instability of the growth of the spatialised economy. The question of innovation deserves to be looked at in more detail, especially in its effects on location and transport.

Several authors provide us with possible points from which to begin. We could for example attempt to apply Wilson's ideas on the growth and evolution of service infrastructure (Wilson, 1981-A) or the work of the Brussels School (Allen et al, 1978) on urban morphogenetic processes to the problem of technological innovation. Alternatively, following the example of Andersson (1983) we could try to extend to the location-transport system the results obtained from non-spatial economic analysis, where the problem of changing production structures is related to a linear combination of intersector matrices each of which represents a different type of technology. In this context the fact that the different production technologies are in competition with each other must be taken into account. Sonis (1983) makes some contributions to the analysis of this aspect of the problem. The problem of technological innovation is also closely connected with the question of diffusion of information especially when we are dealing with a spatial context. Studies in the field of information diffusion, for example Ralston (1983) who considers the dynamics of communications, could be usefully applied to the problem. Last of all technological innovation is linked to the problem of investment in research and development. Here the work of Nijkamp (1983) for example could play a useful part in the analysis.

BIBLIOGRAPHY AND REFERENCES

Abraham-Frois, G., Berrebi, E. (1979) *Theory of Values, Prices and Accumulation: a mathematical integration of Marx, Von Neumann and Sraffa*, Cambridge University Press, Cambridge, U.K.

Aczél, J., Daroczy, Z. (1975) *On Measures of Information and Their Characterization*, Academic Press, New York.

Akinc, C.V., Khumavala, B.M. (1977) An Efficient Branch and Bound Algorithm for the Capacitated Warehouse Location Problem, *Management Science*, *23*, 585-594.

Alfeld, L.E., Graham, A.K. (1976) *Introduction to Urban Dynamics*, Wright-Allen Press, Cambridge, Mass.

Allen, P.M., Boon, F., Sanglier, M. (1980) A Dynamic Model of Interurban Evolution, Report to the Department of Transportation, U.S.A., Under contract TSC-1640, Interim Report II, Department of Transportation, Cambridge, Mass.

Allen, P.M., Deneubourg, J.L., Sanglier, M., Boon, F., de Palma, A. (1978) The Dynamics of Urban Evolution, Volume 1: Interurban Evolution, Volume 2: Intraurban Evolution, University of Brussels, Final Report prepared for U.S. Department of Transportation, Research and Special Programs Administration, Washington, Washington D.C.

Allen, P.M., Deneubourg, J.L., Sanglier, M., Boon, F., de Palma, A. (1979-A) Dynamic Urban Models, I, Report to the Department of Transportation, U.S.A., Under contract TSC-1185, Department of Transportation, Cambridge, Mass.

Allen, P.M., Deneubourg, J.L., Sanglier, M., Boon, F., de Palma, A. (1979-B) Dynamic Urban Models, II, Report to the Department of Transportation, U.S.A., Under contract TSC-1640, Interim Report I, Department of Transportation, Cambridge, Mass.

Allen, P.M., Sanglier, M. (1978) Dynamic Models of Urban Growth, I, *Journal of Social and Biological Structures*, *1*, 265-280.

Allen, P.M., Sanglier, M. (1979-A) A Dynamic Model of Growth in a Central Place System, I, *Geographical Analysis*, *11*, 256-272.

Allen, P.M., Sanglier, M. (1979-B) A Dynamic Model of Urban Growth, II, *Journal of Social and Biological Structures*, *2*, 269-278.

Allen, P.M., Sanglier, M. (1981-A) A Dynamic Model of a Central Place System, I, *Geographical Analysis*, *13*, 149-164.

Allen, P.M., Sanglier, M. (1981-B) Urban Evolution, Self-organization and Decision-making, *Environment and Planning*, *A*, *13*, 167-183.

Allen, P.M., Sanglier, M., Engelen, G., Boon, F. (1982) The Dynamics of Urban Systems: the U.S. experience and further steps towards modelling change, Report DOT/RSPA/DPB - 10/82/4, Systems Analysis Division, U.S. Department of Transportation, Research and Special Programs Administration, Washington, Washington D.C.

Alonso, W. (1960) A Theory of the Urban Land Market, *Papers and Proceedings of Regional Science Association*, *6*, 149-157.

Alonso, W. (1964-A) *Location and Land Use. Toward a General Theory of Land Rent*, Harvard University Press, Cambridge, Mass.

Alonso, W. (1964-B) Location Theory, in Friedmann, J., Alonso, W. (eds.) *Regional Development and Planning. A Reader*, The MIT Press, Mass., 78-106.

Alonso, W. (1967) A Reformulation of Classical Location Theory and its Relation to Rent Theory, *Papers and Proceedings of the Regional Science Association*, *19*, 23-44.

Alonso, W. (1971) The Economics of Urban Size, *Papers of Regional Science Association*, *26*, 67-83.

Alonso, W. (1978) A Theory of Movement, in Hansen, N.M. (ed.) *Human Settlement*, Ballinger, Cambridge, Mass., 197-211.

Amson, J.C. (1974) Equilibrium and Catastrophic Modes of Urban Growth, *Space-Time Concepts in Urban and Regional Models*, *London Papers in Regional Science*, *4*, Pion, London, 108-128.

Amson, J.C. (1975) Catastrophe Theory: a contribution to the study of urban systems?, *Environment and Planning B*, *2*, 177-221.

Amson, J.C. (1977) A Note on Civic State Equations, *Environment and Planning A*, *9*, 105-110.

Anas, A. (1973) A Dynamic Disequilibrium Model of Residential Location, *Environment and Planning*, *5*, 633-647.

Anas, A. (1975) The Empirical Calibration and Testing of a Simulation Model of Residential Location, *Environment and Planning A*, *7*, 899-920.

Anas, A. (1976) Short-Run Dynamics in the Spatial Housing Market, in Papageorgiou, Y.Y. (ed.) *Mathematical and Land Use Theory*, Lexington Books, Toronto, 261-275.

Anas, A. (1978-A) Dynamics of Urban Residential Growth, *Journal of Urban Economics*, *5*, 66-87.

Anas, A. (1978-B) Equilibrium Properties of Logit Models, WP, Northwestern University, Evanston, Ill.

Anas, A. (1979) The Impact of Transit Investment on Housing Values: a simulation experiment, *Environment and Planning A*, *11*, 239-255.

Anas, A. (1980) A Model of Residential Change and Neighbourhood Tipping, *Journal of Urban Economics*, *7*, 358-370.

Anas, A. (1982) *Residential Location Markets and Urban Transportation*, Academic Press, New York.

Anas, A. (1983) From Physical to Economic Urban Models: the Lowry framework revisited, Paper presented at the International Symposium on New Directions in Urban Modelling, University of Waterloo, Waterloo, Ontario, Canada, July 11-15.

Anas, A., Dendrinos, D.S. (1976) The New Urban Economics: a brief survey, in Papageorgiou, Y.Y. (ed.) *Mathematical and*

Land Use Theory, Lexington Books, Toronto, 23-31.

Anderson, D.H., Eisenfeld, J., Reisch, J.S., Shaffer, S.I. (1977) The Mathematical Analysis of a Stochastic Model of Normal-Abnormal Liver Function, in Lakshmikantham, V. (ed.) *Nonlinear Systems and Applications*, Academic Press, New York, 353-372.

Andersson, A.E. (1983) A Theory of Interregional Trade and Location, *Sistemi Urbani*, *5*, 477-497.

Arnold, L. (1974) *Stochastic Differential Equations: theory and applications*, Wiley, New York.

Arnold, L., Lefever, R. (1981) *Stochastic Nonlinear Systems in Physics, Chemistry and Biology*, Springer-Verlag, Berlin.

Artle, R. (1959, 1965 edition) *Studies in the Structure of the Stockholm Economy*, Cornell University, Ithaca.

Atkin, R.H. (1974) *Mathematical Structure in Human Affairs*, Heinemann, London.

Atkin, R.H. (1981) *Multidimensional Man*, Penguin, Harmondsworth.

Aubin, J.P., Cellina, A. (1982) Differential Inclusions and Viability Theory, IIASA, WP-82-51, Laxenburg, Austria.

Aubin, J.P., Cellina, A. (1984) *Differential Inclusions*, Springer Verlag, Berlin.

Aubin, J.P., Naslund, B. (1972) An Exterior Banking Algorithm, Working Paper 72-42, European Institute in Management, Brussels.

Ayeni, M.A.O. (1976-A) A Predictive Model of Urban Stock and Activity: 2. Empirical development, *Environment and Planning A*, *8*, 59-77.

Ayeni, M.A.O. (1976-B) The Development of a Disaggregated Residential Location Model in Nigeria, *Annals of Regional Science*, *10*, 31-54.

Ayeni, M.A.O. (1979) Intraurban Residential Migration: an entropy maximising approach, *Journal of Regional Science*, *19*, 331-343.

Babcock, D.L. (1970) Analysis and Improvement of a Dynamic Urban Model, Ph.D. Dissertation, University of California, Los Angeles, Calif.

Bach, L. (1980) Locational Models for Systems of Private and Public Facilities Based on Concepts of Accessibility and Access Opportunity, *Environment and Planning A*, *12*, 301-320.

Bacharach, M. (1970) *Biproportional Matrices and Input-Output Change*, Cambridge University Press, London.

Bacon, R.W. (1971) An Approach to the Theory of Consumer Shopping Behaviour, *Urban Studies*, *8*, 55-65.

Bahrenberg, G. (1981) Providing an Adequate Social Infrastructure in Rural Areas: an application of a maximal supply dispersion model to elementary school planning in Roteburg/Wumme (FRG), *Environment and Planning A*, *13*, 1515-1527.

Bailey, N.T.J. (1975) *The Theory of Infectious Diseases and its Applications*, Griffin, London.

Barnes, T.J. (1982-A) Theories of Agricultural Rent within the Surplus Approach, University of Minnesota, Department of Geography (manuscript).

Barnes, T.J. (1982-B) Towards a Consistent Regional Trade Theory (manuscript).

Barnes, T.J., Sheppard E. (1984) Technical Choice and Reswitching in Space Economies, in Andersson, A., Isard, W., Puu, T., Schweizer, U. (eds.) *Structural Economic Analysis in Time and Space*, North-Holland, Amsterdam.

Barras, R., Broadbent, T.A. (1974) The Development of an Activity-Commodity Representation of Urban Systems as a Potential Framework for Evaluation, in Cripps, E.L. (ed.) *Space-Time Concepts in Urban and Regional Models*, Pion, London, 207-237.

Barras, R., Broadbent, T.A., Cordey-Hayes, M., Massey, D.B., Robinson, K., Willis, J. (1971) An Operational Model of Cheshire, *Environment and Planning*, *3*, 115-233.

Barratt-Brown, M. (1974) *The Economics of Imperialism*, Penguin, London.

Bartezzaghi, E. (1979) Modelli di Localizzazione Industriale, in Colorni, A. (ed.) *Modelli di Localizzazione e Distribuzione nella Gestione dell'Ambiente e del Territorio*, CLUP, Milano, 139-178.

Bartezzaghi, E., Colorni, A., Palermo, P.C. (1976) Considerazioni su Alcune Classi di Modelli di Localizzazione, in Lombardini, S., Ruberti, A. (eds.) *Teoria dei Sistemi ed Economia*, Il Mulino, Bologna, 45-78.

Bartezzaghi, E., Colorni, A., Palermo, P.C. (1981) A Search Tree Algorithm for Plant Location Problems, *European Journal of Operational Research*, *7*, 371-379.

Bartholomew, D.J. (1973) *Stochastic Models for Social Processes*, Wiley, London.

Bartlett, M.S. (1960) *Stochastic Population Models*, Methuen, London.

Bass, F.M. (1969) A New Product Growth Model for Consumer Durables, *Management Science*, *15*, 215-227.

Batey, P.W.J., Madden, M. (1981-A) An Activity Analysis Approach to the Integration of Demographic-Economic Forecasts, in Voogd, H. (ed.) *Strategic Planning in a Dynamic Society*, Delftsche Uitgevers Maatschappij BV, Delft, 143-153.

Batey, P.W.J., Madden, M. (1981-B) Demographic-Economic Forecasting within an Activity-Commodity Framework: some theoretical considerations and empirical results, *Environment and Planning A*, *13*, 1067-1083.

Batty, M.J. (1969-A) The Development of an Activity Allocation Model for the Notts/Derbys Subregion, Department of Town and Country Planning, University of Manchester, Manchester, England.

Batty, M. (1969-B) The Impact of a New Town. An Application of the Garin-Lowry Model, *Journal of the Town Planning Institute*, *55*, 428-435.

Batty, M. (1970-A) An Activity Allocation Model for the Nottinghamshire-Derbyshire Subregion, *Regional Studies*, *4*, 307-322.
Batty, M. (1970-B) Some Problems of Calibrating the Lowry Model, *Environment and Planning*, 2, 95-114.
Batty, M. (1971-A) Design and Construction of a Subregional Land Use Model, *Socio-Economic Planning Sciences*, *5*, 97-124.
Batty, M. (1971-B) Modelling Cities and Dynamic Systems, *Nature*, *321*, 425-428.
Batty, M. (1972-A) An Experimental Model of Urban Dynamics, *Town Planning Review*, *43*, 166-186.
Batty, M. (1972-B) Dynamic Simulation of an Urban System, in Wilson, A.G. (ed.) *Patterns and Processes in Urban and Regional Systems*, Pion, London, 44-82.
Batty, M. (1972-C) Recent Developments in Land-Use Modelling: a review of British research, *Urban Studies*, *9*, 151-177.
Batty, M. (1973) Concepts of Geographical Aggregation Based on Hierarchical Entropy, Department of Geography, University of Reading, Reading.
Batty, M. (1976) *Urban Modelling*, *Algorithms*, *Calibrations*, *Predictions*, Cambridge University Press, Cambridge, England.
Batty, M. (1978) Ten Years of Modelling in Britain, *Area*, *10*, 111-115.
Batty, M. (1979-A) Invariant-Distributional Regularities and the Markov Property in Urban Models: an extension of Schinnar's result, *Environment and Planning A*, *11*, 487-497.
Batty, M. (1979-B) Paradoxes of Science in Public Policy: the baffling case of land use models, *Sistemi Urbani*, *1*, 1, 89-122.
Batty, M. (1983) Technical Issues in Urban Model Development: a review of linear and nonlinear model structures, Paper presented at the International Symposium on New Directions in Urban Modelling, University of Waterloo, Waterloo, Ontario, Canada, July 11-15.
Batty, M., Bourke, R., Cormode, P., Anderson-Nicholls, M. (1974) Experiments in Urban Modelling for Country Structure Planning: the Area 8 Pilot Model, *Environment and Planning A*, *6*, 455-478.
Batty, M., Foot, D., Alonso, L., Bray, G., Breheny, M., Constable, D., Dugmore, K., Ellender, R., Shepherd, J., Williams, J. (1973) Spatial System Design and Fast Calibration of Activity Interaction-Allocation Models, *Regional Studies*, *7*, 351-366.
Batty, M., Mackie, S. (1972) The Calibration of Gravity, Entropy and Related Models of Spatial Interaction, *Environment and Planning*, *4*, 205-233.
Batty, M., March, L. (1976) Method of Residues in Urban Modelling, *Environment and Planning A*, *8*, 189-214.

Batty, M., Masser, I. (1975) Spatial Decompositions and Partitions in Urban Modelling, in Cripps, E.L. (ed.) *Regional Science - New Concepts and Old Problems, London Papers in Regional Science, 5*, Pion, London, 188-206.
Batty, M., Sidkar, P.K. (1982) Spatial Aggregation in Gravity Models, *Environment and Planning A, 14*, 377-405; 525-583; 629-658; 795-822.
Baxter, R., Williams, I. (1975) An Automatically Calibrated Urban Model, *Environment and Planning A, 7*, 3-20.
Bay Area Simulation Study (1968) Jobs, People and Land, University of California, Office of Real Estate and Urban Economics, Berkeley, Calif.
Beardwood, J.E., Kirby, H.R. (1975) Zone Definition and the Gravity Model. The Separability, Excludability and Compressibility Properties, *Transportation Research, 9*, 363-369.
Beaumont, J.R. (1980) Spatial Interaction Models and the Location-Allocation Problem, *Journal of Regional Science, 20*, 37-50.
Beaumont, J.R. (1981) Location Allocation Problems in a Place: a review of some models, *Socio-Economic Planning Sciences, 15*, 217-229.
Beaumont, J.R. (1982) Towards a Conceptualization of Evolution in Environmental Systems, *Man-Machine Studies, 16*, 113-145.
Beaumont, J.R. (1984) Location, Energy and Environment Interrelationships: a methodological overview, *Sistemi Urbani, 6*, 399-450.
Beaumont, J.R., Clarke, M., Wilson, A.G. (1981-A) Changing Energy Parameters and the Evolution of Urban Spatial Structure, *Regional Science and Urban Economics, 11*, 287-315.
Beaumont, J.R., Clarke, M., Wilson, A.G. (1981-B) The Dynamics of Urban Spatial Structure: some exploratory results using difference equations and bifurcation theory, *Environment and Planning A, 13*, 1473-1483.
Beaumont, J.R., Keys, P. (1981) Combined Heat Power Generation Schemes: a feasibility study, *Environment and Planning A, 13*, 623-634.
Beaumont, J.R., Keys, P. (1982) *Future Cities: spatial analysis of energy issues*, Wiley, London.
Becker, G.S. (1965) A Theory of the Allocation of Time, *Economic Journal, 75*, 488-517.
Beckmann, M.J. (1952) A Continuous Model of Transportation, *Econometrica, 20*, 643-660.
Beckmann, M.J. (1953) The Partial Equilibrium of a Continuous Space Market, *Weltwirtschaftliches Arch., 71*, 73-89.
Beckmann, M.J. (1955) Some Reflections on Lösch's Theory of Location, *Papers and Proceedings of the Regional Science Association*, N1-N9.
Beckmann, M.J. (1957-A) On the Distribution of Rent and Residential Density in Cities, in Interdepartmental Seminar on

Mathematical Applications in the Social Sciences, Yale University, New Haven (mimeo).

Beckmann, M.J. (1957-B) On the Equilibrium Distribution of Population in Space, *Bulletin of Mathematical Biophysics*, *19*, 81-90.

Beckmann, M.J. (1958) City Hierarchies and the Distribution of City Size, *Economic Development and Cultural Change*, *6*, 243-248.

Beckmann, M.J. (1968) *Location Theory*, Random House, New York.

Beckmann, M.J. (1969) On the Distribution of Urban Rent and Residential Density, *Journal of Economics Theory*, *1*, 60-67.

Beckmann, M.J. (1970) The Analysis of Spatial Diffusion Processes, *Papers of the Regional Science Association*, *25*, 109-117.

Beckmann, M.J. (1971) Market Share, Distance and Potential, *Regional and Urban Economics. Operational Methods*, *1*, 3-18.

Beckmann, M.J. (1972-A) Spatial Cournot Oligopoly, *Papers of the Regional Science Association*, *21*, 37-47.

Beckmann, M.J. (1972-B) Von Thünen Revisited: a neoclassical land use model, *Swedish Journal of Economics*, *74*, 1-7.

Beckmann, M.J. (1973-A) Equilibrium Models of Residential Land Use, *Regional and Urban Economics. Operational Methods*, *3*, 361-368.

Beckmann, M.J. (1973-B) The Isolated Region: a model of regional growth, *Regional and Urban Economics. Operational Methods*, *3*, 223-232.

Beckmann, M.J. (1974) Spatial Equilibrium in the Housing Market, *Journal of Urban Economics*, *1*, 99-107.

Beckmann, M.J. (1975) On the Economic Structure of Strictly Hierarchical Central Place Systems, *Environment and Planning A*, *7*, 815-820.

Beckmann, M.J. (1976-A) Equilibrium in a Continuous Space Market, *Operations Research Verfahren*, *14*, 48-63.

Beckmann, M.J. (1976-B) Spatial Equilibrium in the Dispersed City, in Papageorgiou, Y.Y. (ed.) *Mathematical Land Use Theory*, Lexington Books, Lexington, Mass., 117-125.

Beckmann, M.J. (1976-C) Spatial Price Policies Revisited, *The Bell Journal of Economics*, *7*, 619-630.

Beckmann, M.J. (1981-A) Continuous Models of Transportation and Location, *Sistemi Urbani*, *3*, 403-413.

Beckmann, M.J. (1981-B) Continuous Spatial Models of Income Diffusion and Commodity Trade, in Griffith, D.A., Mackinnon, R. (eds.) *Dynamic Spatial Models*, NATO ASI Series D: Behaviour and Social Systems, No 7, Sijthoff and Noordhoff, Alphen aan den Rijn, The Netherlands, 8-19.

Beckmann, M.J., Buttler, H-J. (1980) Design Parameters in Housing Construction and the Market for Urban Housing, *Econometrica*, *48*, 201-225.

Beckmann, M.J., Golob, T.F. (1971) On the Metaphysical Foundations of Traffic Theory: entropy revisited, in *Proceedings of the Fifth International Symposium on the Theory of Traffic Flow and Transportation*, Elsevier, New York, 109-117.

Beckmann, M.J., Marschak, T. (1955) An Activity Analysis Approach to Location Theory, *Kyklos*, *8*, 125-143.

Beckmann, M.J., McGuire, C.B., Winsten, C.B. (1956) *Studies in the Economics of Transportation*, Yale University Press, New Haven.

Beckmann, M.J., McPherson, J.C. (1970) City Size, Distribution in a Central Place Hierarchy: an alternative approach, *Journal of Regional Science*, *10*, 25-33.

Beckmann, M.J., Puu, T. (1982) Continuous Flow Models in Spatial Economics, International Institute for Applied System Analysis, Laxenburg, Austria (manuscript).

Beckmann, M.J., Schramm, G. (1972) The Impact of Scientific and Technical Change on the Location of Economic Activities, *Regional and Urban Economics, Operational Methods*, *2*, 159-174.

Bécus, G.A. (1979) Random Evolution and Stochastic Compartments, *Mathematical Biosciences*, *44*, 241-254.

Beltrami, E.J. (1977) *Models for Public Systems Analysis*, Academic Press, New York.

Beltrami, E.J. (1979) Localizzazione di Servizi e Impiego dei Servizi di Emergenza, in Colorni, A. (ed.) *Modelli di Localizzazione e Distribuzione nella Gestione dell' Ambiente e del Territorio*, CLUP, Milano, 178-210.

Ben-Akiva, M.E. (1974) Structure of Passenger Travel Demand Models, *Transportation Research Record*, *526*, 26-42.

Ben-Akiva, M.E., Lerman, S.R. (1979) Disaggregate Travel and Mobility Choice Models and Measures of Accessibility, in Hensher, D.A., Stopher, P.R. (eds.) *Behavioural Travel Modelling*, Croom Helm, London, 654-679.

Ben-Akiva, M., Lerman, S.R., Damm, D., Jacobson, J., Pitschke, S., Weisbrod, G., Wolfe, R. (1980) Understanding, Prediction and Evaluation of Transportation Related Consumer Behaviour, Centre for Transportation Studies, M.I.T., Cambridge, Mass.

Benassy, J.P. (1975) Neo Keynesian Disequilibrium Theory in a Monetary Economy, *Review of Economic Studies*, *42*, 503-523.

Benito-Alonso, M.A., Devaux, P. (1981) Location and Size of Day Nurseries: a multiple goal approach, *European Journal of Operational Research*, *6*, 195-198.

Berman, O., Odoni, A.R. (1982) Locating Mobile Servers on a Network with Markovian Properties, *Networks*, *12*, 73-86.

Bertuglia, C.S., Gallino, T., Gualco, I., Occelli, S., Rabino, G.A., Salomone, C., Tadei, R. (1982) Alcuni Aspetti della Calibrazione di un Modello Dinamico Spazializzato: il caso del modello dell'area metropolitana orinese, in Atti delle Giornate di Lavoro, AIRO 1982, 200-248.

Bertuglia, C.S., Gallino, T., Gualco, I., Occelli, S., Rabino, G.A., Salomone, C., Tadei, R. (1983-A) Calibrating the Residential Location Submodel of the Simulation Model for the Turin Metropolitan Area, in *Atti delle Giornate di Lavoro AIRO 1983*, Guida, Napoli, 555-573.

Bertuglia, C.S., Gallino, T., Gualco, I., Occelli, S., Rabino, G.A., Salomone, C., Tadei, R. (1983-B) L'Applicazione di un Modello Dinamico a Larga Scala per l'Area Metropolitana di Torino, in Leonardi, G., Rabino, G.A. (eds.) *Scienze Regionali, 1, L'Analisi degli Insediamenti Umani e Produttivi*, Angeli, Milano, 205-227.

Bertuglia, C.S., Leonardi, G. (1979) Dynamic Models for Spatial Interaction, *Sistemi Urbani, 1*, 2, 3-25.

Bertuglia, C.S., Leonardi, G. (1980-A) A Model for the Optimal Location of Multi-Level Services, *Sistemi Urbani, 2*, 283-297.

Bertuglia, C.S., Leonardi, G. (1980-B) Heuristic Algorithms for the Normative Location of Retail Activities Systems, *Papers, Regional Science Association, 44*, 149-159.

Bertuglia, C.S., Leonardi, G. (1982) Localizzazione Ottimale dei Servizi Pubblici, in Bielli, M., La Bella, A. (eds.) *Problematiche dei Livelli Sub-regionali di Programmazione*, Angeli, Milano, 286-313.

Bertuglia, C.S., Leonardi, G., Tadei, R. (1981) Localizzazione Ottimale dei Servizi Pubblici con Esperienze sulle Scuole del l'Area Torinese, Atti Delle Giornate di Lavoro AIRO, Torino, Vol. 1, 67-250.

Bertuglia, C.S., Leonardi, G., Tadei, R. (1983) A Nested Random Utility Model for Multi-Service Systems: an application to the high school system in Turin, *Sistemi Urbani, 5*, 55-105.

Bertuglia, C.S., Occelli, S., Rabino, G.A., Salomone, C., Tadei, R. (1983) The Dynamics of Turin Metropolitan Area: a model for the analysis of the processes and for the policy evaluation, Paper presented at the 23rd European Congress of the Regional Science Association, 29 August-2 September, Poitiers, France, Working Paper 24, IRES, Torino.

Bertuglia, C.S., Occelli, S., Rabino, G.A., Tadei, R. (1980) A Model of Urban Structure and Development of Turin: theoretical aspects, *Sistemi Urbani, 2*, 59-90.

Bertuglia, C.S., Rabino, G.A. (1975) *Modello per l'Organizzazione di un Comprensorio*, Guida, Napoli.

Bertuglia, C.S., Tadei, R., Leonardi, G. (1980) The Optimal Management of Natural Recreational Resources: a mathematical model, *Environment and Planning A, 12*, 69-83.

Bettelheim, P. (1972) Appendix I, in Emmanuel, A. (ed.) *Unequal Exchange*, Monthly Review Press, New York, 271-322.

Beumer, L., van Grameren, A., van der Hee, B., Paelinck, J. (1978) A Study of the Formal Structure of J.W. Forrester's Urban Dynamics Model, *Urban Studies, 15*, 167-177.

Black, J., Conroy, M. (1977) Accessibility Measures and the Social Evaluation of Urban Structure, *Environment and Planning A*, *9*, 1013-1031.

Black, W.R. (1981) The Utility of the Gravity Model and Estimates of its Parameters in Commodity Flow Studies, *Proceedings, Association of American Geographers*, *3*, 28-32.

Blase, J.H. (1979) Hysteresis and Catastrophe Theory: Empirical Identification in Transportation Modelling, *Environment and Planning A*, *11*, 675-688.

Bluestone, B., Harrison, B. (1980) *Capital and Communities: the consequences of private disinvestment*, The Progressive Alliance, Washington.

Bodin, L. (1973) Towards a General Model for Manpower Scheduling, *Urban Analysis*, *1*, 191-208 (part 1), 223-246 (part 2).

Bodin, L., Golden, B., Assad, R., Ball, M. (1981) The State of Art in the Routing and Scheduling of Vehicles and Crews, Working Paper MS/S 81-035, University of Maryland, College Park.

Bonsall, P.W., Champernowne, A.F., Cripps, E.L., Goodman, P.R., Hankin, A., Mackett, R.L., Sanderson, I., Senior, M.L., Southworth, F., Spence, R., Williams, H.C.W.L., Wilson, A.G. (1977) Models for Urban Transport Planning, in Wilson, A.G., Rees, P.H., Leigh, C.M. (eds.) *Models of Cities and Regions*, Wiley, Chichester, 457-519.

Bonsall, P.W., Champernowne, A.F., Mason, A.C., Wilson, A.G. (1977) *Transport Modelling: Sensitivity Analysis and Policy Testing*, Pergamon, Oxford.

Boon, F., de Palma, A. (1979) Boolean-Formalism and Urban Development, in Thomas, R. (ed.) *Lecture Notes in Biomathematics*, *29*, Springer-Verlag, Berlin, 402-439.

Boyce, D.E., Chon, K.S., Lee, Y.J., Lin, K.T., LeBlanc, L.J. (1983) Implementation and Computational Issues for Combined Models of Location, Destination, Mode and Route Choice, *Environment and Planning A*, *15*, 1219-1230.

Boyce, D.E., Hewings, G.J.D. (1980) Interregional Commodity Flow, Input-Output and Transportation Modelling: an entropy formulation (mimeo).

Boyce, D.E., Jansen, B.N. (1980) A Discrete Transportation Network Design Problem with Combined Distribution and Assignment, *Transportation Research*, *14B*, 147-154.

Boyce, D.E., LeBlanc, L.J., Chon, K.S., Lee, Y.J., Lin, K.T. (1981) Combined Models of Location, Destination, Mode and Route Choice: a unified approach using nested entropy constraints, Publication 3, Transportation Planning Group, University of Illinois, Urbana, Illinois.

Boyce, D.E., Southworth, F. (1979) Quasi-Dynamic Urban-Location Models with Endogenously Determined Travel Costs, *Environment and Planning A*, *11*, 575-584.

Broadbent, T.A. (1969-A) Zone Size and Singly Constrained Interaction Models, CES-WN-132, Centre for Environmental Studies,

London.
Broadbent, T.A. (1969-B) Zone Size and Spatial Interaction in Operational Models, CES-WN-106, Centre for Environmental Studies, London.
Broadbent, T.A. (1970) Notes on the Design of Operational Models, *Environment and Planning*, 2, 469-476.
Broadbent, T.A. (1973) Activity Analysis of Spatial-Allocation Models, *Environment and Planning*, 5, 673-691.
Broadbent, T.A. (1977) *Planning and Profit in the Urban Economy*, Methuen, London.
Brotchie, J.F. (1965) A General Planning Model, *Management Science*, *16*, 265-266.
Brotchie, J.F. (1978) A Model Incorporating Diversity in Urban Allocation Problems, *Applied Mathematical Modelling*, 2, 191-200.
Brotchie, J.F. (1979) A Model Based on Non-Homogeneity in Allocation Problems, in Hensher, D.A., Stopher, P.R. (eds.) *Behavioural Travel Modelling*, Croom Helm, London, 355-377.
Brotchie, J.F., Lesse, P.F., Roy, J.R. (1979) Entropy, Utility and Planning, *Sistemi Urbani*, *1*, 3, 33-53.
Bruegel, I. (1975) The Marxist Theory of Rent and the Contemporary City: a critique of David Harvey, in *Political Economy and the Housing Questions*, Paper presented at the Housing Workshop of the Conference of Socialist Economists, CSE, London.
Burdekin, R. (1978) The Construction of the 1973 Scottish Input-Output Tables, UKSC 0091, IBM UK Ltd, Peterlea.
Burdekin, R., Marshall, S.A. (1972) The Use of Forrester's Systems Dynamics Approach in Urban Modelling, *Environment and Planning*, *4*, 471-485.
Burmeister, E. (1980) *Capital Theory and Dynamics*, Cambridge University Press, Cambridge.
Burnett, P. (1974) A Three-State Markov Model of Choice Behaviour within Spatial Structure, *Geographical Analysis*, *6*, 53-67.
Burnett, P. (1980) Spatial Constraints-Oriented Approaches to Movement, Microeconomic Theory and Urban Policy: conceptual issues, *Urban Geography*, *1*, 53-67.
Byler, J.W., Gale, S. (1978) Social Accounts and Planning for Changes in Urban Housing Markets, *Environment and Planning A*, *10*, 247-266.
Camerini, P.M., Colorni, A., Maffioli, F. (1983) Some Experience in Applying a Stochastic Method to Location Problems, Atti del Netflow '83, Pisa.
Capasso, V., Paveri-Fontana, S.L. (1981) Some Results on Linear Stochastic Multicompartmental Systems, *Mathematical Biosciences*, *55*, 7-26.
Casetti, E. (1981-A) Between Growth and Decline: a catastrophe model of regional dynamics, *Annals of the Association of American Geographers*, *71*, 572-579.

Casetti, E. (1981-B) Technological Progress, Exploitation and Spatial Economic Growth: a catastrophe model, in Griffith, D.A., Mackinnon, R. (eds.) *Dynamic Spatial Models*, Sijthoff and Noordhoff, Alphen aan den Rijn, The Netherlands, 215-227.
Casetti, E., Papageorgiou, Y.Y. (1971) A Spatial Equilibrium Model of Urban Structure, *Canadian Geographer*, *15*, 30-37.
Castells, M. (1973) *La Question Urbaine*, Maspero, Paris.
Castells, M. (1978) *City, Class and Power*, Macmillan, London.
Casti, J., Swain, H. (1975) Catastrophe Theory and Urban Processes, RM-75-14, IIASA, Laxenburg, Austria.
Cesario, F.J. (1973) Parameter Estimation in Spatial Interaction Modelling, *Environment and Planning*, *5*, 503-518.
Chalmet, L.G., Francis, R.L., Kolen, A. (1981) Finding Efficient Solutions for Rectilinear Distance Location Problems Efficiently, *European Journal of Operational Research*, *6*, 117-124.
Champernowne, A.F., Williams, H.C.W.L., Coelho, J.D. (1976) Some Comments of Urban Travel Demand Analysis, Model Calibration and the Economic Evaluation of Transport Plans, *Journal of Transport Economics and Policy*, *10*, 3, 267-285.
Charnes, A.W., Cooper, W.W. (1961) *Management Models and Industrial Applications*, Wiley, New York.
Chen, K. (ed.) (1972) *Urban Modelling in Urban Dynamics: extensions and reflections*, The San Francisco Press, San Francisco, Calif.
Chen, K. (1973) An Evaluation of Forrester-Type Growth Models, *IEEE Transactions on Systems, Man and Cybernetics*, *3*, 631-632.
Chiang, C.L. (1968) *Introduction to Stochastic Process in Biostatistics*, Wiley, New York.
Chillingworth, D.R.J. (1976) *Differential Topology with a View to Applications*, Pitman, London.
Chon, K.S. (1982) Testing of Combined Urban Location and Travel Choice Models, unpublished Ph.D. Dissertation, University of Illinois, Urbana, Ill.
Choukroun, J-M. (1975) A General Framework for the Development of Gravity-Type Distribution Models, *Regional Science and Urban Economics*, *5*, 177-202.
Christaller, W. (1933) *Die Zentralen Orte in Süddeutschland: Eine Ökonomisch-Geographische Untersuchung über die Gesetz massigkeit der Verbreiting und Entwicklung der Siedlungen mit Stödtischen Funktionen*, Fischer Verlag, Jena. [English translation: (1966) *Central Places in Southern Germany*, Prentice-Hall, Englewood Cliffs, N.J.]
Christiansen, P.A. (1975) A Version of the Lowry Model and its Use in Practical Planning: An Example from Southern Norway, in Karlqvist, A., Lundqvist, L., Snickars, F. (eds.) *Dynamic Allocation of Urban Space*, Saxon House, Westmead, Farnborough, Hants, England, 311-324.

Christofides, N., Beasley, J.E. (1982) A Tree Search Algorithm for the p-Median Problem, *European Journal of Operational Research*, *10*, 196-204.

Church, R.L., ReVelle, C.S. (1976) Theoretical and Computational Links between the p-Median, Location Set-Covering and the Maximal Covering Problem, *Geographical Analysis*, *8*, 406-415.

Clark, C. (1951) Urban Population Densities, *Journal of the Royal Statistical Society*, *CXIV*, Part IV, 490-496.

Clark, G., Dear, M. (1981) *The State in Capitalism and the Capitalist State*, in Dear, M., Scott, A.J. (eds.) *Urbanization and Urban Planning in Capitalist Society*, Methuen, New York, 45-61.

Clarke, M. (1981) A Note on the Stability of Equilibrium Solutions in Production-Constrained Spatial Interaction Models, *Environment and Planning A*, *13*, 601-604.

Clarke, M., Keys, P., Williams, H.C.W.L. (1981) Micro-Analysis and Simulation of Socio-Economic Systems: progress and prospects, in Bennett, R.J., Wrigley, N. (eds.) *Quantitative Geography: a British view*, Routledge and Kegan Paul, Henley, 248-256.

Clarke, M., Spowage, M. (1982) Specification of a Microsimulation Model of a District Health Service, Working Paper 338, School of Geography, University of Leeds, Leeds, England.

Clarke, M., Wilson, A.G. (1983) The Dynamics of Urban Spatial Structure: progress and problems, *Journal of Regional Science*, *23*, 1-18.

Clarke, M., Wilson, A.G. (1985) The Dynamics and Evolution of Urban Spatial Structure, manuscript.

Cochrane, R.A. (1975) A Possible Economic Basis for the Gravity Model, *Journal of Transport Economics and Policy*, *9*, 34-39.

Coelho, J.D. (1979) A Locational Surplus Maximisation Model of Land Use Plan Design, in Breheny, M.J. (ed.) *Developments in Urban and Regional Analysis*, *10*, Pion, London, 48-60.

Coelho, J.D. (1983) Public Facility Location: a survey of recent developments, *Sistemi Urbani*, *5*, 5-32.

Coelho, J.D., Williams, H.C.W.L. (1978) On the Design of Land Use Plans through Locational Surplus Maximization, *Papers of the Regional Science Association*, *40*, 71-85.

Coelho, J.D., Williams, H.C.W.L., Wilson, A.G. (1978) Entropy Maximizing Submodels within Overall Mathematical Programming Frameworks: a correction, *Geographical Analysis*, *10*, 195-201.

Coelho, J.D., Wilson, A.G. (1976) The Optimum Location and Size of Shopping Centres, *Regional Studies*, *10*, 413-421.

Coelho, J.D., Wilson, A.G. (1977) An Equivalence Theorem to Integrate Entropy-maximizing Submodels within Overall Mathematical Programming Frameworks, *Geographical Analysis*, *9*, 160-173.

Cohon, J.L., ReVelle, C., Current, J., Eagles, T.W., Eberhart, R., Church, R. (1980) Application of a Multiobjective Facility Location Model to Power Plant Siting in a Six-State Region of the U.S., *Comput. & Operations Research*, *7*, 107-123.
Cohon, J.L., ReVelle, C., Shobrys, D.E., Margulies, T.S., Hereford, L.G., Eagles, T.W. (1982) Location Systems Analysis of Away-from-Reactor Spent Fuel Storage Facilities, New Directions in Nuclear Energy with Emphasis on Fuel Cycles, Bruxelles.
Coleman, J.S. (1964) *Introduction to Mathematical Sociology*, The Free Press, New York.
Colorni, A. (1982) Esperienze di Localizzazione di Servizi Collettivi in Italia e all'Estero, Relazione al 3° Corso su Tecniche e Modelli per la Programmazione Regionale, IASI-CNR, Capri.
Colorni, A., Romeo, F., Scattolini, R., Zanoni, M. (1979) Alcuni Programmi di Calcolo per Problemi di Localizzazione e Distribuzione, in Colorni, A. (ed.) *Modelli di Localizzazione e Distribuzione nella Gestione dell'Ambiente e del Territorio*, CLUP, Milano, 397-468.
Conlisk, J. (1976) Interactive Markov Chains, *Journal of Mathematical Sociology*, *4*, 157-185.
Cooke, K.L. (1975) A Discrete-Time Epidemic Model with Classes of Infectives and Susceptibles, *Theoretical Population Biology*, *7*, 175-196.
Cooper, L. (1963) Location-Allocation Problems, *Operations Research*, *11*, 331-343.
Cordey-Hayes, M. (1972) Dynamic Framework for Spatial Models, *Socio-Economic Planning Science*, *6*, 365-385.
Cordey-Hayes, M. (1975) Migration and the Dynamics of Multiregional Population Systems, *Environment and Planning A*, *7*, 793-814.
Cordey-Hayes, M., Wilson, A.G. (1971) Spatial Interaction, *Socio-Economic Planning Sciences*, *5*, 73-95.
Cornuejols, G., Fisher, M.L., Nemhauser, G.L. (1977) Location of Bank Accounts to Optimize Float: an analytic study of exact and approximate algorithms, *Management Science*, *23*, 789-810.
Cox, D.R., Miller, H.D. (1965) *The Theory of Stochastic Processes*, Chapman and Hall, London.
Crecine, J.P. (1964) TOMM (Time Oriented Metropolitan Model), CRP Technical Bulletin 6, CONSAD Research Corporation, Pittsburgh.
Crecine, J.P. (1968) A Dynamic Model of Urban Structure, P-3803, RAND Corporation, Santa Monica, Calif.
Crecine, J.P. (1969-A) Spatial Location Decisions and Urban Structure: a time oriented model, Discussion Paper 4, Institute of Public Policy Studies, University of Michigan, Michigan.

Crecine, J.P. (1969-B) Time Oriented Metropolitan Model, University of Michigan, Michigan.

Cripps, E.L., Foot, D.H.S. (1969) The Empirical Development of an Elementary Residential Location Model for Use in Subregional Planning, *Environment and Planning*, *1*, 81-90.

Cripps, E.L., Foot, D.H.S. (1970) The Urbanization Effects of a Third London Airport, *Environment and Planning*, 2, 153-192.

Cripps, E.L., Macgill, S.M., Wilson, A.G. (1974) Energy and Materials Flows in the Urban Space Economy, *Transportation Research*, *8*, 293-305.

Crosby, R.W. (1983) *Cities and Regions as Nonlinear Decision Systems*, Westview Press, Boulder, Colorado.

Curry, L. (1969) A Classical Approach to Central Place Dynamics, *Geographical Analysis*, *1*, 272-282.

Curry, L. (1978) Position, Flow and Person in Theoretical Economic Geography, in Carlstein, T., Parkes, D., Thrift, N. (eds.) *Time and Regional Dynamics*, Arnold, London, 35-50.

Curry, L. (1982) Recruitment as Diffusion and the Spatial Structure of Occupations, *Journal of Regional Science*, 22, 479-498.

Curry, L. (1983) Inefficiency and Instability of Trade Patterns, in Griffith, D., Lea, A. (eds.) *Evolving Geographical Structures*, Martinus Nijhoff, The Hague, 278-292.

Daganzo, C. (1979) *Multinomial Probit: the theory and its applications to demand forecasting*, Academic Press, New York.

Dalvi, M.Q., Das, T.K. (1983) A Multi-Sectoral and Multi-Regional Transport Model for India - Data Base and Calibration Techniques, *Environment and Planning A*, *15*, 391-403.

Dalvi, M.Q., Martin, K.M. (1976) The Measurement of Accessibility: some preliminary results, *Transportation*, 5, 17-42.

Day, R.H. (1981) Emergence of Chaos from Neoclassical Growth, *Geographical Analysis*, *13*, 315-327.

Day, R.H. (1982) Dynamical Systems Theory and Complicated Economic Behaviour, MRG Working Paper 8215, Department of Economics, University of Southern California.

Dendrinos, D.S. (1977) Short-Run Disequilibria in Urban Spatial Structure, *Regional Science Perspectives*, 7, 2, 27-41.

Dendrinos, D.S. (1978) Urban Dynamics and Urban Cycles, *Environment and Planning A*, *10*, 43-49.

Dendrinos, D.S. (1979) Slums in Capitalist Urban Settings: some insights from catastrophe theory, *Geographica Polonica*, 42, 63-75.

Dendrinos, D.S. (1980-A) A Basic Model of Urban Dynamics Expressed as a Set of Volterra-Lotka Equations, in Catastrophe Theory in Urban and Transport Analysis,

Report DOT/RSPA/DPB-25/80/20, US Department of Transportation, Washington, D.C., 79-103.

Dendrinos, D.S. (1980-B) Dynamics of City Size and Structural Stability: the case of a single city, *Geographical Analysis*, *12*, 236-244.

Dendrinos, D.S. (1981-A) Fast and Slow Equations: the development patterns of urban settings, *Environment and Planning A*, *13*, 819-827.

Dendrinos, D.S. (1981-B) Individual Lot and Neighbourhood Competitive Equilibria: some extensions from the theory of structural stability, *Journal of Regional Science*, *21*, 37-49.

Dendrinos, D.S. (1982) On the Dynamic Stability of Interurban/Regional Labour and Capital Movements, *Journal of Regional Science*, *22*, 529-540.

Dendrinos, D.S., Mullally, H. (1981-A) Evolutionary Patterns of Urban Populations, *Geographical Analysis*, *13*, 328-344.

Dendrinos, D.S., Mullally, H. (1981-B) Fast and Slow Equations: the development patterns of urban setting, *Environment and Planning A*, *13*, 819-827.

de Palma, A. (1981) Modèles Stochastiques des Comportements Collectifs dans les Systèmes Complexes, Ph.D. Thesis, Université Libre de Bruxelles, Bruxelles, Belgium.

de Palma, A., Ben-Akiva, M. (1981) An Interactive Dynamic Model of Residential Location Choice, Paper presented at the International Conference on Structural Economic Analysis and Planning in Time and Space, June 21-26, Umeå, Sweden.

de Palma, A., Ben-Akiva, M., Lefèvre, C., Litinas, N. (1983) Stochastic Equilibrium Model of Peak Period Traffic Congestion, *Transportation Science*, *17*, 430-453.

de Palma, A., Ingenbleek, J.F., Lefèvre, C. (1983) Peak Period Congestion Model with Arrivals in Series, Paper prepared for presentation at the World Conference on Transport Research.

de Palma, A., Lefèvre, C. (1982) Residential Change and Individual Choice Behaviour (mimeo).

de Palma, A., Lefèvre, C. (1983) Individual Decision-Making in Dynamic Collective Systems (mimeo).

Desai, M. (1979) *Marxian Economic Theory*, 2nd Edition, Blackwell, Oxford.

Dickey, J.W., Leone, P.A., Schwarte, A.R. (1971) Use of Topaz for Generating Alternative Land Use Schemes, *Journal of the Institute of Town Planners, India*, *68*.

Dixit, A. (1973) The Optimum Factory Town, *The Bell Journal of Economics and Management Science*, *4*, 637-651.

Dodson, A.J., Muller, E. (1978) Models for New Product Diffusion through Advertising and Word-of-Mouth, *Management Science*, *24*, 1568-1578.

Dokmeci, V. (1979) A Multiobjective Model for Regional Planning of Health Facilities, *Environment and Planning A*, *11*, 517-525.

Domanski, R. (1973) A General Model of Optimal Growth in a System of Regions, *Papers of the Regional Science Association, 31*, 73-82.

Domencich, T., McFadden, D. (1975) *Urban Travel Demand. A Behavioural Analysis*, North-Holland, Amsterdam.

Drèze, J.H. (1975) Existence of an Exchange Equilibrium under Price Rigidities, *International Economic Review, 16*, 301-320.

Drezner, Z., Wesolowsky, G.O. (1980) Single Facility 1_p-Distance Minimax Locations, *SIAM Journal of Algebraic and Discrete Mathematics, 1*, 315-321.

Dynkin, E.B., Yushkevich, A.A. (1969) *Markov Processes: theorems and problems*, Plenum Press, New York.

Eaton, B.C., Lipsey, R.G. (1975) The Principle of Minimum Differentiation Reconsidered: some new developments in the theory of spatial competition, *Review of Economic Studies, 42*, 27-49.

Eaton, B.C., Lipsey, R.G. (1976) The Non-uniqueness of Equilibrium in the Löschian Model, *American Economic Review, 66*, 77-93.

Eaton, B.C., Lipsey, R.G. (1977) The Introduction of Space into the Neoclassical Model of Value Theory, in Artis, M.J., Nobay, A.P. (eds.) *Studies in Modern Economics*, Basil Blackwell, Oxford.

Eaton, B.C., Lipsey, R.G. (1978) Freedom of Entry and the Existence of Pure Profit, *Economic Journal, 88*, 455-469.

Echenique, M., Crowther, D., Lindsay, W. (1969) A Spatial Model of Urban Stock and Activity, *Regional Studies, 3*, 281-312.

Echenique, M., Crowther, D., Lindsay, W. (1971) The Development of a Model of a Town: some considerations, in Wilson, A.G. (ed.) *Urban Regional Planning, London Papers in Regional Science, 2*, Pion, London, 134-156.

Echenique, M., Crowther, D., Lindsay, W., Stibbs, R. (1969) Model of a Town: Reading, Working Paper 12, Centre for Land Use and Built Form Studies, University of Cambridge, Cambridge, England.

Echenique, M., Domeyko, J. (1970) A Model for Santiago Metropolitan Area, Working Paper 11, Centre for Land Use and Built Form Studies, University of Cambridge, Cambridge, England.

Echenique, M., Feo, A., Herrera, R., Riquezes, J. (1973) A Disaggregate Model of a Metropolitan Area: Caracas, Working Paper 9, Land Use and Built Form Studies, University of Cambridge, Cambridge, England.

Efroymson, M.A., Ray, T.L. (1966) A Branch and Bound Algorithm for Plant Location, *Operations Research, 14*, 361-368.

Eilon, S., Tilley, R.P.R., Fowler, T.R. (1969) Analysis of a Gravity Demand Model, *Regional Studies, 3*, 115-122.

Eilon, S., Watson-Gandy, C.D.T., Christofides, N. (1971) *Distribution Management: mathematical modelling and*

practical analysis, Griffin, London.
Einstein, A. (1906) Zur Theorie der Brownschen Bewegung, *Annalen der Physik*, *19*, 371-381.
Eisenfeld, J. (1979) Relationship between Stochastic and Differential Models of Compartmental Systems, *Mathematical Bioscience*, *43*, 289-305.
Elson, D. (1979) *Value: the representation of labour in capitalism*, CSE Books, London.
Emmanuel, A. (1972) *Unequal Exchange*, Monthly Review Press, New York.
Enke, S. (1951) Equilibrium Among Spatially Separated Markets: solutions by electric analog, *Econometrics*, *19*, 40-47.
Erlander, S. (1977) Accessibility, Entropy and the Distribution and Assignment of Traffic, *Transportation Research*, *11*, 149-153.
Erlander, S. (1980) *Optimal Spatial Interaction and the Gravity Model*, *Lecture Notes in Economics and Mathematical Systems*, *173*, Springer-Verlag, London.
Erlander, S., Smith, T.E. (1983) A General Formulation of the Cost-Efficiency Principle (mimeo).
Erlenkotter, D. (1978) A Dual Based Procedure for Uncapacitated Facility Location, *Operations Research*, *26*, 992-1009.
Erlenkotter, D. (1981) A Comparative Study of Approaches to Dynamic Location Problems, *European Journal of Operational Research*, *6*, 133-143.
Ermoliev, Y., Leonardi, G. (1981) Some Proposals for Stochastic Facility Location Models, *Sistemi Urbani*, *3*, 455-470.
Erneux, Th. (1979) Phénomènes de Bifurcation en Cinétique Chimique de Non-équilibre, unpublished Ph.D. Dissertation.
Evans, A.W. (1972) On the Theory of the Valuation and Allocation of Time, *Scottish Journal of Political Economy*, *19*, 1-17.
Evans, A.W. (1975) Rents and Housing in the Theory of Urban Growth, *Papers and Proceedings of the Regional Science Association*, *28*, 49-80.
Evans, S.P. (1973) A Relationship between the Gravity Models for Trip Distribution and the Transportation Problem in Linear Programming, *Transportation Research*, *7*, 39-61.
Evans, S.P. (1976) Derivation and Analysis of Some Models for Combining Trip Distribution and Assignment, *Transportation Research*, *10*, 37-57.
Evans, S.P., Kirby, H.R. (1974) A Three-Dimensional Furness Procedure for Calibrating Gravity Models, *Transportation Research*, *8*, 105-122.
Faddy, M.J. (1977) Stochastic Compartmental Models as Approximations to More General Stochastic Systems with the General Stochastic Epidemic as an Example, *Advances in Applied Probability*, *9*, 448-61.
Feldman, E., Lehrer, F.A., Ray, T.L. (1966) A Warehouse Location under Continuous Economies of Scale, *Management Science*, *12*, 670-684.
Ferguson, C.E. (1969) *The Neoclassical Theory of Production and Distribution*, Cambridge University Press, Cambridge, U.K.

Fife, P.C. (1979) *Lecture Notes in Biomathematics*, Springer-Verlag, Berlin.

Fine, B. (1979) On Marx's Theory of Agricultural Rent, *Economy and Society*, *8*, 241-278.

Fisk, C.S., Boyce, D.E. (1982) A Note on Trip Matrix Estimation from Link Traffic Count Data, Paper No. 5, Transportation Planning Group, Department of Civil Engineering, University of Illinois, Urbana, Ill.

Floor, H., Jong, T. (1981) Testing a Disaggregated Residential Location Model with External Zones in the Amersfoot Region, *Environment and Planning*, *A*, *13*, 1499-1514.

Florian, M. (1977) A Traffic Equilibrium Model of Travel by Car and Public Transit Modes, *Transportation Science*, *11*, 166-179.

Florian, M., Los, M. (1982) A New Look at Static Spatial Price Equilibrium Models, *Regional Science and Urban Economics*, *12*, 579-598.

Florian, M., Nguyen, S. (1976-A) An Application and Validation of Equilibrium Trip Assignment Methods, *Transportation Science*, *10*, 374-390.

Florian, M., Nguyen, S. (1976-B) Traffic Equilibrium Methods, *Lecture Notes in Economics and Mathematical Systems*, *118*, Springer-Verlag, Heidelberg.

Florian, M., Nguyen, S. (1978) A Combined Trip Distribution Modal Split Assignment Model, *Transportation Research*, *12*, 241-246.

Florine, J. (1964) *La Synthèse des Machines Logiques et son Automation*, Dunod, Paris.

Forrester, J.W. (1969) *Urban Dynamics*, M.I.T. Press, Cambridge, Mass.

Forrester, J.W. (1972) *World Dynamics*, Wright-Allen Press, Cambridge, Mass.

Fortak, H.G. (1982) Source Allocation and Design via Simulation Models, in Fronza, G., Melli, P. (eds.) *Mathematical Models for Planning and Control of Air Quality*, Pergamon Press, Oxford, 91-107.

Francis, R.L., Goldstein, J.M. (1974) Location Theory: a selective bibliography, *Operation Research*, *22*, 400-410.

Frankowicz, M., Gudowska-Nowak, E. (1982) Stochastic Simulation of a Bistable Chemical System: the two box models, *Physica*, *116A*, 331-344.

Friesz, T.L., Tobin, R.L., Smith, T.E., Harker, P.T. (1983) A Nonlinear Complementarity Formulation and Solution Procedure for the General Derived Demand Network Equilibrium Problem, *Journal of Regional Science*, *23*, 337-359.

Fujita, M. (1975) On Optimal Development in a Multicommodity Space System, *Regional Science and Urban Economics*, *5*, 59-89.

Fujita, M. (1976-A) Spatial Patterns of Urban Growth: optimum and market, *Journal of Urban Economics*, *3*, 209-241.

Fujita, M. (1976-B) Towards a Dynamic Theory of Urban Land Use, *Papers of the Regional Science Association*, *37*, 133-165.
Fujita, M. (1978) *Spatial Development Planning. A Dynamic Convex Programming Approach*, North-Holland, Amsterdam.
Fujita, M. (1979) Spatial Patterns of Urban Growth and Contraction: problem A, *Geographica Polonica*, *42*, 112-148.
Fujita, M. (1980) A Multiperiod Model of Urban Land Market under Uncertainty, Working Papers in Regional Science and Transportation, 27, University of Pennsylvania, Philadelphia, P.A.
Fujita, M. (1981-A) Location of Firms with Input Transactions, *Environment and Planning A*, *13*, 1401-1414.
Fujita, M. (1981-B) Spatial Dynamics of Urban Land Use, in Griffith, D.A., Mackinnon, R. (eds.) *Dynamic Spatial Models*, NATO ASI Series D: Behavioural and Social Sciences, No. 7, Sijthoff and Noordhoff, Alphen aan den Rijn, The Netherlands, 404-439.
Fujita, M. (1981-C) Urban Land Market under Uncertainty with Infinite Time Horizon, Working Papers in Regional Science and Transportation, 27, University of Pennsylvania, Philadelphia, P.A., Part I: text.
Fujita, M. (1982-A) Spatial Patterns of Residential Development, *Journal of Urban Economics*, *12*, 22-52.
Fujita, M. (1982-B) The Spatial Growth of Tokyo: theoretical and empirical analysis, Working Papers in Regional Science and Transportation, 12, University of Pennsylvania, Philadelphia, P.A.
Fujita, M. (1982-C) Towards a General Equilibrium Model of Urban Land Use, Working Papers in Regional Science and Transportation, 68, University of Pennsylvania, Philadelphia, P.A.
Fujita, M. (1983) Urban Spatial Dynamics: a review, *Sistemi Urbani*, *5*, 411-475.
Fujita, M. (1984) The Spatial Growth of Tokyo Metropolitan Area, in Andersson, A.E., Isard, A., Puu, T., Schweizer, U. (eds.) *Structural Economic Analysis and Planning in Time and Space*, North-Holland, Amsterdam.
Fujita, M., Kashiwadani, M. (1976) A Study on the Theoretical Relation between Market and Optimum Urban Residential Theories, *Annals of Japanese Regional Association*, *5*, 107-135.
Fujita, M., Ogawa, H. (1982) Multiple Equilibria and Structural Transition of Non-Monocentric Urban Configurations, *Regional Science and Urban Economics*, *12*, 161-196.
Furness, K.P. (1965) Time Function Iteration, *Traffic Engineering and Control*, November, 458-460.
Galambos, J. (1978) *The Asymptotic Theory of Extreme Order Statics*, Wiley, New York.
Gallo, G., Pallottino, S. (1982) Introduction and Recent Advances in Shortest Path Methods, 1st Course on Transportation Planning Models, ICTS-CNR, Amalfi.

Gani, J., Jerwood, D. (1971) Markov Chains Methods in Chain Binomial Epidemic Models, *Biometrics*, *27*, 591-603.
Gardiner, C.W., McNeil, K.J., Walls, D.F., Matheson, I.S. (1976) Correlations in Stochastic Theories of Chemical Reactions, *Journal of Statistical Physics*, *14*, 307-331.
Garegnani, P. (1970) Heterogeneous Capital, the Production Function and the Theory of Distribution, *Review of Economic Studies*, *37*, 407-436.
Garey, M.R., Johnson, D.S. (1979) *Computers and Intractability. A Guide to the Theory of NP-Completeness*, W.H. Freeman & Co., San Francisco.
Garfinkel, R.S., Neebel, A.W., Rao, M.R. (1977) The m-Centre Problem: minimax facility location, *Management Science*, *23*, 1133-1142.
Garfinkel, R.S., Nemhauser, G.L. (1972) *Integer Programming*, Wiley, New York.
Garin, R.A. (1966) A Matrix Formulation of the Lowry Model for Intrametropolitan Activity Location, *Journal of the American Institute of Planners*, *32*, 361-364.
Garn, H., Wilson, R. (1970) A Critical Look at Urban Dynamics: the model and public policy, The Urban Institute, Washington, Washington D.C.
Geoffrion, A.M. (1968) Proper Efficiency and the Theory of Vector Maximization, *Journal of Mathematical Analysis and Applications*, *22*, 618-630.
Geoffrion, A.M., Dyer, J.S., Feinberg, A. (1972) An Interactive Approach for Multicriterion Optimization with an Application to the Operation of an Academic Department, *Management Science*, *19*, 357-368.
Geoffrion, A.M., McBride, R. (1978) Lagrangian Relaxation Applied to Capacitated Facility Location Problems, *AIIE Transactions*, *10*, 40-47.
Gibson, B. (1980) Unequal Exchange: theoretical issues and empirical findings, *Review of Radical Political Economics*, *12*, 3, 15-35.
Gillespie, D.T. (1976) A General Method for Numerically Simulating the Stochastic Time Evolution of Coupled Time Evolution of Chemical Reactions, *Journal of Computational Physics*, *22*, 403-434.
Ginsberg, R.B. (1972) Critique of Probabilistic Models: application of the semi-Markov model to migration, *Journal of Mathematical Sociology*, *2*, 63-82.
Glickmann, N.J. (1981) Emerging Urban Policies in a Slow-growth Economy, Conservative Initiatives and Progressive Responses in the U.S., *International Journal of Urban and Regional Research*, *5*, 492-528.
Goldman, A.J. (1971) Optimal Centre Location in Simple Networks, *Transportation Science*, *5*, 212-221.
Goldner, W. (1968) Projective Land Use Model (PLUM): a model for the spatial allocation of activities and land use in a metropolitan region, Technical Report 219, The Bay Area

Transportation Study Commission, Berkeley, Calif.
Goldner, W. (1971) The Lowry Model Heritage, *Journal of the American Institute of Planners*, *37*, 100-110.
Goldner, W., Graybeal, R.S. (1965) The Bay Area Simulation Study: pilot model of Santa Clara Country and some application, Centre of Real Estate and Urban Economics, University of California, Berkeley, Calif.
Goldner, W., Rosenthal, S., Meredith, J. (1971) Theory and Application: projective land use model, Volume II, Institute of Transportation and Transport Engineering, University of California, Berkeley, Calif.
Golob, T.F., Beckmann, M.J. (1971) A Utility Model for Travel Forecasting, *Transportation Science*, *51*, 79-90.
Golob, T.F., Gustafsson, R.L., Beckmann, M.J. (1973) An Economic Utility Approach to Spatial Interaction, *Papers of the Regional Association*, *30*, 158-182.
Goodchild, M.F. (1978) Spatial Choice in Location-Allocation Problems: the role of endogenous attraction, *Geographical Analysis*, *10*, 65-72.
Goodchild, M.F. (1979) The Aggregation Problem in Location-Allocation, *Geographical Analysis*, *11*, 240-255.
Goodchild, M.F., Kwan, M.Y.C. (1978) Models of Hierarchically Dominated Spatial Interaction, *Environment and Planning A*, *10*, 1307-1317.
Goodwin, R.M. (1976) Use of Normalized General Coordinates in Linear Value and Distribution Theory, in Polenske, K.R., Skolka, J.V. (eds.) *Advances in Input-Output Analysis*, Ballinger, Cambridge, MA., 581-602.
Gordon, I.R. (1974) A Gravity Flows Approach to an Interregional Input-Output Model for the U.K., in Cripps, E.L. (ed.) *Space-Time Concepts in Urban and Regional Models*, Pion, London, 56-73.
Gray, P. (1971) Exact Solution of the Fixed Charge Transportation Problem, *Operations Research*, *19*, 1529-1538.
Greenberg, M.R. (1978) *Applied Linear Programming for the Socio-Economic and Environmental Sciences*, Academic Press, New York.
Greenhut, M.L. (1963) *Microeconomics and the Space Economy*, Scott Foresman and Co., Glenview, Ill.
Greenhut, M.L., Ohta, H. (1975) *Theory of Spatial Pricing and Market Areas*, Duke University Press, Durham.
Griego, R., Hersh, R. (1971) Theory of Random Evolutions with Applications to Partial Differential Equations, *Transactions of the American Society*, *156*, 405-418.
Griffith, D.A. (1982) A Generalised Huff Model, *Geographical Analysis*, *14*, 135-144.
Gustafsson, J.R., Harsman, B., Snickars, F. (1978) Medium Term Forecasting Models for the Housing Market, *Papers, Regional Science Association*, *40*, 87-106.
Haag, G., Weidlich, W. (1983) A Non-linear Dynamic Model for the Migration of Human Populations, in Griffith, D.A.,

Lea, A.C. (eds.) *Evolving Geographical Structures*, NATO ASI Series D; Behavioural and Social Sciences, No. 15, Nijhoff, The Hague, 24-61.

Hadley, G., Kempf, M.C. (1971) *Variational Methods in Economics*, North-Holland, Amsterdam.

Hagerstrand, T. (1970) What About People in Regional Science? *Papers, Regional Science Association*, *24*, 7-21.

Hahn, F.K. (1966) Equilibrium Dynamics with Heterogeneous Capital Goods, *Quarterly Journal of Economics*, *80*, 633-646.

Haig, R.M. (1926) Towards an Understanding of the Metropolis, *Quarterly Journal of Economics*, *40*, 197-208.

Haimes, Y.Y. (1977) *Hierarchical Analysis of Water Resources Systems*, McGraw-Hill, New York.

Haken, H. (1977) *Synergetics. An Introduction*, Springer-Verlag, Berlin.

Hakimi, S.L. (1964) Optimum Location of Switching Centres and the Absolute Centres and Medians of a Graph, *Operations Research*, *12*, 450-459.

Hakimi, S.L. (1965) Optimum Distribution of Switching Centres in a Communication Network and Some Related Graph Theoretic Problems, *Operations Research*, *13*, 462-475.

Halpern, J., Maimon, O. (1982) Algorithms for the m-Centre Problems: a survey, *European Journal of Operational Research*, *10*, 90-99.

Handler, G.Y. (1979) Complexity and Efficiency in Minimax Network Location, in Christofides, N. et al (eds.) *Combinatorial Optimization*, Wiley-Interscience, New York.

Handler, G.Y., Mirchandani, P.B. (1979) *Location on Networks Theory and Algorithms*, The M.I.T. Press, Cambridge, Mass.

Hansen, P., Thisse, J.F. (1983) Recent Advances in Continuous Location Theory, *Sistemi Urbani*, *5*, 33-54.

Hansen, W.G. (1959) How Accessibility Shapes Land Use, *Journal of the American Institute of Planners*, *25*, 73-76.

Hanushek, E.A., Quigley, J.M. (1979) The Dynamics of the Housing Market: a stock adjustment model of housing consumption, *Journal of Urban Economics*, *6*, 90-111.

Harcourt, G.C. (1972) *Some Cambridge Controversies in the Theory of Capital*, Cambridge University Press, Cambridge, U.K.

Harris, B. (1964-A) A Model of Location Equilibrium for Retail Trade, Institute for Urban Studies, University of Pennsylvania, Philadelphia, P.A. (mimeo).

Harris, B. (1964-B) A Note on Probability of Interaction at a Distance, *Journal of Regional Science*, *5*, 31-35.

Harris, B., Choukroun, J-M., Wilson, A.G. (1982) Economies of Scale and the Existence of Supply-Side Equilibria in a Production-Constrained Spatial-Interaction Model, *Environment and Planning A*, *14*, 823-837.

Harris, B., Nathanson, J., Rosenburg, L. (1966) Research on an Equilibrium Model of Metropolitan Housing and Locational

Choice, Interim Report, University of Pennsylvania, Philadelphia, P.A.

Harris, B., Wilson, A.G. (1978) Equilibrium Values and Dynamics of Attractiveness Terms in Production-Constrained Spatial-Interaction Models, *Environment and Planning A*, *10*, 371-388.

Harris, C.D., Ullman, E.L. (1945) The Nature of Cities, *Annals of the Academy of Political and Social Sciences*,, *242*, 7-17.

Harris, D.J. (1978) *Capital Accumulation and Income Distribution*, Stanford University Press, Stanford, CA.

Harsman, B., Snickars, F. (1975) Disaggregated Housing Demand Models: some theoretical approaches, *Papers , Regional Science Association*, *34*, 121-143.

Hartwick, J. (1976) Intermediate Goods and the Spatial Integration of Land Uses, *Regional Science and Urban Economics*, *6*, 2, 127-145.

Harvey, D. (1973-A) *Social Justice and the City*, Edward Arnold, London.

Harvey, D. (1973-B) The Space-Economy of Capitalist Production: a Marxian interpretation, in *Proceedings of the Latin American Conference of the International Geographical Union*, Vol. 2, Rio de Janeiro, Fundacao Instituto Brasileiro de Geografia e Estatistica, 378-383.

Harvey, D. (1982) *The Limits to Capital*, Basil Blackwell, Oxford.

Hearon, J.Z. (1953) The Kinetics of Linear Systems with Special Reference to Periodic Reactions, *Bulletin of Mathematical Biophysics*, *15*, 121-141.

Hearon, J.Z. (1963) Theorems on Linear Systems, *Annals of the New York Academy of Sciences*, *108*, 36-68.

Helly, W. (1975) *Urban Systems Models*, Academic Press, New York.

Henderson, J.M. (1958) *The Efficiency of the Coal Industry*, Harvard University Press, Cambridge, Mass.

Herbert, D.S., Stevens, B.H. (1960) A Model of the Distribution of Residential Activity in Urban Areas, *Journal of Regional Science*, *2*, 21-36.

Herman, E. (1981) *Corporate Control*, *Corporate Power*, Cambridge University Press, Cambridge, U.K.

Hewings, G.J.D. (1977) Evaluating the Possibilities for Exchanging Regional Input-Output Coefficients, *Environment and Planning A*, *9*, 927-944.

Hill, D.M. (1965) A Growth Allocation Model for the Boston Region, *Journal of the American Institute of Planners*, *31*, 111-120.

Hill, D.M., Brand, D., Hansen, W.B. (1966) Prototype Development of a Statistical Land Use Prediction Model for Greatest Boston Region, *Highway Research Record*, *114*, 51-70.

Hochbaum, D.S. (1982) Heuristics for the Fixed Cost Median Problem, *Mathematical Programming*, *22*, 148-162.
Hochman, B.F., Pines, D. (1973) Dynamic Aspects of Land Use Patterns in a Growing City, W.P. 17, Centre for Urban and Regional Studies, Tel Aviv University, Tel Aviv.
Hodgson, G. (1980-81) A Theory of Exploitation without the Labour Theory of Value, *Science and Society*, *44*, 257-273.
Hodgson, M.J. (1978) Towards More Realistic Allocation in Location-Allocation Models: an interaction approach, *Environment and Planning A*, *10*, 1273-1285.
Holahan, W.L. (1975) The Welfare Effects of Spatial Price Discrimination, *American Economic Review*, *65*, 498-503.
Holahan, W.L., Schuler, R. (1977) Competitive Entry in a Spatial Economy, Market Equilibrium and Welfare Implications, *Cornell*, August.
Hoover, E.M. (1937) *Location Theory and the Shoe and Leather Industries*, Harvard University Press, Cambridge, Mass.
Hoover, E.M. (1948) *The Location of Economic Activity*, McGraw-Hill Books, New York.
Hoover, E.M. (1967) Some Programmed Models of Industry Location, *Land Economics*, *43*, 303-311.
Hotelling, H. (1929) Stability in Competition, *Economic Journal*, *41*, 41-57.
Hotelling, H. (1938) The General Welfare in Relation to Problems of Taxation and of Railway and Utility Rates, *Econometrica*, *6*, 242-269.
Hoyt, H. (1939) Structure and Growth of Residential Neighbourhoods in American Cities, U.S. Government Printing Office, Washington D.C.
Hubbard, R. (1979) Parameter Stability in Cross-Sectional Models of Ethnic Shopping Behaviour, *Environment and Planning A*, *11*, 977-992.
Huff, D.L. (1963) A Probabilistic Analysis of Shopping Centre Trade Areas, *Land Economics*, *39*, 81-89.
Huff, D.L. (1964) Defining and Estimating a Trading Area, *Journal of Marketing*, *28*, 34-38.
Hurd, R.M. (1903) *Principles of City Land Value*, The Record and Guide, New York.
Huriot, J. (1981) Rente Foncière et Modèle de Production, *Environment and Planning A*, *13*, 1125-1149.
Hymer, S. (1976) *The International Operation of National Firms; a study of direct foreign investment*, M.I.T. Press, Cambridge, Mass.
Hymer, S. (1979) *The Multinational Corporation. A Radical Approach*, Cambridge University Press, Cambridge, U.K.
Ingram, G.K., Kain, J.F., Ginn, J.R. (1972) *The Detroit Prototype of the NBER Urban Simulation Model*, Columbia University Press, New York.
IRES (1976) *Linee di Piano Territoriale per il Comprensorio di Torino*, Guida, Napoli.

Isard, W. (1956) *Location and Space-Economy*, Wiley, New York.

Isard, W. (1960) *Methods of Regional Analysis*, Wiley, New York.

Isard, W., Liossatos, P. (1972) On Optimal Development over Space and Time, *Regional Science Perspectives*, *3*.

Isard, W., Liossatos, P. (1975) Optimal Space Time Development: a summary presentation, in Karlqvist, A., Lundqvist, L., Snickars, A. (eds.) *Dynamic Allocation of Urban Space*, Saxon House, Westmead, Farnborough, Hants., England, 45-70.

Isard, W., Liossatos, P. (1979) *Spatial Dynamics and Optimal Space-Time Development*, North-Holland, Amsterdam.

Isard, W., Smith, T.E., Isard, P., Tze Hsiung Tung, Dacey, M. (1969) *General Theory: social, political, economic and regional*, M.I.T. Press, Cambridge, Mass.

Ive, G. (1975) Walker and the "New Conceptual Framework" of Urban Rent, *Antipode*, *7*, 1, 20-30.

Jacquez, J.A. (1972) *Compartmental Analysis in Biology and Medicine*, Elsevier, Amsterdam.

Jacquez, J.A. (1979) Compartmental Models of Biological Systems: linear and nonlinear, in Lakshmikantham, V. (ed.) *Applied Nonlinear Analysis*, Academic, New York, 185-205.

Jarvinen, P., Rajala, J., Sinervo, H. (1972) A Branch and Bound Algorithm for Seeking the p-Median, *Operations Research*, *20*, 173-178.

Jaynes, E.T. (1968) Prior Probabilities, *IEEE Transactions on Systems, Science and Cybernetics*, *4*, 227-241.

Jefferson, T.R., Scott, C.H. (1979) The Analysis of Entropy Models with Equality as Inequality Constraints, *Transportation Research*, *13B*, 123-132.

Johansson, B., Korcelli, P., Leonardi, G., Snickars, F. (1983) Nested Dynamics of Metropolitan Processes and Policies, IIASA, Laxenburg, Austria (mimeo).

Jordan, D.W., Smith, P. (1977) *Non-Linear Ordinary Differential Equations*, Oxford University Press, Oxford.

Jørgensen, S.E. (1983) State of the Art of Ecological Modelling, *Sistemi Urbani*, *5*, 107-117.

Kadanoff, L.P. (1971) From Simulation Model to Public Policy: an examination of Forrester's *Urban Dynamics*, *Simulation*, *16*, 261-268.

Kahn, D., Deneubourg, J.L., de Palma, A. (1981) Transportation Mode Choice, *Environment and Planning A*, *13*, 1163-1174.

Kahn, D., Deneubourg, J.L., de Palma, A. (1982) Transportation Mode Choice and City-Suburban Public Transortation Service, *Transportation Research B*, *17*, 25-43.

Kain, J. (1969) A Computer Version of How a City Works, *Fortune*, *Nov.*, 241-242.

Kain, J., Ingram, G., Ginn, R. (1972) *The Detroit Prototype of the NBER Urban Simulation Model*, Columbia University Press, New York.

Kalecki, M. (1938) The Determinants of Distribution, *Econometrica*, 6, 97-112.

Kanemoto, Y. (1976) Optimum, Market and Second Best Land Use Patterns in a von Thünen City with Congestion, *Regional Science and Urban Economics*, 6, 23-32.

Kanemoto, Y. (1980-A) Externality, Migration and Urban Crises, *Journal of Urban Economics*, 8, 150-164.

Kanemoto, Y. (1980-B) *Theories of Urban Externalities*, North-Holland, Amsterdam.

Kantorovich, L.V. (1965) *The Best Use of Economic Resources*, Harvard University Press, Cambridge, MA.

Kariv, O., Hakimi, S.L. (1979) An Algorithmic Approach to Network Location Problem. Part I: the p-Centres, *SIAM Journal on Applied Mathematics*, 37, 513-538.

Karlin, S., Taylor, H.M. (1981) *A Second Course in Stochastic Processes*, Academic Press, New York.

Karmeshu, Pathria, R.K. (1980) Stochastic Evolution of a Nonlinear Model of Diffusion of Information, *Journal of Mathematical Sociology*, 7, 59-71.

Karp, R.M. (1972) Reducibility among Combinatorial Problems, in Miller, R.E., Thatcher, J.W. (eds.) *Complexity of Computer Computations*, Plenum Press, New York, 85-103.

Kaufmann, S.A. (1969) Metabolic Stability and Epigenesis in Randomly Constructed Genetic Nets, *Journal of Theoretical Biology*, 22, 437-467.

Kellogg, O.D. (1929) *Foundations of Potential Theory*, Springer Verlag, Berlin.

Kemeny, J.C., Snell, J.L., Knapp, A.W. (1966) *Denumberable Markov Chains*, Van Nostrand, Princeton, NJ.

Kendall, D.G. (1956) Deterministic and Stochastic Epidemics in Closed Populations, *Proceedings of the Third Berkeley Symposium on Mathematical Statistics and Probability*, 4, 149-165.

Kennington, J., Unger, E. (1976) A New Branch and Bound Algorithm for the Fixed Charge Transportation Problem, *Management Science*, 22, 1116-1126.

Keyfitz, N. (1977) *Applied Mathematical Demography*, Wiley, New York.

Khumavala, B.M. (1972) An Efficient Branch and Bound Algorithm for the Warehouse Location Problem, *Management Science*, B718-B731.

King, J.R. (1974) Immigrant Fertility Trends and Population Growth in Leeds, *Environment and Planning A*, 6, 509-546.

Kirby, H.R. (1974) Theoretical Requirements for Calibrating a Gravity Model, *Transportation Research*, 8, 97-104.

Koopmans, T.C. (1949) Optimum Utilization of the Transportation System, *Econometrica*, 17, 136-149.

Koopmans, T.C., Beckmann, M.J. (1957) Assignment Problems and the Location of Economic Activities, *Econometrica*, 25, 53-76.

Koopmans, T.C., Reiter, J. (1951) A Model of Transportation, in Koopmans, T.C. (ed.) *Activity of Production and Allocation*, Wiley, New York, 222-259.

Kornai, J. (1980) *Economics of Shortage*, North-Holland, Amsterdam.

Kornai, J., Weibull, J.M. (1978) The Normal State of the Market in a Shortage Economy: a queue model, *Scandinavian Journal of Economics*, 4, 375-398.

Krarup, J., Pruzan, M.P. (1981) Reducibility of Minimax to Minisum 0-1 Programming Problems, *European Journal of Operational Research*, 6, 125-132.

Kuehn, A.A., Hamburger, M.J. (1963) A Heuristic Program for Locating Warehouses, *Management Science*, 9, 643-666.

Kuhn, H.W. (1973) A Note on Fermat's Problem, *Mathematical Programming*, 4, 98-107.

Kuhn, H.W., Tucker, A.W. (1951) Nonlinear Programming, in Neyman, J. (ed.) *Proceedings of the 2nd Berkeley Symposium on Mathematical Statistics and Probability*, University of California Press, Berkeley, 481-492.

Kurtz, T.G. (1978) Strong Approximation Theorems for Density Dependent Markov Chains, *Stochastics Processes and Their Applications*, 6, 223-240.

Kurtz, T.G. (1981) Approximation of Discontinuous Processes by Continuous Process, in Arnold, L., Lefever, R. (eds.) *Stochastic Nonlinear Systems in Physics, Chemistry and Biology*, Springer-Verlag, Berlin, 22-35.

Kurz, H. (1978) Rent Theory in a Multisectoral Model, *Oxford Economic Papers*, 32, 16-37.

Lakshmanan, T.R., Hansen, W.G. (1965) A Retail Market Potential Model, *Journal of the American Institute of Planners*, 31, 134-143.

Lantner, R. (1974) *Théorie de la Dominance Economique*, Dunod, Paris.

Larson, R.C., Odoni, A.R. (1981) *Urban Operation Research*, Prentice-Hall, Englewood Cliffs.

Launhardt, W. (1885) Mathematische Bergründung der Volkswirtschaftslehre, Leipzig.

Lave, L.B. (1970) Congestion and Urban Location, *Papers and Proceedings of the Regional Science Association*, 25, 133-143.

Ledent, J. (1978) Stable Growth in the Nonlinear Components-of-Change Model of Inter-regional Population Growth and Distribution, RM-78-28, IIASA, Laxenburg, Austria.

Lefeber, L. (1958) *Allocation in Space: production, transportation and industrial location*, North-Holland, Amsterdam.

Lefebvre, H. (1972) *La Pensée Marxiste et la Ville*, Casterman, Paris.

Lefèvre, C. (1982) A General Discrete Time Version of the Simple Epidemic Process (mimeo).

Lehoczky, J.P. (1980) Approximations for Interactive Markov Chains in Discrete and Continuous Time, *Journal of*

Mathematical Sociology, *7*, 139-157.
Lehoczky, J.P., Gaver, D.P. (1977) A Diffusion-Approximation Analysis of General M-Compartment Model, *Mathematical Biosciences*, *36*, 127-148.
Leonardi, G. (1977) Analogie Meccanico-Statistiche nei Modelli di Interazione Spaziale, Atti delle Giornate di Lavoro AIRO 1977, Parma, 530-539.
Leonardi, G. (1978) Optimum Facility Location by Accessibility Maximizing, *Environment and Planning A*, *10*, 1287-1305.
Leonardi, G. (1979-A) Accessibilit e Localizzazione Ottimale dei Servizi Pubblici, *Sistemi Urbani*, *1*, 3, 173-189.
Leonardi, G. (1979-B) Introduzione alla Teoria dell'Accessibilità, *Sistemi Urbani*, *1*, 1, 65-88.
Leonardi, G. (1979-C) Some Mathematical Programming Ideas within a Generalised Spatial Interaction and Activity Framework, in Breheny, M.J. (ed.) *Developments in Urban and Regional Analysis*, Pion, London, 28-42.
Leonardi, G. (1981-A) A General Accessibility and Congestion-Sensitive Multiactivity Spatial Interaction Model, *Papers of the Regional Science Association*, *47*, 3-17.
Leonardi, G. (1981-B) A Unifying Framework for Public Facility Location Problems, *Environment and Planning A*, *13*, 1001-1028; 1085-1108.
Leonardi, G. (1981-C) The Use of Random-Utility Theory in Building Location-Allocation Models, WP-81-28, IIASA, Laxenburg, Austria.
Leonardi, G. (1982-A) The Structure of Random Utility Models in the Light of the Asymptotic Theory of Extremes, WP-82-91, IIASA, Laxenburg, Austria.
Leonardi, G. (1982-B) Transient and Asymptotic Theory of a Random-Utility Based Stochastic Search Process in Continuous Space and Time, Paper presented at the 3rd Annual Meeting of the Regional Science Association, Italian Section, Venice, Italy.
Leonardi, G. (1983) An Optimal Control Representation of a Stochastic Multistage-Multiactor Choice Process, in Griffith, D.A., Lea, A.C. (eds.) *Evolving Geographical Structures*, NATO ASI Series D: Behavioural and Social Sciences, No. 15, Nijhoff, The Hague, 62-72.
Leonardi, G. (1985) Asymptotic approximation of the assignment model with stochastic heterogeneity in the matching utilities, *Environment and Planning A*, *17*, 1303-1314.
Leonardi, G., Campisi, M. (1981) Dynamic Multistage Random Utility Choice Processes: Models in Discrete and Continuous Time, Paper presented at the 2nd Meeting of the Regional Science Association, Italian Section, Naples, 19-21 October.

Leonardi, G., Tadei, R. (1981) Nested Random Utility Models for Multi-Service Systems, Paper presented at the International Conference on Structural Economic Analysis and Planning in Time and Space, June 21-26, Umeå, Sweden.

Leontief, W.W., Strout, A. (1963) Multiregional Input-Output Analysis, in Barna, T. (ed.) *Structural Interdependence and Economic Development*, Macmillan, London, 119-150.

Lerman, S.R. (1975) A Disaggregate Behavioural Model of Urban Mobility Decisions, Ph.D. Thesis, Department of Civil Engineering, M.I.T. Press, Cambridge, Mass.

Lerman, S.R. (1979) The Use of Disaggregated Choice Models in Semi-Markov Process Models of Trip Chaining Behaviour, *Transportation Science*, *13*, 273-291.

Lerman, S.R., Manski, C.F. (1979) Sample Design for Discrete Choice Analysis of Travel Behaviour: the state of the art, *Transportation Research*, *13A*, 29-44.

Leslie, P.M. (1945) On the Use of Matrices in Certain Population Mathematics, *Biometrika*, *33*, 183-212.

Lesse, P.F. (1982) A Phenomenological Theory of Socioeconomic Systems with Spatial Interactions, *Environment and Planning A*, *14*, 869-888.

Li, L.Y., Yorke, J.A. (1982) Period Three Implies Chaos, *American Mathematical Monthly*, *82*, 985-992.

Liaw, K.L. (1975) A Discrete-Time Dynamic Analysis of Interregional Population Systems, *Geographical Analysis*, *7*, 227-244.

Lierop, W. van, Nijkamp, P. (1979) A Utility Framework for Interaction Models for Regional and Urban Systems, *Sistemi Urbani*, *1*, 1, 41-64.

Liossatos, P. (1980-A) Surplus Value, Capitalist Competition and the Intersectoral Distribution of Monetary Income (manuscript).

Liossatos, P. (1980-B) Unequal Exchange and Regional Disparities, *Papers, Regional Science Association*, *45*, 87-104.

Liossatos, P. (1981) Differential Composition of Labour and Uneven Regional Development, Paper presented at the North American Meeting of the Regional Science Association, Montreal, November, 1981.

Lipietz, A. (1982) The So-called "Transformation Problem" Revisited, *Journal of Economic Theory*, *26*, 59-88.

Lippi, M. (1979) *Value and Naturalism in Marx*, New Left Books, London.

Lombardo, S.T., Rabino, G.A. (1983-A) Non-linear Dynamic Models for Spatial Interaction: the results of some empirical experiments, Paper presented at the 23rd European Congress of the Regional Science Association, 29 Aug - 2 Sept, Poitiers, France.

Lombardo, S.T., Rabino, G.A. (1983-B) Some Simulations of a Central Place Theory Model, *Sistemi Urbani*, *5*, 315-332.

Lorenz, E. (1963) Deterministic Non-Periodic Flow, *Journal of the Atmospheric Sciences*, *20*, 130-141.
Loria, A. (1880) *La Rendita Fondiaria e la sua Elisione Naturale*, Ulrico Hoepli, Milano.
Los, M. (1978) Combined Residential Location and Transportation Models, *Environment and Planning A*, *11*, 1241-1265.
Los, M., Nguyen, S. (1981) Spatial Allocation on a Network with Congestion, *Transportation Research*, *15B*, 113-126.
Lösch, A. (1940) *Die Räumliche Ordnung der Wirtschaft; eine untersuchung über standort, wirtschaftsgebiete und internationalen handel*, Fischer, Jena. [English translation: (1954) *The Economics of Location*, Yale University Press, New Haven, Conn.]
Loucks, D.P., Stedinger, J.R., Haith, D.A. (1981) *Water Resource Systems Planning and Analysis*, Prentice-Hall, Englewood Cliffs.
Lovering, J. (1978) The Theory of the "Internal Colony" and the Political Economy of Wales, *Review of Radical Political Economics*, *10*, 3, 55-67.
Lowry, I.S. (1964) *A Model of Metropolis*, RM-4035-RC, Rand Corporation, Santa Monica, Calif.
Luce, R.D. (1959) *Individual Choice Behaviour*, Wiley, New York.
Ludwig, D. (1975) Qualitative Behaviour of Stochastic Epidemics, *Mathematical Biosciences*, *23*, 47-73.
MacArthur, R.H. (1972) *Geographical Ecology: patterns in the distribution of species*, Harper and Row, New York.
Macgill, S.M. (1977-A) Rectangular Input-Output Tables-Multiplier Analysis and Entropy Maximising Principles: a new methodology, *Regional Science and Urban Economics*, *8*, 355-370.
Macgill, S.M. (1977-B) The Lowry Model as an Input-Output Model and its Extensions to Incorporate Full Inter-sectoral Relations, *Regional Studies*, *11*, 337-354.
Macgill, S.M., Wilson, A.G. (1979) Equivalences and Similarities between Some Alternative Urban and Regional Models, *Sistemi Urbani*, *1*, 1, 9-40.
Mackett, R.L. (1974) A Residential Location Model Incorporating Spatial Varying Levels of Information, *Regional Studies*, *8*, 257-265.
Mackie, S. (1971) The Calibration of Spatial Interaction Models, Geographical Paper 14, Department of Geography, University of Reading, Reading.
MacKinnon, R.D., Rogerson, P. (1980) Vacancy Chains, Information Filters and Interregional Migration, *Environment and Planning A*, *12*, 649-658.
Macmillan, W.D. (1979) Some Comments on the Stevens Linear and Quadratic Programming Version of von Thünen's Theory of Agricultural Land Usage, *Environment and Planning A*, *11*, 943-962.
Mahajan, V., Muller, E. (1979) Innovation Diffusion and New Product Growth Models in Marketing, *Journal of Marketing*,

43, 55-68.

Malek-Mansour, M., Nicolis, G. (1975) A Master Equation Description of Local Fluctuations, *Journal of Statistical Physics*, *13*, 197-217.

Mandel, E. (1962) *Marxist Economic Theory*, 2 Volumes, Monthly Review Press, New York.

Manne, A. (1964) Plant Location under Economies-of-Scale. Decentralization and Computation, *Management Science*, *11*, 213-235.

Manski, C.F. (1973) Structure of Random Utility Models, Ph.D. Dissertation, Department of Economics, M.I.T. Press, Cambridge, Mass.

Manski, C.F. (1975) Maximum Score Estimation on the Stochastic Utility Model of Choice, *Econometrics*, *3*, 205-228.

Manski, C.F. (1977) The Structure of Random Utility Models, *Theory and Decisions*, *8*, 229-254.

Manski, C.F., Lerman, S.R. (1977) The Estimation of Choice Probabilities from Choice-based Samples, *Econometrica*, *45*, 1977-1988.

Manski, C.F., McFadden, D. (1979) Alternative Estimators and Sample Designs for Discrete Choice Analysis, in Mansky, C.F., McFadden, D. (eds.) *Structural Analysis of Discrete Data: with econometric applications*, M.I.T. Press, Cambridge, Mass., 2-50.

Maranzana, F.E. (1964) On the Location of Supply Points to Minimize Transport Costs, *Operational Research Quarterly*, *15*, 261-270.

March, L. (1971) Urban Systems: a generalised distribution function, in Wilson, A.G. (ed.) *Urban and Regional Planning*, Pion, London, 157-170.

Marks, D.H. (1976) Modelling in Solid Waste Management: a state of the art review, Proceedings of the Conference on Environmental Modelling and Simulation, Cincinnati.

Marotto, F.R. (1982) The Dynamics of a Discrete Population Model with Threshold, *Mathematical Biosciences*, *58*, 123-128.

Martin, R.L., Thrift, N.J., Bennett, R.J. (eds.) (1978) *Towards the Dynamic Analysis of Spatial Systems*, Pion, London.

Marx, K. (1967) *Capital: a critique of political economy*, *3* Volumes, International Publishers, Moscow.

Mass, N.J. (ed.) (1974) *Readings in Urban Dynamics: Volume 1*, Wright-Allen Press, Cambridge, Mass.

Masser, I. (1970) Notes on Application of the Lowry Model to Merseyside, Department of Civic Design, University of Liverpool, Liverpool.

Masser, I., Batey, P.W.J., Brown, P.J.B. (1975) The Design of Zoning Systems for Interaction Models, in Cripps, E.L. (ed.) *London Papers in Regional Science*, *5*, *Regional Science - New Concepts and Old Problems*, Pion, London, 166-187.

Massey, D.B. (1973) The Basic-service categorization in planning, *Regional Studies*, *7*, 1-15.

Massy, W.F., Montgomery, D.B., Morrison, D.G. (1970) *Stochastic Models of Buying Behaviour*, The M.I.T. Press, Cambridge, Mass.
Matis, J.H., Hartley, H.O. (1971) Stochastic Compartmental Analysis: model and least squares estimation from time series data, *Biometrics*, *27*, 77-102.
Matis, J.H., Wehrly, T.E. (1979) Stochastic Models of Compartmental Systems, *Biometrics*, *35*, 199-220.
May, R.M. (1973) *Stability and Complexity in Model Ecosystems*, Princeton University Press, Princeton.
May, R.M. (1976) Simple Mathematical Models with Very Complicated Dynamics, *Nature*, *261*, 459-467.
May, R.M. (1978) The Evolution of Ecological Systems, *Scientific American*, *239*, 161-175.
May, R.M., Oster, G.F. (1976) Bifurcations and Dynamic Complexity in Simple Ecological Models, *The American Naturalist*, *110*, 573-599.
Mayhew, L.D., Leonardi, G. (1982) Equity, Efficiency and Accessibility in Urban and Regional Health-Care Systems, *Environment and Planning A*, *14*, 1479-1507.
Maynard Smith, J. (1978) The Evolution of Behaviour, *Scientific American*, *239*, 176-192.
Mayr, E. (1978) Evolution, *Scientific American*, *239*, 46-55.
McCarthy, P.S. (1980) A Study of the Importance of Generalized Attributes in Shopping Choice Behaviour, *Environment and Planning A*, *12*, 1269-1286.
McFadden, D. (1973) Conditional Logit Analysis of Qualitative Choice Behaviour, in Zarembka, P. (ed.) *Frontiers in Econometrics*, Academic Press, New York, 105-142.
McFadden, D. (1974) The Measurement of Urban Travel Demand, *Journal of Public Economics*, *3*, 303-328.
McFadden, D. (1976) The Mathematical Theory of Demand Models, in Stopher, P.R., Meyburg, A. (eds.) *Behavioural Travel Demand Models*, Lexington Books, Lexington, Mass., 305-314.
McFadden, D. (1978) Modelling the Choice of Residential Location, in Karlqvist, A., Lundqvist, L., Snickars, F., Weibull, J.W. (eds.) *Spatial Interaction Theory and Planning Models*, North-Holland, Amsterdam, 75-96.
McKeown, P. (1975) A Vertex Ranking Procedure for Solving the Linear Fixed Charge Problem, *Operations Research*, *23*, 1183-1191.
McLean, S.I. (1978) Continuous-Time Stochastic Models of a Multigrade Population, *Journal of Applied Probability*, *15*, 26-37.
McLean, S.I. (1980) A Semi-Markov Model for a Multigrade Population with Poisson Recruitment, *Journal of Applied Probability*, *17*, 846-852.
Merlin, P. (1968) Modèles d'urbanisation, Volume 11, IAURP, Paris.
Metcalfe, J.S., Steedman, I. (1973) Heterogeneous Capital and the Hecksher-Ohlin-Samuelson Theory of Trade, in Parkin,

J.M. (ed.) *Essays in Modern Economics*, Longman, London, reprinted in Steedman, I. (ed.) (1979) *Fundamental Issues in Trade Theory*, St Martin's Press, New York, 64-76.

Metcalfe, J.S., Steedman, I. (1974) A Note on the Gain from Trade, *Economic Record*, *50*, 581-595.

Miehle, W. (1958) Link-Length Minimization in Networks, *Operations Research*, *6*, 232-243.

Miller, E.J., Lerman, S.R. (1979) A Model of Retail Location, Scale and Intensity, *Environment and Planning A*, *11*, 177-192.

Mills, D.E. (1981) Growth Speculation and Sprawl in a Monocentric City, *Journal of Economic Theory*, *11*, 113-146.

Mills, E.S. (1967) An Aggregative Model of Resource Allocation in a Metropolitan Area, *American Economic Review*, *57*, 197-210.

Mills, E.S. (1972) *Studies in the Structure of the Urban Economy*, Johns Hopkins University Press, Baltimore.

Mills, E.S., de Ferranti, D.M. (1971) Market Choices and Optimum City Size, *American Economic Review*, *61*, 360-365.

Mills, E.S., Lav, M. (1964) A Model of Market Areas with Free Entry, *Journal of Political Economy*, *72*, 278-288.

Mills, E.S., Mackinnon, J. (1973) Notes on the New Urban Economics, *Bell Journal of Economics and Management Science*, *4*, 593-601.

Minieka, E. (1970) The m-Centre Problem, *SIAM Review*, *12*, 138-139.

Minorski, N. (1962) *Nonlinear Oscillations*, Van Nostrand, Princeton.

Mirlees, J.A. (1972) The Optimum Town, *Swedish Journal of Economics*, *74*, 114-135.

Miyao, T. (1979) Dynamic Stability of an Open City with Many Household Classes, *Journal of Urban Economics*, *6*, 292-298.

Miyao, T. (1981) *Dynamic Analysis of the Urban Economy*, Academic Press, New York.

Miyao, T., Shapiro, P. (1979) Dynamics of Rural-Urban Migration in a Developing Economy, *Environment and Planning A*, *11*, 1157-1163.

Miyao, T., Shapiro, P., Knapp, D. (1980) On the Existence, Uniqueness and Stability of Spatial Equilibrium in an Open City with Externalities, *Journal of Urban Economics*, *8*, 139-149.

Monaco, R., Rabino, G.A. (1984) A Stochastic Treatment of a Dynamic Model for an Interacting Cities System, in Avula, X.J.R., Kalman, R.E., Liapis, A.I., Rodin, E.Y. (eds.) *Mathematical Modelling in Science and Technology*, Pergamon Press, 326-330.

Moore, G.C., ReVelle, C. (1982) The Hierarchical Service Locations Problem, *Management Science*, *28*, 775-780.

Morishima, M. (1973) *Marx's Economics. A Dual Theory of Value and Growth*, Cambridge University Press, Cambridge, U.K.

Morishima, M. (1976) *The Economic Theory of Modern Society*, Cambridge University Press, Cambridge, U.K.
Morishima, M., Catephores, G. (1978) *Value, Exploitation and Growth*, McGraw-Hill, London.
Morishima, M., Seton, F. (1961) Aggregation in Leontief Matrices and the Labour Theory of Value, *Econometrica*, *29*, 203-220.
Morrison, W.I., Smith, P. (1974) Nonsurvey Input-Output Techniques at the Small-Area Level: an evaluation, *Journal of Regional Science*, *14*, 1-14.
Murchland, J.D. (1966) Some Remarks on the Gravity Model of Trip Distribution and an Equivalent Maximizing Procedure, LSE-TNT-38, London School of Economics, London (mimeo).
Murchland, J.D. (1969) Road Traffic Distribution in Equilibrium, *Mathematical Methods in the Economic Sciences*, Mathematisches Forschungsinstitut Oberwolfach, West Germany.
Murty, K.G. (1968) Solving the Fixed Charge Problem by Ranking the Extreme Points, *Operations Research*, *16*, 268-279.
Muth, R.F. (1961) The Spatial Structure of the Housing Market, *Papers and Proceedings of the Regional Science Association*, *7*, 207-220.
Muth, R.F. (1969) *Cities and Housing*, University of Chicago Press, Chicago.
Muth, R.F. (1976) A Vintage Model with Housing Production, in Papageorgiou, Y.Y. (ed.) *Mathematical Land Use Theory*, Lexington Books, Toronto, 245-259.
Nagelhout, R.V., Thompson, G.L. (1981) A Cost Operator Approach to Multistage Location-Allocation, *European Journal of Operational Research*, *6*, 149-161.
Nakamura, H., Hayashi, Y., Miyamoto, K. (1983) Land Use-Transportation Analysis System for a Metropolitan Area, *Transportation Research Record*.
Nash, D.H. (1979) On the Closeness of Logistic and Normal Distribution Functions: implications for mode choice modelling, Transportation and Urban Analysis Department, GM Research Laboratories, GMR-2120.
NEDO (1970) *Urban Models in Shopping Studies*, National Economic Development Office, London.
Neuburger, H.L.I. (1971-A) Perceived Costs, *Environment and Planning*, *3*, 369-376.
Neuburger, H.L.I. (1971-B) User Benefit in the Evaluation of Transport and Land Use Plans, *Journal of Transport Economics and Policy*, *5*, 52-75.
Nicolis, G., Prigogine, I. (1977) *Self-Organization in Non-equilibrium Systems*, Wiley, New York.
Niedercorn, J.H., Bechdolt, B.V. (1969) An Economic Derivation of the Gravity Law of Spatial Interaction, *Journal of Regional Science*, *9*, 273-282.
Nijkamp, P. (1975-A) Reflections on Gravity and Entropy Models, *Regional Science and Urban Economics*, *5*, 203-225.

Nijkamp, P. (1975-B) Spatial Interdependencies and Environment Effects, in Karlqvist, A., Lundqvist, L., Snickars, F. (eds.) *Dynamic Allocation of Urban Space*, Saxon House, Farnborough, 175-206.

Nijkamp, P. (1977) *Theory and Applications of Environmental Economics*, North-Holland, Amsterdam.

Nijkamp, P. (1983) Technological Change, Policy Response and Spatial Dynamics, in Griffith, A., Lea, A.C. (eds.) *Evolving Geographical Structures*, NATO ASI Series, Nijhoff, The Hague, 75-98.

Nijkamp, P., Rietveld, P. (1980) Recent Development in Linear and Nonlinear Multiobjective Programming for Multilevel Systems, *Ricerca Operativa*, *15*, 5-33.

Nijkamp, P., Spronk, J. (1979) Goal Programming for Decision-Making, *Ricerca Operativa*, *12*, 3-49.

Nijkamp, P., Spronk, J. (1981) Interactive Multidimensional Programming Models for Locational Decisions, *European Journal of Operational Research*, *6*, 220-223.

Offe, C. (1972) Political Authority and Class Structures - An Analysis of Late Capitalist Societies, *International Journal of Sociology*, *2*, 1, 73-105.

Ogawa, H., Fujita, M. (1979) Nonmonocentric Urban Configurations in Two-Dimensional Space, Working Papers in Regional Science and Transportation, 18, University of Pennsylvania, Philadelphia, P.A.

Ogawa, H., Fujita, M. (1980-A) Land Use Pattern in a Non-monocentric City, *Journal of Regional Science*, *20*, 455-475.

Ogawa, H., Fujita, M. (1980-B) Multicentric Urban Configuration: equilibrium and optimum, Working Papers in Regional Science and Transportation, 25, University of Pennsylvania, Philadelphia, P.A.

Okabe, A. (1979) Population Dynamics of Cities in a Region: condition for a state of simultaneous growth, *Environment and Planning A*, *11*, 609-628.

O'Kelly, M.E. (1981) A Model of the Demand for Retail Facilities Incorporating Multistop, Multipurpose Trips, *Geographical Analysis*, *13*, 134-148.

Okishio, M. (1963) A Mathematical Note on Marxian Theorems, *Weltwirtschaftliches Archiv*, *91*, 287-291.

Openshaw, S. (1975) *Some Theoretical and Applied Aspects of Spatial Interaction Shopping Models*, Geo Abstract, Norwich.

Openshaw, S. (1976) An Empirical Study of Some Spatial Interaction Models, *Environment and Planning A*, *8*, 23-41.

Openshaw, S. (1977) Optimal Zoning Systems for Spatial Interaction Models, *Environment and Planning A*, *9*, 169-184.

Openshaw, S. (1978-A) An Empirical Study of Some Zone-Design Criteria, *Environment and Planning A*, *10*, 781-794.

Openshaw, S. (1978-B) *Using Models in Planning: a practical guide*, Retail Planning Associates, Corbridge.

Oppenheim, I., Shuler, K.E., Weiss, G.H. (1977) Stochastic Theory of Non-linear Rate Processes with Multiple Stationary States, *Physica*, *88A*, 191-214.

Ostanello, A. (1980) Evoluzione del Concetto di Ottimalitǎ e sue Prospettive Normative, *Sistemi Urbani*, 2, 257-270.

Paelink, J.H.P., Nijkamp, P. (1975) *Operational Theory and Method in Regional Economics*, Saxon House, Farnborough.

Palander, T. (1935) *Beiträge zur Standortstheorie*, Almqvist and Wiksell, Uppsala, Sweden.

Palermo, P.C. (1981) *Politiche Territoriali e Modelli*, Angeli, Milano.

Pankhurst, I.C., Roe, P.E. (1978) An Empirical Study of Two Shopping Models, *Regional Studies*, *12*, 727-748.

Papageorgiou, Y.Y. (1971) The Population Density and Rent Distribution Models within a Multicentre Framework, *Environment and Planning*, *3*, 267-281.

Papageorgiou, Y.Y. (1974) Spatial Equilibrium within a Hierarchy of Centres with Distributed Incomes, Department of Geography, McMaster University, Hamilton, Ontario.

Papageorgiou, Y.Y. (ed.) (1976-A) *Mathematical Land Use Theory*, Lexington Books, Lexington, Mass.

Papageorgiou, Y.Y. (1976-B) On Spatial Consumer Equilibrium, in Papageorgiou, Y.Y. (ed.) *Mathematical Land Use Theory*, Lexington Books, Toronto, 145-176.

Papageorgiou, Y.Y. (1976-C) Urban Residential Analysis: 1. Spatial Consumer Behaviour, *Environment and Planning A*, *8*, 423-442.

Papageorgiou, Y.Y. (1978) Spatial Externalities. I: Theory; II: Applications, *Annals of the Association of American Geographers*, *68*, 465-476; 477-492.

Papageorgiou, Y.Y. (1979) Agglomeration, *Regional Science and Urban Economics*, *9*, 41-59.

Papageorgiou, Y.Y. (1980) On Sudden Urban Growth, *Environment and Planning A*, *12*, 1035-1050.

Papageorgiou, Y.Y. (1982) Externality Diffusion, *Sistemi Urbani*, *4*, 17-39.

Papageorgiou, Y.Y. (1983) Models of Agglomeration, *Sistemi Urbani*, *5*, 391-410.

Papageorgiou, Y.Y. (1985) Aspetti teorici dell'economia urbana: relazioni tra trasporti e struttura spaziale, Working Paper 53, IRES, Torino, Italy.

Papageorgiou, Y.Y., Mullally, H. (1976) Urban Residential Analysis: 2. Spatial Consumer Equilibrium, *Environment and Planning A*, *8*, 489-506.

Papageorgiou, Y.Y., Smith, T.R. (1983) Agglomeration as Local Instability of Spatial Uniform Steady-States, *Econometrica*, 1109-1119.

Papageorgiou, Y.Y., Thisse, J.F. (1982) Agglomeration as Spatial Interdependencies between Firms and Households, Department of Geography, McMaster University, Hamilton, Ontario.

Park, R.E., Burgess, E.W. (1921) *Introduction to the Science of Society*, University of Chicago Press, Chicago.

Park, R.E., Burgess, E.W., McKenzie, R.D. (1925) *The City*, University of Chicago Press, Chicago.
Parry-Lewis, J., Bridges, M.J. (1974) The Two-Stage Household Shopping Model Used in the Cambridge Subregion Study, *Regional Studies*, *8*, 187-197.
Pasinetti, L. (1962) Rate of Profit and Income Distribution in Relation to the Rate of Economic Growth, *Review of Economic Studies*, *29*, 267-279.
Pasinetti, L. (1974) *Growth and Income Distribution. Essays in Economic Theory*, Cambridge University Press, Cambridge, U.K.
Pasinetti, L. (1977-A) *Lectures in the Theory of Production*, Macmillan, London.
Pasinetti, L. (1977-B) On "Non Substitution" in Production Models, *Cambridge Journal of Economics*, *1*, 389-394.
Pasinetti, L. (1981) *Structural Change and Economic Growth*, Cambridge University Press, Cambridge, U.K.
Phiri, P.A. (1980) Calculation of the Equilibrium Configuration of Shopping Facility Size, *Environment and Planning A*, *12*, 983-1000.
Philips, L., Thisse, J.F. (1982) Spatial Competition and the Theory of Differentiated Markets: an introduction, *The Journal of Industrial Economics*, *31*, September/December, 1-9.
Piasentin, U., Costa, P., Foot, D. (1978) The Venice Problem: an approach by urban modelling, *Regional Studies*, *12*, 579-602.
Pielou, E.C. (1977) *Mathematical Ecology*, Wiley, New York.
Pines, D. (1976) Dynamics Aspects of Land Use Pattern in a Growing City, in Papageorgiou, Y.Y. (ed.) *Mathematical Land Use Theory*, Lexington Books, Toronto, 229-244.
Pollard, J.H. (1967) Hierarchical Population Models with Poisson Recruitment, *Journal of Applied Probability*, *4*, 209-213.
Popkov, Y.S. (1980) Simulation and Analysis of Structural Properties of Human Settlement Systems by Means of Entropy Maximising Models, *Environment and Planning A*, *12*, 1165-1190.
Poston, T., Wilson, A.G. (1977) Facility Size Versus Distance Travelled: urban services and the fold catastrophe, *Environment and Planning A*, *9*, 681-686.
Pred, A.R. (1976) The Interurban Transmission of Growth in Advanced Economies: empirical findings versus regional planning assumptions, *Regional Studies*, *10*, 151-171.
Putman, S.H. (1977) Calibrating a Residential Location Model for Nineteenth-Century Philadelphia, *Environment and Planning A*, *9*, 449-460.
Putman, S.H. (1978) *Urban Residential Location Models*, Martinus Nijhoff, Leiden.
Putman, S.H., Ducca, F.W. (1978-A) Calibrating Urban Residential Models 1: procedures and strategies, *Environment and*

Planning A, *10*, 633-650.
Putman, S.H., Ducca, F.W. (1978-B) Calibrating Urban Residential Model 2: Empirical Results, *Environment and Planning A*, *10*, 1001-1014.
Putman, S.H., Ducca, F.W. (1978-C) Private communication.
Puu, T. (1977) A Proposed Definition of Traffic Flow in Continuous Transportation Model, *Environment and Planning A*, *9*, 559-567.
Puu, T. (1978) Towards a Theory of Optimal Roads, *Regional Science and Urban Economics*, *8*, 225-248.
Puu, T. (1979-A) Regional Modelling and Structural Stability, *Environment and Planning A*, *11*, 1431-1438.
Puu, T. (1979-B) *The Allocation of Road Capital in Two-Dimensional Space*, North-Holland, Amsterdam.
Puu, T. (1981-A) Catastrophic Structural Change in a Continuous Regional Model, *Regional Science and Urban Economics*, *11*, 317-333.
Puu, T. (1981-B) Stability and Change in Two-Dimensional Flows, in Griffith, D.A., Mackinnon, R. (eds.) *Dynamics Spatial Models*, NATO ASI Series D: Behavioural and Social Sciences, No. 7, Sijthoff and Noordhoff, Alphen aan den Rijn, The Netherlands, 242-255.
Puu, T. (1981-C) Structural Stability and Change in Geographical Space, *Environment and Planning A*, *13*, 979-989.
Puu, T. (1982-A) An Interaction Model, CP-82-50, International Institute for Applied Systems Analysis, Laxenburg, Austria.
Puu, T. (1982-B) Long-Run Planning for Capital and Labour Allocation in Space, CP-82-11, International Institute for Applied Systems Analysis, Laxenburg, Austria.
Puu, T. (1982-C) Structurally Stable Transport Flows and Patterns of Location, RR-82-42, IIASA, Laxenburg, Austria.
Puu, T. (1982-D) The General Equilibrium of a Spatially Extended Market Economy, *Geographical Analysis*, *14*, 145-154.
Puu, T. (1983) Equilibrium in the Spatial Production and Exchange Economy. A long-run model, *Sistemi Urbani*, *5*, 499-534.
Quadrio Curzio, A. (1980) Rent, Income Distribution, and Orders of Efficiency and Rentability, in Pasinetti, L. (ed.) *Essay in the Theory of Joint Production*, Columbia University Press, New York, 218-239.
Quandt, R.E. (1968) Estimation of Modal Split, *Transportation Research*, *2*, 41-50.
Rabinowitz, P.H. (1977) *Applications of Bifurcation Theory*, Academic Press, New York.
Ralston, B. (1983) The Dynamics of Communication, in Griffith, D.A., Lea, A.C. (eds.) *Evolving Geographical Structures*, NATO ASI Series D: Behavioural and Social Sciences, No. 15, Nijhoff, The Hague, 130-167.
Ratcliff, R.U. (1949) *Urban Land Economics*, Harvard University Press, Cambridge, Mass.

Rees, P.H. (1980) Multistate Demographic Accounts: measurement and estimation procedures, *Environment and Planning A*, *12*, 499-531.

Rees, P.H., Stillwell, J.C.H. (1982) An Integrated Model of Migration Flows and Population Change for a System of U.K. Metropolitan and Non-Metropolitan Regions: a framework, Working Paper 332, School of Geography, University of Leeds, Leeds.

Rees, P.H., Wilson, A.G. (1977) *Spatial Population Analysis*, Arnold, London.

Reilly, W.J. (1931) *The Law of Retail Gravitation*, Pilsbury, New York.

ReVelle, C. (1982) Lezioni tenute al 3° Corso su Tecniche e Modelli per la Programmazione Regionale, IASI-CNR, Capri.

ReVelle, C., Cohon, J.L., Shobrys, D.E. (1981) Multiple Objective Facility Location, *Sistemi Urbani*, *3*, 319-343.

ReVelle, C., Marks, D.H., Liebman, J.C. (1970) An Analysis of Private and Public Sector Location Models, *Management Science*, *16*, 692-707.

ReVelle, C.S., Swain, R.W. (1970) Central Facilities Location, *Geographical Analysis*, 2, 30-42.

Richardson, H.W. (1969-A) *Elements of Regional Economics*, Penguin, Harmondsworth.

Richardson, H.W. (1969-B) *Regional Economics: location theory, urban structure and regional change*, Weidenfeld and Nicolson, London.

Richardson, H.W. (1971) *Urban Economics*, The Chaucer Press, Suffolk.

Richardson, H.W. (1972) *Input-Output and Regional Economics*, Weidenfeld and Nicolson, London.

Richardson, H.W. (1973-A) *Regional Growth Theory*, Macmillan, London.

Richardson, H.W. (1973-B) Theory of the Distribution of City Size: review and prospects, *Regional Studies*, *7*, 239-251.

Richardson, H.W. (1973-C) *The Economics of Urban Size*, Saxon House, Farnborough, Hants, U.K.

Richardson, H.W. (1977-A) A Generalization of Residential Location Theory, *Regional Science and Urban Economics*, *7*, 251-266.

Richardson, H.W. (1977-B) *The New Urban Economics: and its alternatives*, Pion, London.

Richardson, H.W. (1978) *Urban Economics*, Dryden Press, Hinsdale.

Rijk, F.J.A., Vorst, A.C.F. (1983) Equilibrium Points in an Urban Retail Model and their Connection with Dynamical Systems, *Regional Science and Urban Economics*, *13*, 383-399.

Rinaldi, S., Soncini-Sessa, R., Stehfest, H., Tamura, H. (1979) *Modelling and Control of River Quality*, McGraw-Hill, New York.

Ripper, M., Varaiya, P. (1974) An Optimizing Model of Urban Development, *Environment and Planning A*, *6*, 149-168.

Robinson, I.M., Wolfe, H.B., Barringer, R.L. (1965) A Simulation Model for Renewal Programming, *Journal of the American Institute of Planners*, *31*, 126-134.

Robinson, J. (1953-54) The Production Function and the Theory of Capital, *Review of Economic Studies*, *21*, 81-106.

Roemer, J. (1981) *Analytical Foundations of Marxian Economic Theory*, Cambridge University Press, Cambridge, U.K.

Roemer, J. (1982) *A General Theory of Exploitation and Class*, Harvard University Press, Cambridge, MA.

Rogers, A. (1966) Matrix Methods of Population Analysis, *Journal of the American Institute of Planners*, *32*, 40-44.

Rogers, A. (1971) *Matrix Methods in Urban and Regional Analysis*, Holden-Day, San Francisco, Calif.

Rogers, A. (1975) *Introduction to Multiregional Mathematical Demography*, Wiley, New York.

Rogers, A. (1980) Introduction to Multistate Mathematical Demography, *Environment and Planning A*, *12*, 489-498.

Rogers, E.M., Shoemaker, F.F. (1971) *Communications of Innovations: a cross-cultural approach*, The Free Press, New York.

Round, J.I. (1978) An Interregional Input-Output Approach to the Evaluation of Nonsurvey Methods, *Journal of Regional Science*, *18*, 179-194.

Ross, T.G., Soland, R.M. (1977) Modelling Facility Location Problems as Generalized Assignment Problems, *Management Science*, *24*, 345-357.

Roy, B. (1973) How Outranking Relation Helps Multiple Criteria Decision Making, in Cochrane, J.L., Zeleny, M. (eds.) *Multicriteria Decision Making*, University of South Carolina Press, Columbia, 179-201.

Roy, B. (1974) Criteres Multiples et Modèlisation des Préférences, *Revue d'Economie Politique*, *84*, 1-44.

Roy, B. (1975) Vers une Méthodologie Générale d'Aide à la Décision, Direction Scientifique, Rapport de Synthèse, No. 87, METRA, Paris.

Roy, B. (1976) From Optimization to Multicriteria Decision Aid: Three Main Operational Attitudes, in Thiriez, H., Zionts, S. (eds.) *Multiple Criteria Decision Making*, *Lecture Notes in Economics and Mathematical Systems*, *130*, Springer-Verlag, Berlin, 1-34.

Roy, B. (1977) A Conceptual Framework for a Prescriptive Theory of Decision Aid, in Starr, M.K., Zeleny, M. (eds.) *Multiple Criteria Decision Making*, North-Holland, Amsterdam, 179-209.

Roy, B. (1979-A) *L'aide a la Décision*, *Tome 1: Essai de Méthodologie Générale*, Vrije Universiteit Brussel, Centrum voor Statistick en Operationeel Onderzock, Brussel.

Roy, B. (1979-B) Necessità di una nuova assiomatica in teoria delle decisioni per pensare in modo diverso la Ricerca Operativa, Atti delle Giornate di Lavoro AIRO 1979, Bologna, Volume 1, XI-XLIII.

Roy, J.R. (1980) External Zones in the Gravity Model - Some Further Developments, *Environment and Planning A*, *12*, 1203-1206.

Sa, G. (1969) Branch and Bound and Approximate Solutions to the Capacitated Plant Location Problem, *Operations Research*, *17*, 1005-1016.

Salkin, H.M. (1975) *Integer Programming*, Addison-Wesley, Reading, Mass.

Samuelson, P.A. (1952) Spatial Price Equilibrium and Linear Programming, *American Economic Review*, *42*, 283-303.

Samuelson, P.A. (1966) A Summing Up, *Quarterly Journal of Economics*, *80*, 568-583.

Samuelson, P.A. (1971) Understanding the Marxian Notion of Exploitation: a summary of the so-called transformation problem between Marxian values and prices, *Journal of Economic Literature*, *9*, 399-431.

Sattinger, D. (1973) *Topics in Stability and Bifurcation Theory*, Springer-Verlag, Berlin.

Saunders, R. (1976) On Joint Exchangability and Conservative Processes with Stochastic Rates, *Journal of Applied Probability*, *13*, 584-590.

Scarf, H.E. (1981) Production Sets with Indivisibilities - Part II: the case of two activities, *Econometrica*, *49*, 395-423.

Schaefer, M.K., Hurter, A.P. (1974) An Algorithm for the Solution of a Location Problem with Metric Constraints, *Naval Research Logistics Quarterly*, *21*, 625-636.

Scherer, F.M., Beckenstein, A., Kaufer, E., Murphy, R.D. (1975) *The Economics of Multi-Plant Operation*, Harvard University Press, Cambridge, Mass.

Schinnar, A.P. (1976) A Multi-Dimensional Accounting Framework for Demographic and Economic Planning Interactions, *Environment and Planning A*, *8*, 455-475.

Schinnar, A.P. (1978) Invariant Distributional Regularities of Nonbasic Spatial Activity Allocations: the Garin-Lowry model revisited, *Environment and Planning A*, *10*, 327-336.

Schroeder, W.W. III, Sweeney, R.E., Alfeld, L.E. (1975) *Readings in Urban Dynamics: Volume 2*, Wright-Allen Press, Cambridge, Mass.

Schweizer, U. (1978) A Spatial Version of the Nonsubstitution Theorem, *Journal of Economic Theory*, *19*, 307-320.

Schweizer, U., Varaiya, P. (1976) The Spatial Structure of Production with a Leontief Technology, *Regional Science and Urban Economics*, *6*, 231-252.

Schweizer, U., Varaiya, P. (1977) The Spatial Structure of Production with a Leontief Technology - II: substitute techniques, *Regional Science and Urban Economics*, *7*, 289-292.

Scott, A.J. (1976) Land Use and Commodity Production, *Regional Science and Urban Economics*, *6*, 147-160.

Scott, A.J. (1978) Urban Transport and the Economic Surplus: notes towards a distributional theory, in Karlqvist, A., Lundqvist, L., Snickars, F., Weibull, J.W. (eds.) *Spatial Interaction Theory and Planning Models*, North-Holland, Amsterdam, 335-360.
Scott, A.J. (1979) Commodity Production and the Dynamics of Land-Use Differentiation, *Urban Studies*, *16*, 95-104.
Scott, A.J. (1980) *The Urban Land Nexus and the State*, Pion, London.
Scott, A.J. (1982) Production System Dynamics and Urban Development, *Annals of the Association of American Geographers*, *72*, 185-201.
Scott, C.H., Jefferson, T.R. (1977) Entropy Maximising Models of Residential Location via Geometric Programming, *Geographical Analysis*, *9*, 181-187.
Seidmann, D.R. (1964) Report on the Activities Allocation Model, P.J. Paper 22, Penn Jersey Transportation Study, Philadelphia, Pennsylvania.
Seidmann, D.R. (1969) The Construction of an Urban Growth Model, Plan Report 1, Technical Supplement, Vol. A, Delaware Valley, Regional Planning Commission, Philadelphia, Pennsylvania.
Seneta, E. (1981) *Non-Negative Matrices and Markov Chains*, Springer, New York.
Senior, M.L. (1973) Approaches to Residential Location Modelling: urban ecological and spatial interaction approaches, *Environment and Planning*, *5*, 165-197.
Senior, M.L. (1974) Approaches to Residential Location Modelling 2: urban economic models and some recent developments, *Environment and Planning A*, *6*, 369-409.
Senior, M.L. (1977) Residential Location, in Wilson, A.G., Rees, P.H., Leigh, C.M. (eds.) *Models of Cities and Regions*, Wiley, Chichester, 282-321.
Senior, M.L. (1979) From Gravity Modelling to Entropy Maximising: a pedagogic guide, *Progress in Human Geography*, *3*, 175-210.
Senior, M.L., Wilson, A.G. (1974-A) Disaggregated Residential Location Models: some tests and further theoretical developments, *Geographical Analysis*, *6*, 209-238.
Senior, M.L., Wilson, A.G. (1974-B) Exploration and Syntheses of Linear Programming and Spatial Interaction Models of Residential Location, *Geographical Analysis*, *7*, 209-238.
Shamos, M.I., Hoey, D. (1975) Closest Point Problems, Proceedings of the 16th Annual Symposium on Foundations of Computer Science, I.E.E.E., Berkeley, 151-162.
Shannon, C., Weaver, W. (1949) *The Mathematical Theory of Communication*, University of Illinois Press, Urbana.
Sharpe, R., Brotchie, J.F., Ahern, P.A. (1975) Evaluation of Alternative Growth Patterns for Melbourne, in Karlqvist, A., Lundqvist, L., Snickars, F. (eds.) *Dynamic Allocation of Urban Space*, Saxon House, Westmead, Farnborough, Hants,

U.K., 259-285.

Sharpe, R., Brotchie, J.F., Ahern, P.A., Dickey, J.W. (1974) The Evaluation of Alternative Growth Patterns in Urban Systems, *Computers and Operations Research*, *1*, 345-362.

Sheffi, Y., Daganzo, C.F. (1977) On Stochastic Models of Traffic Assignment, *Transportation Science*, *11*, 253-274.

Sheffi, Y., Daganzo, C.F. (1980) Computation of Equilibrium over Transportation Networks: the case of disaggregate demand models, *Transportation Science*, *14*, 155-173.

Shell, K. (1973) Discussion of the Paper by F.H. Hahn, in Mirlees, A., Stern, N.H. (eds.) *Models of Economic Growth*, Methuen, London, 193-206.

Sheppard, E. (1974) A Conceptual Framework for Dynamic Location-Allocation Analysis, *Environment and Planning A*, *6*, 547-564.

Sheppard, E. (1976) Interaction Feedback Modelling, unpublished Ph.D. Thesis, University of Toronto.

Sheppard, E. (1979-A) Geographical Potentials, *Annals of the Association of American Geographers*, *69*, 438-447.

Sheppard, E. (1979-B) Spatial Interaction and Geographic Theory, in Olsson, G., Gale, S. (eds.) *Philosophy in Geography*, Reidel Dordrecht, 361-378.

Sheppard, E. (1980-A) Interaction and Potential in Spatial Systems, *Ontario Geography*, *13*, 47-60.

Sheppard, E. (1980-B) The Ideology of Spatial Choice, *Papers of the Regional Science Association*, *45*, 197-213.

Sheppard, E. (1981-A) Public Facility Location with Elastic Demand: users' benefits and redistribution issues, *Sistemi Urbani*, *3*, 435-454.

Sheppard, E. (1981-B) Spatial Economic Development in Capitalistic Economies, Paper presented at the Annual Meeting of the North American Regional Science Association, Montreal, November.

Sheppard, E. (1983-A) Commodity Trade, Corporate Ownership and Urban Growth, *Papers of the Regional Science Association*, *52*, 175-186.

Sheppard, E. (1983-B) Economic Development in Capitalist Spatial Economies (mimeo).

Sheppard, E. (1983-C) Growth, Conflict and Crisis in the Urban System: a neo-Marxian approach to modelling inter-urban economic dynamics, WP 83-00, IIASA, Laxenburg, Austria.

Sheppard, E. (1983-D) Pasinetti, Marx and Urban Accumulation Dynamics, in Griffith, D.A., Lea, A.C. (eds.) *Evolving Geographical Structures*, NATO ASI Series D, No. 15, Nijhoff Publishers, The Hague, 293-322.

Sheppard, E. (1983-E) Urban System Population Dynamics: incorporating non-linearities, WP-83-34, IIASA, Laxenburg, Austria.

Sheppard, E., Curry, L. (1982) Spatial Price Equilibria, *Geographical Analysis*, *14*, 279-304.

Shoukry, T.R., Scott, A.J. (1981) The Urban Land Question, in Dear, M., Scott, A.J. (eds.) *Urbanization and Land Planning in Capitalist Society*, Methuen, London, 123-157.
Sikdar, P.K., Karmeshu (1982) On Population Growth of Cities in a Region: a stochastic non-linear model, *Environment and Planning A*, *14*, 585-590.
Simon, H.A. (1955) A Behavioural Model of Rational Choice, *Quarterly Journal of Economies*, *69*, 99-118.
Sisson, R.L. (ed.) (1974) *A Guide to Models in Governmental Planning and Operations*, U.S. Environmental Protection Agency, Washington.
Sistemi Urbani (1981) *3*, 3 (special issue).
Smeed, R. (1964) Road Pricing: the economic and technical possibilities, Her Majesty's Stationery Office, London.
Smith, A.P., Whitehead, P.J., Mackett, R.L. (1977) The Utilisation of Services, in Wilson, A.G., Rees, P.H., Leigh, C.M. (eds.) *Models of Cities and Regions*, Wiley, Chichester, 323-403.
Smith, P., Morrison, W.I. (1974) *Simulating the Urban Economy*, Pion, London.
Smith, T.B., Leigh, C.M. (1977) Regional Economic Models, in Wilson, A.G., Rees, P.H., Leigh, C.M. (eds.) *Models of Cities and Regions*, Wiley, Chichester, 405-456.
Smith, T.E. (1975-A) An Axiomatic Theory of Spatial Discounting Behaviour, *Papers of the Regional Science Association*, *35*, 31-44.
Smith, T.E. (1975-B) A Choice Theory of Spatial Interaction, *Regional Science and Urban Economics*, *5*, 137-176.
Smith, T.E. (1976-A) A Spatial Discounting Theory of Interaction Preferences, *Environment and Planning A*, *8*, 879-915.
Smith, T.E. (1976-B) Spatial Discounting and the Gravity Hypothesis, *Regional Science and Urban Economics*, *6*, 331-356.
Smith, T.E. (1978-A) A Cost-Efficiency Principle of Spatial Interaction Behaviour, *Regional Science and Urban Economics*, *8*, 313-337.
Smith, T.E. (1978-B) A General Efficiency Principle of Spatial Interaction, in Karlqvist, A., Lundqvist, L., Snickars, F., Weibull, J.W. (eds.) *Spatial Interaction Theory and Planning Models*, North-Holland, Amsterdam, 97-118.
Smith, T.E. (1981) The Minimum Information Principle as a Conditional Law of Large Numbers, Working Paper No. 54, Working Papers in Regional Science and Transportation, Department of Regional Science, University of Pennsylvania, Philadelphia, PA.
Smith, T.E. (1982-A) A Choice Probability Characterization of Generalized Extreme Value Models, Working Paper No. 66, Department of Regional Science, University of Pennsylvania.
Smith, T.E. (1982-B) Random Utility Models of Spatial Choice: a structural analysis, Paper presented at the Workshop on

Spatial Choice Models, April, IIASA, Laxenburg, Austria.
Smith, T.E. (1983-A) A Cost-Efficiency Approach to the Analysis of Congested Spatial Interaction Behaviour, *Environment and Planning A*, *15*, 435-464.
Smith, T.E. (1983-B) Dispersed Network Equilibria for Strongly Cost-Efficient Spatial Interaction Behaviour (mimeo).
Smith, T.E., Papageorgiou, Y.Y. (1982) Spatial Externalities and the Stability of Interacting Populations Near the Centre of a Large Area, *Journal of Regional Science*, *22*, 1-18.
Smolka, M. (1980) Location Theory and Urban Economics: a spatial extension of Sraffa's critique of neoclassicism, unpublished Ph.D. Dissertation, Department of Regional Science, University of Pennsylvania.
Snickars, F. (1978) A Dynamic Stock-Flow Model of a Regulated Housing Market, in Karlqvist, A., Lundqvist, L., Snickars, F., Weibull, J.W. (eds.) *Spatial Interaction Theory and Planning Models*, North-Holland, Amsterdam, 157-175.
Snickars, F., Weibull, J.W. (1977) A Minimum Information Principle, *Regional Science and Urban Economics*, *7*, 137-168.
Soland, R.M. (1974) Optimal Facility Location with Concave Costs, *Operations Research*, *22*, 373-382.
Solow, R.M. (1972) Congestion, Density and the Use of Land for Streets, *Swedish Journal of Economics*, *74*, 161-173.
Solow, R.M., Vickrey, W.S. (1971) Land Use in a Long Narrow City, *Journal of Economic Theory*, *9*, 418-448.
Sonis, M. (1983) Competition and Environment: a theory of temporal innovation diffusion, in Griffith, D.A., Lea, A.C. (eds.) *Evolving Geographical Structures*, NATO ASI Series D: Behavioural and Social Sciences, No. 15, Nijhoff, The Hague, 99-129.
Southworth, F. (1978) A Highly Disaggregated Modal-Split Model. Some tests, *Environment and Planning A*, *10*, 795-812.
Spaventa, L. (1970) Rate of Profit, Rate of Growth and Capital Intensity in a Simple Production Model, *Oxford Economic Papers*, *22*, 129-147.
Spaventa, L. (1973) Notes on Problems of Transition between Techniques, in Mirlees, J.A., Stern, N.H. (eds.) *Models of Economic Growth*, Macmillan, London, 168-187.
Spicer, C.C. (1979) The Mathematical Modelling of Influenza Epidemics, *British Medical Bulletin*, *1*, 23-28.
Spielberg, K. (1969) Algorithms for the Simple Plant Location Problem with Some Side Conditions, *Operations Research*, *17*, 85-111.
Spitzer, F. (1964) *Principles of the Random Walk*, Van Nostrand, New York.
Sraffa, P. (1960) *The Production of Commodities by Means of Commodities*, Cambridge University Press, Cambridge, U.K.
Steedman, I. (1977) *Marx after Sraffa*, New Left Books, London.

Steedman, I. (ed.) (1979-A) *Fundamental Issues in Trade Theory*, St. Martin's Press, New York.

Steedman, I. (1979-B) *Trade Amongst Growing Economies*, Cambridge University Press, Cambridge, U.K.

Steedman, I., Metcalfe, J. (1972) Reswitching and Primary Input Use, *Economic Journal*, *82*, 140-157.

Steedman, I., Metcalfe, J. (1977) Reswitching, Primary Inputs and the Hecksher-Ohlin-Samuelson Theory of Trade, *Journal of International Economics*, Reprinted in Steedman, I. (ed.) (1979) *Fundamental Issues in Trade Theory*, St. Martin's Press, New York, 38-46.

Steedman, I., Sweezy, P. (eds.) (1981) *The Value Controversy*, New Left Books, London.

Steenbrink, P.A. (1974) *Optimisation of Transport Networks*, Wiley, London.

Sternberg, W.J., Smith, T.L. (1946) *The Theory of Potential and Spectral Harmonies*, University of Toronto Press, Toronto.

Steuer, R.E. (1977) An Interactive Multiple Objective Linear Programming Procedure, in Starr, M.K., Zeleny, M. (eds.) *Multiple Criteria Decision Making*, North-Holland, Amsterdam, 225-239.

Stevens, B.H. (1961) Linear Programming and Location Rent, *Journal of Regional Science*, *3*, 15-25.

Stevens, B.H., Rydell, P. (1966) Spatial Demand Theory in Monopoly Price Policy, *Papers, Regional Science Association*, *17*, 195-204.

Stewart, J.Q. (1947) Empirical Mathematical Rules Concerning the Distribution and Equilibrium of Population, *Geographical Review*, *37*, 461-485.

Stewman, S. (1976) Markov Models of Occupational Mobility: theoretical development and empirical support - Part 1: Careers/Part 2: Continuously Operative Job Systems, *Journal of Mathematical Sociology*, *4*, 201-245, 247-278.

Stillwell, J.C.H. (1978) Interzonal Migration: some historical tests of spatial-interaction models, *Environment and Planning A*, *10*, 1187-1200.

Stone, R. (1966) *Mathematics in the Social Sciences and Other Essays*, Chapman and Hall, London.

Stone, R. (1970) *Mathematical Models of the Economy and Other Essays*, Chapman and Hall, London.

Strotz, R.H. (1965) Urban Transportation Parables, in Margolis, J. (ed.) *The Public Economy of Urban Communities*, Johns Hopkins University Press, Baltimore, 127-169.

Stubbs, J.R., Barber, B. (1970) Spatial Policies for Regional Development, Technical Report 10: the Lowry model, American-Yugoslav Project, Ljubljana.

Swain, R.W. (1974) A Parametric Decomposition Approach for the Solution of Uncapacitated Location Problems, *Operations Research*, *22*, 189-198.

Sweezy, P. (1946) *The Theory of Capitalist Development*, Monthly Review Press, New York.

Takayama, T., Judge, G.G. (1964) Equilibrium Among Spatially Separated Markets, *Econometrica, 32,* 510-524.
Takayama, T., Judge, G.G. (1971) *Spatial and Temporal Price and Allocation Models,* North-Holland, Amsterdam.
Teitz, M.B., Bart, P. (1968) Heuristic Methods for Estimating the Generalized Vertex Median of a Weighted Graph, *Operations Research, 16,* 955-961.
Thom, R. (1972) *Stabilité Structurelle et Morphogenese,* Benjamin, New York.
Thomas, R. (1973) Boolean Formalization of Genetic Control Circuits, *Journal of Theoretical Biology, 42,* 563-585.
Thomas, R. (1979) Kinetic Logic: a Boolean approach to the analysis of complex regulatory systems, in Thomas, R. (ed.) *Lecture Notes in Biomathematics, 29,* Springer-Verlag, Berlin.
Thrift, N. (ed.) (1981) *The Geography of Multinationals,* Croom Helm, London.
Thünen, J.H. von (1826) *Der isolierte Staat in Beziehung auf Landwirschaft und Nationa-ökonomie,* Hamburg. (3rd Vol., and new edition: (1963), Hamburg.) [English translation: (1966) *The Isolated State,* Pergamon Press, New York.]
Thurstone, L. (1927) A Law of Comparative Judgement, *Psychological Review, 34,* 273-286.
Tobler, W.R. (1979) Estimation of Attractivities from Interactions, *Environment and Planning A, 10,* 121-127.
Tomlin, S.G. (1979) A Kinetic Theory of Urban Dynamics, *Environment and Planning A, 11,* 97-106.
Traffic Research Corporation (1964) Review of Existing Land Use Forecasting Techniques, Boston Regional Planning Project, Boston.
Turner, J.W., Malek-Mansour, M. (1978) On the Absorbing Zero Boundary Problem in Birth and Death Processes, *Physica, 93A,* 517-525.
Tyson, J.J. (1976) The Belousov-Zhabotinskii Reaction, *Lecture Notes in Biomathematics, 10,* Springer-Verlag, Berlin.
Urban, G., Hauser, J.R. (1980) *Design and Marketing of New Products,* Prentice-Hall, Englewood Cliffs.
Urry, J. (1981) Localities, Regions and Class, *International Journal of Urban and Regional Research, 5,* 455-474.
Vajda, S. (1978) *Mathematics of Manpower Planning,* Wiley, Chichester.
Van Roy, T.J., Erlenkotter, D. (1982) A Dual-Based Procedure for Dynamic Facility Location, *Management Science, 28,* 1091-1105.
Van Vliet, D. (1976-A) Road Assignment I: principles and parameters of model formulation, *Transportation Research, 10,* 137-143.
Van Vliet, D. (1976-B) Road Assignment II: the GLTS models, *Transportation Research, 10,* 145-150.
Van Vliet, D. (1976-C) Road Assignment III: comparative tests of stochastic methods, *Transportation Research, 10,* 151-157.

Varaprasad, N. (1980-A) A Dynamic Accounting Model of Intra-metropolitan Household Relocation, *Environment and Planning A*, *12*, 1301-1315.
Varaprasad, N. (1980-B) An Interactive Strategic Model of Transport Costs in Metropolitan Population Dynamics, *Environment and Planning A*, *12*, 1009-1034.
Varian, H.R. (1975) On Persistent Disequilibrium, *Journal of Economic Theory*, *10*, 218-228.
Vassiliou, P-C.G. (1982) On the Limiting Behaviour of a Non-Homogeneous Markovian Manpower Model with Independent Poisson Input, *Journal of Applied Probability*, *19*, 433-438.
Vernon, R.B. (1972) Structure and Growth of a von Thünen Economy, Ph.D. Thesis, Brown University, Rhode Island.
Volterra, V. (1927) Variazione e Fluttuazione del Numero di Individui in Specie Animali Conviventi, Regio Comitato Talassografico Italiano, Memoria 131, 1-142.
Von Barh, B., Martin-Löf, A. (1980) Threshold Limit Theorems for Some Epidemic Processes, *Advances in Applied Probability*, *12*, 319-349.
Von Neumann, J. (1945) A Model of General Economic Equilibrium, *The Review of Economic Studies*, *13*, 1-9.
Voogd, H. (1984) Transportation Policy Analysis, *Sistemi Urbani*, *6*, 355-398.
Walker, R.A. (1974) Urban Ground Rent: a new conceptual framework, *Antipode*, *6*, 1, 51-57.
Walker, W.E. (1976) A Heuristic Adjacent Extreme Point Algorithm for the Fixed Charge Problem, *Management Science*, *22*, 587-596.
Walsh, P.K., Gibberd, R.W. (1980) Developments of an Entropy Model for Residential Location with Maximum Zonal Population Constraints, *Environment and Planning A*, *12*, 1253-1268.
Walsh, V., Gram, H. (1980) *Classical and Neoclassical Theories of General Equilibrium*, Oxford University Press, New York.
Waltman, P. (1974) Deterministic Threshold Models in the Theory of Epidemics, *Lecture Notes in Biomathematics*, *1*, Springer-Verlag, Berlin.
Warszawski, A. (1974) Pseudo-Boolean Solutions to Multidimensional Location Problems, *Operations Research*, *22*, 1081-1085.
Watson, R.K. (1972) On an Epidemic in a Stratified Population, *Journal of Applied Probability*, *9*, 659-666.
Weaver, W. (1958) A Quarter Century in the Natural Sciences, *Annual Report*, The Rockefeller Foundation, New York, 7-122.
Webber, M.J. (1978) Spatial Interaction and the Form of the City, in Karlqvist, A., Lundqvist, L., Snickars, F., Weibull, J.W. (eds.) *Spatial Interaction Theory and Planning Models*, North-Holland, Amsterdam, 203-226.

Webber, M.J. (1979) *Information Theory and Urban Spatial Structure*, Croom Helm, London.
Webber, M.J. (1981-A) Location of Manufacturing and Operational Urban Models, Paper presented at the Annual Meeting of the North American Regional Science Association, Montreal, November, 1981.
Webber, M.J. (1981-B) Operational Models in Urban Planning, *Environment and Planning A*, *13*, 763-779.
Webber, M.J., Joseph, A.E. (1978) Spatial Diffusion Processes 1: a model and an approximation method, *Environment and Planning A*, *10*, 651-665.
Webber, M.J., Joseph, A.E. (1979) Spatial Diffusion Processes 2: numerical analysis, *Environment and Planning A*, *11*, 335-347.
Weber, A. (1909) *Uber den Standort der Industrien*, Verlag Mohr, Tubingen. [English translation: (1957) *The Theory of the Location of Industries*, University of Chicago Press, Chicago.]
Wegener, M. (1981) The Housing Market in the Dortmund Region: a micro simulation, in Voogd, H. (ed.) *Strategic Planning in a Dynamic Society*, Delftsche Uitgevers Maatschappij, Delft, 127-138.
Wegener, M. (1982) A Multilevel Economic-Demographic Model for the Dortmund Region, *Sistemi Urbani*, *4*, 371-401.
Wegener, M. (1983) Description of the Dortmund Model, Arbeitspapier 8, Institut für Raumplanung, Universität Dortmund, Dortmund.
Weibull, J.W. (1976) An Axiomatic Approach to the Measurement of Accessibility, *Regional Science and Urban Economics*, *6*, 357-379.
Weibull, J.W. (1984-A) A Dynamic Simulation Model of Disequilibrium in the Housing Market, *Sistemi Urbani*, *6*, 325-354.
Weibull, J.W. (1984-B) A Stock-Flow Approach to General Equilibrium with Trade Frictions, *Applied Mathematics and Computation*, *14*, 63-76.
Weidlich, W., Haag, G. (1980-A) Dynamics of Interacting Groups with Application to the Migration of Population, *System for Schung und Neuerungs-Management*, *11*, 114-123.
Weidlich, W., Haag, G. (1980-B) Migration Behaviour of Mixed Population in a Town, *Collective Phenomena*, *3*, 89-102.
Weidlich, W., Haag, G. (1983) *Concepts and Models of a Quantitative Sociology*, Springer-Verlag, Berlin.
Weintraub, E.R. (1979) *Microfoundations: the compatibility of microeconomics and macroeconomics*, Cambridge University Press, Cambridge, U.K.
Wendell, R.E., McKelvey, R.D. (1981) New Perspectives in Competitive Location Theory, *European Journal of Operational Research*, *6*, 174-182.
Wesolowsky, G.O., Truscott, W.G. (1975) The Multiperiod Location-Allocation Problem with Relocation of Facilities,

Management Science, *22*, 57-65.
Westaway, J. (1974) The Spatial Hierarchy of Business Organization and its Implications for the British Urban System, *Regional Studies*, *8*, 145-155.
Wheaton, W.C. (1972) Income and Urban Location, Ph.D. Dissertation, University of Pennsylvania, Philadelphia, PA.
Wheaton, W.C. (1974) Linear Programming and Locational Equilibrium: the Herbert-Stevens Model Revisited, *Journal of Urban Economics*, *1*, 278-288.
Wheaton, W.C. (1982) Urban Spatial Development with Durable but Replacable Capital, *Journal of Urban Economics*, *12*, 53-67.
Wheaton, W.C., Harris, B. (1970) Linear Programming and Residential Location: the Herbert-Stevens model revisited, University of Pennsylvania, Philadelphia PA. (mimeo).
White, R.W. (1977) Dynamic Central Place Theory: results of a simulation approach, *Geographical Analysis*, *9*, 226-243.
White, R.W. (1978) The Simulation of Central Place Dynamics: two sector systems and the rank-size distribution, *Geographical Analysis*, *10*, 201-208.
Wiener, N. (1923) Differential Space, *Journal of Mathematics and Physics*, *2*, 131-174.
Williams, H.C.W.L. (1976) Travel Demand Models, Duality Relations and User Benefit Analysis, *Journal of Regional Science*, *16*, 147-165.
Williams, H.C.W.L. (1977-A) On the Formation of Travel Demand Models and Economic Evaluation Measures of User Benefit, *Environment and Planning A*, *9*, 285-344.
Williams, H.C.W.L. (1977-B) The Generation of Consistent Travel-Demand Models and User-Benefit Measures, in Bonsall, P.W., Hills, P.J., Dalvi, M.Q. (eds.) *Urban Transportation and Planning*, Abacus Press, Tunbridge Wells, 161-176.
Williams, H.C.W.L., Ortuzar, J.D. (1976) Some Generalisations and Applications of the Velocity Field Concept: trip patterns in idealised cities, *Transportation Research*, *10*, 65-74.
Williams, H.C.W.L., Senior, M.L. (1977-A) A Retail Location Model with Overlapping Market Areas: Hotelling's problem revisited, *Urban Studies*, *14*, 203-205.
Williams, H.C.W.L., Senior, M.L. (1977-B) Model Based Transport Policy Assessment 2: removing fundamental inconsistencies from the models, *Traffic Engineering and Control*, *18*, 464-469.
Williams, H.C.W.L., Senior, M.L. (1978) Accessibility Spatial Interaction and the Spatial Benefit Analysis of Land-Use Transportation Plans, in Karlqvist, A., Lundqvist, L., Snickars, F., Weibull, J.W. (eds.) *Spatial Interaction Theory and Planning Models*, North-Holland, Amsterdam, 253-288.
Williams, H.C.W.L., Wilson, A.G. (1978) Dynamic Models for Urban and Regional Analysis, in Carlstein, T., Parkes,

D.N., Thrift, N.J. (eds.) *Time and Regional Dynamics of Timing Space and Spacing Time*, Volume 3, Edward Arnold, London, 81-95.

Williams, H.C.W.L., Wilson, A.G. (1980) Some Comments on the Theoretical and Analytic Structure of Urban and Regional Models, *Sistemi Urbani*, *2*, 203-242.

Williams, I.N. (1976) A Comparison of Some Calibration Techniques for Doubly-Constrained Models with an Exponential Cost Function, *Transportation Research*, *10*, 91-104.

Williams, I.N. (1979) An Approach to Solving Spatial Allocation Models with Constraints, *Environment and Planning A*, *11*, 3-22.

Wilson, A.G. (1967) A Statistical Theory of Spatial Distribution Models, *Transportation Research*, *1*, 253-269. Reprinted in Quandt, R.E. (ed.) (1970) *The Demand for Travel. Theory and Measurement*, Heath Lexington, Boston, 55-82; and reprinted in Angel, S. and Hyman, G.M. (eds.) (1976) *Urban Fields*, Pion, London, 162-178.

Wilson, A.G. (1969-A) Developments of Some Elementary Residential Location Models, *Journal of Regional Sciences*, *1*, 377-385.

Wilson, A.G. (1969-B) Entropy, CES-WP-26, Centre for Environmental Studies, London.

Wilson, A.G. (1969-C) Notes on Some Concepts in Social Physics, *Papers of the Regional Science Association*, *22*, 159-193.

Wilson, A.G. (1970-A) *Entropy in Urban and Regional Modelling*, Pion, London.

Wilson, A.G. (1970-B) Interregional Commodity Flows: entropy maximising methods, *Geographical Analysis*, *3*, 255-282.

Wilson, A.G. (1971-A) A Family of Spatial Interaction Models and Associated Developments, *Environment and Planning*, *3*, 1-32. Reprinted in Wilson, A.G. (ed.) (1972) *Papers in Urban and Regional Analysis*, Pion, London, 170-201.

Wilson, A.G. (1971-B) Generalising the Lowry Model, in Wilson, A.G. (ed.) *Urban and Regional Planning*, Pion, London, 112-123. Reprinted in *Papers in Urban and Regional Analysis*, 58-70.

Wilson, A.G. (1972) Recent Developments in Macro-Economic Approaches to Modelling Household Behaviour with Particular Reference to Spatio-Temporal Organisation, Presented to the Centre for Environmental Studies Conference on Urban Economics, Keele. Reprinted in Wilson, A.G. (ed.) (1972) *Papers in Urban and Regional Analysis*, Pion, London, 216-236.

Wilson, A.G. (1974) *Urban and Regional Models in Geography and Planning*, Wiley, Chichester, U.K.

Wilson, A.G. (1976-A) Catastrophe Theory and Urban Modelling: an application to modal choice, *Environment and Planning A*, *8*, 351-356.

Wilson, A.G. (1976-B) Non-linear and Dynamic Models in Geography: towards a research agenda, Working Paper, 160,

School of Geography, University of Leeds, Leeds, U.K.

Wilson, A.G. (1976-C) Retailer's Profits and Consumers' Welfare in Spatial Interaction Shopping Models, in Masser, I. (ed.) *Theory and Practice in Regional Science*, Pion, London, 42-59.

Wilson, A.G. (1977) Recent Developments in Urban and Regional Modelling: towards an articulation of systems' theoretical foundations, Atti delle Giornate di Lavoro AIRO 1977, Parma, Volume 1, 1-28.

Wilson, A.G. (1978-A) From Comparative Statics to Dynamics in Urban Systems Theory, Working Paper 218, School of Geography, University of Leeds, Leeds, U.K.

Wilson, A.G. (1978-B) Spatial Interaction and Settlement Structure: towards an explicit central place theory, in Karlqvist, A., Lundqvist, L., Snickars, F., Weibull, J.W. (eds.) *Spatial Interaction Theory and Planning Models*, North-Holland, Amsterdam, 137-156.

Wilson, A.G. (1978-C) Towards Models of the Evolution and Genesis of Urban Structure, in Martin, R.L., Thrift, N.J., Bennett, R.J. (eds.) *Towards the Dynamic Analysis of Spatial Systems*, Pion, London, 79-90.

Wilson, A.G. (1979-A) Aspects of Catastrophe Theory and Bifurcation Theory in Regional Science, Working Paper 249, School of Geography, University of Leeds, Leeds, U.K.

Wilson, A.G. (1979-B) Criticality and Urban Retail Structure: aspects of catastrophe theory and bifurcation, in Prigogine, I., Schrive, W.C. (eds.) *Proceedings International Conference on Dissipative Structures*, University of Texas Press, Austin, Tex.

Wilson, A.G. (1979-C) Equilibrium and Transport Systems Dynamics, in Hensher, D., Stopher, P. (eds.) *Behavioural Travel Modelling*, Croom Helm, London, 164-186.

Wilson, A.G. (1980) Comments on Alonso's Theory of Movement, *Environment and Planning A*, *12*, 727-732.

Wilson, A.G. (1981-A) *Catastrophe Theory and Bifurcation. Applications to Urban and Regional Systems*, Croom Helm, London.

Wilson, A.G. (1981-B) *Geography and the Environment: systems analytical methods*, Wiley, Chichester.

Wilson, A.G. (1981-C) Some New Sources of Instability and Oscillation in Dynamic Models of Shopping Centres and Other Urban Structures, *Sistemi Urbani*, *3*, 391-401.

Wilson, A.G. (1981-D) The Evolution of Spatial Structure, in Bennett, R.J. (ed.) *European Progress in Spatial Analysis*, Pion, London, 201-225.

Wilson, A.G. (1982) New Developments in Location Theory (mimeo).

Wilson, A.G. (1983) Transport and the Evolution of Urban Spatial Structure, in *Atti delle Giornate di Lavoro AIRO 1983*, Guida, Napoli, 7-27.

Wilson, A.G., Clarke, M. (1979) Some Illustrations of Catastrophe Theory Applied to Urban Retailing Structures, in

Breheny, M. (ed.) *Developments in Urban and Regional Analysis*, *London Papers in Regional Science*, *10*, Pion, London, 5-27.

Wilson, A.G., Coelho, J.D., Macgill, S.M., Williams, H.C.W.L. (1981) *Optimization in Locational and Transport Analysis*, Wiley, New York.

Wilson, A.G., Macgill, S.M. (1978) A Systems Analytic Framework of Comprehensive Urban and Regional Modelling, Working Paper 209, School of Geography, University of Leeds, Leeds, U.K.

Wilson, A.G., Oulton, M.J. (1983) The Corner-Shop to Supermarket Transition in Retailing: the beginnings of empirical evidence, *Environment and Planning A*, *15*, 265-274.

Wilson, A.G., Pownall, C.E. (1976) A New Representation of the Urban System for Modelling and for the Study of Micro-Level Interdependence, *Area*, *8*, 256-264.

Wilson, A.G., Senior, M.L. (1974) Some Relationships between Entropy Maximizing Models, Mathematical Programming Models, and their Duals, *Journal of Regional Science*, *14*, 205-215.

Wilson, S.R. (1976) Statistical Notes on the Evaluation of Calibrated Gravity Models, *Transportation Research*, *10*, 343-345.

Wingo, L. (1961) Transportation and Urban Land, Resources for the Future, Washington, D.C.

Wootton, H.J., Pick, G.W. (1967) A Model for Trips Generated by Households, *Journal of Transport Economics and Policy*, *1*, 137-153.

Yu, P.L. (1973-A) Introduction to Domination Structures in Multicriteria Decision Problems, in Cochrane, J.L., Zeleny, M. (eds.) *Multicriteria Decision Making*, University of South Carolina Press, Columbia, 249-261.

Yu, P.L. (1973-B) A Class of Solutions for Group Decision Problems, *Management Science*, *19*, 936-946.

Zalai, E. (1981) Eigenvalues and Labour Values, CP-81-17, International Institute for Applied Systems Analysis, Laxenburg, Austria.

Zeeman, E.C. (1977) *Catastrophe Theory*, Addison-Wesley, Reading, Mass.

Zeleny, M. (1974) *Linear Multiobjective Programming*, Springer-Verlag, Berlin.

Zeleny, M. (1976) The Theory of the Displaced Ideal, in Zeleny, M. (ed.) *Multiple Criteria Decision Making-Kyoto 1975*, Springer-Verlag, Berlin, 151-205.

Zimmermann, H.J., Sovereign, M.G. (1974) *Quantitative Models for Production Management*, Prentice-Hall, Englewood Cliffs.

Zipf, G.K. (1941) *National Unity and Disunity*, Indiana Press, Bloomington.

INDEX

For Product Safety Concerns and Information please contact our EU
representative GPSR@taylorandfrancis.com
Taylor & Francis Verlag GmbH, Kaufingerstraße 24, 80331 München, Germany

www.ingramcontent.com/pod-product-compliance
Lightning Source LLC
Chambersburg PA
CBHW070613270326
41926CB00011B/1678

9780415714617